SEXUALITIES AND IRISH SOCIETY

SEXUALITIES AND IRISH SOCIETY

A Reader

Edited by

Máire Leane and Elizabeth Kiely

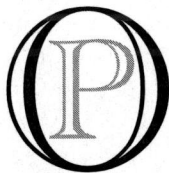

ORPEN PRESS

Published by
Orpen Press
Lonsdale House
Avoca Avenue
Blackrock
Co. Dublin
Ireland

e-mail: info@orpenpress.com
www.orpenpress.com

Paperback ISBN 978-1-909518-47-6
Kindle ISBN 978-1-909895-10-2
ePub ISBN 978-1-909895-11-9
PDF ISBN 978-1-909895-14-0

Printed in Dublin by SPRINT-print Ltd

Acknowledgments

We would like to thank the contributors, without whose time, hard work and goodwill the book would not have been possible.

We would like to extend our thanks to the anonymous reviewer, who gave positive feedback and encouragement and whose critical comments we used to improve the work.

We thank Jennifer K. deWan for her professional proofreading.

Our gratitude is extended to Elizabeth Brennan, Jennifer Thompson and Eileen O'Brien of Orpen Press for their advice and assistance to us throughout.

We wish to acknowledge the financial assistance provided by the College of Arts, Celtic Studies and Social Sciences in University College Cork and the National University of Ireland.

Contents

Contents

Contents

About the Contributors

Alison Afra has recently completed her PhD with the School of Psychology at Trinity College Dublin. Her thesis, which foregrounds primary school children's constructions of 'childhood sexuality', is situated in critical social psychology and aims to contribute to scholarship that unsettles what is 'taken-for-granted' about 'gender' and 'sexuality' in 'childhood'.

Cliona Barnes lectures at the University of Limerick. She is a sociologist and her research focuses on the critical study of masculinities, and specifically on understanding the lives and experiences of young men as they relate to broader issues around sex and gender, social class, education and youth culture. She has published several articles and book chapters in this area.

Selina Bonnie is an Indian/Irish disabled woman who holds a Masters Degree in Disability Studies from the University of Leeds. She has been an activist, lecturer and trainer in the international disabled people's movement for the past twenty years. Her particular research interests centre on sexuality, sexual expression and reproductive rights for disabled people. For further information visit <http://www.sexualcitizens.com>.

Natalie Delimata is a lecturer in the Department of Social Science in the Institute of Technology, Sligo, where she lectures in Creative Practice and Social Pedagogy. She is currently completing her PhD thesis, entitled 'Articulating Intersex: A Crisis at the Intersection of Science and Society'. Her research interests include biology, ethics, the sociology of medicine, and the construction of gender identity. She is a practicing artist and art teacher in the community and educational sectors.

Christine Gaffney is completing her PhD (Social Science) GREP in University College Cork, where she is researching the experiences of women who 'come out' as lesbian in mid-life. She also teaches on the MA in Women's Studies there. Christine is an ISSP-funded scholar under PRTLI4.

Ben Hughes is a Government of Ireland Scholar (IRCHSS) in the School of Social Policy and Social Work, Trinity College Dublin. His research interests include counselling psychology, particularly interventions for behaviour change. He has extensive experience in education, spirituality and integrative psychotherapy. He holds a MSc in Counselling and Therapeutic Communication (University of Ulster) and a Higher Diploma in Education (Trinity College Dublin).

Grace Kelly is a National Disability Authority Scholar undertaking a PhD in the School of Applied Social Studies at University College Cork, where she is researching sexuality and intellectual disability. Grace is also on the committee of the Connect People Network, a charity organisation that is led by people with extra support needs and that promotes their rights around friendships, relationships and sexuality.

Elizabeth Kiely (e.kiely@ucc.ie) (M.Soc.Sc., PhD) is a senior lecturer in social policy in the School of Applied Social Studies, University College Cork. She has published work in the fields of youth policy and practice, sex education, drug education and women's studies. She is the principal investigator on an IRCHSS RDI-funded project on the commercialisation and sexualisation of children in Ireland. She is co-editor of *Youth and Community Work in Ireland: Critical Perspectives* (Dublin: Blackhall Publishing, 2009) and co-author of *Irish Women at Work 1930–1960: An Oral History* (Kildare: Irish Academic Press, 2012).

Máire Leane (m.leane@ucc.ie) (MA, PhD) is Associate Dean of the Graduate School in the College of Arts, Celtic Studies and Social Science at UCC and is a senior lecturer in social policy in the School of Applied Social Studies, University College Cork. Her core research interests relate to the social construction of sexuality and womanhood in both historical and contemporary contexts and she has a range of publications in these areas. She is co-author of *Irish Women at Work 1930–1960: An Oral History* (Kildare: Irish Academic

Press, 2012). *See* <http://research.ucc.ie/profiles/A012/mleane/Publications>.

Sandra McAvoy (PhD) co-ordinates the Masters in Women's Studies programme in University College Cork. Her research interests include the history of sexuality, the history and politics of reproductive rights, and women and political representation. Recent publications include 'Vindicating Women's Rights in a Fetocentric State: The Longest Irish Journey' in Noreen Giffney and Margrit Shildrick, *Theory on the Edge* (New York: Palgrave Macmillan, 2013), and '"Its Effect on Public Morality Is Vicious in the Extreme": Defining Birth Control as Obscene and Unethical, 1926–32', in Elaine Farrell, *'She Said She Was in the Family Way': Pregnancy and Infancy in Modern Ireland* (London: Institute of Historical Research, 2012).

Tanya Ní Mhuirthile is a senior lecturer at Griffith College Dublin. Tanya's research investigates the impact of the law's understanding of corporeality on certain types of bodies. Her doctoral research, entitled 'Intersex Individuals, Gender and the Limits of Law', was conducted under the joint supervision of Dr Mary Donnelly and Professor Siobhán Mullally at UCC. Tanya is a legal consultant to both Transgender Equality Network Ireland (TENI) and Intersex UK. An expert in the field of gender recognition, Tanya has written opinions for newspapers, including the *Irish Times* and *Irish Examiner*, has been a guest on radio shows, including *Today with Pat Kenny*, and has been an expert consultant on a BBC/Oprah Winfrey Network documentary entitled *Me, My Sex and I*.

Angela O'Connell is a lesbian, a mother and, amongst other things, a researcher. She is currently working on a project, Advancing Children's Rights in Ireland, in the Child Law Clinic Department of Law, University College Cork, and has previously worked on other children's research projects, community development and adult education. She was awarded a fellowship in Women's Studies, National University of Ireland, Galway, where she completed her PhD in 2010. In her thesis she used a feminist standpoint approach to critically examine the Irish family from the standpoint of lesbian families in contemporary Ireland.

Fiachra Ó Súilleabháin (DSocSc) is a social worker based in Cork. He currently manages a child sexual abuse assessment unit in the Health Service Executive and is a part-time lecturer in University College Cork. He has also worked in child protection social work and in voluntary sector youth organisations. His research interests include GLBT studies, parenting issues, child sexual abuse issues, direct work with children and young people, self-care for practitioners and elderly care.

Jean Quigley is a lecturer in the School of Psychology in Trinity College Dublin. She teaches social psychology and qualitative research within the discipline of psychology. Her research expertise and publications are mostly in the psychology of language, with particular reference to early first language acquisition and developmental language disorders. She is the author of *The Grammar of Autobiography* (New Jersey: Erlbaum, 2000).

Fergus Ryan LL.B. (Dub.), PhD. (Dub.) is a lecturer in law at the Dublin Institute of Technology. From 2003 to 2009 he served as acting Head of the Department of Law at DIT. A former President of the Irish Association of Law Teachers, he has written and spoken extensively on civil partnership, non-traditional families and LGBT rights.

Paul Ryan is a lecturer in the Department of Sociology at the National University of Ireland, Maynooth. His research interests are located within the sociology of personal life, specifically families, intimacy, sex work, and gay and lesbian studies. He is author of *Asking Angela Macnamara: An Intimate History of Irish Lives* (Dublin: Irish Academic Press, 2011).

Sara Stokes (BA, MA, PhD) is a feminist sociologist who graduated in 2012 with a PhD from NUI Galway. Since then she has gone on to work in a research capacity for a number of public bodies and is currently working as an independent researcher. While undertaking her MA dissertation on the subject of 'Neo Burlesque', Sara became fascinated with female sexuality and the ways in which it is represented culturally. This led to her doctoral research into raunch culture's impact on Irish female sexuality and her immersion in the often contradictory fields of pop-culture and feminism.

Teresa Whitaker (BA, M. Soc. Science, PhD) is Programme Director of the Masters in Teaching and Learning in Hibernia College (MATL). She has worked as a sociologist for the past twenty years, either teaching sociology in higher-level institutions (Hibernia College, UCD, DCU, TCD, SNMCI, CMI) or conducting research (UCD, NACD). Teresa has worked for Hibernia College for the past three years, teaching and assessing modules (Interculturalism, Sociology of Education and Research Methods), and is also involved in programme and curriculum development. Teresa worked for the National Advisory Committee on Drugs, where she was lead researcher on a study entitled *Drug Use, Sex Work and the Risk Environment in Dublin*. She has been an advocate for a harm reduction approach to sex work for the past four years with Sex Workers Alliance Ireland (SWAI).

Introduction

Máire Leane and Elizabeth Kiely

This book takes as its starting point the cultural shifts that have occurred in Ireland in recent decades and have led to a multiplicity of ways of thinking about sexuality and an extension of ways of being sexual. The *Irish Study of Sexual Health and Relationships*, the first large-scale study of sexual attitudes and behaviour in Ireland, reveals significant changes in sexual attitudes and behaviour since the early 1980s (Layte et al., 2006: 280). It indicates decreased age at first sex, increased numbers of sexual partners, more frequent contraceptive use and a reduction of negative attitudes towards pre-marital sex, homosexuality and abortion. Increased legal recognition has been won by lesbian and gay people (Civil Partnership and Certain Rights and Obligations of Cohabitants Act, 2012), while the rights of transgender people are, at the time of writing, moving onto the political agenda (Gender Recognition Advisory Group, 2011). However, differentiated sexual rights continue to be a challenge for these and other groups, such as people with disabilities and intersex people, and certain sexualities continue to be denied, problematised and subjected to regulation. At the same time globalisation, new technologies and commercialisation (Hawkes, 2004) are changing the cultural context in which sexualities are shaped and experienced.

The impact of such changes in terms of lived experiences of sexuality and in terms of legislative, policy and practice developments is a core consideration of this reader. The ongoing exchanges between real-life sexualities and the social contexts in which they are forged and moulded provide the key focus of the essays gathered here. All of the contributors to this text understand sexuality as a socially constructed phenomenon, which is continually shaped and re-shaped within specific political, socio-cultural and historical contexts. Furthermore, the focus is on 'sexualities', rather than sexuality, to deliberately acknowledge the diversity, fluidity and richness in sexual activities, interactions, identities and relationships.

Notwithstanding some excellent scholarship concerned with the broad canvas of Irish sexual politics (Inglis, 1987; Hug, 1999; Ferriter, 2009), this much-needed text showcases new and exciting insights deriving from contemporary research into diverse sexualities in Irish society. While acknowledging the peculiarities of the Irish context, the following chapters demonstrate the relevance of an increasingly internationalised sexual landscape. The contributors come from a range of disciplines, including history, social policy, sociology, psychology, disability studies, law and women's studies. Some are young scholars completing innovative doctoral work, more have a history of campaigning in relation to specific issues pertaining to sexuality, while others are 'insiders' with personal experience of the topics under discussion.

The authors employ diverse methodological approaches, engage with both theoretical and empirical material and pay attention to the relations of power within which sexualities are constructed, resisted and reconstructed. Key themes, concepts, theories, controversies and developments are explored in interesting and accessible ways; examples are used to illustrate important points; and the extensive references section at the end of the book directs readers to other sources, with the potential to deepen their understanding of the many issues raised. There is no attempt to provide a totalising overview of the issues explored in this cross-disciplinary collection of seventeen individual chapters. Some of the topics addressed are familiar, while others remain relatively neglected in existing Irish scholarship. All of the chapters are academically engaging and politically challenging and will provoke the reader to think about sexualities in new, innovative and possibly controversial ways.

Structure of the Book

The seventeen chapters are organised into eight sections, which reflect the key themes shared among the articles in each section. The first section, 'Historical Sexualities', contains chapters that explore how contraception was constructed in nineteenth-century texts (Sandra McAvoy) and the ways in which sexuality was understood, embodied and negotiated by a cohort of Irish women born between 1914 and 1955 (Máire Leane). The interconnections between discourse and practice, and power and resistance are highlighted in these contributions. The section entitled 'Sexual Rights and Activism' tracks political activism (Paul Ryan) and legislative responses (Fergus Ryan) in the sphere of non-traditional sexual orientations and critically analyses legal responses to the issue of gender recognition in Ireland (Tanya Ní Mhuirthile). Parenting experiences in non-heterosexual families are considered in 'Lesbian and Gay Parenting', which contains a chapter on gay fathers (Fiachra Ó Súilleabháin) and a chapter on lesbian mothers (Angela O'Connell).

Sexual orientation and the construction of sexual identities receive attention in Section 4, 'Sexual Identities: Becoming and Unbecoming Heterosexual'. Cliona Barnes focuses on the nature and experience of young male heterosexuality, arguing that because of its status as a privileged identity it remains under-researched, while Christine Gaffney engages with the instability and fluidity of sexual categories in her exploration of women who transition to lesbianism mid-life. The roles played by scientific discourses, professional expertise and popular culture in creating and reinforcing sexual meanings, norms and behaviours are examined in the section entitled 'Sexualities: Medical and Therapeutic Interventions'. In this section, interactions between socio-cultural and biomedical paradigms are critically interrogated in chapters on sexual addiction (Ben Hughes) and the medical diagnosis and treatment of intersex or ambiguous sexual differentiation (Natalie Delimata).

'Children and Young People's Sexualities' draws attention to how sexualities are actively manufactured in and by schools. Elizabeth Kiely's chapter explores the politics of sex education and critically analyses the formal sex education curriculum in the Irish context. Alison Afra and Jean Quigley question the often presumed sexual innocence of young school children in their ethnographic exploration of a 'porn' incident that occurred in an Irish primary school.

The inequalities and limitations created by sexual stereotypes and the push to dismantle them provide the focus for chapters in the section on 'Sexualities and Disabilities: Rights and Recognition'. The extent, nature and impact of sexual stereotyping in the spheres of physical and intellectual disability are highlighted by Selina Bonnie and Grace Kelly, as are contemporary challenges to the inequalities and the lack of recognition that prevails. The final section, 'Commercialised and Commodified Sexualities', explores the economic and cultural dynamics that provide the backdrop to contemporary debates about how 'raunch' culture (Sara Stokes) and prostitution/sex work (Teresa Whittaker) might be understood and addressed in the Irish context.

The organisation of the chapters into the sections described above is designed to help the reader identify material relating to her or his personal area of interest. There are, however, a number of core conceptual themes that traverse these various sections. The social construction of sexuality, for example, is addressed in numerous chapters, as are the processes through which certain sexual subjectivities are privileged while others are denied. The contested nature of sexual identities and practices, as evidenced in moral panics, political clashes and professional disputes, also receives frequent attention throughout the anthology. So too does the theme of sexual citizenship and the recognition and status afforded to different sexual subjects. The chapters in their entirety draw attention to the ways in which individuals and collectives continue to challenge understandings of sexuality, to name and resist inequitable practices and to extend the range of sexual identities that are considered acceptable.

This book is intended to be useful to diploma, degree and postgraduate students in a range of disciplines where the study of sexualities is important. It is also intended as a useful resource for activists, campaigners and professional practitioners.

Section 1

Historical Sexualities

CHAPTER 1

'Bring Forth Abundantly in the Earth, and Multiply Therein' (Genesis 9:7): Aspects of Irish Discourse on Contraception (1837–1908)

Sandra McAvoy

Introduction

Whether a society permits access to reliable fertility control goes to the core of how it thinks about women's identity, the hetero-sexual family, and female and male sexuality. Coming to terms with the idea that sexual relations can be non-reproductive may challenge deeply imbedded cultural norms and assumptions. Most importantly, a society's understanding of the status of women will define its approach to reproductive rights and the development of social, cultural and legal freedoms or restraints. Ireland is one country in which access to reproductive rights has been staunchly resisted. The Roman Catholic Church condemns artificial methods of birth control and abortion in any circumstance, and its influence on Irish legislation and public policy regulating reproduction has been significant. For example, the role played by the Church in the censorship of publications advocating birth control, under the Censorship of Publications Act (1929), and in the prohibition on the import or sale of contraceptives, under the Criminal Law Amend-ment Act (1935), has been well documented (Whyte, 1971; Keogh, 1986; Inglis, 1987, 1998a; Hug, 1999; Earner-Byrne, 2007; Ferriter, 2009; Curtis, 2010).

This chapter examines three treatises on birth control by Irish writers, all published during the century before the introduction of the 1935 ban on the import and sale of contraceptives. Material in these works suggests that the parameters of pro- and anti-birth-control discourse, and a focus on female sexuality as dangerous, were established long before they surfaced in political debate in post-independence Ireland. They provide a range of insights into contemporary thinking.

The first treatise, *The Philosophy of Marriage in its Social, Moral, and Physical Relations* (1837) [see full title in References], was written and published in London by an Irish medical doctor, Michael Ryan (d. 1840), who is regarded as one of the founding fathers of British medical ethics (Brody et al., 2009: 3[1]). It was a substantial medical textbook (364 pages) covering a range of related issues. Ryan opposed birth control and abortion, sometimes drawing on biblical sources to support his arguments (Brody et al., 2009: 233–4).

The second treatise, *The Marriage Problem* (1868), is the first known Irish pamphlet to promote contraceptive methods. It was published by feminist, suffragist, free-thinker and former Quaker Thomas Haslam (1825–1917), written under the pseudonym 'Oedipus'. The 'problem' encompassed the effect on marital relationships, children, health and wellbeing of inability to control fertility and also the perceived relationship between enforced celibacy and vice.

The final work examined is an early twentieth-century pamphlet, *Murderess of the Unseen: A Tract on Race-Suicide* (1908), by Rev. Samuel Hemphill (1859–1927). Born in Killanaule, County Tipperary in 1859, Hemphill was a Church of Ireland clergyman, a respected scholar, a Professor of Biblical Greek at Trinity College Dublin (1888–1898) and a Royal Irish Academician. He was twice chaplain to the Lord Lieutenant of Ireland, first in 1891 and then from 1918 to 1920. When his tract was published Hemphill was Rector of Birr, County Offaly. In 1909 he was appointed Canon of St Patrick's Cathedral, Dublin (Neill, n.d.: ch. 4). As the title suggests, Hemphill condemned both abortion and contraception.

Population Control

English birth control 'propaganda' – texts promoting contraceptives, such as those discussed below – originated in the early nineteenth century. Even into the twentieth century, it is difficult to measure the extent to which the ideas propounded in such texts percolated into the consciousness of Irish readers, particularly as limiting fertility was, from the outset, condemned by the main

Christian churches and medical organisations as contrary to divine and natural law, as subversive, obscene or likely to deprave – factors that inhibited public discussion. Why was birth control perceived in this way? As discussed below, it was regarded as a violation of divine law because it ran counter to biblical guidance, such as 'bring forth abundantly in the earth, and multiply therein' (Genesis 9:7) or Psalm 127's declaration that 'children are an heritage of the Lord: and the fruit of the womb is *his* reward' (verse 3). The story of Onan (Genesis 38: 8–10) was read as implying that both *coitus interruptus* and masturbation were deeply sinful. Birth control may also, from the outset, have been perceived as politically subversive because the earliest texts were produced by secular, free-thinking, working-class English political radicals, such as Francis Place (1771–1854) and Richard Carlisle (1790–1843). More importantly, by promoting female contraceptive methods, such writers challenged not only contemporary religious and moral understandings that sexual relations must always be open to the possibility of conception but also gendered assumptions about women's subordination within marriage and the inevitability of intensive motherhood.

Advocacy of birth control arose from concerns to limit population growth. Place's *The Principles of Population* (1822), for example, was the first English text to relate contraception and Malthus's 1798 theory that the wretchedness of the poor resulted from unrestrained population growth, which kept wages low and stretched food supplies. Place used the misery resulting from Irish potato crop failures of 1816 and 1817 as one illustration of the consequence of overpopulation in periods when resources were limited (Place 1822: 263–8). Where Malthus called for late marriage, celibacy before it and self-restraint within it – arguments in tune with dominant discourses on morality – Place posited that, though some would regard the idea with 'abhorrence' and 'repugnance', contraception would alleviate poverty and, by encouraging early marriage, would reduce vice (Place 1822: 173–9). Why did Place use such words as 'repugnance'? Not only was the idea of using artificial means of limiting fertility controversial in itself, use of contraceptives also had associations with prostitution and protection against venereal disease.

Richard Carlisle's book, *Every Woman's Book: or, What is Love?* (1826), went much further than Place's text in addressing 'an ill-founded notion current that to produce an unlimited number of children is beneficial to society' (Carlisle, reprinted in Bush, 1998: 98).[2] It spoke of the 'mental misery and bodily suffering' that might be alleviated if contraception were employed but, most controversially, challenged contemporary sexual mores and Christian teaching that sex outside marriage was sinful. Carlisle linked birth control and women's emancipation, arguing that their subordination within current sexual norms allowed women to be 'most brutally used by some men' (Carlisle, cited in Bush, 1998: 17). Carlisle, an atheist, was anti-clerical and anti-aristocracy. Bush points to his observation that women 'denied sex became especially devoted to religion'. His hope for the liberation of women from religious superstition rested on a new philosophy of free thought and free love, within which sex would be considered a 'virtue' and extra-marital sex, using the methods of contraception Carlisle hoped to popularise, would not be condemned (Bush, 1998: 17 and 99–104).

Carlisle's was the first book to provide information on contraceptive use. He detailed the use of the vaginal sponge – a female barrier method intended to prevent sperm passing through the cervix – which he implied was used by the English aristocracy and by French and Italian women (Carlisle, reprinted in Bush 1998: 99). He also promoted the 'skin', or condom, and that most ineffectual of methods, partial withdrawal (Carlisle, reprinted in Bush, 1998: 100). His ideas on sex were considered scandalous; a threat to the family and a revolutionary challenge to a patriarchal social order in which women's fear of pregnancy outside marriage was regarded as an essential social control. Nonetheless, the book sold well but, as Bush (1998: 139) explains, Carlisle gradually revised future editions until its focus became 'the responsible mission of poverty prevention'.

Substantial texts putting forward economic and social arguments on birth control would have reached only those middle- and upper-class readers who could afford them. Into the twentieth century, the greatest problem for proponents of birth control was how to bring this knowledge to the class whose lives they were most intended to improve: the working class. Place, a self-made man with a successful business, paid for handbills (leaflets) carrying pro-birth-control arguments and promoting the sponge and withdrawal to be distributed in English industrial cities during the 1820s (Cook, 2004: 56; Quinlan, 2002: 27). A feature of the later birth control movement was the production of cheap information pamphlets – describing contraceptive methods and providing the information necessary for their use – which were sold by mail order through advertising in the press.

Opposition to the Doctrine of Limiting Population

Michael Ryan's *Philosophy of Marriage* (1837) appears to be the first detailed condemnation of birth control by a medical doctor. Brody et al. (2009: 17–19) suggest that Ryan was born in Borrisoleigh, Tipperary, during the last decade of the eighteenth century and that, after training as a physician in Dublin and Edinburgh, he practised in Tipperary and Kilkenny before moving to London around 1827. There is no confirmation of Ryan's religious affiliation, but the authors cite evidence suggesting that he may have been a member of the Church of Ireland and note that it might have been more difficult to establish his career in London had he been Catholic. They acknowledge, however, that aspects of his writing on medical ethics reflect understanding of Catholic teaching (Brody et al., 2009: 62, n.72) and that some commentators suggest he had had a Catholic education.

Like the other two tracts discussed in this paper, Ryan's comments on contemporary society reflected personal perception more than scientific knowledge. For example, he expressed concerns that 'the passions are strong, modern morals too lax, and temptations in all large cities and towns very great' (Ryan, 1837: 16). His work may, however, have carried weight not only because of its author's profession but also because his publications were directed at medical students and therefore may have had some influence on future generations of doctors. Ryan addressed the question of female sexual activity early in the text, implying that women are by nature promiscuous and are restrained only by fear of pregnancy:

> None can deny that, if young women in general were absolved from the fear of consequences, the great majority of them, unless the comparatively few who are strictly moral and highly educated, would rarely preserve their chastity: illicit amours would be common and seldom detected – seduction would be facilitated, and prostitution become almost universal, unless among the virtuous and small class already excepted. (Ryan, 1837: 10)

Developed as a series of lectures, delivered at the North London School of Obstetrics, Ryan's work put forward arguments that were repeated into the twentieth century. Among them was that material advocating birth control runs counter to divine and natural law. Apparently unaware of their authorship, he decried the 'grossly immoral men' who distributed Place's handbills in major industrial cities. He suggested few would practise the 'abominable' methods they recommended, 'for all were contrary to the dictates of nature, to the precepts of revealed religion, to morals, to the divine and primitive demand to "go forth and multiply"' (Ryan, 1837: 9). He emphasised that the Christian position was 'that it is sinful in married persons to wish not to have a family, or to use any means of prevention, or to procure abortion at any period from the moment of conception' (Ryan, 1837: 16).

Ryan agreed that 'increase of family without means of sustenance' was a 'source of anxiety and pauperism', but noted that there was evidence neither of overpopulation 'in any civilised country' nor of food resources being insufficient (Ryan, 1837: 8). He also insinuated that those who feared overpopulation lacked faith in the power of the Almighty:

> It must be scarcely necessary to observe, that the doctrine of limiting population is based upon a most irregular doubt in the conservative power of the divine creator; which regulates, preserves, and reproduces the illimitable number of organised beings in the animal and vegetable kingdoms. (Ryan, 1837: 19)

Though expressing a concern that contraception would 'facilitate the prostitution of our daughters, sisters and wives', in that it would encourage sexual excess (Ryan, 1837: 9–10), he confidently predicted that birth control would be rejected by the population because:

> ... it is contrary to nature to wish that offspring should not be conceived or born, although a spurious modern philosophy of our day inculcates the contrary, and has even suggested unnatural means for the limitation of offspring. Such precepts and checks to population, being contrary to the dictates of nature and reason, will never be prioritised by the great mass of mankind. (Ryan, 1837: 118–19)

Ryan (1837: 118) rejected abstinence as well as contraception, arguing that '[t]hose united in wedlock cannot lawfully abstain from rendering conjugal rights on account of poverty or a multiplicity of children' and suggested that adultery – presumably by husbands – 'would be the common result'. He also cast cold water on the idea that early marriage would prevent sexual permissiveness (Ryan, 1837: 52), and was of the opinion that 'premature exertion of the genital function, or marriage at too early an age, must not only be injurious to the parents, but also to the constitution of the offspring' (Ryan, 1837: 31). Believing *coitus* depleted one's 'moral and physical powers', he suggested that 'the state of morals' was central to the well-being of empires (Ryan, 1837: 157).[3]

In a section of the book on marriage and mores in pre-Famine Ireland, however, Ryan related early marriage and Irish women's high reputation for 'chastity' (Ryan, 1837: 61). He suggested that such marriage customs among Ireland's close-to-destitute labouring class were 'in strict accordance with nature, though often injurious to health, population, and national prosperity' (Ryan, 1837: 59). He also appeared to accept the necessity of population control, but considered that 'the only effectual check to surplus population (that is, to the progress of population outstripping that of employment and comfortable maintenance) is the attachment of the working classes to the comforts and decencies of civilised life' (Ryan, 1837: 59–60). The words are interesting because they imply that Ryan's experience was that the comfortably-off had fewer children. He reported that farmers' sons and 'the few labourers who are in better circumstances than the generality of their class' delayed marriage until they met 'a woman who has also some little property or other means of assisting to maintain a family' (Ryan, 1837: 60). He appears to imply that if the poorest delayed marriage and conformed to the middle-class custom of marrying only when the means of keeping a family were available, their condition might improve. This is the regime we associate with the decades following the Famine of 1845–1848, when both late marriage and remaining single became alternative norms in Ireland. In 1837, however, Ryan presented the lives of the majority of the labouring classes as a picture of wretchedness:

> ... the hopes and ambition of the labouring class confined, as in Ireland, to the mere absence of hunger and cold ... the

labouring population will be found marrying when little more than children, though without a blanket to cover them, or a potatoe [*sic*] for the next day's meal, reckless imprudence and callous despair thus filling the land with hopeless destitution. (Ryan, 1837: 60)

Looking at why the Irish working class had large families, Ryan reported reasons that retained their validity into the twentieth century and throw light on why working-class couples did not consider birth control advantageous:

They say that their only support in old age, or in illness and under infirmities, are their children, and that they, therefore, marry young in order that their children may be old enough to maintain them, before their own strength begins to fail, which, in consequence of insufficient food, clothing, and other hardships, takes place at a much earlier age than in Great Britain. (Ryan, 1837: 60–61)

Ryan clearly recognised in Ireland the same extreme poverty among the poorest that had galvanised pro-birth-control arguments in England. The strength of his moral and religious position against contraception and belief that women were naturally promiscuous, his doubts that early marriage, with access to contraceptives, would reduce vice but might instead drain couples' strength, and his recognition that children were a valuable support in old age all contributed to his strident opposition.

On Irish female sexuality, Ryan provided one indication of how women's sexual behaviour was controlled. When referring to seduction and illegitimacy, he cited the 'severe denunciations of the Catholic clergy, the personal danger to women from their brothers and their relations for such offences, and the utter ruin of the women for having disgraced their family; unless their seducers marry them, which they are generally compelled to do both by their clergy or relations' (Ryan, 1837: 58–9). He added that:

The Roman Catholic doctrine enforced from the pulpit, in books and in the confessional, that impure thoughts and words are sinful and lead to violations of chastity, has the most powerful influence in preventing licentiousness, seduction, illegitimacy, and destruction of female virtue and happiness. (Ryan, 1837: 59)

Access to Birth Control Literature

The strictures described by Ryan must have inhibited engagement with birth control literature in Ireland, but Daly's (2012) reading of an Irish medical journal, the *Dublin Medical Press* (*DMP*), identified concern about its availability, at least in specific periods. In 1845, for example, she found that the journal estimated that as many as 120 advertisements relating to birth control appeared weekly in just seven daily newspapers in circulation in Ireland, representing three advertisements per day in each newspaper (Daly, 2012: 30). Some may have been imported papers, but if the publications were Irish, it would suggest that advertisers felt there might be some Irish interest in birth control. Daly also highlights an 1865 action by the *DMP* when it named Irish papers considered to be 'stained with obscenities' because they carried such advertising. She includes the *Dublin Evening Mail*, *Irish Times*, *Freeman's Journal* and some provincial papers amongst those listed (Daly, 2012: 31). Her research implies that by the mid-nineteenth century, readers of Irish publications may have had ready access to information on birth control, if they wished to investigate further.

Is there further evidence on access? Quinlan (2001:790) identified a 1921 letter to Marie Stopes, the twentieth-century birth control pioneer, from Irish feminist, Quaker and proponent of birth control Anna Haslam (1829–1922), who was by then in her nineties (British Library). It laid out a list of the literature she and her husband Thomas had collected, after their marriage in 1854, naming works published between 1856 and 1896. Titles of some works mentioned, such as *Life to Women* (1896) by Ellis Ethelheimer, gave little hint that they included information on contraception. Annie Besant's *Law of Population* (1884) was a publication the author updated as new contraceptive methods became available (Jütte, 2008: 121). Quinlan (2002: 52) mentions that the Haslams owned Albutt's *The Wife's Handbook* (1885), the first text to recommend the diaphragm (Jütte, 2008: 121–2). The example of the Haslams, taken in conjunction with Daly's findings, suggests that a middle-class, Irish-based couple with an interest in the issue could access a range of literature on marriage and birth control, at least between the 1860s and 1890s.

This is a reminder that Ireland did share in England's print culture, even if such material had to be requested by mail order.

Medical Knowledge or Obscenity?

Radical ideas on sexuality, on motherhood as oppressive to women and on the benefits of contraception were condemned as immoral, but there were additional concerns. Quinlan's biography of Anna and Thomas Haslam quotes a complaint made to Thomas Haslam by Cardinal Newman's brother, Francis S. Newman, regarding an advertisement in an English periodical for medical doctor Russell Thacher Trall's *Sexual Physiology* (1866), which promised 'drawings of the secret parts of men and women and what not beside' (Quinlan, 2002: 37). For example, it contains anatomical drawings of male sex organs (Trall, 1866: 15), of the vulva (Trall, 1866: 24) and cross-sections of the breast that one would expect to find in a medical textbook (Trall, 1866: 35). Having some understanding of physiology and of *coitus* was necessary for the practice of birth control, but material providing this information could also be regarded as obscene. While a British Obscene Publications Act – which applied also to Ireland – was passed in 1857, Heath (2010) observes that it was targeted at the 'penny papers and ephemera' considered dangerous to the moral welfare of the working class (Heath 2010: 59–60), rather than at substantial and expensive volumes, such as Trall's, which were available to the middle and upper classes.

Daly describes how the *DMP* had to grapple with the question of obscenity. It arose in connection with an important 1877 English prosecution, the Besant–Bradlaugh case, in which Annie Besant and Charles Bradlaugh were found guilty of publishing obscene material, and then acquitted on appeal. They had reissued American medical doctor Charles Knowlton's 1831 birth-control treatise, *The Fruits of Philosophy*, which recommended the condom, sponge and douching with a spermicidal solution of 'sulphate of zinc, alum or pearl ash' (Knowlton, 1891: 73[4]). The version produced by Besant and Bradlaugh was an affordable sixpenny pamphlet, potentially available to a wide, even a working-class, audience (Jütte, 2008: 120–21). Daly quotes the *DMP*'s argument, in a June 1877 edition, that works like Knowlton's might be read by a doctor or medical student with impunity, but that the same material would be obscene and likely to deprave in the hands of a youth with 'prurient curiosity' (Daly, 2012: 32–33). It was, as Daly suggests, a statement that positioned information on reproduction as a medical matter, but also as potentially dangerous in the wrong hands. It also reflected the definition of 'obscene' material, arrived at in a British 1868 legal ruling, that applied to Ireland as well as England. This held that whether printed matter was obscene depended on whether it was likely to 'deprave and corrupt those whose minds are open to such immoral influences'; and vulnerable groups, as Heath (2010: 51) points out, were considered to include 'children, women, the working-classes'.

An Irish Birth Control Pamphlet

Thomas and Anna Haslam owned Trall's *Sexual Physiology* (1866) and Quinlan (2002) has demonstrated that it influenced Thomas's own sincere and socially concerned 1868 birth control pamphlet: *The Marriage Problem*, by 'Oedipus', a pamphlet 'for gratuitous circulation amongst Adult Readers only' (Haslam, 1868: cover). In it he promoted the sponge as 'undoubtedly one method of preventing the birth of offspring that has long been known to medical men, and which has largely been put into practice in several countries in Europe, as well as in the United States of America' (Haslam, 1868: 6). As inserting the sponge might be 'revolting to the feelings of highly refined and conscientious women' (Haslam, 1968: 6), Haslam (1868: 7) also detailed something he considered ranked with the great discoveries of modernity: a 'safe' period method. Unfortunately, it was based on the misunderstanding that conception was most likely to occur during menstruation.

Haslam presented the safe period as 'nothing more offensive than the highest notions of propriety, – than the *entire abstinence from sexual intercourse during a certain limited portion of every month*' [Haslam's italics] (Haslam, 1968: 7) and an 'easy, inoffensive, and practical solution to one of the most urgent problems of the past generation' (Haslam, 1968: 7). He credited Trall (1866) as the source of his information (Haslam, 1868: 8) and footnoted an 'authority' who found that 'the exceptions to the rule, that conception occurs immediately before or after, or during menstruation, are not more than six or seven per cent' (Haslam, 1868: 8n). Haslam wrote confidently, but utterly wrongly, that:

The menstrual disturbance is the signal which nature herself gives that woman has become liable to impregnation. That impregnation may possibly take place either within a day or two of commencement of the menstrual discharge, or during its continuance, or during the subsequent period of greater or less extent throughout which the Ovum continues in the womb; but in ordinary circumstances it can take place at no other time. (Haslam, 1868: 8–9)

Quinlan (2002: 31) suggests that the circulation of Haslam's pamphlet was probably small, but that there is evidence it was distributed by J. Burns's Progressive Library in Camberwell, London. An English publisher friend wrote telling him about the flaw in his advice and enclosing a sample condom (Quinlan, 2002: 44). His mistake as to when conception was most likely to occur may, however, have been commonly made in this period when guesswork and unreliable information appear to have been wide-spread. As Quinlan (2002: 30) points out, approximate dates of the 'safe' period were not established until the 1920s. Jütte (2008: 151), for example, points to an 1873 work by Catholic theologian Auguste Joseph Lecomte of the University of Louvain, *Spontaneous Ovulation and Moral Theology*, that carried erroneous advice similar to Haslam's, and the publication of which was criticised by those within the Church who opposed birth control in any circumstances, including during a 'safe period'. The fact that such misinformation circulated is one reason why demographic statistics may tell us little about the extent to which attempts at birth control may have been made.

Like many who promoted birth control, the Haslams were deeply socially concerned. Quinlan (2002: 43) makes clear, first, that Thomas's aim was to improve the situation of 'the poor, the unhealthy and those young men "who are unable to control their passions"' and, second, that he sought to bring about moral, as much as physical, improvement in living conditions and saw the prac-tice of birth control as involving self-restraint. His 1868 pamphlet does sum up a range of social, moral and medical concerns. Central to the 'marriage problem' were parents whose 'pecuniary means' could not educate even one child, and those who might 'main-tain two or three children in health and comfort' but not carry 'the burden of eight or ten' (Haslam, 1868: 5). When it was impossible to maintain children without 'sinking into the condition of irretrievable pauperism' (Haslam, 1868: 13) – he placed wage-earners on ten to twelve shillings a week in this category[5] – he suggested parenthood should be delayed:

> Let them marry by all means as soon as they can support a wife; a good thrifty wife will be no material burden so long as she is not herself overloaded with the cares of an infant family; but let them have no children until they have saved some fifty or one hundred pounds for future wants, or until they have secured an advance of wages to fifteen shillings or one pound per week. (Haslam, 1868: 13)

Accumulating such savings would have been no mean feat for a working-class couple.

Haslam's work reflected a positive view of women and men, which contrasted with Ryan's, when he wrote of birth control making marriage more attractive and reducing vice, prostitution, the seduction of women and 'the deplorable prevalence of unnatural celibacy, which is the great fountainhead of this horrible evil' (Haslam, 1868: 14–15):

> When women are more generally shielded from the temptations of seduction by the reasonable prospect of a life of wedded happiness, there will not be one in a hundred – perhaps not one in a thousand – who will deliberately sacrifice that happiness to the brutal licence of a vicious life. And on the other hand, when men discover that they can obtain a virtuous sphere for the satisfaction of their sexual instincts, without condemning themselves to the misery of cheerless pauperism, the number of the systematic seducers of female innocence will be greatly diminished. (Haslam, 1868: 15)

The final lines of Haslam's pamphlet promoted birth control in terms of *'moral progress'* [Haslam's italics] (Haslam, 1868: 14) and summed up its benefits for 'so many sections of the human family': 'innocent victims of congenital disease'; 'young men of ardent passions'; 'men of narrow incomes' of all classes; the 'vast majority of workingmen'; 'an immense proportion of our female population'; and for the 'physical health and moral well-being of our whole future posterity' (Haslam, 1868: 15). His closing words called for birth control information to be 'speedily disseminated amongst all classes of our fellow-men' (Haslam, 1868: 15). Quinlan (2002: 58–61), however, explains how Haslam's 1872 book, *Duties of Parents*, promoted a different regime. It focused on abstinence, moral purity and social engineering (that society would benefit if those considered morally or physically unfit did not have children). In essence, it promoted repression of sexuality as character-building and sexual indulgence as inevitably resulting in degeneracy. This was thinking that appeared in tune with the sexual mores of the latter decades of the nineteenth century.

Haslam (1868: 14) had suggested that women would find birth control, 'almost without exception', a matter of 'universal interest'. Quinlan (2002: 33) makes the point that contraception may have been perceived as a mixed blessing by women in the nineteenth century, with feminists divided on the subject and some considering 'it made it more difficult for women to refuse husbands' unreasonable demands for sexual intercourse'. Considerations such as whether one experienced sexual relations as pleasurable, or as a marital duty to be endured, were presumably relevant to the attitudes of those women who had knowledge of contraception. In addition to religious and moral constraints, such personal concerns must have existed in Ireland and remained current into the twentieth century. As late as 1923 they were articulated by Professor (later Dame) Louise McIlroy, of the London School of Medicine for Women, a County Antrim-born Presbyterian, and the first woman to hold a chair of Obstetrics and Gynaecology in the United Kingdom. She argued that '[c]ontraceptives will not bring to women freedom but worse slavery in sexual matters, for they will remain the instruments of men's uncontrolled desires' and that '[b]irth control does not mean sex control, but rather unlimited indulgence without its responsibilities and consequences' (McIlroy, 1923: 34).

Fin de Siècle: Competing Discourses

Significantly, the Irish fertility transition (fall in birth rates) was not discernable until the early twentieth century (Ó Gráda and Duffy, 1995: 89–93), though a question may arise about whether this means that birth control was little practised or that methods attempted were so ineffective as not to register in statistics. The decline in the English birth rate is traceable to the period follow-ing the Besant–Bradlaugh trial, when British contraceptive retailers produced what Leathard referred to as an 'avalanche' of advertis-ing material, leaflets and pamphlets, a process that also deepened an association of birth control with commercialism (Leathard, 1980: 5). The methods recommended earlier in the century were free or cheap, if not particularly reliable. By the 1880s effective, though expensive, commercially manufactured contraceptives for women and men were available, including vaginal pessaries, the diaphragm, cervical caps and spermicides (Jütte, 2008: 121–2). These were effective provided one understood how to use them. Evidence suggests, however, that in England withdrawal remained the most commonly used method (Cook, 2004: 42). It seems likely that it was also attempted by some in Ireland.

Co-operation between partners in the use of contraception involved an adjustment to more equal gender roles, though female contraceptives, in particular, may have provided some women with a new level of personal control, even when husbands would not co-operate. Cultural taboos around having access to material considered obscene and lack of knowledge of how to obtain them must, however, have inhibited their use. Hardly an expert on female sexuality, Thomas Haslam had acknowledged that 'large numbers of our most elevated women' might have an 'invisible repugnance' to the use of 'artificial preventatives' (Haslam, 1868: 33). There may have been truth in the statement, but it gives rise to unanswerable questions about attitudes of women and networks of knowledge about contraception. Did those whose husbands refused to abstain, for example, and for whom pregnancy might mean death, passively await the inevitable or take steps – perhaps homemade – to protect themselves?

Other competing discourses and concerns came into play in Britain in the final decades of the nineteenth century that must have had some impact on Ireland. As Cook points out, radical arguments relating contraception and female sexual freedom had disappeared from pro-birth-control literature by this period (Cook, 2004: 61). It was an era of growing concern about venereal disease, prostitu-tion and the nation's health, and saw the establishment of vigilance associations and other pressure groups to campaign for amend-ments to legislation on vice and public morality and for greater protection of children and young women, who were perceived as under threat from male sexual aggression (Jackson, 2000). These campaigns brought concrete concerns about public morality to the fore, and demands for amendments to legislation on sexual crime and prostitution continued into the twentieth century. Heath's (2010) study of developments in nineteenth-century Britain, India and Australia places discussion of both sexuality and birth control in a context of imperial expansion, during which motherhood was increasingly represented as women's duty and healthy children as a national resource, particularly as concern grew about falling birth rates among the middle and upper classes, who practised birth control more than the working class – issues reflected in the Hemphill tract discussed below.

The Murderess of the Unseen: A Tract on Race-Suicide

In the early twentieth century a number of concerns were conflated in a 'race-suicide' scare. The term was used in a 1905 anti-birth control speech, 'On American Motherhood', delivered by President Theodore Roosevelt at that year's US National Congress of Mothers (Roosevelt, 1905). Gordon (2007: 87) suggests that this issue was current in the period 1905–1910. She identifies four strands of concern: that birth control was 'sinful'; that growing populations and 'large, stable families' were a national resource depleted by family limitation; that as birth control was practised by Northern European races they would become a minority, swamped and politically dominated by non-white races and the working class; that women's practice of fertility control constituted a 'rebellion' against their allocated gender role of motherhood.

Samuel Hemphill's 1908 treatise, *The Murderess of the Unseen: A Tract on Race-Suicide*, was published in Dublin and London and referred to the Roosevelt speech (Hemphill, 1908: 4). Though directed at both English and Irish readerships, this pamphlet contains what may be one of the earliest acknowledgments of the practice of birth control in Ireland. Hemphill's views on this matter are expressed in what today would be considered immoderate and racist language. The reference follows expressions of anxiety about falling population rates, the likely extinction of the French, American 'failure to propagate', Australia's being 'in a bad way' and 'appalling' English statistics (Hemphill, 1908: 3–4). It goes to the core of contemporary anxieties about 'race-suicide':

In Ireland, where this kind of thing might least be expected, I am informed that there is a certain amount of interference with the birth-rate. In all these and many other lands, certain practices, as expounded by a late M.P. [Charles Bradlaugh] and an equally leprous female [Annie Besant], are doing incalculable harm. Indeed, the Chinese and the Negroes will yet have this world to themselves, if we don't look out. (Hemphill, 1908: 4)

Hemphill (1908: 1) condemned those 'wicked doctors and druggists' who assured women that birth control was safe and quoted a range of ailments attributed to contraception, including 'nervous enfeeblement, impaired mental vigour, fibrous tumours, ovarian diseases, uterine cancer …'. He similarly reproved 'mealy-mouthed clergymen' who failed to speak against its practice (Hemphill, 1908: 2). Instead of scholarly argument on natural law, he used simplistic terms, perhaps drawn from a sermon. Positing that the 'generative process' of 'vegetables or animals' remained utterly natural, he suggested it was 'repulsive' that 'artifices unknown to all other orders of God's creatures' were being employed by couples whose marital responsibility and duty to state and race was procreation:

Coition is one of the ordinary laws of nature; therefore we would draw the conclusion that it ought to be quite natural. But when we take marriage into consideration, how much more enhanced is this process. It is then regulated by religion. It is for the most exalted ends. Married people are doing their duty, and a religious duty. They are also doing a duty to the State and to the Race. The pleasure annexed to this is a subordinate idea. (Hemphill, 1908: 5)

Giving some indication of the class to which his arguments were addressed, and his distance from the reality of working-class lives, Hemphill (1908: 7) recommended that 'self-denial as regards amusements, travelling, food, drink, servants, carriages, and other such expenses' would allow couples to support larger families. He reassured readers that 'God never creates a need without creating the means of supplying it' (Hemphill, 1908: 7). Hemphill did, however, approve of abstinence – which he characterised as 'living apart' – as a means of fertility control and rejected as 'a lie' the argument that this involved 'just as much an interference with nature' as contraception (Hemphill, 1908: 7).

Hemphill was particularly dismissive of women's concerns about intensive motherhood. He considered *'thoroughly selfish'* [Hemphill's italics] arguments about pregnancy resulting in ill-health or *'life-long debility'* [Hemphill's italics] (Hemphill, 1908: 8). To the view that childbearing *'tied down'* [Hemphill's italics] a woman, he responded, 'And what else is her destiny? Does not St. Paul advise wives to be "keepers at home"?' (Hemphill, 1908: 9). Hemphill (1908: 10) accepted fear of parturition as 'the only really colourable excuse for a woman wishing to avoid her obligations, especially if she has had several very bad confinements' and as one reason why 'a man should spare her, as far as he can'. The latter words are a reminder of women's subordination and disempowerment in a period when being sexually available to her husband was considered a wife's duty. Still, he urged such women to 'be brave, and go through what so many countless millions of other women have had to go through. Let her leave herself in the hands of God, and hope for the best' (Hemphill, 1908: 10).

Making clear his disapproval of the activities of a younger generation of women, the generation whose rebellion against assigned gender roles caused concern, Hemphill wrote: 'I dislike nothing so much as to see young mothers jumping about at rough and boisterous games, rushing in automobiles, careering on bikes, and generally laying aside a matronly appearance and behaviour' (Hemphill, 1908: 9). Citing 'wearing of high-heeled boots, tight lacing, too much bicycling, and so forth ...' as threats, he recommended that schoolgirls be trained to avoid activities that would 'interfere with maternity at a later age' (Hemphill, 1908: 16). Hemphill also recorded an argument that women found it humiliating to appear pregnant in the presence of men, presumably because pregnancy implied sexual activity and a degree of shame attached to this. He suggested that 'no man of proper feeling would take notice of such things' and, indeed, that most would not notice at all (Hemphill, 1908: 9). Presumably reflecting contemporary middle-class practice, he added that 'in any case ... ladies in that way naturally keep aloof from much male society. They do not deliberately choose to promenade before club windows where unemployed gentlemen are idly gazing'[6] (Hemphill, 1908: 9).

The discussion of contraception concluded by naming users as 'race murderers' and un-Christian and calling on God to 'forgive and convert them' (Hemphill, 1908: 11). As the title of the treatise suggests, however, the full weight of his wrath and direst warnings were kept for those contemplating back-street abortions – a position that may imply contemporary concern about these matters. He suggested that abortionists should be 'hanged publicly', that *fifty per cent* [Hemphill's italics] of their clients died and that 'most of the others lose their health permanently' (Hemphill, 1908: 13). Hemphill characterised women who sought abortions as:

> Wives who have got tired of conception: who love dress, good figures, and gaiety? Or else ... the unfaithful wife, who is not exactly in a position to welcome her husband home after a prolonged absence ... And what shall I say of deflowered maids? They are the most numerous class of 'patients.' They will do anything to avoid disgrace. (Hemphill, 1908: 13)

As with Ryan, Hemphill's professional standing as a churchman gave him licence to speak as an expert on matters of reproduction and women's behaviour. Yet his treatise also reflects personal opinion, contemporary race and class prejudices and anxieties about emancipated women rejecting motherhood. Most notably, it appears directed at an upper- and middle-class readership, completely ignoring the impoverished groups that advocates of birth control believed might benefit most from contraception. This focus presumably reflected both the social circles in which Hemphill moved and those within which expensive but effective contraception was most likely to be practised. It is a reminder, too, that concomitant with concern about race suicide was an anxiety that limiting family size might result in a form of class suicide, depleting the middle and upper classes and making them vulnerable to being over-run by the working classes.

Conclusion

From its beginnings in the 1820s, knowledge of birth control and the literature through which it was disseminated was condemned as sinful, evil and obscene, as permitting the shirking of marital duties, as facilitating promiscuity and as a danger to social and moral order. Ryan's treatise reflected these concerns. The dissemination of information on contraception did threaten a patriarchal social hierarchy in which women were defined as subordinate and their sexuality and reproduction controlled by religious and social strictures, enforced by the families of unmarried girls and the husbands of married women. Modest challenges to women's assigned gender roles in the late nineteenth and early twentieth centuries coincided with declining European populations, and provoked a panic that restricting births would endanger the family, the State and the white upper and middle classes. Hemphill's pamphlet, with its criticisms of contemporary arguments for limiting family size, reflected these anxieties and implies that they were current in some circles in Ireland in the early twentieth century. Research by Daly (2012) and Quinlan (2002) suggests that some Irish readers may have had access to birth control information during the nineteenth century, while Hemphill's reference to some Irish couples restricting family size by the early twentieth century may be significant. So too may have been the influence in Ireland of publicity around the Bradlaugh and Besant case, referred to by both the *DMP* and Hemphill. Haslam's pamphlet indicates awareness, in the 1860s, of arguments that had circulated in England since the 1820s on the benefits of limiting family size for the poor and for women, and of information on contraceptive methods – even if he repeated inaccurate information on the safe period. An understanding that much of the information on birth control in circulation before the late 1870s was unreliable, and that effective contraceptives were expensive, strongly suggests that demographic statistics may not reflect attempts to restrict pregnancies. Further research is required to establish the extent to which pro-birth control discourse may have percolated into Irish consciousness.

Notes

[1]   Brody et al. (2009) is a jointly authored commentary on selected works by Ryan. It places these works in historical perspective and provides a useful biographical summary (Brody et al., 2009: 17–33).

[2]   Carlisle's texts of the 1825 essay 'What Is Love?' and an 1826 edition of *Every Woman's Book*, with notes on changes made in an 1828 version, are reproduced in full in Bush (1998: 55–80 and 81–104), and Bush examines

both the influences on Carlisle's writing and the contemporary impact of the text.

3   Ryan does offer contrasting opinions on early marriage in the book. At a later point, he relates it to healthy offspring when the parties have been chaste prior to marrying (Ryan, 1837: 157).

4   The edition cited is an 1881 San Francisco 'Readers' Library' edition, but the introduction implies that it is a copy of a reprint issued immediately after the 1877 trial. *See:* <http://archive.org/stream/fruitsphilosoph00 knogoog#page/n42/mode/2up> [accessed 4 October 2012].

5   A rough calculation of the purchasing power of 10–12 shillings in 1868 in today's values suggests figures of £37–£44. (This was calculated using Officer and Williamson, Measuring Worth website, which is available at <http://www.measuringworth.com> [accessed 4 October 2012].)

6   He means 'gentlemen's' clubs here and in this context the word 'unemployed' means unoccupied rather than jobless.

CHAPTER 2

Embodied Sexualities: Exploring Accounts of Irish Women's Sexual Knowledge and Sexual Experiences, 1920–1970

Máire Leane

Introduction

This chapter explores the ways in which sexuality has been under-stood, embodied and negotiated by a cohort of Irish women through their lives. It is based on qualitative data generated as part of an oral history project on Irish women's experiences of sexuality and reproduction during the period 1920–1970.[1] The interviews, which were conducted with 21 Irish women born between 1914 and 1955,[2] illustrate that social and cultural discourses of sexuality as secretive, dangerous, dutiful and sinful were central to these women's interpretative repertoires around sexuality and gender. However, the data also contains accounts of behaviours, experiences and feelings that challenged or resisted prevailing scripts of sexuality and gender. Drawing on feminist conceptualisations of sexuality and embodiment (Holland et al., 1994; Jackson and Scott, 2010), this chapter demonstrates that the women's sexual subjectivities were forged in the tensions that existed between normative sexual scripts and their embodied experiences of sexual desires and sexual and reproductive practices. While recollections of sexual desire and pleasure did feature in the accounts of some of the women, it was the difficulties experienced around sexuality and reproduction that were spoken about in greatest detail.[3] What emerges clearly from the data is the confusion, anxiety and pain occasioned by the negotiation of external demands and internal desires and the contested, unstable nature of both cultural power and female resistance.

Theoretical and Contextual Framework

Social constructionist accounts of sexuality have challenged notions of sexuality as a product of innate drives and replaced them with conceptualisations of sexuality as historically and culturally constructed.[4] This has prompted explorations of the processes through which language and culture provide the raw material of sexual subjectivity and of the frames of reference through which experiences are understood and interpreted.[5] Conceptualisations of sexuality as socially constructed have impacted on feminist theorising, most significantly by challenging essentialist understandings of the body and sexuality as pre-given or pre-determined. In her analysis of feminist theorising of the body, Brook (1999: 2) associates the early 1990s with an explosion of feminist work on the body, the aim of which was to understand how female bodies are inscribed with and constituted by cultural discourses of what it means to be sexual.[6] This type of feminist scholarship, frequently described as corporeal feminism, promotes an approach that eschews a mind/body split and explores instead how a sense of self is produced through discourse.[7] Canning, writing in 1999, points out that the discursive body featured prominently in the previous decade of gender history, influenced in no small part by the work of Michel Foucault (1981) and by the increasing dominance of post-structuralist and postmodern approaches.[8] Foucault's (1981: 152) understandings of the body as a site where power both operates and is resisted and his conceptualisation of the micro techniques through which power plays out in localised sites have provided feminists with useful insights into the ways in which individual bodies in specific locations are regulated and disciplined.[9]

Some feminists express concern about how a focus on the discursive or symbolic body may limit our potential to understand the embodiedness of the material body. Holland et al. (1994: 21) challenge the conceptual dualism between the material, the biological and the socially constructed female body and argue that, in practice, the social and physical bodies are entwined in complex ways. Examining how young women negotiate sexuality, they argue that sexuality is gendered, embodied and social (Holland et al., 1994: 22). Jackson and Scott (2010) provide a similar critique of more abstract, philosophically informed postmodern considerations of sexual subjectivities and the reflexive project of making the sexual self (see also Giddens, 1991; 1994). They suggest that such work can take attention away from the very mundane practices, activities and relationships of everyday social life within which embodied sexuality actually occurs. They contend that sexuality is 'not limited to "sex acts" or to sexual identities but involves feelings and relationships, the ways in which we are or are not defined as sexual by others and the ways in which we so define ourselves' (Jackson and Scott, 2010: 2). As such, they call for a multidimensional understanding of the 'sociality of sexuality (structure, practice, meaning, subjectivity)' (Jackson and Scott, 2010: 3).

Their approach is heavily influenced by the work of Gagnon and Simon (1974), and in particular they draw on Gagnon and Simon's concept of 'sexual scripts' (Gagnon and Simon, 1974: 23). Gagnon and Simon suggest that bodies, feelings and acts are not in themselves sexual and only become so when socio-cultural scripts confer sexual significance on them. Three dimensions of scripting have been identified.[10] The first refers to cultural scenarios that indicate what any given culture interprets as sexual, in other words a culturally specific, shared body of knowledge about sexuality. The second dimension focuses on interpersonal scripts, defined by Simon (1996: 41) as 'scripts for behaviour in specific contexts'. These scripts were described by Jackson and Scott (2010) as emerging from and being deployed within everyday encounters, discussions of sex and negotiation of sexual activities. Finally, intrapsychic scripting (Simon, 1996: 44) refers to the individual, reflexive processing of sexual thought and desire and is informed by and informs interpersonal scripts. In this chapter we will draw on these various dimensions of cultural scripts to explore the interviewees' accounts and try to make sense of how they experienced and negotiated their material, biological bodies in the context of prevailing discursive/social constructions of female sexuality.

Identifying sources that offer insights into individual, lived, embodied experiences of sexuality is, as Canning (1999: 501) pointed out, challenging for the researcher. In contrast, a wide range of written sources (religious, medical, legal, scientific, etc.) exists that can facilitate the charting of discursive constructions of the body, and indeed of sexuality. The discursive construction of female sexuality in Ireland has been considered in a number of contexts, including: in explorations of constructions of femininity and female sexuality in colonial discourses (Moane, 1996; Thapar-Bjorkert and Ryan, 2002); in discourses of nation-building (Valiulis, 1995; Gray and Ryan, 1997; McAvoy, 1999; Ryan, 2002a, 2002b, 2008; O'Connor, 2003); and in policy-making and governance practices (Smith, 2004; Luddy, 2007a; Crowley and Kitchin, 2008). To date, fewer studies have been undertaken that provide data about the ways in which sexuality was experienced, enacted and discussed in concrete social situations. Drawing on qualitative interviews with thirteen women born in Ireland between 1923 and 1940 and the biographies of Irish women who grew up in that period, Lyder (2003) considers girls' pre-courtship experiences of sexual exploration. Hilliard's (2003) interviews with 32 women chart their perceptions of changes in family life in Cork City between 1975 and 2000, and also provide extensive insights into the women's experiences of and attitudes to fertility control, marital sexuality and clerical attitudes towards women. These studies are utilised throughout this essay to provide a contextual background for discussion of the data presented.[11]

Cultural Scenarios: Dominant Discourses and Interpretative Frameworks

Gagnon and Simon's (1974) concept of cultural scenarios calls attention to what any given society interprets as sexual, and in this section of the chapter we will explore what the women's accounts reveal about the shared knowledge of sexuality that prevailed in their youth. In other words, what socio-cultural discourses or resources did the women have to help them make sense of the sexual?

As discussed by Kiely in Chapter 12, 'Lessons in Sexual Citizenship: The Politics of Irish School-Based Sexuality Education', the narratives clearly indicate that during their adolescence the women were denied explicit information about sexual matters. A lack of concrete knowledge about menstruation, copulation, conception and pregnancy was reported by all but two of the 21 women interviewed. Hilliard's work (2003: 31–5) and Lyder's work (2003: 77–9) reveal a similar lack of knowledge about sexual matters.[12] The absence of a vocabulary with which to speak about sexual matters was mentioned in many of the interviews. Alice,[13] a working-class woman born in the early 1930s, commented that 'there wasn't even a word for sex', while Hannah, a woman of similar age to Alice, noted that 'you couldn't mention sex' and that 'there was a big mystery about all of it'.[14] Mothers and other female relatives and neighbours conspired to exclude young women from conversations and experiences that might provide information about sexual or reproductive issues. Joan, who was born in 1932, recalled that: 'If our mothers or grandmothers were talking about somebody who was about to produce a baby or whatever, we were put out straight away and told to go and play.' Nuala, again of similar age, eloquently described the impact that the absence of clear information about sexual matters had on her early understandings of sexuality.

> My mother was a very direct woman but one of the things my mother was not very good at, was talking about sexuality ... I was never really told anything, nothing from the nuns, nothing, occasional inferences that were actually more confusing than anything and I can tell you that was fairly common. I suppose the way I can best summarise it, what I learnt, I learnt from a *negative* perspective rather than a positive one, in the sense that, I pieced together from people, *not talking* about what *actually happened* but talking about the *implications* or the dangers of the whatever it was, you know.[15]

[Italics indicate the emphasis put on certain words by the narrator.]

Despite the lack of empirical information, inferences to sexual and reproductive issues were commonplace and most of the respondents recalled ways in which risk or danger was alluded to by mothers, teachers and clerics. For many of the narrators the vague warnings to 'mind themselves', issued primarily by mothers, served only to generate confusion. Anne recalled her mother's caution about engagement with boys: '"you are grown up now and don't let the boys interfere with you." I didn't know what she meant but I couldn't ask.' Rose's reaction to her mother's instruction in the late 1950s revealed a similar naïvety: 'All she ever said was mind yourself and we were on the bike and we thought it was mind yourself in case you'd fall off, that is true.' Lyder (2003: 79) found similar evidence of obtuse warnings and noted the anxiety that the lack of clarity caused for some of her interviewees. Implicit in the maternal warnings was the attribution of responsibility for sexual control to young women, who were admonished to conceal and indeed control the sexual allure or sexual dimensions of their own bodies. Rose recalled a clerical warning against looking in the mirror too many times as this gave rise to vanity, while Ellie remembered being taught at school in the 1960s that 'you weren't to wear a dress that would expose your cleavage' and that:

> ... you had to make sure you were clean and that touching certain parts of your body was a sin and I'll never forget – I was very naïve – I was in the bathroom and looking at my body, I was examining myself and wondering what were they talking about! Nothing was set out, but you learnt what was allowed and not acceptable.

Discourses promoting the need for modesty and highlighting the risk associated with the sexualised female body were paralleled by a vociferous religious discourse of extra-marital sexual activity as sinful. Inglis (1997) has noted that in Ireland, up until the last three decades of the twentieth century, sexuality was deployed through a thematic of sin. All of the narrators had clear memories of the clerical pronouncements disseminated through the mass, the mission, the confessional and the school, with a view to regulating practices, and indeed thoughts, of a sexual nature. References to 'company keeping', 'occasions of sin', 'close dancing', 'passionate kissing', 'impure thoughts' and 'immoral thoughts' punctuate the women's descriptions of clerical pronouncements on sexual matters. The confessional, as noted by Inglis (1997: 11), was a key site for the deployment of clerical power and almost all of the narrators recounted stories that highlighted the interrogatory nature of clerical questioning about sexual behaviour.

The revelation of sexual misconduct in the semi-public forum of the confessional was a source of anxiety, not primarily because of the sinfulness of the behaviour itself but because of the loss of social standing that would follow public revelation of it. Joan specifically highlights this dimension of confession:

> They [priests] would say, 'were you kissing? or were you doing this, were they touching you? …what kind of kiss?' The

priest would ask you in the confessional so you'd be ashamed of your life, like, telling your confession to the priest because there'd be a crowd outside ... if the least thing was wrong, they would embarrass you in front of people.

The clerical castigation of extra-marital sexual activity as sinful was reinforced by a parental discourse, which further depicted such practices as dangerous and a potential source of family shame and individual ruin. Madge, referring to her adolescence in the 1940s, emphasised the importance of paternal and, in particular, maternal surveillance: 'Most of my friends that time feared their mothers. Mother was the one you feared, more than God.' Significantly, all of the respondents recalled being aware of stories about young women who became pregnant outside marriage and disappeared from the community. Indeed, they could all identify the mother-and-baby home in their region. As Nancy noted: 'If a girl got into trouble, they were taken away to a home. You were put away and nobody knew about it.'

The culture of clerical regulation of sexual practices was not limited to the unmarried. Catholic dictates relating to the use of contraception within marriage and to the practice of churching were hugely significant in influencing sexual and gender scripts available to married women.[16] Sheila highlighted the strength of clerical discourses around contraception: 'It was a mortal sin if you avoided having children, you were condemned. Everybody told us that.' As discussed later in the chapter, fertility control was a key area of anxiety and stress for women, while churching was experienced as a demeaning practice.

These memories described by the narrators indicate that as young women they were exposed to a culturally specific, shared body of knowledge about sexuality. The prevailing set of discourses imbued sexuality and the female body with meaning, and this social construction of sexual meaning underpinned a range of material practices that were central to the social management of female sexuality. As Holland et al. (1994: 22) observed: 'The material body and its social construction are entwined in complex and contradictory ways which are extremely difficult to disentangle in practice.' However, Gagnon and Simon's (1974) exhortation to examine the interpersonal scripts that emerge from and are deployed within everyday encounters, discussions of sex and negotiation of sexual activities provides the opportunity to explore the extent to which the women internalised, accepted and acted upon prevailing constructions of sexuality.

Interpersonal Scripts: Negotiating Sexual Discussion and Behaviour

In their discussion of interpersonal scripting, Gagnon and Simon (1974: 23) emphasise that cultural scripts, while providing an interpretative framework within which individuals make sense of sexuality, are not fixed or limited. Each person engages with such scripts from their unique biographical position and in their everyday social interactions and relations they construct their individual, personal sense of their own sexual body and sexual self. In this section we will consider the ways in which individual women engaged with cultural scripts in their own lives. Drawing on the conception of the body as a site for the effects of power and as a site for the exercise of power (Foucault, 1981: 152), we shall consider the ways in which women negotiated the power relations that surrounded sexuality.

Sexual Knowledge

The very limited nature of the information women had regarding conception, sexual practices and giving birth was highlighted in their narratives. Young women did, however, seek out information from a myriad of sources and in a variety of contexts. Helen recalled her efforts to gain information about sexual issues through newspaper reports in the early 1950s: 'If the paper was hidden from me, I knew there was something on it then that wasn't suitable for my eyes. I used to root it out and read about it, but didn't understand anything about it.' For most women, what information they received came from older cousins, friends or work colleagues; acquaintances who had been to England were also a good source of information. One woman recalled getting a book from her cousin that explained menstruation, sexual intercourse and reproduction and another was conscious that 'books would have been circulating'. Overall, though, the narratives suggest that prior to their marriages most of the women were unclear about how sexual intercourse, or indeed conception, occurred.

This lack of information had quite profoundly negative implications for some. Joan's level of knowledge about reproduction was so limited that when she became pregnant at the age of 28 and experienced morning sickness, she did not realise she was pregnant:

> When I got married and when I got pregnant, I was three months pregnant and I said to this woman, 'it must have been the turnips I ate' and I didn't know, she knew, I never knew what was going to happen at 28 years [of age]. You had terrible concepts about going into hospital and the fear of the unknown.

Like most of the narrators, Joan attributed her mother's reluctance to discuss the body and sexuality to embarrassment and noted that the deference to parents in that era precluded questioning by young people:

> Your mother would be too embarrassed to discuss it and you wouldn't ask, you weren't frightened of them, you just didn't ask ... It was tough-going 'cause I had no one to ask and even after getting married had no one to ask, you didn't have anyone to share your problems.

Robinson et al. (2004: 419), in their study of attitudes to and experiences of sexuality among English women between the wars, found a similar reluctance among families to discuss or provide information about sexuality. They argue that maintaining 'a reserve, or even coyness with respect to sexual talk and practice' was seen as a sign of respectability. In this way the potential of home and family to provide a resource for women in relation to sexuality and reproduction was constrained.

Two narrators did identify key adult figures in their lives who not only provided them with information about sexuality but did so in a way that challenged prevailing cultural portrayals of it as shameful and dangerous. While on a social work course in London in the mid-1950s, Nuala was provided with a lot of information by the mother of a classmate. This woman was Irish, but had been living in London for many years and working as a journalist: 'She told me a lot of things that I didn't know ... and was very open and ... I think I learned more from her, albeit that she was an Irish woman, but she was a liberated Irish woman.' Ellie, who was born in the early 1950s, explained that her attitude to sexuality was strongly influenced by her father, despite the fact that he was absent during most of her childhood and adolescence because he worked in England:

> ... he was always proud that I was a girl, you know, taking awful good care of me and I remember it was to do with menstruation ... I saw the blood and I nearly died ... and I came home and I told my mother and my mother was making it an awful big secret, I'll always remember that ... and my father was in the kitchen and he asked what all the fussing was about and I heard him say, 'but isn't that beautiful', he said, 'she's growing to be a young woman' ... and I was boosted by that ... And that was good because otherwise, coming from my mother, it would have been awful because my mother would have been very negative by the way, a very negative person ... My father took me aside after that, and he explained a few things to me and you know that really normalised it for me. That was unusual now, remember ... but you remember he had been in England.

The positive impact of Ellie's father's attitude towards menstruation was undermined by another encounter that damaged Ellie's confidence in her body. Her uncle's reaction to her pubescent body provides a striking example of patriarchal power and of the male appropriation of the right to define what constitutes a suitable female body: 'I had hairy legs and my uncle said to my mother that I should have stockings on those hairy legs and I was awfully self-conscious about it and I thought it was an awful thing, and I mean they probably weren't that bad at all.'

The extracts above highlight how denial of information about the workings of the body and the ascription of negative meaning to physical changes in the developing female body constitute practices of power through which femininity and female sexuality are constructed (Holland et al., 1994: 24). The reaction of Ellie's uncle incited her to lose confidence in and become embarrassed by her body, which was subsequently subjected to regulation through concealment under tights. The ways in which such practices can inscribe a particular model of femininity and sexuality on the female body become apparent in the following section.

Negotiating Embodied Sexuality

There is much evidence in the women's accounts to suggest that the cultural valorisation of modesty and the incitement to conceal the body and diminish its sexual attractiveness impacted on the ways in which they perceived and managed their emerging sexuality. So, too, did the attribution of responsibility to women in relation to upholding standards of sexual propriety. Deirdre, who was born into a middle-class family in Limerick in 1923, explained that she was advised by her mother to 'keep her dignity', while the nuns teaching her recommended that she remain 'Mary-like'. These instructions resulted in Deirdre developing what she described as 'an artificial preciousness about modesty and virginity' and 'a scared ignorance' about sexual matters. This ignorance made her very wary of engaging in relationships and when she did so, her keen sense that 'the girl was the one who had to draw the line' hindered her engagement in and enjoyment of sexual practices. Ellie, who was born almost thirty years later, acknowledged that she too was keenly conscious of the responsibility of women to resist male sexual advances. She pointed out that the discourses around sexuality to which she was exposed in her youth resulted in her perceiving that '… women were the sex object' and had to take responsibility for rebuffing male sexual advances. Ellie emphasised in her account how strongly she was aware of the perception that 'the girl was the sinner, the man was following his natural tendencies'.[17] Nancy, commenting on extra-marital pregnancy, also acknowledged the double standard in terms of the treatment of women who were found to have transgressed: 'And I mean, the fellow could be local and all, but the girl had to go away, the girl had to go away, that was very sad, I think.'

For Nuala, the cultural imperative to conceal and desexualise the body and the understanding of sexuality as a negative and dangerous force was challenged when she moved to London in the mid-1950s at the age of twenty. She was attending college and sharing accommodation in a London hostel with young Italian women, and they possessed a very different understanding of femininity and sexuality:

It was totally different. What was riveting about them [the Italian women] was, you know, as far as they were concerned, sexuality was something brilliant ... it was *absolutely wonderful*, and you as a woman would benefit greatly ... you know, you exploited your sexuality – they didn't use those kind of words – and you put all this effort into enhancing your femininity in order to acquire all of these *wonderful* men, and they thought men were really wonderful.

[Italics indicate the emphasis put on certain words by the narrator.]

Nuala's description of the Italian women's enthusiastic attitude towards sexuality and their enjoyment of their femininity and sexual allure is in marked contrast with the sense of negativity and prohibition that had shaped her perceptions of sexuality in Ireland. Furthermore, her amazement at the effort the Italian women put into the enhancement of their physical appearance suggests that such practices of self-beautification conflicted with the cultural practices of female self-presentation in Ireland:

I was fascinated, at *how long* the Italian girls took getting ready before they went out on a date. [Laughter] It was hilarious, and they were *super-looking* girls, but they spent *all day nearly*. I mean, they curled their hair ... they *both* spent absolutely *hours, hours and hours* getting ready, you know, and everything had to be perfect.

[Italics indicate the emphasis put on certain words by the narrator.]

Nuala's experience provides an example of what Robinson et al. (2007: 418), drawing on Nast (1998), refer to as the naturalisation of heterosexuality through space. National, regional and indeed family spaces construct and reproduce norms of sexuality, and shifting between such spaces can serve to highlight differences in the prevailing paradigm of what is considered acceptable and normal sexual, and indeed gender, behaviour. This understanding of the spatial dimension of sexuality will be drawn on later to make sense of perceptions of the sexual behaviour of Irish women who emigrated to England.

Negotiating Sexual Desire and Sexual Behaviour

Despite the negativity of the dominant sexual scripts described by the narrators, their stories also articulate discourses of sexual desire, curiosity and pleasure. Alice described the attraction she and her peers had to the local young men: 'we used to be coming down from the park and we used to admire the guys'. All of the women recounted stories of courtships, which in many cases were conducted without the knowledge of parents. However, while the narrators clearly resisted many clerical and parental dictates around sexual practices, many of them emphasised that sexual expression was often accompanied by anxiety. Limited information about sexual and reproductive matters, the absence of reliable contraception, clerical dictates against its use and a generalised sense of fear about sexual activity becoming public knowledge all impacted on decisions about engagement in sexual activity and hampered sexual enjoyment. As Molly observed: 'Fear used to keep us on the straight and narrow and I don't think that's healthy. You would be going out with a lad for weeks before you'd even let him kiss you.' The keen awareness that had been instilled in the narrators of the fate that would befall anyone who got pregnant outside marriage was a particularly strong disincentive to pre-marital sexual intercourse. Dolores recalled, with sorrow, the consequences of extra-marital pregnancy for a woman who was on her midwifery course in Dublin in the early 1950s: 'That was the end of her course … She defied everything, you know. She was always defying the rules … yeah, that was her. So what happened to her after, I don't know.'[18]

Even engagement in restrained sexual practices, such as kissing, was not unproblematic. Ellie recalled that when she was dropped home by the young man who had been approved by her uncles and her mother to take her to her first dance, she '… wouldn't even let him kiss me'. At a subsequent dance she recalled that 'the guy kissed me and I thought I was pregnant! I was as innocent, I am not joking you. Somebody must have said, you know how they instil fear in you and we all got that. I enjoyed the kiss!' This tension between pleasure and fear featured in many accounts of sexual behaviour, with sexual expression frequently being tempered with anxiety. Two months before her wedding, in the late 1950s, Patricia confessed to a visiting priest during the parish mission that she was 'passionate kissing' with her boyfriend. The priest refused to give her absolution unless she promised to terminate the relationship: 'I came out of confession without absolution and came home in floods of tears'. Patricia's father, upon hearing the story, declared her to be 'a bloody fool' for confessing such information and took her to the local priest, who gave her absolution without dispute. Patricia's account is instructive in that it reveals the mechanisms of power that translated the private sexual behaviour of a young woman into a clerical and parental matter. It also provides insights into the willingness of some parents to challenge clerical power.

While Patricia was distressed over the refusal of absolution, most of the women indicated that fear of sinning was not a strong deterrent to engaging in a certain amount of sexual activity with boyfriends. Concern about sinfulness did appear to dominate in one area of sexual conduct, however, namely the prevention of pregnancy within marriage, and it proved a significant factor in women's decision-making about birth control. Abstinence from sexual relations appears to have been a common form of birth control, but one older interviewee indicated that abstinence was not an unproblematic option. Sheila, who married in the early 1930s at the age of eighteen, highlighted how for herself and her contemporaries, religious, legal and patriarchal forces combined to limit the control they had over their sexual lives:

> ... it was a *mortal sin* if you avoided a family, you were *condemned, absolutely* ... they [women of her generation] knew nothing about contraception, what to do or what not to do, they just had them [children], you had to have them, if you avoided, you were nearly *excommunicated* from the Church at that time, *you just had to,* there was no two ways about it, even if you didn't want to, you had to, ... *you had to obey your husband* ... that was one of the vows you took at marriage, you see.[19]

[Italics indicate the emphasis put on certain words by the narrator.]

The imperative to obey one's husband was also alluded to by some respondents in Hilliard's study (2003: 36), who reported the reluctance of certain husbands to co-operate with the period of abstinence required when using the Billings, or 'safe period', method of contraception.[20] As one would expect, the behaviour of husbands appears to have varied in this regard. While acknowledging the strain abstinence or use of the 'safe period' could put on a marriage, Alice noted that in her experience husbands were accepting of the situation: 'Nobody's husband wandered off anywhere. They never went with anybody else. They were the same as ourselves.'

What the women's accounts of birth control also reveal is chang-ing practices regarding fertility control. The majority of the younger women interviewed, whose children were born between the early and mid-1960s, indicated that they were actively seeking to limit their families and that in some cases, surprisingly, it was their mothers or mothers-in-law who advised and encouraged them to do so. As Alice remarked: 'I remember my mother-in-law telling me to abstain and I remember my mother would say, "you've enough now".' It would appear that at least some of the older generation of women, who had experienced the hardship associated with lack of fertility control and the rearing of large families, did not desire the same conditions for the next generation of women.

It is noteworthy, however, that all of the women who were practising fertility control – primarily through abstinence, *coitus interruptus* (described by the women as 'withdrawal') and the use of the Billings or safe period/rhythm method – continued to attend confession and to face the censure of priests who castigated such behaviour. Hilliard (2003: 38) found similar behaviour among her respondents. Awareness that their actions constituted sin in the eyes of the Church was a significant source of stress among the women interviewed for this study. As Noreen noted: 'In the early days of my marriage, I didn't know about the Billings method, contracep-tion was withdrawal, but that was a sin then.' A priest 'blew the ears off' Joan in the mid-1960s when she confessed to avoidance of pregnancy. Even Rose, who had lost two children and was under medical advice to avoid further pregnancies, was told by her confes-sor in the late 1960s that it was her duty to have children. Following a third pregnancy and the loss of another baby at an advanced stage, Rose and her husband considered using the contraceptive pill. She consulted a different priest before taking it and was assured by him that he would give her absolution, on medical grounds. A priest who was willing to give absolution to women taking the pill was also identified by a number of the interviewees from Cork City. Respondents in Hilliard's study (2003: 38) recalled similar variation in the attitudes and practices of priests. Commenting on a priest who was less censorious than his colleagues, Christine noted: 'If you went in and said that you were on the pill, he'd say that God would love you anyway. So everybody went to him, including myself. You'd queue there for hours just for the sake of that.' Only two of the 21 women interviewed indicated that they had taken the pill and a similarly low rate of usage was found in Hilliard's study (2003: 35), in which only one of the 32 women interviewed reported taking it.

The publication of the papal encyclical *Humanae Vitae*[21] in 1968, which staunchly reiterated Catholic opposition to any form of artificial birth control, was a source of distress and disappointment to some women, who had been hoping for a change in Catholic teaching on the topic of contraception. Christine described her neighbour's reaction to the encyclical: 'I remember when the Pope spoke out against the pill, meeting a neighbour and she was crying 'cause she had been on the pill and whatever the Pope had said, she was damned. She wasn't going to be able to take it again and she had a lot of children.' Alice also highlighted how difficult a decision it could be to oppose the Church on the issue of artificial birth control:

> I remember going with a friend to the (Cork) family planning clinic when it started and I suppose it was after my third child.[22] I got all the information on the Billings method and she got the pill. We walked home and she threw the pills over the hedge, she wouldn't take it.

The lack of access to fertility control and the sanctions around its use undoubtedly hindered sexual pleasure. Molly, who was advised after her first pregnancy not to become pregnant again for health reasons, was obliged to use abstinence as her primary form of contraception: 'I had no safe period 'cause I used to get my period every three months and nobody would advise me, you couldn't ask anyway, so we just abstained. Several times I thought I was pregnant and I wasn't. It was terrible.' Anne had similar memories of the fear occasioned by the unreliability of the safe period method she was using: 'when I was a young married woman, you would be waiting to know if you were pregnant, the fear of it was with you the whole time. I used to have the calendar on the wall marked, like the Billings method.' Anne's description of how reliance on the 'safe period' method hampered sexual pleasure for herself and her husband is underpinned by a discourse of sexual desire: 'it was very hard on everyone, it was very hard for ourselves, you couldn't be together, we were young and in love and wanted to be together and couldn't.' Dolores, who worked as a district nurse in a Cork town in the mid-1950s, also described the stress imposed on women by lack of contraception. She regularly visited married women who were struggling to raise families in poor conditions and recalled that the women used to tell her: '"I'm only going from month to month", that was their saying ... That was a great worry of theirs.' She also noted that the conditions in which many women lived would have mitigated against privacy and that, combined with the fear of pregnancy, would have inhibited sexual enjoyment: 'More poverty then and sure they'd no privacy anyway, so they wouldn't have any pleasure out of it [sex].'

The pregnant body, which is a definitive physical manifestation of sexual activity, was subjected to strict regulation and the women recalled many specific instances in which their pregnant bodies were disciplined. Vera, who was born in the late 1930s, noted: 'I don't ever remember seeing any obviously pregnant woman, they kept it very quiet and private.' Similarly, Dolores, referring to her pregnancies in the 1950s, explained '... being pregnant, you didn't get the pleasure that they're getting out of it now, d'you know'. Many women noted the association between pregnancy, sexuality and shame. The pregnant body was a physical testament to sexual activity and as such was constructed as shameful. As Betty observed: 'sex was always taboo. I can remember my mother saying to me, when I was expecting my first child and I was married, my coat blew open and she told me to cover myself up.' Others, like Hannah, highlighted the tension they experienced between their joy and excitement at being pregnant and the need to conceal, rather than celebrate, their condition:

> I remember I was married a few years before I had mine and I was so excited about being pregnant. I went home to tell my mother and she said, 'we won't say anything about it to your father today. I'll catch him at a good time to tell him.' It was like shame. I had a single brother at home and my mother used to say, 'Don't come up now while he's there,' and we didn't go up.

The construction of the pregnant body as offensive to the public gaze impacted on pregnant women in very concrete ways and most recalled consciously excluding themselves from public spaces and ensuring that when they did venture out, they wore a loose-fitting coat that covered their body. Alice's account clearly reveals these strategies of self-management of the body:

> I remember in the sixties when I was pregnant with Christine, I kept it quiet all through that summer. I remember going into a shop and an elderly woman asking me if I went into town like that. I was supposed to wear a coat. I remember I had a royal blue coat and I had to wear that coat all the time, you couldn't go out with your bump, you had to hide it.

Churching was a practice that required women who had given birth to receive a blessing from a priest before they could attend mass again, and it represented another form of body regulation. The woman had to attend the church at a prescribed time and kneel in front of the priest, holding a lighted candle while he said prayers over her. The practice was recalled with displeasure and sometimes anger by many of the narrators, but none reported that they refused to subject themselves to the practice. As Alice explained: 'You couldn't go out until you were churched … A week later, when you came out of hospital, you had to go to church straight away, then you were all right. You were unclean until then. It was terrible.'

The social symbolism attributed to the pregnant body and the practices of power that surrounded it can be read as efforts to discipline the female body and to disembody and conceal the reality of female sexual activity. The women's accounts of pregnancy and churching also indicate a high degree of compliance with existing customs and practices and the strong role that older generations of women had in the surveillance of younger pregnant women.

Sexuality, Subversion and Emotion

The material above reveals that in both marital and extra-marital situations, engaging in sexual activity and exercising fertility control could constitute subversive practices because they challenged religious, social and, in some cases, legal dictates. Such practices involved an emotional strain for many women, however, a reality that was also attested to by the women interviewed by Hilliard (2003: 31), who identified that fear inhibited questioning and dissent. The narrators' accounts reveal a keen consciousness of the power and status differentials that existed between women and the clergy, and indeed of the subordinate status of women in Irish society at the time. Sheila, born in 1914, had clear memories of the clerical attitude towards women, describing it as 'very, very, stern then, very, very, stern, yeah, very stern'. Other narrators expressed the view that the Church was disdainful of women. Joan, who was born in a rural area in 1932, described the Church's attitude to women as 'very haughty and taughty, the Church was the Church and women were only women, like, you know, they kind of looked down on the woman of the house … they looked down on you, the priests did … They were cruel, like, they really were.'

Ellie, who was born twenty years later in the early 1950s, provided an insightful analysis of the gender hierarchy within which female sexuality was constrained: 'At that stage, women were less than men, priests were the highest authority at the time, after that it was the people who got married because they were linked to a man and that made it valid, but the woman was still very inferior in that situation.' Even Pauline, born in 1955 and the youngest woman interviewed, remembered priests having a condemnatory attitude towards women: 'very strict, very strict … years ago [if] you went to a priest with a problem, he would say it was your fault'. These descriptions of priests as harsh and contemptuous provide insights into the narrators' emotional encodement of the religious discourses around sexuality. They also suggest the way in which gendered power and status differentials were experienced by women. Hilliard's (2003: 32) interviews with older married women in 2000 revealed similar perceptions of the power of the priest, and she asserts that women in the era under study experienced a habitus informed by an institutional discourse of control and submission.

Nuala's experiences as a social worker on a project for unmarried mothers in London during the late 1960s and early 1970s provide further insights into the emotional impact on women of clerical and social dictates regarding sexual propriety. Although she worked with women from many Catholic countries, including Spain and Italy, Nuala noted that it was the Irish women who expressed the greatest sense of shame about their situation:

> … lots of Irish women, the biggest numbers we had were the Irish and Spanish, both Catholic countries and they [Irish women] were the most difficult to deal with, you know, because they had all the … they had all the baggage. A huge

amount of it. And the *contortions* that a number of Irish girls went through ... the sense of being ... of having misbehaved, was a very strong reflection of Irish attitudes then and that was the sixties into seventies ... they had an awful lot of guilt about it, dreadful stress, you know ... And the ones who considered termination went through agony.

[Italics indicate the emphasis put on certain words by the narrator.]

The data discussed above suggests that it was difficult for women living in Ireland to experience sexuality as a celebratory, pleasurable, vital dimension of their lives. The remainder of the chapter will explore the ways in which the narrators retrospectively made sense of their sexual desires and actions and consider how cultural context and individual biography impacted on this process.

Intrapsychic Scripts: Reflecting on the Social Shaping of the Material Body

Intrapsychic scripting (Simon, 1996: 44) refers to the individual, reflexive processing of sexual thought and desire, which is informed by and informs interpersonal scripts. This section considers the women's conscious reflections on the ways in which social forces and discourses shaped their biological bodies, their practices in managing their sexuality and their resistance to or critique of prescribed ideals of femininity and sexuality.

A common theme in the women's reflections was a reframing of their youthful sexual activities as natural and 'innocent'. Many strongly rejected the clerical definitions of their sexual behaviour and fertility practices as sinful. Christine articulated a discourse of sexual desire, which she framed as normal, while simultaneously rejecting the clerical edicts of the day as unrealistic:

If you were company keeping, totally wrong, totally wrong. If you done anything that wasn't right, you were for it. It had to be kind of just to their specification and just so, you lived the life of a saint, a saint, like, which normally that wouldn't happen if you were going out with someone ... you daren't do this and you daren't do that and it was always a mortal sin and now like the biggest of things aren't mortal sins like, but that is the way it was.

Joan expressed her resentment of the clerical attitude to sexuality and acknowledged that while some of her contemporaries challenged it, fear always surrounded and restrained any sexual experimentation in which she engaged:

> The more they got on to people about it, the more people do it, you know, they weren't going to stop because [of] the priest … but at the same time, you had the dread … the dread was there … and you often after would resent it, because you have said to yourself, like, well what did you do wrong that warranted all of that? You didn't really, you wouldn't be after doing … God knows compared to today's living, like, you know, ours was completely different, totally kind of innocent in ways, you know, 'tisn't that we mightn't have committed the sins alright! [Laughs]

Joan's narrative also reflected regret for her lack of courage in seeking out more information about bodily and sexual matters and her subsequent efforts to make sense of how such a silence was maintained:

> … you just didn't ask those questions, you know, which is a pity. When you look back through the years now and you say, like, 'oh we didn't ask the things'. Why didn't we, like, you know? But we didn't at the time … when you look back now, you say it's a pity that people were afraid to ask questions, you know they were afraid to query the things, the facts of life, you didn't know them.

Similar expressions of hurt and anger were expressed by respondents in Hilliard's study (2003: 40–41). The other issue that prompted the women in this research to express strong resentment was the practice of churching. Dolores castigated the Church's attitude to women's fertility and sexuality, which demanded that married women be fecund while simultaneously defining their post-partum bodies as polluted:

It should never have been there ... It was a ridiculous thing. It wasn't a blessing, it was a cleansing ... We were unclean because we had a baby and then you were told to go out and multiply. I used *to dread it* ... we felt we had done something wrong. We felt we were guilty, guilty! It was nearly as bad as having a baby out of marriage.

[Italics indicate the emphasis put on certain words by the narrator.]

Rejection and resentment of the prevailing cultural scripts regarding sexuality and acknowledgment of the ways in which fear made resistance difficult were the sentiments expressed most often by the women. However, two of the narrators provided quite distinctly different accounts of how they interpreted cultural scripts and everyday interpersonal experiences. Ellie acknowledged that she rejected Catholicism at an early age because of its teachings regarding sexuality and gender: 'Religion was against sex because it seemed to be a dirty thing altogether and the priests were so pure standing up there and the rest of us were lesser humans, particularly women, and actually, I turned against religion very early on because of that.' She also noted that her attitude to sexuality was not negatively impacted by the cultural scripts of her childhood and adolescence: 'I have no hang-ups now about sexuality, oddly enough, and I should have, considering the guarded way I was brought up.' Ellie recalled becoming conscious of the gendered power relations that framed courtship practices and how objectified she felt by them: 'I *hated the dances*, I really did ... I felt it was so demeaning, I always had that sense, it was like women being demeaned. ... I had a *very strong* sense of that from *a very young age*.' Her narrative reveals a strong tension between her framing of sexuality as something natural and pleasurable and her rejection of what she perceived to be the sexually predatory nature of men and the unequal position of women in sexual and, particularly, marital relationships during her youth in the early 1960s:

E: I'm quite a bit anti-marriage, you can see where it's coming from, you know, because that would only still use women, you know, chattels, the word chattels, they were used. I saw that very early on, God knows but it wasn't a difficult thing to perceive ... I remember thinking to myself,

in frustration, well, men … they were looking at you like …
something to be …

I: A kind of sex object?

E: Yeah, I got an awful lot of that.

Ellie described how she formed a brief relationship with a man she met when working away from home at the age of seventeen, only to discover subsequently that he was married. She noted that this experience compounded her negative view of men: 'I wouldn't have, deep down, I wouldn't have an awful lot of respect for men. And I've to work at it. I really have to work at it. Because, you can see why … I remember with him now, I mean, he was only after one thing ....'

When she moved to London in the late 1960s to train as a nurse, Ellie became conscious of a difference in the sexual climates that prevailed in Ireland and in England at that time. She perceived that in Ireland, despite her experience with the married man: 'It wasn't a free-for-all, like. I mean, if I was out with somebody … they wouldn't expect sex, d'you know what I mean, it wasn't part of the social thing at the time, you know. Unless you were a real lower class.'[23] In contrast, she described the English scene as much more liberal and commented negatively on the sexual behaviour of Irish women in London: 'The Irish were wicked. They were terrible. They were so suppressed, you see, I think they went mad.' Ellie disassociated herself from this behaviour, which she perceived as sexually promiscuous, and recalled that she 'went the opposite way round, I kept my snobbery! [Laughs] All my empty snobbery … that they were less than me, more inferior, you know.' Evident in this account is an 'othering' of sexually active women, with the collectivist stereotype of social class being used to demarcate sexual behaviour. It would appear that in Ellie's case, her rejection of gendered power differentials, her negative understanding of male sexuality and her socialisation into norms of respectability that castigated extra-marital female sexual expression influenced her reaction to the sexual opportunities London presented.

Nuala emigrated to London in the mid-1950s and in common with Ellie she had an awareness of the gender inequities that could underpin sexual relations. In describing the attitude of her Italian roommates to relationships with men, she noted that in 'their whole kind of image of their relationships … they had a very *feminine,* definitely as opposed to a *feminist* approach'. Notwithstanding this awareness, she described how living in London facilitated her development of a much more positive attitude to sexuality:

> The whole ... the *positive* side of sexuality, you know, certainly was *blooming* in London ... so, you know, the whole thing changed dramatically, you know, a process of changing. It just changes the way one develops in the social context one has.

[Italics indicate the emphasis put on certain words by the narrator.]

In Nuala's case, London provided a space that disrupted the idealised, asexual femininity into which she had been socialised in Ireland and thereby afforded opportunities for a rethinking and revising of attitudes and beliefs about sexuality. In contrast, for Ellie it appeared to reinforce her prevailing belief that an unmarried woman with an active sexual life fell short of the ideals of appropriate female behaviour. A comparison of Ellie's and Nuala's experiences highlights the possibility for women to challenge and reject beliefs and practices into which they were socialised, while also demonstrating the enduring impact of cultural scenarios on sexual subjectivities and sexual agency.

Conclusion

The conceptual matrix of cultural, interpersonal and intrapsychic scripts (Gagnon and Simon, 1974) provides a useful way of exploring both the discursive/corporeal body and the empirical/material body and, indeed, of highlighting the multiple dimensions (structure, practice, meaning, subjectivity) of the 'sociality of sexuality'(Jackson and Scott, 2010: 3). The attribution of meanings to sexuality through the discursive construction of the female body as a desexualised yet fecund entity, and of sexuality as a dangerous and shameful force, are clearly manifest in the narrators' accounts. So too are the myriad regulatory and disciplinary practices that operated at the level of mundane, everyday interactions to incite compliance with this prescribed ideal. The structural inequalities that shaped women's lives are also evident, in particular the institutional power of the Catholic Church and its gendered, patriarchal practices that constrained women.

The key insights from this chapter come from consideration of the subjectivities of the women. Their accounts of sexuality support the contention of Robinson et al. (2004: 417) that heterosexuality is 'an embodied, spatially located emotional experience'. The data reveals that women displayed agency in their engagement with the discursive, material and structural factors that shaped the sexual climate in the period under discussion. Unmarried women engaged in various forms of sexual expression during courtship, while married women practised fertility control and resented the concealment of their pregnant bodies and the churching of their post-partum bodies. Such behaviour did not, in most cases, constitute a conscious, concerted or collective challenge to prevailing norms, and yet this behaviour had an emotional cost. Accounts of the fear and anxiety that accompanied most sexual experiences and resentment about the restrictions that limited enjoyment of their sexual and fecund bodies are central to the women's retrospective reflections. Furthermore, their narratives keenly emphasise how difficult it was for women to assert a sexual persona that did not comply with prevailing norms and practices. Holland et al. (1994: 22) contend that 'When women are able to take control of their sexuality in an active femininity, they can bring the social shaping of their material bodies into consciousness, and govern their own sensuality.' Becoming conscious of the social shaping of the body, and resisting the elements of its construction that are not desired, was profoundly challenging and, as this chapter has shown, was not easily achieved.

Notes

[1] The research was funded by an award from the Royal Irish Academy/ British Council Research Network Scheme. The interviews were conducted with women in counties Cork and Tipperary in 1998/99. For more details of the sample and research process, *see* Leane et al. (2002). My colleague Helen Duggan (R.I.P.), who specialised in research with older people and was a skilled qualitative researcher, conducted seven of the oral history interviews. The empirical accounts collected in the interviews are not objective accounts, but rather constitute personal memories and interpretations of the past reconstructed through the prism of the present. All remembering has a social dimension, however, and the accounts provided by the women contain both individual stories and information about collective cultural attitudes and practices of the time. For a discussion of

memory in oral history and life-story research, *see* Green (2004), Summerfield (2000) and Beiner (2004). For a discussion of memory in the context of life history accounts of sexuality, *see* Robinson et al. (2007: 457–8).

[2]   Ten of the oral histories were collected through individual interviews, with the remaining eleven being collected through two group interviews of five and six women, respectively. Each study participant received a transcribed copy of the interview proceedings and a subsequent follow-up interview was held with nine of the ten individual participants and with the two groups involved in the research. Nineteen of the women were married or widowed at the time of interview; two had remained single throughout their lives. All but one of the married women had children; neither of the single women had a child. The women were drawn from urban and rural backgrounds in Cork and Tipperary, with the majority from working-class backgrounds and three from more prosperous farming families.

[3]   The narrators discussed sexual activity in a very general way, with none providing detailed information on their sexual practices. This is unsurprising and is consistent with the experience of Meah et al. (2008), who interviewed women in England about sexuality in the period between the two world wars. As Meah et al. (2008: 459) observe: 'If sex was absent from public discourses of heterosexuality, could interviewees realistically recall and describe it in the present?'

[4]   Social constructionist theorising of sexuality rejects the view of sexuality as natural or innate and highlights instead its construction at a cultural and historic level. Researchers using this approach seek to identify how processes of representation and regulation imbue bodies, actions and feelings with sexual meaning. For a discussion of the emergence of the social constructionist approach, *see* Jackson and Scott (2010: 11–23).

[5]   For an analysis of discursive constructions of sexuality in Irish society, *see* Inglis (1997).

[6]   The work of Elizabeth Grosz (1994) exemplifies this trend in feminist theorising. For a discussion of feminist work reflecting the essentialist perspective, *see* Brook (1999: 6–8).

[7]   For a discussion of corporeality, *see* Brook (1999: 2–4).

[8]   The shift from modernist to postmodernist paradigms of understanding reflects a move away from a modernist belief that the truth, or reality of all things, could be named or defined, and a move towards a more fluid understanding of the world as consisting of multiple truths or realities and shifting meanings. In the context of sexuality, it has seen a move away from efforts to categorise sexuality into narrow, predefined typologies and towards an understanding of sexuality that takes into account both collective and individual experiences. For a discussion of postmodernism and sexuality, *see* Simon (2003). For a discussion of the impact of postmodernist ideas on feminism, *see* Nicholson (1990) and McLaughlin (1997).

[9] For a discussion of feminist appropriations of Foucault's ideas about the operation of power on the body, *see* Sawicki (1991).

[10] For a more detailed discussion of these, *see* Jackson and Scott (2010: 15–16).

[11] This chapter focuses exclusively on Irish sexual attitudes, practices and behaviours, but it is acknowledged that Irish experiences of the regulation of sexuality share many parallels with practices in other Western countries. *See* Inglis (2005) for a discussion of Irish sexual prudery in the context of international material and *see* Robinson et al. (2007), Meah et al. (2008) and Hockey et al. (2009) for insights into experiences of and attitudes to sexuality in England between the world wars.

[12] Similar exclusion of young women from information about sexual knowledge was found in life history interviews with English women who reached adulthood in the period between the wars. *See* Robinson et al. (2007: 425) and Meah et al. (2008: 459).

[13] Pseudonyms have been assigned to the participants.

[14] Many of the participants identified the late 1960s as the time when issues around sexuality began to be raised in public forums, primarily through the efforts of the women's movement and the media.

[15] Life history interviews with English women who reached adulthood in the period between the wars revealed a similar finding. *See* Robinson et al. (2007: 425).

[16] Churching refers to a practice whereby a woman attended a church after giving birth and a priest made the sign of the cross on her and recited some prayers. Opinion varies as to whether the rite of churching constituted a blessing and a thanksgiving for the safe arrival of the baby or a purification of the post-partum woman. Undoubtedly, the women in the study on which this chapter is based understood it as a purification ritual. *See* Pope (nd).

[17] Catholic discourses in Ireland between 1920 and 1940 contain many examples of the construction of female sexuality as passive and reactive, while male sexuality is portrayed as a vital, active force. *See* Leane (1999).

[18] A narrator in the research conducted by Meah et al. (2008) recounted a similar incident, where an unmarried nursing colleague became pregnant in the early 1950s. In that instance, however, the narrator noted that while the woman was not 'shunned', her situation was unusual for the time (Meah et al., 2008: 459).

[19] It is noteworthy that Sheila's account shifts between the use of the generic 'they' to the more personalised 'you', but at no point does she speak in the first person. Errante (2004) describes this pattern of narration as a 'verbal hiding' strategy. Such strategies, she suggests, are 'patterns of communication that try to diminish the speakers' actual sense of vulnerability regarding a particular topic of speech' (Errante, 2004: 423). The increase in volume and the emphasis Sheila placed on certain words in the

account also indicate the strength of emotion and depth of feeling associated with the topic.

[20] The Billings method was a form of natural family planning developed by Dr John Billings in 1953. It involves women relying on bodily signs, such as vaginal secretions, to determine the days in each cycle during which they are fertile. This method is compliant with the teachings of the Catholic Church.

[21] The publication of *Humanae Vitae* followed much speculation as to whether or not the Catholic Church would allow some form of contraceptive use. When the contraceptive pill was made available in 1960, this led to some within the Church seeking reconsideration of the Church's position. In 1963 a commission of six European non-theologians was established by Pope John XXIII to consider the issue of birth and population control. This commission met intermittently in 1963 and 1964, was subsequently enlarged to 58 members, including married people, laywomen, theologians and bishops, and it reported its findings in 1965. The final majority report of the commission, in 1966, proposed that some form of contraception be approved for married couples. A minority report opposing this view was issued by some members. The support of contraception in the majority report had raised expectations of a change in Church teaching, but the publication of *Humanae Vitae* reiterated very clearly Church opposition to any form of artificial contraception. For further details, *see* Paul VI (1983).

[22] The Cork Family Planning Clinic was established in 1975. *See* Cork Family Planning Clinic (nd).

[23] Skeggs has argued that the working class and, in particular, working-class women have always been classified in relation to an ideal of respectability and that working-class people themselves have also engaged in this process of self-classification. *See* Skeggs (1997: 1–8).

Section 2

Sexual Rights and Activism

CHAPTER 3

'We'll Have What They're Having': Sexual Minorities and the Law in the Republic of Ireland

Fergus Ryan

Introduction

This chapter concerns the law as it relates to sexual orientation in the Republic of Ireland. The law in this context has changed in recent decades in a manner and to an extent that offers a particularly vivid insight into the evolution of attitudes to people who are lesbian, gay and bisexual (LGB) in modern Ireland.[1] Indeed, there are few areas of the law that reflect so emphatically the transformation of Irish society in the course of the last three decades.

Even a cursory observation of the evolution of the law in the past thirty years reveals how dramatic the change has been. Robson (1995: 47) describes the Republic of Ireland in 1988 as '...on paper at least, the worst legal regime in Western Europe for lesbians and gay men. There was no recognition or protection of any sort, and gay men faced a total ban on any type of sexual activity.' In the interim years, Ireland has witnessed not only the introduction of broadly equal treatment in the context of the criminal law (Criminal Law (Rape) (Amendment) Act 1990; Criminal Law (Sexual Offences) Act 1993; and Criminal Law (Sexual Offences) Act 2006) but also the inception of equality laws that ban sexual orientation discrimination in the context of employment (Unfair Dismissals (Amendment) Act 1993; Employment Equality Acts 1998–2011), in relation to the supply of goods and services (Equal Status Acts 2000–2011), pensions (Pensions Act 1990, as amended by Part 3 of the Social Welfare (Miscellaneous Provisions) Act 2004) and health insurance (Health Insurance Act 1994), as well as the express formal recognition of LGB asylum-seekers (Refugee Act 1996). The most notable reform, however, has arguably been the inception, from 2011, of a substantial scheme of registered civil partnership for same-sex couples, together with the legal recognition of cohabiting couples, both same-sex and opposite-sex. (*See* Civil Partnership and Certain Rights and Obligations of Cohabitants Act 2010.)

These legal innovations reflect, and in certain respects have served to reinforce, the radical shift evident in the social and cultural acceptance of sexual minorities and, in particular, of same-sex couples. Legal change has removed most of the barriers to full and open participation in Irish society by sexual minorities. While chronicling and welcoming these extraordinary changes, this chapter also sounds a note of caution. Significant gaps in legal protection remain, particularly in relation to parenting and guardianship (*see* Chapters 6 and 7), while employment protections for some gay and lesbian employees are qualified by a religious ethos exemption that detracts from the protection otherwise afforded by these reforms. In addition, same-sex marriage is not currently recognised in Irish law (section 2 (2)(e), Civil Registration Act 2004 and *Zappone and Gilligan v Revenue Commissioners* [2008] 2 I.R. 417). On a more critical level, the recognition of same-sex couples has proceeded largely by unquestioning reference to a template of relationship recognition that is itself arguably in need of reform and reconsideration. The goal of equality with heterosexuals has obscured, in certain respects, considerations as to what models of family recognition best suit modern and diverse manifestations of family life, a point that is addressed further in the Conclusion.

Criminalisation of Male Homosexual Activity

Given what has happened since, it is remarkable to consider that the decriminalisation of male homosexual sexual acts took place in the Republic of Ireland (henceforth 'Ireland') only in 1993. This was eleven years after equivalent legislation was enacted in Northern Ireland[2] and 36 years after decriminalisation had taken place in England and Wales.[3] Up to 1993, the criminal law in Ireland banned anal intercourse and all manifestations of male-to-male sexual conduct of a 'grossly indecent' nature, whether such acts took place in a private or public context and regardless of the age or willingness of the parties. Notably, these sanctions were inherited rather than home-grown, having been a colonial over-hang carried over, without modification, from an era of Victorian British rule.[4]

The first statute of relevance is the Offences Against the Person Act 1861, section 61 of which penalised 'the abominable Crime of Buggery', which included anal intercourse between persons.[5] Technically, section 61 did not itself create the crime of buggery but instead set penalties for the already long-established common law offence.[6] This offence addressed (as well as sexual intercourse with an animal) penile penetration of the anus of either a man or a woman,[7] and applied even if the couple were married to each other. The maximum penalty that could be imposed on conviction was a life sentence of penal servitude, a mark of just how seriously the offence was taken.[8]

While the offence of buggery applied equally to heterosexual and homosexual activity, a later statutory provision – section 11 of the Criminal Law (Amendment) Act 1885, which created the offence of 'gross indecency between males' – was addressed specifically to homosexual activity between males.[9] A notable feature was that it expressly related to sexual conduct of a male *'with* another male' [emphasis added]. The use of the term 'with' was judicially interpreted as requiring that the parties 'act in concert',[10] and thus presupposed the willing participation and consent of both parties.[11] Otherwise, the 1885 Act left the offence of gross indecency undefined. In *Norris v Attorney General* ([1984] I.R. 36), Justice McWilliam observed that the Act had left it to the courts to determine what was grossly indecent, adding that what constituted gross indecency would depend on the context in which it occurred. Intriguingly, he adds that '… changing attitudes must affect such decisions' (*Norris v Attorney General* 1984: 48). The Wolfenden Report (1968: para.105) indicates that, in practice, gross indecency typically involved oral-genital contact and mutual masturbation, though it appears from the case law that physical contact between the parties was not required.[12]

A notable feature of the criminal law framework of the time was that it did not address female homosexual acts, which from 1935 onwards attracted no criminal sanction once both parties consented and were aged fifteen or older.[13] In *Norris v Attorney General* (1984: 36), the Supreme Court concluded that Parliament was constitutionally entitled to consider male homosexual sexual activity a greater threat to society than like female acts. As Chief Justice O'Higgins rather unconvincingly observed:

> ... The legislature would be perfectly entitled to have regard to the difference between the sexes and to treat sexual conduct or gross indecency between males as requiring prohibition because of the social problem which it creates, while at the same time looking at sexual conduct between females as being not only different but as posing no such social problem. (*Norris v Attorney General*, 1984: 59) [14]

That is not to say that lesbianism has universally escaped the attention of the criminal law nor that it has been universally considered more socially acceptable than male homosexuality. Crompton (1981) challenges what he terms the standard 'myth of lesbian impunity', documenting, in a survey spanning from 1270 to 1791, a series of mainland European laws imposing criminal sanctions, including the death penalty, in respect of lesbian sexual acts. It is clear, nonetheless, that in the English common law tradition inherited by Ireland, lesbianism has not attracted the same level of legal opprobrium as male homosexuality (Sherwin Bailey, 1955). Ryan notes, however, that the different treatment of lesbians:

> ... cannot be put down to any greater tolerance of lesbians than of gay men; in fact it is the clearest indication of an attitude that sees the female as the sexual subject of the male. Thus women, although being spared the stigma of criminality, were denied recognition in law of a sexuality independent of that of the male. (Ryan, 1997: 39, fn. 4)[15]

Certainly, there is no evidence (in spite of the unconvincing hypothesis of the Supreme Court in *Norris*) that, socially or culturally, lesbianism was (pre-decriminalisation) considered more acceptable than male homosexuality.[16]

Impact of Enforcement

The terminology used to describe the former offences addressing male homosexual conduct was particularly condemnatory. Buggery was described as '*the* abominable Crime' [emphasis added], even when consensual, while activity between males was deemed not just indecent[17] but 'grossly indecent'. For the purpose of crime statistics, moreover, both buggery between persons and gross indecency were often grouped together with bestiality (intercourse with an animal – also a form of buggery) under the heading 'unnatural offences'. Yet despite this language, in practice there appeared to be comparatively little enthusiasm to enforce these laws comprehensively. A review of Garda statistics from the two decades immediately preceding decriminalisation reveals, as Ryan (1997: 46) has observed, an exceptionally low rate of detection and prosecution of homosexual offences.[18] Indeed, the government's own evidence before the European Court of Human Rights in *Norris v Ireland* ([1988] 13 E.H.R.R. 186) indicates that, from at least 1974 onwards, no prosecutions had been pursued in respect of consensual sexual activity between adult males, provided it occurred in private (*Norris v Ireland* [1988]: §§19–20).[19]

Thus, while Irish society was not particularly tolerant of homosexual acts, neither did there appear to be any great zeal to enforce the relevant laws (at least directly) in respect of private, consensual behaviour. The discretion of individual gay men and the development of 'survival strategies' possibly played a part in concealing consensual adult activity, such that it did not typically come to the attention of the authorities. Nonetheless, as Ryan (1997: 46) has observed, while not directly enforced, the ban on male homosexual activity was often employed to justify official and quasi-official practices – such as media censorship – that sought to suppress public discussions and other public manifestations of homosexuality. In this regard, Ireland prior to decriminalisation possibly exemplified *in practice* what Andrew Sullivan (1995: 94ff) terms the 'conservative' approach to homosexuality, typified by informal tolerance of private homosexual activity coupled with disapproval of public manifestations thereof and the rejection of claims for public recognition and rights.

In fact, criminalisation often operated to sanction discriminatory practices, offering the implicit backing of the law to those who sought to target homosexuals. For instance, Rose (1994: 19–20) documents the harassment of gay men by police investigating the murder of Charles Self, a gay man, in 1982. The investigation led to almost 1,500 gay men being questioned by Gardaí. Rose observes that much of the questioning did not relate to the murder but sought instead to scrutinise the sexual lives of the interviewees. Thus while the relevant laws were not being directly enforced with any great zeal, homosexuality did attract many informal, extra-legal sanctions, for which the formal ban on male homosexual acts provided a justificatory backdrop (Ryan, 1997).[20]

Challenging the Ban

Whether they were enforced or not, the relevant laws stood as visible symbols of society's condemnatory views of homosexuality. In substance, the law labelled gay men as 'criminal' and 'deviant', whether or not they were the subjects of prosecution. As Robson has observed, by their very existence these laws 'insulted and marginalised' the gay population in Ireland (Robson, 1995: 47).

In *Norris v Attorney General* ([1984] I.R. 36) and *Norris v Ireland* ([1988] 13 E.H.R.R. 186) the plaintiff, Senator David Norris, who is openly gay, challenged the ban on male homosexual acts before, first, the Irish High and Supreme Courts, and subsequently the European Court of Human Rights.[21] In his litigation before the Irish Courts, Norris sought a declaration that the aforementioned provisions of the 1861 and 1885 Acts penalising homosexual conduct infringed his constitutional rights to equality, privacy, free expression and free association. By a majority of three to two, the Supreme Court (upholding the earlier High Court verdict) rejected his claim, ruling in 1983 that the laws were constitutionally valid.[22] In particular, Chief Justice O'Higgins (with whom Justices Finlay and Griffin agreed) concluded that any rights enjoyed by the plaintiff could validly be subordinated in this context with a view to safeguarding public morality, family life and the common good.

Speaking for the majority, Chief Justice O'Higgins placed particular emphasis on the long-standing condemnation of homosexual activity in Christian theology. Pointing to aspects of the Constitution that exhibit a strongly Christian tenor,[23] he rejected the proposition that there could, without express words to that effect, be a constitutional right to engage in conduct deemed contrary to Christian teaching dating back to biblical times. The Chief Justice also pointed to various deleterious effects that he believed arose from homosexuality, for both the individual homosexual and for society. In particular, he claimed that '… [e]xclusive homosexuality, whether the condition be congenital or acquired, can result in great distress and unhappiness for the individual and can lead to depression, despair and suicide ...' Exploiting the commonly deployed discourse of the male homosexual as 'diseased' (*cf.* Stychin, 1995: 50–51, 134–8), he noted what he viewed as the negative implications of male homosexual behaviour for public health, as well as what he saw as its harmful impact on family life and on marriage. The Chief Justice placed particular emphasis on the risk of 'contagion', hypothesising that the 'congenitally and irreversibly homosexual' (for whom homosexuality was fixed) would, if unchecked, potentially lead a '... mildly homosexually orientated person into a way of life from which he may never recover' (*Norris v Attorney General*, 1984: 64). (This may possibly reflect a concern to dissuade bisexual men from engaging in same-sex relations.) The Chief Justice thus concluded that the plaintiff's right to privacy could validly be subordinated to the overriding concern to maintain public morality, public health and the integrity and wellbeing of marriage and the family:

> I regard the State as having an interest in the general moral wellbeing of the community and as being entitled, where it is practicable to do so, to discourage conduct which is morally wrong and harmful to a way of life and to values which the State wishes to protect. (*Norris v Attorney General*, 1984: 64)

The minority judges, Justices Henchy and McCarthy, disagreed with this verdict, finding that the relevant laws did breach the plaintiff's constitutional right to privacy. The dissenting judges both focused on the breadth of the ban. While noting that the State may be entitled, even constitutionally *obliged*, to prohibit some homosexual activity (for the protection, for instance, of young and vulnerable parties), Justice Henchy criticised the extensive and undifferentiated nature of the ban, which, he concluded, condemned it to unconstitutionality. In his view, the State had failed to establish that public order and morality demanded and warranted such an extensive intrusion into the private lives of gay men. Justice Henchy reasoned, in particular, that the ban worked a significant injustice in the case of those men who were exclusively gay, effectively denying them any lawful sexual outlet, contrary to their constitutional privacy rights.[24] With this judgment Justice McCarthy concurred, noting that:

... a very great burden lies upon those who would question personal rights in order to justify State interference of a most grievous kind (the policeman in the bedroom) in a claim to the right to perform sexual acts or to give expression to sexual desires or needs in private between consenting adults, male or female. (*Norris v Attorney General*, 1984: 102)[25]

In Justice McCarthy's view, the State had signally failed to satisfy this burden.

Success in Europe

Senator Norris lost his case in the Irish Courts and proceeded to the European Court of Human Rights (ECHR).[26] The ECHR found in his favour, ruling in October 1988 that Ireland was in breach of his right to privacy under Article 8 of the European Convention on Human Rights (*Norris v Ireland*, [1988] 13 E.H.R.R. 186). In doing so, the Court was following its earlier verdict in *Dudgeon v United Kingdom* (*Dudgeon v United Kingdom*, [1981] 4 E.H.R.R. 149), a case concerning the application of the exact same laws, this time in Northern Ireland. While noting that states were entitled to place limits on homosexual activity to protect, for instance, young and vulnerable people, the Court in *Dudgeon* concluded that the relevant law, '... by reason of its breadth and absolute character' (*Dudgeon v United Kingdom*, 1981: para. 61), was disproportionate to the legitimate aim of protecting public morality. The Court reasoned that the law was overreaching, going further than was necessary to protect public morals. The Court was influenced, in particular, by the trend in Council of Europe states (most of which, by the early 1980s, had decriminalised consensual adult homosexual activity) towards greater tolerance of private homosexual behaviour. Noting that, for some decades before the judgment, the authorities in Northern Ireland had not, in fact, enforced the law in respect of consensual private activity between adults aged 21 or over, the Court concluded that insufficient evidence had been presented to show that non-enforcement had been or would be '... injurious to moral standards in Northern Ireland or that there [had] been any public demand for stricter enforcement of the law' (*Dudgeon v United Kingdom*, 1981: para. 60). Any justification for the maintenance of such legislation was, the Court ruled:

... outweighed by the detrimental effects which the very existence of the legislative provisions in question can have on the
life of a person of homosexual orientation like the applicant.
Although members of the public who regard homosexuality as immoral may be shocked, offended or disturbed by the
commission by others of private homosexual acts, this cannot
on its own warrant the application of penal sanctions when
it is consenting adults alone who are involved. (*Dudgeon v
United Kingdom*, 1981: para. 60)

The application of these laws in the Republic met a similar fate
in *Norris v Ireland* (1988). The ECHR determined, in particular,
that Ireland had failed to demonstrate a 'pressing social need' to
maintain such an extensive ban on consensual male homosexual
sexual conduct. While it found that the State had a legitimate aim
in protecting public morals (and a wide degree of latitude in deciding what was necessary to achieve this end), the Court nonetheless
concluded that the relevant laws went further than was necessary in a democratic society to uphold such morals, and were thus
disproportionate to the legitimate aim of the legislation. The laws in
question impinged to an extensive degree on an area of particular
personal intimacy, with no apparent benefit or social good arising
from such broad and far-reaching sanctions.

Decriminalisation

The judgment of the European Court of Human Rights, while politically embarrassing for the State, did not have the immediate effect of
changing the law in Ireland.[27] Indeed, it took some five years before
the issue of decriminalisation was tackled. In the interim, however,
the green shoots of reform were beginning to sprout. Notably, the
Prohibition of Incitement to Hatred Act 1989 banned public speech
inciting members of the public to hatred on the ground, among
others, of sexual orientation. The Video Recording Act 1989 placed
restrictions on video recordings that encouraged hatred on this
and other grounds. The Criminal Law (Rape) (Amendment) Act
1990 further reflected this growing trend towards equalisation,
with rape laws being extended to address forced anal intercourse
(homosexual or heterosexual) and non-consensual penile-oral
penetration, regardless of the gender of the victim.[28] Previously,

the Criminal Law (Rape) Act 1981 had equalised the maximum penalties for indecent assault (now sexual assault) upon a male and upon a female respectively; formerly penalties for indecent assault had been less severe where the victim was female.[29] The report of the Law Reform Commission on Child Sexual Abuse, published in 1990, also signalled a sea change in attitudes. The Commission recommended that as there was no good reason to posit a higher age of consent for homosexual sexual activity, the same legal regime should apply to consensual sexual activity, whether same-sex or opposite-sex (Law Reform Commission, 1990: 45–9).

The Criminal Law (Sexual Offences) Act 1993 finally addressed the issue of decriminalisation.[30] The Act abolished the old offences of buggery (except as it related to animals)[31] and gross indecency. It replaced them with new provisions that banned buggery of persons (anal intercourse with a man or woman), and gross indecency between males, but in both cases *only* where one of the participants[32] was either under the age of seventeen or mentally impaired. Effectively, this served to legalise consensual adult male homosexual activity in private, where both parties were aged seventeen or over. The choice of seventeen as the age of consent was notable, given that it was also, at the time, the age at which girls could lawfully consent to heterosexual sexual intercourse (Criminal Law (Amendment) Act 1935, section 2). This did not quite create an equal age of consent (boys, for instance, prior to 2006 could still lawfully consent to heterosexual sexual intercourse at the age of fifteen), though the fact that male homosexual sexual activity was not made subject to an age of consent higher than seventeen was widely considered progressive.[33] That said, a curious protective regime emerged, under which the precise age of consent differed depending on the gender of the parties and the acts in which they engaged.[34] Most of these anomalies were removed by the Criminal Law (Sexual Offences) Act 2006, which created a new offence of 'defilement of a child'. The 2006 Act treats homosexual and heterosexual sexual activity with minors in a largely identical fashion and imposes a uniform age of consent of seventeen for penetrative 'sexual acts', as defined.[35]

The 1993 and 2006 Acts reflect a broader shift in legal policy relating to sexual activity. Notably, the Criminal Law (Rape) (Amendment) Act 1990 removed the marital rape exemption, whereby a man could formerly not be convicted of raping his wife. The criminalisation of rape in this context, coupled with the decriminalisation of consensual sexual activities in the 1993 Act, signalled a broad realignment of the criminal law away from penalising consensual activities regarded as morally wrongful *per se* and towards a policy targeted more specifically at non-consensual and exploitative sexual activities, such as sex with minors and prostitution. This realignment reflects a broader 'retreat from the bedroom' of consensual adult parties, coupled with greater vigilance in respect of unwanted and exploitative sexual acts. The early 1990s, for instance, also saw the culmination of moves away from the regulation of contraceptive use based on moral concerns.[36] The sale of condoms, which had for a long time been the subject of contentious debate, was largely deregulated in 1993, while the legislative focus of the law on contraception shifted decisively from the realm of morality to the exclusive domain of the medical safety of such devices.[37]

Combating Discrimination

Even before decriminalisation was achieved, considerable inroads were already being made in the context of discrimination law, with several measures being passed proscribing discrimination on the basis of sexual orientation. As early as 1988, some five years before decriminalisation, a Department of Finance Circular banned discrimination in the civil service on the basis of sexual orientation and HIV status (Department of Finance, 1988). Broader reform came in 1993, just two months prior to decriminalisation, with the enactment of the Unfair Dismissals (Amendment) Act 1993. This measure added sexual orientation to the list of grounds in relation to which a dismissal from employment would be automatically deemed unfair (and thus unlawful). This was a profoundly significant step that attracted, at the time, relatively little attention or controversy. It meant that a person could not legally be dismissed from employment simply because of their sexual orientation. In many respects this was as important an innovation as decriminalisation, perhaps even more so. It meant – crucially – that lesbians, gay men and bisexuals no longer needed to conceal their sexual orientation in the workplace. While this did not necessarily herald an immediate emptying of closets, this step and decriminalisation together removed two very significant barriers to the open participation of lesbians, gay men and bisexuals in society – the risk of criminal sanction (specifically in the case of men) and the prospect of dismissal from employment.

The Employment Equality Act 1998 extended the principle of non-discrimination on the ground of sexual orientation to discrimination in the context of hiring, the terms and conditions of employment, training for employment, and promotion within the workplace. The basic outcome is that in making employment-related decisions, the sexual orientation of employees should be treated as irrelevant. The Act also bans harassment on the basis of sexual orientation.[38] Since 2011, it is also unlawful to discriminate against or harass an employee on the basis that he/she is or was (among other things) a civil partner.[39]

The Equal Status Act 2000 similarly bans discrimination on the ground of sexual orientation in relation to the provision of goods and services. While some exceptions apply,[40] the Act prevents a person, as a recipient of goods or services, from being treated less favourably on account of his/her sexual orientation or, since 2011, on account of the fact that the person is currently or was formerly in a civil partnership. The Health Insurance Act 1994 expressly proscribes sexual orientation discrimination in the specific context of health insurance provision, while the Social Welfare (Miscellaneous Provisions) Act 2004 (amending the Pensions Act 1990) bans sexual orientation discrimination in relation to pensions.[41]

The enactment of the Refugee Act 1996 is a measure of the progress made in relation to matters of sexual orientation in such a short period of time. That Act expressly recognises a right to asylum in Ireland where a person can demonstrate a reasonable fear of persecution on grounds of his/her sexual orientation if returned to his/her home country. Although this entitlement can be problematic (Brazil, 2011; O'Leary, 2008),[42] the principle that a person may seek asylum in Ireland based on their sexuality illustrates the dramatic reversal in official attitudes to sexual orientation in the space of a few years.

The importance of these measures – particularly in the context of workplace discrimination – cannot be understated. Even into the mid-1990s, workplace discrimination and the fear thereof caused significant social and economic strain for lesbians and gays. A groundbreaking report by GLEN/Nexus (1995) for the Combat Poverty Agency revealed the effects of discrimination and social exclusion on gay and lesbian respondents in the mid-1990s. It evidenced, in particular, the widespread deployment by gays and lesbians of defensive workplace strategies that involved either remaining discreet about sexual orientation in the workplace, or avoiding certain types of employment. A majority of respondents, for instance, were not 'out' at work.

In some cases these defensive strategies diminished the career prospects of respondents, with 21 per cent indicating that fear of discrimination had prompted them to avoid pursuing employment opportunities for which they felt qualified. Based on their sexual orientation, 39 per cent overall had self-selected out of applying for jobs where there was a greater perceived prospect of harassment or discrimination. Furthermore, 7 per cent and 14 per cent of respondents, respectively, reported having been sacked or having left a job due to their sexual orientation, while others had left school early due to anti-gay bullying (GLEN/Nexus, 1995).[43] This experience in turn contributed to significant levels of economic strain among gay and lesbian respondents at that time.[44]

Instinctively, this experience jars with the standard national narrative depicting the Irish as a people who – at home and abroad – have experienced discrimination. Emigrant stories of 'no blacks, no dogs, no Irish' form an integral part of the lore of the Irish experience abroad. At home, the narrative of the penal laws and sectarian oppression sat uneasily with charges of discrimination and social exclusion in the modern Republic. (The Irish perceive themselves as the traditional victims of discrimination, rather than the perpetrators thereof.) This may explain, in part, why bans on workplace discrimination and dismissals on the basis of sexual orientation were in place in Ireland long before equivalent British legislation and why they had been passed with relatively little opposition. Rose suggests, for instance, that '... these changes stem from positive traditional Irish values arising from the anti-colonial struggle reinvigorated and amplified by the new social, cultural and economic influences of the 1960s onwards' (Rose, 1994: 3). He posits that the experience of colonial oppression in Ireland had left a lasting legacy of distaste for inequality and had engendered 'a tradition of tolerance, which was benign, and based on a belief in fairness and justice' (Rose, 1994: 3).[45]

It is important, however, not to overstate the impact of these changes. Legal change of this nature often belies the social reality, which does not always reflect the ideal posited by official policy. Anti-gay bullying in schools, for instance, remains a serious concern. Even in the workplace, 26 per cent of the LGB workers recently surveyed by McIntyre (2011) were 'out' only to some work colleagues; 12 per cent were 'out' to none. McIntyre indicates that while there were diverse and complex reasons for this discretion, at least some of these respondents chose to conceal their sexuality for fear of negative repercussions, including reputational damage and curtailment of career opportunities. Kenji Yoshino (2002; 2007) suggests that, despite increasing gay visibility, even openly lesbian and gay people still adopt workplace strategies of what he terms 'covering', with a view to downplaying aspects of their homosexuality. Yoshino observes that many lesbian and gay employees who are 'out' to their work colleagues carefully manage their presence in the workplace (and elsewhere) by suppressing aspects of their lives that might serve to emphasise or draw attention to their minority sexuality.

That said, the new laws have served to institutionalise – and to some extent internalise – the notion that ill-treatment of LGB work colleagues and customers is no longer considered acceptable behaviour. It is notable that exceptionally few instances of sexual orientation discrimination are reported annually to the Equality Tribunal, which may in itself be indicative of a seismic change in attitudes (though the Tribunal has ruled that a small number of applicants have been discriminated against on this basis). Nonetheless, while there is no doubt that the experience of gays and lesbians has improved immeasurably, it would be erroneous to assume that law reform has wiped away all instances of discrimination and harassment in the workplace or elsewhere.

The International Dimension

The influence of international legal developments has already been demonstrated in the discussion of *Norris* and *Dudgeon*, above. The European Court of Human Rights, while generally affording states a wide 'margin of appreciation' in morally delicate issues, has in more recent years proved decidedly more robust and proactive in addressing the equality rights of gays and lesbians. In *Karner v Austria* (2003, Applic. 40016/98, 24 July),[46] for instance, the ECHR found that tenancy legislation affording a right of succession for surviving opposite-sex partners of a tenant but not for same-sex partners infringed Article 14 of the Convention read in conjunction with Article 8,[47] in that such treatment discriminated against the applicant on grounds of sexual orientation in relation to his right to respect for his home life. Similarly, laws banning gays from the military[48] and laws setting different ages of consent and legal conditions for heterosexual and homosexual sexual activity[49] have been deemed in breach of the Convention. Additionally, prospective sole adopters (where permitted to adopt as individuals) and homosexual parents cannot be discriminated against on the basis of sexual orientation (*Salgueiro da Silva Mouta v Portugal* [1999] 31 E.H.R.R. 47 and *E.B. v France* Applic. 43546/02, 22 January 2008), though the Convention still permits more favourable treatment for married couples in the context of adoption (*Gas and Dubois v France* Applic. 25951/07, 1 August 2010).[50] Although initially reluctant to do so, the Court has recently recognised same-sex couples (and same-sex couples with children) as coming within the scope of 'family life' protected by Article 8 of the Convention (*Schalk and Kopf v Austria* Applic. 30141/04, 24 June 2010 and *Gas and Dubois v France* Applic. 25951/07, 1 August 2010).[51] Nevertheless, the Court has declined to find that the exclusion of same-sex couples from marriage infringes the Convention's terms, ruling that the right to marry under the Convention does not extend to same-sex marriage (*Schalk and Kopf v Austria*, 2010).

Although the effects of the Convention in Irish law are somewhat limited,[52] as a signatory thereto, Ireland is obliged in international law to comply with the Convention. The Irish courts are required in the domestic realm to read Irish law in a Convention-compliant manner, where possible (European Convention on Human Rights Act 2003, sections 2 and 4), while certain State organs may be sued for non-compliance with Convention norms (European Convention on Human Rights Act 2003, section 3). The Irish courts may also make a 'declaration of incompatibility' in respect of laws that breach the Convention, although this does not invalidate the relevant laws or prevent them from being enforced pending reform by the Oireachtas (Parliament) (European Convention on Human Rights Act 2003, section 5).

The impact of European Union law in this context has been more limited, though a 2000 Directive on employment equality (European Union, 2000),[53] which banned discrimination in the employment context on grounds that included sexual orientation, led to some changes in pensions and employment equality legislation in Ireland.[54] Notably, the European Union's Charter of Fundamental Rights (which binds the EU and the member states when implementing EU law) expressly prohibits discrimination on the basis of sexual orientation (*Charter of Fundamental Rights of the European Union*, Article 21) and guarantees a right to marry in terms that avoid any reference to gender (*Charter of Fundamental Rights of the European Union*, Article 9).[55] In the arena of immigration, EU law also secures to civil partners and same-sex partners of EU nationals a right to move with the EU national to another member state, subject to certain conditions (European Union Directive 2004/38/EC, 2004).[56]

Tensions – Religion and Homosexuality

Significant tensions have arisen in relation to religious exemptions from anti-discrimination measures. These tensions illustrate the uneasy conflict between the need to respect the free practice of religion and the egalitarian concern to combat discrimination and prejudice against lesbians, gay men and bisexuals. A prominent example of this tension is evidenced by section 37(1)(b) of the Employment Equality Act 1998. This provision allows a religious institution, school or hospital run or controlled by a body established for religious purposes, or 'whose objectives include the provision of services in an environment which promotes certain religious values', to discriminate with a view to preventing its religious ethos from being undermined, notwithstanding other provisions of the 1998 Act. In particular, section 37(1)(b) stipulates that a religious-run school or hospital will not be deemed to have discriminated under the 1998 Act where it takes '… action which is reasonably necessary to prevent an employee or a prospective employee from undermining the religious ethos of the institution'.[57] (This exemption does not apply to some specific gender equality provisions in the Act.) Where such institutions adhere to religious beliefs that hold negative views of homosexuality, section 37 potentially allows the employer to deny employment and/or promotion to openly gay prospective employees on ethos grounds or, as appears more common in practice, to grant employment conditional upon the understanding, implicit or explicit, that the employee will refrain from challenging the organisation's ethos.[58] Given that over 90 per cent of primary schools (Coen, 2008: 461), a majority of secondary schools and a great many hospitals in the State are run in accordance with a religious ethos, the potential impact of such an exemption is significant.

It is unclear whether this exemption has ever been *directly* invoked against gays or lesbians. In *Flynn v Power* ([1985] I.R. 648) a religious order was found to have acted lawfully when dismissing a female teacher from her employment in a Roman Catholic girls' secondary school. The teacher was living openly with and had become pregnant by a married man who was not her husband, a lifestyle that the High Court agreed was inimical to the values that the school wished to inculcate.[59] Notably, this case arose under the Unfair Dismissals Act 1977, in respect of which there is *no* express religious exemption. Given that that Act has since been amended expressly to ban dismissal on the grounds of sexual orientation (with no religious exemption),[60] it is unlikely that a gay or lesbian teacher could meet a similar fate today simply because they are gay or lesbian. The outcome in *Flynn* nonetheless suggests that open *behaviour* inimical to the ethos of a religious employer may feasibly result in lawful dismissal. Thus, while it would be unlawful under the 1977 Act (as amended) to dismiss a teacher specifically because of his/her sexual orientation, a school might be able to take action where the teacher's outward behaviour or expression represented a 'threat' to the school's ethos.

Notably, under section 37 the onus is on the establishment to demonstrate that its action is reasonably necessary to prevent the undermining of its religious ethos. Arguably, an establishment may be reluctant to engage in litigating the point, particularly given the negative publicity that would ensue. It appears, however, that the legislative exemption is already highly effective in practice: it is evident that section 37 has had a significant 'chilling effect' on LGB professionals, who 'play safe' in order to minimise the risk of their conduct being regarded as prejudicial to a school or hospital's religious ethos.[61] Indeed, the prevailing impact of section 37 seems to be the enforced silencing and self-censorship of gay and lesbian employees of religious-run institutions. Section 37 thus operates as a species of 'don't ask, don't tell', pushing gay and lesbian teachers and health professionals working in religious-run institutions back into the closet, at least in the context of their working lives.[62]

Some commentators, such as Coen (2008: 460–61), have suggested that the breadth of section 37 may infringe EU law, in that it goes beyond what is permitted by the much more narrowly drawn religious ethos exemption contained in EU Directive 2000/78 EC. This permits discrimination where religion or belief is a genuine, legitimate and justified occupational requirement for a post.[63] Notably, the Directive does not permit this exemption to be used to justify discrimination on grounds of disability, age or sexual orientation.[64] The jurisprudence of the ECHR also suggests that dismissals for engaging in private relationships considered immoral by a religious employer may only be acceptable where religious adherence is integral to the post in question, given the nature of the post.[65] While there appears to be some willingness on the part of the government to restrict sexual orientation discrimination in this context,[66] a delicate balance is required so as not to undermine the constitutional protection afforded to religious practice.[67]

These tensions resurfaced in the context of the introduction of civil partnership. During debates on the Civil Partnership Bill 2009, some TDs and Senators pressed for exemption clauses for public officials and private business people who object on religious grounds to homosexual unions (*see* Ryan, 2011: 32–3). These calls were successfully faced down by the government, which refused to dilute the effect of equality laws protecting gays and lesbians and civil partners from discrimination.[68] Nonetheless, the concern not to antagonise the Churches did have one notable outcome. The Civil Partnership and Certain Rights and Obligations of Cohabitants Act 2010, in making provision for civil partnerships, did not permit the formalisation of civil partnerships by religious ministers, who are permitted to celebrate legally recognised marriages (Civil Partnership and Certain Rights and Obligations of Cohabitants Act 2010, section 16; Civil Registration Act 2004, Part 7A). Nor can civil partnerships be registered in venues with any recent or continuing connection with religion, thereby underlining that civil partnership is strictly a *civil* matter.[69]

Marriage and Relationship Recognition

A distinct feature of the legal landscape as it stood prior to 2011 was that while offering very strong protections to lesbians and gays as *individuals*, Irish law rarely addressed the legal implications of the relationships formed by such persons (Ryan, 2007: 13–8). In one sense this was not surprising: the law at the time offered scant recognition even to *heterosexuals* in non-marital cohabiting relationships. Insofar as the Constitution of Ireland (1937) is concerned, there is only one acceptable template for family formation, namely marriage. The Supreme Court, in particular, has been consistent in confining the constitutional protection afforded by Article 41 of the Constitution to the family based on marriage (*State (Nicolaou) v An Bord Uchtála* [1966] I.R. 567; *G. v An Bord Uchtála* [1980] I.R. 32; *W.O'R. v E.H.* [1996] 2 I.R. 248; and *J.McD. v P.L. and B.M.* [2009] I.E.S.C. 81).[70] As late as 2009 the Supreme Court confirmed emphatically that the Constitution did not recognise family life outside the context of the family based on marriage (*J. McD. v P.L. and B.M.* [2009] I.E.S.C. 81). This approach was reflected, until very recently, in legislation that (pre-2011) almost universally failed to recognise any intimate cohabitation arrangements between unmarried couples.

This had significant implications for same-sex couples, given that they are legally excluded from marriage. As Tobin (2008: 10) notes: '… while non-marital opposite-sex couples may escape the legal quagmire by marrying, same-sex cohabitants simply cannot because this option is currently closed to them' (*see also* Ryan, 2007). At common law, marriage has long been defined as the union of one man and one woman to the exclusion of all others (*Hyde v Hyde* [1866] L.R. 1 P. and D. 130 at 133; *Talbot (orse. Poyntz) v Talbot* 111 Sol. Jo. 213 (1967, HC (Eng.)); *Corbett v Corbett* [1971] Probate 83). This view has been confirmed repeatedly in both Supreme Court and High Court decisions (*Murray v Ireland* [1985] I.R. 532 at 536; *B. v R.* [1995] 1 I.L.R.M. 491 at 495; *T.F. v Ireland* [1995] I.R. 321; *D.T. v C.T.* [2003] 1 I.L.R.M. 321; *Foy v An tArd Chláraitheoir* [2002] I.E.H.C. 116 (9 July 2002); *J.McD. v P.L. and B.M.* [2009] I.E.S.C. 81),[71] and was copper-fastened in legislation by section 2(2)(e) of the Civil Registration Act 2004, which stipulates that the parties' identity of sex is an impediment to the celebration of a marriage.

The constitutional validity of the refusal to recognise same-sex marriage was confirmed by the High Court in *Zappone and Gilligan v Revenue Commissioners* ([2008] 2 I.R. 417).[72] This case involved a lesbian couple who sought recognition of their Canadian marriage in Ireland, ostensibly for the purpose of gaining certain tax benefits, which at that time were confined to married couples.[73] Justice Dunne ruled, however, that the marriage was not entitled to such recognition either under the Constitution or the European Convention on Human Rights. She concluded, in particular, that 'marriage' in Article 41 of the Constitution of Ireland (1937), though not expressly defined in that Article, meant and continued to mean a heterosexual marriage only. Adopting a historical interpretative approach, Justice Dunne concluded that at the time the Constitution was enacted, the term 'marriage' could only have meant a heterosexual union. This understanding of marriage had not, moreover, changed over time, as evidenced by the enactment, in 2004, of legislation preventing the solemnisation of same-sex marriages (Civil Registration Act 2004, section 2(2)(e)). Justice Dunne also pointed to several contemporary judicial pronouncements confirming the essentially heterosexual nature of marriage in Irish law.[74]

Whether this precludes the Oireachtas (the legislature, that is, Parliament) from legislating for same-sex marriage is a contested point. In certain respects – though the point is unclear – Justice Dunne's decision suggests that the traditional constitutional understanding of the concept of marriage as a heterosexual union may not be subject to change through an 'updating' judicial interpretation of the Constitution, as is possible with some other aspects of the Constitution.[75] (An 'updating' judicial interpretation involves judges applying the Constitution in the light of modern-day conditions as opposed to historical considerations.) In particular, she appears to doubt whether the courts can alter the definition of the concept of marriage as a heterosexual union. From this, one might surmise that the constitutional 'right to marry' cannot be extended to same-sex couples, at least by judicial decree. Given that marriage (as defined by the judge) is protected by the Constitution (*see* Article 41.3.1, Constitution of Ireland 1937), introducing same-sex marriage in Ireland (if Justice Dunne is correct) might thus possibly require a popular referendum to alter the Constitution.[76] More recently, Justice Denham (now Chief Justice) in the Supreme Court in *J.McD. v P.L. and B.M.* ([2009] I.E.S.C. 81) appeared to confirm this view, noting that '[u]nder the Constitution it has been clearly established that the family in Irish law is based on a marriage between a man and a woman.'[77] If this is the case, it is difficult to see how the Oireachtas could enact same-sex marriage legislation without provoking a constitutional challenge.

On the other hand, the courts in Ireland (and, in particular, the Supreme Court) tend to defer heavily to the legislature on points of social policy,[78] considering the Oireachtas as having greater democratic legitimacy than the courts to progress social reforms. The courts are thus very reluctant to overrule the Oireachtas on a sensitive point of political controversy. Indeed, in her judgment in *Zappone*, Justice Dunne suggested at one point that the recognition of same-sex couples was essentially a legislative and not a judicial matter, hinting heavily that the courts would defer to whatever policy the legislature considered best in this context.[79] This suggests that if the Oireachtas were to legislate for same-sex marriage, the courts would more than likely uphold such a move. In a similar vein, Carolan (2007), Tobin (2012), O'Mahony (2010; 2012) and Daly (2012) have all argued compellingly that it is constitutionally possible to legislate for same-sex marriage without requiring a constitutional referendum. Nonetheless, the government's steadfast and consistent view appears to be that same-sex marriage is not possible without a referendum altering the Constitution.[80] Notably, in April 2013 the Constitutional Convention recommended by a significant majority that a referendum be held to extend civil marriage to same-sex couples; in November 2013 the government announced that this would take place in 2015.

Recognising Relationships Outside Marriage

The ban on same-sex marriage was formerly compounded by the traditional lack of legal recognition for couples outside the context of marriage. Prior to 2011, non-marital couples enjoyed only very limited recognition in law. Ironically, in the few contexts in which non-marital unions were addressed in legal instruments, such recognition was often confined to opposite-sex couples. The few rights and obligations that were extended to non-marital couples were usually confined in remit to couples who, while not married, lived together 'as husband and wife'. While the point is debatable, the prevailing view appeared to be that this formula implied an opposition of gender and thus excluded same-sex couples, a view confirmed by both case law[81] and parliamentary comment (*see* Ryan, 2011: 9). Same-sex couples thus appeared to be excluded, prior to 2011, from seeking barring orders and suing for wrongful death,[82] as well as from automatic succession to a private residential tenancy.[83] (Since 2011, these rights have been extended to civil partners and, subject to certain conditions, to same-sex cohabitants.)[84]

Throughout the 2000s, the impetus grew to introduce some framework for the recognition of same-sex couples. Initially, debate focused on the legal position of non-marital couples generally, both same-sex and opposite-sex, although the particular position of the same-sex couple increasingly came to prominence. With the growing visibility of same-sex couples (itself a product, in part, of earlier legal reforms) came a heightened appreciation of the very precarious legal position of such couples. In areas such as immigration, taxation and succession, in particular, same-sex couples experienced significant legal disabilities and disadvantages. In most respects these difficulties matched those experienced by unmarried opposite-sex couples, though the inability of same-sex couples to marry compounded this disenfranchisement, setting same-sex couples apart from their heterosexual counterparts who could at least remedy their legal difficulties by marrying (*see* Ryan, 2007: 31–7).

The introduction of civil partnership in Northern Ireland in 2004 provided a particularly significant impetus to reform in the Republic. The terms of the Good Friday Agreement require equivalence of human rights protections north and south of the border, an international legal commitment that some commentators suggested required at least comparable, if not identical, legal recognition for same-sex couples south of the border (Ó Cinnéide, 2005). Several reports, meanwhile, highlighted the lack of legal recognition for non-marital couples and, in particular, same-sex couples, and recommended reform (Ronayne and Mee, 2000; Equality Authority, 2002; Law Reform Commission, 2004; 2006b; Walsh and Ryan, 2006; Irish Council for Civil Liberties, 2006; the Working Group on Domestic Partnership, 2006).[85] Notably, the case for greater protection for cohabitants was made by the Law Reform Commission in its 2006 report, *The Rights and Duties of Cohabitants*. The recommendations contained therein included protection on an equal basis for both same-sex and opposite-sex cohabitants (Law Reform Commission, 2006b).

While the government initially proved resistant to recognising same-sex couples (as evidenced by measures in the Social Welfare (Miscellaneous Provisions) Act 2004 denying recognition to same-sex partners in the context of various administrative social welfare schemes), over time it gradually softened its stance. The Parental Leave (Amendment) Act 2006 extended parental leave to the same-sex partners of parents and *force majeure* leave to same-sex cohabitants.[86] From 2006 onwards, the State gradually began to recognise the non-EU national, same-sex partners of Irish citizens for the purpose of immigration, first on an *ad hoc* basis, but culminating in the adoption of a formal policy recognising *de facto* partners, provided certain conditions are met.[87]

In late 2006 a high-level Working Group set up by the Minister for Justice, Equality and Law Reform published an Options Paper, setting out proposals for law reform in relation to same-sex couples. While not definitively recommending any one option, the report suggests that given possible constitutional complications with same-sex marriage, a comprehensive scheme of civil partnership would best address the needs of same-sex couples. Private members' bills proposing civil partnership – namely Senator David Norris's Civil Partnership Bill 2004 and the Labour Party's Civil Unions Bill 2006 – while not adopted by Parliament, added further pressure for reform.

Civil Partnership

The passage of law reform for same-sex couples proved painfully slow, but the ultimate result of these efforts was a civil partnership regime for same-sex couples that was arguably as comprehensive as possible, politically and constitutionally. This came courtesy of the Civil Partnership and Certain Rights and Obligations of Cohabitants Act 2010, a significant milestone in the development of lesbian and gay rights in Ireland. The Act – which came into force in January 2011 – departs significantly from the pre-existing legal situation for same-sex couples, though it also has implications for opposite-sex couples. It introduces two new schemes for relationship recognition outside of marriage: the first relating to what is called 'civil partnership'; and the second addressing 'cohabitation'. The cohabitation provisions of the Act[88] apply to couples in intimate and committed cohabiting relationships who are not closely related to each other, not married to each other and not in a civil partnership with each other. Applying to both same-sex and opposite-sex couples, the cohabitation provisions provide certain basic and limited rights for cohabiting couples, including the right to enter into cohabitation agreements addressing the financial and proprietary aspects of the couple's relationship.[89] The Act also offers certain financial remedies to 'qualified cohabitants' on the break-up of a long-term relationship (where the couple have lived together at least two years if they have children in common, otherwise five years), provided the applicant for relief is financially dependent as a result of the relationship or its termination.[90] A person may also seek provision from the estate of his/her deceased qualified cohabitant if the deceased has not otherwise made proper provision for the survivor (subject to certain conditions).

While these measures provide important protections, particularly for financially vulnerable long-term cohabitants, the bulk of the Act addresses civil partnership, that is an exclusive, registered union, potentially for life, between two unrelated adults[91] who must be of the same sex. While the law does not require any sexual basis for the relationship, it is clear that it is a conjugal-style, as opposed to a consanguineous, union that is envisaged and as such civil partnership is intended to address the specific position of gay and lesbian couples. Notably, parties who are closely related to each other – such as sisters, an aunt and niece, or a father and son – are not permitted to enter into a civil partnership with each other.[92]

The process for registering a civil partnership is remarkably similar to the steps that are required for the celebration of a legally recognised marriage, the key exception being that a civil partnership may only be registered in the presence of a state-employed registrar of civil partnerships, and not before a religious minister.[93] Once 'civilly partnered', the couple are treated to a large degree as they would be if they were married. Indeed much of the Act comprises a 'copy and paste'-style replication (or, in the alternative, amendment) of the equivalent provisions of legislation applying to married couples.[94] Most of the legal remedies that are available to married couples are now extended to civil partners, and usually on the same basis. While there are some differences in the application of some remedies to spouses and civil partners, respectively (*see* Fagan, 2011), it is clear from the Act that the template for civil partnership is marriage. The Act broadly achieves equality as between spouses and civil partners in the context of mutual obligations of financial support (maintenance), shared home protection, succession, pensions, domestic violence, wrongful death and housing. The legal remedies available on the dissolution of a civil partnership are identical to those available on divorce. In practice, civil partners are now treated the same as spouses for the purpose of immigration, while civil partners of Irish citizens (in the same manner as spouses of Irish citizens) may apply for citizenship of Ireland two years earlier than would be the case if they were not in a civil partnership with an Irish citizen.[95]

Taxation (Finance (No.3) Act 2011 and Finance Act 2012) and social welfare legislation (Social Welfare and Pensions Act 2010) have also been amended to provide taxation exemptions and social welfare benefits to civil partners, on largely the same basis as spouses. Civil partners are now entitled to share tax bands and credits for the purpose of reducing their collective income tax burden, while transfers and bequests between civil partners are entirely exempt from stamp duty, capital gains tax[96] and – crucially – capital acquisitions tax (the tax on inheritances and gifts). Survivors' social welfare benefits (such as the widow's/widower's pension), previously confined to spouses, have also been extended to civil partners. Meanwhile, both civil partners and same-sex cohabitants are now recognised as couples for the purpose of the social welfare code on the same basis as spouses and heterosexual cohabitants, respectively. (Social welfare law had previously recognised only spouses and opposite-sex cohabitants.) While in many instances this will benefit same-sex couples,[97] equality in the social welfare context may result in a reduction in some social welfare payments for some same-sex couples, as these couples are now considered as a unit with shared resources.[98] As Colker (1991) has astutely observed, it is often the case that the poorer the family unit, the less, in financial terms, it has to gain from recognition and the more (potentially) it has to lose.[99]

Gaps in Protection for LGB Families

While civil partnership is, in most respects, extensive and comprehensive, some significant gaps remain in the protection offered to LGB families. The most notable of these relate to couples with children (Ryan, 2011: 24–9; *see also* Chapters 6 and 7). While a civil partner retains full rights and obligations in respect of children *naturally born to or adopted by her*, the civil partner of such a parent has next to no rights or obligations in respect of that child. In particular, a child cannot claim to be supported by the civil partner of his/her natural or adoptive parent, and cannot inherit property on the death of his/her parent's civil partner, unless expressly named in the latter's will. Although a person may be made a guardian of a civil partner's child on the death of an existing guardian,[100] there is no straightforward legal mechanism whereby *both* civil partners may jointly and simultaneously exercise parental responsibility (called 'guardianship')[101] in respect of the same child. Exceptionally, on the removal of an existing guardian by a court, a person may apply to the court to be made a guardian alongside the remaining guardian(s). Yet such removals happen very rarely, if at all, and there can be no removal of a biological mother or marital father as guardian. Notably, civil partners and same-sex couples (unlike married couples) may not jointly adopt a child.[102] Additionally, a person who has played a parenting role in respect of their civil partner's child may seek access (visitation rights) in respect of that child, but not custody thereof.

To some extent this situation reflects the privileged position in Irish law of biological parenthood over social parenthood. While spouses of parents have some rights and obligations in respect of their step-children, even marriage to a parent does not confer parental rights (though spouses, unlike civil partners, may jointly adopt a child, and step-parents may be obliged to support their step-children).[103]

The Civil Partnership Act did little to ameliorate these gaps. While the relationship between a child and its natural or adoptive parent is recognised for some purposes in the legislation (for instance, as a factor in determining the amount of financial provision for civil partners on dissolution of the civil partnership), the Act generally avoids conferring any parental obligations or rights on the civil partner of a biological parent in respect of the biological parent's child, even where the couple is jointly raising the child.[104] The Law Reform Commission (2010) has recommended permitting the extension of parental responsibility (guardianship) to the spouses and civil partners of parents,[105] a recommendation the government looks likely to follow.[106] Nonetheless, as the law stands at present, a same-sex couple (be they civil partners or not) generally cannot in law simultaneously share guardianship/parental responsibility in respect of a child.

The precarious situation of same-sex couples raising children (and whether or not they are civil partners makes no difference) was very ably demonstrated by the decision of the Supreme Court in *J.McD. v P.L. and B.M.* ([2009] I.E.S.C. 81). In this case, a male friend of a lesbian couple had agreed to help them father a child, confirming in writing that he would not act as a parent of the child, but would instead play the role of a 'favourite uncle'. When the child was born, however, the father realised that he wanted an increased role and sought guardianship (parental responsibility) of and access (visitation rights) to the child through the courts. While not awarding him guardianship, the Supreme Court granted the father a right of access to his child, believing this was in the best interests of the child. The court ruled that the environment in which the lesbian partners were raising their child was a loving and caring environment, a factor regularly referred to in the judges' decisions. Nonetheless, the court emphatically concluded that the lesbian couple and their child were not a family for the purpose of the Constitution or under the European Convention on Human Rights, and thus were not entitled to protection as a family under the Constitution or (at that time) the Convention.[107] The mother's partner, moreover, had no independent rights to guardianship or custody of the child. The decision provides a rather chilling and unsettling reminder to the growing number of same-sex couples (particularly lesbian couples) raising children of the very precarious legal position in which they are parenting. In particular, it underlines that, even with civil partnership, same-sex couples are not and cannot be 'families' for the purpose of the Constitution, a stance that excludes same-sex couples and their children from the protective ambit of Article 41 thereof (which safeguards the family based on marriage).

Differences between Civil Partnership and Marriage

While largely equivalent to marriage, some differences remain between marriage and civil partnership. Some of these differences are technical and relatively minor, and some are apparently inadvertent, but some differences are significant and profound in their impact.[108]

One major area of difference relates to the criteria for separation and dissolution. First, while civil partners may enter into a separation agreement, a court-ordered remedy of judicial separation[109] – which formally permits the parties to live separate lives but not to remarry – is confined to married couples.[110] Second, a court may order the dissolution of a civil partnership (allowing the civil partners to marry or enter into new civil partnerships) where the couple have been living apart for two of the previous three years and where proper provision (in terms of property and financial arrangements) has been or will be made for both civil partners. These requirements differ from the criteria for dissolution of a marriage (divorce) in several respects, most notably that a marriage will be dissolved only where the spouses have lived apart from each other for *four of the previous five years*. The most likely reason for this difference, as suggested by Mee (2007: 208–10), is that too long a waiting period for civil partnership dissolution might be considered as unduly fettering the constitutional right to marry of a separated civil partner who wishes to marry a person of the opposite sex.

For a divorce to issue, moreover, the court must be satisfied that there is no reasonable prospect of reconciliation between the spouses, which is not a requirement for civil partnership dissolution.[111] The court must also be satisfied that proper provision on divorce has been or will be made not only for both spouses but also for *any dependent children*. Civil partnership dissolution, by contrast, may be granted regardless of its impact on either partner's child. Given the best interests principle – which foregrounds the welfare of the child as the paramount consideration in the context of child law[112] – this disregard for the interests of children seems remarkable.

Thus, while the remedies available to civil partners following dissolution are largely identical to those available to divorced spouses, the criteria for dissolution are significantly less robust in the case of civil partnership.[113] While it may well be argued that the shorter living-apart requirement for civil partnership is, on balance, more reasonable than that for divorce, and that a requirement to prove irreconcilability would amount to superfluous window-dressing, one cannot escape the uncomfortable conclusion that civil partnership is not officially viewed quite as seriously as marriage.

Challenging the Marriage/Civil Partnership Binary

It is arguable that – even if it were identical in every respect to marriage – the inception of civil partnership creates a new binary in Irish law that, despite the monumental improvement in the legal position of same-sex couples, serves to emphasise the State's official view that same-sex couples and opposite-sex couples are substantively different in some important way.[114] This differentiation in turn signals to gays and lesbians as individuals – even those who do not wish to marry or enter into a civil partnership – that there is something essentially different about gay relationships, and indeed about homosexuality itself, that merits such differential treatment. For what other reason would the State go to the bother of creating a separate legal regime for relationship recognition for a minority of couples when it already has a functioning regime in place, namely marriage?

A growing body of foreign case law challenges this binary. The overall tenor of these judgments is exemplified by the ruling of the US (Federal) District Court for Northern California in *Perry v Schwarzenegger* (704 F. Supp. 2d 921 (N.D. Cal. 2010)),[115] where Justice Walker concluded that a constitutional ban on same-sex marriage in the state constitution of California (commonly known as 'Proposition 8') infringed the equality and due process guarantees of the US Constitution. While ruling that laws discriminating against homosexuals could only be upheld where there was a particularly compelling justification for such measures, Justice Walker proceeded to conclude that the ban was not rationally connected to any legitimate state interest:[116]

> Proposition 8 fails to advance any rational basis in singling out gay men and lesbians for denial of a marriage license. Indeed, the evidence shows Proposition 8 does nothing more than enshrine in the California Constitution the notion that opposite-sex couples are superior to same-sex couples ... (*Perry v Schwarzenegger*, 2010: 135)

Moral viewpoints, Justice Walker added, were not sufficient (in isolation) to justify this discrimination (*Perry v Schwarzenegger*, 2010: 132–5). In particular, he concluded that arguments relating to the upbringing of children had no currency in this context, given that same-sex couples were already entitled to raise children in California, and indeed were facilitated in doing so by the state, just not within the context of marriage (*Perry v Schwarzenegger*, 2010: 127–9).[117] In sum, he could find no evidence that same-sex couples should be treated as the inferiors of opposite-sex couples: 'The evidence shows that, by every available metric, opposite-sex couples are not better than their same-sex counterparts; instead, as partners, parents and citizens, opposite-sex couples and same-sex couples are equal' (*Perry v Schwarzenegger*, 2010: 132). The decision was upheld on appeal to the Ninth Circuit Court of Appeals in February 2012 (albeit on a somewhat narrower basis) (*Perry v Brown*, 2012), while in 2013 the US Supreme Court rejected a challenge to the original verdict of Justice Walker (though on purely technical grounds).[118]

Similar conclusions have been reached in the courts of individual US states and other jurisdictions. In *Varnum v Brien* (763 NW 2d 862 Iowa, [2009]), for instance, the Supreme Court of Iowa concluded[119] that the ban on same-sex marriage infringed the equal protection clause of that state's constitution in that it did not '... substantially further any important governmental objective' (*Varnum v Brien*, 2009: 906). The court placed particular emphasis on the fact that gays and lesbians were '... a historically disfavored class of persons ... excluded from a supremely important civil institution without a constitutionally sufficient justification' (*Varnum v Brien*, 2009: 906). The Supreme Court of California's verdict in *In re Marriage Cases* ([2008] 43 Cal.4th 757), which preceded the enactment of Proposition 8 in that state, also noted the historic disparagement of gays and lesbians, a factor that made the ban on same-sex marriage, in its view, all the more invidious. That ban is, indeed, most problematic in that it substantially affects a category of persons who historically have experienced considerable stigmatisation, discrimination and (as discussed at the start of this chapter and in Chapter 4) criminalisation on account of innate and immutable human characteristics.

Querying the Equality Agenda

There is much merit in the proposition that same-sex couples should be entitled to be treated the same as opposite-sex couples. While civil partnership delivers most, though not all, of the same rights and obligations as marriage – and indeed is largely modelled on marital legislation – it remains a union distinct and separate from marriage. The inescapable implication is that same-sex couples are considered not to be the same as opposite-sex couples, that there is some qualitative difference between the two functionally similar situations. This stance is particularly problematic given the historic stigma attached to homosexuality.

There is, however, a risk in arguing unthinkingly for identical treatment in this context without allowing for scrutiny of the benchmark for equal treatment, in particular the content and processes of marriage law. Like the diner in *When Harry Met Sally* (1989) who witnesses Meg Ryan's character faking an orgasm in the middle of a crowded restaurant, the standard discourse of the marriage–civil partnership debate seems to be, 'I'll have what she's having.' This involves rating the worth or otherwise of civil partnership by reference to how closely it equates same-sex couples and married, heterosexual couples. The underlying assumption is that the more closely civil partnership is equated with marriage, the better for same-sex couples.

Marriage is thus the unquestioned touchstone for determining the value of what is offered to same-sex partners, regardless of whether the content of marriage in fact universally serves the interests of same-sex couples, or any couples for that matter. For instance, civil partnership dissolution, like divorce, is granted on a 'no clean break' basis (Ryan, 2011: 180–82). Under the relevant legislation, former civil partners and spouses may seek provision from a court at the time of divorce or dissolution *or at any time thereafter* (though, in practice, the courts have indicated a preference for finality, where feasible). While certain exceptions apply,[120] this potentially creates an open-ended right to be supported indefinitely by a former spouse or civil partner. There has been comparatively little analysis as to whether this policy is appropriate to the situation of the average same-sex couple. Is a potentially life-long obligation of support for a former partner – and corresponding dependency of the latter – either necessary or useful in all cases, in particular where the parties have no children? Indeed, the extension of this policy proceeded in spite of several prominent court decisions underlining the value of finality and certainty in divorce settlements, and suggesting a less-than-enthusiastic judicial attitude to the prospect of open-ended litigation between divorced parties (*see* Ryan, 2011: 180–82).

On the converse side, at least some instances of inequality could be to the advantage of same-sex couples. It may well be, for instance, that the shorter living-apart requirement for civil partnership dissolution is, in fact, more reasonable than that applicable to marriage. Notably, the former discrimination in the context of social welfare entitlements often financially benefited poorer same-sex couples; these social welfare advantages have been eliminated by legal recognition.

The discourse of equality thus tends to under-problematise existing policy and law on marriage. In the rush to be treated the same as heterosexuals, comparatively little attention has been directed to whether the laws and practices that apply to heterosexuals in the context of marriage are, in fact, universally of merit or work well. It is arguable, in this regard, that a unique opportunity to reconceptualise and reconsider the foundations of marriage law has been missed. It is important to note, in particular, that access to marriage on its own will not resolve all of the legal difficulties experienced by same-sex couples with children, given the continued prioritisation of biological parenthood over social parenthood.

This experience may reflect a broader de-radicalisation of gay and lesbian discourses (*see also* Chapter 4, 'The Pursuit of Gay and Lesbian Sexual Citizenship Rights, 1980–2011'). Ryan (2007) charts how the discourses of gay community activism have shifted markedly from the radical disestablishmentarianism of the 1970s, which rejected, in particular, marriage as a 'one size fits all' model for relationship formation. Modern activist discourses, by contrast, focus predominantly – though not exclusively – on achieving equality of treatment with heterosexuals, and in particular seek assimilation into the institution of marriage rather than its modification or reform. While such equality is crucially important for same-sex couples, both symbolically and in practice, the push for same-sex marriage has arguably diverted attention from the need for widespread reform of family law and the institution of marriage itself. Stychin (2000) warns that these assimilationist tendencies also risk playing into a discourse of 'acceptable homosexualities', separating 'good homosexuals' – those responsive to the demands of the State, civil society and the market – from gays and lesbians who challenge this order, leading to the further marginalisation of the latter. Kamikaze (1995: 117) makes a similar claim in the Irish context, noting the concern of the Irish gay community '… with projecting a "respectable" image of homosexuality', which in turn has led to more radical perspectives and more marginalised segments of the LGB community being sidelined.

Conclusion

None of the above is intended to detract from the enormous achievements of the past three decades. That such extraordinary change could occur in a comparatively short period of time is a testament to the determination of a great many activists and campaigners, many of whom suffered greatly for their bravery. The passage of the Civil Partnership Act is, perhaps, the most substantial and momentous of these achievements, made all the more remarkable by the fact that it passed with so little opposition – by universal acclaim in Dáil Éireann and by 48 votes to 4 in Seanad Éireann. Yet the earlier reforms are equally crucial, not least because they removed significant barriers to the open participation of gay and lesbian citizens in Irish society. It is arguable that these extraordinary achievements provide a firm platform from which to press for further reform, particularly in relation to families with children, and ultimately for equal marriage rights. It is important, nonetheless, to ensure that LGB discourses move beyond the equality agenda and towards more substantive and critical examination of the outcomes of proposed reforms, with particular emphasis on the needs of diverse family types (*see also* Chapters 6 and 7) and, in particular, those of poorer and marginalised parts of the LGB community.

Notes

[1] For reasons of space, this chapter deals exclusively with the law as it applies to lesbians, gay men and bisexuals and does not address the particular position of transgender persons. For an excellent review of the experience of transgender persons in Ireland, *see* McIlroy (2009) and also Chapter 5 in this book.

[2] Homosexual Offences (Northern Ireland) Order 1982.

[3] The Sexual Offences Act 1967, section 1, decriminalised private sexual acts between males aged 21 or over in England and Wales. The initial age of consent was later lowered to 18 and then, in 2000, to 16. The Sexual Offences Act 2003 imposes an equal regime for heterosexual and homosexual sexual activity.

[4] *See* Article 50 of the Constitution of Ireland 1937. In *Norris v Attorney General* [1984] I.R. 36 at 102, McCarthy J. makes reference to these sanctions as a legacy of the moral hypocrisy of Victorian England: 'The Acts of 1861 and of 1885 were passed during the long reign of a British monarch whose name is identified with many human virtues — those of duty, responsibility, love of family and country and so on — but a less attractive quality of that age was the gross hypocrisy that frequently prevailed, even amongst the ranks of the legislators.'

[5] Section 61 also applied to sexual intercourse with an animal ('bestiality'), a ban on which remains in force. Additionally, section 62 of the Offences Against the Person Act 1861 set a maximum penalty of ten years

of penal servitude for attempted buggery and indecent assault upon a male, though a constitutional challenge to section 62 succeeded in *S.M. (Mitchell) v Ireland* [2007] I.E.H.C. 280.

[6] In *DPP v Judge Devins and M. O'M* ([2012] I.E.S.C. 7) the Supreme Court concluded that the offence of buggery addressed by section 61 was a common law offence (an offence developed in the courts rather than created by Act of Parliament), the *penalties* for which had been set by Act of Parliament.

[7] If both were willing participants, each party to the act was potentially liable to prosecution.

[8] The Penal Servitude Act 1891 and the Probation of Offenders Act 1907 allowed lesser sentences to be imposed.

[9] 'Any male person who, in public or private, commits, or is a party to the commission of, or procures or attempts to procure the commission by any male person of, any act of gross indecency with another male person, shall be guilty of a misdemeanour, and being convicted thereof shall be liable at the discretion of the court to be imprisoned for any term not exceeding two years.'

[10] *R. v Hornby and Peaple* ([1946] 2 All E.R. 487) and *R. v Preece and Howells* ([1977] Q.B. 50).

[11] An unwanted sexual act, on the other hand, constitutes an indecent or sexual assault.

[12] Knowingly committing a solo sexual act in the presence of another male, which the other male willingly observes, may, for instance, have constituted an offence. *See R. v Preece and Howells* ([1977] Q.B. 50) and *R. v Hunt and Badsey* ([1950] 2 All E.R. 291).

[13] Until the enactment of the Criminal Law (Sexual Offences) Act 2006, women were generally treated less rigorously in this context. While a man could not have sexual intercourse with a woman under the age of 17, a woman could, until 2006, have sexual intercourse with a male aged 15 or over. Meanwhile, for all other heterosexual conduct and for lesbian sexual acts the age of consent was, prior to 2006, 15 years, although in the case of lesbians this was probably an inadvertent consequence rather than the result of a deliberate policy choice. The minimum age limit of 15 arises from s. 14 of the Criminal Law (Amendment) Act 1935, which provides that consent is not a defence to a charge of indecent assault (now sexual assault) against a person aged under 15. Since 2006 the age of consent for penetration of the vagina by an object is 17 (it is unclear whether 'object' in this context includes a body part), though for all other lesbian sexual activities the age of consent remains 15.

[14] A similar line of reasoning was employed in *Somjee v Attorney General* ([1981] I.L.R.M. 324), where the High Court upheld an exemption from rules relating to citizenship by naturalisation, where the exemption applied only to women (and not men) marrying Irish citizens. Keane J. reasoned that the State was entitled to assume that women were less likely

than men to engage in activities that might justify a refusal of citizenship, and thus the court found that the Oireachtas was entitled to grant this exemption exclusively to women.

[15] *See also* Norris, who suggests that '[i]t simply did not occur to the legislators that women might possess a sexuality independent of the male' (Norris, 1977: 32).

[16] Byrne (1995: 164), for instance, recounts the verbal and physical abuse she suffered following her appearance on the *Late Late Show* (Irish television chat show) in the early 1990s to discuss her experience as a lesbian. This included receiving a death threat and being physically attacked by three adult males.

[17] At the time, a non-consensual sexual assault on a person was deemed an 'indecent assault'.

[18] The average number of recorded 'unnatural' or homosexual offences between 1970 and 1991 inclusive stood at just under 43 recorded offences per year, not all of which were prosecuted. These figures varied from year to year, the highest number of recorded offences for the period being 88 in 1970, the lowest being 7 in 1979. In some years, the statistics specifically addressed 'homosexual offences'. In others, however, the figures embraced all 'unnatural offences', which may possibly have included some incidents of bestiality and heterosexual buggery (thus possibly reducing further the rate of detection of specifically homosexual offences). *See Report of the Garda Síochána Commissioner on Crime* (Dublin: Stationery Office) for the years 1970–1991, available from: <http://www.garda.ie/Controller.aspx?Page=8824&Lang=1> [accessed 21 January 2013].

[19] Given the number of prosecutions per annum documented in the text, it appears that there was no particular zeal to address even public activity, though some prosecutions certainly did occur. Nell McCafferty (1975: 13) recounts a prosecution involving two consenting male adults engaged in a sexual act in a public toilet.

[20] Another example was the fate of Declan Flynn, a gay man killed by five teenagers in Fairview Park in 1982. In their defence, the teenagers alleged that they were acting as vigilantes, targeting gay men cruising in the park. It appears this line of argument was influential in the judge's decision to impose suspended sentences on the offenders, despite their conviction for manslaughter. *See* Cashin (2008; 2011).

[21] Ironically, part of the State's lines of defence in this litigation was that the plaintiff had no grounds for complaint, as he had not been the subject even of an investigation, let alone prosecution, in respect of homosexual offences. Although the outcomes in the Irish and European courts respectively were different, both sets of courts agreed that even if they were not being robustly enforced, the plaintiff was entitled to challenge the laws in question. The Supreme Court reasoned that the laws effectively had a chilling effect on gay males as they held out the prospect of being prosecuted for consensual adult sexual activity (*see* O'Higgins CJ. [1984] I.R. 36

at 59). The European Court determined likewise, concluding that Senator Norris was a 'victim' for the purpose of the Convention, entitled to challenge the legislation notwithstanding the lack of direct enforcement by the authorities to his particular situation.

[22] For a further analysis of the narrative of the judgments in *Norris, see* Ryan (2012b: 427–35).

[23] The Constitution contains multiple prominent references to religion, God and specifically to Jesus Christ, most notably in the Preamble, Article 6 and Article 44. In *Quinn's Supermarket v Attorney General* ([1972] I.R. 1 at 23), Walsh J. (in the Supreme Court) invoked these constitutional references, noting the Constitution's '… firm conviction that we are a religious people' and, notably, 'a Christian people'.

[24] *See* Ryan (2012b: 432–5).

[25] Justice McCarthy's decision primarily addressed the contention that the ban on anal intercourse infringed the privacy rights of marital couples. He concluded that it did so, but the remaining four judges declined to consider this contention. They reasoned that the plaintiff was not himself married, nor likely to be, and thus had no standing to put forward an argument on behalf of married couples who were not party to the case.

[26] The ECHR adjudicates upon claims that a contracting state (there are 47 such contracting states, all members of the Council of Europe) is in breach of the terms of the European Convention on Human Rights. Individuals may (once they have exhausted all domestic remedies) take proceedings before the court, alleging a State's breach of Convention rights.

[27] Until 2003, decisions of the ECHR had no direct legal impact within Ireland as a matter of domestic Irish law, though they often proved to be of persuasive effect before the Irish courts. The European Convention on Human Rights Act 2003 now requires that Irish courts interpret national law, where possible, in a manner consistent with the Convention (s. 2). Certain public bodies may, moreover, be sued for breach of convention rights (s. 3), while in cases where a clear breach of the Convention can be established, Irish law may be declared incompatible with the Convention (s. 5), an outcome that nonetheless does not invalidate the relevant law, which remains operative until repealed by the Oireachtas (Parliament).

[28] The 1990 Act also deemed the penetration of the vagina (but not the anus) by an object to be a rape under s. 4 of the Act. Whether the term 'object' includes a body part, such as a finger or the mouth, remains unclear.

[29] A constitutional challenge to this disparity succeeded in *S.M. (Mitchell) v Ireland* [2007] I.E.H.C. 280.

[30] The Act arguably owes as much to political as it does to legal factors, the measure having been introduced by the Fianna Fáil–Labour coalition formed in early 1993. Decriminalisation was a major plank of the more liberal Labour Party's agenda for law reform.

[31] The Criminal Law (Sexual Offences) Act 1993 abolished the former offence of buggery between persons with no saving provision for offences committed before the commencement of the Act. This meant, remarkably, that offences of buggery, even against children, committed before 1993 can no longer be prosecuted. (The new offences created by the 1993 Act could only be applied prospectively.) *See* the Supreme Court decision in *DPP v Judge Devins and M. O'M* [2012] I.E.S.C. 7.

[32] Theoretically, an offence could also have been committed where *both* parties were underage, each committing an offence in respect of the other participant.

[33] These liberalising provisions were offset by the imposition of new legal restrictions on and penalties for prostitution in ss 6–9 of the Criminal Law (Sexual Offences) Act 1993. Even in this latter respect, however, the Act represents a general move towards equality, the legislation removing the former distinction between male and female prostitution.

[34] For instance, prior to 2006, 17 was the age of consent for all acts of anal intercourse (whether heterosexual or homosexual) and for most sexual acts between two or more males. While heterosexual sexual intercourse with a girl aged under 17 was also illegal, prior to 2006 heterosexual intercourse between a female aged 17 or over and a boy was permitted once the boy was aged 15 or more. Meanwhile, all heterosexual acts falling short of anal or sexual intercourse, as well as lesbian sexual acts, attracted an age of consent of 15.

[35] The 2006 Act posits a uniform age of 17 for all penetrative 'sexual acts', which are defined as comprising penetration by the penis of the vagina, mouth or anus, and penetration of the vagina by an object. For sexual activity that involves violence or the threat of violence, or that causes injury, humiliation or degradation of a grave nature, the age of consent is also set at 17. It is unclear whether oral sex performed on a female or digital penetration *per vaginam* is a 'sexual act' for this purpose, though the better view may be that the term 'object' in this context means an inanimate object as opposed to a part of the body. For all sexual contact falling short of a 'sexual act' as defined, the age of consent is 15, through some activities involving a person under 18 may constitute 'sexual exploitation' under the Criminal Law (Human Trafficking) Act 2008. Where a girl under the age of 17 engages in sexual intercourse with a boy under the age of 17, the girl is exempted from criminal liability by s. 5 of the Criminal Law (Sexual Offences) Act 2006. The Supreme Court upheld this controversial exemption as constitutional in *M.D. (A Minor) v Ireland* ([2012] I.E.S.C. 10), reasoning that it was justified by the risk of pregnancy for girls, a risk unique to women. The 2006 Act abolished the offence of gross indecency with a male under 17. Some but not all of the activities covered by this old offence were criminalised by the 2006 Act, though for acts falling short of a 'sexual act' as defined above, the age of consent is 15.

[36] The Health (Family Planning) Act 1979, for instance, allowed access to contraception (including condoms) solely on the prescription of a doctor, who could prescribe contraception only for *bona fide* family planning purposes or for 'adequate' medical reasons. The requirement of a prescription for condoms was dropped by the Health (Family Planning) (Amendment) Act 1985, though strict restrictions on the venues for the sale of condoms (which generally could only be sold in a pharmacy, doctor's clinic, family planning clinic or hospital) remained in place until 1993.

[37] Health (Family Planning) (Amendment) Act 1993 and the Irish Medicines Board Act 1995.

[38] The Equality Act 2004 amended these provisions also to outlaw discrimination and harassment by association (where a person is treated less favourably because of their relationship or association with someone of a particular sexual orientation) and discrimination and harassment by imputation (where a person is discriminated against because they are wrongly believed to be of a particular sexual orientation).

[39] Civil Partnership and Certain Rights and Obligations of Cohabitants Act 2010, s. 102.

[40] In the context of sexual orientation, one of the most notable exemptions is s. 5(2)(d) of the Equal Status Act 2000, a provision that allows insurance (other than health insurance) and pension providers, among others, to discriminate based on actuarial evidence of risk. This, for instance, would potentially allow an insurer to set higher life insurance premia (or refuse such insurance policies) for categories of persons (such as gay men) with a higher per capita risk of contracting medical conditions such as HIV.

[41] Though subject to a caveat that allowed widows and widowers to be treated more favourably than other parties – *see* discussion in Ryan (2011: 162–3). The same Act closed off the recognition of same-sex couples for the purpose of certain social welfare administrative schemes, though the Social Welfare and Pensions Act 2010 has reversed this step. Additionally, the Civil Partnership and Certain Rights and Obligations of Cohabitants Act 2010 requires that in relation to pension schemes, civil partners must now be treated the same as spouses.

[42] Gay and lesbian asylum-seekers often experience difficulties establishing a credible case for their claims. The likelihood of discrimination *per se* is not sufficient to ground a claim, while, additionally, applicants are sometimes turned down on the basis that they can avoid persecution by remaining 'discreet' about their sexuality on their return to their home country. The UK Supreme Court, however, has rejected this approach in cases where a person would be forced to remain discreet with a view to avoiding persecution: *see HJ (Iran) and HT (Cameroon) v Secretary of State for the Home Department* [2010] UKSC 31.

[43] Moane (1995: 87), for instance, documents one case where a female worker was allegedly dismissed from work for kissing another woman in the workplace.

[44] Notably, 21 per cent of respondents reported living in poverty, while 57 per cent indicated that they had experienced some financial difficulty in their lives. A remarkable one-third of respondents had, at some point in their lives, left home in circumstances where they were unsure where next they would live (GLEN/Nexus 1995).

[45] Rose reprises this argument in Rose (1995: 75–6).

[46] *See also Kozak v Poland* Applic.13102/02, 2 March 2010.

[47] Article 14 of the Convention bans discrimination specifically in the application of other Articles of the Convention, on various grounds, including sex, race and religion. It is not, as such, a general ban on discrimination, but proscribes discrimination in relation to the application of Convention rights. While Article 14 does not expressly refer to sexual orientation discrimination, the grounds listed in Article 14 are non-exhaustive and have been interpreted to include sexual orientation discrimination. Article 8 addresses the right to respect for one's privacy, family life, home life and correspondence.

[48] *Lustig-Prean and Beckett v United Kingdom* ([2000] 29 E.H.R.R. 538) and *Smith and Grady v United Kingdom* ([2000] 29 E.H.R.R. 493).

[49] *A.D.T. v United Kingdom* ([2000] 2 FLR 697); *L. and V. v Austria* Applics. 39392/98 and 39829/98, 9 January 2003; *Woditschka and Wilfling v Austria* Applics. 69756/01 and 6306/02, 21 October 2004; and *B.B. v the United Kingdom* Applic. 53760/00, 10 February 2004). But *see also Fernando dos Santos Couto v Portugal* (Applic. 31874/07, 21 September 2010), where criminal law provisions addressed at protecting minors were upheld, despite the fact that the conditions applicable to homosexual and heterosexual activity were different.

[50] In *Gas and Dubois v France* (Applic. 25951/07, 1 August 2010), where the court ruled that measures that confined second-parent adoption to married couples did not infringe the Convention.

[51] In *Gas and Dubois*, for instance, a chamber of the court found, in an admissibility decision, that the common life of a lesbian couple and their child constituted 'family life' for the purpose of the Convention.

[52] The Convention may, since 2003, be invoked in the Irish courts, by virtue of the European Convention on Human Rights Act 2003, though it may only be relied upon under the conditions laid down in the Act. *Cf.* endnote 27 above. Because it was incorporated at a sub-constitutional level, moreover, where there is a conflict between the Convention and the Constitution, the Constitution will always prevail. *See J.McD. v P.L. and B.M.* [2009] I.E.S.C. 81.

[53] European Union Council Directive 2000/78/EC of 27 November 2000, establishing a general framework for equal treatment in employment and occupation.

[54] *See* Equality Act 2004 and Social Welfare (Miscellaneous Provisions) Act 2004.

[55] Contrast this with Article 12 of the European Convention on Human Rights, which refers to the right of 'men and women' to marry, which has been interpreted as being confined to heterosexual unions.

[56] European Union Directive 2004/38/EC has been implemented in Ireland by the European Communities (Free Movement of Persons) (No. 2) Regulations 2006 (S.I. No. 656 of 2006) as amended by the European Communities (Free Movement of Persons) (Amendment) Regulations 2008 (S.I. No. 310/2008).

[57] Additionally, under s. 37(1)(a), an employee or prospective employee may be treated more favourably on the basis of his/her religious belief, which includes religious background or outlook, where 'it is reasonable to do so in order to maintain the religious ethos of the institution'. While this does not expressly permit sexual orientation discrimination, a person who is gay or lesbian may possibly be deemed to have a different religious belief or outlook from that to which the employer is committed, if the employer's religious outlook is opposed to homosexual activity.

[58] A similar religious exemption was expressly examined in *In the Matter of the Employment Equality Bill 1995* ([1997] 3 I.R. 321) and upheld as constitutional, the Supreme Court reasoning that the measure represented a fair balance between the need to prevent discrimination and the constitutional requirement to respect the free practice of religion (Article 44, Constitution of Ireland 1937).

[59] The court found that Ms Flynn had not been dismissed because of the pregnancy *per se* but because of her conduct in openly living with a married man outside of marriage (the pregnancy simply having confirmed that relationship). Notably, the Unfair Dismissals Act 1977 made it unlawful to dismiss a person on the ground of pregnancy.

[60] By the Unfair Dismissals (Amendment) Act 1993. Notably, s. 37 of the 1998 Act does not apply to claims under the Unfair Dismissals Act 1977. There is no religious exemption in the latter Act. The 1998 Act allows a dismissal to be challenged as discriminatory, and s. 37 would apply to such a challenge, though s. 37 does not excuse a dismissal deemed unfair under the 1977 Act.

[61] For a telling personal testimony outlining the impact of s. 37, *see Irish Times* (2011). *See also* Faller (2012).

[62] For further analysis of the impact of s. 37 for teachers in denominational schools, *see* Lynch (2001), Gowran (2004) and Neary (2012). Neary (2012) examines, in particular, the experience of LGB teachers who have chosen to 'come out' in the workplace. While noting that many have felt this as a positive experience, she nonetheless records the teachers' ongoing concerns regarding the possible impact of s. 37.

[63] Article 4(2) of the Directive allows states to permit a difference of treatment based on religion or belief where the post in question requires, as a genuine, legitimate and justified occupational requirement, that such religion or belief be held by the employee. This is much narrower than what

is permitted by s. 37(1)(b) of the Employment Equality Act 1998, which in theory applies to any post in a religious institution, school or hospital run in accordance with a particular religious ethos, and is not confined to discrimination on the basis of religious belief. Article 4(2) expressly precludes a wider exemption than is permitted by the Article itself.

[64] The clear EU Commission view is that Article 4(2) of the Directive does not permit discrimination on the basis of sexual orientation. (Doward, J. (2009) 'Brussels Says Churches Must Lift Ban on Employing Homosexuals', *Observer*, 22 November.) The EU Commission appears, however, to have accepted that s. 37 complies with the Directive, though it did so preceding the Lisbon Treaty referendum, where political sensitivities may have prompted the Commission to take a more conciliatory, cautious line. *See* 'Religious Bodies Win Right to Hire Based on Ethos', *Irish Examiner*, 8 May 2008.

[65] *See Schüth v Germany* Application no. 1620/03 and *Obst v Germany* Application no. 425/03, both decided 23 September 2010.

[66] *See Irish Times* (2012). In 2012, Senator Averil Power tabled a private member's bill, the Employment Equality Bill 2012, proposing to preclude sexual orientation discrimination in religious-run schools and hospitals. While the bill was rejected, both the Minister for Justice and Equality and the Minister for Education and Skills, speaking in the Seanad, accepted the principle that LGBT teachers should be protected in all workplaces. The Minister for Justice and Equality, in particular, proposed that a distinction should be made between sexual orientation as an inherent characteristic (on the basis of which discrimination should not, he suggested, be permitted) and behaviour inimical to religious ethos, which a religious body should be entitled to address. He also distinguished between wholly private institutions and those funded in part by the State, suggesting that tougher equality requirements might be imposed on the latter. *See* Vol. 215, No. 3 *Seanad Éireann Debates* 152–5, 2 May 2012, available at http://debates.oireachtas.ie/seanad/2012/05/02/00007.asp [accessed 21 January 2012].

[67] *See In the Matter of Article 26 and the Employment Equality Bill 1995* [1997] 2 I.R. 321 at 358.

[68] *Cf. Ladele v London Borough of Islington* ([2009] EWCA Civ. 1357), where the English and Welsh Court of Appeal upheld as lawful attempts to discipline a marriage registrar who had refused, for religious reasons, to officiate at civil partnerships. In *Eweida and Others v United Kingdom* (Applics. 48420/10, 59842/10, 51671/10 and 36516/10, 15 January 2013), the ECHR found that Ms Ladele's treatment had not breached the European Convention on Human Rights.

[69] *See* the venue guidelines issued by Minister Éamon Ó Cuív, January 2011, available from <http://www.groireland.ie/civil_partnership_process. htm#venues-for-civil> [accessed 14 June 2012]. These are discussed in further detail in Ryan (2011: 75–6).

[70] *See also* Ryan, 2012a.

[71] Most recently, Denham J. (now Chief Justice), in the Supreme Court in *J.McD. v P.L. and B.M.* ([2009] I.E.S.C. 81), reaffirmed this view, noting that '[u]nder the Constitution it has been clearly established that the family in Irish law is based on a marriage between a man and a woman' (para. 77).

[72] *See further* Tobin (2012), Ryan (2012a) and Ryan (2012b).

[73] These tax benefits have since been extended to civil partners by the Finance (No. 3) Act 2011 and the Finance Act 2012.

[74] *See*, for instance: Costello P. in *B. v R.* ([1995] 1 I.L.R.M. 491, (HC) at 495); McKechnie J. in *Foy v Registrar of Births, Marriages and Deaths* ([2002] I.E.H.C. 116 (9 July 2002) at para. 175); and Murray J. in *D.T. v C.T.* ([2003] 1 I.L.R.M. 321).

[75] *See further* Ryan (2012b: 448–51).

[76] Though several commentators maintain that such a referendum is not required: *see* Carolan (2007), Tobin (2012), O'Mahony (2010; 2012) and Daly (2012).

[77] [2009] I.E.S.C. 81, judgment of Denham J., at para. 77.

[78] *See*, for instance, *MhicMhathúna v Ireland* ([1995] 1 I.R. 484), *T.D. v Minister for Education* ([2001] 4 I.R. 259) and *M.D. v Ireland* ([2012] I.E.S.C. 10 at para. 49).

[79] [2006] I.E.H.C. 404; [2008] 2 I.R. 417 at 513.

[80] *See* O'Mahony (2010: 88) and O'Brien, C. (2007), 'Lenihan Rules Out "Divisive" Referendum on Gay Marriage', *Irish Times*, 5 December. While supporting same-sex marriage, the Minister for Justice and Equality, Alan Shatter TD, has also suggested that a constitutional referendum would be required to permit its introduction. *See* Freeman, M. (2012), 'Gay Marriage: Shatter Joins Gilmore in Support', *the journal.ie*, 2 July, available from: <http://www.thejournal.ie/gay-marriage-ireland-shatter-gilmore-506853-Jul2012/> [accessed 22 January 2012].

[81] *See Harrogate Borough Council v Simpson* ((1984) 17 H.L.R. 205) and *Fitzpatrick v Sterling Housing Association* ([2001] 1 A.C. 27). The House of Lords, however, reversed this stance in *Ghaidan v Godin-Mendoza* ([2004] UKHL 30), ruling that the phrase 'living together as husband and wife' could be read as extending to same-sex partners, as this was necessary to give the relevant legislation an interpretation compliant with the European Convention on Human Rights under the UK's Human Rights Act 1998.

[82] The Domestic Violence Act 1996 extended the right to seek a barring order (excluding a violent or abusive partner from the shared home) to opposite-sex partners who were living together outside marriage, subject to certain conditions. The Civil Liability (Amendment) Act 1996 extended the right to sue for wrongful death to the cohabiting opposite-sex partner of the deceased, where the deceased and her partner had lived together for at least three years prior to the death.

[83] Section 39 of the Residential Tenancies Act 2004 extended the automatic right to succeed to a Part 4 tenancy to an opposite-sex partner of

a deceased tenant. A surviving same-sex partner who had lived with the tenant could apply to take over the tenancy, but was excluded from the automatic right afforded by s. 39. *See* Ryan (2011: 9).

[84] Civil Partnership and Certain Rights and Obligations of Cohabitants Act 2010 and the Civil Law (Miscellaneous Provisions) Act 2011.

[85] The All-Party Oireachtas Committee on the Constitution (2006) also recommended a limited form of civil partnership.

[86] Employees may now seek parental leave if acting *in loco parentis* (in the place of a parent) in respect of a child, and need no longer establish that they are the natural or adoptive parents of the child for this purpose. Meanwhile, employees may now also seek exceptional or *force majeure* leave in respect of an injury or illness to a same-sex partner that requires the immediate presence of the employee.

[87] For details, *see* <http://www.inis.gov.ie/en/INIS/Pages/WP07000278> [accessed 14 June 2012].

[88] *See* Part 15 of the Civil Partnership and Certain Rights and Obligations of Cohabitants Act 2010.

[89] Prior to the enactment of the Act, such agreements were regarded as unenforceable: *see Ennis v Butterly* [1996] 1 I.R. 426.

[90] A further condition applies: two people will not be treated as qualified cohabitants if either cohabitant is married to another person, unless the married parties have been living apart for four of the previous five years.

[91] The parties must be aged 18 or over.

[92] *See* the Civil Partnership and Certain Rights and Obligations of Cohabitants Act 2010 (henceforth 'Act of 2010'), s. 26.

[93] Section 16 of the Act of 2010. A marriage, by contrast, may be celebrated before a registered solemniser, including (as well as a state marriage registrar) a religious minister appointed for that purpose on the request of a religious body: *see* Part 6 of the Civil Registration Act 2004. Representatives of secular not-for-profit bodies may also be appointed as registered solemnisers for marriage but not for civil partnership: *see* the Civil Registration (Amendment) Act 2012.

[94] For instance, the provisions on maintenance (financial support) for civil partners largely replicate those applicable to spouses as set out in the Family Law (Maintenance of Spouses and Children) Act 1976, as amended.

[95] Civil Law (Miscellaneous Provisions) Act 2011, s. 33 amending s. 15A of the Irish Nationality and Citizenship Act 1956.

[96] Though in the case of capital gains tax, the parties must not be living apart.

[97] Social welfare recipients may now claim, for instance, an extra payment to support a same-sex partner (civil partner or cohabitant) as a 'qualified adult' who is dependent on the recipient.

[98] Recognition means, for instance, that a civil partner's or same-sex cohabitant's income may be taken into account in assessing social welfare entitlements, while the recognition of same-sex couples excludes parents

living with civil partners or same-sex cohabitants from accessing the One Parent Family Payment (prior to 2011, a parent living with a person of the same sex was nonetheless entitled to access this payment, as same-sex cohabitation was not recognised in social welfare law).

[99] Colker (1991: 326) '… [f]or poor people marriage may offer few economic advantages. It should not surprise us that marriage is a less popular institution in poor communities than in middle-class communities'.

[100] This can be either by will made by a parent who is an existing guardian of the child or by order of the court. *See* ss 7 and 8 of the Guardianship of Infants Act 1964.

[101] A guardian of a child is entitled to make major decisions regarding the child's upbringing, including where the child attends school, whether the child undergoes surgery and the religion in which the child will be raised. Guardians may also veto the adoption of a child, and must generally consent to the issuing of a passport in respect of a child. Guardianship does not automatically guarantee custody, though as against all those who are not guardians, a guardian has a *prima facie* right to custody. If married to each other, both parents of a child are its guardians. If the parents are not married to each other, the mother alone is automatically a guardian, though the biological father may become a guardian either by agreement with the mother or by court order. *See* the Guardianship of Infants Act 1964, as amended.

[102] Section 33, Adoption Act 2010 allows only married couples to adopt a child jointly. Other persons, including civil partners, may adopt as individuals but not jointly with another person.

[103] The spouse of a parent, while not automatically entitled to parental rights, may be required to maintain his spouse's children, if knowing that he is not the parent he accepts the child as a child of the family. A step-parent and parent, if married to each other, may also jointly adopt a child of the parent, rendering the couple jointly responsible for the child, though legally this may prove very difficult if the child was born to parents who were married to each other. While none of this means that a step-parent automatically acquires parental rights through marriage to a parent (in particular, there is no provision, absent joint adoption, for the couple sharing guardianship of the child of one of them), the legal position is nonetheless considerably better than for civil partners.

[104] Some notable exceptions are in the context of domestic violence, where a person who is parenting a child of their civil partner (i.e. caring for the latter's child) may seek a barring order against their civil partner for the protection of that child. Additionally, in the context of ethical conflicts of interest, social welfare and capital acquisition tax liability, the relationship between a child and its parent's civil partner is also generally recognised. A person parenting a child may also seek access to (contact with) the child, should the person's relationship with the child's parent end.

[105] This would allow a civil partner or spouse to obtain parental responsibility either by agreement with all those who already have parental responsibility or by court order, if it would be in the best interests of the child. This recommendation is complicated, however, by the Commission's further recommendation that all fathers should automatically be given parental responsibility, meaning that a lesbian couple might have to share parental responsibility with the father, even if he was a sperm donor.

[106] The Minister for Justice and Equality, at the Annual Conference of the European Gay Police Association, 28 June 2012, indicated his intention to reform the law to allow joint parenting arrangements by same-sex couples. *See* <http://www.justice.ie/en/JELR/Pages/SP12000196> [accessed 18 July 2012]. In a speech to Fine Gael LGBT on 19 November 2012, the Minister repeated this commitment. *See* <http://www.justice.ie/en/JELR/Pages/SP12000321> [accessed 21 January 2013].

[107] The ECHR, however, has since progressed beyond this restrictive view. In *Gas and Dubois v France* (Applic. 25951/07, 1 August 2010), the court concluded that the common life of a lesbian couple and their child constituted 'family life' for the purpose of the Convention.

[108] For a full discussion of these differences, *see* Ryan (2011: 24–32) and Fagan (2011).

[109] Judicial Separation and Family Law Reform Act 1989 as amended by the Family Law Act 1995 and the Family Law (Divorce) Act 1996.

[110] The key difficulty for civil partners is that judicial separation affords access to a range of remedies that are only available to civil partners on dissolution of a civil partnership.

[111] Notably, solicitors are obliged to advise divorcing clients of the alternatives to litigation – mediation and counselling, for instance – an obligation not imposed on the legal representatives of civil partners. *See* Family Law (Divorce) Act 1996, ss 6 and 7. The absence of similar requirements from the Act of 2010 may reflect a realisation that these measures are largely ineffective or – in the case of the requirement of 'no reasonable prospect of reconciliation' – redundant.

[112] *See* s. 3, Guardianship of Infants Act 1964 and Article 3 of the UN Convention on the Rights of the Child. *See also* the 31st Amendment to the Constitution Bill 2012.

[113] The tougher criteria for divorce are constitutionally mandated and cannot be changed without a referendum. *See* Article 41.3.2 of the Constitution of Ireland 1937, inserted by the Fifteenth Amendment to the Constitution Act 1995.

[114] Arguably, this binary has also served, in part, to reify the homosexual–heterosexual binary, at the expense of the bisexual population. Although civil partners need not be gay or bisexual, a marriage may be voidable if one of the parties is gay: the marriage–civil partnership binary thus

implicitly categorises partners as 'gay' or 'straight', eliminating the validity of the bisexual experience.

[115] For the original judgment, *see* <http://documents.nytimes.com/us-district-court-decision-perry-v-schwarzenegger#document/p137> [accessed 14 June 2012].

[116] In the USA various tests are used to assess the constitutionality of discrimination claims, ranging from a particularly high standard of strict scrutiny, whereby the state must demonstrate that the discrimination is strictly necessary to achieve a compelling state interest, to a weaker 'rational basis' test, which requires that the measure be upheld unless it can be shown that it serves no rational legitimate purpose. While different tests have been used in various states in same-sex marriage cases, Walker J. employed the strict scrutiny test but, referring also to the rational basis test, found that the ban did not survive even this, the weakest of the applicable tests.

[117] Same-sex couples in California are entitled to adopt and foster children, and to access assisted human reproductive services. The judge noted, indeed, that approximately 18 per cent of same-sex couples in California are raising children.

[118] *Perry v Brown*, Judgment of 7 February 2012, available from: <http://www.ca9.uscourts.gov/datastore/general/2012/02/07/1016696com.pdf> [accessed 14 June 2012]. On 26 June 2013, the US Supreme Court, in *Hollingsworth v Perry* 570 US (2013), refused to overrule the original decision of Walker J. in the Federal District Court in *Perry v Schwarznegger*. The Supreme Court ruled that the parties who had appealed Walker J.'s earlier decision lacked legal standing to do so, both before the Ninth Circuit and before the Supreme Court itself. This effectively means that Proposition 8 has now been overturned, with the result that same-sex couples may once again marry in California. On the same day, in *United States v Windsor* 570 US (2013), the Supreme Court declared parts of the Federal Defense of Marriage Act unconstitutional. The Act had precluded federal recognition of marriages between same-sex couples recognised in individual states. The court found that the federal government's failure to recognise such marriages denied married same-sex couples equal protection in the application of liberty and due process rights under the Fifth Amendment to the US Constitution.

[119] Using a test of intermediate scrutiny, halfway between the rational basis test and the strict scrutiny test discussed above in endnote 116.

[120] The right to seek further provision (and, in particular, the right to ongoing financial support) ends where the applicant or recipient of relief marries or enters into a civil partnership after a dissolution or divorce. Similarly, the surviving civil partner's right to relief ends where either civil partner dies.

CHAPTER 4

The Pursuit of Gay and Lesbian Sexual Citizenship Rights, 1980–2011

Paul Ryan

Introduction

On 5 April 2011 Barry Dignan and Hugh Walsh became the first Irish gay couple to register their civil partnership. The ceremony was made possible by the passage of a Civil Partnership Act (discussed in detail in Chapter 3) that bestowed a range of marriage-like provisions and obligations on couples in the areas of taxation and social welfare.[1] The passage of the Act was an extraordinary achievement. When Dignan and Walsh first met, almost twenty years earlier, their sexual relationship constituted a criminal offence under sections of the Offences Against the Person Act 1861 and the Criminal Law Amendment Act 1885 (Weeks, 1996: 48). The passage of the Act marked the culmination of nearly forty years of gay rights campaigning and opened a new phase in the pursuit of equal marriage rights for gay and lesbian couples. The slow pace with which gay couples moved from being outlaws in their own land to being granted almost full sexual citizenship rights raises important questions. It highlights how the tempos of sexual liberation movements are determined by and intersect with a changing political and cultural milieu. It reminds us that sexual liberation is not an automatic perquisite of modernisation, moving in a linear direction towards equality. There are starts and stops. There are false dawns.

This chapter charts the journey of gay men and lesbians seeking vindication of their rights in Ireland and the European Union.

The three decades from 1980 to 2011 reveal two distinct cycles of mobilisation. The successful case taken by Jeffrey Dudgeon to the European Court of Human Rights (ECHR) in 1981, which led to the decriminalisation of homosexuality in Northern Ireland in the face of strong opposition from Ian Paisley's 'Save Ulster from Sodomy' campaign, set the stage for a similar change in the law south of the border (McLoughlin, 1996: 36).[2] The Irish State resisted such a move, forcing then Trinity College lecturer and senator David Norris to embark on a lengthy and costly legal campaign through the same European court in order to achieve the same judgment some eight years later.[3] In this chapter we will explore whether this was the result of a counter-sexual revolution or whether, more fundamentally, the idea of a sexual liberation in Ireland during the 1960s and 1970s was greatly exaggerated. We will consider this victory in the ECHR and the campaign for civil partnership rights in the context of an extension of sexual citizenship identified by Diane Richardson (1998; 2000) and Ken Plummer (2001), among others, to illustrate the transnational dimension of sexual rights in late modern societies.

The development of the gay movement in Ireland in the 1970s was occurring within a wider process of informalisation. Identified by Dutch sociologist Cas Wouters (2004: 2–4), informalisation refers to a trend of growing permissiveness in the rules of social conduct that govern emotions and contact between the sexes and within social hierarchies, in other words an informal approach that supersedes the formal rules that previously governed social interactions. People expressed this growing freedom through fashion, dancing, music and hairstyles. Wouters (2004: 80–84) argues that the greater use of first names in social introductions and the spread of social kissing between virtual strangers in the 1960s were indicative of a greater intimacy and familiarity. Informalisation provides a useful framework for understanding a broader cultural flux that enveloped the gay rights movement and the ordinary gay lives within it. Informalisation brought a relaxation of manners, etiquette and deference towards elders and authority figures. It brought greater equality between the sexes, with wider public discussion of such topics as pre-marital sex, cohabitation and contraception. Gay men and lesbians were the unintended beneficiaries of this relaxed climate.

Setting the Stage: Battles Won and Lost

Our story begins in 1980, a landmark year in Irish sexual politics. The Fianna Fáil government's Health (Family Planning) Act 1979 had just come into force, providing for the provision of contraceptives to married couples on prescription from their doctor (Hug, 1999: 114; Ferriter, 2005: 666; Ryan, 2011: 72). The 1979 Act, which decriminalised the importation and sale of contraceptives, was required under a 1973 Supreme Court judgment in the *McGee* case, which ruled that the ban was unconstitutional because it breached the right of marital privacy (Connolly, 2003: 159; Ryan, 2011: 18). The political establishment grappled with the consequences of the Supreme Court judgment for the following seven years and attempts to enact the ruling, such as the Fine Gael government's proposals to legislate in 1974, were repeatedly brought down by a combined Fianna Fáil opposition and divisions within the government frontbench. From the moment a cohort of gay men and lesbians gathered together in Trinity College Dublin, in the early 1970s to form the Sexual Liberation Movement (SLM) – a forerunner to the Irish Gay Rights Movement (IGRM), founded in 1974 – overturning the ban on contraception was high on their agenda. Those within the gay movement recognised the importance of severing the association between sex and procreation (Ryan, 2006: 88). Throughout the 1970s there had been a wider discussion of sexuality outside the confines of the marital bed; a new narrative that described sex for pleasure, for recreation, for self-fulfilment. This development has been conceptualised by sociologist Anthony Giddens (1994: 2) as marking the emergence of *plastic sexuality*, where contraception and women's greater economic independence from men contributed to the liberation of sexuality from the modernist constraints under which it had laboured. In this late modern era, a greater mutability emerged into intimate relationships once they were freed from the traditional binaries of marital or pre-marital sex, heterosexual or homosexual, committed or promiscuous. Giddens also sees the decline in viewing homosexuality as a perversion and subsequent 'coming out' stories as linked to the removal of sexuality from the realm of nature (Giddens and Pierson, 1998: 145).

The 1970s was also a decade of second-wave feminist movement agitation, which had done much to bring about a situation where this greater mutability and self-fulfilment within sexual life became evident in Ireland. Groups like the Irish Women's Liberation Movement (IWLM) and Irish Women United (IWU) had adopted the protest strategies of a new social movement culture sweeping across Europe and the USA. Direct action strategies, like bringing contraceptives through Dublin's Connolly Train Station in defiance of the prohibition on their importation, both raised the media profile of their activities and contributed to splits that would eventually lead to the IWLM's demise (Connolly, 2003: 120–21). Legislative progress on women's rights did continue slowly through the 1970s with the passage of a number of Acts that represented a redistribution of power between the sexes.[4] Women also achieved greater economic independence through the 1973 repeal of the marriage bar, which had prevented married women holding positions in the civil service, and the passing of the Anti-Discrimination (Pay) Act the following year (Connolly, 2003: 106; O'Connor, 1998: 32–80).

The gay movement also made significant progress during the 1970s. A new social and political climate that facilitated the emergence of fresh social movements throughout Europe and the USA contributed to the tentative emergence of the Irish gay movement (Ryan, 2006: 88; Rose, 1994: 4–5). Future leaders of the gay movement, for example David Norris and Edmund Lynch, emerged through Trinity College Dublin and the State broadcaster, RTÉ, both institutions offering vital security in employment at a time when public involvement in gay rights threatened livelihoods, family relationships and, in acts of violence and arson, life itself. The aims of the IGRM were twofold: providing a legal service to men charged under gross indecency legislation; and providing a social space in a newly acquired building in Parnell Square, Dublin, that allowed men and women to socialise openly (Ryan, 2006: 97–8; Rose, 1994: 11). A tension emerged within the IGRM as some members felt that increased political agitation focused greater Garda attention on gay men. This situation had previously occurred in Britain, where in the first four years after the passage of the 1967 Reform Bill, convictions for gross indecency increased by 160 per cent (Kinsman, 1987: 143).

The IGRM split and more politically motivated members like Norris left to form the Campaign for Homosexual Law Reform (CHLR), whose single focus was to seek the decriminalisation of homosexuality through the Dáil (Irish Parliament) or the courts. This movement would parallel the establishment of the Campaign for Homosexual Equality in Britain, which shared a commitment to an extension of social services and strategies to woo the political establishment to help it achieve its aims (Marshall, 1980: 78). It quickly became apparently that seeking change through the Houses of the Oireachtas (the house of political representatives and the Senate) would be futile. When asked if the government intended to re-examine the legislation, Minister for Justice Gerry Collins responded that it did not (Dáil Éireann, 1977). Attention turned to a High Court challenge that came before the court in November 1977. It invoked that a right to privacy was denied to gay men – an argument previously successfully made in the *McGee* case – and claimed that the criminalising legislation made homosexuals unequal citizens before the law (Hug, 1999: 212). The High Court made its judgment in October 1980 when Judge McWilliam ruled against Norris, declaring that the legislation was not unconstitutional and that it was 'reasonably clear that current Christian morality in this country does not approve of buggery or any sexual activity between persons of the same sex' (Ferriter, 2009: 497). Bizarrely, the judge believed homosexuality to be a contagion, whereby people with mere tendencies would be enticed into a more habitual sexual identity as a result of contact with gay men and would be forced to endure the 'sad, lonely and harrowing life' of the exclusively homosexual man (Rose, 1994: 36).[5]

Norris's appeal to the Supreme Court in 1983 also ended in failure. The court's judgment revealed how pervasive the power of both religious and medical discourses remained in the Irish State. The judgment claimed that homosexual acts were unnatural, given that the State, which was founded on a Judeo-Christian tradition, believed the use of sexual organs should be for reproductive purposes only (Flynn, 1995: 37–42). Furthermore, the judgment found that homosexuality should be criminalised due to a belief that the resultant increased promiscuity would contribute to the spread of venereal disease. This part of the Supreme Court decision specifically showed an inability to comprehend that same-sex relationships could be based on monogamy, love or companionship (Ryan, 2011: 180). The final ground on which the Supreme Court rejected Norris's application rested on the belief that homosexuality was an individual disorder that made the afflicted prone to unhappiness, despair, loneliness and suicide. Significantly, the minority judgment of the court observed correctly that it may have been the legal regime existing in Ireland that had contributed to that despair and unhappiness (Hug, 1999: 214).

Counter-Sexual Revolution

If we are to understand the development of the gay movement in Ireland, we must be cognisant of the wider international context. While Ireland may have been influenced by and have benefited from a relaxation in sexual attitudes, particularly in the USA and Britain, events at home and abroad throughout the 1980s would illustrate how the global would continue to exert and find voice in the local, shaping both the political objectives of the gay movement and the timeline to achieve them. While Western industrial democracies entered into the contentious sexual politics of the 1980s bolstered by significant gains in the advancement of sexual rights in such areas as divorce, abortion and homosexual law reform (Wouters, 2004: 149), Ireland faced a rising tide of conservatism, with just a limited contraceptive bill passed at the opening of the decade. Even Northern Ireland had seen the passage of the Homosexual Offences (Northern Ireland) Order in 1982, following Jeffrey Dudgeon's successful case before the ECHR (McLoughlin, 1996; Hug, 1999: 216). While there were evident successes, however, the extent of the sexual revolution in Britain has been questioned, with Diarmaid Ferriter (2009: 337) claiming that its effects were largely confined to London and the South East, while Jeffrey Weeks (1989: 253–4) points out that British sexual behaviour had remained sexually conservative, with births outside marriage only rising modestly from 5 per cent in 1955 to 8 per cent in 1967.

Time magazine reported in 1984 that the sexual revolution was over (McLaren, 1999: 193). This declaration coincided with an economic downturn on both sides of the Atlantic that marked the end of the post-war boom and the beginning of a wave of economic austerity, strikes and pessimism. Voters turned to conservative leaders, like Reagan and Thatcher, who offered not just an economic but a moral readjustment that would see governments attempt to row back on what was perceived as the excesses of the permissive society (McLaren, 1999: 194). The 1980s represented the outbreak of a culture war, seeing a resurgent campaign against pornography, a rise in conservative men's movements and a rise in campaigns against abortion, culminating in attacks on and bombings of clinics in the USA. Gay men and lesbians were among the first victims of this backlash, with the advent of HIV/AIDS providing the political cover. The disease was presented by conservatives as evidence that the sexually promiscuous were now paying a terrible price for their transgression, and that the cure lay in a return to faith, monogamy and marriage. American conservatives like Patrick Buchanan saw AIDS as nature 'exacting an awful retribution' (Seidman, 1992: 158). Liberals seized the opportunity to strategically remarket the gay community, with Steven Seidman (1992: 156) arguing that to gain a place within the acceptable moral boundaries of the nation, an image of the 'respectable homosexual' had to be constructed. This involved placing sex firmly within a context of monogamy and romance and a greater assimilation of homosexuality within the dominant values of the USA. There was a similar response in Scandinavian countries, where gay movements now agitated for a return to domesticity, resulting in the introduction of marriage-style rights for lesbians and gay men in Denmark in 1989 (McLoughlin, 1996: 89).

In Britain, the Thatcherite political response resulted in measures such as section 28 of the Local Government Act 1988, which prevented local authorities 'promoting' homosexuality through educational resources as a valid family relationship of equal status to the traditional family unit (Weeks, 1990: 240–42; Weeks, 2000: 155; Richardson, 1998: 91). International gay movements struggled to withstand a conservative onslaught, which, emboldened by the fear generated by HIV/AIDS, sought to roll back legislative gains or justify existing criminalising legislation. The state of Georgia in the USA successfully argued in a federal civil rights case that the criminalisation of homosexuality was vital to protect public health in the context of HIV/AIDS (O'Connor, 1995: 185).

Against this backdrop the prospect of law reform in Ireland seemed remote. O'Connor (1995: 185–6) argues that the advent of HIV/AIDS did not, in fact, hamper or delay the Irish gay movement from achieving decriminalisation in 1993. Research from the World Health Organisation (WHO) proved helpful in this regard, with the WHO's argument that decriminalising measures would actually contribute to greater education about the risk of infection, making the case for decriminalisation more compelling. HIV/AIDS also mobilised a small number of gay activists in organisations such as Gay Health Action (GHA), bringing them into close contact with a range of government agencies and strengthening institutional contacts (Hug, 1999: 219). This early HIV/AIDS activism led to the establishment, in 1992, of the Gay Men's Health Project, on a statutory basis, within the Health Board, later the HSE (Ferriter, 2009: 504). Efforts were also made to bring greater information about the disease and its sufferers into the public domain in an attempt to lessen the stigma attached to it. In 1989 *Magill* magazine published a diary written by a Dublin man, describing his experience of his diagnosis and grim prognosis of a life expectancy of three to five years. RTÉ's flagship current affairs programme, *Today Tonight*, also carried an interview with a Dublin-born man with AIDS, providing the public with a rare insight into lives that were secret and feared (Ferriter, 2009: 505).

Gay men and lesbians also faced other dangers at this time. Sexually active gay men faced prosecution under gross indecency legislation, with 455 convictions between the years 1962 and 1972 (Hug, 1999: 270). Careers and family relationships were destroyed when newspapers printed the names of those convicted. Nell McCafferty's (1987: 32–3) report on Dublin District Court cases gave a look inside the somewhat bizarre legal situation facing gay men at the time. Her report from 12 September 1975 described two men, one married, observed leaving a cubicle of a public toilet by a Garda. They subsequently found themselves in court, being charged under gross indecency legislation. A psychiatrist was called to give evidence for the younger man, while the solicitor of the married man claimed that 'his wife says they are happily married' (McCafferty, 1987: 33). The judge summed up: 'The law's the law and they broke the law. One answer is prison obviously. If they had been dealt with before a jury, they could have gotten penal servitude.' The men were bound to the peace for a year.

The murder of Declan Flynn in 1982, in an area of Dublin's Fairview Park known to be frequented by gay men, created a climate of fear and distrust of the judiciary. When suspended sentences were handed down to his killers, widespread outrage and protests followed (Ferriter, 2009: 499; Rose, 1994: 20–21). In his summing up of the case, the judge said that 'this could never be called murder' (Crone, 1995: 67). Confidence in the Gardaí was undermined following the murder of another Dublin man, Charles Self, in the same year as Flynn was killed. The investigation into Self's murder led to over 1,500 gay men being interviewed, photographed and fingerprinted in an exercise that appeared to have more interest in personal surveillance than genuine investigation. No one was charged for the murder (Rose, 1994: 19). Acts of violence continued into the 1990s, with two gay activists, Suzy Byrne and Junior Larkin, attacked after an appearance on the Irish television chat show, the *Late Late Show* (Moane, 1995: 87).

In spite of this hostile background, progress was being made. The National Gay Federation (NGF) was set up in 1979, with a subgroup established to document the history of the movement and the experience of ordinary gay lives. This became the forerunner to the Irish Queer Archives (IQA), now housed in the National Library of Ireland.[6] In 1981 the NGF participated in the first national gay conference, which was organised by the Cork Gay Collective, a group of mainly gay, left-wing men keen to embrace a more radical sexual politics (Rose, 1994: 16–17). The NGF changed its name to the National Lesbian and Gay Federation (NLGF) in 1991.

The cultural wars fought in the USA about sexuality found a more local and nuanced voice in Ireland. The exaggerated fears of the spread of a permissive society mobilised anti-abortion activists to campaign for the insertion of a constitutional amendment to outlaw its practice (Hesketh, 1990: 5–6; Fahey, 1999: 63). The 1983 abortion referendum was marked by a divisive campaign and the ambiguous wording of the amendment led to a further four constitutional referenda. Furthermore, in 1986 the Irish electorate substantially rejected a referendum to remove the constitutional ban on divorce (Fahey, 1999: 64; Ferriter, 2005: 718–19). It was 1995 before the ban was lifted, following a referendum, by the slightest margin: 50.3 per cent for and 49.7 per cent against.

Sexual Citizenship and the European Court of Human Rights

After exhausting all legal avenues in Ireland, Norris and the campaign for decriminalisation moved, as Jeffrey Dudgeon had done earlier, to Europe. The vindication of Irish sexual citizenship on a European stage raises some interesting questions. While citizenship debates had previously been confined to the public sphere, there was a growing interest in the everyday and private lives of individuals. Ken Plummer (2001: 238) argues that this new form of citizenship 'examines the rights, obligations, recognitions and respect around those most intimate spheres of life'. For Plummer, core issues would include who to live with, how to raise children and, crucially in the context of this chapter, how to be an erotic person.

This transition in the way sexual citizenship was thought about was evident in Ireland in the period under discussion. Individuals came to understand their intimate choices within a context of a self-fulfilment, rather than through the paradigm of repression of the self and denial of the body as a source of multiple pleasures, as promoted in the teachings of the Catholic Church (Ryan, 2011: 39). This individualism, not to be misunderstood as selfishness, manifested itself in greater intimate choice in Ireland – the opportunity to 'come out' as gay to one's family and friends; the opportunity to deny parental expectations and move beyond one's parish, city or country; the opportunity to chart a new life, independent of the community and family ties that previously exerted so much pressure. This choice of *who* to have an intimate relationship with – whether heterosexual or homosexual – was central to this individualism, and the process by which these choices became publicly recognised was central to the extension of sexual citizenship. By extending this concept of citizenship, questions are raised about rights and responsibilities and the mechanisms by which people should be included or excluded from the extension of the benefits it bestows. In Plummer's analysis (2001: 248–9), globalisation is key to understanding what appear to be two contradictory forces at work moulding intimate lives. One is the *local*, which contributes to a distinct cultural footprint on sexualities around the world. In Ireland, throughout the 1970s, there was a curious blend of allegiances – to family, religion and community – that contributed to 'coming out' stories that were different from those told in Europe or North America (Ryan, 2003).

The second element of the new form of citizenship identified by Plummer is a '*McDonaldisation of intimacies*' (Plummer, 2001 [original italics]), whereby there is a sameness in sexual identity and, I would argue, in the rights bestowed through the extension of a sexual citizenship by globalising entities like the ECHR. In 1988 the ECHR ruled that an individual's sexual life was part of his/her private life under Article 8 of the European Convention on Human Rights, and that Ireland stood in contravention of this Article in its denial of homosexual privacy (Ryan, 1997; Hug, 1999: 217). The focus then turned to how successive Irish governments would seek to formulate a legislative solution that would appease the ECHR, the newly formed Gay and Lesbian Equality Network (GLEN) and an increasingly radicalised lay Catholic movement that would certainly oppose any change to the existing legislation.

Diane Richardson (2000: 107) identifies three broad themes within the sexual citizenship discourse that are also helpful in tracing the campaign for gay rights in the Irish context. The first – the right to participate in sexual activity – is the most relevant to this part of the campaign, where gay men sought the right to engage in sexual relations, invoking an essentialist belief that the physical need for a sexual life is a fundamental right. Given that gay sex remains illegal in many states in America and in other jurisdictions, it is a right that is still being contested.[7] These minimal rights to have sex without fear of prosecution have traditionally come with privacy exceptions – such as Britain's Reform Act 1967– where recognition is given dependent on no further rights being given in the public sphere, or what Richardson (2000: 110) calls the 'I don't care what they do in their own homes as long as I don't have to see it or hear about it' approach.[8] We will return to Richardson's (2000: 126) other theme – the right to publicly recognised sexual relationships – later in the chapter, when discussing the fight for civil partnerships, marriage and the recognition of foreign same-sex marriages in Ireland.

Decriminalising Homosexuality: The Reform Options

As highlighted in Chapter 3, despite the ECHR judgment in 1988, the Irish State showed a distinct lack of urgency to comply with the ruling. The government asked the Law Reform Commission to examine various legislative reform options. The Commission reported back in 1990 that the 'same legal regime should obtain for consensual homosexual activity as for heterosexual and that, in particular, no case has been established that the age of consent (seventeen years) should be any different' (Robson, 1995: 52). At the time it may have seemed unlikely that the Commission's recommendations would be heard, but three years later the political climate changed when a Fianna Fáil–Labour coalition came to power. The new government was eager to promote a reform agenda through the establishment of a Minister of Equality and Law Reform, and to capitalise on the election of Mary Robinson as the first female President of Ireland (Dunphy, 1997: 249).[9] Gay reform was, Dunphy argued, a low risk for both political parties as it did not require a constitutional referendum and would help court an urban middle-class vote that had been mobilised during the Robinson election campaign (Dunphy, 1997).

The tactics employed by GLEN also facilitated this reform agenda. It located its campaign within existing political structures while courting high-profile allies. Since its inception, the Irish gay movement rejected a politics of confrontation that had been the hallmark of campaigns in Britain and the USA in the 1970s (Ryan, 2006: 96). Groups like the Gay Liberation Front (GLF) in the USA campaigned on a broad platform of racial and sexual exploitation, with a loose organisational structure. This was not a strategy suited to the contours of Irish politics. GLEN's campaign strategy best suited the still parochial, close-knit nature of Irish politics. Furthermore, like the previous campaigns of the CHLR, the numbers involved in GLEN remained small (Dunphy, 1997: 252), which meant that confrontation was not really a viable option. The strategy adopted delivered results, with GLEN forging alliances and garnering the support of the Irish Congress of Trade Unions (ICTU) and the Irish Council for Civil Liberties (ICCL). ICTU had launched a policy document on lesbian and gay rights in the workplace in 1987, while the ICCL had published a document in 1990 calling for the decriminalisation of homosexuality (Rose, 1994: 25–7; Robson, 1995: 50). By locating its campaign within a wider context of social exclusion and human rights, GLEN garnered support from 40 organisations, as various as those representing the Travelling community and persons with disabilities.

GLEN also grounded its campaign in a subversion of the concepts of family and nationalism, which were particularly close to the Fianna Fáil heartland. GLEN continued to emphasise that the legislation criminalising homosexuality was, in fact, a remnant of Ireland's colonial past. Rose (1994: 3–4) describes how there 'were real and positive traditional Irish values, arising from the struggle against colonialism ... and that the demand for equality was attuned to this heritage'. Rose also recognises that such recourse to a more tolerant and egalitarian past was political opportunism, unsupported by the historical record. Indeed, the nationalist press had been the most ferocious in capitalising on a series of homosexual scandals that had beset the Dublin Castle regime in 1884 (Ryan, 2005: 40–42).

The government faced two choices when considering decriminalisation: one was to follow the British model of retaining an unequal age of consent with a restrictive proviso that such sexual activities take place 'in private'; the other was to introduce equality between both sexual orientations (Weeks, 1990: 176). It was a choice that Norris repeatedly emphasised to his fellow parliamentarians (Hug, 1999: 225). The use of the word 'family' in the GLEN campaign was also significant. This was not a by-product of the growing individualism discussed earlier; rather, through the use of terms such as 'sons and brothers' and 'daughters and sisters', it emphasised how decriminalisation would be in keeping with Ireland's traditional respect for the institution of the family. Dunphy (1997: 256) argues that the subtext of the campaign centred on the message that individual families had shown compassion to their gay relatives and now 'Ireland as family' should do the same.[10] Not everyone was convinced that a change in the law posed no danger to the traditional family. The Archbishop of Dublin, Desmond Connell, had described homosexuality in 1990 as 'a disorder and an affliction' (Rose, 1994: 27). The Catholic hierarchy issued a statement outlining its objections to the proposed legislation to decriminalise homosexuality, stating that 'new laws cannot make what is wrong right' (Hug, 1999: 225).[11] The most vocal opposition to the decriminalisation proposals came from lay Catholic groups such as Family Solidarity (1990), which had circulated its pamphlet to every TD (member of Parliament). The organisation warned against decriminalisation in a time of AIDS and suggested that decriminalisation would mark the beginning of a series of liberal legislative gains in the fields of adoption and education (Hug, 1999: 226). Other organisations, for example the Knights of Columbanus, played a more secretive role in attempting to influence the direction of public policy with regard to sexuality, particularly homosexuality (Ferriter, 2009: 465; Rose, 1994: 29).

The Criminal Law (Sexual Offences) Bill 1993 repealed sections 61 and 62 of the 1861 law and section 11 of the 1885 law, putting in its place an equal age of consent of seventeen years old, with no privacy exceptions and with no exemptions within the armed forces (Ryan, 1997; Rose, 1994: 57–8; Hug, 1999: 227). Given that the Fianna Fáil–Labour government had a majority of 41, the passage of the bill was not in dispute, but it was the ease with which it passed, without a vote being taken, that was extraordinary (Ryan, 1997).

A vote would have been required if ten deputies requested it; only one did. While there were some rumblings within Fine Gael (put forward by Gay Mitchell, Norris's presidential campaign adversary some eighteen years later) about an amendment that would seek a higher age of consent, such pressure was resisted within the party.

During the campaign for decriminalisation, David Norris had emerged as both a public figure able to communicate the aspirations of the gay community to a wider audience and as a role model within the gay community. No such similar figure emerged within the lesbian movement, contributing to a continued perceived invisibility. The reasons for this are complex. Some, like writer and journalist Nell McCafferty, have felt uncomfortable with the term 'lesbian'. The collective energies of Irish lesbians had also been spilt across a diverse range of activism, most obviously women's liberation, but also pro-choice and anti-nuclear Greenpeace campaigns (Crone, 1995: 61). The result was often unsatisfactory, leading lesbians to feel they had committed themselves to campaigns for reproductive rights within the broad church of the women's movement, while believing that their sexual rights were not fully embraced or even named in return, particularly in the Irish Women's Liberation Movement (IWLM) (Connolly 2003: 122). Groups like Irish Women United (IWU) did call for the right of women to have a 'self-determined' sexuality, yet the commitment to lesbian rights remained opaque; although according to Mary Dorcey, 40 per cent of the IWU was lesbian (Dorcey, 1995: 37). According to Connolly (2003: 132), the IWU struggled to find agreement on issues because of the divergent feminist ideological commitments of its members. The disbandment of IWU brought about the emigration of the most radical lesbians from the group (Crone, 1988: 342). By the 1980s lesbian activists had splintered from the mainstream women's movement, with Crone (1988) pointing to a women's conference on lesbianism in 1978 as a significant milestone in carving a unique space outside the confines of the traditional women's movement. Crone's (1995: 66) own appearance on the *Late Late Show*, though seen as inspirational by a generation of Irish lesbians, came at a high personal cost, bringing her familial rejection and threats of violence. Other women also splintered from IWU, creating new groups like Women's Right to Choose and the Rape Crisis Centre (Connolly, 2003: 141).

Several lesbian groups made written submissions to the Second Commission on the Status of Women (1993). Dublin Lesbian Line's oral presentation outlined the priorities for the lesbian community, including funding, legislative change and educational programmes that would include realistic portrayals of lesbians in education and training (Moane, 1997: 440). In 1991 Lesbians Organising Together (LOT) was founded and became the first national network, complete with office, archive and outreach services for talks with schools or other groups. Groups affiliated with LOT included the Dublin Lesbian Line, First Out and the Lesbian Equality Network (Moane, 1995: 93–4). The following year Mary Robinson invited members of LOT to a reception in Áras an Uachtaráin for the gay and lesbian community, although those who attended chose not to release their names to the press (Ferriter, 2009: 515), a sad reminder that there were still high personal costs to be paid for public visibility.

Back to the Courts: The Status of Foreign Same-Sex Marriages in Ireland

A key catalyst in the development of the gay movement in Ireland was the harnessing of individual resources and, more important, the willingness of individuals to bear personal, emotional and financial costs in the pursuit of collective aims (Ryan, 2006: 93–4). After their marriage in Canada in 2003, Ann Louise Gilligan and her wife, Katherine Zappone, returned home to Ireland to seek recognition of their marriage in respect of a range of tax allowances made available to married heterosexual couples. Gilligan and Zappone wrote to the Revenue Commissioners to request that their tax status be changed to reflect their marital status. The letter of reply, addressing the couple as 'Dear Ladies', made it clear that the Revenue Commissioners would not become an agent of transformative change (Gilligan and Zappone, 2008: 256). Following this rejection by the Commissioners, the couple applied for and were granted a judicial review.

This next phase in the legal battle for same-sex rights raises some important issues. First, given the earlier discussion of the invisibility of lesbians in the history of the gay movement, it was significant that this phase was spearheaded by two women. Gilligan and Zappone (2008: 253) reviewed cases in other jurisdictions and realised that similar cases had been taken by a number of couples, thus sharing the personal and financial risks and the media attention involved in such a case. The search for similar couples to participate in their court case ended in failure, with candidates discouraged by the notoriety the case would likely generate. Like Norris before them, Gilligan and Zappone were forced to head the campaign alone in the absence of any national organisation campaigning for gay marriage in Ireland (Gilligan and Zappone, 2008: 254).[12] The couple concluded that 'while we clearly took the case on our own behalf, we also took it on behalf of those who might not be able to withstand the human cost – financial and otherwise – of engaging in such democratic action' (Gilligan and Zappone, 2008: 251–2).

Some feminist writers have been critical of lesbians who have pursued equal marriage rights, arguing that it is middle-class gay men who are most likely to be in a position to support the cost of pursuing legal action and indeed are more likely to be the beneficiaries of a range of rights that gay marriage can bestow (Ettelbrick, 1989; Auchmuty, 2004). They argue the legal campaigns for same-sex marriage serve the interests of middle class men more than women, with men being more likely to hold jobs that provide spousal health benefits or pension entitlements (Ettelbrick, 1989: 166). Auchmuty (2004: 111) goes further, claiming that the debate for gay marriage has been driven in the USA and Britain by gay men, both in the public sphere and in academia. Given such a male focus it is unsurprising, Auchmuty (2004: 105) argues, that the radical feminist critique of marriage is now conveniently seen to be obsolete. These critiques, she believes, have consistently revealed that marriage has 'been shown to endow men with a better lifestyle, greater freedom and power, while it has the opposite effect on women, limiting, impoverishing, and rendering them vulnerable to abuses of power by their husbands'.

The judgment of the High Court in the Gilligan–Zappone case came in October 2006, when Judge Elizabeth Dunne ruled that the couple did not have the right to marry in Ireland under the 1937 Irish Constitution, which defines marriage as between a man and a woman. In October 2011 the Supreme Court refused to include a challenge to the Civil Registration Act 2004 as part of their appeal to the Supreme Court, and this appeal was subsequently withdrawn. Zappone and Gilligan then initiated a new High Court appeal to challenge the constitutionality of the provisions of the Civil

Registration Act 2004 and the Civil Partnership Act 2010, both of which prohibit marriage for same-sex couples. It is this new challenge which is currently before the High Court. To understand the presentation of the case before the High Court and the wider court of public opinion, we must return to the concept of sexual citizenship. Citizenship rights are garnered, or denied, through bureaucratic and political manoeuvring, 'through rituals of modern political debate', a process that has the potential to identify 'good' and 'bad' citizens (Hubbard, 2001: 53). Gay men and lesbians have traditionally found themselves in the latter category, in the company of the sex worker, the pornographer or the single mother, among others. Indeed, the Criminal Law (Sexual Offences) Act 1993 combined the decriminalisation of homosexuality with what many would consider regressive measures against prostitution. Richardson (1998: 90) argues that these 'partial' citizenship rights, for example the right to engage in sex, as discussed earlier, are dependent on gay men and lesbians not seeking public recognition and remaining within the private sphere; as Sylvia Walby (1994: 389) points out, the concept of citizenship is rendered obsolete in a private setting.

The traditional heterosexual, married, middle-class, nuclear family is the model of good citizenship (Richardson, 1998: 92). Gilligan and Zappone's relationship was, arguably, recasting the image of the gay and lesbian couple in the public imagination, and bringing it closer to the desirable model. No longer were gay men and lesbians viewed as a contagion that presented a threat to public health through multiple sexual partners and a defiance of monogamy, as outlined in the High Court judgment against Norris in 1980. In this stage of the campaign, Gilligan and Zappone represented the desire of many in the gay and lesbian community for recognition of relationships built upon domesticity, fidelity and, in their case, a 23-year commitment to each other. Gay men and lesbians wanted to come in from the cold, to become 'good citizens' and to embrace a world of joint tax assessment, inheritance and divorce. There was cross-party agreement within the political establishment that they should be allowed to do so. Gilligan and Zappone represented a cohort of gay and lesbian people who wanted to move from being what Richardson (1998: 88) describes as 'partial citizens' – in that they pay the same taxes as heterosexual people yet are denied key entitlements from the distribution of those taxes and the ability to marry and foster children – to being people included within a traditional model of citizenship embracing civil, political and social rights.

Gilligan and Zappone explained their rationale for choosing marriage after considering the implications for themselves as feminist women familiar with the feminist critique of marriage, which viewed it as an institution beyond redemption. The couple understood marriage to be a changing institution, not exclusively confined to any one cultural or historical interpretation: 'understanding the purpose and consequences of marriage, aspiring to live as best we could the ideals of this time-honoured institution, we wished to avail of this opportunity, to celebrate our love and have full legal recognition' (Gilligan and Zappone, 2008: 239–40).

Gilligan and Zappone were not the only feminists to have grappled with a critique of marriage as a heteropatriarchal institution. Prominent gender and sexuality academics Celia Kitzinger and Sue Wilkinson (2004) outlined their rationale for choosing marriage in Canada instead of a civil partnership in Britain in an autobiographical article published in 2004. Like Gilligan and Zappone, the couple married in 2003 and wanted the British authorities to recognise their Canadian marriage in a similar manner to heterosexual couples. Kitzinger and Wilkinson (2004: 130) reject the cohabitation requirement implicit in many civil partnership models, including the UK, arguing that gay men and lesbians are pressurised to prove that their relationships are 'real'; a burden not borne by heterosexual married couples. Such a requirement also exists in relation to immigration criteria in countries like Australia, where gay couples do have marriage rights equal to heterosexual couples' but the onus on proving a 'genuine' relationship for the three categories of partner visa (i.e. married, prospective marriage and interdependent) is based on traditional heterosexual relationship criteria, such as a shared home and a merging of financial resources (Holt, 2004: 32).[13] Gay men and lesbians, whether married or not, must furnish evidence of a long-term, committed, exclusive relationship, shared financial obligations and proof, too, that the relationship has been socially recognised by wider family, peers and colleagues. More fundamentally, though, Kitzinger and Wilkinson state that 'from a human rights perspective, equal access to marriage for all citizens is a straightforward human right' (Kitzinger and Wilkinson, 2004: 132), and despite a similarity in entitlements, the exclusion of gay men and lesbians from marriage is hugely symbolic.

This 'rebranding' of the civil partnership exercise that separates gay men and lesbians from marriage is, of course, politically expedient, deflecting criticism from LGTB groups about the exploitative nature of marriage, while conservative critics are happy that the 'sacredness' of marriage is retained for heterosexuals. Kitzinger and Wilkinson (2004: 135–6) argue that while early feminist critiques of marriage have now been made redundant by a range of equality measures secured through feminist agitation, there has been no comparable critique of inequalities existing within civil partnership relationships, which are based on similar exclusivity and cohabitation expectations of heterosexual marriage. The couple argue (Kitzinger and Wilkinson, 2004: 140), as do Gilligan and Zappone (2008), that socially constructed institutions of family and marriage are not the preserve of any one social group; they can be reimagined and divested of their gendered connotations.

The Civil Partnership Bill: Enshrining Inequality or a First Step to Full Civil Marriage?

The publicity surrounding the Gilligan and Zappone case forced a wider societal debate on the rights of same-sex couples in Ireland. It was a debate that was occurring within an international context, because an increasing number of European states had extended sexual citizenship rights to create new citizens who may, in the future, seek to have those rights upheld in Ireland (Eskridge and Spedale, 2006). Richardson (2000: 126–7) develops three broad themes within sexual citizenship discourse. The first of these are claims made based on relationships and, more specifically, the right to publicly recognised sexual relationships. The ideological difficulties within gay and lesbian communities in embracing a legislative model that would provide for social and legal benefits have been discussed earlier in the chapter. Newly married same-sex couples, like Gilligan and Zappone, provided the courts and legislators with a conundrum as they sought to try to define these rights and obligations within constitutional parameters. This forced politicians to take a stand. Taoiseach Bertie Ahern, for example, speaking in 2004, supported the extension of tax and inheritance rights to gay and lesbian couples, stating that he thought this was the 'fairest, caring and Christian way to deal with this' (BBC News, 2004).

There had been a number of reports published since 2000 that were critical of government inaction in dealing with the issue of partnership recognition for lesbians and gay men. In 2000 the Equality Authority published a report that catalogued a list of discriminations faced by same-sex couples with regard to children, property entitlements, workplace benefits and taxation. A further report, two years later, formally called on the government to legislate to give full recognition to same-sex couples (Equality Authority, 2002). In 2003 the National Economic and Social Forum (NESF) issued a report expressing concern that the absence of such formal recognition for gay and lesbian couples would become an impediment to achieving LGBT equality (NESF, 2003). It recommended to the government that the 'Law Reform Commission should include consideration of the feasibility of different models to achieve equal rights for same-sex partnerships, drawing on the experiences of other countries which have recently legislated' (NESF, 2003: 12). The Law Reform Commission had also been asked by the government to advise on the issue of partnership recognition, and its 2004 report suggested a partnership scheme bestowing marriage-style rights to couples cohabiting for a minimum of three years, albeit the scheme could not be referred to as marriage for constitutional reasons (Law Reform Commission, 2004). In 2006 the Irish Human Rights Commission suggested that a constitutional referendum to overcome these difficulties in granting full civil marriage would be feasible, but that the minimum requirement would be a partnership registration scheme (Walsh and Ryan, 2006). In the same year the ICCL published *Equality for all Families*, a report that was sharply critical of the treatment of non-traditional families in Ireland (Irish Council for Civil Liberties, 2006). It suggests that recognition for same-sex partnerships should be a key concern for the country in supporting relationships of love and care.

When a Fianna Fáil–Green Party coalition government came to power in June 2007, a commitment to pass civil partnership legislation was included in the negotiated Programme for Government. This decision was based, in part, on the report of the Working Group on Domestic Partnership, established in 2005 by the Minister for Justice, Equality and Law Reform, Michael McDowell TD, which recommended a civil partnership scheme as opposed to gay marriage, which would be 'vulnerable to constitutional challenge' (Working Group on Domestic Partnership, 2006). Even this limited civil partnership was threatened with legal challenge when the Catholic Primate of Ireland, Cardinal Sean Brady, stated in June 2008 that the Catholic Church would consider supporting a constitutional challenge to any proposed partnership legislation (RTÉ, 2008). The following year the government published the Civil Partnership Bill, to allow same-sex couples to register their partnerships and thereby avail of a range of protections and rights and also comply with significant obligations to financially support each other during and after the dissolution of the civil partnership. Courts were empowered to make orders in respect of maintenance, property and pensions. The bill gave civil partners the option of having a joint tax assessment, similar to married couples. There is no residency requirement attached to the civil partnership scheme and couples with foreign marriages are automatically recognised under the conditions of the scheme. As highlighted in Chapter 3 and discussed in more detail in Chapter 7, there is no provision that a civil partner's relationship with their non-biological child would gain any greater legal status.

While the Minister for Justice, Dermot Ahern TD, believed the legislation 'struck the right balance', it was criticised by the Director of Amnesty International in Ireland, Colm O'Gorman, who said he believed it enshrined in law discrimination against gay men and lesbians, particularly in its failure to offer protection to the children of same-sex couples (RTÉ, 2009). The chairperson of the National Lesbian and Gay Federation (NLGF, 2009), Ailbhe Smyth, stated that 'civil partnership will fuel anti-gay sentiments by signalling: "Yes, you are different."' Ordinary gay and lesbian people voiced their displeasure with the bill, too, and five thousand members of the public joined a protest march in Dublin on 9 August 2009. The suggestion by the Catholic bishops that TDs should be allowed a free vote on the issue was greeted with derision by Minister of the Environment and Green Party leader John Gormley TD, who stated that 'he thought we had left the era of Church interference behind us' (RTÉ, 2010). The bill passed all stages in the Dáil on 2 July 2010, without a vote. Minister Dermot Ahern noted in the Dáil that 'This is one of the most important items of civil rights legislation that has come before the House for some time. It makes a clear and powerful statement to gay people that they will never again have their status or relationship ignored' (Dáil Éireann, 2010: 12). John Gormley described it as 'truly an historic day. It is a joyous day for so many same-sex couples throughout the country. I convey my thanks to the organisations which campaigned so hard for this, including the Gay and Lesbian Equality Network, Marriage Equality, LGBT Ireland and others' (Dáil Éireann, 2010: 12).

The debate about civil partnership versus gay marriage played out very differently in Britain. Leading gay rights advocacy group Stonewall argued strongly for the introduction of civil partnership, seeing it as a twenty-first-century means of recognising modern relationships that was preferable to expanding the concept of marriage to incorporate gay and lesbians, as had been done in Canada, for example (Shipman and Smart, 2007: 2). The Stonewall strategy was designed to avoid criticism of aping a patriarchal institution while at the same time being able to differentiate partnerships from marriage in debates with the religious right. Similarly, Peter Tatchell of gay lobby group OutRage! argued for a 'queer' rejection of marriage in its entirety, seeking instead an alternative means of recognising the relationships of both gay and straight couples that would be equal in status and rights to marriage. A Cabinet Office questionnaire revealed that the civil partnership proposals had huge support among the gay and lesbian community, with 86 per cent of respondents stating that they would consider registering (Kitzinger and Wilkinson, 2004: 128–9). The ordinary gay and lesbian couples whom Shipman and Smart (2007: 4) interviewed were concerned less with the ideological status of civil partnership versus marriage and more with pressing everyday and personal concerns. Couples identified different motivations for their decision to embark upon a civil partnership, which included love, acknowledging mutual responsibility, the importance of family recognition, legal rights and a public statement of commitment.

Marriage Equality: The Next Phase

Ironically, it was the decision to legislate for civil partnership that galvanised the first national campaign for gay marriage in Ireland. Marriage Equality was founded in 2008 and campaigns for the extension of full civil marriage rights to gay and lesbian couples. The organisation disputes the view put forward by the Working Group on Domestic Partnership (2006) that a constitutional referendum would be required to legislate for the extension of civil marriage rights to gay men and lesbians. Notwithstanding debates about whether gay marriage undermines gay and lesbian identity (Herman, 1993: 250), or reinforces a patriarchal social organisation based an exclusive binary relationship (Auchmuty, 2004: 122), or promotes assimilation into a model of sexual citizenship that has traditionally proved so hostile for gay men and lesbians, there remains little doubt that civil marriage will be the next stage of the campaign. It will also be challenging. With legal opinion suggesting that the instigation of gay marriage would require a referendum to change the Irish Constitution, any future government would approach the issue with great trepidation. Although surveys report high levels of support for gay marriage, a campaign would be undoubtedly divisive (O'Brien, 2010). Reynolds' analysis (2007) of the media coverage in Ireland following the publication of a photograph of a German couple at their civil partnership revealed that many readers were aggrieved, particularly by the appropriation of the symbolism of traditional marriage, in this case the cutting of a wedding cake.

In Britain, Auchmuty (2004: 116) argues that full marriage rights for gay men and women is now only a matter of time, partly because marriage has been divested of all religious and social status, becoming merely a lifestyle choice, and partly because of its dwindling popularity as an institution. Marriage in Britain is now so unfashionable that numbers getting married have fallen to their lowest level for more than a century (Carter, 2003). The same cannot be said for Ireland. The 2011 Census in Ireland revealed that between 2002 and 2011 the marriage rate had remained stable at 37 per cent (Central Statistics Office, 2011: 21). It would also be naïve to believe that the introduction of civil partnership, although a significant development, will change the everyday lives of gay men and lesbians in schools, workplaces or on the streets. Despite the progress witnessed in this country, the decision of young people to 'come out' is still fraught with fear of rejection. Research into the experience of Irish second-level students by Norman et al. (2006: 26) revealed a high level of tolerance among teachers of pervasive homophobic name-calling in the classroom, while some parents expressed 'sadness and disappointment' if they discovered their child to be gay. A majority of students had a fear of anything associated with homosexuality being discussed within the school (Norman and Galvin, 2006: 27).

The same year as the Civil Partnership Act was passed, Cork Senior hurler Dónal Óg Cusack published his autobiography, *Come What May* (published by Penguin Ireland in 2009), describing his three All-Ireland victories and his decision to come out as a gay man to his teammates and family. Cusack's father greeted the news with incredulity, telling him, 'but you don't, you're into hurling' (2009: 156), as if the sport that had so embodied a vision of Gaelic masculinity would preclude any sexual diversity among the starting fifteen players.

While the passage of the Civil Partnership Act, although limited in provision, was momentous, for a time in 2011 it appeared that Ireland would go even further and elect David Norris as President of Ireland. If this had happened, he would have been the first openly gay man to hold the office. Early polls consistently showed that Norris was the people's favourite candidate (Drennan, 2011). Revelations that Norris had sought clemency from an Israeli court for his ex-partner, who stood guilty of the statutory rape of a fifteen-year-old boy in 1997, led to his withdrawal from the race. Although Norris re-entered the race in September and reclaimed a leading position in the polls, he struggled in television debates to put behind him his clemency or his refusal to publish all of his correspondence to the Israeli court (Taylor, 2011). On election day, he received 6.2 per cent of the vote.

Conclusion

This chapter has put forward the argument that the progress of the gay movement in Ireland over the last 31 years has been dependent on local and global cultural and political factors, which have fashioned both standardised and unique campaign outcomes. At a time when the Christian Right exercised greater influence over sexual politics in the USA, for example, the institutional power of the Catholic Church in Ireland came under increasing pressure from secularisation and experienced diminished authority arising from clerical sexual abuse scandals. The concept of sexual citizenship (Richardson, 2000) was employed to illustrate how homosexual individuals sought a vindication of a range of rights, from the right to have specific forms of sex to recognition for same-sex relationships in a political climate where citizenship claims would increasingly be contested in the private, as opposed to the public, domains. This would manifest itself in legal claims to the High and Supreme Courts in Ireland and to the ECHR, illustrating the transnational scope of sexual rights in the late modern age.

We also discussed the differing opinions on civil partnership, both in Ireland and Britain and within gay and lesbian communities. These differences reveal the tensions within lesbian feminism over the extent to which the very concept of marriage can be embraced or rehabilitated, with contributors offering academic but also autobiographical accounts to explain why the intangible, symbolic nature of marriage matter. For those committed to full civil marriage in Ireland, this aspiration now rests on the outcome of the Gilligan and Zappone case, currently before the High Court, and the willingness of subsequent governments to legislate accordingly. Both outcomes are uncertain. Nonetheless, sexual citizenship rights in Ireland continue to be influenced by the global as much as by the local. In this context, commitments by the British Conservative–Liberal Democrat coalition government and by French President François Hollande to the introduction of gay marriage may prove significant.

Notes

[1]   The full title of the Act is the Civil Partnership and Certain Rights and Obligations of Cohabitants Act 2010. Read the Act at <http://www.irish statutebook.ie/2010/en/act/pub/0024/index.htm>.

[2]   Jeffrey Dudgeon was made an MBE by Queen Elizabeth II in the 2012 New Year's Honours list for services to the lesbian, gay, bisexual and transgender communities.

[3]   *See* Freedman (1995) for an overview of Norris's life.

[4]   Core pieces of legislation included: the Maintenance Orders Act 1974; the Family Law (Maintenance of Spouses and Children) Act 1976; and the Social Welfare Act 1974, which transferred the legal right of children's allowance from fathers to mothers. All of these legislative changes represented a redistribution of power between the sexes (Connolly 2003: 108).

[5]   I have argued in my analysis of problems about homosexuality written to 'Agony Aunt' Angela Macnamara that it was this distinction between a homosexuality that could be determined as 'transient' or 'congenital' that remained key in determining what advice was dispensed (Ryan 2011: 170–78).

[6]   *See* <http://www.nlgf.ie> and <http://www.irishqueerarchive.com>

[7]   Other groups, for example disability campaigners, similarly argue for the right to a sexual life often denied within domestic and residential care

home settings (Richardson, 2000: 109). (*See also* Chapters 14 and 15 in this book.)

[8]   Even in liberal democracies not all of these claims are realised: a group of British men involved in consensual sadomasochistic acts were convicted under the Offences Against the Person Act, a conviction upheld in the ECHR, which ruled that the right to protect health had primacy over the right to privacy in this case (Richardson, 2000: 112).

[9]   Robinson had been a key campaigner for reproductive rights while in the Senate and had, in a legal capacity, represented Norris during his ECHR appeal.

[10]   Indeed, it had been much reported that the rapport between Phil Moore, representing the parents of gay and lesbian children, and the Minister for Justice, Máire Geoghegan-Quinn TD, was influential in persuading the government to reject British-style 'reform' compromises (Robson, 1995: 55).

[11]   However, the Church's power and its position as moral adjudicator of the Irish nation had been weakened since the resignation of the Bishop of Galway, Eamon Casey, the previous year when it became known he had fathered a child with an American woman (*see* Hilliard, 2003: 42). It was a decline in power that would continue throughout the decade when far more devastating allegations of clerical child sex abuse and institutional collusion emerged.

[12]   Although Gilligan and Zappone stood before the court alone, they received support from a wide range of individuals and organisations, such as the Human Rights Commission, National Lesbian and Gay Federation and Labour LGBT, among others.

[13]   Australia recognises three categories of partnership visa: spouse, prospective marriage and interdependent. The last refers to mutually dependent relationships and is the visa most often applied for by gay men and lesbians.

CHAPTER 5

Legal Recognition of Preferred Gender Identity in Ireland: An Analysis of Proposed Legislation

Tanya Ní Mhuirthile

Introduction

In order to come *sui juris*, to be recognisable by the law, one must define oneself in a manner the law can comprehend. At present, the law divides people into two categories: male and female (Civil Registration Act, 2004, Schedule 1). However, nowhere in legislation are these terms defined. Nor is it clearly explained whether an individual must be male in order to be legally recognised as a man. This chapter investigates the question of legal gender recognition in Ireland. It teases out the manner in which Irish case law has defined male/female and man/woman for legal purposes. Emerging debates in international human rights discourse are analysed to provide a critique of the current legal situation in Ireland, and the report of the Irish Gender Recognition Advisory Group (GRAG) is examined to ascertain how this position might be reformed (Gender Recognition Advisory Group, 2011).

Terminology

Prior to engaging in an analysis of the question of legal gender recognition, it is first necessary to clarify some terms that will be used repeatedly in this chapter.

The first terms to explain are 'sex' and 'gender', which are often used interchangeably. For the purposes of this chapter, 'sex' refers to biological considerations, while 'gender' refers to social considerations. With this as a framework, 'male' and 'female' are terms referring to sex. They refer to the biology and bodily characteristics of a person. 'Man' and 'woman' are social terms and indicate a person's gender. Where this chapter specifically employs either of the terms 'sex' or 'gender', it does so with these particular meanings in mind. Where the chapter refers to discussions where the terms are used interchangeably, the term 'sex/gender' will be employed to indicate that the terms have been treated as synonymous. It is not a given that people's sex will correspond with their gender. Although a person who considers himself to be a man might have male biology, this is not necessarily always the case. Where there is a conflict between a person's biological sex and the social gender adopted, for example a male who identifies as a woman, the term 'preferred gender identity' will be employed to prevent confusion. Likewise, in deference to a person's perceived sense of self the pronouns used will correspond to that person's preferred gender identity. Thus the person born male who identifies as a woman will be referred to using female pronouns, so that her preferred gender identity is acknowledged.

'Sexual orientation' is a term that connotes a pattern of emotional, romantic, and/or sexual attractions to men, women, both genders, neither gender or another gender. According to the American Psychological Association, 'sexual orientation' can also refer to a person's sense of identity arising from these attractions, related behaviours and membership of a community of others who share these attractions (American Psychological Association, 2012). This is quite distinct from 'gender identity', which is defined as one's own innate sense of self as either male, female or ambivalent (Money, 1965a; 1973). One's internal sense of self as a gendered being is in no way linked to one's sexual orientation.

The term 'transgender' is a fluid term that includes and implies many different identities. It refers to those people who challenge 'norms' of sex and gender. It is intended as an all-encompassing term to indicate those who cross-dress, whether occasionally or frequently, those who live in a gender other than that implied by the sex in which they were born, including both those who do not seek medical or surgical treatments/assistance and those who do, or anyone else whose sex and gender identity do not cohere as the 'norm' suggests. Thus, 'transgender' will be used throughout this chapter to mean those who engage in a generic questioning of the correlation between sex and gender. The term 'trans' is a more recent take on the term 'transgender'. Although it had been about for a while, the term 'trans' was first formally approved when it was used by a parliamentary discussion group in the UK with the specific intention of it being as inclusive as possible in equality legislation (Whittle, 2006: xi). Throughout this chapter the term 'trans-man' will be used to identify a person whose preferred gender identity is as a man, and likewise 'trans-woman' will be used to indicate a person whose gender preference is to be a woman.

'Transsexual' refers quite particularly to those who have undergone some form of medical and/or surgical procedures or treatment to bring their bodily sex into congruence with their preferred gender identity. Generally, transsexuals experience a conflict between their bodily sex and their preferred gender identity and receive a medical diagnosis of gender identity disorder. In fact, such a diagnosis is essential for a person to qualify as eligible for treatment.

Finally, 'intersex' is an umbrella term for a variety of physical conditions where a person's body simultaneously combines traits of both males and females. (*See* Chapter 10 in this book for a discussion of intersex in the Irish context.)

Current Paradigm for the Determination of Legal Gender Recognition

As stated above, in order to be legally recognised, an individual or entity must assume a form with which the law is familiar and which the law can categorise in a manner enabling that individual or entity to access all the rights and privileges pertaining to that categorisation. One of the criteria for legal recognition is that a person's sex be declared. This requirement can be seen in Irish domestic legislation, in the Civil Registration Act 2004. Under section 19(1) of that Act, all births must be registered no more than three months from the date of birth. Such registration involves providing the Registrar with the required particulars, including the child's name, the date, time and place of birth and the sex of the child (Civil Registration Act 2004, Schedule 1). The Act is silent on the meaning of the term 'sex'. It neither discusses nor mentions any potential conflict between a person's biological sex and social gender identity. Nor does it define sex, or delineate how many possible sexes there might be.

Despite increasing equality, the law maintains differences between men and women. Thus the sex as which one is legally recognised can have a profound effect on the rights and respon-sibilities available to a person under the law. It determines who one can marry, as marriage is defined as the union of one man and one woman (*Hyde v Hyde* [1866] LR 1 P & D 130). In addition to mandating that one must marry a person of the opposite sex, the law also restricts which members of that sex one can marry. The list of prohibitive degrees is therefore gendered and different for both men and women (Marriage (Prohibited Degrees of Relationships) Acts 1907, 1921). Prisons are divided along gender lines, therefore the experience of incarceration can vary significantly depending on whether one is a woman or a man.[1] In Ireland a significant number of schools are single sex, which means the educational experience may also differ depending on sex, as, for example, few girls' schools offer subjects like construction studies or technical drawing.[2] Deter-mining one's sex/gender is thus crucially important not only to the establishment of one's legal identity but to a whole range of aspects of one's life.

Two-thirds of the member states of the European Union have an official identity card system.[3] Neither the UK nor Ireland has an identity card system, although there is some debate in the UK about its potential introduction. In these countries, to establish one's current identity and acquire legal status an individual must resort to official documentation that was not designed exclusively for identification purposes, such as driver's licence, passport and birth certificate.

In Ireland, to apply for either a driver's licence or a passport, the birth certificate is required as proof of identification. Thus the birth certificate becomes the document by which legal status is definitively determined. Birth certificates can, under the Civil Registration Act 2004, be altered in three ways: first, to add or change the forename of the child (Civil Registration Act 2004, s. 25); second, to include the name of the father where the parents were not married at the time of the birth (Civil Registration Act 2004, s. 23); and third, to reflect the subsequent marriage of the parents (Civil Registration Act 2004, s. 24). Altering an individu-al's name is a relatively simple procedure, requiring the swearing of an affidavit that is witnessed by a Commissioner of Oaths and registered in the High Court. Registering an alteration of sex is not so simple. Ireland does not have a formal procedure for offi-cial recognition of such an alteration. Thus it has fallen to the courts to elucidate how the legal gender of a person ought to be determined.

In the common law world, there are two schools of thought as to how the sex of an individual ought to be determined. The first school deals with the question of sex as a matter of law. It defines sex within the confines of biology and medicine, focusing on birth as the crucial moment when the sex of an individual is set for life. In Sharpe's words, this first school of thought deploys a '(bio)logic approach to constructing sex' (Sharpe, 2002: 39). The second school, by contrast, combines considerations of medicine and biology with the individual's psychological and social identity and treats the question of sex as one of fact. In essence, the difference between these two schools is that by deeming sex to be legally determined at birth, the first school cannot accommodate those who would wish subsequently to alter that sex. By contrast, deeming sex to be a matter of fact facilitates such a desire, as a legal determination can be reached in consideration of the changing facts. A quick description of the leading case of each school illustrates the point.

The English case *Corbett v Corbett (Corbett v Corbett (otherwise Ashley)* ([1970] 2 All E.R. 33) concerned the validity of the marriage of a man and a male-to-female trans woman. The husband, who was the petitioner in the case, sought to have the marriage annulled and thereby avoid maintenance payments. Thus the essential question to be determined by the court was whether Mrs Corbett was a man or a woman for the purposes of marriage. The judge in the case, Justice Ormrod, was uniquely well placed to adjudicate as in addition to being a judge he was a qualified doctor. His Lordship evaluated the available expert medical evidence. He noted that the medical experts agreed on four criteria for assessing the sex of an individual: chromosomal, gonadal, genital and psychological. Some of the experts, he noted, would add a fifth criterion: the hormonal factor (*Corbett v Corbett*: 44). Such criteria, he remarked, had been evolved by doctors to systemise medical knowledge and to assist unfortunate patients who suffer either physically or psychologically from sexual abnormalities. However, he stated that: '[t]hese criteria are, of course, relevant to, but do not necessarily decide, the legal basis of sex determination' (*Corbett v Corbett*: 44).

Ormrod J. found that it was common ground between the medical experts that the biological sexual constitution of an individual is fixed at birth (at the latest) and cannot be changed, either by the natural development of organs of the opposite sex, or by medical or surgical means (*Corbett v Corbett*: 47). Having thus found, his Lordship concluded that the law should adopt the first three of the doctor's criteria, i.e. the chromosomal, gonadal and genital tests. Where all three are congruent at birth, this determines the sex of an individual for the purposes of marriage and any operative interventions can be ignored (*Corbett v Corbett*: 48). Accordingly, the respondent was deemed to be legally male and the marriage was a nullity on the basis of *Hyde v Hyde*. Although Ormrod J. attempted to confine this test to the context of marriage, in *R v Tan* ([1983] QB 105) the test was applied in the context of criminal law and thus became the *de facto* legal test for the determination of the sex/gender of an individual in England and Wales.

The key case for the second school of thought is *MT v JT* ([1976] 140 NJ Super 77) from the Superior Court of New Jersey. The plaintiff was a male-to-female transsexual who was seeking an order of maintenance from her ex-husband. The respondent asserted that MT had been born a male, therefore the marriage was void and he was not liable for maintenance payments. The court examined *Corbett* as the only case that had previously considered the legal status of transsexuals as regards marriage. The court considered that the decision in *Corbett* had been reached incorrectly (*MT v JT*: 86). The *Corbett* judgment viewed sex and gender as disparate phenomena, meaning that its conclusion was rooted in the premise that 'true sex' was required to be ascertained, even for marital purposes, by biological criteria. The court in the instant case found that if the anatomical sex of a transsexual is made to conform to the psychological sex, then identity by sex must be governed by the harmonisation of these standards (*MT v JT*: 87). For the purposes of marriage it is the sexual capacity of the individual that must be scrutinised. Handler J. stated: 'Sexual capacity or sexuality in this frame of reference requires the coalescence of both the physical ability and the psychological and emotional orientation to engage in sexual intercourse as either a male or a female' (*MT v JT*: 87). Thus the court concluded that MT was a woman, the marriage was legally valid and her claim for maintenance was successful.

These two contrasting cases demonstrate the very different outcome for parties before the courts depending on whether a biological or a harmonisation approach is adopted by the courts. Interestingly, this is not a debate that emerged in the first cases to come before the Irish courts demanding a consideration of the question of the legal sex/gender of a person.

Determining Legal Gender Before the Irish Courts

This issue first arose before the Irish courts in *Foy v An tArd Chláraitheoir & Ors (No 1)* ([2002] I.E.H.C. 116). The plaintiff in this case, Dr Lydia Foy, was a male-to-female transsexual. As a child she experienced a strong and persistent gender dysphoria. Marriage and the birth of two children notwithstanding, she continued to feel thus and in 1992, after extensive consultations with various medical professionals, she underwent gender reassignment surgery. At its core, her argument alleged that the refusal of the Register General to alter her birth certificate to reflect her preferred gender amounted to a breach of her constitutional rights to equality, dignity and privacy, as well infringing her constitutionally protected right to marry.

In support of these arguments, Dr Foy adduced medical evidence from Professor Gooren that male and female brains differ and that the size and shape of the hypothalamus in a male-to-female transsexual is the same as that to be found in 'normal' females and smaller than that found in 'normal' males.[4] Thus Professor Gooren concluded that there is a neuro-scientific basis to transsexuality, and it should therefore be considered as a form of intersexuality (*Foy v An tArd Chláraitheoir & Ors (No 1)*: paras 52–4). This argument did not find favour with the court. McKechnie J. concluded:

> I am of the opinion that the evidence to date is insufficient to establish the existence of brain differentiation as a marker of sex and accordingly I do not believe that this court in such circumstances could give to it the legal recognition which is sought. (*Foy v An tArd Chláraitheoir & Ors (No 1)*: para. 121)

He therefore held that the biological indicators enunciated by Ormrod J. should continue to be decisive for this case (*Foy v An tArd Chláraitheoir (No 1)*: para. 121). As much of the evidence presented to the court concerned medical developments, and given that it largely ignored the effects of transsexuality, this conclusion was not surprising, particularly in light of the disagreements within the medical community as to the cause of transsexuality. There is no mention in the judgment of any consideration being given to alternative approaches to the question of legal sex/gender determination. Thus it is unclear whether the court was of the opinion that the *Corbett* test was the most suitable vehicle to employ or whether it was simply the only vehicle seemingly available.

Flowing from this conclusion, McKechnie J. then considered the effect of Article 8 of the European Convention on Human Rights (ECHR).[5] Given that the decision in the instant case was handed down a mere two days before that in *Goodwin v United Kingdom* ((2002) ECHR 583),[6] Mr Justice McKechnie concluded that confining the determining criteria to those which are biological was not inconsistent with principles of the Convention (*Foy v An tArd Chláraitheoir & Ors (No 1)*: para. 122). Thus in consideration of the medical evidence, the Strasbourg case law,[7] UK case law and the domestic legislation, McKechnie J. concluded that when responding to Dr Foy's request, the Registrar General had no alternative but to refuse to issue an amended birth certificate (*Foy v An tArd Chláraitheoir & Ors (No 1)*: para. 125).

The court then moved to a consideration of the constitutional issues raised in the case. As the rights that were allegedly infringed are not absolute, the court found that a balance had to be achieved between the rights of Dr Foy and the rights of anyone who would be impacted by a change in her status, in addition to the interests of society in general (*Foy v An tArd Chláraitheoir & Ors (No 1)*: para. 169). McKechnie J. concluded that the State had a legitimate interest in operating a functioning system of registering births that occur within the jurisdiction. Given that marriage and succession rights, rights of motherhood and other rights flow from such a determination, McKechnie J. found that the recording of the sex of a person is a 'a vital element of society's legitimate interest in a registration system' (*Foy v An tArd Chláraitheoir & Ors (No 1)*: para. 170). Such a record constitutes a historical recoding of the facts, '"a snap shot" of matters on a particular day' (*Foy v An tArd Chláraitheoir & Ors (No 1)*: para. 170). The entire system would be 'inoperable' if a confirmation of whether a person might subsequently present as transsexual had to be awaited prior to filling in the entry as regards sex. The absence of a provision permitting possible amendment at some unspecified time in an adult's life, to take effect retrospectively from the moment of birth, was not, the court held, unconstitutional. According to McKechnie J., the current system is 'reasonable in reach and response': criteria the State can legitimately expect of such a system (*Foy v An tArd Chláraitheoir & Ors (No 1)*: para. 171).

In his concluding remarks, the judge, demonstrating his sympathy for the plaintiff's plight, admitted that 'many of the issues raised in this case touch the lives, in a most personal and profound way, of many individuals and also are of deep concern to any caring society' (*Foy v An tArd Chláraitheoir & Ors (No 1)*: para. 177). Accordingly, he called on the Oireachtas to review the matters urgently (*Foy v An tArd Chláraitheoir & Ors (No 1)*: para. 177).

Two days later the Strasbourg Court handed down the landmark decision in *Goodwin v United Kingdom*. This ground-breaking decision changed entirely the approach of the Strasbourg Court to the issue of the recognition of the rights of transgendered persons. It held that the persistent refusal of the law in the UK to recognise the preferred gender identity of transgender people amounted to a breach of the privacy rights of such people under Article 8 of the Convention. Thus the *Foy (No 1)* case was appealed to the Irish Supreme Court.[8] By the time the appeal was heard, the legal landscape had been further altered by the introduction of the European Convention on Human Rights Act 2003 and the Civil Registration Act 2004, which established a new system of civil registration and repealed all previous legislation on the issue. As these developments had not been considered as part of the original hearing, the Supreme Court remitted the case back to the High Court. Unusually, by agreement of the parties, the remitted action was again heard by Justice Liam McKechnie, on the basis that he was familiar with the medical evidence and understood the issues involved. Given the absence of any new evidence, the Court found that the principle of *res judicata* (it is already decided) applied (*Foy v An tArd Chláraitheoir & Ors (No 2)* [2007] I.E.H.C. 470, at para. 12). Having analysed the then legislative framework in detail, McKechnie J. reiterated the findings of *Foy (No 1)*. He then had to consider what impact, if any, the *Goodwin* judgment might make on these findings.

Prior to the enactment of the ECHR Act 2003, Ireland operated a dualist approach regarding the ECHR. Thus only those judgments of the Strasbourg Court in which Ireland was a party were binding on Irish courts. Therefore the *Goodwin* case, having been handed down in 2002, was not binding on Ireland. Furthermore, the court noted that *Goodwin* was prospective in nature, as confirmed by the Strasbourg Court in *Grant v UK*, where it held that the *Goodwin* decision did not apply at any point in time prior to 11/7/2002 (*Grant v UK* [2006] ECHR 548, at paras 42–3). Finally, given that the *Goodwin* decision post-dated the judgment in *Foy (No 1)*, the decision reached on the day was correct both in light of the then case law of the Strasbourg Court and the margin of appreciation afforded to member states.[9] Thus the plaintiff lost the remitted action. That was not the conclusion of events, however.

Independently, a second application for the amended birth certificate was made to the Registrar in light of the events outlined above. This was refused. This second refusal was brought to the High Court for judicial review – hence the second set of pleadings. The two cases were heard jointly.

In essence, the core of the argument in the second *Foy* case was that if the new system of registration introduced under the Civil Registration Act 2004 did not permit an amendment of the birth certificate to reflect her preferred gender identity, then this amounted to a breach of the plaintiff's rights under Article 8 of the ECHR. In considering this argument, McKechnie J. found that there are currently no legal formalities required prior to undergoing gender reassignment surgery (*Foy v An tArd Chláraitheoir & Ors (No 2)* [2007] I.E.H.C. 470, at para. 64(1)). He reiterated that legal sex is determined by the biological temporal test outlined in *Corbett* and reinforced under the 2004 Act (*Foy v An tArd Chláraitheoir & Ors (No 2)* [2007] I.E.H.C. 470, at para. 64(4–5)). He further stated that the fact that a person's psychological gender may differ from his/her biological sex is not a ground for issuing a corrective birth certificate (*Foy v An tArd Chláraitheoir & Ors (No 2)* [2007] I.E.H.C. 470, at para. 64(6)). Finally, he found that the birth register is a record of historical fact: 'It is not intended to and does not record any other major event in a person's existence or even in death. In particular it is not intended to be a document of current identity although in practice this has not always been the case' (*Foy v An tArd Chláraitheoir & Ors (No 2)* [2007] I.E.H.C. 470, at para. 64(8)). Thus a person's legal sex is determined by the entry on the birth register and no subsequent event, including gender reassignment surgery, can alter the sex recognised by the law.

Consequently, McKechnie J. found that the case before him raised two questions: do the rights contained in Article 8 include a right to have one's acquired gender legally recognised? If so, has the Irish State provided an effective means for upholding that right

(*Foy v An tArd Chláraitheoir & Ors (No 2)* [2007] I.E.H.C. 470, at para. 94)? Answering these questions, McKechnie J. stated that if he was prepared to follow the *Goodwin* case, then unless Dr Foy's case was distinguishable from that case, he would be obliged to find that she had a right to legal recognition of her acquired gender. Responding to submissions from the State, he found that at the time of the *Goodwin* case, the legal situation in the UK was 'virtually identical' to the present Irish position (*Foy v An tArd Chláraitheoir & Ors (No 2)* [2007] I.E.H.C. 470, at para. 96). Thus McKechnie J. concluded that the two domestic legal frameworks were so 'strikingly similar' that the *Goodwin* decision should be considered highly influential in the Irish context, and subject to the margin of appreciation doctrine, the *Goodwin* decision reflects the law in Ireland (*Foy v An tArd Chláraitheoir & Ors (No 2)* [2007] I.E.H.C. 470, at para. 96).

McKechnie J. commented on the differing reaction of the UK and Irish authorities to the *Goodwin* decision. In the UK, two years after the decision, the Gender Recognition Act 2004 (GRA) was passed. This legislation set up a scheme whereby those who have been diagnosed with gender identity dysphoria and intend to live forever in the gender opposite to that in which they were born can have that preferred gender legally recognised. The legislation concerns not only those personally affected by transsexualism but all those who might be affected by a person's change of gender. Furthermore, from a judicial perspective, in 2003 the House of Lords issued a declaration that section 11(c) of the Matrimonial Causes Act 1973 was incompatible with Articles 8 and 12 of the Convention in *Bellinger v Bellinger* [2003] UKHL 21), thus giving practical effect to the *Goodwin* decision. Therefore within two years of the decision, the UK had responded both legislatively and judicially to the *Goodwin* case (*Foy v An tArd Chláraitheoir & Ors (No 2)* [2007] I.E.H.C. 470, at para. 99).

By contrast, Ireland had failed to respond at any level, even the most exploratory, to the issue of gender recognition. McKechnie J. noted that the silence from the government on the issue indicated that it had taken no significant steps to address the difficulties that continue to exist. He considered that the Civil Registration Act 2004 would have been a most suitable legislative vehicle for this purpose, and that the failure to include any consideration of these issues in that legislation must cause one to question whether the State is deliberately refraining from addressing these problems.

Concluding that Ireland was 'disconnected from mainstream thinking', he stated: 'Indeed it could be legitimately argued that Ireland's right to stand on the margin of appreciation is, as of today, significantly more tenuous than the position of the United Kingdom was, at the time of the *Goodwin* decision' (*Foy v An tArd Chláraitheoir & Ors (No 2)* [2007] I.E.H.C. 470, at para. 100).

Therefore, on 14 February 2008, Justice McKechnie formally issued an order declaring that sections of the Civil Registration Act 2004 were incompatible with the ECHR because they do not make any provision for recognising the new gender identity of transgendered persons.

The initial response of the State was to appeal the case to the Supreme Court. However, in June 2010 it was announced that the State was to withdraw this appeal. This followed the establishment, in May of that year, of an interdepartmental committee known as the Gender Recognition Advisory Group (GRAG), 'to advise the Minister for Social Protection on the legislation required to provide for legal recognition by the State of the acquired gender of transsexuals' (Gender Recognition Advisory Group, 2011: 6). The GRAG report was delivered to the Minister in June 2011. Prior to analysing some of the recommendations contained in that report, this chapter will very briefly turn to a consideration of the evolving human rights discourse on this issue, which provides a lens through which the report will be analysed.

Human Rights Discourse on the Right to Gender Recognition

The past twenty years have seen a growth in the number of claimants petitioning the courts for legal recognition in their preferred gender identity (Sharpe, 2002; Whittle, 2002). In the European context, a notable trend in these cases, particularly since the adoption of the Human Rights Act 1998 in the UK, has been the assertion, by plaintiffs, of a right to legal recognition in their preferred gender identity (Ní Mhuirthile, 2008). More recently, with the publication of the *Yogyakarta Principles* (2007), the discussions surrounding draft UN Declarations (2008) and the Resolution of the UN Human Rights Council (2011), evidence moves towards explicitly recognising gender identity rights, including that to legal recognition in one's preferred gender, as normative human rights. This chapter now turns to an examination of these international developments.

In March 2007, the *Yogyakarta Principles* were launched by an international group of human rights experts. The *Yogyakarta Principles* consist of 'a set of principles on the application of international human rights law in relation to sexual orientation and gender identity' (ICJ, 2007). The Principles 'collate and clarify State obligations' (ICJ, 2007: 7) by relating sexual orientation and gender identity rights issues to established human rights norms, and thereby seek to establish a legal framework for assessing such claims. The Principles also urge UN bodies to integrate sexual and gender rights issues into their procedures through the inclusion of specific recommendations for the UN (ICJ, 2007: 32). They were celebrated as a crucial tool (O'Flaherty & Fisher, 2008: 238), but without official sponsorship from sovereign states or a multilateral organisation, the Principles were non-binding and did not immediately address the legal status of those who question the heteronormative understanding of sex/gender. Nonetheless, the Principles use existing international human rights conventions to insist that states are obliged to protect sexual minorities from the vast majority of abuses that they face – not as a minority, but as human beings entitled to human rights.

The *Yogyakarta Principles* are the most comprehensive statement on sexual and gender rights yet produced. They encompass a wide range of issues, including non-discrimination, legal recognition, security of person, privacy, access to justice, work, social security, housing, education, health, freedom of expression, immigration and refugee issues, founding a family, public participation and effective redress. Furthermore, the Principles are not designed as an abstract or theoretical statement, but rather are intended for practical implementation. As Sanders argues, the drafters of the Principles 'did not want an aspirational document. They did not want to produce a "where we should be going" sermon' (Sanders, 2008: para. 7). Instead, the Principles clearly 'affirm the primary obligation of States to implement human rights', and specifically aim to 'bring greater clarity and coherence to States' human rights obligations' (Sanders, 2008: para. 7). Each broad human rights provision enshrined by the Principles is accompanied by detailed information on the responsibilities of potential state parties, and recommendations for the practical implementation of the Principles at a domestic level.

The Principles have 'met with a surprising degree of success' in international fora (O'Flaherty & Fisher, 2008: 239). Since their launch in 2007, the Principles have significantly influenced discussions and interpretations of sexual and gender rights at the UN. Several states have drawn on the Principles in domestic policy-making (O'Flaherty & Fisher, 2008: 238; Sanders, 2008). Additionally, the Principles have been endorsed by several human rights organisations, including those representing the interests of sexual and gender minorities. Therefore, they have relevance to the individuals and communities affected by sexual and gender rights violations, are sufficiently detailed to have potential for practical implementation, and their congruence with the existing human rights framework has resulted in a considerable level of international acknowledgment and acceptance.

Similarly, the inclusion of sexual orientation and gender identity rights, including the right to legal gender recognition, has been the subject of debate by both the UN General Assembly and the UN Human Rights Council. On 18 December 2008, a landmark statement was issued by Argentina at the UN General Assembly (United Nations General Assembly, 2008b). Supported by 66 member states, the draft UN *Declaration on Sexual Orientation and Gender Identity* affirmed that 'all human rights [must] be applied to all human beings, regardless of their sexual orientation or gender identity' (United Nations General Assembly, 2008b: para. 3), and 'condemned all human rights violations based on sexual orientation or gender identity, whenever or wherever they might occur' (United Nations General Assembly, 2008b: para. 6). This was a milestone in UN history. For the first time, the issue of gender identity had been formally placed on the General Assembly's human rights agenda. However, immediately following the Declaration, an Alternative Statement was issued by Syria on behalf of 57 member states, opposing the mention of the 'so-called notions of sexual orientation and gender identity' (United Nations General Assembly, 2008a). As a result, there was no definitive statement from the UN on the issue. However in 2011, the UN Human Rights Council passed a resolution that expressed its '*grave concern* at acts of violence and discrimination, in all regions of the world, committed against individuals because of their sexual orientation and gender identity' (United Nations Human Rights Council, 2011). Consequently, it commissioned the UN High Commissioner on Human Rights to undertake a study documenting such incidents and to make recommendations that it undertook to implement. Furthermore, the

Council decided to 'remain seized of this priority issue' (United Nations Human Rights Council, 2011).

The *Yogyakarta Principles*, together with the debates on the issue at the UN, confirm the approach by the ECHR in *Goodwin* that there is a right to be legally recognised in one's preferred gender, and that this right exists as part of the normal human rights of all people. With this in mind, this chapter now turns to a consideration of the proposals put forward in the GRAG report to ascertain whether the potential scheme for gender recognition in Ireland would respect and vindicate the rights of trans people.

Recognition of the Preferred Gender Identities of Trans People: Recommendations from the GRAG report

As stated above, the GRAG report was published on 15 June 2011. The report proposes establishing a scheme where a person whose birth is registered in Ireland, is at least 18 years of age, has a clear and settled intention to live in the preferred gender permanently and has lived in that gender for at least two years can apply to be legally recognised. In addition to these criteria, the applicant must supply evidence of diagnosis of gender identity disorder (GID), or evidence of having undergone gender reassignment surgery, or evidence of legal recognition of preferred gender identity by another jurisdiction. Furthermore, persons in an existing valid marriage or civil partnership are excluded from the scheme (Gender Recognition Advisory Group, 2011).

Effectively, this amounts to an adoption of the scheme available in the UK under the Gender Recognition Act 2004. There are a number of difficulties with these proposals. This chapter will critique the two most controversial aspects of the proposed scheme: the requirement for medical diagnosis or surgical intervention; and the marriage issue.

The Diagnosis Issue

The GRAG report proposes that in order to be recognised, one must either have a diagnosis of GID, or have undergone gender reassignment surgery, or be legally recognised in another jurisdiction. Encapsulated in this requirement are two issues that cause tension: surgical alteration; and diagnosis. The question of the requirement for surgical alteration has long been a bone of contention. Gender reassignment requires more than one surgical intervention, thus the question of when sufficient surgeries have been undertaken to enable recognition is relevant. For example, in *Rees v UK* ((1986) 9 EHRR 56) the dissenting judgment made much of the pain and anguish that Rees had undergone to acquire a male body and that this evidenced 'how real and intense was his desire to adopt a new sexual identity as far as possible' (*Rees v UK* 1986: 69). Sharpe criticises this judgment for inexorably linking 'authenticity' of trans-sexual identity to bodily change: '[T]hose unwilling and/or unable to undergo surgical procedures are depicted as "inauthentic" and therefore undeserving. In other words, surgical intervention is important not only for the bodily change it effects in the present but also for what it signifies about the past' (Sharpe, 2002: 54).

Sharpe's comments illustrate the difficulty that might arise where a person has not completed all possible surgeries to effect a gender reassignment. Male phalloplasty is a particularly difficult procedure and therefore is not always undergone by trans men.[10] Thus the success of an application for gender recognition from a trans man under the scheme as proposed by the GRAG may depend on whether he has undergone phalloplasty, which in practical terms may result in the exclusion from the scheme of a significant number of trans men. It was the exclusive requirement of a diagnosis of GID that resulted in the almost universal acclaim for the Gender Recognition Act 2004 in the UK. Dispensing with any requirement for medical or surgical intervention, '[T]he G.R.A., intentionally or otherwise, interrupts the orthodoxies of gender that the law has peddled to a greater extent than any other development in recent times' (Sandland, 2005: 44). The GRA does not include a definition of GID. In practice, the Gender Recognition Panels have turned to definitions from the medical community and particularly that from the *Diagnostic and Statistical Manual of Mental Disorders* (DSM), which defines GID as a registered mental disorder evidenced by the congruence of five criteria.[11]

1. There must be evidence of a strong and persistent cross-gender identification.
2. This cross-gender identification must not merely be a desire for any perceived cultural advantages of being the other sex.

3. There must also be evidence of persistent discomfort about one's assigned sex or a sense of inappropriateness in the gender role of that sex.

4. The individual must not have a concurrent physical intersex condition (e.g. androgen insensitivity syndrome or congenital adrenal hyperplasia).

5. There must be evidence of clinically significant distress or impairment in social, occupational or other important areas of functioning.

There are a number of difficulties with this as a definitional determinate. First, it problematises those people who wish for recognition in a gender other than male or female. Recognition depends on diagnosis, therefore unless an applicant is willing to be labelled or stigmatised as mentally ill, recognition will not be forthcoming. Second, it perpetuates by implication the binary gender paradigm, that one must have cross-gender identification, i.e. one must want to be of 'the other sex' (criterion 2 from the DSM definition of GID). Finally, one must 'not have a concurrent physical intersex condition' (criterion 4 from the DSM definition of GID). Thus the right to recognition, expressed in the *Goodwin* case as grounded in a common humanity and thus accessible to all regardless of their gender, is frustrated because intersex individuals cannot exercise this right under this piece of legislation. As is evidenced in the *Yogyakarta Principles*, the Committee of Ministers of the Council of Europe Recommendation CM/Rec(2010)5, and the recent report of the Council of Europe Commissioner for Human Rights (Council of Europe Commissioner for Human Rights, 2011), within international human rights discourse there is a move away from the requirement to have undergone some form of medical and/or surgical intervention prior to being granted recognition. Furthermore, those EU member states that have most recently introduced, or amended, their legal gender recognition mechanisms have dispensed with the need for such interventions (ILGA Europe, 2011). Most recently, the Senate of Argentina passed a Gender Identity law that specifically states that '[i]n no case will it be needed to prove that a surgical procedure for total or partial genital reassignment, hormonal therapies or any other psychological or medical treatment has taken place [for recognition to be granted]' (Global

Action for Trans Equality, 2012: Article 4). The Argentinian law simply relies on a self-declaration by the applicant as to their gender identity (Global Action for Trans Equality, 2012: Article 4). Thus the proposal put forward by the GRAG requiring medical evidence is out of step with best international practice on this question. Recognition of preferred gender that follows the Argentinian example and that relies on a declaration from the person seeking recognition as to their gender identity would better ensure the vindication of the rights of trans people.

The Marriage Question

The second, and more problematic, issue among the GRAG recommendations that this chapter will focus on is the requirement that an applicant be single prior to making an application. This is not a unique requirement and mirrors that contained in the UK's GRA (Gender Recognition Act 2004: s. 5).

The difficulty arises because, at present, marriage in Ireland is available only to opposite-sex couples (*Hyde v Hyde*). Same-sex couples can formalise their relationships by civil partnership, which does not enjoy the same status as marriage (Civil Partnership and Certain Rights and Obligations of Cohabitants Act 2010). Therefore, the concern is that if married trans people were to be legally recognised in their preferred gender, this would result in what would ostensibly be a same-sex marriage and thereby would create an inequality for same-sex couples where one party is not a trans person.

The exclusion of those applicants who are married or in a civil partnership raises clear constitutional questions. It is arguable that to effectively mandate that a happily married couple divorce prior to granting recognition is a direct interference with the special constitutional position of the family based on marriage, as contained in Article 41.3.1 of the Constitution. The GRAG report, however, was of a different opinion. It contends that as same-sex marriage is currently not provided for in Irish law, any attempt to introduce legislation that would have as an effect the acknowledgment of the legality of same-sex marriage would be vulnerable to constitutional challenge (Gender Recognition Advisory Group, 2011: 30). Furthermore, the GRAG draws support for the decision of the Strasbourg Court in *Parry v UK* ([2006] ECHR 1157) to argue that it is within the margin of appreciation afforded to member states on this issue to exclude married applicants from recognition. Regarding those in an existing civil partnership, the GRAG stated that the effect of transition would be the recognition of opposite-sex civil partners whose relationship 'does not benefit from the full protection afforded to marriage' (Gender Recognition Advisory Group, 2011: 31). Furthermore, it expressed the opinion that failure to require dissolution of a civil partnership when dissolution of a marriage is mandated would potentially result in a constitutional challenge. Additionally, this exclusion seems to run contrary to the second guiding principle purportedly underpinning the proposed scheme that '[t]he terms and conditions of the scheme should not deter potential applicants from applying' (Gender Recognition Advisory Group, 2011: 52). It is submitted that the requirement to divorce or dissolve a civil partnership can only have the practical effect of deterring potential applications.

The situation is further complicated by the provisions governing divorce in Ireland. As enshrined in Article 41.3.2(i), to be granted a divorce, the spouses must have lived apart from one another for a period of, or periods amounting to, at least four years during the five years prior to the commencement of proceedings. Furthermore, under Article 41.3.2(ii), in order to grant a divorce there must be no reasonable prospect of reconciliation between the spouses. The proposal that recognition be extended only to single persons, together with the provisions governing divorce, combine to create a situation that is very invidious. Essentially, it requires a trans spouse to apply for a divorce, against their wishes and where the marriage has not broken down, as a condition of recognising their preferred gender. It is submitted that this would be a clear violation of the pledge contained in Article 41.3.1 of the Constitution 'to guard with special care the institution of marriage, on which the family is founded, and to protect it against attack', as the couple would presumably be in a validly contracted and subsisting marriage. It would also, of course, constitute an interference with the rights of the non-trans spouse who wants to continue in the marriage. It is also debatable whether a divorce could ever be granted to such a couple because there has been no irreconcilable breakdown of the relationship. Thus married trans people remain caught in a quagmire where, potentially, they can never be recognised in their preferred gender.

A solution would be to abandon the requirement that a person be single prior to being recognised in their preferred gender. This would result in an apparent legal anomaly, as identified by the GRAG (Gender Recognition Advisory Group, 2011), but would affect only a small number of people. As to the concern that it might create a precedent enabling a challenge to either the Civil Registration Act 2004 or the Civil Partnership and Certain Rights and Obligations of Cohabitants Act 2010 in the hope of a result in favour of same-sex marriage, it is submitted that such a challenge would not arise as the anomaly would extend only to those who have contracted a valid heterosexual marriage and one of whom had subsequently transitioned to the opposite gender with the agreement of the non-trans spouse. Thus the anomaly is confined to a very particular situation.

The anomaly can be legally justified by drawing an analogy with the legal age for capacity to enter a marriage. In determining whether a person is old enough to marry, it is the age of the party at *the time of marriage* that counts (Civil Registration Act 2004, section 2(2)(c); Family Law Act 1995, section 31(1)). The fact that an underage party has, subsequent to the marriage, reached the age of majority does not render the marriage retrospectively valid. Correspondingly, an incapacity (such as impotence or a mental infirmity) that develops only *after* a marriage has been validly formed, and that was not present at the time of marriage, does not technically render a marriage invalid. Similarly, it is suggested that where a couple contracts a marriage as opposite-sex partners at the time of the marriage, it is validly constituted and is not rendered invalid because one spouse subsequently transitions to the opposite gender.

Conclusion

The issue of whether and how to recognise the preferred gender identity of trans persons has been under consideration in Ireland, either by the courts or the Oireachtas (Irish houses of parliament), since 1997. During that time, huge advances have been made in international human rights discourse, such that the right to legal recognition in one's preferred gender is generally accepted as existing within international human rights law. In introducing a scheme for legal gender recognition in Ireland, it is important to be cognisant of this obligation and to introduce legislation that respects and vindicates all the rights of trans people. Viewed from this perspective, the scheme proposed by the GRAG represents a missed opportunity to learn from problems and challenges exposed elsewhere, particularly concerning the UK scheme, to produce proposals that would ensure respect for the rights of all those, whether transsexual, transgender or intersex, who might benefit from gender recognition legislation.

At the time of writing, two Private Members' Bills on this issue have been introduced in the Oireachtas: Aengus Ó Snodaigh's Gender Recognition Bill 2013, introduced in the Dáil in June 2013; and Katherine Zappone's Legal Recognition of Gender Bill 2013, introduced in the Seanad in July 2013. Both these bills have been drafted in light of international human rights norms and are inspired by the Argentinian legislation. Yet the government-sponsored Gender Recognition Bill remains on the 'C list' of the legislative programme for the summer session 2013, with publication not expected until 2014. As such it is a low priority, as bills on this list have yet to have 'heads of bill' approved by the government.[12] Transgender Equality Network Ireland (TENI) is the major NGO in this area and it has advocated strongly in favour of a legislative framework that is in keeping with international human rights law. Whether this strategy will bear fruit remains to be seen.

Notes

[1] In Ireland, for example, in the biggest male prison in the State, Mountjoy, cells are overcrowded and there is no in-cell sanitation, necessitating the use of chamber pots. The women's prison, known as the Dóchas Centre, has single rooms with toilet, shower and wash-hand basin. The centre is arranged as six house units and each house has its own kitchen facilities, which inmates can use freely. *See* Kinlen (2003).

[2] *See* Department of Education and Science (2007), which provides a gender analysis of selection and performance in all subjects covered by State examinations, based on the 2003 State examination results. This survey revealed that following gender distribution of students sitting the following Leaving Certificate exams: Construction Studies, 93.8% male; Technical Drawing, 94.1% male; Engineering, 95.3% male; Agricultural Science, 75.5% male; Home Economics (General), 87% female; Home Economics (Social and Scientific), 86.3% female; Music, 77.4% female.

[3] The following states all have an identity card system, although it is not compulsory to carry the card in all of the states and in some possession of the card is voluntary: Belgium, Bulgaria, Republic of Cyprus, Czech

Republic, Denmark, Estonia, Finland, France, Germany, Greece, Hungary, Italy, Poland, Portugal, Romania, Slovakia, Spain and Sweden.

[4] Professor Louis J. Gooren is an Emeritus Professor of Medicine at the Hospital of the Vrije Universiteit of Amsterdam, the Netherlands. An endocrinologist, he is internationally renowned as an expert on transgender and was one of the first physicians to treat transgender youth.

[5] For the sake of clarity, throughout this chapter the European Convention on Human Rights will be referred to as ECHR, while the European Court of Human Rights will be referred to as the Strasbourg Court.

[6] *Goodwin v United Kingdom* ((2002) ECHR 583) was the case in which the Strasbourg Court held that the right to be recognised in one's preferred gender identity is to be found within the privacy rights contained in Article 8 ECHR. More important, it held that the margin of appreciation on this issue had now vanished due to the consensus within the Council of Europe member states in favour of affording recognition.

[7] Strasbourg case law refers to case law originating from the European Court of Human Rights, which is based in Strasbourg. Prior to the enactment of the European Convention on Human Rights Act 2003, such judgments were not binding on the Irish courts unless Ireland was a party to a particular case. Since the introduction of the 2003 Act, Irish judges are obliged to interpret legislation or case law in a manner compatible with the ECHR (ECHR Act 2003, s. 2).

[8] There is a hierarchy of courts in Ireland. When dealing with non-criminal cases it is as follows, in descending order of importance: Supreme Court, High Court, Circuit Court and District Court. Each court is bound by decisions of the courts further up the hierarchy. In other words, it must follow the precedent or legal decisions of a higher court. It is, however, free to depart from its own previous decisions and the decisions of lower courts.

[9] The margin of appreciation is a doctrine of the Strasbourg Court whereby, in the absence of a broad consensus throughout the member states of the Council of Europe on an issue, each state retains 'wriggle room' to decide the matter for itself.

[10] Phalloplasty is the term for surgical alteration of the phallus or penis. In the context of female-to-male trans men, it means the creation of a penis.

[11] The Gender Recognition Panels established under the GRA 2004 in the UK administer the system of gender recognition. In other words, they review applications and decide whether or not an individual has met the criteria for recognition. Each panel consists of at least one person with medical expertise and one lawyer.

[12] Heads of bill is the term used for the outline of the items to be covered in the bill.

Section 3

Lesbian and Gay Parenting

CHAPTER 6

Out at the School Gate:
Visibility, Sexuality and the Lesbian Mother

Angela O'Connell

Introduction

> Familia is cross-generational bonding, deep emotional ties
> between opposite sexes, and within our sex. It is sexuality,
> which involves, but is not limited to, intercourse or orgasm.
> It springs forth from touch, constant and daily. The ritual of
> kissing and the sign of the cross with every coming and going
> from the home. It is finding familia among friends where blood
> ties are formed through suffering and celebration shared.
> (Moraga, 1994: 41)

The family has been the location from which women's sexuality
has historically been analysed, as mothers and daughters within
families, or as 'mistresses and whores' who threaten the sanctity of
the family (Jackson and Scott, 2010: 24). The family itself received
little attention, however, until the latter decades of the twentieth
century, when feminists began to frame questions about women's
sexuality, and the role of the family in defining sexuality, in terms
of public, political issues.

In this chapter, through the lens of the 'lesbian mother', I will
explore how states and societies utilise the ideology of the family
in order to control the expression of sexuality and thus preserve
particular, gendered, balances of power. I draw on original research
with ten lesbian couples who are, or plan to become, parents, in
order to explore sexuality from an 'outsider' (Collins, 2004: 103)
perspective, in this case from a lesbian family standpoint:

… many lesbians, and certainly lesbian intellectuals, are not just outsiders, but 'outsiders within.' The perspective from their lives, which are located not only on the margins of the social order but also in certain respects at its center, can reveal the causal relations between the margins and the center. (Harding, 1991: 265)

This chapter will not be a lesbian sex manual, nor will it delve too deeply into the sexual lives of the women who participated in the research. Like Gabb, who conducted research on LGBT-parent families, I found that, paradoxically, sexuality was 'notably absent' in the participants' accounts in this study – perhaps related to the taboos around both adult and child sexuality within the family, which are evident in society and academia (Gabb, 2013: 333) – although some oblique references are apparent. Instead, this chapter looks at where the sexual and the social intersect, from the perspective of the families these women are creating. Feminist standpoint theory is based on the premise that social structures can best be understood by those engaged in struggles against them. My contention is that a lesbian family standpoint provides a basis from which to develop knowledge claims that are unique yet accessible, mapping 'how a social and political disadvantage can be turned into an epistemological, scientific, and political advantage' (Harding, 2004: 7). Knowledge arising from this standpoint has the potential to impact upon women's relationships with other women, as well as to inform family policy, children's rights and other social and policy areas where gender and sexuality intersect. This was addressed by one interviewee, Rebecca,[1] who suggested the political potential of lesbian visibility:

But in actual fact, another thing I'm saying is, the more strengths we have in ourselves as lesbians, to be out there, in the public eye, as mothers … the more straight women get back. Because they're all mothers. You know, hell-bent or something. [Laughs] They're all a bit afraid to be themselves. [...] I mean, you just have to go to a school, simply stand at the gate. You know, that's how you learn. Stand at the gates, all these different mothers, all with their different children, all with their different angles, and notions about life, and blah,

blah, blah. And all separate. And all terrified of each other. And that's really sad. (Rebecca: interview 2005)

The Family as the Problem

Feminists have long critiqued the hegemonic family as unsustainable and unfulfilling for women, and have focused on the family as a central site of gendered inequality and oppression. Okin asserts that 'the family presents a problem' (Okin, 1989: 16). Almost two decades ago, Jackie Stacey, like Adrienne Rich before her, accused feminism of ignoring *heterosexuality* altogether, as if this were not a problematic category itself (Stacey, 1993: 62; Rich, 1980b: 79). Notably, Stacey also pointed out that lesbian issues were the subject of less research than might be expected, given the centrality of sexual identity to feminism in general (Stacey, 1993: 62).

Imelda Whelehan argues that lesbian politics as a faction arose in the 1960s because lesbians did not feel that the women's movement was responsive to their concerns (Whelehan, 1995: 88). Rich had attempted to address the perceived gulf between lesbian and heterosexual concerns by pointing to the political necessity of female bonding for women, and to how patriarchal systems work to prevent this, in part by recruiting women to stigmatise woman-identification. This is achieved through erasing the (politically necessary) distinction between female and male experience, by considering the 'lesbian continuum' – the range of women's relationships with each other – as a female version of stigmatised, male homosexuality (Rich, 1980b: 136). In an Irish context, Anne Byrne notes that lesbianism is recognised as a stigmatised identity by her (female, heterosexual) research participants. Byrne observes that societal homophobia can serve to silence straight women's identification with other women, and impact upon their expression of female solidarity (Byrne, 2000: 21).

Within academic feminism, too, lesbians have felt marginalised. In recent years feminism has been criticised for being ethnocentric and heteronormative, based on the experiences of white, heterosexual, middle-class women and excluding the experiences of other groups, such as lesbians and women of colour (Harding, 1991; hooks, 2000; Collins, 2004; Combahee River Collective, 1994; Narayan, 2004; Sandoval, 2004). An example of this can be found in Irish feminist debates on reproductive rights, which revolve almost exclusively around contraception and abortion, and do not consider how exclusion from fertility treatment, denial of custody and adoption rights, and social disapproval act as extreme forms of reproductive control over the lives of lesbian women (*cf.* Ryan-Sheridan, 1994; Daly, 1997; Galligan, 1998; O'Connor, 1998; Bacik, 2004; Kennedy, 2004). By including lesbian experiences in these accounts, a different perspective would be provided from which to analyse the control that dominant structures exercise over all women's sexuality through control over their reproductive bodies.

On the other hand, work that centrally features 'lesbian experience' can be accused of essentialism, unless care is taken to reveal that a lesbian standpoint is not a representation of a fixed identity category, but rather a particular critical, socially constructed location (Harding, 1991: 266; Moya and Hames-Garcia, 2000: 10; Sandoval, 2004: 204). Following from this, a lesbian standpoint does not necessarily confine the researcher to generating insights about lesbians (Harding, 1991: 252), but plays a vital role in offering a unique perspective on the ways society in general functions, in how discourses are constructed and in how social controls operate.

Defining Research Parameters

Although scholars have moved away from monolithic identity politics to more sophisticated intersectionality approaches, Fineman (2008) argues that some theorists of intersectionality still mistakenly focus on the *identities* of those who are suffering from discrimination and inequality. She proposes that it is their *relationship* to the institutions, i.e. their place in the web, which in fact creates their identities and results in their marginalisation (Fineman, 2008: 16). While public attitudes have softened in recent years, showing greater tolerance of homosexuality in general, including towards lesbian families, laws and policies have consistently failed to recognise the ties between lesbian mothers and their children in these families. In my research, I adopted the term 'lesbian' as a descriptor for individual women in same-sex relationships who were sharing similar experiences in trying to form families with children in contemporary Ireland. Lesbian couples in Ireland have used a wide variety of means to have children within their relationships. These include, but are not confined to, self-insemination (with a known or unknown sperm donor), sex with a man, insemination with medical assistance, adoption, fostering (formal or informal), and guardianship of relatives. Currently in Ireland, female same-sex couples encounter a number of obstacles to having children that they would not have to negotiate if they were heterosexual. Lesbian couples have no legally established rights to avail of fertility treatments,[2] and have no rights to jointly adopt a child. Lesbian families in this sense 'are part of the whole but outside the main body' of the family in Ireland (hooks, 2000: xvi). It is this 'everyday problematic' (Smith, 2005: 39) that was the focus of my research, in order to explore those laws, policies and social mores surrounding the 'traditional' heterosexual family protected by the Irish Constitution. The omission of other types of family, such as gay male families, single-parent families, families without children, 'Families We Choose' (Weston, 1991) and others, reflects a particular emphasis on Irish family policy in my research. Obviously, these types of family are also rich sites for future exploration in Irish research on sexuality and families, but were beyond the scope of this research.

Within this remit, all of the couples I interviewed had experienced some level of exclusion from fertility or adoption services, or anticipated difficulties accessing such services in the future, on the basis of their same-sex relationship status. Although most of the women I interviewed used the term 'lesbian' when referring to themselves, some refused this moniker, perhaps because, as Gabb notes, the label *lesbianism* appears to focus attention on sexuality as the defining characteristic of a woman who adopts, or to whom is ascribed, this identity: 'We actually know very little about the ordinary experiences of *sexuality practices* in families per se, while the *sexual identities* of LBGT parents are afforded an excess of significance, determining parenthood through queer sexuality' (Gabb, 2013: 325).

This paradoxical presence/absence of explicit reference to sexuality is precisely the point of interest here, exposing as it does tensions women in general experience about being both 'woman' and 'mother'. The term 'lesbian' exposes female sexuality in a very particular way. However, even those women I interviewed who did not use the term 'lesbian' to describe themselves accepted the shorthand that this term afforded me to refer to the group I was researching: 'Well, actually we don't ever identify as lesbian, just to say that. We don't really identify, particularly, in terms of sexual orientation. But, yes, the children will be raised by two women and we are perceived as lesbians, and that's grand' (Mamie: interview 2005).

Researching Hidden Populations

Lesbians are a marginalised, hidden and dispersed population, and research that seeks to explore their lives can be fraught with difficulties with regard to gaining access to them (Flood, 2003: 117). Quite early in the research process I decided to confine my study to interviewing a relatively small number of lesbian couples (*see also* Hesse-Biber, 2007), given the scale of the research and taking into account its other empirical requirements. As I recruited partic-ipants, it was clear that although socially rather homogeneous,[3] the variety of different situations they represented appeared to provide a broad range of experiences, and I finally decided that ten couples would be optimal. At the time of interviewing, between the ten couples, there were seven children born or adopted within their relationships, aged between one year and eight years (three boys, four girls). Three of these children were born through donor insemination at a UK clinic; three were born after inseminating with sperm from a known donor; and one child was adopted in the UK.

In order to recruit participants, I had planned to advertise in the gay media, to visit a recently established lesbian, gay and bisexual (LGB) parenting network, to ask permission to include a mail shot in a widely circulated lesbian newsletter, as well as asking lesbian friends to take part and 'snowball' with other couples they knew. But within a few weeks, after the visit to the parenting network and having raised the subject among friends and acquaintances who then 'snowballed' for me, I had a full cohort of participants. After talking with these women, I concluded that they see themselves as social actors and construe their experiences as having a significance that goes beyond the personal:

> Living your life, and, you know, parenting together, and, you know, living in the way that we're living, is, is such a powerful thing to do, you know? [...] And I think that, something about doing the research draws the people together under one story, and I think that can be quite significant. (Harriet: interview 2006)

Reflexively recording the voices of silenced groups can be invaluable as a means of producing unique insights into problematic situations. My research starts from lesbian mothers' lives and critically theorises how these lives intersect with, resist and challenge dominant discourses on sexuality.

'The Family'

Connell argues that 'far from being the basis of society, the family is one of its most complex products' (Connell, 1987: 121). In practice, the term 'the family' is used to describe actual social configurations and to denote a normative ideal. The family in Western societies is frequently alluded to as a natural and pre-social institution arising from the innate sexuality of men and women (Nussbaum, 1999: 78). This model owes much of the legitimacy it has acquired to the prevalence of natural law thinking among law-makers and policy-makers (Nussbaum, 1997: 326).

The natural law tradition is ancient and widespread, but critics point out that what natural law presents as objective fact can, on deeper investigation, prove to be knowledge constructed by vested interests in various historical settings (Fahey, 1995: 207). Its 'natural' status is established by habit and repetition (Nussbaum, 1997: 329), as well as by the forcing out of dissent (Connell, 1987: 145). The Irish Constitution explicitly appeals to natural law and calls the family 'the natural primary and fundamental unit group of society' and places it as 'antecedent and superior to all positive law' (Article 41.1.1).

The influence of natural law can further be detected in early, supposedly secular anthropological definitions of who counts as family from influential theorists such as Radcliffe-Brown (1952), Lévi-Strauss (1996) and Murdock (cited in Hantrais, 2004). These analyses of family and kinship were based on fixed patterns of consanguinity and affinity, or blood and marriage, which, these theorists claim, together with the incest taboo, define kinship and maintain bloodlines in every society. However, these accounts overlooked ties based on economic necessity, spirituality or sociality and thus, unsurprisingly, resulted in accounts of family framed purely in terms of recognisable, Western, kinship patterns – what Fineman calls 'The Sexual Family' (Fineman, 2009b).

In contrast, Gillis (1996) illustrates how before the nineteenth century the term 'family' was used in two quite different ways. In one usage, 'family' referred to huge networks of blood- and marriage-related kin who were not co-resident. The other usage of the term referred to a co-resident household, including unrelated servants, as well as those tied by blood and marriage (Gillis, 1996: 13). The ideal of the co-resident, biological, nuclear family, based on marriage, started to become firmly established in its current hegemonic form only after the Second World War (Nicholson, 1997: 27).

The State of the Family

The role of the State in bringing about such changes in understandings and practices of family has been explored by a number of theorists, such as Connell (1994; 1987) and Foucault (1990). Importantly, these theorists illustrate the ways in which states operate at the level of embodied individuals, channelling sexuality, desire and a myriad of aspirations into a particular model of the family, thus diminishing and concealing the role of explicit state force in regulating social behaviour. Feminist accounts of the State in particular emphasise the gendered nature of the State's interests, interests that have significant implications for women's sexuality within and outside the family (Okin, 1989: 129; Connell, 1994: 159; Nussbaum, 1999: 140; Butler, 2004: 104).

Connell (1987) proposes that gender relations are shaped by the State using three underlying structures. The first two, the division of labour along gender lines and the assumption of power as a masculine attribute, are well documented in sociological literature (Connell, 1987: 96). The third, 'cathexis', characterised as 'the daily conduct of emotional relationships' (Connell, 1987: 97), explains how the interpersonal lives of citizens are ordered by socially constructed relations designed to maintain a status quo that privileges the (predominantly heterosexual, male) holders of social power (Connell, 1987: 104). Within this order, gender struggles, such as domestic violence, are portrayed as crises, aberrations of what – utilising natural law discourses – the State presents as the natural order (Connell, 1987: 159).

Foucault posits implicit, psychic regulation and intervention by the State, focusing on individuals at a bodily level – whereby the State began to rely on 'the manner in which each individual made use of his sex' (Foucault, 1990: 26). He suggests that the obsession with sex that appeared during the eighteenth century was instituted by states that were motivated to ensure that the population continued to grow, in order to feed the demand for labour and reproduce conservative social relations (Foucault, 1990: 36–7). The resulting discourses of sex became integral to the State's exercise of its power, 'a bio-politics of the population' (Foucault, 1990: 139). From the eighteenth century onwards, norms increasingly replaced laws as mechanisms to control the workings of society. Consequently, the State forged a new, life-affirming identity for itself based on the subtle and implicit appearance of popular consent, rather than relying on the explicit force of the law 'in its murderous splendour' (Foucault, 1990: 144).

Sexuality as Identity

As the State situated each person within a society saturated with sex, 'a continuum of apparatuses (medical, administrative, and so on) whose functions are for the most part regulatory' (Foucault, 1990: 144) began to have at their disposal a whole series of powerful mechanisms of control over every individual.

As these mechanisms were deployed, the wider interpretations of family, as described by Gillis (1996), above, gave way to what Foucault describes as the norm of the 'family cell' (Foucault, 1990: 108), composed of two parallel strands of husband–wife/parents–children, which became the primary location for the deployment of sexuality. Norms that regulate and oversee the personal, emotional and sexual aspects of individuals have the potential to both create and control individuals' sense of innermost identity:

> The sexual area may be precisely that realm wherein the superordinate position of the sociocultural over the biological level is most complete. (Gagnon and Simon, in Jackson & Scott, 2010: 13)

The family, insofar as it was insular and appeared different from other mechanisms of power, provided essential support to states intent on controlling population, labour and social power (Foucault, 1990: 100). The rise of sexology and the subsequent spread of influence of the Freudian model of 'natural' sexual development within the heterosexual nuclear family further inscribed the centrality of 'sexuality' in Western culture. As the State came to be seen as the donor of respectability, rather than of subjugation, citizens began to look to it, as Butler puts it, 'for redemption, for belonging, for eternity' (Butler, 2004: 111). In doing so, the State and its citizens instituted 'a new hierarchy of legitimate and illegitimate sexual arrangement' (Butler, 2004: 111) whose foundation was the biologically based, heterosexual, nuclear family.

The Family – Private or Public?

As indicated above, the nuclear model of the family has come under scrutiny from a range of critics, including sociologists, legal and social policy scholars and feminist theorists, who see not only that it serves the ideological purposes of a patriarchal capitalist state but also that the privacy it affords provides a dense site where inequality and injustice can go unchecked (Connell, 1987: 130; Okin, 1998: 130; Gabb, 1999: 12; Nussbaum, 1999: 274; Sevenhuijsen, 1998: 140; Conrad, 2004: 65; Fineman, 2008: 3). For instance, Okin (1997) suggests that, first, within the private sphere of families, issues of differential power directly reflect unequal power relations between the sexes in the public sphere. Second, the public sphere, through political action and social practice, defines what constitutes the private sphere and which activities will be included in that definition. Third, families are the places where the gender of public citizens is constituted, both psychically and socially, through sex-role conditioning, education and gendered parenting practices (Okin, 1997: 17–18).

In the psychoanalytic tradition, Chodorow critiques Freudian models of sexual development, which frame the natural sexual development of the individual along biologically determined pathways. Chodorow argues that adult sex roles thus defined are simply part of the psychodynamics of early childhood development within (*hetero*)sexual families. When the family is analysed in feminist psychoanalytic terms, the clear traditional distinctions drawn between men's and women's 'normal' (Chodorow, 1994: 70) sexual and psychical development can be understood more accurately as manifestations of complex anatomical, cultural, familial and social forces. Chodorow argues that what classical Freudians talk about as the vital importance of the *symbolic* role of the father in the psycho-sexual and emotional development of the child in fact stems from cultural values and practices that are inscribed on the developing psyche through dominance and repetition of particular behaviours and attitudes (Chodorow, 1994: 76). Similarly, Butler argues that the symbolic is itself 'the sedimentation of social practices' (Butler, 2004: 44), implying that psychoanalysis, rather than providing universal explanations of psychic and sexual patterns, is instead culturally located: if family structures were to be altered, there would have to be a corresponding alteration in psychoanalytic understandings of sexuality.

In fact, family structures are indeed altering, creating alarm among those who believe that the 'traditional family' is an immutable, natural entity. As Zack (1997: 43) notes, this need not entail either rejecting family itself, or allowing anything to pass as a family regardless of its efficacy in producing good outcomes for its members. Rather than jettisoning the institution itself, critics point to the need to identify those aspects of family that embody its positive potentialities (Bradford & Sartwell, 1997: 125). For example, safety and emotional needs, such as intimate relationships, caring and kinship, are widely acknowledged as basic human needs, the satisfaction of which is often sought within families.

Moving away from a model of family that sees it as based on co-residence and biological kinship, David Morgan (1996) argues that we need to rethink family in terms of what families actually do, focusing on their practices rather than on an institution called 'the family' (cited in Smart & Neale, 1999: 181–2). Focusing specifically on the welfare of children within families, many critics argue that we need to focus on the importance of intimate relationships for children's development and sense of identity, rather than on how families are structured (Shanley, 2001). Fineman, too, argues for a rethinking of the institution of the family, to prioritise the caring and dependency roles of family members, and to give children's and other dependants' interests and vulnerabilities equal consideration alongside those of dominant adults (Fineman, 2009a: 453). Smart and Neale (1999) posit that UK family policy in the 1990s was driven by an ideology based on a set of assumptions about the primacy of genetic ties and their ensuing economic responsibilities and dependencies. They note, however, that people protested against many of the resulting policies, arguing that they did not reflect their actual daily family practices. Recognising the political importance of emotions echoes Connell's and Foucault's argu-ments that the State operates, to a large extent, by manipulating and exploiting people's sexual, emotional and relational affiliations. The post-modern family that emerges from seeing the family as a set of practices (Morgan, 1996) reveals a multitude of fluid forms, no longer based solely on tradition, but encompassing a mixture of 'experimental and nostalgic elements' (Stacey, 1991, cited in Featherstone, 2004: 51). Such a 'bottom up' approach (Featherstone, 2004: 53) implies that public policy should attend both to the inter-nal structures and workings of families, as well as to their social environments.

The preceding critiques of the heteronormative family converge on one point: that as an institution, it is an ideological construct developed and sustained by discourses. These discourses are vari-ously said to support male dominance and the State's, as well as society's, economic interests, while powerfully shaping women's sexuality, in particular (but also children's and men's), to serve these ends. Inequalities within families, arising from differences in biology, psychology, or the exercise of social or economic power, are exploited by states that use the family as a bridge between capitalism and patriarchy to produce a two-tiered, overlapping system of workers and carers. Heteronormativity subsists by the exclusion of viable practical, sexual and emotional alternatives (*cf.* Gabb, 2005: 422), and by the erasure, exposure and exploitation of women's sexuality, regardless of orientation. The norm of gender is crucial to these processes.

Lesbian Families

Due to its centrality, gender has been the subject of a range of femi-nist analyses of family and heterosexuality. Butler contends that gender does not exist prior to regulation, but rather is produced by the regulations surrounding its performance, through a process of subjection (Butler, 2004: 41). She also suggests that the homosocial bonds between men that underlie civil society actively separate women from each other, while at the same time excluding women from benefiting equally with men from the masculine social order (Butler, 1990: 54). Rich argues that male interests use incentive, persuasion and even coercion to tie women's gender identities to a 'compulsory heterosexuality' that subjugates them in marriage and maternity (Rich, 1980b: 68–71; Rich, 1992: 42). The reiteration of 'compulsory heterosexuality' becomes a powerful norm that upholds the economic, emotional and sexual dependence of women upon men.

Accordingly, visible, non-hegemonic families can pose a threat to the capitalist–patriarchal status quo by challenging gender norms and other social and economic roles. States have historically reacted to this threat by silencing, ignoring, or excluding these families from a varying range of social benefits, a strategy that is legitimated by marginalising and stigmatising them as unnatural, abnormal or deviant. Bar On, in her study of Jewish lesbianism, contends that it is not the transgressive sexuality of the lesbian but rather her refusal of social roles that is seen as posing a threat to Jewish-Israeli society (Bar On, 1997: 229). Rich asserts that it is because lesbians, and particularly lesbian mothers, are seen as a menace to the homogeneity of the heterosexual ideal, and as a challenge to the dominant heterosexual identity, that they become the target of social control (Rich, 1992: xxxvi). Okin suggests that the traditional longing for distinct sex roles underlies much of the hostility directed towards lesbian and gay parenting, which many perceive as blurring these 'natural' roles (Okin, 1997: 21). Similarly, Gabb suggests that the lesbian family is perceived as a threat to the heteronormative family by its very existence, before it ever demands equal rights (Gabb, 1999: 15). Lesbianism is seen as a hazard to both gender and dependency: 'The refusal to become (or to remain) heterosexual always meant to refuse to become a man or a woman, consciously or not. For a lesbian this goes further than the refusal of the *role* "woman". It is the refusal of the economic, ideological, and political power of a man' (Wittig, 1981: 47 [emphasis in original]).

Like Wittig, and echoing Irigaray (1985), Gabb refuses the binarism of the heteronorm and states that the lesbian family is 'neither normal, nor alternative, but *essentially different*' (Gabb, 2001: 13 [emphasis in original]). Turner similarly states that heterosexual hegemony is constituted by binarism and by the resulting expulsion of deviant homosexuals from the heterosexual community, while at the same time claims to the 'essential' or 'natural' character of their own sexual identity enables the heterosexual community to remain oblivious to its active part in this process (Turner, 2000: 164). Calhoun suggests that the hypersexualised lesbian figure as 'outlaw' (Calhoun, 1997: 137) is utilised by societies keen to hold on to privileges attaching to failing heteronormal structures, such as marriage, parenting and family.

I argue that lesbian mothers are experienced as a threat to Irish society as much because of their disruption of prescribed social and gender roles as because of the ostensible problem of their deviant sexuality, and it is from this dense matrix that their marginalised status originates. Butler asks: 'What departures from the norm disrupt the regulatory process itself?' (Butler, 2004: 53). I argue that situating the 'examples' of lesbian families in this research within a critical examination of the 'regulatory powers (medical, psychiatric, and legal, to name a few)' (Butler, 2004: 52) disrupts the regulatory power of the heterosexual family: '... lesbianism, in any form, and male homosexuality which openly avows both the sexual and emotional elements of the bond, challenges the very foundation of la familia [...] Family is *not* by definition the man in a dominant position over women and children' (Moraga, 1994: 41).

Motherhood and Lesbian Identity

Given the density of these debates, the actual embodied lives of lesbian mothers must be explored. If, as has been suggested, lesbianism subverts the family, where does the lesbian mother stand – inside or outside? For Pippa, becoming a mother brought with it the unforeseen consequence of domestication:

> And I mean, there's been ways as a mother which I just, I've hated about myself, I just couldn't stand, you know. I was crying to Rebecca one day, saying, I never wanted to be a harpy, d'you know. Giving out about the kitchen, or the dishes, or, you know, the washing, all this kind of stuff. Like, to be a domestic creature. I have never been a domestic creature, I never have. (Pippa: interview 2005)

Lewin questions whether motherhood affects the lesbian's outsider status, by assimilating lesbians into conventional expectations for women, validating and intensifying 'the long-standing division of women into mothers and non-mothers that has been one of the sources of their exclusion from the category "woman"' (Lewin, 1995: 116–17). Lewin recommends a critical awareness of the conflicts of adopting this dual identity, which for many obscures their deviant sexuality under the more acceptable mantle of their maternity (Lewin, 1995: 116–17).

> As I said, it's not a big, we don't see being parents as kind of a big political, or any kind of statement. It's only the natural thing that we would be doing with our lives if we weren't gay. We don't see gay as changing that ... It's the same thing as all my straight friends when they have kids. We're not any different, really. (Debbie: interview 2005)

Pippa talks about the 'naturalness' of becoming a mother and about how, after her daughter was born, she became immersed in motherhood and lost interest in other relationships, including her relationship with her partner:

> I just wanted to be with my baby. D'you know what I mean? I just want to be with her, and that's all I want. And, ehm, I've found it quite, eh, hard in terms of, like, having any energy for, or really any interest in anyone else, or any energy for it: for my relationship, for my friendships, or, ehm, ehm, gardening is the exception. [Laughs] (Pippa: interview 2005)

For Jean, becoming a mother impacted negatively on her identity as a lesbian. Rather than seeing it as indicating a closer identification with straight mothers, she felt it was more closely allied to the loss of sexual identity she saw as tied to becoming a mother for all women:

> You know, most mothers, whether straight or heterosexual or whatever, you know, ehm, lesbian, would all probably say, what's happened to my identity, you know? [...] because I think our lesbian identity really gets a backseat, you know. Both by myself as well as society. I mean, I put it in the back seat because I can hardly, hardly *think* lesbian, never mind [both laughing] *be* lesbian. You know, so, something happens in all of that, that's why I think it would be an interesting discussion with heterosexual women on that, d'you know? (Jean: interview 2005)

Some writers have argued that the very act of becoming a mother disempowers lesbians by assimilating them into the mainstream

(Weeks, 1990: 99). Furthermore, because it drains the pool of available lesbian activists, its wider negative political significance must be acknowledged (Polikoff, 1987: 51). Jean said that despite her activist past, where she had worked to promote lesbian rights and visibility, she now had to consciously struggle to maintain an autonomous identity 'as a lesbian' (Jean: interview 2005), distinct from her maternal identity, and that an important part of that was reclaiming an active sex life with her partner, Viv:

> Because I am a lesbian [laughing], I went to a lot of trouble and made a lot of decisions in my life being lesbian, as lesbian, and I'm damned if it's all going down the tubes now, you know? I mean, it was always important to me, I did a lot of work around it, I had a family deliberately as a lesbian, so why the hell should I disappear now? [...] Here I was becoming a mother and then everything else got obliterated, you know? And that's still true. Even though we're on a bit of a 'campaign' to get it back [both laughing]. We've decided, it's time to get it back. So that's good. We're beginning to get a bit of a fighting spirit into it again. (Jean: interview 2005)

Mamie commented on how becoming a mother at once renders you invisible as a sexual being, while at the same time repeatedly forcing you to own your lesbian sexuality, which, once recognised, becomes the main focus, over and above your motherhood:

> Because it's a pain in the arse having to come out all the time. You think you do it, and you just do it for the rest of your life. [...] So, your private life is very, very much brought into the public spheres all the time, as of course it always is anyway as a same-sex couple, you are sexualised, and seen. (Mamie: interview 2005)

Jean just wanted to reclaim a lesbian identity, whether or not it was seen: 'I would like to be a lesbian again. Just a bit more visibly, and I don't care about anybody else seeing it, it's about me seeing it, you know?' (Jean: interview 2005).

There is clearly a tension evident in the narratives between the identities of mother and lesbian. Many of the participants in my study also reported that they felt, and wanted to be accepted as, what they often described as 'ordinary' (Charlotte: interview 2005). Wanda celebrates the social acceptability she and Sally experience in their comfortable, middle-class life, where they divide work and care in ways that seem to mirror heterosexual norms: 'We're a very palatable sort of lesbian couple, d'you know? [...] Because we have people saying, ye're the most unlesb-, apart from the fact that ye're dykes, you're the straightest people we know' (Wanda: interview 2006). In fact, in many cases, rather than seeking accept-ance as being different, some lesbian parents sought assimilation and were prepared to work extremely hard to achieve this. In some couples, this created tensions in itself. For example, Pippa sought support from other, heterosexual mothers, while Rebecca wanted the couple's lesbianism to be a central part of their parenting:

> Like, she's got a baby group, and they've all been together since Ella was born, which is a great, but it's all straight women, and I find that really hard. And I wanted to join a lesbian parenting group, and I could still do it for myself, but ehm, I don't know. Anyway, there was all that, and there was places we never kind of, got back together as *lesbians*, I don't know. (Rebecca: interview 2005)

Having a child brought many of the women into closer quar-ters with their heterosexual counterparts. Rebecca said that a lot of Pippa's 'wandering, out there, in the motherhood wilderness [laughs], is with straight mothers' (Rebecca: interview 2005), while Pippa explained: 'Since being a mother, since having Ella, I'm much more involved in the heterosexual community than, you know, than before, when I lived in a lesbian world, really' (Pippa: inter-view 2005).

Significantly, although many of the interviewees said that they identified more with heterosexual women or couples after they had children, in some cases an awareness of differences became even more apparent. Pippa talks about how, when she was in hospi-tal after giving birth to Ella, she suddenly had an insight into the culturally inscribed lack of touch and physical intimacy in the heterosexual world:

> But that was the most kind of, I don't know, where I kind of felt that kind of isolation and that, you know. [...] That's the

place where I felt eh, kind of not normal, you know what I mean? Kind of, everyone's there, and they've got their families, and they're, most of them are feeding their babies with bottles, and I was breastfeeding, and they were in the cots, and my baby was in the bed, and that's nothing to do with being a lesbian, but I mean, it all kind of feeds into it a bit, d'you know? (Pippa: interview 2005)

Pippa said that heterosexual women appeared to be separated from each other and that she felt she was expected to adjust to the expectation of lack of touch between the women in her mothers' group:

It's, part of it's to do with being a lesbian, and it's being with women and being a certain way with women, being very free and very open with women, and, ehm, you know, I found it very strange that they don't touch each other, you know, there's lots of kinds of things which are really different, you know. (Pippa: interview 2005)

Gender roles also emerged as an explicit identity issue, particularly among non-biological mothers, some of whom felt they were often (unwillingly, in most cases) compared with (male) fathers, with whom they shared aspects of a role but with whom they rarely identified. While some of the women played with the idea of being a 'dad', they still maintained a strong identity as a mother to their children. For example, Bríd described Kay as 'the dad' to her younger sister after their mother and father divorced, while Wanda laughingly described herself as her son's 'lesbian Daddy' and saw her primary role at the time of the interview as that of provider, but she still insisted she would be called Mammy by her son. Pippa talked about how she and her daughter played with the idea of dads – sometimes Ella says Pippa looks like a dad because she has short hair or because she 'does dad things', and they sometimes played 'mums and dads and babies' and took turns being the dad.

Rebecca explicitly said, however, that as the non-biological parent, she was angered by lesbian friends who teased her: '"Oh, so you're going to be a daddy, are you?" Who are these women? What, what's, where's their heads? Up their arses? No, I'm bloody not going to be a dad!' (Rebecca: interview 2005). For Rebecca, this analogy was felt as a negation of her identity as a woman, even though she struggled with the idea of calling herself by the term 'Mum' because of its biological connotations, and because by doing so she would have to challenge the perception that there can be only one mother, not two 'lesbian parents, mothers, I don't know how to name them' (Rebecca: interview 2005).

Rebecca felt that for mothers, the presence of a father can actually lock them further into domesticity, where fathers refuse to engage in the daily work of caring. For her, and for many of the women interviewed, the flexibility and equity of roles permitted by being in partnership with a woman allowed greater scope for the expression of their individual identities. However, Pippa, her partner, felt that the lack of clearly defined roles threw into relief the differences between the parenting styles of two women while providing no alternative scripts: 'Differences, I think that's the hard thing about bringing up a child with another woman' (Pippa: interview 2005).

Work and Care

De-gendered work and care practices among the women in my study notably challenged the gendered stereotypes of the 'male provider' family model. Working practices among the couples varied, with the majority being engaged in full-time work outside the home, while others worked part-time or stayed at home with full-time care responsibilities. 'An awful lot of the decisions that we've made in the last, you know, four years, have been with having Zach in mind [...] and decisions around how we set up our work stuff – all of that was around our plan to have a child' (Sally: interview 2006). Sally (the biological mother) was at home minding Zach, but decisions around who would stay at home with children did not always correspond to who was the birth or adoptive mother. For example, Jo (non-birth mother) stayed at home looking after her elderly mother and daughter, Phoebe; Lydia (non-birth mother) worked full-time while Niamh (birth mother) worked part-time; Jean and Viv each had flexible work schedules, with Bob, the boys' (gay) father, helping out with childcare on a regular basis; and Harriet and Florence both worked full-time. Ita said that when she and Yvonne were considering fostering, what most influenced their decision to go ahead was the fact that they would share the work involved, in contrast to what they saw among their heterosexual friends, 'even ones with [male] partners who are helpful' (Ita: interview 2006).

As parents and partners, roles were said to change frequently in response to current needs and capabilities, rather than along gendered lines. Florence was clearing plumbing tools from the table when I arrived for our interview: she was in the middle of installing central heating in her house while simultaneously watching the movie *Bambi* with her daughter, Beth. Indeed, many of the women suggested that their sexuality freed them from many of the gendered constraints felt by heterosexual women in performing traditionally 'masculine' tasks for fear that they would be seen as less 'feminine'. 'There I'd be ironing clothes, and I'd be out chopping wood with a 10-pound sledge ... I suppose it's a bit kind of funny, but to me it's kind of very natural' (Pippa: interview 2005).

However, although a great degree of fluidity of roles was recounted, Jean felt that a male presence was important in helping her sons develop confidence in themselves as males, but it was the quality of that presence, not just the fact of it, that was salient. She wanted caring and involved males for her sons to relate to, in order to counteract the more harmful models of masculinity they would be exposed to in society, although she stressed it did not have to be a father who filled that role: 'There's a lot of things not to feel good about in terms of being male, really and truly, and certainly from my perspective, so, I want them [two sons] hopefully to be, you know, feel good. Because it would be easy not to actually, you know?' (Jean: interview 2005).

Conclusion

Lesbians engaging in struggles to form families with children in contemporary Ireland have stories to tell that illuminate areas often hidden from view in mainstream accounts of family life. When reflecting on the place such stories have in generating knowledge and engaging in social critique, however, Wise and Stanley challenge approaches that focus simply on 'telling better stories' rather than on 'understanding the stories that are told, which ones are dominant, and what people do with them' (Wise and Stanley, 2003: 1.24). Smith similarly criticises such approaches for seeming to lack political commitment to engage in actively effecting social change through critique of social structures (Smith, 2005: 43). Lynch decries approaches that present detailed accounts of marginalised lives without paying attention to the social forces that maintain their subordination (Lynch, 2000: 78).

My use here of a feminist standpoint approach explores specific subjective experiences of opposition to, compliance with and resistance to social structures. Critically, this opens up new ways of thinking about an invisible and minority group who none-theless provide significant insight into the highly regulated forms of personal and public lives of lesbians and mothers. This chapter shows the heteronormative family to have developed in response to a range of historical factors and to have been shaped by particular social, cultural and political conditions, resulting in its privileged position in contemporary Western societies. This 'sexual family' (Fineman, 2009) bridges state capitalism and patriarchy, and relies primarily on silence and exclusion in order to maintain its image as the natural, basic building-block of society.

Lesbian families are marginalised in society because they disrupt both sexual and gender roles, thus challenging patriarchal family forms. They are at once hypersexualised and rendered invisible, in an effort to sustain the centrality of the heteronormal family. In this they shed light on the family, but also on the control of all women within this matrix. Like Wittig (1981), Rich (1992), Bar On (1997), Calhoun (1997), Okin (1997), Gabb (1999) and others, many of the women I interviewed stressed that they felt that gender, rather than sexuality, was the primary cause of social unease about their families. These narratives recounted experiences of loss of sexual identity in motherhood, through physical exhaustion, and through assimilation into the heterosexual mainstream, but also as a result of the desexualising of all mothers. Furthermore, as highlighted in the narratives, children forced the visibility of these women's sexu-ality precisely through its co-presence with the very constricted traditional, gendered mother role.

Lesbian parents make public what is usually kept private or ignored: women's own sexuality and desire. Sexuality is simultane-ously erased and exposed. Being 'Out at the School Gates' exposes the political nature of sexuality and the various socio-political functions of repression and denial, focusing attention on public structures that shape sexuality, such as the State and contempo-rary systems of the family, not least among which is the system of motherhood. The lesbian family standpoint provides evidence that for all citizens to flourish equally, family policy in Ireland must incorporate a pluralistic model of the family based on a variety of relationships that include social bonding and voluntary commitment, in addition to biological and legal ties. Such an approach now has even greater potential for impact since the passing at referendum of the Thirty-First Amendment of the Constitution (Children) Bill in 2012. This Amendment paves the way for children's rights to be treated independently of the sexual orientation or relationship status of the parents who care for them, although numerous legislative and policy changes will still need to follow. A further referendum, to remove references to the 'natural' family and to the primacy of marriage in defining family, could further push legislation and social protection policies towards reflecting and supporting actual family practices across the wide range of families that exist, in fact, in Ireland.

Notes

[1]   Pseudonyms are used throughout this chapter.
[2]   Although a number of private fertility clinics in Ireland have begun to provide services for openly lesbian couples, there is no legislation governing who may avail of services in this area. In the absence of legal precedent establishing a right to access on the grounds of equality, it remains up to individual clinicians (including GPs) as to whether they will engage with lesbian clients seeking services such as donor insemination.
[3]   All were white, with English as their first language, and were broadly middle class.

CHAPTER 7

Vigilant Dads: Exploring Gay Men's Parenting Experiences in Contemporary Ireland

Fiachra Ó Súilleabháin

Introduction

Personal politics, sexual politics and politics of the family are entering a new era in Ireland, where paths to parenthood, models of parenting and family structures are no longer following the dominant traditional nuclear family model of the mid-twentieth century. Seward et al. (2005) have charted the demographic changes that have taken place in Ireland over recent decades, which include a sharp increase in co-habitation, lone-parenting and children born outside of marriage. These novel types of kinship arrangement have changed the notion of family in Ireland. As the notion of families becomes redefined, we find more non-traditional parents playing active roles in families (Better, 2005). The focus in this chapter is to explore one example of non-traditional parent groups: gay fathers.

As Peterson, Butts and Deville (2000) have remarked, research concerning gay fathers is particularly sparse. Families headed by lesbians and gay men, for which I will use the term 'lesbi-gay families', have been a hidden section of Irish family life and this chapter aims to address this. First, I will outline the contested nature of parenting by gay people and how it challenges heterosexual family norms. Second, I will discuss the marginalisation of lesbi-gay families from the 'Irish' family. Finally, I will discuss some key findings from the research I conducted with gay fathers in Ireland as a part of my doctoral studies in social science. I examine how these men co-construct their sexual and parenting identities, and highlight the implications of parenting for their sexual identities and their sexual expression. I also explore the strategies these men employ, which in their view are designed to protect their families and to better negotiate a largely heterosexist society.

Lesbi-Gay Parenthood: Challenging, Embattled and Controversial

The heteronormative assumptions about appropriate parenthood, gender norms and parenting practices that continue to underpin the hegemonic view of family are challenged by the very existence of gay-headed families. Lesbi-gay families 'occupy the vanguard of the post-modern family condition because they make the denaturalised and contingent character of family and kinship impossible to ignore' (Stacey and Davenport, 2002: 357). According to Bornstein (2005), lesbians and gay men are inventing new family forms because there is no pre-existing model for lesbi-gay families. She holds that in the absence of an established model of how a lesbi-gay family looks or should be formed, lesbians and gay men can exercise agency in determining the gender, number and role of the people who will be included in their families. While there is no uniform, distinctive pattern of relationships, structure or parenting among lesbi-gay families (Berkowitz, 2006), what unifies these diverse families is their everyday struggle with an array of '... psychic, social, legal, practical, and even physical challenges to their very existence that institutionalized hostility to homosexuality produces' (Stacey, 1996: 108). Gay male sexual culture is used by those opposed to lesbi-gay parenting to construct gay men as 'risks' to children. Fears about such risks are evident in the Muintir na hÉireann submission to the All-Party Oireachtas Committee on the Constitution in Ireland, which states:

> It [same-sex marriage] would also give homosexual couples the right to adopt children up to 18 years of age. I do not think any parent surrendering their child for adoption in this or any other jurisdiction would give up their child for adoption if they believed they would be adopted by homosexuals. It would also mean that a sixteen year old, who could be homeless, could be adopted by a homosexual couple for perverted reasons. (All Party Oireachtas Committee on the Constitution, 2006: A193)

Beliefs about the perceived threat gay men pose to children prevail, despite long-standing literature (Finkelhor, 1986; McGee et al., 2002) clearly showing that heterosexual men are the primary perpetrators of child sexual abuse.

Lesbi-gay parenting provokes strong anxieties within a heteronormative society and significant segments of society devalue non-heterosexual communities, same-sex relationships and gay-headed families (Hicks, 2005a). The Irish Catholic Bishops' Conference, for example, has argued against any change to the Irish constitutional understanding of marriage and family because they believe it would suggest that a lesbi-gay household is an equally valid context for raising children as a heterosexual home. Its submission to the All-Party Oireachtas Committee on the Constitution states, 'What is at stake here is the natural right of children to the presence normally of a mother and father in their lives' (All-Party Oireachtas Committee on the Constitution, 2006: A120). This argument serves to ostracise families that are not headed by a heterosexual couple and draws into question the ability of a same-sex couple to provide a stable upbringing for children. Lesbi-gay parenting is at times seen as a form of social engineering and an expression of political correctness. Hicks (2005b: 301) identifies what he calls a 'Frankenstein' discourse, which is used '… to assert that lesbian and gay families are artificial, unnatural, political and a threat, where the 'family' is genuine, natural, neutral and safe'. The consequence of this Frankenstein discourse is the exclusion by the State and its institutions of gay men, lesbians and the children raised by them from the protective legislation surrounding families. The concern about the risks posed to children by lesbi-gay parenting has been an important impetus for research in the area of parenting by both gay men and lesbians. The purpose of this type of research is to address any negative assumptions that have been expressed in judicial opinions, legislative initiatives or public policies relevant to lesbian and gay parents and their children (Patterson & Redding, 1996). This research and literature has been reviewed in a number of American articles, two of the more recent being Tasker and Patterson (2008) and Patterson (2009). Tasker and Patterson (2008) conclude that the many studies examining developmental outcomes report few significant differences between children with lesbian or gay parents and children with heterosexual parents, in terms of gender or sexual identity or the many aspects of personal identity development so far considered. They also state that the results of research to date suggest that children in lesbi-gay families have positive relationships with peers, family members, adults of both sexes and their wider community, although lesbians and gay men who are not biologically related to their children sometimes have to struggle for recognition outside the family (Tasker and Patterson, 2008). Due to a paucity of research, however, far less is known about the development of the children of gay fathers than is known about the development of children of lesbian mothers.

The 'Irish Family' and the Marginalisation of Lesbi-Gay Families in Ireland

Despite demographic changes and diversity in 'family' practices, the 'nuclear' family continues to be idealised and celebrated as a stabilising, respectable force in Irish society. It is enshrined in Article 41 of the Irish Constitution, which recognises the family as the 'natural primary and fundamental unit group' of society and guarantees to protect the family as the 'necessary basis of social order'. This support for the nuclear family model has ensured that heterosexist notions of family prevail in Ireland and that other family formations (such as lesbi-gay families) are, at least, held in less esteem and, at most, excluded. However, the last decade has seen a particular drive for equality for LGBT people in the area of marriage and the legal recognition of same-sex relationships in Ireland. It began in 2004 with the *KAL* case, when a lesbian couple, Katherine Zappone and Ann Louise Gilligan, applied to the High Court to have the Revenue Commissioners (the Irish tax and customs office) recognise their legal Canadian marriage for the purpose of filing joint tax returns. The High Court decided that the Irish Constitution had always meant for marriage to be between a man and a woman and could find no reason to change that. However, the *KAL* case, along with the government's Working Group on Domestic Partnership (2006) and the report on the family by the All-Party Oireachtas Committee on the Constitution (2006), prepared the way for the introduction of legislative recognition of same-sex couples.

The Fianna Fáil–Green Party coalition introduced the Civil Partnership and Certain Rights and Obligations of Cohabitants Act in 2010. This Act provides for a civil partnership registration scheme for same-sex couples and represents, both practically and symboli-cally, real and substantial progress in the recognition and protection of non-traditional families in Ireland (Ryan, 2009). The rights and obligations of civil partners mirror those of a married couple in most cases, but Ryan (2009) has pointed out that the civil partnership legislation generally avoids describing civil partners as a family. This symbolic exclusion serves to differentiate same-sex relation-ships from marriage and family.

The Act is also largely silent on the issue of children being raised by same-sex couples (as already mentioned in Chapter 4). It does not give the children of civil partners the same rights as the chil-dren of married people, and does not recognise the relationship between a child and its non-biological, civil-partnered parent. Under the Act, a child living with civil partners will not have any legal right to claim from the non-biological parent's estate on death or to claim a death benefit for orphans in respect of a non-biological parent. Custody and guardianship rights continue to be denied to non-biological parents. Although the non-biological parent may be nominated as a guardian in the will of the biological parent, the non-biological parent cannot acquire guardianship during the life-time of the biological parents (Ryan, 2009; Elliott, 2010). Making a distinction between civil partnership and marriage and family therefore has direct effects on children, a point made by Emily Logan, the Ombudsman for Children in Ireland, in her advice to the Irish government before the Act was signed into law. She said: 'The omission of robust protections for the children of civil partners will have real consequences for the young people concerned and it is in their interests that the law reflect and provide for the reality of their lives' (Ombudsman for Children, 2010: 2). In the focus group she conducted with adult children of lesbian parents in Ireland, Elliott (2010) spoke about their shame and embarrassment at the lack of legal recognition of lesbi-gay families in Ireland. (This lack of legal recognition is covered in more detail in Chapter 4 in this book.)

There are, broadly, two types of gay father: those who become parents from a sexual encounter or relationship with a person of the opposite sex and subsequently come out as gay; and established gay men who choose parenthood. Similar to other jurisdictions, for Irish gay men 'possibly the most common scenario is where a person who has had children in a previous heterosexual relation-ship subsequently enters into a same-sex relationship' (Ryan, 2009:

90). Gay men who choose parenthood confront a range of challenges and difficult options, including adoption, fostering, surrogacy or co-parenting with women. None of these options is without considerable legal, social, emotional and financial barriers that must be overcome somehow. It is hardly surprising that most gay men are childless. The Adoption Act 2010 does not allow same-sex couples to adopt children together and only married couples can adopt jointly. Neither can a gay person legally adopt his/her partner's child or children. The only option available for gay adoption applicants is for one of the partners to apply as a single person to adopt a child born outside Ireland, which means that only one partner is the legal parent of the adopted child. While gay couples are not entitled to adopt jointly, there is nothing in law precluding a couple from fostering a child, although one Irish gay foster carer has written an article in the *Irish Times* about the significant difficulties he and his partner encountered during the assessment process (Thomas, 2011).

Donor insemination and surrogacy are two paths to parenthood that can result in legal quagmires for parents in Ireland. Gay men who become parents through surrogacy may not be in a position to protect their parenting rights because they are not married to the child's mother and any agreements signed by parties are not enforceable in Irish law. Despite the publication of the report of the Commission on Assisted Human Reproduction in 2005, there is a lack of regulation and legislation around surrogacy in Ireland. The particular difficulty for gay men in Ireland who use donor insemination or surrogacy to become parents is that the woman who gives birth to a child is automatically recognised as the child's legal guardian. It was against this social and legal backdrop that I conducted my research with gay fathers in Ireland, which is discussed in the following section of this chapter.

Gay Fathers' Experiences in Ireland

I sought to explore the parenting experiences and practices of gay men in Ireland, to seek insight into how gay fathers manage their gay and father identities and how they accept or challenge heterosexual family norms. The research method used in this study was in-depth semi-structured interviews with seven gay men (five individuals and one couple). I accessed these men through purposive, convenience and snowballing sampling strategies (utilising personal and social networks, as well as *Gay Community News*, a free nationwide newspaper/website resource for LGBT people). Recruitment was a time-consuming endeavour, which often involved conducting 'meet and greet' sessions with potential participants to enable them to make informed decisions about partaking in the study. I have used pseudonyms in this chapter to protect the privacy of these men and their families.

The seven men interviewed had a largely homogenous profile, as men who are Caucasian, well-educated, middle to high income earners, although there was a roughly equal urban/rural divide. Four of the seven gay fathers interviewed became parents while in an intimate heterosexual relationship and subsequently established themselves as gay. One gay father interviewed chose to become a father by donor insemination with a heterosexual acquaintance. The last two fathers, the couple, became parents when they were made the legal guardians of the children in their care. Whatever path led the participants to parenthood, all of them placed significant meaning on their parenthood status. During each interview, these men talked about their children in loving, tender ways, and about the joy that their children brought to their lives. For example, Alan (a divorced biological father to four children) said: 'I absolutely adore my four kids. I mean, I couldn't imagine my life without my kids.' The parents in this study frequently emphasised that their children's interests are their paramount consideration. The importance these men place on fatherhood is reminiscent of Mallon's American study (2004) of gay men who chose parenthood. He found that his participants described parenting as 'a rich opportunity in which they were privileged to participate' (Mallon, 2004: 137), and they reported that the most meaningful dimension of their lives was the daily pleasure of parenting. The findings in my research, and in Mallon's study, about the pride and apparent joy these men have from being parents counter arguments put forward by social/religious conservative writers, such as Patricia Morgan (2002), who state that gay men have little interest in children.

Coming Out, Letting Go

Brinamen and Mitchell (2008) maintain that when a man identifies as gay he internalises heteronormative values, which dictate that fatherhood is for heterosexual men only. This assertion appeared to hold true for six of the gay fathers in this study, who viewed their individual coming-out processes as synonymous with accepting that that they would not have children. For example, in the early stages of his personal identification of being gay, George (father of one child through donor insemination) thought doing so would mean he would not become a parent: 'Kids were a big thing on my mind. Like, if I went down the road of being gay, I thought I wouldn't get the chance of having kids.' Similarly, in his interview, Conor (a biological father of one child from a heterosexual relationship) said: 'A big part of the discovery that I was gay for me was that I wouldn't have children. That was a major issue for me more than anything really [...] because, well, gay men didn't have children.' These experiences of 'letting go' demonstrate how culturally embedded the traditional family model is within Irish society and the impact heteronormative hegemony can have on the procreative consciousness of men when they identify as gay. They are also similar to the experiences of many researched gay fathers in the USA, who reported that when they first 'came out', they believed that being gay automatically meant being childless (Mallon, 2004; Berkowitz and Marsiglio, 2007; Berkowitz, 2008a and 2008b; Gianino, 2008).

Bozett (1980, 1981 and 1982) and Armesto (2002) have highlighted how the process of admitting to being gay is so stressful that some gay men try to cope by passing as heterosexual, marrying and having children. This certainly was a strategy applied by the three men who had married in the sample studied, who all spoke about having some sexual attraction and feelings for men prior to becoming involved with the mothers of their children and getting married. David described the pressure he felt to conform to the heterosexual norm at the stage when all his friends were marrying. When asked if he knew he was gay at the time, David responded: 'Yeah I did. But I thought I would beat it. I seriously thought I could beat it.' The decisions of these men to conform to prevailing heterosexist hegemony demonstrate the 'culture of silence' (Wilton, 2000) that surrounds non-heterosexual norms in Ireland.

Expanding Understandings of Sexuality

The accounts of the gay fathers in my study also serve to expand understandings of sexuality beyond simplistic binary (homosexual/

heterosexual) categorisations. As Weeks (2003) has argued, the gay/straight categorisation does not exhaust the actual lived experiences of sexuality. Understanding sexual practices as fluid rather than static, as socially constructed rather than objectively known (Klein, Sepekoff and Wolf, 1985; Patterson, 2000; McPhail, 2004) has been more helpful in understanding the experiences of the gay men who participated in this research and who became fathers in the context of heterosexual marriages.

Since publicly identifying as gay, both Alan and Ben have been questioned about their sexual behaviour during their marriages. Both of them stated that some people assume that their fatherhood status means they are bisexual, not gay. Alan said: 'A lot of people, gay people, make an assumption that if you have had sex with a woman, you must have some sexual attraction. Certainly if you have four children there is no way you can be anything other than bisexual at least. But [...] that, for me, was never the case.' Their accounts suggest that the traditional binary model of sexual identity is not necessarily helpful in trying to understand the past heterosexual behaviour of gay men who have become parents through a heterosexual relationship. So while Martin and Knox (2000: 53) note that 'not all men who engage in sex with other men identify themselves as gay', it is also the case that not all men who have engaged in sex with women identify as heterosexual or even bisexual. On the contrary, they may identify themselves as gay men who have had sexual intercourse with a woman. Therefore, examining the experiences of gay fathers in Ireland adds to the debates about whether sexuality is best understood as identities or practices, orientations or lifestyles (Epstein, 2003). It could also be argued that the past heterosexual behaviour of these men demonstrates how culturally embedded heterosexism is in Irish society. These men sought first to comply with a 'heteronormative master narrative' (Hammack and Cohler, 2011) before they began to see the possibility of expressing a gay identity.

Co-Constructing Sexual and Parenting Identities

In terms of constructing an integrated gay father identity, children's awareness of their father's gay identity is central to the balance between and/or co-existence of both gay and fathering identities for the men in this study. Bozett (1980, 1981 and 1982) and Armesto

(2002) have found that some gay fathers endure an enforced dishonesty with their children by not identifying as gay, and they suggest that full integration of both identities is only possible when they are openly manifested to others. While five of the seven gay fathers interviewed in this study are open with their children about their sexual identity, two participants live compartmentalised lives, whereby they separate their parenting and gay worlds. Ben said he had one life with his son and another life in the urban area where he socialises on the gay scene: 'There's just an hour in the difference.' Only one of the participants was fully 'closeted' about his sexual identity with his children. David stated that he does not plan to tell his three children, who range from six to ten years of age, until they are much older. He said that he would lie outright if asked directly by any of them at present because he wants 'to protect their innocence'. During his interview, David described strategies he uses to protect his children from becoming aware of his sexual orientation. He 'de-gays' his house before his children come to stay with him and he also made a conscious decision not to introduce his one gay male friend to his children because this person is 'too camp' and this might compromise his closeted status with his children. The strategies David employs to exclude his gay identity from his parenting identity serves to create what Arnesto (2002: 70) has called an 'enforced dishonesty' within his family.

I also found, like Better (2005), that dissonance between father and gay identities is particularly pronounced around relationships and dating. The gay fathers in this study described a variety of responses from other gay people and partners in relation to their parenthood. Four of the men mentioned that having children influenced the way they dated. Ben, who described himself as having a 'double life', stated that his parent identity blocks him from having a full relationship: 'I still have this double life and I have to stop looking into the future, because we have to enjoy now. I can't have a proper relationship. […] I couldn't be bothered. […] I've no interest in being in a relationship for a few years.' Similarly, David is not looking for a full-time relationship and does not see himself doing so for the foreseeable future. He stated that any boyfriend would have to realise that he will spend all personal and family celebrations with his children, to the exclusion of that partner, which he believes would not be fair to any long-term partner. As a consequence, he has decided that it is easier not to pursue a relationship now because doing so would mean that he would have to come out fully.

The accounts given by Alan and Conor also revealed a dissonance between parent and gay identities around relationships, but it seems that this dissonance has been resolved by the presence of a partner who accepts, respects and even shares these men's fathering identity. Alan stated that he was initially very open about being a father when he started dating men after his marital separation, and noted that while all his dates/boyfriends were intrigued by the fact that he was a father, some were scared off. Alan's experiences show a diversity of reactions in gay men towards the issue of gay parenting, which is something that has been commented upon by gay fathers in American research (Mallon, 2004; Brinamen and Mitchell, 2008; Gianino, 2008). When Alan met his current partner of two and a half years, he waited for 'a number of dates' before telling him that he is a father. Alan's partner has been 'fantastic' about him being a parent. Alan also said that his partner had always wanted children and his quasi-stepfather role with Alan's children has somewhat fulfilled that yearning: 'He's always loved kids and wanted kids. So it's provided something for him. Okay they're not his kids, but he's able to benefit from a family life.'

Conor described himself as the 'marrying kind of gay man' and being involved in a relationship has always been very important to him. While he never received negative reaction from partners around his parent identity, the commitments (time and financial) that parenthood brings did impact on Conor's relationships. He said: 'It's often been difficult for me to reconcile the two issues [...] but as [my son has] grown up, it's not been an issue because I eventually did start going out with a partner who has participated fully as a father, well, a parental figure.' Conor also said that he went through a process of 'letting go' of his search for a partner who would be a co-parent with him and described it as 'ironic' that in letting go he met his current partner, who has been so actively involved in parenting his son. The fact that Alan and Conor have both found partners who have embraced their families is another example of how gay parenting can expand care and family arrangements and repertoires, where children can have multiple parental figures in their lives.

The findings demonstrate the complex processes gay fathers can face in co-constructing and negotiating their gay and father identities. All of the men are involved in complex, individualised negotiations of their roles, identities and practices as gay fathers, and 'identity' alone does not fully capture the complexity of their lives. In order to really understand how they negotiate their identities, we have to look at their lifestyles, in relation to how they manage their relationships with children and partners, how they compartmentalise or integrate these relationships, and even whether they are open to new relationships. These findings are reminiscent of what Hammack and Cohler (2011) call 'experiential compartmentalization', where gay men navigate carefully negotiated boundaries and finely demarcated roles in their lives. The findings in this study also suggest that gay fathers can prioritise their children's needs over their own relationship practices or desires. As Better (2005: 10) states: 'many gay fathers find that their role as father comes before their role as gay men.' The findings also show that when gay men do find partners, they can expand care repertoires by including their partners in their children's lives, and some of these partners play stepfather roles. As such, gay fatherhood and parenting practices can serve to expand notions of family beyond the traditional bi-parent, heterosexual norm.

Gay Fathers in a Heterosexual World: Responses, Negotiations and Strategies

In his research on gay men who choose parenthood, Mallon (2004) found that 'many men shared anecdotes about being put on the spot by well-meaning but intrusive questions' (Mallon, 2004: 109). Similarly, the adoptive gay fathers in Gianino's study (2008) also reported their apprehension about the possibility of unwelcome public curiosity. In the study I conducted, community and public responses to their gay father identity have been an issue for many of the participants. Two of the men perceived that they were each the subject of much speculation and rumour in their communities. Nevertheless, the participants in this study who experienced initial community interest in their family lives because of their sexual orientation stated that this changed over time; now, they are no longer the topic of rumours, speculation or gossip. This suggests that while the idea of gay fatherhood can seem 'surprising or even exotic' (Patterson, 2000), awareness of it and observing and witnessing gay fathering over time can serve to normalise it.

Berkowitz (2008b) maintains that families who do not mirror the traditional nuclear model must employ tactics to ensure that outsiders accord them the validation of a family. In my study, this issue of 'family validation' appears to be central to how much public intrusion participants will accept in their lives. For example, George, who became a father through donor insemination, has experienced intrusive questioning and rude jokes from people, including friends, about how he and his child's mother conceived through non-heterosexual means. He explained: 'If people ask, I always say, "We did it with love." If it's someone who has a genuine interest, particularly gay people, I will tell them. But if people are just being nosey, that's what I say. I haven't told too many people.' George challenges the inherent heterosexism in the jokes about his path to parenthood by asserting that love makes a family. In this way, George and other gay fathers challenge the primacy of the traditional two-parent heterosexual family in familial discourses.

Despite some intrusive questioning by people about the validity of their families, most of the participants state that they have not experienced overt discrimination in their communities. Conor says that his fear about being judged was greater than the reality: 'The fear has been greater than the reality about the reaction of the straight world to me as a father.' In his study of American adoptive gay couples, Gianino (2008) also found that in most instances the anticipation of discrimination far exceeded the reality. In his interview, George said that while gay people face discrimination from the law and the Catholic Church, he believes that in everyday life Irish people do not marginalise gay parents. Conor also said that people are supportive on a one-to-one basis, but he sees that it is the shared experience of parenting that makes other people supportive. He said: 'Individually, on a one-to-one basis, people are very supportive, you know. Particularly parents are supportive of each other. Parents know what it is to be a parent and all of the heartache and joy and whatever that's connected to it.' One of the other participants, Eoin, believes that social acceptance comes over time and when gay parenting is normalised: 'I think that when people have an experience that they can humanise and can connect with, and engage with, then the difference suddenly starts to disappear.' Conor's and Eoin's experiences of support seem to suggest that, over time, gay fathers establish their 'credentials' as parents in their communities. Thus, community acceptance seems to be gained when the focus shifts from these men's sexuality to their parenting practices and the commonality of that between all parents.

Vigilant Parenting – Strategically Protecting their Families

Despite stating that they have not encountered significant discrimination, it is clear from this research that the fathers anticipate negative reaction towards their families and make conscious, strategic decisions to try to avoid such reaction. This vigilance about possible discrimination has also been reported by gay fathers in the USA (Mallon, 2004; Brinamen and Mitchell, 2008; Gianino, 2008). I found evidence of what I call strategic, or vigilant, parenting practices. One couple, Eoin and Frank, practice strategic/vigilant parenting in a number of ways, such as by self-regulating themselves in public places by not holding hands or demonstrating their affection for each other, in case this causes a reaction. Eoin said:

> We would never walk around holding hands like another couple would and in the same way we wouldn't do that as a family because that is a statement that draws attention and scrutiny to us as a family […]. So that's one way we […]. That's one way that we are conscious of the external and would be careful of the external and be protective of the children.

They also do not attend religious services because of concerns that members of the clergy may speak in a discriminatory manner about non-traditional families.

These examples from Eoin and Frank's narrative suggest that gay fathers can make purposeful decisions about protecting their children from potential hurt that may arise for them in the 'outside world' because of their fathers' sexual orientation. Studies by Berkowitz (2008b) and Schacher, Auerbach and Silverstein (2005) have shown that gay fathers work to create a supportive environment for their children and that they teach their children strategies for responding to or ignoring homophobic comments. Some of the participants in this study also reported that they employ a similar range of strategies to protect their children from the potential risk of being harmed as a result of their fathers' sexual identities. The school is a particular 'flash-point', a public site where gay parenting can be challenged and problematised. Eoin and Frank wanted to ensure that their two children could attend a school where diversity was respected and the potential for homophobic and discriminatory ideas/comments would be minimised. This resulted in them becoming involved in the establishment and development of a non-denominational primary school in their locality. Even though George's son is only an infant, George has researched potential schools and plans to send him to a non-denominational school. Conor discussed ways of dealing with school bullies and role-played scenarios with his son, in order to reduce the risk of his son being bullied. His decision to do this was also based on his own experiences of being bullied when he was at school. The conscious decisions and actions taken by these gay fathers in relation to schooling demonstrate their efforts to protect their children from institutional homophobia and are understandable when considered in the context of an abundance of Irish data documenting the existence of homophobia in schools (GLEN/Nexus, 1995; Equality Authority, 2002; Mayock et al., 2009; O'Higgins Norman, Goldrick and Harrison, 2010). It also shows that while these gay fathers can manage and negotiate their parenting at the micro/familial level, there is greater potential for negative reaction to them and their children in the macro/public realm because of institutional homophobia.

Mallon (2004) and Tasker and Patterson (2008) have contended that the dilemmas a person faces in deciding whether or not to publicly identify as gay become more complex if that person is a parent. Tasker and Patterson (2008) have noted that parents and children in lesbi-gay families may have different levels of comfort about how publicly the parents' sexuality is known. For the gay fathers I interviewed, their children's safety and wellbeing is uppermost in their minds when deciding whether to publicly disclose their sexuality. Weeks, Heaphy and Donovan (2001) have noted that gay parents do make compromises about how openly they identify as gay. This has been the case for Alan, who said that he has never forced his children to tell their friends about his sexual identity. Eoin and Frank told me that in the past they felt the need to have 'the conversation' with the parents of their children's friends, in which they would disclose their sexual identities. However, they have now decided it is not their responsibility to do this. Eoin said: 'I think we've got to the point now where we don't manage it for other people. If somebody has got to the stage where they're coming to our house or getting into a relationship with our family in some way, we're not going to manage it for them.' This may suggest that as gay fathers become increasingly confident in their parenting practices and as they build positive relationships with other families, they begin to claim a 'right' to parent, which then results in a decrease in efforts to manage their public interactions. This could be a hopeful signal that gay fathers can become less vigilant in their parenting.

Conclusion

To my knowledge, this study is the first piece of academic research that focuses on gay fathers' experiences in Ireland and, as such, I have tried to break the cultural silence that surrounded gay parenting and to shed some light on this previously hidden part of contemporary Irish life. The findings from the research demonstrate the complex processes gay fathers in Ireland must engage in when co-constructing and negotiating their sexual and father identities.

First, the narratives of their 'coming out' stories have highlighted the impact that cultural and institutional heterosexism has on their parenthood consciousness. They believed at some point in their coming out journey that the acceptance of their sexual identity would mean 'letting go' of a parent identity. These men had to overcome their own internalised homophobia in order to step out of the closet. Second, the findings have also shown that binary categorisations of sexual orientation are not sufficient for understanding the life experiences of gay fathers in Ireland, particularly those who were previously married. Third, the findings suggest that children's awareness and acceptance of their father's sexual orientation is integral to the possibility of full integration of both gay and parenting identities. Fourth, it appears from the research that to really understand how gay fathers negotiate their identities, we have to look at the interplay between many different elements. These include their lifestyles and their parenting and relationship practices, particularly how they manage their relationships with their children and partners, and whether or not they choose to integrate or compartmentalise these aspects of their lives. It appears that gay fathers make compromises about how, when and where they express their sexuality and that they prioritise their parent identity above their sexual identity.

Contrary to institutional homophobic discourses, this research shows that gay men want to parent, can parent and enjoy parenting. More importantly, how they *do* family life contributes to the diversification of family constellations and expands 'family' beyond the traditional heterosexual norm. The findings highlight how gay parenting arrangements can serve to transform what it means to be a family. Some of the partners of the gay fathers have assumed a quasi-stepfather role, demonstrating that gay parenting arrangements can extend relationship repertoires to include novel kinship networks that are based on care/emotional relationships, as distinct from legal or biological relationships. Rather than viewing these blended families as examples of the demise of the 'family', they need to be recognised as new manifestations of committed, nurturant relationships, which transcend the hegemonic model of family life in Ireland. Recognition of the potential for relationships of care/emotion between children and adult men to whom they are not biologically or legally related can pave the way for social, and indeed legislative, acknowledgment of the potential of men, and in particular gay men, to be independent and exclusive carers for children.

Acknowledgments

I would like to express my gratitude to the men who participated in this research, particularly given that the topic centred on their personal and family lives.

Section 4

Sexual Identities – Becoming and Unbecoming Heterosexual

CHAPTER 8

Hiding in Plain Sight? Male Heterosexuality in the Irish School Context

Cliona Barnes

Introduction

This chapter explores the embodiment and expression of hetero-sexuality among young Irish men in a classroom setting. In doing so, it raises questions about the establishment and maintenance of the normative status of heterosexuality among young people, and across wider Irish society. A key concern here is to address the often hidden nature and experience of young male heterosexuality. Indeed, it is precisely due to its familiarity and 'normalness' that everyday heterosexual identities among young men have remained, for the most part, critically unquestioned, while non-heterosexual identities have been the focus of both public and scholarly discourse (Hubbard, 2000). Alongside this, there has been much attention paid to the impact of young heterosexual masculinities on young women and on young gay men, particularly in the classroom setting (Mac an Ghaill, 1994b; Epstein and Johnson, 1998; Francis and Skelton, 2005 and 2001; Martino and Pallotta-Chiarolli, 2005). Nonetheless, a significant gap remains in our knowledge of embodied young Irish heterosexual masculinities. Research exploring young masculinities in Ireland tends to be focused on an educational context and related questions (Lodge, 2005; Lynch, 1999) or on broader cultural issues about gender inequality (O'Connor, 2008; 2009). Specific studies on young Irish masculinities remain hard to find.

Background

This chapter presents a case study drawn from fieldwork data collected as part of a small-scale, qualitative study completed in 2010 in Limerick.[1] This research critically engaged with understandings of social class and gendered identities through an exploration of differences and similarities between constructions, expectations and experiences of young working-class and middle-class masculinities. Participants, aged fifteen and sixteen, were drawn from fourth-year classes at two co-educational schools: Forthill School and St Pious' School.[2] Forthill School serves a number of long-established, geographically dispersed, middle-class neighbourhoods. Academically, it is rated highly. Consequently, places at the school are heavily oversubscribed and numbers are rising; currently, about one thousand students attend. St Pious' School is undersubscribed and numbers are falling rapidly each year; currently about three hundred students attend. St Pious' is situated close to a disadvantaged social housing estate that has been blighted by drug use, criminal activity, poverty and unemployment. As a result, it bears a reputation as a 'rough' school and parents are unwilling to send their children there. Fourteen young men from Forthill took part in the study, and six from St Pious'. This reflects both lower student numbers in fourth year at St Pious', but also relates to broader concerns about over-research in particular working-class areas of Limerick city and county. This has left many community members less willing to take part in research studies (Barnes, 2011; Clark, 2008).

For this study, fieldwork was participant-led and task-based, seeking to engage young men on an active and enjoyable footing. This approach was informed by a growing body of work that focuses on participatory research as a way of acknowledging the power inequalities existent in research with young people (Conolly, 2008; Dentith et al., 2009; Hopkins, 2010).[3] Two semi-structured discussion groups were held in each school. The first session used media images selected by the researcher to facilitate general discussion about masculinities and representation. The second drew on the principles of photo-elicitation, using images produced by the participants themselves to facilitate a more localised, personal discussion of gendered and classed identities.[4] This photo-work actively engaged the participants in an enjoyable activity; it gave them control over the research in terms of the images they produced and chose to share with the researcher; and it provided the impetus for a series of richly detailed, illustrated discussions about masculinity across different social class contexts (Bloustein and Baker, 2003; Conolly, 2008; Packard, 2008).

Key findings from the study demonstrate that social class has a defining impact on the understandings and expressions of masculinity among young men in school, giving rise to differences as to what is considered appropriately or inappropriately masculine. Across both contexts, however, the centrality and necessity of an 'assertive' heterosexuality (Epstein, 1997: 113) emerged as both unspoken and non-negotiable in the construction of young masculine identities. Both groups continually made reference to familiar markers of heterosexuality, referring to sex and (hetero)sexual activity at any opportunity and urgently censuring each other at the slightest possible deviation from a normative, heterosexual male identity.

Hiding in Plain Sight

In his classic discussion of youth as the object of official surveillance, Hebdige (1988: 17) proposed that both in public discourse and in academia 'youth is present only when its presence is a problem'. This chapter makes a similar proposition, suggesting that young people's sexualities are the focus of discussion primarily when they are seen as being deviant or problematic. This is, arguably, why we can read a considerable amount about perceived problems arising as a result of heterosexual activity among young people, such as teenage pregnancy or the occurrence of sexually transmitted diseases, as well as about the identities, sexualities and experiences of lesbian, gay, bisexual and transgender (LGBT) young people and others who resist dominant discourses of heterosexuality (Allen, 2003). This focus is understandable when we consider the institutionalised homophobia faced by young people who do not identify as solely heterosexual. A consequence of this, though, is that our knowledge of the construction and maintenance of less obviously problematised or disruptive heterosexual identities has been less to the fore. Yet, as this chapter will make clear, there are a number of key consequences arising from the very 'ordinariness' and unseen nature of heterosexuality that have a significant impact on all young people.

In seeking to address this relative invisibility, the chapter presents a critical questioning of male heterosexuality in three key ways. First, male heterosexuality is explored as a powerful, resilient and dominating social norm from which all other sexual identities are understood to deviate. Second, it explores the way in which heterosexuality is tightly bound to long-established understandings of what constitutes a successful or hegemonic young male identity. Third, heterosexual masculinity is discussed as a privileged but also, crucially, as a limiting identity (Heasley and Crane, 2012: 100–2), wherein, due to its powerful social positioning, young men feel socially and culturally obligated to embody and express traditional, hegemonic, heterosexual masculinity, a situation that becomes particularly acute in a group setting (Frosh et al., 2002: 32; Robb, 2007: 124). There are important societal consequences attached to this social and cultural pressure to conform to a narrow and limiting gendered identity. These consequences exist for those young men who seek to live up to the standards of an idealised form of masculinity and also for those young men who, for a variety of reasons, cannot or do not. Phoenix and Frosh (2001: 29) note how a typically popular form of young masculinity operates as a powerful social regulator, 'narrowing the range of gendered behaviours seen as open to them [young men]'. An exchange at the end of the first session at Forthill highlights the restricted roles allowable in the group context. Jamie, who appears shy and quiet and who contributed little to the general group discussion, was encouraged to speak by Ronan:

Ronan: C'mon, Jamie, you haven't said nothing [puts arm around him and draws him forward].

Fergal: Ronan! You should stop touching Jamie *right now*.

The combination of gentleness and thoughtfulness with the act of physically touching another boy is immediately conflated with femininity and homosexuality, and sees Ronan and Jamie become subject to laughter, whistling and mocking whispers of 'mammy Ronan' and 'gay boys'. Swain (2003) also details how, and why, many boys feel compelled to publicly align themselves to the dominant and collective form of 'normal' masculinity in operation around them. This 'being normal' (Martino and Pallotta-Chiarolli,

2005) is required in order to achieve social acceptance (Epstein and Johnson, 1998) or, at the very least, as Jackson (2006) discusses, to avoid unpopularity.

Heterosexuality, Gender Binaries and 'Appropriate' Masculinities

Active and assertive heterosexuality is at the heart of what is understood to constitute a successful male identity (Francis and Skelton, 2005; Mac an Ghaill and Haywood, 2012). It is regarded as the 'natural' and proper form of sexual desire, and there are powerful and resilient social and cultural expectations at work to maintain it as such. Jackson and Scott (1996) argue that we learn to be sexual beings in a social context that defines 'normal' sexual attraction and activity as occurring only between a man and a woman. Within this definition men are understood to be active and aggressive in the pursuit of sex and sexual activity, while women are understood to be passive and in receipt of male attention (Allen, 2003: 218). This widespread understanding of sexual relationships not only positions heterosexuality as a normative identity, thus positioning all others as abnormal or as deviant, it also perpetuates understandings of gender as a 'natural' binary structure within which individuals can be divided neatly into male and female, and then a whole range of gendered characteristics, attributes, behaviours, emotions and appearances can, thereafter, be expected from them. This binary structure powerfully links masculinity and certain socio-cultural characteristics (strength, assertiveness, emotional reticence, etc.) to the male body and links femininity (nurturing, passivity, gentleness) to the female body. This 'certainty' about the rightness or gender-appropriateness of particular ways of being makes it more difficult and more socially disruptive for young men to embody characteristics or to enact behaviours seen as feminine – as 'belonging' or as 'attached to' the female.

As will be discussed in the next section, this normative discourse of heterosexuality positions men and masculinities and women and femininities as direct opposites. This continuation of a historically resilient gender binary (Kehily, 2001: 117) helps to maintain the dominance of heterosexuality as 'natural', and thus homosexuality as unnatural. The dominance of heterosexuality both depends on and reinscribes powerful social constructs that understand successful masculinities as aggressive, tough and strong and, in direct contrast, positions appropriate femininities as nurturing, gentle and fragile. These binaries 'lock' young men and young women into narrowly drawn, gendered identities that seek to position only one form of masculinity or femininity as appropriate or desirable (Heasley and Crane, 2012). Individuals who resist or step outside of this binary division, or whose sexual orientation, desires and behaviour can be seen to transgress or to deviate from this heterosexual norm, can be positioned as abnormal and may be socially and culturally marginalised to varying extents, depending on their cultural context.

In spite of this, many individuals and groups work to resist the dominant discourse of heterosexuality (Hubbard, 2000; Allen, 2003). It is essential to understand and document the experiences of those groups and individuals who have been pushed to the margins and who have suffered, at best, social exclusion and, at worst, violence, criminalisation and death because of their sexual orientation. It is equally important, however, that we study the experience of the majority and, in doing so, that we question and seek to unsettle or problematise dominant discourses around sexuality.

Normative Identities, Masculinity and Heterosexism

The term 'normative' is related to the concept of social norms that can be understood as the rules of social behaviour, which are shared widely and adhered to in any given society. Norms are contextually specific and will differ from place to place and across different cultural contexts. They are also often reflected in a country's laws, lending them extra weight with regard to the structuring of understandings and behaviours. For example, in many countries the social norm of heterosexuality has been enshrined by laws that criminalise homosexual acts between consenting adults. Homosexuality was decriminalised in Ireland only in 1993 and it continues to be illegal in many African and Asian countries, where same-sex relationships are punishable by fines and prison sentences. A position that regards heterosexuality as being 'more normal', 'more right' or 'more natural' than homosexuality can be referred to as heterosexism (Wilton, 2000: 7) (also Herek, 2004: 15–16). Heterosexist discourse is powerfully evident in contemporary society and is reproduced on a daily basis through what Kitzinger (2003: 478) identifies as '... mundane quotidian actions that result in the routine achievement of a taken-for-granted world that socially excludes or marginalizes non-heterosexuals'.

It is important to note, as emphasised by both Kitzinger (2003) and Wilton (2000), that heterosexist language, constructions and assumptions are often used without homophobic intent, although they have the same effect, i.e. marginalisation of the non-heterosexual. Wilton (2000: 7) uses the example of hospital admission forms, which assume heterosexuality by asking about marital status, while Kitzinger (2003) highlights the way in which the 'taken-for-granted' nature of heterosexuality is both the source and the expression of its power. This is, both authors note, often a problem of omission or unthinking, rather than overt, hostility on the part of the majority. Nonetheless, it is exactly this 'unthinking-ness' that reinforces conventional gender relations and that requires challenge. This is asserted powerfully by Kitzinger, who states that her analysis of heterosexism:

> ... is motivated by my strong sense that while LGBT activists are campaigning against blatant oppression and overt discrimination, at the same time all around us a heteronormative social fabric is unobtrusively rewoven, thread by thread, persistently, without fuss or fanfare, without oppressive intent or conscious design. (Kitzinger, 2003: 478)

This unobtrusive reinscription of the norm of heterosexuality highlights the need to critically examine heterosexual identities and experiences. Indeed, the questioning of the familiar or of the norm is at the heart of sociological inquiry. Bauman and May (2001: 10) note that 'the familiar is seen as self-explanatory: it presents no problems and may arise no curiosity'. In this way heterosexuality, as the most familiar and most 'normal' sexual identity, has flown under the radar. This presents a paradox, whereby male heterosexuality is, simultaneously, both a normative, privileged identity that is embedded in key social structures, relationships and institutions, such as the family, parenthood or the legal system (Hubbard, 2000: 192; Kitzinger, 2003: 478), while at the same time remaining unseen, hiding in plain sight. This oversight is evident both in academic terms and in everyday life, as noted by Nelson (2009: 101): 'Although heterosexuality is pervasive, it is rarely constructed as (hetero)sexual identity, so it often remains unmarked, at least among heterosexuals. Straight people often fail to see the myriad ways in which heterosexuality permeates daily conversation.' Indeed, it has been argued consistently, by a range of theorists, that a key characteristic and a key marker of the power of hetero-sexuality is the lack of obligation to admit to it (Weeks, 1987; Mac an Ghaill, 1994a; Hubbard, 2000; Nelson, 2009) because it is auto-matically assumed. For heterosexuals, sexuality is something that other(ed) people have to think about. Hubbard states: 'From this mainstream perspective, sexuality is something that is seen to impact on people other than heteronormal – they are the deviations that need explaining – with "normal" heterosexuality seeming unworthy of investigation' (Hubbard, 2000: 206).

Heterosexuality, while it does not necessarily have to be spoken – 'Not many, perhaps, say, "I am a heterosexual" because it is the taken-for-granted norm, the great unsaid of our sexual culture' (Weeks, 1987: 31) – is still an identity that must be worked at. That is to say, heterosexuality must be clearly evident or else its absence is noted. There is a powerful impetus for such demonstration among young people, and particularly young men, something Kimmel links with fear arising from the belief '... that others might perceive us as homosexual propels men to enact all manner of exaggerated masculine behaviours and attitudes, to make sure that no one could possibly get the wrong idea about us' (Kimmel, 1994: 133). This fear drives the urgent need to repeatedly reference heterosexual activity and prowess. Although sex and sexualities were not raised by the interviewer, conversations, particularly at Forthill, were continu-ally punctuated with references to sex, regardless of relevance. For example, any mention of computers was immediately linked to pornography:

Fergal:	[showing his next photo] ... and that's my computer. I do my homework there and spend a lot of time on it.
Anthony:	Oh go easy on that now [mimes masturbation].
David:	Just on the sexiest ones [i.e. websites].

A conversation about family pets led to comparisons between dogs and girlfriends, with Ronan's girlfriend, Melanie, being referred to as a 'sexy dog'. Discussion about clothing and appearances included reference to the 'pimp' style of one of the boys, Sean, who was described as a 'pimp with no ho's'. A photograph of a bedroom led to comments about how much 'action' each bed saw. The fear behind this continual reference to sex is particularly marked in inter-actions in the classroom and among groups of young men, where projecting heterosexuality is essential in order to avoid marginali-sation, stigmatisation (Herek, 2004) and social exclusion. It is at the very heart of 'being normal' (Martino and Pallotta-Chiarolli, 2005). Young men who fail to enact or to embody an assertive heterosexu-ality are pushed to the group margins, ridiculed and subjected to name-calling, mockery and even physical violence. Such ridicule and exclusion can be seen in the experience of two young men attending St Pious' School. Keith and Kyle both resist the dominant discourse of masculinity at play in their school and community and both are subsequently positioned as 'queers', as social-class traitors and as outsiders.

Keith's marginal status is immediately visible. He is a death metal fan and displays his fandom through his appearance. His long hair, bracelets and self-drawn marker tattoos visibly and purposely mark him as different from his peers, all of whom sport the same hair cut (very short on top and shaved on the sides), like soccer and rap music, talk loudly about girls and take part in the same youth club activities at weekends and in the evenings. Keith never goes to the youth club or hangs out with any member of the group after school, preferring to listen to 'his own' music at home. Kyle also looks different, being plump where the others are skinny; his hair is not shaved and he wears his uniform neatly, with his shirt tucked in and his tie knotted correctly. Kyle has little inter-est in sport or hanging out and firmly states his intention to 'get away' from St Pious' and to study art at college. Both these young men openly disassociate themselves from the norms of masculine appearance, speech, stance and interests that prevail at the school, and both are marginalised as a result. This marginalisation is a normalised process shared by the other boys as a means of high-lighting difference and maintaining distance. For example, in our opening conversation about media use, Kyle is immediately posi-tioned as feminised:

Interviewer: *Teens in the Wild* – did you watch that?
Tony: Yeah.
Interviewer: And what did you think of that?

Tony:	They were all babies …
Interviewer:	Does anybody else think anything about … did you see *Teens in the Wild*?
Kyle:	No.
Tony:	Kyle was watching Living (a female-oriented television station).

Marking the distance between Keith and Kyle's 'failed' masculinities and the more appropriate masculinities of the other boys is part of the maintenance of the acceptable boundaries of gendered identities. A further, interesting example comes in an unusual instance of total subversion of the norms of behaviour among the Forthill boys. This occurred in discussion about a series of photographs:

Fergal:	This is a picture of the lads just messing [pictures of two boys with pants rolled up above their knees].
Interviewer:	Why are your pants rolled up?
David:	We were comparing legs!
Fergal:	Yeah, we were comparing legs!
Gavin:	It was a total contest!
Interviewer:	Why were you comparing legs?
Gavin:	Coz I have got more muscly legs.
David:	No! I had nicer legs.
Gavin:	But I had more muscly legs.
David:	No you don't, I had more hairy – I had way more nice legs!
Fergal:	OK, OK – we were very bored! We were that bored.
Evan:	Gavin has sexy legs, you have stronger legs.
Gavin:	No! I had the stronger legs!
David:	No, I had stronger legs, then he has nice legs.
Fergal:	That's enough of that.

This suspension of normal rules regarding suitability of discussion topics, language and scrutiny of each other is unusual and, ultimately, very brief. Fergal's warning draws a line under the exchanges and talk turns back to television and sport. The flouting of the normal rules in such an extreme manner by the group acts as a reaffirmation of their shared heterosexuality. Although in apparent opposition to the function of exaggerated displays of hyper-masculinity (Kimmel, 1994: 133), this exchange performs the same role. It is conducted deliberately as a farce, with Gavin and David displaying exaggerated concern and fierceness. Such farce functions to undermine even the suggestion of homosexuality or homosexual desire among the group. By flagging homosexuality in this way, it is established that this is not an issue for serious consideration. Important here is the participation in this by the most popular and 'masculine' young men in the group. Their status allows them this brief interlude, leeway that would not be granted to other, less well-positioned young men who are lower down in the gender order (Connell, 1995).

The Social Impact of Normative Heterosexuality

The consequences of the dominance of one form of masculinity can be seen in a number of ways. First, on a macro level, they can be seen in the difficulties encountered in the fields of education and health, whereby young men are obliged to actively resist structures of classroom learning and discipline and to engage in risky behaviours that denote 'manliness' (Jackson, 2006; Heasley and Crane, 2012). This has contributed hugely to the rise in concern about the performance of young working-class men in school, something strongly linked to the association of study or academic labour with femininity or feminised identities. Concern about risk-taking behaviour, such as alcohol or drug use, dangerous driving or fighting are also clearly linked to understandings and constructions of manliness among young men. Fighting, in particular, is of great interest to all participants. At St Pious', a lively debate about the 'realness' of fights uploaded to the content-sharing website YouTube highlighted both the act of fighting as a marker of masculinity and the way in which refusal to accept that marker positions some young men as outsiders:

> **Interviewer:** '... has anybody come across this on YouTube? [Images of schoolboy fights recorded on mobile phones]

Kyle:	It's fake … they just decide to fight … there's no real reason like … just to be on cameras [rolls eyes].
Patrick:	Yeah there is [a reason]. How do you know he didn't get smart with him in school?
Kyle:	But sure there's no reason for fighting, you'll just get hurt.
Patrick:	There is too. It's organised, somebody says it during school that they are going to fight somebody and then, like, everyone … then it spreads around the whole school and then everyone *normal* waits for it.
Joe:	Yeah [indicating the photo], look at all the people around him, like, in the photo.
Patrick:	You wouldn't be able to find that many people, like, if you just started fighting there and then, like.

Interviewer:	Okay, so … does this kind of thing happen?
Kyle:	It barely happens.
Patrick:	Unless when some people are smart [to Kyle].

The boys at Forthill also express interest in fights, again linking such behaviour to the expression of appropriate young masculinities:

Michael:	It's only a fight or messing, like …
Justin:	There's fights all the time.
Michael:	Sure, we are young boys, like [laughter].
Fergal:	We are so full of energy …
Ronan:	… and hormones, like!

The need to express 'laddish' (Jackson, 2006), 'super-heterosexual' (Epstein, 1997: 113) or 'exaggerated' masculinities emerges to prevent what Kimmel (1994: 133) identifies as the fear of being seen as gay or insufficiently masculine. This well-documented fear means that young men are often reluctant to be seen to work too hard or comply too easily with classroom discipline and requirements, where to do so is to risk being seen as 'uncool' and 'soft'. Young men who are considered 'soft' are assimilated to the low-status and interlinked positions of feminised masculinity or homosexual masculinity.

The fear of being marginalised is inextricably linked to the consequences seen in the treatment meted out to boys who are deemed to be insufficiently masculine in appearance, demeanour, behaviour and/or interests (Epstein, 1997; Frosh et al., 2002). Jackson notes that at school, young people interact with the dominant discourses of popularity in different ways: some seek to be popular or high up in the classroom hierarchy; some seek to simply not be 'unpopular'; while others will seek to actively resist the discourse (Jackson, 2006: 1–2). Resistance is the least common response because overt rejection of, or opposition to, the norms in place can lead to bullying and marginalisation. At St Pious', Keith and Kyle resist the dominant interlinked discourses of masculinity and popularity in place at their school and as a result both boys are unpopular and subject to ridicule and marginalisation. This overt resistance is not seen at Forthill, although several young men embody what Connell calls 'complicit masculinity' (*see next section*) and what Jackson (2006) refers to as seeking to 'not be unpopular'. These young men do not offer a visual or verbal challenge to the masculine norms in place at Forthill, as Keith and Kyle do at St Pious'.

The Gender Order

It can be understood that in order for some young men to be classified as insufficiently masculine in any given context (such as school, sport or the street), there needs to be a broadly agreed measure against which masculinity can be evaluated. Connell (1995) offers a critical discussion of this ranking process via her gender order construct. In illustrating this construct, she positions a dominant, or high-status, masculinity at the top of the gender order or hierarchy. This high-status form of masculinity can be termed *hegemonic* and is seen to be the most desirable, most popular or most 'culturally exalted' (Connell, 1995: 77) form of masculinity in any particular context. Hegemonic masculinity is, importantly, understood to be relational and is identified alongside two categories that Connell (1995) terms 'complicit masculinities' and 'subordinated masculinities', both of which are placed lower down in the gender order. As an idealised form, very few men will achieve hegemonic masculinity in its entirety. Rather, the bulk of men are understood to embody a complicit masculinity, which sees men demonstrate a willingness to strive for and to value aspects of hegemonic masculinity. They are seen as complicit because they are in receipt of the advantages wrought and maintained by a powerful masculinity, but do not have to work to defend these advantages. Complicit masculinity does not demonstrate or entail any active challenge to the unequal positioning of women and of groups of subordinated men who may be marginalised due to their sexuality, their race, their ethnicity or their physicality (Connell, 1995: 77–80).

Working with Connell's gender order, homosexual, bisexual and transgender men can be considered to possess subordinated masculinities. Because they do not identify as heterosexual, they are regarded as incomplete or insufficiently masculine. Reflecting their subordination, these masculinities are regularly assimilated with the less powerful feminine and positioned alongside women as what Epstein (1997: 113) calls 'dual Others'. The disparagement of femininity is a key element of heterosexual masculinity, which is commonly defined against what it is not, i.e. passive, soft, etc. (Epstein, 1997). Young men who do not project a macho masculinity or an assertive heterosexuality can be, as Connell (2000: 31) discusses, 'symbolically assimilated to femininity' wherein they are ridiculed by their 'properly "masculine"' peers (Phoenix and Frosh, 2001: 27) (also Linneman, 2008; Barnes, 2011). Critically engaged discussion of the gender order makes explicit the disparity in social power between heterosexual masculinity and the multiple categories of heterosexual and homosexual femininities, as well as feminised masculinities. This lack of power associated with the feminine is strongly critiqued by Connell (1987), who makes no provision for a hegemonic femininity, arguing that there can be no such expression as femininities remain subordinated to masculinity.

The usefulness of the gender order as a concept is seen in the clarity it brings to the interactions between different gendered identities. It is important, however, to understand that the gender order is not static, nor is it replicated directly across different social and cultural contexts. The categories of hegemonic and subordinate masculinities are continually contested and are continually in flux. What is considered to be appropriately masculine can, and does, shift and change. Different expectations, associations and experiences are incorporated or phased out, sometimes in response to challenges from below. Indeed, the long history of political and academic activism by feminists and LGBT activists can be seen as a direct and ongoing challenge to dominant discourses of gender and heterosexuality.

This concept of a gendered hierarchy, alongside the understanding that masculinity is contextual and thus can and will differ across place and time, provides a key paradigm for the critical study of masculinities. It allows us to understand that what constitutes a successful male identity will differ across different contexts. For example, the interaction between social class background and gender identities has been widely studied and key differences can be seen in the expression, embodiment and understandings of what is appropriate for young, classed masculinities (Willis, 1977; Phoenix and Frosh, 2000; Frosh et al., 2002; Jackson, 2006; Barnes, 2011). This has been shown to be particularly powerfully in studies of young masculinities at school. Key differences that illustrate the influence of social class background on young men's understandings of masculinity have been identified, particularly in relation to the incorporation of academic labour into young men's understandings of successful masculinities, as well as different valuing of physical strength and toughness as key markers of appropriate manliness (Frosh et al., 2002; Jackson, 2006; Barnes, 2011). At Forthill, studying hard and expressing anxiety about academic performance have been fully incorporated into the dominant form of masculinity at play. This reflects the young men's middle-class concerns for their future careers (as engineers, doctors, architects and lawyers), a concern expressed by Will:

Will:	... I like Transition year, but I know I am screwed for fifth year.
David:	You are not, you are going to be grand! Just buckle down now.
Will:	I am screwed.
Evan:	Don't worry about it.
Interviewer:	Is that because you feel you didn't get time to do the work?
Will:	If I don't study, I won't be able to do anything, EVER!

At St Pious', due to their severe economic marginalisation and the associated experience of early school leaving and joblessness as local norms, the young men (apart from Kyle) are not focused on third-level entry or career prospects. As a result, being seen to study too hard, to worry about exams or to be too eager in class are viewed negatively by the peer group. This again reflects the narrowness of what constitutes 'adequate' masculinity and the continuing need for this to be broadened.

Plural Masculinity/ies

A key contribution of men's studies to critical discourse on men's lives was to open up discussion and debate around the concept of plural *masculinities* rather than the singular construction of *masculinity*. In their influential *Theorizing Masculinities*, Brod and Kaufman (1994: 4–5) asserted:

> … we cannot study masculinity in the singular, as if the stuff of man were a homogenous and unchanging thing. Rather we wish to emphasize the plurality and diversity of men's experiences, attitudes, beliefs, situations, practices, and institutions, along lines of race, class, sexual orientation … and various other categories …

This assertion – that different forms, embodiments and experiences of masculinities must all co-exist contemporaneously, that there is no one, single ideal form that can be representative of all men – encourages us to critically question the dominance of heterosexuality as a defining aspect of gendered identities. Brod and Kaufman emphasise the difficulty of separating out masculinity from the other elements of men's social identities, most essentially from the impact that social class, race and ethnicity have on gender identity, as well as the impossibility of seeking to study any one element in isolation (*see also* Connell, 1995: 76–7). A balance is thus required in our understanding of masculinity and masculinities. We now know that, given the diversity of men's experiences, backgrounds, histories and life chances, one form of masculinity, or indeed one aspect, cannot be representative of all. And yet, both in the past and in our present, the concept of masculinity has been, and continues to be, socially and culturally synonymous with active and obvious heterosexuality (Mac an Ghaill and Haywood, 2012). Following this, we understand that at any given time one form of masculinity will dominate, or be positioned as a more desirable expression and embodiment of maleness, and be presented as something to which all men must aspire. Where men do not or cannot aspire to this form, we see a hierarchical order emerge that is replete with contestation and inequalities between the different forms, embodiments and experiences of masculinities.

Successful or Hegemonic Young Masculinities

While understanding that a dominant or hegemonic form of masculinity takes different shape and form at different times, in different places and within different cultures, we must balance that with what we have seen in our recent past and what we continue to see today in the West, whereby a particular form of masculinity has achieved hegemony and remains powerfully influential in the lives of young men. This form has been shown repeatedly to include a number of key characteristics, which have become inextricably associated with the expression and embodiment of a successful young masculinity. These characteristics have been outlined usefully by, among others, Francis and Skelton (2005: 29) to include 'humour, daring, resistance, competition, physical strength and prowess, assertive heterosexuality, homophobia, aggression and derision'. Indeed, the majority of studies of young masculinities at school have demonstrated the existence of a definable and identifiable form of high-status young masculinity that is based around these characteristics (Mac an Ghaill, 1994b; Connell, 1995; Martino, 1999; Frosh et al., 2002; Francis and Skelton, 2005; Martino and Pallotta-Chiarolli, 2005; Jackson, 2006; Swain, 2003; Nayak and Kehily, 1996, 1997; Barnes, 2011; Heasley and Crane, 2012; Mac an Ghaill and Haywood, 2012). The most important for our purposes is 'assertive heterosexuality' (Epstein, 1997: 113). In the context of young masculinities, it is not enough to simply *be* heterosexual; it must be continually asserted and reinscribed in speech, stance, appearance, interests and aspirations. The importance of being demonstrably 'straight' cannot be overstated in relation to young masculinities in the school setting.

Frosh et al. (2002: 10–16) outline a series of what they refer to as 'canonical narratives', adherence to which is required for young men in the school setting in order to avoid marginalisation or bullying. These narratives include establishing and maintaining an observable difference from femininity and from behaviours, interests and appearances associated with females (*see also* Connell, 2005: 13). They also include demonstrating the expression of appropriately masculine characteristics, such as those outlined by Francis and Skelton, above, and the awareness of a gendered hierarchy that entails the understanding that 'some boys are "more masculine" than others' (Francis and Skelton, 2002: 10). The existence of gendered hierarchies in the school setting is well documented (Willis, 1977; Mac an Ghaill, 1994b; Connell, 1995, 2000), and young men, where they are asked, are keenly aware of their own position and that of their peers in their immediate context (Frosh et al., 2002; Jackson, 2006). In response to this, the majority of young men define and express their own masculinity in relation to this hierarchy, with the majority defining themselves by seeking to demonstrate their difference and distance from less masculine, or subordinated, masculinities (Epstein, 1997). This is deeply problematic, not just for young men who feel compelled to aspire to one form of masculinity but also for young women, who must be the targets of such assertive heterosexuality, and for non-conforming young men.

The consequences faced by teachers, by young women and by non-conforming young men can make the classroom a difficult and unequal space (Jackson, 2006). This was identified by Willis in his classic study (1977) of young working-class men at school, and later at work. In Willis' study the 'lads' who embodied tough, aggressive and domineering heterosexual masculinities did so against the quieter, less physical masculinities of the 'swots' or 'ear'oles'. Their masculinity was deeply homophobic and deeply misogynistic, the objects of each having blurred into one despised 'other'. The tensions between what are positioned as diametrically opposed expressions of masculinity continue to raise concerns, as can be seen throughout the works cited in this chapter, which span almost three decades of dedicated research. It seems that the power of this deeply problematic form of hegemonic masculinity has continued unabated, despite multiple attempts to derail or at least mitigate its negative effects. In the Irish context, these efforts include the *Exploring Masculinities* programme, an important educational intervention that was first piloted in 1995 and is designed to assist and encourage young men to explore and question established understandings of masculinity as part of the curriculum. However, in a demonstration of the power of normative heterosexual masculinity in the public sphere, a combination of public outrage and negative media focus on the programme saw it phased out from 2001 onwards. This withdrawal of the programme occurred amidst media-driven fears that boys were being feminised through being asked to question the powerful norm of hegemonic masculinity (Barnes, 2011: 6–7).

Conclusion

The moral panics and anxieties that periodically emerge in relation to challenges to gender norms, sexual norms and widely shared public understandings of what constitutes appropriate and socially desirable masculinities and femininities both highlight and reinforce the prevailing power of the binary construct of gender. Where male and female, masculine and feminine, man and woman are defined only in opposition to one another, there can be no movement or leeway permitted for either to change (Connell, 2005: 13). This lack of flexibility is applied very stringently to men and masculinities. As Lees notes (1993), for a female to aspire to male characteristics is considered a positive move – something that simply does not apply in reverse. The higher social value placed on the male/masculine allows for greater freedom for young women in terms of stretching and bending gendered boundaries. This shows us that while normative, heterosexual masculinity confers, on the one hand, a position of great social power and advantage, at the same time it remains powerfully restrictive and limiting, confining young men to narrowly drawn identities in which the expression of dissent carries the high price of likely social exclusion or marginalisation. It is essential, therefore, that we vigorously question and challenge these norms, seeking to unsettle not just their dominance but also their 'rightness'. This is necessary in order to dismantle dominant discourses of heterosexuality from the inside out, critically questioning the experiences of those who embody, express, protect and maintain those norms. If we question and challenge the everyday, the familiar and the norm, we will continue to draw attention to the experiences of the subordinated and excluded masculinities and femininities, while also revealing the limitations inherent within the narrow confines of the normative.

Notes

[1] This project was part of post-doctoral research funded by the Irish Social Sciences Platform (ISSP) under the Irish government's Programme for Research in Third Level Institutions, Cycle 4 (PRTLI4). It was undertaken at the Department of Sociology and the Institute for the Study of Knowledge in Society (ISKS) at the University of Limerick, Ireland.

[2] Both schools and all individuals have been assigned pseudonyms.

[3] *See* Hopkins (2010: 28–34) for an introductory outline of different approaches.

[4] A full discussion of photo-elicitation cannot be provided here, but in the most basic terms it involves the active engagement of participants in research through taking photographs that are then discussed in individual interview, or, as in this study, in group settings. For more discussion, *see* Bloustein and Baker, 2003; Conolly, 2008; Packard, 2008.

CHAPTER 9

Coming Out of Heterosexuality, Coming Into Lesbianism in Ireland

Christine Gaffney

Introduction

Women who 'come out' mid-life experience a radical, deeply emotional and profoundly significant change in their sense of identity. The transition from identifying as a heterosexual (an identity held for the majority of one's adult life) to identifying as lesbian has an impact that cannot be overstated. It is a life-changing event. I interviewed nine women who have made this transition.[1] The interviews were conducted between 2009 and 2010 in the Munster region, and all the participants were Irish. The age at which the women came out was quite varied. Martina was the youngest, at age 27; Deirdre was the oldest, at 51.[2] The mean age at coming out was 38 years. Seven of the women (Anne, Mary, Eileen, Orla, Linda, Maura and Joan) had been married; Mary had married twice; Deirdre had had two long-term relationships with men; and Martina had had no long-term significant heterosexual relationship. Of those women who had been married, all had children. Without exception, for each woman the process of coming out was a prolonged and difficult experience.

So, why did these women come out and identify as lesbian following an extensive period of heterosexual identity and, in most cases, following a marriage? After all, transitioning from identifying as heterosexual to identifying as lesbian is no small thing. It has profound personal and social consequences, not least of which are the repercussions that result from identifying as what many people still think of as a sexual deviant. Obviously a large-scale shift in these women's self-perception, and their self-identification, must have taken place to warrant such a profound identity change. Was there one particular event or cause of this shift; or were there several causes; or, indeed, no cause at all?

The very short answer to this question is that for five of the women (all of whom had been married), the initial cause was becoming sexually attracted to a particular woman, entirely unexpectedly, falling in love with her and starting a sexual relationship. One woman, Martina, had a 'lightbulb moment'. Three women found that they had to acknowledge, primarily to themselves and to significant others, their same-sex attraction; what Anne described as the 'truth' of that aspect of her sexuality that she had 'hidden' away.

Aside from the wider issues with which they had to cope, such as the issues surrounding marital breakdown and the reactions of family and friends, most of the women really struggled with coming to terms with finding themselves sexually attracted to a woman. They couldn't understand *how* they could be sexually attracted to a woman. They had *never* doubted their sexual orientation: '[I] had never questioned my sexuality, ever, never.' And questioning their sexuality raised particular problems for the women because the socially available ways of looking at sexual orientation are essentialist. Heterosexuality and homosexuality are, for the most part, represented as binary (although not equal) opposites, with bisexuals somewhere in the middle.[3] People are either one or the other. So, having never previously questioned her heterosexuality, Linda recalled asking herself: '*how* can I *be* gay?' Eileen asked herself: '[am] I *really* a lesbian?'

On the question of the *authenticity* of their sexuality, the women weren't alone. Their families of origin, their husbands and their friends usually had the same question. As Maura's mother put it: 'you were married with three children, you couldn't be lesbian.' Given the prevailing models of sexuality available in the public sphere, the confusion surrounding the women's sexuality is not surprising. In society at large it is generally assumed that individuals are either straight or gay. So for most of their family and friends the available options for assessing the women's sexuality were: (a) the women are really lesbian and have always been lesbian, but were living with a false belief about their sexuality for most of their adult lives; (b) the women are really heterosexual and are going through some sort of phase, or 'illness' – more than one woman's parents recommended she see a doctor; (c) the women are really bisexual; (d) none of the above.

In this chapter it is my intention to demonstrate that to ask what the women 'really' are with regard to their sexuality is to fundamentally misunderstand women's sexuality. The 'categories' of sexual identity available to us here in Ireland are narrow cultural constructions and do not represent the vast range of the human experiences of sexuality that have existed historically (*see*, for example, Weeks, 2000), or that still exist today in different cultures around the world (*see*, for example, Blackwood & Wieringa, 1999).[4]

At the heart of the questions that arise with regard to the women's sexuality – that is to say, what the women 'really' are – are those 'commonsense' notions about human sexuality that are widely held in society. Primarily, 'sexual orientation' is portrayed as being innate and immutable; a predisposition we are born with, fixed from early childhood and which, like our eye colour, cannot be changed. The contingent nature of human sexuality, and the fact that much of the biological research on human sexuality is 'fraught with internal contradictions' (Jordan-Young, 2011: 144), remains an invisible narrative in the public sphere (Waites, 2005). Commonsense notions about sexuality have a significant impact on the individual, particularly when the individual's personal experience runs contrary to those notions, as is the case with the women interviewed for this study.

In order to explore some of the complexities of sexuality raised by the women's experience of transitioning from one sexual identity to another, I shall first review the overwhelming emphasis on biological determinism in the public sphere, before moving to an in-depth discussion of sexual fluidity in women. In that section I will focus on Lisa M. Diamond's (2009) particular thesis of 'sexual fluidity'. I shall demonstrate how, in an otherwise excellent exploration of women's sexuality, she too has tended toward a 'commonsense' conception of sexual orientation – surprisingly, a not uncommon feature amongst scientists researching both sexuality and gender (Jordan-Young, 2011). Following this, I will correlate the traditional 'coming out story' to the women's experience of coming out mid-life. Then I will examine bisexuality, and ask why the women do not claim a bisexual identity. Finally, before my conclusion, I will frame the women's experience of coming out as a 'rite of passage', and explore the importance of having a 'community of meaning'.

Sexuality in the Public Sphere

To ask the question how one could *be* lesbian, or if one was *really* straight is, of course, to assume that there are distinct types of human – homosexual or heterosexual. It is hardly surprising that both the women and their families found themselves confused, with some even denying the possibility that a woman could genuinely identify as heterosexual for years and then genuinely identify as lesbian. This is because the popular discourses on sexuality, those that are available in the wider social world, are those bioreductive discourses that 'triumph in the public sphere' and inform the commonsense understandings of sexuality and gender in society (Lancaster, 2006).[5]

The media abounds with 'just so' stories of 'gay brains', 'gay genes' and the evolutionary 'function' of homosexuality. As Lancaster (2006: 102) puts it, bioreductivism joins 'the question of origins with evolutionary fables that are scarcely distinguishable from creationist myths'. He states that 'genomania (the reduction of social traits to genetic causes) and evolutionary psychology (the justification for supposedly universal institutional arrangements via speculative evolutionary scenarios)' (Lancaster, 2006: 101) are both deployed in mutually supportive discourses in the public sphere. The media hype surrounding the 'discovery' of the biological basis for homosexuality is a case in point. A great deal of publicity was generated by the 'discovery' of the 'gay gene' by geneticist Dean Hamer (Hamer et al., 1993), and by neuroscientist Simon LeVay's (1991) 'discovery' that the brain structures of gay and heterosexual men differ – with gay men's being more like women's. Despite the fact that Hamer and his colleagues 'used fairly cautious' language (Fausto-Sterling, 2000: 236), and that LeVay's research was subject to considerable valid technical criticism[6] – ultimately, his results could not be independently replicated – their 'discoveries' were trumpeted as unequivocal demonstrations proving the biological basis of sexuality.[7] The critiques of LeVay's (1991) and Hamer et al.'s (1993) research that contested their findings never gained the visibility and presence in the public sphere that would have allowed them to also become a part of the social discourse.

Setting aside the issue of men's sexuality, the case for the biological underpinning of women's sexuality is even more tenuous. In a review of the scientific and empirical research on women's sexuality and sexual orientation conducted by Peplau and Garnets, they conclude that research 'has so far failed to identify major biological or childhood antecedents of women's sexual orientation' (Peplau and Garnets, 2000: 329). Citing empirical research to support their claim, they challenge 'biological models' of women's sexuality, noting that empirical research 'has failed to demonstrate that biological factors are a major influence in the development of women's sexual orientation', adding, however, that genetics research is the most promising of those biological approaches (Peplau and Garnets, 2000: 331). They conclude that 'there is no reason to expect that biological factors play anything other than a minor and probably indirect role in women's sexual orientation' (Peplau and Garnets, 2000: 332).

Sexual Fluidity

Since the second half of the twentieth century concepts of human sexuality in the humanities have shifted radically from earlier conceptions of human beings as 'sexual types' and homosexuals as 'sexual inverts'. In 1948, Kinsey, Pomeroy and Martin advocated conceptualising human sexuality as being on a continuum, rather than as distinct categories. Feminist psychologists have been writing about 'fluidity' and 'choice' with regard to women's sexuality since the 1970s. Based on the data they generated, Blumstein and Schwartz (1977: 37) concluded that '(a) sex-object choice and sexual identification can change in many ways and many times over the lifecycle, (b) the individual is often unaware of his or her ability to change, and (c) childhood and adolescent experiences are not the final determinants of adult sexuality.' And in a major review of scientific literature on women's sexuality, Peplau and Garnets (2000: 332) advocated a 'new paradigm' for thinking about women's sexuality, concluding that: 'Scholars from many disciplines have noted that women's sexuality tends to be fluid, malleable, and capable of change over time.' Golden's research, which involved interviewing over one hundred women of all sexual orientations, also supports the conceptualisation of women's sexuality as fluid. She notes that the concept of sexual fluidity is absent in mainstream contemporary psychological literature, which relies instead on 'prevailing essentialist models of sexual orientation' (Golden, 2003: 625). More recently, Lisa M. Diamond's research on women's sexuality, which will be discussed in greater detail later in this chapter, concludes that for many women sexuality is fluid rather than fixed, but that this scientifically supported finding has yet to enter public consciousness (Diamond, 2009: 9).

In fact, the experience of most of the women I interviewed of undergoing a sudden, unexpected shift in their sexual orientation is not that unusual. Far from being 'the only one', the phenomenon of their experience is specifically noted in the work of Blumstein and Schwartz (1977: 42): ' … previously heterosexual women who developed deep attachments to other women … ultimately shifted these feelings into the erotic arena and began long-term homosexual relationships.' The experience of the women who participated in this study supports the thesis of sexual fluidity. Most of them had never questioned their sexuality prior to developing an overwhelming erotic attraction to a particular woman. As Orla put it: 'I have to say, I had absolutely no idea that I had any inclination, any conscious awareness that I was, or could possibly be, a lesbian.'

Lisa M. Diamond's book, *Sexual Fluidity: Understanding Women's Love and Desire* (2009), is the result of her longitudinal research carried out in the USA, primarily on sexual minority women's experiences of their sexuality. In addition to her book, Diamond has produced an impressive range of articles in peer-reviewed journals based on this research (e.g. Diamond, 2000; 2003; 2004; 2005; 2006). I have chosen to focus on aspects of Diamond's book, *Sexual Fluidity*, as it is a recent exposition on the subject of women's sexual fluidity, is widely available outside academia and received widespread coverage in the media.[8] I intend to explore both how her conceptualisation of sexual fluidity coheres with and how it contradicts the experiences of the women who participated in my research project.

Diamond's research was carried out over a ten-year period and focuses on the experiences of 89 sexual minority women and eleven women who identified as heterosexual. The sexual minority participants in her study identified variously as lesbian, bisexual and unlabelled. The participants were largely middle class; 85 per cent were white; and they had an average age at the initial interview of twenty years. According to Diamond, 'one of the fundamental, defining features of female sexual orientation, is its *fluidity*'

(Diamond, 2009: 3). She goes on to explain that sexual fluidity 'means situation-dependent flexibility in women's sexual responsiveness' (Diamond, 2009: 3). Sexual fluidity is made possible by 'three inter-related phenomena' (Diamond, 2009: 202). The first phenomenon Diamond invokes is based on non-human primate research and relates to the distinction between two different types of sexual desire: 'proceptivity' and 'arousability' (Diamond, 2009: 202–15). The second phenomenon is the 'unorientation' of romantic love and draws on neurobiological research (Diamond, 2009: 215–31); and the third phenomenon is the connection between romantic love and sexual desire (Diamond, 2009: 231–4). Her analysis allows her to argue that although women seem to be born with 'distinct sexual orientations, these orientations do not provide the last word on their sexual attractions and experiences' (Diamond, 2009: 3). She observes that women of all orientations 'may experience variation in their erotic and affectional feelings as they encounter different situations, relationships and life stages' (Diamond, 2009: 3).

As already stated, Diamond differentiates the capacity for sexual fluidity from sexual orientation, holding (for the most part) that one's sexual orientation cannot change. However, Diamond's concept of 'sexual orientation', as she utilises it in her book, is prob-lematic. Conceptualising sexual orientation as an essentialist trait results in significant contradictions within her book. It contradicts the research mentioned above and it contradicts the experiences of the women who participated in the study that is the focus of this chapter.

Diamond defines 'sexual orientation' as 'a consistent, enduring pattern of sexual desire for individuals of the same sex, the other sex, or both sexes, regardless of whether this pattern of desire is manifested in sexual behaviour' (Diamond, 2009: 12). She believes that we are 'born with' distinct sexual orientations (Diamond, 2009: 3), which she explicitly states cannot change (Diamond, 2009: 11).

Diamond points out 'that a woman's sexual orientation is not the only factor determining her attractions … [And that a] predomi-nantly heterosexual woman might, at some point in time, become attracted to a woman, just as a predominantly lesbian woman might at some point become attracted to a man' (Diamond, 2009: 11). She concludes, however, that 'Despite these experiences, the women's overall orientation remains the same' (Diamond, 2009: 11). Diamond's analysis of her research participants' experiences led her to conclude that although 'novel' attractions may arise for an individual woman, these are 'short-term fluctuations' (Diamond, 2009: 245), and that women's overall level of sexual attractions – be they heterosexual, lesbian or bisexual – remain within too narrow a range to be considered as changes in sexual orientation. She concludes that women's sexual fluidity can result in 'short-term variability and long-term regularity' (Diamond, 2009: 244).

In her book, Diamond specifically notes the phenomenon of heterosexual women who experience a dramatic shift in their sexual attractions. She reviews, briefly, research by Freud Lowenstein (1985), Kitzinger and Wilkinson (1995) and Golden (1987), all of whom conducted studies on 'late-life transitions' of women from heterosexuality to lesbianism. All of these researchers concluded that some women could, and did, make a 'novel', 'unprecedented', 'sudden' and 'surprising' 'shift in love object orientation' (*see* Diamond, 2009: 142–3).

In her discussion of the experiences of women who develop a same-sex attraction in the context of an emotionally intense bond to one specific woman, Diamond (2009: 252–3) dismisses 'traditional understanding of sexual orientation [that] allow only two possible interpretations of such experiences' – that either such women '[A] had same-sex attractions all along but had repressed them, or [B] they did not really have them now; they were simply misinterpreting their feelings' (2009: 253). She states that 'it is possible for specific relationships to spark the emergence of authentic and authentically novel sexual attractions that might contradict a person's sexual orientation' (Diamond, 2009: 253). However, this raises the question of what exactly she means by the term 'sexual orientation'. If one's 'pattern of sexual desire' undergoes the most radical of shifts, then either one's 'sexual orientation' has *de facto* changed, or else there is a problem with Diamond's (2009: 12) definition of sexual orientation as one that involves a '... consistent enduring pattern ...'. As Carr notes: 'Diamond's insistence on a reified "sexual orientation", made problematic by her own interview data, seems awkward, and leads to some clumsy propositions, such as referring to (essentially) heterosexual women in sexual relationships with other women' (Carr, 2009: 132). In her effort to defend her thesis of women's sexual fluidity leading to 'short-term variability and long-term regularity' (Diamond, 2009: 244), Diamond overlooks the experiences of those women whose sexual orientation did undergo a profound and permanent shift. Of the five women I identified as having started to question their sexual orientation in the context of having fallen in love with a particular woman, none of them was still in a relationship with that original woman. Those relationships had all ended, but the women had all continued to identify as lesbian and had proceeded to have relationships with other women. This contradicts Diamond's thesis, which would indicate that the women should have reverted back to heterosexuality.

In Diamond's writing there is an absence of a thoroughgoing *social* analysis of the power of sexual categories to define the conceptual framework. Diamond does not acknowledge that the concept of 'sexual orientation', which she describes as an innate biological predisposition, is central to the social construction not only of sexuality but of society itself. She acknowledges socio-cultural influences, but only at the personal/situational level. Had she stood back and questioned her deployment of 'sexual orientation' – the deployment of which is, after all, central to how we categorise sexual identities in the first place – she would not have been forced to effectively deny the validity of the experiences of those women who do experience a significant shift in the pattern of their sexual attractions, or 'sexual orientation'. In Diamond's terms, their experience is rendered as a logical impossibility. As noted by Peplau and Garnets (2000: 336): 'One of the most profound ways in which society shapes sexual orientation is by providing the social identities and institutions available to individuals.' Reflecting the reciprocal nature of social meaning, one might also say that the representation of 'sexual orientation' as an innate disposition returns the favour, and shapes the 'social identities and institutions' that are available. As Carr asks: '[g]iven the frequent changes in sexual attractions evidenced by Diamond's participants, why posit a stable sexual orientation that may run counter to both behaviour and identity?' (Carr, 2009: 132).

Prior to Diamond's recent research on the subject of women's sexual fluidity, other researchers explored the subject, primarily in the context of the lesbian feminist politics of the 1970s and 1980s when some women – 'political lesbians' – identified as lesbian out of feminist solidarity with other women. Golden, in her discussion of sexual fluidity, alludes to the 'tensions and antagonisms' during the 1970s between 'primary' lesbians and 'elective' lesbians (Golden, 2003: 638). Describing primary lesbians as women 'who experienced their sexuality as fixed and inborn', she describes as elective lesbians those women 'who had chosen to explore relations with women and eventually to adopt a lesbian identity' (Golden, 2003: 638). However, she makes it clear that those divisions do not *necessarily* entail a direct correlation between the 'type' of lesbian and essentialism and fluidity of sexuality, respectively. Some primary lesbians, in confidential interviews, claimed a fluidity of sexuality and admitted that they were 'really bisexual lesbians'. Some elective lesbians retrospectively narrated an essentialist story of an unchanging sexuality.

Golden emphasises that there are a variety of experiences of sexual fluidity amongst women. She also clarifies that for some women, no matter at what life-stage they experience sexual fluidity, it is not 'something sought or solicited as part of feminist self-exploration' (Golden, 2003: 636). For others, however, 'fluidity is a possibility they specifically seek to explore' (Golden, 2003: 636). Some women deny sexual fluidity exists at all. Golden observes that '[f]luidity can occur by conscious choice, independent of such choice, and via explicit denial of such choice' (Golden, 2003: 636).

Golden's (2003) and Kitzinger and Wilkinson's research (1995) into the experience of women who made the transition from heterosexuality to lesbianism focused primarily on those women who made the transition in the context of a strong ethos of lesbian separatist feminism and feminist awakenings. For the majority of those women, the transition to the sexual identification as lesbian was a conscious choice. This was not the experience of the women I interviewed. Not one of them came to their lesbian identity in the context of a feminist awakening. They did not choose to explore sexual relationships with women as part of a political separatist agenda. As I noted above, for five of the women it was the unexpected development of a sexual attraction towards a particular woman that triggered their sexual questioning. Was it an 'awakening' of their sexual attraction towards women or a resurgence? In the case of three of the women, they considered it to be inevitable rather than a choice they had made. As Anne puts it, coming out 'was a very necessary thing. It wasn't something I had a choice about. If there was an element of choice at all, I wouldn't have, 'cause of the life that I had that I was comfortable with.'

Setting aside the discussion of essentialism and any possible biological underpinning of 'sexual orientation' and its intersection with the issue of 'sexual fluidity', let us focus now on the women's own experiences of their sexual transition.

The 'Coming Out' Story

The act of publicly identifying as homosexual is usually considered one of the most significant events in a person's lifetime. It is often described euphemistically as 'coming out of the closet'. This is commonly represented as revealing the 'truth' of one's same-sex sexual orientation – an orientation that has often been hidden until that admission. First, one comes out to oneself, then one comes out to significant others, family, friends, work colleagues, etc. These events can occur repeatedly over one's lifespan because, given the universal presumption of heterosexuality, coming out as other than heterosexual is regularly required. The coming out story also serves a necessary function for the individual. Sociologist Ken Plummer (1995: 85–6) has written that:

> Ultimately, the coming out story is a tale concerned with establishing a sense of who one really is – an identity which ideally exists not just for oneself alone, but which is also at home in the wider world. In coming out to him or herself, to the gay community and to the wider environment, the lesbian and gay can develop a consistent, integrated sense of a self.

The coming out story is at the intersection between self and society. Like all modernist narratives, it allows an individual to tell a story of identity that resonates with the wider social world. The coming out story joins the ranks of other 'sexual stories' that have become a feature of late modernity, and which 'perform political tasks' (Plummer, 1995: 17). They both enable participation in and are foundational to the creation of a 'community of meaning'. This can give rise to problems for those whose coming out story does not run along traditional lines because the 'dominant narrative' of the coming out story 'affirms an essential and deterministic causality – a fixity of desire' (Plummer, 1995: 93). However, 'fixity of desire' is precisely what the women I interviewed do *not* have.

For women who come out mid-life, their coming out story includes all those elements mentioned above, but telling the story of 'who one really is' is complicated by the fact that one has a dichotomous 'who'. One is the new 'who' – the 'lesbian who' – but there is also the *old* 'who' – the 'heterosexual who'. And as the 'commonsense' understanding of sexualities holds that one is *either* one or the other, it can be difficult to reconcile both formulations of identity. Can one authentically claim the identity of 'lesbian' if one previously authentically claimed the identity of 'heterosexual'? I named this chapter 'Coming Out of Heterosexuality, Coming Into Lesbianism' to call attention to the fact that one doesn't just 'come out' as lesbian. One has to come *out of* heterosexuality first because for most of the women they had *never* questioned their sexuality *as heterosexuals*. It wasn't so much that they were uncovering an inner lesbian identity as they found they had a *new* identity. Adrienne Rich may have written about the 'lesbian continuum' (Rich, 1980a) and radicalesbians[9] may have claimed that any woman could be lesbian, but that discussion is part of a radical feminist past that bears no connection to the women I interviewed. As mentioned above, none of the women in this study came to her lesbian identity through radical feminism.

The nine women interviewed did not disavow having *been* heterosexual, but they had to reconcile having identified as heterosexual for a long period of their lives with their lesbian identities. Of those who had been in long-term relationships with men, all except one said that they had enjoyed what they perceived to be 'normal' sexual relationships with their partners. Three of the women had recognised at an earlier age that they had a sexual attraction towards women, but they had put away 'that part', one way or another. In Anne's case, she explained her prolonged heterosexual identification by saying that she 'fell in love' with her husband of sixteen years because he was 'fabulous'. She elaborated: 'he has a very strong feminine side, and he had everything that I thought was perfect in a man. And because we were programmed to these are your options for falling in love with, I picked the absolute best one.' She said that she had 'really loved him' with 'every single part' of herself she was being 'truthful about'. She continued: 'but not for the section that you weren't being truthful about, the part of you that was hidden you just kept away … In a drawer … And with that part of you, it wasn't engaged in any relationship.'

Five of the nine women had no recognition whatsoever of any same-sex attraction prior to falling in love with a woman. Yet still, they needed to explain their long-term heterosexual identification to themselves. They made sense of their heterosexuality with reference to the pervasive social pressure to identify *as* heterosexual; they averred to the fact that they felt they had no choice in the matter of their sexuality. Linda described it in the following way:

> Like most people in the world I was born a girl, so I was put on a conveyor belt for a girl, and I followed that conveyor belt all my life and the world assumed I was straight and so did I. So I assumed the role of heterosexual woman and I got married and I did all those things and I suppose if I had maybe had time to reflect within it, then maybe I would have recognised it myself earlier on, but I didn't, I just went along the road and this is what I do and now I'm eighteen, I need to start dating guys and I need to, you know … I just assumed the role that was given to me.

The women had reassessed heterosexuality and now viewed it as a limit that had been placed on their own sexuality. Seven of the women expressed anger and/or regret that they had never been made aware that there was any other option *except* heterosexuality. Mary explained that she:

> … went through a period of anger, angry at the world that I had come from, angry that people had influenced my thought process to such a fucking extent that I could not see the wood for the trees, that I was disabled, emotionally disabled, intellectually disabled, and how dare they, how fucking dare they not give me the choices that I deserved in my life.

Like many women, they accepted unquestioningly and behaved according to the social and familial expectations that they would date men, get married and have children. None of the women regretted having children. In fact, for those who do have children, the children were their primary concern. They worried for them as they were going through the coming out process, and they expressed concern at the time of interview that their coming out may have negative repercussions for their children in the long term.

Plummer (1995: 85–6) says that '[u]ltimately, the coming out story is a tale concerned with establishing a sense of who one really is.' And so it is for the women in this study. For most of them, unable or unwilling to deny their former heterosexuality, the story they tell is not one of an unchanging 'core' hitherto denied and now freshly revealed. Who they 'really' are has broadened to encompass their same-sex sexual attractions. They identify as lesbian because that label best described, at the time of interview, their relationship with their sexuality.

Bisexuality

It may be asked why these nine women don't identify as bisexual. After all, this might be considered to provide an answer to the issue of being sexually attracted to both women and men. I specifically asked each woman if she identified as bisexual; none of the women did. The women recognised that they had complicated relationships with the sexual categories available to them and they tried to reconcile their experiences of their sexuality – undergoing a dramatic shift in their sexual orientation – with the 'commonsense' notion of sexual orientation as an innate, immutable trait. Yet they rejected bisexuality as an identity. The primary reason the women gave for rejecting bisexuality as an identity is because it would imply that they still maintained an interest in having intimate relationships with men, which they explicitly did not. Maura's response gets to a core issue of bisexual identification:

> So I remember going through at the time, I suppose very early on in my lesbian days, I was thinking, I must be bisexual. I slept with men. Again this whole ignorance around, how can I be lesbian? I slept with men, I was married to one for ten years and I had no issue at the time in saying, 'I'm bisexual', but the reality is I have zero interest in sleeping with a guy and I really feel, I mean I can be attracted to a guy, absolutely, I really enjoy men's company and everything, I find them really attractive. But have I ever wanted to sleep with one in the eleven years I've been out, no, not for a second. So, I suppose based on that I don't feel, I never felt bisexual, which is very strange and I personally struggle with that, thinking, but I slept with guys, but no, no.

Paula Rust has extensively researched, and written about, bisexuality (e.g. 1992, 1993, 2000a, 2000b, 2002). She observes that there is considerable overlap between lesbian and bisexual women in terms of both their sexual attractions and their sexual histories. Golden's research (2003) reveals that 'one cannot simply predict, on the basis of sexual attractions and experiences, whether a woman considers herself to be lesbian, bisexual, or heterosexual' (Golden, 2003: 628). Ultimately, for many women identifying as lesbian rather than as bisexual hinges on whether or not they are open to having sexual relationships with men. Women who identify as lesbian have foreclosed on that possibility, whereas women who identify as bisexual remain open to it (Rust, 1992).

In keeping with the above research, for most of the women I interviewed the issue of lesbian identity versus bisexual identity came down to the issue of whether they *wanted* to have a sexual relationship with a man. Linda considered identifying as bisexual 'for about two minutes … once I realised, really, what bisexual meant, it meant that I actually had to be interested in being with a man, I thought, no thanks very much. No, I wouldn't consider myself bisexual at all.' Joan recognised that she might be described (by others) as bisexual, having had a long marriage, but she doesn't identify as such. In answer to the question of whether she would consider describing herself as bisexual, she responded: 'No. Only because I'd just never, ever again go near a man.'

Most of the women have foreclosed on any possibility of ever having a sexual relationship with a man, either now or in the future, because they have no desire to do so. However, two women, Eileen and Mary, acknowledged that their life histories had taught them that you can 'never say never'. Eileen would not consider describing herself as bisexual. She is 'very clear' that she is lesbian, and she has 'no desire to be with a man again'. But 'life' has taught her that she cannot say that she would never be with a man again, given her experiences.

Anne is exceptional in that she believes that 'we're all bisexual, somewhere along the scale', and so she has no problem with saying that she *is* bisexual. Nonetheless, she describes her sexuality as 'more lesbian than bisexual or straight'. Having 'experimented with all the words', she has 'no problem with using lesbian or dyke', but she doesn't particularly like the *word* lesbian, preferring to call herself a 'dyke' or 'gay'. For Anne, her lesbian identity does not hinge on an exclusive attraction to women – she identifies as lesbian because she 'prefers' to be with a woman. Anne's position, that we are 'all bisexual', does not restrain her from identifying as lesbian. For her, electing to describe herself as lesbian reflects the significance that her preference for relationships with women has for her sense of identity.

Transitions

Primarily, the women framed their transition to lesbianism as a 'truth'-telling, both painful and necessary. As Eileen tells it, for example:

> There's a cost not being true to yourself, and there's a cost being true to yourself. I am so glad that I have come out, there wasn't a choice. I was dying, I was dying in it and I nearly died when I came out because I got to the stage I didn't want to live like that. The pain was too horrific.

For the women I interviewed, once they became aware of their capacity to be sexually attracted towards women, having hitherto been unaware of it, they found that it was something they could not ignore. As Linda expressed it: 'I couldn't shove it away, it was like the light coming out of the cave and recognising the light, you can't deny the light if it's there.' For those who had had some previous awareness, their sexual attraction towards women came to assume a greater significance, demanding recognition. But with accepting their sexuality, coming out both to themselves and to others, eventually a resolution is at hand. For Martina: 'I feel much lighter. I feel like I'm living from the inside out.' For Deirdre: 'I felt whole. I had never in my life experienced that sense of wholeness.'

There is no doubt that coming out as non-heterosexual is a very difficult process at any age. Research among young lesbian, gay, bisexual or transgender (LGBT) persons indicates some of the difficulties that they face; in particular, they fear the prospect of isolation and rejection by family and peers.[10] Women who come out mid-life share those fears. For these women there is an added dimension to the process, in that there is a shattering of an already lived identity. There is a severe discontinuity in one's own sense of self. The women have a lot to lose. As one woman described it: as a teenager, 'you don't have anything to lose, when you experience that as an adult, you lose everything.' As an adult woman, a 'middle-aged' woman even, one already has a clearly defined sense of self: 'You know who you are.' To start the process of questioning one's sexuality is to start the process of questioning one's self at the most profound level. Unsurprisingly, it is profoundly destabilising. The period of adolescence is a time when one is coming into one's sense of self; it is a time of transition between childhood and adulthood. For many LGBT youth, in particular, this is a difficult journey. Chet Meeks (2006: 64–7) has posited the process of coming out as a 'rite of passage'. The elements of the 'rite of passage' provide a broad schemata with which to frame the experience for women who come out mid-life.

The concept of 'liminality' is central to the concept of the 'rite of passage'. Victor Turner developed the concept of liminality from the anthropologist Van Gennep's work. Van Gennep (1909) demonstrated that rites of passage have three phases, which he defines as: separation; margin [*limen* – 'threshold' in Latin]; and reaggregation (Turner, 2009 [1969]: 94). Liminality both names and describes the middle phase of rites of passage – the phase of being 'betwixt and between' two cultural states, or two positions in the social structure (Turner, 2009 [1969]: 95). Separation, the first phase of a rite of passage, 'involve[s] the removal of the individual from the everyday world. This removal can be real or imaginary, partial or total, but some separation of the individual from the usual world he or she inhabits must occur' (Meeks 2006: 65). In the second phase, or the liminal phase, the characteristics of the 'ritual subject' are 'ambiguous' (Turner, 2009 [1969]: 94). It is during this time that, as Meeks (2006: 65) describes it, 'there is refashioning of the self and identity'. In reaggregation, the third phase, the 'ritual subject … is in a relatively stable state once more', albeit with their 'very being' 'refashion[ed]' (Turner, 2009 [1969]: 94–103). This is when the subject re-enters the social world with her new status/identity.

'Separation' is the phase that signifies 'the detachment of the individual or group either from an earlier fixed point in the social structure, from a set of cultural conditions (a "state"), or from both' (Turner, 2009 [1969]: 94). Women who come out mid-life can find themselves detached from their former position in the social structure – physically, psychologically and emotionally. Their iden-tification as heterosexual women is shattered; they may be newly separated from their husbands; they can be facing rejection from their families. Their whole sense of self can be dismantled. As Eileen put it: 'I just completely and utterly fell apart.'

The liminal phase, as experienced by the women I interviewed, does not have the clearly defined boundary that marks rites of passage in tribal societies – indeed, the boundaries may be multiple and fluid – but it is still a time of transition. It is a period of time when one is 'betwixt and between' two different social states; a period when one has 'ambiguous and indeterminate attributes' (Turner, 2009 [1969]: 95). It is a time before one resolves (*if* one resolves) the ambiguity of one's sexual identity by clearly defining one's self *as* lesbian – and situating one's self as lesbian both in the lesbian 'community' as well as in wider society. All the women spoke of a period of liminality – a prolonged period of time when they were 'betwixt and between' their identity as heterosexual women and their identity as lesbian. Mary explained it as follows:

> It definitely destabilises you. It does bring everything you were into question. And that's the kind of shock that kind of, like, my world didn't just, you know, change, it just exploded on me. Totally, exploded on me. So I was in shock.

In a very real sense the women found themselves removed from 'the everyday world' – emotionally and psychologically – and in a place of instability, where they were unsure of exactly who they were. According to Martina: 'I was very unsettled. Because when I was going to counselling, my emotions were all over the place and I was depressed. I suppose I didn't really identify it as depression. I was sometimes unstable, like my body was unstable, I couldn't concentrate, I couldn't concentrate at work.' Some of the women likened it to being teenagers again; as Maura put it: 'you do have these adolescent feelings of madness.'

The women also reported transitioning to the final stage of 'the rite of passage'. It can take years, but they manage to progress to a more stable sense of themselves. Deirdre spoke of her need to 'settle in, settling into my own skin'. And now, she's 'still settling'. Most of the women I interviewed were fortunate indeed in that they had help in reaching that final stage of the 'relatively stable state' – the reaggregation phase. They had access to a 'community of meaning'.

There was, for example, a lesbian resource centre [LINC][11] available to them. As Mary put it:

> I think … for me, the best thing that ever happened was walking into LINC, and those wonderful women who didn't judge me, who validated me first and foremost as a woman, and that's the first time it ever happened to me in my life. As I told you, the [first] relationship didn't work out. And I found the strength to say, right, no, I think I can do this, with the support of these women with me, I can do it.

LINC started a 'married women's group', which was an 'essential' support for Linda, who described it as her 'oxygen'. A 'community of meaning' was, for these women, a community of support – a community of belonging. The importance of a community of belonging cannot be underestimated. Meeks (2006) argues that the availability of a community can shape the coming out process itself. A dialectical process operates between lesbian and gay individuals and the lesbian and gay 'cultural' communities (*see* Plummer, 1995: 86–7).

Lesbian and gay culture 'is a culture creating its own essentialist story of identity' (Plummer, 1995: 86–7). The prevailing essentialist discourse of sexuality as innate and fixed in the public sphere is often echoed within the lesbian and gay communities themselves. This strategic essentialism (Spivak, 1990) has been effectively deployed as a political tool to gain rights for lesbian women and gay men. But it has also been used as a tool to silence those 'queer others' who do not fit so easily into a simplified story of innate sexualities. Various campaigns for same-sex marriage have tended to obscure those 'others' whose coming out stories do not fit within an essentialist narrative of an innate sexuality. Rendering the 'queer' invisible, pretending that sexuality is a simple 'just so' story undoubtedly makes it harder for those whose experience of their sexuality is more complicated. The women who went into LINC were fortunate indeed that they met other women who shared the same story as them. More broadly, they also found, as has been long observed in the literature, that there are very few women in the lesbian community whose sexual history is exclusively lesbian. Discovering that they were *not* 'the only one' was significant because it allowed them to claim the identity 'lesbian'.

Conclusion

The experience of women who come out mid-life asks questions of our commonly held ideas about sexuality. The concept of sexual orientation as an inbuilt, unchanging disposition that is directed towards either men or women or (to a lesser extent) both is widely held in the public sphere. This concept is reinforced by research on sexuality that lacks a thoroughgoing, reflexive approach. Furthermore, this essentialist concept of sexual orientation is supported by some LGBT groups in an effort to attain rights and equalities. Whilst it is true that many individuals do experience their sexuality as something they feel is innate and that remains unchanged (in any fundamental way) for the duration of their lives, this is not true for everyone.

Women coming out mid-life are faced with trying to explain – both to themselves and to others – a personal experience that is absolutely contrary to the prevailing social norms of sexuality. They need to tell an intelligible story that reflects their experiences, but they are limited by the sexual identity categories that are available. So they 'make do' with the existing labels, and tell their story as best they can. Identifying as lesbian coheres most closely with how the women see their sexuality at the time of interview, but the transition to that identity was not an easy task and was made all the more difficult by the narrow categorisation of sexualities. The findings of the research indicate that as a society, we need to broaden our understanding of sexualities and recognise the complexity and diversity of human sexual experience. We must find a place in the public sphere for academic research that challenges the binaries of sexuality and contests the bioreductive discourses that at present so loudly dominate.

Notes

[1] In order to recruit the participants for this study, I first sent out an email describing my research project to a lesbian community and resource centre's (LINC) email list. Five of the participants responded directly to that email. One of the women volunteered to participate having been informed of the research by her partner, who was also a participant. Three of the women knew me personally, knew about my research and volunteered to be interviewed. The sample group is small, which had the advantage of allowing in-depth interviews that generated a lot of 'rich

data'. However, it must be noted that research on such a small group is necessarily limited in its diversity. The interviews were semi-structured. I initially asked the women to 'tell me about your coming out', having made it clear that they should speak about any, and all, aspects of that experience that they so wished. They were free to take as much or as little time as they wanted. I followed on the initial open-ended question with a short series of specific questions, two of which were: 'Do you identify as lesbian?' and 'Do you identify as bisexual?' The shortest interview lasted for twenty minutes and the longest was just over two-and-a-half hours. The average duration of an interview was 73 minutes.

[2]   In order to preserve the anonymity of the participants, all the women's names have been changed.

[3]   For a discussion and exploration of essentialism in gender and sexuality, see Fuss, 1989; Stein, 1992; Rust, 1993; Fausto-Sterling, 2000; Jordan-Young, 2011.

[4]   All sexual categories in every human society are, of course, cultural constructions.

[5]   By 'society', broadly speaking I mean North America and Europe – the West. Concepts of sex, gender and sexuality, and the multiplicity of ways in which they can intersect, vary hugely around the world. Western hegemonic concepts that construe gender as a 'natural' outcome of biological sex, and posit an absolute binary divide between being a man and being a woman, have had great impact worldwide in the wake of colonisation.

[6]   Indeed, even if the purported brain differences had been demonstrated conclusively, such differences would not have 'proved', one way or another, whether those differences are 'innate', that is biologically 'hard-wired', or a result of developmental processes.

[7]   LeVay's 'unquestioning use of gender dichotomies' was problematic, both for feminists and for those scientists working in neuroscience who are critical of the 'old-fashioned' approach, which holds that function can be 'located in particular parts of the brain' and that ultimately 'function and anatomy [are] one' (Fausto-Sterling, 2000: 27). 'Connectionist models', by contrast, argue that 'function emerges from the complexity and strength of many neural connections acting at once … responses are often non-linear … not easily predictable, and information is not located anywhere – rather, it is the net result of the many different connections and their differing strengths' (Fausto-Sterling, 2000: 27). With regard to the understanding of human sexual development, Fausto-Sterling points out that: 'we could easily be looking in the wrong places and on the wrong scale for aspects of the environment that shape human development. Furthermore, a single behaviour may have many underlying causes, events that happen at different times [and to different effect] in development.' She agrees with those connectionists who argue that 'the developmental process itself lies at the heart of knowledge acquisition. Development is a process of emergence' (Fausto-Sterling, 2000: 27). '[B]rains and nervous systems are

plastic … early physical and cognitive experiences shape the brain's struc-ture' (Fausto-Sterling, 2000: 239–40).

[8]   Diamond's book was widely cited in newspaper articles discussing the phenomenon of women coming out later in life, including articles in the *Irish Independent* (August 2010) and the *Guardian* (July 2010).

[9]   In 1970 a group calling themselves *Radicalesbians* produced a mani-festo, 'The Woman-Identified Woman', and distributed it in New York City at the Second Congress to Unite Women to protest at the exclusion of lesbian organisations and issues from the conference (Faderman, 1991). In the manifesto the women explained that 'as lesbian-feminists' they were "women-identified-women"', putting women first in their lives in all ways, including the sexual, and that all feminists must become "women-identified" … [they] expanded the meaning of lesbianism so that it applied to a far greater number of women' (Faderman, 1991: 206).

[10]   Recent research (Mayock et. al., 2009) on the lives of young lesbian, gay and bisexual (LGB) people, funded by the National Office for Suicide Prevention, showed that LGBT people face specific challenges in relation to questioning and disclosing their identity. They encounter homophobic bullying in schools, at work or on the street and they fear coming out and negative reactions from families and friends. The research also showed that many LGBT people have had negative experiences when using health and social services and feel that healthcare professionals need more under-standing of LGBT issues. Specific findings included:

- Most young people know they are LGBT at age 12 and start 'coming out' at 17
- The period prior to coming out was particularly stressful because of fears of rejection and isolation
- 27 per cent had self-harmed and 85 per cent did so more than once
- 40 per cent of females and 20 per cent of males had self-harmed
- 18 per cent had attempted suicide and 85 per cent of these saw their first attempt as being related in some way to their LGBT identity
- Over a third of those aged 25 years and under had seriously thought about ending their lives within the past year
- 80 per cent had been verbally abused because of their LGBT identity
- 40 per cent had been threatened with physical violence
- 25 per cent had been punched, hit, kicked or beaten

[11]   LINC (Lesbians in Cork) is a resource and community centre for lesbian and bisexual women, based in Cork City. They advocate for lesbian and bisexual women; and run a helpline and a range of support groups. Their website is www.linc.ie.

Section 5

Sexualities – Medical and Therapeutic Interventions

CHAPTER 10

Disorders of Sex Development (DSDs) and the Elimination of Sexual 'Ambiguity'[1]

Natalie Delimata

Introduction

At the moment of birth, the first pronouncement made to signal our entry into the world is our sex. 'It's a girl' or 'It's a boy' begins the process of relating meaningfully with a person. With this pronouncement, anticipation ends and we begin building a picture of who this little person is and who they might become. Gender assignment, the pronouncement of a baby as being a girl or a boy, is based on the apparent sex or, more specifically, genitalia of the newborn. A penis signifies a boy and a vagina signifies a girl. However, not all newborns have genitalia that allow such a pronouncement. Some babies are born with 'ambiguous' genitalia. That is, their genitals cannot be clearly defined as either a penis or a vagina. In such a situation there is no gender-neutral term available to usher a newborn into the world. The pronouncement 'It's an it' is dehumanising and demonstrates how sex is a prerequisite for signifying human. A child without a sex is culturally unintelligible. As clinical researchers Money, Hampson and Hampson stated as early as 1955, '[t]he language dictates that they refer to the child as he or she, and they cannot sit on the fence indefinitely before announcing the birth of a son or daughter' (Money et al., 1955: 289). Not surprisingly, this situation is viewed as an emergency, not because there is anything necessarily medically wrong with the baby but because ambiguity ruptures the very fabric of our cultural framework. Staff must be mobilised in order to exercise their expertise in repairing this rupture by assigning a sex and restoring order. Ambiguity makes us uncomfortable by opening up a disturbing void in our perception of reality, which must be resolved in order to maintain the internal coherence of our cultural paradigm. For decades the resolution has taken the form of surgical 'correction' of the genitalia, which allows an assignment of 'girl' or 'boy'. More recently, the medical ethics of consent and full diagnostic disclosure have led to a more subtle resolution through the manipulation of meaning.

Figures on the prevalence of ambiguity vary enormously depending on how it is being framed. At the narrower end of the spectrum, looking just at genital ambiguity, the figures are estimated at about 1:4,500 births (Hughes et al., 2006: 554). Biomedical science, however, describes sex 'differentiation' as a cascade involving four physiological stages: chromosomes, gonads, hormones and morphology:[2] ambiguity can occur at any or all of these stages (Nelson, 2000). A study covering eleven different ambiguous conditions, and incorporating all four stages of sex differentiation, estimated that 1.7 per cent of people globally do not conform to the biomedical binary male/female (Fausto-Sterling, 2000: 51–4). Drawing on feminist and postmodern social theory, this chapter will explore the management of 'ambiguity' in the regulation of sex within Western culture.

Theoretical Perspective

In her book *Sexing the Body*, feminist and biologist Anne Fausto-Sterling provides a detailed historical account of how scientific knowledge of sex has been interpreted and organised in accordance with our cultural ideas about gender. As a scientist, Fausto-Sterling does not contest the existence of chromosomes, hormones, genitalia or any of the other biological objects associated with sexing the body, though she does dispute the reductive biomedical interpretation of sex as dualistic. According to Fausto-Sterling, 'sex is too complex' to conform to such a dualism (Fausto-Sterling, 2000: 3). Fausto-Sterling therefore promotes a more complex, developmental systems approach to understanding sex, which incorporates a range of biological, psychological and environmental factors. These factors include: cells, the psyche, personal relationships, culture and history; she views all of these as impacting sex.

In his book *The History of Sexuality, Volume 1*, Michel Foucault uses the term 'sexuality', which integrates the body, behaviour, orientation and identity, as a means of exploring what he views as a discursive unity regulating society. According to Foucault, sexuality represents 'an especially dense transfer point for relations of power [...] serving [...] the most varied strategies' (Foucault, 1976: 103). For Foucault, sex can be understood as a power strategy, as a kind of structural framework that regulates individuals. Foucault does not view these strategies as developed by powerful individuals, but rather as emerging within discourse. While individuals may engage in regulatory practices in the maintenance of sex, they are also subject to it and cannot be understood as the authors of these practices. Though Foucault argues that there is no neutral ground from which these power strategies can be contested, an examination of the internal coherence of knowledges relating to sex, as well as consideration of subjected knowledges, can provide a means of disrupting such power strategies (Foucault, 1980).

This chapter takes the position that scientific knowledge of sex is produced in accordance with social ideals. This is not to say that biological products, such as chromosomes and hormones, do not exist, but rather that they are viewed through a lens that organises knowledge in accordance with the preconceived or *a priori* belief that sex is dichotomous. This dualistic interpretation of sex has emerged within Western society and operates through a series of regulatory mechanisms to maintain the social order. Sex 'ambiguity', i.e. bodies that do not conform to this dualism, disrupts the social order. Within Western societies, biomedical science has long been engaged in regulatory practices aimed at eliminating or framing ambiguity.

The Elimination of 'Ambiguity'

Prior to the twentieth century, hormone and surgical 'treatments' did not yet exist to render ambiguity invisible. On the contrary, some individuals even made a living from displaying their ambiguity at sideshows and carnivals as bearded ladies, breasted men or hermaphrodites (Nelson, 2000: 176). Early medical practitioners were not surprised by ambiguity but understood sex to fall on a continuum, with men at one end, women at the other and 'hermaphrodites' somewhere in the middle (Fausto-Sterling, 2000: 33). Before the Enlightenment, regulation of ambiguity was not the realm of any particular discourse; physicians, religious personnel, the legal profession and politicians all contributed often contradictory directions of what to do in the case of ambiguity (Fausto-Sterling, 2000: 34).

By the late eighteenth and early nineteenth centuries changing social values and a growing enthusiasm for science were generating a preoccupation with sex difference as it emerged as a site for signifying social status. Within a cultural climate that embraced the social ideals of liberty and equality, it became necessary to find a method of justifying the different rights, roles and social statuses of men and women; for example, women's domestic role was described as an effect of physiology (Schiebinger, 2000: 25–7). Londa Schiebinger argues that 'Rousseau was instrumental in initiating the view that the inherent physical, moral, and intellectual differences of women suited them for roles in society vastly different from those of men' (Schiebinger, 2000: 46). Schiebinger describes how Rousseau understood woman in binary oppositional terms, 'not as man's equal but his complement' (Schiebinger, 2000: 46). The hermaphrodite disrupted this dualistic trope and the concept of a 'natural' binary order. During the nineteenth century science emerged as the authority on the body, and as such attempted to construct sex in accordance with the cultural dualism necessitating the elimination of ambiguity. Towards the end of the twentieth century this was almost achieved when German microbiologist Theodore Albrecht Klebs identified gonads as *the* sex signifier (Money et al., 1955: 284; Fausto-Sterling, 2000: 38). People whose bodies were sexually ambiguous but possessed testes were 'male pseudo-hermaphrodites'; people whose bodies were sexually ambiguous but possessed ovaries were 'female pseudo-hermaphrodites' (Money et al., 1955: 284). Thus, the vast majority of previously ambiguous individuals could now be accommodated within a two-sex system. The fly in the ointment was the 'true-hermaphrodite', who was an individual possessing both ovarian and testicular tissue, but this was sufficiently rare as to not cause a major disruption (Money et al., 1955: 284; Dreger, 1998; Fausto-Sterling, 2000).

It was not long before it emerged that the true-hermaphrodite was not the only anomaly in Klebs' system. Individuals with complete androgen insensitivity syndrome[3] have the morphological appearance of 'normal' females, usually identify as women, but possess XY chromosomes and functioning testes. Due to their bodies' insensitivity to androgens, they do not masculinise but are born looking like 'normal' females. According to Klebs' system, they would have been defined, and at that time forced to live, as men (Dreger, 1998). By the beginning of the twentieth century clinicians such as William Blair Bell in Britain and Hugh Hampton Young in the USA argued that this system was too simplistic, making the body a problematic site for sex and the maintenance of the social order (Fausto-Sterling, 2000: 42). Of course, by the 1950s the first sex reassignment surgeries were being performed. This technology, combined with a shift in locus from sex dualism to gender dualism, provided an entirely new mechanism for constructing sex and eliminating ambiguity (Fausto-Sterling, 2000; Money, 2002).

Psychosocial Sex

In 1952 psychologist John Money, together with psychiatrists John and Joan Hampson, set up the first clinic for the study and treatment of hermaphroditism: the Psychohormonal Research Unit (PRU) at the Johns Hopkins University Hospital. Here they conducted research into a large group of hermaphrodite babies, children and adults, in order to ascertain what factors were responsible for gender identity differentiation (Preves, 2003: 52). Money, Hampson and Hampson concluded that 'sex of assignment and rearing is consistently and conspicuously a more reliable prognosticator of a hermaphrodite's gender role and orientation' than physical sex (Money et al., 1957: 333). Thus the body's sex was no longer viewed as an essential element informing gender; gender was acquired through the psychosocial process of learning. Genitals no longer acted as external markers signifying an innate or internal gender, but instead acted as social signifiers that elicited gender-appropriate behaviours in parents. This represented a profound shift in thinking about sex/gender. Prior to this, no distinction was made between sex and gender. By situating gender identity in the mind, Money, Hampson and Hampson effectively eliminated the body from the picture. Though genitals acted as behaviour cues, they had no direct impact on gender identity and could therefore be manipulated (within the confines of hormonal and surgical technology) to produce either gender. Providing the genitals looked, or could be made to look 'normal', a child would develop a healthy gender identity. In brief, Money, Hampson and Hampson asserted that:

- Children are born psychosexually neutral.
- Children's genitals are the key social signifier, prompting their parents and carers to respond to them in gender-appropriate ways. Through interaction with their parents, children then learn gender-appropriate behaviour.
- In the case of ambiguous genitalia, surgical 'correction' is necessary in order to ensure that the child receives the appropriate social cues and thereby develops a healthy psychosexual identity (Money et al., 1957: 336).
- Ambiguous language is to be strenuously avoided when talking with parents as this would interfere with the parents' conviction regarding the child's gender assignment (Money et al., 1955: 291).

For over four decades Money, Hampson and Hampson's theory of psychosexual development and model of intersex treatment became 'the standard practice' of 'virtually all physicians' (Nelson, 2000: 176–8). In 1965, however, Milton Diamond wrote a paper in which he critiqued Money, Hampson and Hampson's theory. Diamond suggested that a hermaphrodite's gender plasticity might be related to their physiology and that Money had 'no examples of a normal individual being successfully reassigned' (Diamond, 1965: 158). In 1972 John Money and Anka Ehrhardt published *Man & Woman, Boy & Girl*, which provided the 'evidence' Diamond's criticism demanded (Money & Ehrhardt, 1972).

In 1965 Bruce Reimer had his penis destroyed during a botched circumcision as a baby (Preves, 2003: 95). Following Money's recommendation, Bruce underwent 'corrective' surgery, including the removal of his testes, and was reassigned a girl (Diamond & Sigmundson, 1997a: 299). Money and Ehrhardt describe the child as 'quite gender-differentiated from her identical twin brother', thereby convincing both feminists and biomedical practitioners that gender is learned rather than innate (Money & Ehrhardt, 1972: 18; Kessler, 1998). Two decades later Milton Diamond and Keith Sigmundson published a paper detailing how Money's patient had not made a successful transition to living as a female and was now living as a man (Diamond & Sigmundson, 1997a). The collapse of this case, combined with increasing numbers of intersex patient advocates dissatisfied with their medical care, precipitated a crisis in treatment practices and a re-emergence of 'ambiguity'.

Intersex Patient Advocacy Movement

The Intersex Society of North America

In 1993 intersex advocate Cheryl Chase founded the Intersex Society of North America (ISNA). Although the ISNA was not the first organisation to offer information and support to intersexed people, it was the most politicised and among the first to identify with the term intersex (Fausto-Sterling, 2000: 81).[4] In 2002 Cheryl Chase presented a paper outlining the agenda of the intersex patient advocacy movement at the First World Congress on Hormonal and Genetic Basis of Sexual Differentiation Disorders in Tempe, Arizona. The agenda was organised into five main points.

1. Intersexuality is primarily a problem of stigma and trauma, not gender. (It is not the ambiguity that harms the patient, but the stigma and trauma of disrupting a binary social system.)
2. The child is the patient, not the parents. (Parents should be supported through interaction with peers and specialist psychologists, not through surgically 'correcting' their child's genitalia.)
3. Professional mental health care is essential. (Treatment centres should have specialist psychologists/psychiatrists available to support, advise and inform patients and parents, particularly when first receiving a diagnosis.)
4. Honest, complete disclosure is good medicine. (Patients and their parents should be told the truth about their condition and not have information that 'contradicts' their gender assignment withheld or delivered in the form of euphemisms.)
5. All children should be assigned as male or female, without surgery. (Western culture requires conformation to a two-sex system, therefore the trauma and stigma of not doing so would be an enormous burden for a child.) (Chase, 2002 initially; my explication in parentheses)

Intersex Experiences

Due to a lack of long-term outcome research, there is little clinical information evaluating treatment practices (Sytsma, 2006: xix). Information regarding intersex treatment experiences comes from a variety of first-hand and anecdotal accounts. Some are web pages designed to give voice to these experiences (AISSG, 1997–2012; Beck, 2001). Others feature as chapters in books written by people with intersex conditions (Dreger, 1998; Sytsma, 2006). Authors writing on intersex occasionally provide transcripts of interviews (Preves, 2003; Harper, 2007). More recently, online fora such as Facebook and YouTube have provided an opportunity for many individuals with intersex conditions to give voice to their medical, social and psychological experiences. The three major themes that emerge from these accounts can be summed up in ISNA's mission statement to 'end shame, secrecy and unwanted genital surgeries' for intersexed people (ISNA, 1993–2008). Intersex experiences will be explored under these three headings.

Shame

In her book *Intersex and Identity*, Sharon E. Preves presents several experiences of shame caused by intense clinical curiosity and scrutiny (Preves, 2003). One individual describes finding the shame more damaging than the surgery: 'the biggest challenge is not the genital mutilation, but the psychic mutilation' (quoted in Preves, 2003: 65). The message of freakishness conveyed by the sheer volume of genital examination is evident from the following accounts. Doctors 'would line up shoulder to shoulder all the way around [...] the bed [...] everybody got a peek and a poke between my legs' (quoted in Preves, 2003: 66). Another woman describes how, at age nine, a 'parade' of doctors came to look, touch and comment on her genitals: 'I stopped counting after one hundred' (quoted in Preves, 2003: 67). These examinations are described not just as embarrassing but painful, 'really painful' (quoted in Preves, 2003: 67). Intersex advocate Max Beck describes how the constant genital investigations and his mother's shame 'all served to distance me considerably from my body' (Beck, 2001: unpaged). Similarly, Sherri Groveman describes how her experiences of being examined 'instilled in me a sense of freakishness that I have only recently shaken' (Dreger, 1998: 26).

In addition to intensive genital scrutiny, some individuals were subjected to invasive naked photography. In many clinical texts there are photographic images of naked intersexed adults, children and babies. Some show genitals being manipulated for the camera by the hands of clinicians. Others are of individuals, both adults and children, with their arms held out, usually standing against height charts with only their eyes blacked out. Preves makes the point that blocking out the eyes does not hide the identity of the person in the photograph, but saves the viewer the discomfort of having the subject stare back (Preves, 2003: 69). This kind of non-consensual intimate touch and naked display has been described as akin to sexual abuse (Dreger, 1998; Preves, 2003).

Secrecy

In an effort to follow the treatment model and avoid using ambiguous language, many clinicians engaged in different degrees of deceit with patients and their parents regarding their diagnosis and treatment. Ethicist Sharon Sytsma explains, in relation to parents, how this practice was justified on the grounds that it would be too traumatising for them to hear the truth (Sytsma 2006). Thus doctors often took it upon themselves to make 'decisions regarding infant genital surgery [...] without informing the parents about the child's intersexed condition' (Sytsma, 2006: xviii). Where parents were informed, they were 'often advised not to inform their children of their intersexed condition or medical history' (Sytsma, 2006: xviii). Preves provides several accounts by intersexed people who tried to find out more about their medical background, but found their efforts were met with silence. One of Preves' interviewees reports, '[t]hey wouldn't tell me anything' (Preves, 2003: 73). Martha Coventry describes how she gathered the courage to ask her father whether she was really a boy after overhearing a conversation about her condition; her father responded by criticising her for being 'so self-examining', which silenced her for 25 years (Coventry, 1998: 72). Howard Devore gives a clear account of the isolation and fear that such secrecy generates; it is worth quoting him at length:

> I asked doctors questions all the time, but they would never tell me anything except to be careful and not to complain. They never told me that there were any other children like me. [...] The privacy of my hell was something that I had to deal with on my own, and I was very withdrawn and depressed. By the time I was a teenager, I was hopeless, suicidal. (Devore, 1998: 80)

Surgery

A central feature of the established treatment model was to surgically 'correct' ambiguous genitalia in order to provide appropriate gender signifiers. However, anecdotal accounts suggest that these surgeries left people with scarred, numb and occasionally painful genitalia. Harper quotes one intersexed woman, who had a clitoral amputation as a baby. She has been unable to experience orgasm in adulthood: '[t]here was no medical problem with my clitoris, no disease, just an offence to somebody else' (Harper, 2007: 100). Max Beck, *né* Judy Beck, described sensation in the genital area following vaginoplasty as 'a maze of unfeeling scar tissue' (Beck, 2001: unpaged). Though most accounts of surgical outcome relate to adults, there have been a few from concerned mothers, related to post-operative pain, scar tissue and infections. One mother, discussing her daughter's treatment, stated that '[a]side from two other reconstructive surgeries, she has been for repeated day surgeries [...] She just keeps saying it hurts [...] we still don't know what's wrong' (quoted in Kessler, 1998: 62). Growing numbers of intersex patient advocates dissatisfied with their medical treatment and an almost total lack of supporting evidence eventually forced clinicians to reconsider their practices.

Maintaining Ethics and the Invisibility of Ambiguity

By 2000 the growing criticism of clinical practice in relation to the treatment of intersex patients and the almost total absence of long-term outcome data led to the establishment of several advisory groups and consortia, which attempted to integrate the perspectives of clinicians and intersex advocates (ISNA, 1993–2008; Diamond & Sigmundson, 1997b; Dreger, 1998; Kessler, 1998; Kipnis & Diamond, 1998; Diamond, 1999). The first attempt to integrate the perspectives of both clinician and patient advocates came in January 2000, with the formation of the North American Task Force on Intersex (NATFI) (Preves, 2003). The task force was set up by paediatric urologist Ian Aaronson of the Medical University of South Carolina and comprised medical specialists from a variety of fields, ethicists and patient advocates (Preves, 2003). The aim of the task force was to follow up long-term outcomes of intersex treatment and management, in order to provide an evidence base for future treatment (Harper, 2007). Unfortunately, clinicians' reluctance to inform patients of their medical history rendered it impossible to gather follow-up data, as doing so ethically and practically would require full diagnostic disclosure (Dreger, 2006). According to Harper (2007), differences between critics and advocates of the established treatment model and a lack of unbiased access to institutional records eventually led to the group's collapse (Harper, 2007).

The American Academy of Pediatrics and the British Association of Paediatric Surgeons announced, in 2000 and 2001 respectively, a shift in their treatment practices in recognition of the new evidence regarding the established treatment model (Harper, 2007: 82). While both the US and UK bodies acknowledged recommendations for change, neither was prepared to accept a moratorium on non-consensual infant genital surgery, though the need for further review was recognised (Harper, 2007). In 2006 two in-depth reviews were published. The 'Consensus Statement on the Management of Intersex Conditions' (Hughes et al., 2006) was first published in the *Archive of Disease in Childhood* in April 2006. The second, *Clinical Guidelines for the Management of Disorders of Sex Development in Childhood* (Consortium on Disorders of Sex Development, 2006a), was first published by ISNA in August 2006.

The 'Consensus Statement on the Management of Intersex Disorders' (henceforth referred to as the Consensus Statement) was a collaboration between 50 participants of the International Consensus Conference on Intersex, including the four authors (all paediatricians) Ieuan Hughes, Christopher Houk, Faisal Ahmed and Peter Lee. The conference was held in Chicago in October 2005, and was jointly organised by the Lawson Wilkins Pediatric Endocrine Society (USA) and the European Society for Paediatric Endocrinology (Hughes et al., 2006: 554). Barbara Thomas was one of only two intersex patient advocates invited to participate in the conference. Her report sheds some light on the proceedings (Thomas, 2006).

Participation in the conference was by invitation only. Participants were divided into working groups based around six themes relating to intersex treatment: molecular genetics, brain programming, medical management, surgical management, psychosocial management and outcome data. Information forwarded had to be evidence-based; no suppositions or anecdotal evidence were admissible. Feedback from these working groups was compiled into a single document, which was later published as the Consensus Statement. In listing the limitations of the conference, Thomas includes a lack of transparency regarding invitation criteria. This is problematic because it makes it difficult to identify if particular interests or perspectives are being served through selection of particular participants. Thomas also mentions that discussions were constrained by the themes and questions posed to groups. Thus, despite claiming to recognise and accept the place of patient advocacy and 'to review the management of intersex disorders from a broad perspective' (Hughes et al., 2006: 554), the methodology underpinning the Consensus Statement greatly delimited what kind of knowledge could be produced. Though Thomas reservedly agrees that intersex patient advocates should participate in such conferences, she concludes that there is need for greater dialogue between support groups and medical professionals (Thomas, 2006).

In 2005 ethicist and Director of Medical Education for ISNA, Alice Domurat Dreger, organised a group comprising 45 intersex people, parents and clinicians, called the Consortium on Disorders of Sex Development, in order to provide advice and support for people with intersex conditions, their parents and clinicians (Consortium on Disorders of Sex Development, 2006a, 2006b). In 2006 the Consortium on Disorders of Sex Development (henceforth referenced as the Consortium) produced two documents: the *Clinical Guidelines for the Management of Disorders of Sex Development in Childhood* (henceforth referred to as the Clinical Guidelines) (Consortium, 2006a) and the *Handbook for Parents* (Consortium, 2006b), published by ISNA. The *Handbook for Parents* is designed to empower parents by providing advice on how to support their child in dealing with the social, emotional and psychological implications of growing up with an intersex condition (Consortium, 2006b). The Clinical Guidelines forwards a 'patient-centred care' model and provides clinical information on a variety of intersexed conditions, as well as guidance on how to advise and support patients/parents from a patient-centred perspective (Consortium, 2006a).

Though the Clinical Guidelines was published after the Consensus Statement, it was the Consortium that first forwarded the term 'disorder of sex development' and its acronym, 'DSD'. The forwarding of this term by ISNA disappointed many intersexed people because few outside the leadership of ISNA were consulted and the use of the term 'disorder' left many feeling betrayed (Koyama,

2008). Much of what has been written, particularly from the patient advocacy perspective, regarding the Consensus Statement and, to a lesser extent, the Clinical Guidelines relates to the new nomenclature and the highly contested use of the term 'disorder'. It is this controversy that will be explored before we examine the treatment practices advocated by the two documents.

Ordering by Disordering

In an effort to find a replacement for the term 'hermaphrodite', with its inaccurate connotations of two sexes in the one body, and 'intersex', which by referring to the whole person implies a third gender, the members of the Consortium forwarded the term 'disorder of sex development' (Reis, 2007). The term was later adopted by the International Consensus Conference on Intersex and incorporated into the Consensus Statement.

The Clinical Guidelines describe 'disorders of sex development' as including 'anomalies of the sex chromosomes, the gonads, the reproductive ducts, and the genitalia' (Consortium, 2006a: 2). The Consensus Statement proposed that 'disorders of sex development' be defined by 'congenital conditions in which development of chromosomal, gonadal, or anatomic sex is atypical' (Hughes et al., 2006: 554). Thus the term 'DSD' incorporates not just genital ambiguity but all physiological forms of ambiguity. However, use of the term 'disorder of sex development' and its acronym 'DSD' remain highly controversial and divisive. On the opening pages of the Clinical Guidelines, three of its contributors, David Cameron, Peter Trinkl and Esther Morris Leidolf (all intersex advocates), 'make it known that they do not support the term "Disorders of Sex Development"' (Consortium, 2006a: ii).

Following the publication of the Consensus Statement online there were nineteen rapid responses (*British Medical Journal* ADC Online, 2006). Eighteen of the nineteen respondents were writing in relation to the new nomenclature. Of these, four were in favour of it; fourteen were opposed to it. In their letter, Milton Diamond and Hazel Glenn Beh argue that 'disorder is far too narrow and too pathological' and propose instead 'variation of sex development' (Diamond & Beh, 2006). Of the fourteen predominantly intersex advocate respondents opposed to the new nomenclature, nine were in favour of 'variation of sex development'. Another forum where opposition to the new nomenclature has been aired is the Organisation Intersex International (OII) website (Hinkle, n.d.a). The OII, which has chapters in sixteen countries, has compiled a list of ten objections to the new nomenclature. In addition to rejecting the term DSD as reductive and pathologising, the OII is particularly concerned that by describing intersexed bodies as disordered, and therefore undesirable, 'disorder' of sex development justifies research designed to eliminate intersex (Hinkle, nd–a).[5]

Though many intersex advocates appear to be opposed to the new nomenclature, there are those in favour of it. In clarifying her position, Chase argued that the new terminology is a shift in focus from who the patient *is* to what they *have*. Chase argues that terms like 'male pseudohermaphrodite' or 'intersex' may imply a gender identity that does not reflect the person (Chase, 2006). Though one can appreciate Chase's point that 'intersex' or 'hermaphrodite' may be inappropriate or uncomfortable for people who see themselves unambiguously as men or women, the problem of sex reflecting gender can also be applied to the term 'disorder of sex development'. If intersex is rejected on the grounds that it suggests gender ambiguity, then 'disorder' of sex development might also be rejected on the grounds that it signifies gender pathology.

Emi Koyama, Director of the advocacy organisation Intersex Initiative, which has chapters in the USA and Japan, cautiously agrees with Chase's position. Though she recognises that DSD is not perfect, it is an acceptable term within the context of biomedicine and by reassuring parents that their child has a recognised medical disorder, rather than being a 'gender outcast', may even reduce incidences of 'normalising' surgeries (Koyama, 2008).

Gender theorist Elizabeth Reis argues that while the word 'disorder' makes sense to clinicians and insurance companies, 'this new nomenclature contradicts one of intersex activism's central tenets: that unusual sex anatomy does *not* inevitably require surgical or hormonal correction' (Reis, 2007: 538). As an alternative, Reis suggests retaining the acronym DSD, but have it stand for '*divergence of sex development*', which would still compel clinicians to check for underlying health problems, but would de-emphasise the need for correction or repair (Reis, 2007: 541). Reis also suggests that divergence of sex development 'would satisfy those who want to minimise the emphasis on genitals, gender identity, and sexual orientation that the intersex label may encourage' (Reis, 2007: 541).

The German Intersex Society similarly subverted the meaning of the first 'D'. In a letter to the Archives of Sexual Behaviour, Milton Diamond endorsed the German Intersex Society's (Intersexualle Menschene e.V.) subversion of the meaning of DSD, in which it reinterprets the first 'D' as standing for 'difference' rather than 'disorder' (Diamond, 2009).

Margaret Simmonds of the UK Androgen Insensitivity Syndrome Support Group, though in favour of eliminating androgynous terms, is opposed to the term 'disorder of sex development' and, more particularly, to 'DSD'. Simmonds argues that not only is the new nomenclature pathologising, but by reducing a diverse range of conditions to a three-letter acronym, it allows 'DSD' to be used as a 'cover-up' term or euphemism that limits patient access to full and honest disclosure (Simmonds, 2006).

Though presented as transparent and therefore satisfying the requirement of full disclosure, this terminology seems akin to Money, Hampson and Hampson's more opaque approach. When talking with parents or patients, Money, Hampson and Hampson instructed clinicians to refer to the child as having a male or female sex, but one that was developmentally 'unfinished' (Money et al., 1955: 291). Disorder of sex development implies something similar: that a person can be viewed as having a 'sex', but an under- or mal-developed one. Thus DSD can be used as a regulatory mechanism, maintaining sex as a dualism within social discourse, while simultaneously signifying ambiguity to clinicians and the initiation of 'treatment' practices. Although many organisations seem to be increasingly successful in subverting the meaning of the DSD acronym from 'disorder of sex development' to either 'divergence of sex development' or 'difference of sex development', the continued use of a three-letter acronym obscures ambiguity and maintains the sex dualism.

Treatment for 'Disorders' of Sex Development

The Consensus Statement on Management of Intersexed Conditions

Though the Consensus Statement reflects much of the agenda of the intersex patient advocacy movement outlined above, its position on surgery seems somewhat normative. In brief, the recommendations of the Consensus Statement are:

- Use of the new nomenclature disorder of sex development or DSD
- Clinical management by an experienced multidisciplinary team, including a psychologist/psychiatrist
- Expedient gender assignment
- Long-term evaluation in order to generate more precise diagnostic algorithms
- That medical photography should be undertaken while the patient is under anaesthesia and with consent (Hughes et al., 2006)

Though the Consensus Statement attempts to address many of the concerns of the intersex patient advocacy movement, its approach seems to be informed as much by social norms as clinical evidence. With regard to female assignment, clitoral surgery is still considered in 'cases of severe virilisation', i.e. a small phallic structure is permissible for a girl, but a large one is not (Hughes et al., 2006: 557). A vagina that is too short to accommodate a penis is referred to as 'inadequate' and 'requires a vaginoplasty' (Hughes et al., 2006: 557). With regard to male assignment, acknowledging the difficulty in surgically constructing a penis, Hughes et al. argue that in cases of male assignment, 'this may affect the balance of gender assignment' (Hughes et al., 2006: 557). Thus, on balance, male assignment is synonymous with having a penis. The reduction of gender to 'normal'-looking genitals is again highlighted with regard to treatment of 'ovotesticular DSD'. Hughes et al. recommend that the assignment decision be taken 'assuming the genitalia are, *or can be made*, consistent with the chosen sex' (Hughes et al., 2006: 556 [my emphasis]).

The Consensus Statement recognises that 'causes of gender dissatisfaction are poorly understood', 'interpretation of sex differences is complicated' and 'information across a range of assessments is insufficient in DSD', which highlights a lack of clinical evidence for their treatment practices (Hughes et al., 2006: 554–8). Conversely, there is evidence that children raised with ambiguous anatomies are no more at risk of psychosocial problems than the general population (Money et al., 1956: 53[6]; Consortium, 2006a: 28). Thus the clinical practice of assigning gender would appear to be informed more by social norms than by clinical evidence.

Consortium on the Management of Disorders of Sex Development – Clinical Guidelines for the Management of Disorders of Sex Development in Childhood

The Consensus Statement was predominantly devised by medical practitioners, whereas the Clinical Guidelines draw from what it terms the 'DSD clinical triad', comprising clinicians, patients and parents (Consortium, 2006a: 3). The authors argue that this methodology 'has helped to address the substantial evidentiary gaps in the medical literature' (Consortium, 2006a: 3). The main difference between the Consensus Statement and the Clinical Guidelines is that the former emphasises clinical management, whereas the latter emphasises psychosocial management. The Clinical Guidelines provide a seven-step definition for what it terms 'Patient-Centred Care for DSDs' (Consortium, 2006a: 2). In brief, these steps are as follows.

1. Provide medical and surgical care when dealing with a complication that represents a real and present threat to the patient's physical wellbeing.
2. Care providers should not seek to force the patient into a social norm, for example, phallic size or gender-typical behaviour.
3. Minimise shame by promoting openness and positive connections with others. Avoid repetitive genital examinations.
4. Delay elective and hormonal treatments until the patient can actively participate in decision-making. Where treatment is considered, healthcare professionals must evaluate whether the procedures are 'truly needed for the benefit of the child or are being offered to allay parental distress' (Consortium, 2006a: 3).
5. Respect parents by addressing their concerns and distress.
6. Directly address the child's psychosocial distress through professional psychosocial and peer support.
7. Always tell the truth to the family and child.

With regard to assigning gender, the Clinical Guidelines acknowledge that gender identity 'is the result of a complex interaction between genes and environment' (Consortium, 2006a: 25). They point out that it is not possible to predict in advance the gender of *any* child, including children with 'DSDs'. They describe gender assignment as a social and legal process that should only be undertaken by parents who have been fully informed of test results and what is known about the gender identity of children with similar conditions. They stress the importance of the multidisciplinary team's support 'of atypical anatomy and behaviour' and the need for flexibility (Consortium, 2006a: 26). They suggest that in addition to clinical staff, the multidisciplinary team should include a social worker and child psychiatrists/psychologists to provide social and psychological advice and support. They also provide a list of 21 'DSDs and Related Concerns', giving advice on gender assignment in most cases (Consortium, 2006a: 5–7). Finally, where a child is undecided about their gender identity as they approach puberty, they suggest delaying puberty with leuprolide and exploring the issues with counselling.

Unlike the Consensus Statement, the Clinical Guidelines oppose *all* non-essential surgery until puberty, allowing the patient to participate fully in and consent to the decision. The Clinical Guidelines describe how '[g]enital cosmetic surgeries are sometimes offered to relieve parental distress, but parental distress should instead be addressed directly through peer support and competent mental health care' (Consortium, 2006a: 28). With regard to parental requests that health care providers withhold information from their children, they recommend that the parents may need support for their own concerns and that all parents receive counselling on how to speak truthfully to their children. The Clinical Guidelines emphasise that full disclosure is not a passive exercise of not telling lies, but actively involves 'not withholding critical information like karyotype, diagnosis and crucial facts about medical history' (Consortium, 2006a: 34).[7] The Clinical Guidelines argue that attempts to protect patients through the use of euphemisms 'may inadvertently harm the patient and the doctor-patient relationship' (Consortium, 2006a: 34). They argue that withholding information can risk trauma either by emerging at some unexpected, and therefore unsupported, time later on, or by making the patient feel ashamed that they have something that is so awful it can't even be talked about.

With regard to surgery, it is interesting to note that in a section entitled 'Helping Parents Think About Elective Surgery' they suggest the 'clinicians make vivid the option of waiting by introducing adults who have lived without the intervention' (Consortium, 2006a: 30). They highlight the 'consistent and growing body of evidence that children raised with "ambiguous" sex anatomy are at no greater risk for psychosocial problems than the general population' (Consortium, 2006a: 28).

Consortium on the Management of Disorders of Sex Development – Handbook for Parents

In supporting its 'Patient-Centred' approach, the Consortium on the Management of Disorders of Sex Development also produced a *Handbook for Parents*, which provides information about 'DSDs'; advice on giving age-appropriate, honest information to a child; tips on what to tell friends and family; and advice on interacting with teachers, care providers and religious groups (Consortium, 2006b). Interestingly, the document consistently acknowledges ambiguity. Parents are encouraged to tell friends and family that 'sometimes babies are born with a body type that is not either the average male or female' (Consortium, 2006b: 40). However, parents are also advised that 'a few people may find your child's DSD very frightening, because DSDs challenge their ideas about human sex and sexuality' (Consortium, 2006b: 42).

A Comparison of the Consensus Statement and the Clinical Guidelines

Both the Consensus Statement and the Clinical Guidelines provide novel approaches to treating 'ambiguity', integrating many of the concerns highlighted by the intersex patient advocacy movement, but they do so from two significantly different perspectives. The perspective in the former is predominantly biomedical, whereas in the latter it is primarily psychosocial. However, the lack of clinical evidence and the apparent normativity of its approach renders the Consensus Statement less convincing as an authority in ordering and disordering sex. By expressly integrating ambiguity into its paradigm the Clinical Guidelines provide an internally coherent and therefore more authoritative approach. Within this context, however, their advocating of the new nomenclature seems inconsistent. First, the term 'disorder of sex development' seems somewhat pathologising given the expressed aim to de-medicalise ambiguity. Secondly, given its recommendation to use direct language and avoid euphemisms, the use of the acronym 'DSD' seems counterproductive.

Impact of the Consensus Statement

Impact of the Consensus Statement in Europe

In 2009 V. Pasterski, P. Prentice and I. A. Hughes wrote an article in which they evaluated the impact of the Consensus Statement throughout Europe (Pasterski et al., 2010a). In conducting their evaluation Pasterski, Prentice and Hughes draw on their previous study (Pasterski et al., 2010b), which looks at 60 DSD centres spanning 23 European countries, in order to 'review the Consensus Statement and its impact on clinical practice' (Pasterski et al., 2010a: 189). With regard to the new nomenclature and classification, Pasterski, Prentice and Hughes state that '[w]hile the uptake of the new nomenclature appears to be almost universal, the taxonomic classification system has met with some dispute' (Pasterski et al., 2010a: 190). They are referring to a different taxonomic system, proposed by the European Society for Paediatric Endocrinology (ESPE), which removed Turner syndrome and Klinefelter's syndrome from the DSD category (Pasterski et al., 2010a; Vilain & Sandberg, 2009). Pasterski, Prentice and Hughes also argue against proposals to use the term 'variation' on the grounds that it is inaccurate, suggesting that DSD 'conditions represent an abnormal pathophysiology, rather than a simple variation' (Pasterski et al., 2010a: 190). Thus, although they describe the uptake of the new nomenclature as 'unparalleled', they recognise that it is not entirely unproblematic (Pasterski et al., 2010a: 193).

With regard to the Consensus Statement recommendation for increased psychosocial support, Pasterski, Prentice and Hughes found that 'approximately 95 per cent of centres reported to offer support from a child psychiatrist or paediatric psychologist for newly diagnosed cases', which they view as a 'remarkable advancement in the psychosocial management of DSD' (Pasterski et al., 2010a: 191). However, in relation to offers of psychosocial support for parents in making decisions regarding their child's gender, only 80 per cent took advantage of the support (Pasterski et al., 2010a: 192). With regard to offers of psychosocial support in cases of 'sex dissatisfaction', only 57 per cent took advantage of the psychosocial support. Though Pasterski, Prentice and Hughes' study clearly suggests that patients and parents are being offered psychosocial support, reasons for the low levels of uptake are not known.

Pasterski, Prentice and Hughes did not look at practices of diagnostic disclosure, but instead drew on a variety of sources to reassert the Consensus Statement's recommendation that 'full disclosure, conducted appropriately, is the optimal approach' (Pasterski et al., 2010a: 193). With regard to disclosure, they recommend that research be conducted into how 'to devise appropriate disclosure strategies for parents and for child patients as they develop both emotionally and psychologically' (Pasterski et al., 2010a: 194). This would seem to suggest a lack of established protocol in dealing with DSD disclosures.

With regard to surgical practices, the only one mentioned is clitoroplasty. Pasterski, Prentice and Hughes found that of the 60 centres, 52 per cent reported reduction in the practice of clitoroplasty, 44.8 per cent reported no change and 3.4 per cent reported an increase in practice (Pasterski et al., 2010b: 618). Though they describe this trend away from clitoroplasty as 'remarkable' (Pasterski et al., 2010b: 622), given the prevalence of literature highlighting the harm done by clitoral surgeries, it is more remarkable that so few have changed their practices (Kessler, 1998; Dreger, 1998; Fausto-Sterling, 2000). Though Pasterski, Prentice and Hughes describe the Consensus Statement as 'transformative', this is qualified as applying 'particularly to a major change in the medical lexicon' (Pasterski et al., 2010b: 622). Thus, though much can be said about the impact of the Consensus Statement in relation to clinical language, very little is known about its impact on patients.

Impact of the Consensus Statement Cross-Culturally and Socio-Economically

In their article, paediatricians Garry Warne and Jamal Raza compare resource-rich and resource-poor countries in the management of DSDs, focusing on countries in Asia and Africa (Warne & Raza, 2008). They point out that although cultural values inform different trends in treatment practice, poverty is the greatest impediment in the implementation of Consensus Statement guidelines in resource-poor countries. The significance of poverty in intersex treatment is reiterated by Curtis Hinkle, founder of the OII. He states that '[a]lmost all intersexed people who contact OII from less affluent regions have contacted us because they do not have access to treatments, surgeries and counselling' (Hinkle, nd–b). Thus it would appear that economic status is a significant factor affecting the level of DSD treatment a patient can expect to receive.

Ireland and 'DSD' Treatment

The Health Service Executive (HSE) describes its position in relation to DSDs in a series of information sheets (HSE, 2012a–g). In what appears to be a recognition of the obscurity of the term, the HSE describes DSDs not under the heading 'DSD' but under the headings 'ambiguous genitalia' and 'intersex conditions' (HSE, 2012b).[8] The HSE has adopted many of the Consensus Statement's recommendations, including the new nomenclature, and defines DSD as 'a mix or blend of male and female sexual characteristics' (HSE, 2012a). In addition to describing some of the possible characteristics of DSDs, the HSE suggests that individuals with a DSD may need hormone therapy and psychological support, directing anyone who thinks they have a DSD to visit their GP (HSE, 2012a). In relation to a multidisciplinary team approach, the HSE suggests that anyone looking for advice or support for a DSD will be referred to a 'team of healthcare professionals who will work together to understand your condition and offer you support and advice' (HSE, 2012a). The HSE gives congenital adrenal hyperplasia, androgen insensitivity syndrome and Turner syndrome as examples of a DSD (HSE, 2012a).

The HSE provides details on the symptoms, causes, diagnosis and treatment of androgen insensitivity syndrome (AIS) (HSE, 2012b). With regard to AIS and disclosure, the HSE suggests that 'it is best to explain the basic facts about the condition to the child as soon as possible [...who can then] be given more detailed information as their ability to understand increases' (HSE, 2012c, my insertion). It further recommends that 'a child fully understand their condition before they reach puberty' (HSE, 2012c). With regard to timing of surgeries, the HSE reflects the Consensus Statement line and advocates that 'surgery be postponed until the child is old enough to make their decision' (HSE, 2012c). The HSE also emphasises the importance of psychosocial support for affected children and their parents, and highlights the availability of genetic counselling (HSE, 2012c). In relation to diagnosis, the HSE suggests that partial androgen insensitivity syndrome (PAIS) is usually obvious due to genital difference at birth, but that complete androgen insensitivity syndrome (CAIS) may go unnoticed until puberty. The HSE also describes a range of prenatal tests that can be conducted early in pregnancy, enabling identification of foetuses with AIS (HSE, 2012d).

With regard to Turner syndrome, the HSE provides a variety of information on symptoms, causes, diagnosis and treatment (HSE, 2012e). The only link to a peer support group provided by the HSE in relation to any DSD relates specifically to Turner syndrome.[9] Various methods of diagnosing Turner syndrome, both prenatally and postnatally, are described (HSE, 2012g).

The HSE would appear to be informed by the Consensus Statement with regard to its use of nomenclature and recommendations regarding full disclosure, delaying surgery, adopting a multidisciplinary team approach and offering psychological support. Though the information provided is detailed and frank, it represents a narrow range and does not reflect the diversity of conditions labelled DSD. However, as the HSE website was being updated at the time of writing, it is possible that a greater breadth of information will be incorporated at a later date.

Irish Support and Advocacy

At the time of writing there are no official DSD/intersex advocacy or support groups based in Ireland dealing with DSDs in general, though there would appear to be some private groups communicating via Facebook, Twitter and YouTube, which have Irish members or are based in Ireland. Most advocacy and support groups operate under the specific title of the condition that unites their members, for example the UK-based Androgen Insensitivity Syndrome Support Group (AISSG). With the exception of the Turner Contact Group Ireland,[10] which supports women with Turner Syndrome, Ireland has very few specific support organisations. The likely cause for this is low population density; there may be too few individuals in Ireland with any one DSD condition to make forming an official group viable. There are, however, several UK-based organisations that welcome Irish members and/or enquiries from Ireland.

For people with congenital adrenal hyperplasia (CAH), the UK organisation Living With CAH Support Group has a group based in Northern Ireland; the Living With CAH Support Group (Ireland) welcomes members from all over Ireland.[11] The Klinefelter's Syndrome Association UK provides support, information and advice for people from the UK and Ireland in relation to Klinefelter's syndrome.[12] The UK-based Androgen Insensitivity Syndrome Support Group, or AISSG UK, provides support for people with AIS and welcomes members from Ireland.[13] The organisation DSD Families is an online information and support resource for parents of children, teens and young adults with a DSD and it provides links to several other support organisations dealing with specific DSD conditions.[14] For people looking for support and advocacy, the Organisation Intersex International (OII) has a UK branch.[15] The US-based Accord Alliance website[16] provides general information, including two online books: *Clinical Guidelines for the Management of Disorders of Sex Development in Childhood* (Consortium on the Management of Disorders of Sex Development, 2006a) and *Handbook for Parents* (Consortium on the Management of Disorders of Sex Development, 2006b). For people experiencing doubts or discomfort in relation to their gender assignment there is an Irish organisation, the Transgender Equality Network Ireland (TENI), which provides information and support for people experiencing gender dysphoria.[17] It should be emphasised, however, that TENI is not a DSD/intersex support organisation, but deals specifically with gender dysphoria and gender transitioning, which affects both the general and DSD/intersexed population. Anyone seeking information in relation to DSD/intersex should explore a broad variety of sources so that when deciding who to approach or what to do, they are well informed of the issues from a range of perspectives.[18]

Current Trends in DSD Research

In 2008 a new research consortium was established, called EuroDSD, which was funded by the European Commission under the 7th European Framework Programme (FP7) and comprised thirteen member universities: four German, four UK, two French, one Dutch, one Italian and one Swedish (Hiort, 2010: 6). According to the project's co-ordinator, Dr Olaf Hiort, EuroDSD aims were the 'development of novel diagnostic strategies to identify currently unknown causes of DSD [and to…] design and validate a DSD GeneChip to offer the opportunity for rapid genetic analysis in DSD' (Hiort, 2009, my insertion). To this end EuroDSD members have been gathering and exchanging 'biological material (blood or its derivatives, tissue, urine)' (EuroDSD, 2008: 1) and extracting DNA from patients for 'identification of novel genetic markers for DSD' (EuroDSD, 2009a). In relation to urine and plasma, EuroDSD requested that regular samples be taken from patients at 3–5 days old, 30 days old, 60 days old, 6 months, 12 months and annually thereafter (EuroDSD, 2009b). Clinical information drawn from these samples has been compiled in a 'tightly controlled' registry (Ahmed, 2009: 6).

The concern here for many intersex patient advocates is that the current focus on using genetic information in the prevention of DSDs resonates with the 'eugenic' practices of the past (Hinkle, nd–a). Sophia Siedlberg, who is both a geneticist and intersex advocate with OII, suggests that many patient groups 'fear that EuroDSD will be motivated more by social cleansing than actually providing a framework for healthcare' (Siedlberg, 2009). This may sound alarmist, but for decades clinicians have been administering a drug called dexamethasone to pregnant mothers thought to be carrying a baby 'at risk' of being born with ambiguous genitalia (Sytsma, 2006).[19] In resource-poor regions where dexamethasone is prohibitively expensive, mothers simply terminate the pregnancy (Warne & Raza, 2008). Thus, the combination of social ideals and biomedical technology is already eliminating ambiguity before birth.

In addition to clinical aims EuroDSD also had commercial aims to generate 'added value for Europe; […] and [bring] new products to the market' (EuroDSD, nd–a). It also sought and obtained sponsorship of its events, which suggests a model increasingly attractive to economic interests (EuroDSD, nd–b).

Though the funding for EuroDSD finished in 2011, maintenance and collection of data continue under a new body, the International DSD, or I-DSD, Registry. Funded by the UK Medical Research Council until 2016, I-DSD suggests that 'this seems to be the right moment to consider extending the use of the registry' (Ahmed, 2012: 3). Access to the registry remains 'tightly controlled', however (Ahmed, 2012: 6). Prospective users of the registry must apply to the I-DSD Panel for approval. Only two categories of user are permitted: clinical partners and research partners (Ahmed, 2012:

4). Clinical partners must be able to prove that they are 'members of a national or international clinical professional society' (Ahmed, 2012: 4). Prospective research partners must provide the I-DSD panel with 'details of their proposed study' (Ahmed, 2012: 4). If satisfied, the panel will 'approve the use of the Registry by the research partner for a fixed period of time' and an 'administration fee may be levied' (Ahmed, 2012: 4).

Biomedical discourse has long been central in the social practice of maintaining and regulating the sex dualism. The gathering of such a vast repertoire of data and the privileging of access within biomedicine means that not only does ambiguity become invisible but any emergent practices aimed at eliminating ambiguity are also rendered invisible and therefore difficult to contextualise.

Conclusion

At the outset of this chapter sex was described as a regulatory mechanism employed in a variety of power strategies. An underlying premise of these power strategies involves the strict dualistic ordering of sex through the socially informed trope of heterosexual copulation. This trope has informed the structure of biomedical knowledge for almost two centuries as it has endeavoured to regulate and maintain the social order through the elimination of 'ambiguity'. Initial attempts by biomedicine focused on identifying a key sex signifier. When gonads were viewed as inadequate for this purpose, attention shifted to the surgical elimination of ambiguity and the construction of gender, but this too was contested. Current biomedical practices involve the manipulation of meaning, with two consequences. First, the use of obscure terminology and acronyms means that only the initiated will understand what is signified. Thus, ambiguity is effectively rendered invisible, even perhaps to those individuals to whom the term is applied. Second, the disordering of ambiguity positions it firmly within the biomedical discourse of the undesirable and justifies the development of prenatal genetic and hormonal technologies aimed at its elimination. While the term 'disorder of sex development' or 'DSD' might allow individuals to seek treatment without feeling that they must subscribe to an ambiguous gender identity, perhaps we should ask who is benefiting from these disordering practices. The recent emphasis on the economic potential of DSD research, the involvement of corporate entities and the privileging of access to data suggests that the elimination of ambiguity is gaining recognition as a prestigious and potentially lucrative enterprise, which may lead to the emergence of new power strategies. In a society that maintains a sex dualism, mechanisms to eliminate 'ambiguity' will proliferate.

Notes

[1]   The term 'ambiguity' is understood here as a bio-social construct that emerges at the boundaries of the sex/gender dualism. Much in the same way that Judith Butler, in relation to psychoanalysis, describes 'the law as productive of the very phenomenon it later claims to channel or repress' (Butler, 1990: 88), 'ambiguity' is understood as a product of biomedical discourse as it engages in the maintenance and regulation of sex. It is the 'other' category that emerges with the delineation of two sexes.

[2]   Morphology is a branch of biology dealing with the form of organisms. In this context morphology refers to the body's form (Kirkpatrick, 1990: 870).

[3]   Androgen insensitivity syndrome (AIS) describes an individual who has XY chromosomes and testes, which produce 'masculinising' hormones, but due to a gene alteration the cells in the body do not respond to these hormones and feminise rather than masculinise. There are degrees of AIS: complete AIS (CAIS) 'is a condition in which the external genitalia are completely female in appearance, but the internal female reproductive structures are missing' (Warne, 1997: 7); Partial AIS (PAIS) 'is a variant of AIS in which affected children are born with [varying degrees of] masculinised genitalia' (Warne, 1997: 7), commonly referred to as Prader stages (Sytsma, 2006: 242). For an illustration of genital variation, *see* the *Handbook for Parents* (Consortium, 2006b: 73).

[4]   It should be mentioned that many people with conditions described in the literature as 'intersexed' do not identify with the term. For a further discussion, *see* Chapter 12, Sex Chromosome variations: Klinefelter's Syndrome and Chapter 13, Sex Chromosome Variations: Turner Syndrome, in Catherine Harper's book *Intersex* (Harper, 2007: 143–82).

[5]   Some clinicians in the USA have been prescribing dexamethasone to mothers pregnant with foetuses with congenital adrenal hyperplasia thought to be 'at risk' of developing ambiguous genitalia. However, dexamethasone has not been approved for this purpose by the Institutional Review Board (IRB) or the Food and Drug Administration (FDA) (Feder, nd). Research indicates that '[c]hildren exposed prenatally to dexamethasone for CAH show problems with working memory, verbal processing, and anxiety' (Feder, nd). Given the lack of proper regulation, many bioethicists are concerned that these mothers are not in a position to give

fully informed consent and that children are being put at medical risk to alleviate cosmetic concerns (Feder, nd).

[6] As early as 1951 Money conducted research that suggested a healthy gender identity was not reliant on 'normal' genitalia. This document formed Money's senior dissertation for PhD and can only be accessed through writing to the Widener Library at Harvard University. For a discussion of this document, *see* John Colapinto's book *As Nature Made Him: The Boy Who Was Raised as a Girl* (Colapinto, 2000: 233–5).

[7] Karyotype generally refers to a person's chromosomal makeup. In this context karyotype refers primarily to the sex chromosomes, e.g. XY, XX, XO, XXY, etc.

[8] The information sheets – which provide a range of information on a wide variety of medical conditions, arranged in alphabetical order – are available on the Irish Health Service Executive's website.

[9] The group identified is the Turner Contact Group Ireland: <http://www.tcgi.ie> (*see* HSE, 2012g).

[10] *See* <http://www.tcgi.ie>.

[11] *See* <http://www.livingwithcah.com>.

[12] *See* <http://www.ksa-uk.uk>.

[13] *See* <http:// www.aissgg.org>.

[14] *See* <http:// www.dsdfamilies.org>.

[15] *See* <http://www.oiiinternational.com/oiiuk/>.

[16] *See* <http:// www.accordalliance.org>.

[17] *See* <http://www.teni.ie>.

[18] In seeking support, information or advice in relation to DSD/intersex, there are several channels an Irish person can explore. First, anyone looking for medical/diagnostic information or psychological support can go to their general practitioner, who may then refer the person to a specialist clinician or psychologist/psychiatrist. Second, there are many different support organisations relating both to specific conditions and to DSD/intersex in general. Those mentioned in the text of this chapter represent a small sample of what is available. Some of these organisations have Irish members and may be in a position to put enquirers in touch with people based in Ireland who have the same condition or similar concerns. Many organisations have online chat rooms or blog spots, which allow members to explore questions or discuss issues and experiences. Finally, it should be mentioned that there is no single guiding principle uniting all these organisations. There are many different opinions and approaches.

[19] For more on the ethics of using dexamethasone, *see* Sharon Sytsma's article, 'The Ethics of Using Dexamethasone to Prevent Virilization of Female Fetuses' (in Sytsma, 2006), and also Fetaldex.org (2012).

CHAPTER 11

'Sexual Addiction': Medical Diagnosis or Social Construct? An Irish Perspective

Ben Hughes

Introduction

The concept of 'out-of-control' sexual behaviour has been popularly referred to as 'sexual addiction' since the 1970s. The concept emerged in the USA in the post-sexual revolution period of the 1960s and is associated with the socio-cultural context of that era. A lack of consensus exists, however, regarding the concept itself and the terminology and criteria surrounding it, all of which remain highly debated (Kingston and Firestone, 2008).

While Orford (1978) was one of the first to propose the conceptualization of out-of-control sexuality in terms of addiction, popular recognition of the term 'sexual addiction' is more commonly associated with Patrick Carnes' (1983) descriptive publication *Out of the Shadows: Understanding Sexual Addiction*. His work ignited a debate about whether or not out-of-control sexuality should be viewed as an addiction. Contemporary terms to describe out-of-control sexuality (Giugliano, 2009) include impulsive sexuality, sexual behaviour disorder and hypersexuality (Manley and Koehler, 2001; Kafka, 2010). The terms 'sexual addiction' or 'compulsive sexual behaviour' (Carnes, 1983; Coleman, 1986) are frequently used simultaneously and the choice of term used often indicates the individual's philosophical beliefs or professional background. Despite the ongoing debate regarding how best to describe this issue, all the descriptions have more similar traits than differences (Raymond et al., 2003). For the purposes of this chapter, the term 'sexual addiction' will be used because it is the term that corresponds with the description used by the participants in the study on which this chapter is based.[1]

The study forms part of PhD research funded by the Irish Research Council for the Humanities and Social Sciences (IRCHSS) and reports on ongoing Irish research into the lived experience of self-identified 'sexual addicts' and the experiences of treatment providers working in clinical practice in the area of sexuality. A qualitative method of investigation was used, involving 88 participants. Individual interviews were conducted with 43 self-identified sexual addicts and with 45 treatment providers who work with this phenomenon in clinical practice.[2] The treatment providers come from medical, social work, educational and other therapeutic settings. The sexual addicts come from a variety of social, professional and age backgrounds; they self-identified their own behaviour as being addictive.[3] Throughout the chapter, quotations taken from the participants' interviews are used to illustrate points. The term (TP) after a name indicates that the quotation belongs to a treatment provider; the term (SA) indicates that the quotation belongs to a self-identified sexual addict. Pseudonyms are used throughout to preserve the participants' anonymity.

The primary purpose of this chapter is to analyse and critique the concept of sexual addiction from two perspectives, namely the self-identified sexual addict and the treatment provider, within an Irish context. The chapter begins with an examination of the concepts of addiction and behavioural addiction, the category into which sexual addiction is designated. The concept of sexual addiction is examined in terms of Carnes' (1983) theoretical framework and the socio-historical context from which the concept has arisen. Alternative explanations for 'dysregulated' sexuality (Winters et al., 2010) are outlined and discussed. How these explanations challenge the concept of sexual addiction is also considered. The remainder of the chapter focuses on sexuality in Ireland and the concept of sexual addiction as understood by the research participants. Particular attention is given to the expression and function of sexual addiction as it is perceived and experienced in the Irish context. The therapeutic supports and challenges that arise when responding to this issue are analysed and the concept of sexual addiction is considered in relation to contemporary sexual health policy in Ireland.

Sexual Addiction

The Socio-Historical Context of Sexual Addiction

The 1960s were characterised by a sexual revolution that marked a radical shift in sexual attitudes and behaviours (Irvine, 1995). Klassen et.al. (1990) argue, however, that the metaphor of a sexual revolution exaggerates the actual sexual changes that happened during the 1960s. Despite disagreement on how best to describe such social changes, Smith (1990) claims that significant attitudinal and behavioural shifts occurred regarding issues such as pre-marital sex, birth control and homosexuality, among others.

Many people embraced the sexual freedom of the 1960s, but opposition to it also emerged. The radical changes in the area of sexuality could be difficult to accept, especially for those who wished to retain traditional social values. Opponents of the liberal sexual agenda argued that sexual freedom resulted in social upheaval, arguments that were expressed by political, moral and social lobbies.[4] For example, the AIDS epidemic in the 1980s was frequently linked to sexual permissiveness and the sexual activity of bisexual and gay men and was used by conservatives to argue against non-traditional sexual behaviours (Rotello, 1998). Due to the social anxiety and change of attitudes towards sexuality, Smith (1990) argues, a number of liberal sexual trends did slow down and some reversed during the 1980s, culminating in the emergence of what has been described as a sexual counter-revolution (Smith, 1999).[5] It was in this anxiety-filled context that Carnes (1983) published his book on sexual addiction.

While there was little scientific evidence to suggest that sexuality could be addictive, a social and moral climate existed where the concept of sexual addiction became an acceptable explanation for out-of-control sexual behaviour (Schwartz and Brasted, 1985). The concept of sexual addiction grew in tandem with the sexual counter-revolution, which Cohen (2012) argues was a well-structured ideological campaign that was socially divisive and politically influential, polarising social conservatives and liberals on the issue of sexuality, among other issues.

Opinion remains divided on the validity of the concept of sexual addiction, ranging from Reay et al. (2012), who believe that it is a pseudo-scientific moral construct that disapproves of non-traditional sexuality, to Carnes (1983), who claims that it is an authentic addictive disorder. The development of the concept has been aided by the increasing medicalisation of sexuality (Tiefer, 2007) and the celebrity status associated with sexual addiction (Reay et al., 2012). Despite the growing popularity of the concept, it remains a contested issue that has invoked scholarly disagreement.[6]

The Conceptualisation of Sexual Addiction and its Controversies

Sexual addiction, as proposed by Carnes (1983), is typically conceptualised in terms of an individual who has lost control over his/her sexual behaviour, but who continues to engage in the behaviour despite the recurrence of significant negative consequences. The reason why 'excessive' sexual behaviour is perceived as a possible 'addiction' is that it contains some of the observable traits typically associated with addiction to psychoactive substances, such as craving, impaired control and high rates of relapse (Wines, 1997).

Carnes (1983) describes sexual addiction as any sexually related compulsive behaviour that interferes with normal living and causes severe stress on family, friends, loved ones and one's work environment. He identifies the following characteristics as indicators of sexual addiction.

1. A pattern of out-of-control sexual behaviour despite adverse consequences
2. Persistent pursuit of self-destructive or high-risk behaviour
3. Ongoing desire to limit sexual behaviour
4. Sexual obsessions become a primary coping mechanism
5. Increasing amounts of sexual experience required
6. Severe mood changes around sexual activity
7. Neglectful of other aspects of life

These characteristics are frequently used in clinical practice and in popular literature. They are deemed useful in the absence of clearly defined criteria for the diagnosis of the concept in either the DSM (*Diagnostic and Statistical Manual of Mental Disorders*) or the International Classification of Diseases (ICD).[7] The concept enjoyed preliminary recognition when it was included in the *Diagnostic and Statistical Manual of Manual Disorders* (DSM-III-Revision in 1987) (American Psychiatric Association, 1987), but since its removal from the DSM-IV in 1994 (American Psychiatric Association, 1994), its validity remains questionable. This lack of agreed criteria is viewed as a hindrance to the recognition, diagnosis and treatment of this behaviour (Finlayson et al., 2001).

The pattern of sexual behaviour is typically characterised by out-of-control behaviour, secrecy, shame, compulsion and high-risk behaviour. Despite the consequences, the 'addict' is driven to satisfy their sexual needs and gradually this pattern becomes more frequent, and more intense sexual experiences are required. The predisposing factors associated with sexual addiction are often linked to early formative experiences, family of origin and child-hood sexualisation, which have fractured the individual's ability to develop and maintain satisfactory relationships. It is argued that sexual addiction is not measured on the amount or type of sexual involvement, but is more concerned with the individual's disposi-tion, their motivation, the impact of the behaviour on their lives and their inability to stop (Goodman, 1998). However, as outlined in the next few paragraphs, the concept of sexual addiction remains contentious and lacks consensus regarding classification, definition, diagnostic criteria and treatment (Gold and Heffner, 1998; Kingston and Firestone, 2008; Kaplan and Krueger, 2010).

In addition to the explanation offered by proponents of the concept of sexual addiction (Carnes, 1983; Griffin-Shelley, 1993; Goodman, 1998; Giuglino, 2006; Kafka, 2010), excessive or dysregu-lated sexual behaviour is associated with a variety of physiological and psychological issues. The out-of-control sexuality may be a manifestation of underlying or co-morbid conditions, which when treated ease the condition and regularise the sexual behaviour (Chughtai et al., 2010). The primary medical syndromes associated with dysregulated sexuality include conditions such as depression, especially bi-polar disorder, dementia, frontal lobe dysfunction, Kluver-Bucy syndrome (KBS) and Klein Levine syndrome (KLS) (Finlayson et al., 2001; Chughtai et al., 2010; Samenow & Finlay-son, 2010).[8] Dysregulated sexuality is also associated with head traumas, invasive surgery, impulse control disorder and medica-tions, particularly those used for Parkinson's disease (Chughtai et al., 2010). Out-of-control sexual behaviour may also be indicative of childhood sexual trauma and is reported as a common conse-quence of child sexual abuse, arising from the assumption that sex is the only way to be loved (Herman and Hirschman, 2000).

It may be a way of re-enacting or resolving the childhood sexual trauma (Parsons et al., 2008) as Elaine (TP), a psychotherapist I interviewed, explains:

> They continue searching for something through sex: trying to make sense of feelings that they were left with – from sexual abuse ... it's like the child trying to make sense of something and they keep doing it again and again and again and so they keep getting into this and they're still not making sense.

Excessive sexual behaviour has also been observed among those recovering from substance abuse (Washton and Boundy, 2000). Different substances exert positive and negative influences on sexuality, which may result in behaviours such as inhibited desire or hypersexuality (Finlayson et al., 2001). Furthermore, sexual addictive behaviour may represent a compensation for the loss of a substance, as Warren (TP), a medical doctor in this study explains: 'I find if somebody had been addicted to alcohol and then, you know, gets into recovery, I think what happens then they switch addictions and they become addicted to sex.'

Participants in this study state that sexual addictive behaviour was used in order to deal with a multiplicity of emotional needs. Similar to Torres and Gore-Felton's (2007) findings, some of the participants used sexual addictive behaviour to increase feelings of psychological and emotional wellbeing, and to manage loneliness and low self-esteem. Sexual addictive behaviour is also associated with relationship insecurity and anxiety linked to attachment styles in early childhood (Zapf et al., 2008).

There are also social scientists, philosophers and civil rights activists who view the concept of 'the sexual addict' as a social construct rather than a clinical entity. It is generally understood in terms of 'a historical character constructed from the sexual ambivalences of a particular era' (Irvine, 1995: 429). This view is echoed by a participant in this study, Dara (TP), a psychotherapist who has worked for many years with individuals presenting with substance abuse. In clinical practice he recognises out-of-control sexuality among some of his clients, and he believes that there is a need to address this issue. However, he is also of the opinion that the label 'sex addiction' is an American construct that is not particularly useful. He says: 'I would have thought it's a bit of a myth and a bit of a construct; it's an American thing to label things, but that's my inclination to feel that way.'

In contrast to those who consider the term 'sexual addiction' beneficial, there are those who consider it to be a restrictive social construct. In conceptualising excessive sexual behaviour, Yvonne (TP), a clinical psychologist, prefers to view the issue from a behavioural perspective:

> I don't think that labelling it as a sexual addiction is particularly helpful ... It's not the sexual addiction that's the problem. The sexual addiction is a response to a person's story that they have lived and the sense that they have made of it and also how their lived experience predisposes them in particular ways. So, I think there's something kind of depersonalising about the term 'sex addict'.

The proposal to explain the concept of sexual addiction in terms of a culturally specific social construct does not mean that the experience of sexual addiction is not real and deserving of attention. In fact, the concept of sexual addiction has helped many people to achieve a better understanding of their behaviour and has led them to beneficial therapeutic help. It is equally important to note that the views on sexual behaviour are constantly evolving and that while sexual addiction may have been a popular concept from the 1970s onwards, as Hawkes (2004: 21) observes, 'what is defined and experienced as acceptable and unacceptable presentations of sex is highly contingent.'

The medicalisation of sexuality is increasingly noticeable, for example in the emergence of issues such as erectile dysfunction or premature ejaculation (Tiefer, 1996), but also in the increasing list of psychosexual disorders in the DSM, including Kafka's proposal (2010) for hypersexuality.[9] The medicalisation of sexuality is also observable in the field of addiction medicine, which is a generic term describing the medical speciality and process of dealing with individuals who are seeking help with a substance or behavioural addiction (Latt et al., 2009). In terms of sexual addiction, treatment recommendations involve a range of approaches, including psychological, educational and pharmacological inputs (Coleman, 2003). Despite the scepticism among some professionals, there has also been increased discussion and training regarding professional competence in relation to sexual addiction, particularly in the addiction and counselling fields (Hagedorn, 2009).

The medical dimension of sexuality has been further affirmed as the concept of sexual addiction has developed in the twelve-step movement, based on the pre-existing model of Alcoholics Anonymous (AA), whereby self-identified sexual addict claimants understand their behaviour in terms of the medical model of addiction (Irvine, 1995). Internationally there are at least eight twelve-step groups in existence, which offer support for those with sexual addiction; there are two of these groups in Ireland. The Irish groups are Sexaholics Anonymous (SA) and Sex and Love Anonymous (SLAA). In recent years a sexual addiction industry has emerged, primarily in the USA, evident in specialised treatment centres, sexual addiction professionals and literature providing a multifaceted 'treatment' package for sexual addiction. The study participants explained that this pattern is reflected on a smaller scale here in Ireland.

Professional awareness of sexual addiction occurred at a later stage in Ireland in comparison to the USA, and has been mainly confined to mental health professionals, especially psychotherapists, particularly those working in the addiction field. The initial development of the twelve-step groups for sexual addiction began in the 1980s. Professional training became available in Ireland two decades later, in 2000, providing training and resources to professionals, mainly focusing on psychotherapists, medical doctors, psychiatrists and psychologists. Subsequently, a growing number of psychotherapists began to advertise professional therapeutic support for sexual addiction. It is only in the past three years, however, that the availability of professional help has been offered to sexual addicts in the residential treatment sector, which traditionally deals with addiction to psychoactive substances, in Ireland. While professional training has been sought by many clinicians (Hagedorn, 2009), the idea of developing sexual addiction into a medical specialism monopolised by the trained expert is viewed suspiciously by some. Fergal (TP) is a social worker who once worked in America in the area of sexual health and addiction and now works in Ireland. He is currently working with individuals who present with sexual addiction issues. While Fergal (TP) acknowledges that individuals encounter problems in terms of sexual behaviour, he is also mindful of how the construct of sexual addiction facilitates the growth of an addiction industry:

I haven't participated in the addiction industry stuff, but I'm aware that people are going around saying they're experts in sexual addiction and also in the States when I was there, there were twelve-step movements around sexual addiction and they became very popular and then they kind of fell back, as in, people weren't going. It was kind of like the sexy topic. Do you know, the sexy addiction in some way.

In comparison to the right-wing moralists who equally facilitate the concept of sexual addiction, Zola (1972) observes that the medical, as opposed to the moral, explanation of out-of-control sexuality is presented as being 'morally neutral'. Zola (1972) warns, however, that medical language frequently masks a combination of moral and social judgements. Indeed, Szasz's (1991) view is that psychiatry, in particular, stigmatises people with moral judgements while camouflaging them as authentic diagnoses.

Levine and Troiden (1988) argue that the concept of sexual addiction is a moral label, not an authentic scientific entity. They argue that the concept merely symbolises a rejection of the liberal sexual behaviour that resulted from the sexual revolution, which was perceived as immoral by right-wing religious conservatives. As a result of changing moral values the term 'sexual addiction' became synonymous with morally objectionable behaviour (Giles, 2006). This is confirmed by the fact that the majority of the designated sexual behaviours viewed as potentially addictive, such as masturbation or cybersex, are behaviours that are not typically associated with procreation. Consequently, the procreative morality of the Judeo-Christian model is encouraged and the recreational script of sexuality is rejected. Furthermore, the emergence of the concept of sexual addiction in the USA took place during a period in which the traditional religious institutions declined, resulting in a moral vacuum. Arguably, when the concept of sexual addiction became known in Ireland, the country was transitioning from being a traditional, Catholic and conservative nation to becoming a more modern and pluralist society (Inglis, 2002a). Religious-based moral undertones are noticeable in some of the treatment programmes available for sexual addiction in the USA, particularly among evangelical Christians, such as the one entitled Every Man's Battle (Edger, 2012), where treatment of sexual addiction is presented in terms of a battle against lust and sexual temptation.[10]

Sexuality and the Socio-Religious Context in Ireland

Sexuality in Ireland has been predominantly understood in terms of the Judeo-Christian tradition.[11] A number of socio-historic factors facilitated the powerful position of control which the Catholic Church assumed in Ireland for centuries, including a near monopoly on morality and sexuality (Corish, 1981; Inglis, 1998b). The Catholic Church's influence was observed in the 'formal and informal enforcement of Catholic social teaching particularly in the area of sexuality' during the establishment of the Free State, and especially noticeable after Éamon de Valera assumed power in 1927 (Howes, 2002: 924). One distinguishing feature of this recent era was the 'architecture of containment' expressed by the creation of a plethora of institutions, such as Magdalene laundries, industrial schools and adoption agencies, which served to hide what was considered 'sexual immorality' (Smith, 2004: 209). As stated in other chapters in this book, this culture of sexual suppression continued through the decades. Gerry (TP), a psychologist working with individuals in the area of sexual abuse, explains how the suppression of sexuality created a culture of silence that allowed problematic sexual issues to be pushed underground: 'In the old style Ireland, sex just didn't get talked about and therefore it was pushed underground and therefore if you had a problem, whether it was even erectile dysfunction to sexualised behaviour to compulsion, it was difficult to get help for it.'

Fergal (TP), a social worker with training in psychotherapy, describes the legacy of the traditional socio-sexual climate in Ireland as follows:

> We've come a long way in Ireland, but we still have a long way to go around attitudes towards sex and comfortableness about talking about sex ... I know in my own training, you know, sex was hardly ever mentioned and people did not feel comfortable talking about it. So there is a whole shame and guilt and phobia around sex as an issue and the role and the place of sex in our lives as human beings.

While the notion of the sexual revolution remains contested (Scott, 1998), the 1960s are correctly, or incorrectly, perceived as a watershed period for Irish sexuality (Howes, 2002). Noel (TP), a psychotherapist working with a generic clientele and trained in sexual addiction counselling, observes the shift from sexual suppression to sexual promiscuity that he associates with the sexual revolution of the 1960s in Ireland:

> On the one hand there was the repression-suppression that we had for so long. Nobody talked about it but people were sexual. Then we had the 60s flower-power and all of that and the whole thing swung, the pendulum swung totally the other way, and now we have promiscuity and the huge mushrooming of STIs. There's all of that, so you have to get the balance.

Noel's assertion regarding the mushrooming of STIs in Ireland is consistent with the increase in STIs as reported by the Health Protection Surveillance Centre (HPSC, 2010).

Ferriter (2009), on the other hand, claims that the sexual-revolution did not happen in Ireland until the 1970s, and even then it should not be over-exaggerated because sex remained a taboo issue for years to come.[12] He claims that the sexual discourse remained focused on controversial issues, such as contraception, for the next thirty years, highlighted by the 'condom train' excursion to Belfast in 1971 and debates over divorce and abortion, culminating in the abortion referendum in 1983. Ardagh (1995) argues that Ireland experienced some type of sexual revolution in the 1990s when people increasingly rejected the power exercised by the Church on sexual matters. As highlighted in Chapters 4 and 5 of this book, significant decisions were made in relation to the decriminalisation of homosexuality, in 1993, and the recognition of same-sex unions, in 2011. Inglis (2006) argues that in the context of the gradual transition from a traditional society to a Celtic Tiger economy, sexuality has moved from being characterised by self-denial to being characterised by self-indulgence. According to Salazar (2008), Ireland is going through a major transition, involving a shift from obedience-sexuality to knowledge-sexuality. This entails a move from reliance on indoctrination to a cognitive model involving personal learning, a transition that is both challenging and complex (Inglis, 2006). Inglis argues that the transition from the obedience model to the self-regulation model is challenging for those who cannot negotiate sexuality successfully.

Another contextual factor related to the development of sexual addiction that is particularly pertinent to the Irish context is the issue of shame. Inglis (1998a) claims that sexuality, which was controlled by the Church and spoken about only in terms of confession, generated feelings of shame and guilt. Shame is believed to be one of the strongest predictors of sexual addiction (Reid, 2010; Gilliland et al., 2011), and may offer an insight into understanding sexual addiction in Ireland. This corresponds with what Hanna (TP), a psychotherapist with specialist training in sexual addiction, encounters in her Irish practice: 'Sex addiction is the most shame-based. There's a toxic shame around it and I don't know if that's partly to do with our culture, our Irish culture, but it's really, really difficult. I can't tell you how difficult it is for clients around sex.'

Another factor associated with the creation of sexual addiction is the experience of poor emotional and affectionate relationships (Zapf et al., 2008). Inglis (1998b) explains that the repressive sexual culture in Ireland often included the denial of physical and emotional affection between children and parents, which was often justified as a preparation for emigration or postponed marriage. The individual has a desire for intimacy, but is inhibited from achieving this due to their poorly developed attachment skills and a learned fear of relationships (Zapf et al., 2008), resulting in many sexual experiences without emotion or affection. Rose (SA), a sexual addict, associates her sexual addictive behaviour with a poorly developed relationship with her father:

> At about thirteen or fourteen I became sexually active without really knowing what I was doing, but I suppose it stemmed back from my relationship with my father, where I didn't have a relationship with him. He was very cold, very unaffectionate, and very tyrannical in the way he behaved so I sought that affection from somebody else. But the issue was, I mixed sex up with affection and intimacy. I would look at other people who were in relationships and really craved that intimacy with somebody, but then I would do the complete opposite and go out and sleep with somebody who I didn't know. So I suppose the trigger events were things not going well in other parts of my life.

Furthermore, as a result of the Catholic Church's control of sexuality in Ireland (Whyte, 1980; Whelan and Fahey, 1996; Inglis, 1998b; Hug, 2001; Ferriter, 2009), a culture of religious-driven rigidity emerged, which is associated by some commentators with the creation of sexual addictive behaviour (Edger, 2012). Participants reported that this culture of rigidity was experienced in formal church settings, in schools and in their homes, indicating its prevalence in many aspects of Irish society. Gerry (TP), a psychologist working with individuals in the area of sexual trauma, commented:

> Religion, first and foremost, pushed sex underground. You know it just was never going to be talked about and the only time it was talked about it was in the context of marriage and making babies ... I mean, it was up to the late eighties, early nineties that priests were still teaching sex education ... It didn't make sense and therefore the way it was taught was probably not going to be the best way to pass on the information or else, alternatively, it was a science teacher who taught it within biology, so the whole concept of emotional connection and sex were never brought together.

Addictive sexual behaviour is often construed as a maladaptive response to prolonged experiences of sexual negativity (Bergner, 2002); such experiences were commonplace in Irish society, as indicated in the data.

Sexual Addiction in Ireland

The concept of sexual addiction, primarily associated with the USA, emerged in Ireland during the 1980s and followed a similar developmental pattern to that which occurred in the USA. Initially, it was accepted by individuals who identified themselves with out-of-control sexual behaviour and formed self-help groups. At a later stage interest began to grow among professionals, and subsequently specialised training became available, which was mainly accessed by mental health professionals and psychotherapists. Since then, professional interest in Ireland has grown to such an extent that it can sustain occasional courses run by American sexual addiction specialists, such as Dr Susan Campling (Gantly, 2011). Despite the interest in some quarters, the concept of sexual addiction is debated among Irish treatment providers and arguments are often presented in the popular press and in professional journals. While some claim that sexual addition is increasing in clinical practice and that the increase may be associated with factors such as the economic recession – and also linked to media coverage, such as the recent screening of the movie *Shame*, which is based on sexual addiction (Coleman, 2011; Bramhill, 2012) – others argue that the concept lacks scientific validity. Michael (TP), an addiction therapist specialising in sexual addiction, explains:

> Part of the difficulty among professionals is that there's some justified theoretical disagreement as to whether there is such a thing as sexual addiction. That's more of an issue for what might be called our mainstream professionals. I mean, psychotherapy is a relatively mainstream profession and becoming more so, but you know, you could say that social work and psychiatry and even psychology are more mainstream and within those professions I think part of the difficulty is that sexual addiction might be seen as a fairly woolly concept that's not in the DSM and therefore not an official condition.

In Ireland many professionals, mainly psychotherapists, offer support for sexual addiction in the context of individual psychotherapy in private practice. However, professionals in this study state that there is a lack of specialised help available, which is a challenge when referring patients for help. Unlike the USA, Ireland has no specific residential treatment centres offering sexual addiction treatment, although treatment has recently become available as part of the services provided by treatment centres that cater for those addicted to psychoactive substances.

Expression of Sexual Addictive Behaviour: The Irish Context

There are multiple behavioural expressions of sexual addiction and the common ones include paid-for sex, internet and phone sex, anonymous sex, pornography, exhibitionism, voyeurism, masturbation and fantasy (Carnes, 1992). One recurrent pattern is the pursuit of continuous sexual relationships by individuals hoping that the physical act of sexual engagement will create an intimate relationship, as explained by Angela (SA), a sexual addict who is recovering from substance addiction: 'I think with the men that I was with, I thought that by giving them kind of what they wanted, they would give me what I wanted, and they would stay with me and fill the need I was missing. It never happened'. Pursuing what she wanted, Angela (SA) developed a pattern of unsatisfactory casual sexual relationships in her place of work:

In the nightclub that I worked in, I was with just two or three of the people that were there, do you know what I mean, and I still had to work there … and even the job I got after that, I was only there about two weeks and I was with the boss, do you know what I mean?

Paid-for sex is identified as a behavioural expression of sexual addiction used mostly by men. Masturbation is also a common expression of sexual addiction, with some reporting genital injury and obsessive masturbation. Edward (SA), a sexual addict who is also addicted to gambling, explains:

My masturbation would have increased and I would have done it maybe twice before I saw her [girlfriend] and I saw her most evenings and we would have sex and I would masturbate maybe once or twice when I went home … but that relationship, it was unhealthy, because I knew that sometimes I was nearly too tired to see that particular girl, but I would still do it because of the sex.

The internet has become a popular medium for the sexual addict because of features such as accessibility, anonymity and the seductive nature of the material. Darren (SA), sexual addict and recently divorced, explains his experience:

There was a slow distancing from each other in our marriage relationship and internet porn replaced the void … It became more and more of an issue after the birth of our second child. My wife became more and more withdrawn. I in turn became more withdrawn from the relationship and it was a vicious circle and I turned more and more to escape. My form of escape was either staying up late at night watching TV until you became oblivious and eventually, I suppose, when internet came in and broadband came into the house, it was much easier just to access internet pornography, and that in turn becomes a vicious circle, you become so withdrawn from the other person.

Many of the behaviours that the addict participants have described are also behaviours that other people use to enjoy healthy, pleasurable sexual lives. Goodman (1998) claims that such behaviours, which are commonly associated with sexual addiction, are not necessarily addictive but are identified as addictive or problematic when the impact of the behaviour on the individual's life is examined.

Function of Sexual Addiction: Irish Perspectives

Participants say that sexual addictive behaviour serves a range of different needs. Many say that sex provided attention, acceptance and happiness, which had frequently been missing in their lives. For others, it was their primary source of 'escape' from painful circumstances, such as fear, loss, or anxiety, and it promised the possibility of emotional security. Rose (SA), a sexual addict, recounts her feelings:

> It allowed me to think that I had been accepted in some way for me and in that moment, it meant that I wouldn't be rejected … it was kind of a security. Once I was attracted to a man or once I was involved with a man, then everything was okay and I felt validated in some way.

Sexual addiction is also linked to experiences of sexual abuse. For some, it was a compensation for the experience of being sexually abused, a means to make up for what had been stolen; for others, it was a subconscious effort to re-enact the abuse in order to resolve it. There were some participants who spoke of their sexual addiction in terms of power and control: they could choose where, how and who to engage with sexually. Others perceived their high-risk sexual behaviour as an act of self-sabotage, an expression of self-hatred. Gary (SA), a gay sexual addict in recovery from substance abuse, explains:

> Like, to have sex in a toilet with somebody, there's something crude about it. It wasn't a classic sexual situation. It was

almost as if I needed to compound what I was feeling about myself by acting out in a situation that represented that for me ... I think that is probably a rejection of me, an element of me being disgusted with myself and I don't want to present that disgusting or disgusted side to somebody else ... So it just appeared to be easier to have numbing sex.

Gary (SA) describes his experience of sex as a punishing behaviour that continually reinforced a negative self-image. Sexual addiction was also a means of human survival for those who found themselves in bleak situations, as Ciaran (SA), a gay sexual addict with a history of child sexual abuse and substance abuse, explains: 'I knew very well that this type of sexual behaviour was soul-destroying. It was shameful and embarrassing and made me feel desperate. In a strange way, it was also a lifeline in a very lonely world. It provided human touch and warmth.'

Therapeutic Support

A range of therapeutic supports is used by individuals to help them manage their addictive sexual behaviour, including psychological, medical and psycho-educational approaches (Kaplan and Krueger, 2010). Psychotherapy is one of the main supports discussed among participants and is deemed more effective when it is specific, focused and involves tasks such as journaling, reading and worksheets. Generally, they claim that it is particularly beneficial when it addresses related issues, like depression and sexual abuse, in clinical situations where this is appropriate. Griffin-Shelley (1993) believes that the combination of individual and group psychotherapy plus psycho-educational and twelve-step groups can be effective and can be used simultaneously or as individual components of treatment.

Nathan (1995) claims that there is a certain level of resistance among some professionals to deal with sexual addiction, ranging from incredulity to anger. Participants in this research believe that resistance among Irish professionals is associated with discomfort regarding sexuality. Yvonne (TP), a psychologist working with a cross-section of issues and populations, states that professional competency in the area of sexuality could be enhanced if therapists undertook personal therapeutic work on their own sexuality, attitudes, values and related issues:

> I think that some counsellors skirt around it rather than dealing with it because of their personal discomfort in the area of sexuality or sexualities, you know. So I think that there is space for more training. More training in this area and also in the area of LGBT [lesbian, gay, bisexual and transgender], the whole spectrum of sexuality for a sense of comfort and understanding.

Additional therapeutic support for sexual addiction is available from the twelve-step sexual fellowships (Schneider, 2005) mentioned earlier in the chapter. Participants report various benefits, including the spirit of solidarity that emerges among individuals who have had similar experiences. The fellowships have a spiritual dimension, but are not affiliated with any specific religious organisation. Issues of safety and confidentiality are seen as particularly important, as Finbar (SA), a gay sexual addict, explains:

> It's important to feel safe, so that you can say how it is for you. It's important to feel you can trust the other person and you can say it, confidentially. That comes across in the fellowships. In the one that I have experienced, I got a sense of very decent people who have different degrees of struggles; good days, bad days and that creates the solidarity, you don't feel as alone.

Nathan (1995) claims that there are mixed responses to the usefulness of the twelve-step model. Some perceive the model as being more evangelical than medical, whereas others recommend it and view it as a supplementary component in treatment, and particularly useful when used in conjunction with psychotherapy. Additional therapeutic support for sexual addiction is available in residential treatment centres. As mentioned previously, in the USA there are dedicated treatment centres for sexual addiction, but in England and Ireland sexual addiction treatment is available only in centres established to deal with substance abuse, which have recently developed facilities to treat sexual addiction as well. In Ireland there are currently three residential addiction centres where specific treatment for sexual addiction is offered, while many professionals, mostly psychotherapists, who work in private practice offer non-residential treatment for sexual addiction. Some participants state that the issue of sexual addiction frequently arises when dealing with other substance abuse issues. An individual may initially present for help with substance abuse or anxiety, and it is during the therapeutic process that sexual addiction emerges, confirming the complex combination of interrelated issues (Black et al., 1997; Samenow and Finlayson, 2010). Brian (SA), a sexual addict, who is bisexual and recovering from addiction to psycho-active substances, explains that the close and complex connection between sexual addiction and substance abuse became clear during his treatment in a residential addiction centre:

> I ended up in a treatment centre and my family thought I was going there for drink or drugs but no one knew about the sex and when I got out there, I just spewed it all up. It was like there was this huge weight that I had been carrying on my shoulders for twenty years was gone. It was a huge pressure release because even in the first few weeks in that treatment centre I was suicidal and I just sat for two weeks. I just got to grips with it and just let it all out and said this is what I have been doing since I was a kid.

Problematic sexual behaviour can frequently remain hidden underneath addiction to psychoactive substances (Siegel, 2011), and unresolved sexual issues can be injurious to recovery from psycho-active substances. Group and family psychotherapy for sexual addiction, not commonly available in Ireland, is usually offered by, but not limited to, residential treatment centres. Hook et al. (2008) argue that group therapy is particularly useful for those who are dealing with relationship difficulties and can be used effectively in conjunction with individual psychotherapy. Group therapy provides learning about interpersonal relationships, which is particularly helpful for the sexual addict who struggles with inti-macy and relationships (Swisher, 1995); this requires competent facilitation.

The use of medical support is also a common feature, particularly for those who contract STIs and HIV, which are a common conse-quence of sexual addictive behaviour. Treatment can be sourced from GPs, but is mostly sought from sexual health clinics. Warren (TP), a medical doctor working in the area of sexual health and addiction, emphasises the value of being aware of sexual addiction within a clinical setting:

> If somebody is repeatedly coming in for a treatment for sexual health, you know, with chlamydia one day and gonorrhoea the next, you have to be aware that that there might be an addictive trait and an addictive problem and maybe it is something that needs to be addressed. I'm not a counsellor and I don't have counselling skills, but I would know counsellors and I'd refer appropriately.

Medical support was also discussed in the interviews in terms of using pharmacologic interventions to manage hypersexuality or for co-morbid issues, such as depression (Raymond et al., 2010). A low level of awareness about the relationship between sexuality and other medical conditions was noted among the Irish participants in comparison to the American clinicians, who recommend a bio-psychosocial model requiring a multidisciplinary approach (Samenow and Finlayson, 2010).

In addition, psycho-educational supports (Griffin-Shelley, 1997), such as literature and the internet, were deemed useful by some participants and typically included non-specialist recovery literature and websites in the area of self-help, popular psychology and recovery. Some sexual addicts also acknowledge the support they received from their family members. Alternative supports included homeopathy, mediation, yoga, exercise, diet, helplines and spirituality.

Participants state that therapeutic support is challenging and that its effectiveness may be lessened by a number of factors, such as client motivation, denial, shame and withholding of significant information (Fearing, 1998). As noted by Griffin-Shelley (2009), treating sexual addiction is challenging as many individuals who seek help frequently present with a complex set of issues, such as trauma histories, multiple addictions and strong psychological defences. Griffin-Shelley (2009) also argues that the therapeutic process is more effective when issues such as professional competency, value clarification and ethical guidelines are addressed. From his clinical experience, Coleman (2003) acknowledges that the presenting issues among sexual addicts are complicated and he suggests that awareness and use of a variety of treatment approaches may be beneficial.

Therapeutic Challenges in Sexual Addiction

A multitude of therapeutic challenges are identified and include issues such as the professional's competence and the therapeutic relationship, among others. Treatment providers state that difficulties arise with clients who display issues such as ambivalence, denial or dishonesty. Treatment providers may demonstrate resistance, incompetence or unprofessionalism, as Elizabeth (TP), a psychotherapist explains: 'Even if a client wants to talk about it, it might be the therapist who is uncomfortable with the issue or with listening to what the person might have to say to them.'

In addition, Hagedorn (2009) claims that clinicians experience added difficulties due to lack of a recognised diagnosis in the DSM, which limits agreement on issues such as assessment, diagnosis, referral and treatment. Brid (TP), a cognitive behavioural therapist (CBT) specialising in sexual addiction counselling, identifies the problem of abstinence where sexual addiction is concerned: 'With the help of treatment or fellowships, you can decide that you are not going to use drugs and that you are not going to gamble and that you are not going to use alcohol, but what do you do with your sexuality? Do you remove it from yourself?'

Another challenging area involves the client–professional relationship and it requires skill to create a relationship where trust is established and where caring can be negotiated ethically. The sexual addict may have difficulties recognising and maintaining sexual and emotional boundaries in treatment (Herring, 2001). Additional challenges are associated with legal concerns regarding issues such as child sexual abuse, prostitution, the transmission of HIV and disclosure, among others. Moreover, there is a general misperception or confusion as to the nature of sexual addiction. Darren (SA), a sexual addict and recently divorced, explains:

> I've been called a pervert and a paedophile by my wife and it's that immediate association that anything to do with sex is immoral and illegal. It's a problem, nobody wants to speak about it or talk about it. It's becoming a little more open in

Ireland, but it's still very much a taboo subject. It may be more open talking about sexual issues and sexual relationships, but not about sexual addiction. So there's no acceptable forum for it publicly and without that, it's driven underground. So it's harder for people to seek help and it's harder for people to accept it as a true addiction.

The concept of sexual addiction is also challenging among those who are gay or bisexual. Suggestions have been made that the prevalence of sexual addiction is higher among this group (Baum and Fishman, 1994), and consequently concerns have been raised regarding sexual disease, especially HIV, among this population (Benotsch et al., 2001). These concerns are linked with a variety of sexual-risk behaviours associated with this group, often involving non-monogamous sexuality (Grov et al., 2010). Hoff and Beougher (2010) explain that there is often a higher tolerance for non-monog-amous or recreational sex, particularly among gay men, which frequently does not entail any emotional involvement, patterns which are typical indicators of sexual addiction (Carnes, 1983). Blumstein and Schwartz (1983) draw attention to the fact that there are different cultural traditions regarding sexual behaviours within the gay community, and Bell and Weinberg (1978) explain that behaviours such as anonymous sexual encounters have a significant meaning among this group. Yvonne (TP), a psychologist who has worked extensively with the gay community, summarises some of the complex issues that arise in relation to sexual addiction among this population:

> Some people, perhaps within the gay community, might fear being labelled negatively with this particular term. And rightfully so ... however, within the community it would be important that there is an understanding of the differ-ence between 'sexual addiction' and sexual choice. All sexual encounters need to be encounters on the basis of sexual choice and if someone is having an encounter with someone who is a sexual addict and they don't know it, then that interferes with the sexual choice of partner. But I think that while celebrat-ing freedom of sexuality, it is important also to recognise the potential for abuses within that. Think of your responsibility within the community to protect the people who are sexual

addicts from continuing, just like you do if your friend is an alcoholic. You try to create other social experiences that don't involve drink, so I think that it's a conversation that would be very valuable to have.

Ley (2012) acknowledges that the issue of sexual addiction within the gay community is complex and opinion remains divided. Nonetheless, he argues that it is not the casual dimension of the behaviour that is creating a vulnerability to disease, but rather the high-risk element where self-control is relinquished.

Sexuality and Sexual Health Policy in Ireland

There is currently no national sexual health strategy in Ireland, despite continuous calls for a strategy that would co-ordinate policy and service provision regarding sexuality (Layte et al., 2006; O'Shea, 2007; Lynch, 2009; Department of Health and Children, 2009). If there were a national strategy, it would be expected to include a focus on sexual addiction. Internationally, there is a proposal to reconsider addictive sexual behaviour as a hypersexuality disorder, which was to be included in the 2013 edition of the DSM (Kafka, 2010). This proposal was rejected due to a lack of unity about how this concept is to be understood. While the debate continues about the concept, some of the participants in this study called for assistance on this issue. Martin (TP), a social worker working in the area of addiction, acknowledges the lack of scientific and diagnostic agreement on sexual addiction and the need for guidance:

> From a professional point of view, a diagnostic tool for counselling or for assessment would be helpful. It might open up a few things that we wouldn't normally look for. I'd have no problem with that as a tool being used because these things come up anyhow and it would be as well for me to be better informed and to get a proper understanding or diagnosis of the problem if it existed ... So for me to have some tools and interventions to diagnose, that would probably be useful.

More is known about sexual knowledge, attitudes and practices in Irish society as a result of increasing research in this field.[13] In the absence of any data directly relating to sexual addiction, data gathered by agencies in the field of sexual health and addiction are worth measuring as potential proxy measures. While it would be inaccurate to conclude that an increase in STIs, for example, is an indication of an increase in sexual addiction, it is not unreasonable to expect that there is an association. A report from the Health Protection Surveillance Centre (HPSC) on sexually transmitted infections (STIs) in Ireland draws attention to the steady increase of STIs since 1995 (HPSC, 2011a).[14] Yvonne (TP), a psychologist working in the area of sexuality, argues that the Irish sexual health clinic setting might be a useful site to investigate how to respond to persons in attendance, whose sexual behaviours may be addictive:

> People who are coming in regularly with sexually transmitted infections, there needs to be someone available who will enquire into the sexual behaviour and whether it is addictive or whether it is normal, but either way how it is that this person is not protecting himself or herself within the sexual encounter and explore what that is about … I think that there is an opportunity for education and provision within the GUM[15] clinics.

In terms of human immunodeficiency virus (HIV), the HPSC's (2011b) Annual Report of 2010 states that the number of new infections has decreased in recent years, and this is largely due to fewer infections occurring heterosexually. However, transmission continues and concern is expressed about the increased number of new cases among men who have sex with men (MSM), which is currently the principal means of transmission. This pattern corresponds with the evidence from other Western European countries (HPSC, 2011b). The relationship between sexual disease and sexual addiction, particularly among the MSM population, is discussed frequently (Dodge et al., 2008) in the literature and remains a concern among treatment providers. Warren (TP), a medical doctor working in sexual health, describes this with reference to a patient he has treated:

> I have a patient who goes to a sauna[16] and he knows what he's doing is very, very wrong. He has unprotected sex with men one after the next and he's going to get HIV. There's no doubt in my mind and he knows he will, but there's nothing he can

do to stop it. He just feels totally disempowered … I think part of him wants to punish himself.

Recommendations have been made, including those of the Royal College of Physicians of Ireland (RCPI, 2011), to respond more effectively to the threat of HIV and other sexually transmitted infections. Renewed attention is required regarding the predisposing factors associated with sexual health, such as social, educational and economic factors, among others (RCPI, 2011). It may also be beneficial to include the concept of sexual addiction for consideration when examining STIs. Professional training about sexual addiction increases awareness, provides skills and equips the clinician to identify underlying issues and related co-morbid disorders. Training also provides knowledge regarding the treatment options available (Hagedorn, 2009). Accurate diagnosis of out-of-control sexual behaviour, particularly in a sexual health clinic, impacts positively on the patient's and the public's sexual health (Goldmeier and Petrak, 2011). Increased training and education in this area will assist professionals, such as general practitioners, who find the concept of sexual addiction a challenging issue in clinical practice (Fleury et al., 2012). Professional training in sexuality should enable the delivery of the Department of Health's aspiration that the barriers to health service usage and the deliverance of sexual education programmes are addressed (Department of Health and Children, 2009).

Conclusion

The contested concept of sexual addiction remains a controversial issue in Ireland and elsewhere. There are those who reject the concept and see it as a social, moral or medical construct. Many see the concept in terms of a contemporary expression of the commercially driven addiction industry. In contrast, there are others who testify to the existence of the concept from their personal or professional experience. Despite the continuing controversy regarding the validity of the concept, there is an increase in the number of individuals who seek therapeutic help, some of whom are satisfied with the professional help they seek, while others remain dissatisfied. An increasing number of professionals are also seeking help, so as to understand and assist individuals to manage out-of-control sexual behaviour. Further research and policy development is required to determine the exact nature of this issue, to develop diagnostic criteria and additional information in order to make a differential diagnosis, and to offer the appropriate help to those who require it.

Despite the scholarly controversy associated with out-of-control sexuality, the data discussed in this chapter suggests a clear need for continuing professional development and education in this area. Treatment providers would benefit from information on assessment procedures and interventions, and from specific training in sexual addictive behaviours. Additional information on the identification of early signs, preventive measures and resources would also be useful. Knowledge about the alternative explanations for dysregulated sexuality would be equally valuable in a clinical context. Professional training would also help the treatment provider explore his/her own sexuality, thereby increasing his/her competence in clinical practice.

When faced with problematic sexual behaviour, a balance is required so as to accurately identify the cause and access appropriate help, while resisting the premature application of inappropriate labels. It is equally important to recognise the variety of sexualities that exist and to allow space for sexual creativity, freedom and enjoyment. The question remains, however: 'How much sex is too much? How much is enough? And who decides?' (Groneman, 2001: 15).

Notes

[1] It is understood that the term 'sexual addiction' can be viewed as pejorative, but no such meaning is ascribed to it in this research. Even though this term is used, it is also understood that there are many other terms used to describe out-of-control sexual behaviour and that the concept is highly contested.

[2] The interviewees represent a geographical spread throughout Ireland and include a gender mix.

[3] Interviews were recorded where consent was given; otherwise, notes were taken. In relation to data collection, the approach was qualitative and focus groups, individual interviews and questionnaires were used. Recorded interviews were later transcribed. Interpretative phenomenological analysis (IPA) (Smith et al., 2009) and thematic analysis (TA) (Braun and Clarke, 2006) informed the analysis of the data. Questionnaires were analysed using the Statistical Package for the Social Sciences (SPSS).

⁴ Sexual disease and teenage pregnancies, for example, were frequently debated topics in many Western countries. In the USA the emergence of the New Christian Right movement in the 1980s represented a new political conservatism, which filled the vacuum created by the decline in religious institutions (Irvine, 1995). Groups such as the Moral Majority and Citizens for Decency began to agitate against the perceived liberal sexual agenda. As a result, budgets for school-based sexual education were lowered, restrictions on abortions were increased and political consideration was given to laws such as the Family Protection Act, all of which created a cultural negativity against non-traditional sexual expression (Rubin, 2007).

⁵ The counter-revolution was characterised by a questioning and, ultimately, a rejection of the sexual behaviours and liberal attitudes celebrated during the 1960s. An observable indication of public concern regarding sexuality was captured on the front cover of *Time* magazine, which in 1984 announced that the sexual revolution was over (Smith, 1999).

⁶ The concept of sexual addiction has attracted continuous controversy from a variety of perspectives. Those opposed to the concept of addiction include: Levine and Troiden, 1988; Irvine, 1995; Rinehart and McCabe, 1997; Keane, 2004; Klein, 2006; Levine, 2010; Winters et al., 2010; Reay et al., 2012; and Ley, 2012.

⁷ The International Classification of Diseases (ICD) is a medical manual designating disease classifications. It is published by the World Health Organization (WHO), is more frequently used outside the USA and is similar to the DSM.

⁸ Finlayson et al. (2001) explain that a number of general medical conditions, such as neurological, endocrine and psychiatric conditions, are associated with sexual dysregulation. Bi-polar disorder, commonly referred to as manic depression, is a psychiatric condition characterised by mood swings ranging from high to low and associated with risky sexual behaviour (Ramrakha et al., 2000). The endocrine system is connected to a complex structure of glands, which produce hormones. These hormones regulate body functions and human development and are often associated with hypersexuality (Swyer, 1975). The frontal lobe dysfunction, associated with an impairment of the frontal lobe, can occur as a result of brain trauma, causing hypersexuality (Miller et al., 1986), and is also associated with degenerative diseases or psychiatric disorders, such as schizophrenia. Furthermore, dementia is a generic term used to describe a degenerative condition typified by the loss of brain function and affecting faculties such as memory, judgement, social skills and intellect and is often related to excessive sexual behaviour. Alzheimer's and Huntington's are typical diseases associated with this condition (Dhikav et al., 2007). Kluver-Bucy is a neurobehavioural condition associated with brain damage and expressed by hypersexuality and diminished fear, mood fluctuations and dementia (Hayman et al., 1998). Klein-Levin syndrome

(KLS) is another neurological disorder characterised by excessive sleepiness and uninhibited sexual behaviour (Chughtai et al., 2010). Finlayson et al. (2001) recommend that careful assessment will assist the clinician to diagnose the presenting condition accurately and ensure the provision of appropriate treatment.

[9] Tiefer (2000) complains that there is an excessive medicalisation of sexuality, often motivated by the self-interest of the pharmaceutical industry, which offers generous funding and professional opportunities in return for drug development and marketing. Medicalisation of the issue has, it can be argued, resulted in the development of a system of diagnostic classifications designating healthy and unhealthy sexuality and a reductionist perspective of sexuality.

[10] This programme was developed by Steve Arterburn, a Christian evangelist counsellor who runs New Life Ministries and who owns a multi-million-dollar business selling sexual addiction treatment (Ley, 2012).

[11] The development of cultural attitudes to sexuality can be viewed in terms of a few major influences, namely the theology of St Augustine, the influence of early Irish monasticism and the impact of Jansenism (*see* Inglis, 1998b). The Christian belief is that sexuality is essentially for the purpose of procreation and consequently all other expressions of sexuality are perceived as sinful (*see* DeLamater, 1981).

[12] During this period a number of changes signalled a new era, such as the retirement of Prime Minster Éamon de Valera in 1959 and of Archbishop McQuaid of Dublin in 1972, both of whom had presented Ireland as an icon of sexual purity. The role of the media, and especially the opening of Raidió Teilifís Éireann (RTÉ) in 1961, provided further opportunity to discuss sexuality (Keating, 2004). Garvin (2005) argues that the availability of contraception brought new sexual freedoms and indicated an end to the powerful control of the Church regarding sexuality. The publication of the papal encyclical, *Humanae Vitae,* in 1968, and the proposals to reject it laid the groundwork to further abandon traditional sexuality as presented by the Church. This also facilitated the establishment in 1969 of the first family planning clinic in Ireland. Despite the public discourse regarding sexuality, the issue of homosexuality remained largely unspoken about, while imprisonments continued into the 1970s against men convicted of having sex with men (*see* Hug, 2001).

[13] The Health Service Executive (HSE) Crisis Pregnancy Programme is a government-associated programme addressing the issues of crisis pregnancy in Ireland. In addition to the support services it provides to those in crisis, the organisation, in collaboration with other bodies such as the Royal College of Surgeons of Ireland (RCSI) and the Department of Health, has undertaken extensive research in the area of sexuality in Ireland. The *Irish Contraception and Crisis Pregnancy (ICCP) Studies* 2003 and 2010 (Rundle et al., 2004; McBride et al., 2012) and the *Irish Study of Sexual Health and*

Relationships (IRSSHR) (Layte et al., 2006) contain information on issues such as sexual knowledge, attitudes and behaviours and sexual trends in Irish society. Additionally, other agencies, such as the Health Protection Surveillance Centre (HPSC), an affiliate of the HSE, collect data on infectious disease, including sexual disease, which informs strategic planning and treatment provision. A number of other statutory and non-statutory bodies, such as the National AIDS Strategy Committee (NASC), Dublin AIDS Alliance (DAA) and Gay and Lesbian Equality Network (GLEN), among others, contribute to the collection of data, which cumulatively provides a growing database of information on sexuality in Ireland.

[14] The high number of STIs in Ireland has been interrupted occasionally by slight decreases, as shown in 2009, when a decrease of 4.1 per cent occurred in comparison to 2008 (HPSC, 2010: 86).

[15] The term 'GUM' refers to genito-urinary medicine and is the faculty that specialises in sexual health and the treatment of sexual disease.

[16] The term 'sauna' in this context refers to a commercial bathhouse where men usually meet other men for sex.

Section 6

Children and Young People's Sexualities

CHAPTER 12

Lessons in Sexual Citizenship: The Politics of Irish School-Based Sexuality Education

Elizabeth Kiely

Introduction

The first part of this chapter will trace the evolution of school-based sexuality education in the Irish context, focusing particularly on the shifting discourses that have constructed Irish students' sexual subjectivities in different ways over time. After outlining the background to the chapter, we shall narrow the focus to look more closely at the life skills programmes that became popular in Irish schools in the 1970s and 1980s, and the Child Abuse Prevention Programme Stay Safe, introduced into schools in the early 1990s. Both of these interventions paved the way for relationships and sexuality education (RSE), which was the first State-led initiative taken in the field of school-based sexuality education. It was rolled out in Irish schools from the mid-1990s onwards and gave rise to some intense public debate.

The chapter will chart the development of the RSE programme and its implementation to date. Using the lens of sexual citizenship, we will consider how the RSE programme constructs students' sexual subjectivities in particular ways. It will be argued that what was amplified and silenced in the official discourses of RSE and in the public debate makes visible operations of power in Irish society, but also reveals insights into the dominant conceptions of students as sexual citizens. Finally, the latter part of the chapter will consider how students' sexual citizenship might be afforded greater recognition and how this relates to the teaching of sexuality education in Ireland. It is hoped that this final discussion will prompt exploration into how schools in Ireland might improve how they teach sexuality education.

Background

This chapter is based on an IRCHSS-funded PhD study, which set out to examine the politics of Irish sexuality education from the 1960s onwards (Kiely, 2004). Informed by a poststructuralist approach[1] and employing the tools of critical discourse analysis,[2] the PhD study sought to interrogate the politics and practice of Irish school-based sex education in order to reveal its disciplinary and regulatory intent. It also sought to explore the potential to open up to young Irish people new possibilities, choices and ways of being sexual.

Increasingly we have seen the concept of citizenship, typically concerned with the rights and obligations within the nation state, being broadened and problematised[3] to generate new and exciting questions in the social sciences. For example, feminists (Phillips, 1991; Lister, 1997; Walby, 1997) have argued that though the concept of citizenship sounded inclusive, it was traditionally conceptualised in ways that implied the existence of a tacitly male, but presumed universal, citizen. As the concept was expanded, its gendered, cultural, ethnic and sexual dimensions, for instance, became emphasised and the notion of sexual citizenship was also formulated. First introduced by Evans (1993), the concept of sexual citizenship has proved difficult to define clearly, but it has often been used to refer to the rights and duties accorded or denied to individuals on the basis of their sexual identities and practices (Richardson, 2000). To flesh out the meaning and value of the notion of sexual citizenship, Richardson elucidates three elements of a sexual rights discourse as involving conduct-based, identity-based and relationship-based rights claims (Richardson, 2000). For example, with reference to children's rights, the age of consent legislation defines seventeen years as the age when individuals in Ireland are legitimately regarded as sexual citizens, with the right to engage in sexual conduct in personal relationships. However, in recognition of the substantial minority of persons under the age of consent who are sexually active consensually, and some of whom access sexual health services, it appears that the age of consent may be reduced to sixteen years in Ireland.[4] Sexual citizenship has been further theorised and critically analysed by other scholars in terms of both the promise and limitations it holds for understanding sexual politics in contemporary society (Weeks, 1998; Bell and Binnie, 2000; Hubbard, 2001; Plummer, 2003). While it is generally recognised as a slippery concept (Richardson, 2001), particularly pertinent to discussions of sexual citizenship is an emphasis on the rights of free sexual expression and bodily autonomy (Richardson, 2001), on inclusion of issues pertaining to institutional and spatial inclusion (Hubbard, 2001) and on connections between the public and private spheres of life (Bell and Binnie, 2000).

At various points in this chapter we will utilise a sexual citizenship lens to analyse changing conceptions of children's sexualities in Irish society and how this has influenced changing approaches to children's formal sexuality education. As noted by others (Roche, 1999; Howe and Covell, 2005; Robinson, 2012), childhood has a difficult relationship to citizenship discourse and this difficulty is even more pronounced when it is sexual citizenship that is being considered (Robinson, 2012). Children tend to be subjected to numerous forms of surveillance and regulation, often defended with reference to discourses of childhood (sexual) innocence and children's need to be protected from (sexual) harm (Robinson, 2012). What is made evident in this chapter is that in Ireland we have moved away from a perspective that denied children and young people any form of sexual expression or sexual identity, either by refusing to acknowledge its existence or by acknowledging its existence but locating it under the auspices of the Church, the State and parents in order to rigorously suppress and control it. In recent decades children have increasingly come to be acknowledged as sexual citizens in Ireland, but they are permitted only a limited sexual citizenship. They are seen as entitled to protection against sexual exploitation by others and to information they need to protect themselves against the perceived negative implications (e.g. sexually transmitted infections, pregnancy) of engagement in sexual practices when they fail to abstain from full sexual relations. In Irish society it has become increasingly evident that children are not sexually innocent (*see also* Chapter 13) and that not all young people wait to engage in full homosexual or heterosexual relations until after they have reached the legal age of consent, which is presently seventeen. However, childhood sexuality in the Irish context is conceptualised in ways that pathologise the sexual subjectivity of children and bolster prevailing, unequal power relations. The argument being made here is that this is evident in the delivery of sex education in Irish schools.

Sex Education in Ireland Prior to the 1990s

According to Kiernan (1992), initiatives in sex education were being put in place in Irish schools by individual teachers from the 1960s onwards. In Irish society education in general, and sex educa-tion in particular, was traditionally subsumed within a Catholic discourse designed to fulfil Catholic objectives. What is consistent in the Catholic approach to sex education is that it affirms sexual relations when they happen within marriage for the purpose of procreation. Catholic moral precepts provide the point of reference for deciding what constitutes acceptable and unacceptable sexual conduct. In relation to the provision of sex education historically in Ireland, the Catholic approach was that it need not be imparted in a strongly Catholic society (Inglis, 1998a) or, if it were to be imparted, it should be clearly guided by a Catholic moral framework and directed at young people only when they had reached their teenage years. There is evidence that in the middle decades of the twentieth century Catholic authorities thought it best that sexual references be kept oblique, in the interests of promoting chastity, and that consistent segregation of the sexes and close supervision by their parents and others until they were close to marrying rendered a sex education unnecessary (Inglis, 1998a; Scheper-Hughes, 2001).

The social anthropologists Arensberg and Kimball (1968) observed, as a result of their study of rural life in the west of Ireland in 1932, that only married people engaged in sex for procreation were considered to be entitled to have a sexual interest. For others in the community, it was supposed the interest did not exist or, in the case of young people, existed only as an evil and powerful force in need of constant control. Among the Catholic community, sex education was sometimes only considered important for those young people who might emigrate to countries where attitudes to sex were considered more secular in orientation. Fitzgerald, a priest, wrote in 1956:

> The Christian teaching on matters of sex should also be given in our secondary and vocational schools. When the place of sex

is seen in the framework of God's plan, the beauty of the plan itself will become clear to the minds of the pupils, and once they reach that stage, the proper attitude towards sex should naturally follow. This is about as much as we can reasonably do to prepare those who ... will have to live in an environment in which the prevailing attitude towards sex is anything but Christian; and we know that many of our emigrants have to live in such an environment. (Fitzgerald, 1956: 350)

Indeed, this concern, which was shared by Church, State and the media, about how migrating from Ireland could potentially threaten Irish Catholic moral standards was very evident during times of high female emigration (Gray, 2004; Ferriter, 2009). Emigration was viewed as an avenue that facilitated the pursuit of sexual pleasure (Gray, 2004), engagement in sexual misconduct (Arensberg and Kimball, 1968) and the exploitation of sexual ignorance (Ferriter, 2009).

That young people in Ireland were denied a factual, scientific type of sex education and deliberately kept ignorant or confused about sexual issues throughout the twentieth century has been well documented (Inglis, 1998; Ferriter, 2009).[5] Calls to educate from professionals and women's organisations were resisted by Catholic Church authorities and fundamentalist Catholic organisations, who maintained a watchful eye and sought to stamp out anything they perceived as a threat to Catholic moral standards (O'Reilly, 1992; Ferriter, 2009). Responsibility for sexuality education was a matter the Catholic Church was not prepared to cede to any other civil authority or to the State (Ferriter, 2009). In the 1960s the minimal sex instruction given by religious authorities[6] was a kind of instruction that, according to many testimonies, left a damaging legacy.[7] It was shrouded in mystery (Inglis, 1998), made strong associations between sex and sin (see Filas, 1964: 7) and put the responsibility squarely on women to be the enforcers of Catholic morality (Inglis, 1998), as discussed in Chapter 2 of this book. Indeed, the work of an agony aunt in the 1960s, Angela Macnamara, has been considered important because she took an approach consistent with Church teaching, but also provided access to factual details about matters sexual and was more frank in her delivery (Ferriter, 2009; Ryan, 2011b).

In the 1970s the American anthropologist Scheper-Hughes's ethnographic study (2001: 208) of a rural village in the south of Ireland found parental resistance to be strong with regard to sex education for their adolescent children because they feared frank discussion might awaken dormant sexual appetites. Nonetheless,a survey in the 1970s revealed that attitudes to sexuality in Irish society were becoming less conservative (Mac Greil, 1978). This was a decade of significant social change (Ferriter, 2009), when new discourses of sex and romance filtered through the public sphere (Ryan, 2011a).[8] In 1981 the Catholic Archdiocese of Dublin issued a programme for use in secondary schools, *Education in Sexuality*, which accorded parents the main responsibility for sex education, but support from schools for parents' endeavours was also permissible. The sexuality/relationships sections of the religious texts, *The Christian Way,* used in post-primary schools in the early 1980s, were considered adequate to cover the basic requirements of a sex education for post-primary students (O'Mahony, 1987). It is evident that up until the 1980s children and young people in Ireland were perceived predominantly as having little or no right to sexual expression or consumption. This was reflected in the perception that a formal sex education would destroy their innocence and possibly arouse sexualities that were best left latent. Emigration of young people was perceived to present the biggest threat to the status quo, prompting some of the Catholic sex education initiatives aimed at those in their teenage years. In the 1970s and 1980s, however, the dominance of this approach to sex education started to come under some pressure.

The introduction of what became known as life skills programmes in schools in the 1970s and 1980s presented a challenge to the dominant Catholic approach to sex education. Life skills programmes became popular in Irish education in the 1970s and 1980s, for a range of reasons, and although they were not sex education programmes *per se*, they did have as their *raison d'être* the development of young people's personal and social skills, to enable them to live and cope in what was considered a fast-changing world. What is significant about life skills programmes is that they were not State-led, but were supported by a range of statutory organisations and agencies operating in civil society and were not particularly prescriptive.[9] Life skills programmes were adapted and modified for use in different post-primary schools and youth work settings around the country. While there was some support for the employment of life skills education among authorities in the Catholic Church and among Catholic educators, who believed that life skills could be taught in a manner that did not threaten Catholic teaching on sexuality,[10] this view was not universally held by all Catholics. In fact, life skills programmes offended a small number of conservative, Catholic, campaigning individuals and groups in Irish society, who vociferously opposed life skills model of education (Kirby, 1987). They did so for such reasons that it contravened Catholic parents' rights, as enshrined in the Irish Constitution, that it permitted teacher intrusion into aspects of students' lives that should not concern them and that the values clarification process,[11] a key aspect of life skills pedagogy, was not appropriate for schools or for school children, who needed to be educated in accordance with Catholic teaching on matters sexual (Manly, 1986; McCarroll, 1987). They argued that life skills programmes were inspired by knowledge and techniques drawn from the discipline of psychology, which lacked verification, but due to the proliferation of life skills programmes were being tried out on school children (McCarroll, 1987). Some of the agencies, such as the Health Education Bureau (HEB)[12] and the Irish Family Planning Association (IFPA),[13] which provided resources and support for the teaching of life skills, were also viewed with suspicion by Catholic conservatives because of their association with the promotion of what they perceived as a more secular and liberal social agenda in Irish society.[14]

Following an initiative taken by the Irish National Teachers' Organisation (INTO), the Child Abuse Prevention Programme Stay Safe was introduced into Irish schools in 1992. It, too, generated similar controversy among a small section of conservative Catholic groups and individuals.[15] The Stay Safe programme was designed for primary school children and the overall aim of the programme was to educate school children for the purpose of reducing their vulnerability to abuse and bullying. An active learning strategy underpinned the programme, and it was intended that its introduction would make it easier for children to disclose abuse to their teachers and to enable teachers respond appropriately and effectively to such disclosures. The programme's introduction challenged traditional notions of the family in Irish society as a juridicially private domain, instead reconfiguring it as a site for intervention and regulation by professionals (Kiely, 2004). While there was reluctance on the part of successive government ministers to make the programme mandatory, it was supported by the necessary infrastructure to provide teacher training, information and resources for school authorities and parents, as well as programme piloting and evaluation to explore programme implementation, effectiveness and outcomes (Kiely, 2004).

The Catholic campaigners who organised to resist the introduction of Stay Safe identified a range of reasons why they were opposed to it. They argued that it was unnecessary, dismissing the statistics on child abuse and child sexual abuse in Irish society that were used to justify the programme's introduction as inaccurate and inflated (Irish Branch of the Responsible Society, Family and Youth Concern, 1992a; 1994). The issue of false accusations of abuse was raised on the grounds that the programme's contents and methods would confuse students, induce false memories and increase the risk that teachers and other professionals could potentially over-react in detecting and reporting abuse, with a consequent negative impact on the parents and families concerned (Irish Branch of the Responsible Society, Family and Youth Concern, 1992b). The programme, it was claimed, would psychologically damage children, reducing their feelings of security in their families, and introduce them to information and psychotherapeutic techniques that were not appropriate for children so young (Irish Educational Research, 1995). A hidden purpose of the programme, it was argued, was the teaching of sex education under the guise of abuse prevention without properly informing parents (Irish Educational Research, 1995).

Life skills and the Child Abuse Prevention Programme Stay Safe undoubtedly helped pave the way for the introduction of the State-led Relationships and Sexuality Education Programme, which was introduced into Irish schools in the mid-1990s. Both of these initiatives were grounded in active modes of learning in school environments and were more informed by the discourses of the human and health sciences than the Catholic moral discourse, which had been the dominant discourse in this field of learning for so long. The introduction of the Stay Safe programme signalled greater recognition of children's right of protection from sexual exploitation, and it also challenged the prominence given to the private sphere in keeping children safe. Indeed, children were coming to be increasingly identified as sexual citizens. Stay Safe, in particular, by being introduced into primary schools, by having a significant infrastructure and by being accompanied by a set of governmental technologies legitimating it as an intervention (Rose and Miller, 1992: 175) was significant in enabling the State take the first steps toward developing a framework for school-based relationships and sexuality education in the early 1990s (Kiely, 2004).

The 1990s – The State Takes the Initiative

Prior to the early 1990s, there was no definitive action taken by the State on the issue of school-based sexuality education. Indeed, in 1992 Kiernan found in her study of school-based sex education provision that it ranged from comprehensive programmes in a few Irish schools to limited or no provision in many other schools. As noted earlier, while it seemed in the early 1980s that this might change and that a State-led initiative in sex education was about to be introduced, by the mid-1980s a change of government and a consolidation of the Catholic conservative lobby in Irish society had made this prospect increasingly remote (Kiely, 2004).[16] However, as in other contexts and at the same time, challenges posed by AIDS and HIV transmission gave increasing priority to a discourse of sexual citizenship (Weeks, 1998) informed by a public health pragmatism, which increasingly exercised an influence on the Irish social and political climate.[17]

By 1992 the Green Paper on Education (Department of Education, 1992) indicated that a comprehensive, school-based sex education programme was a requirement in the Irish context. In 1993 the *Fianna Fáil/Labour Programme for a Partnership Government* (Fianna Fáil, 1993) stated its commitment to providing an adequate and comprehensive programme of sex education for second-level students. In 1994 Niamh Breathnach, Minister for Education in the Fianna Fáil/Labour government, appointed a small Expert Advisory Group. The purpose of this group was to inquire into current sex education provision in Irish schools and, following consultation with members of the public, to report its findings after a two-month period. The small, closely drawn Expert Advisory Group made the important first steps in the RSE policy-making process predictable and speedy by keeping the process within the boundaries of a small, State-selected, reliable group of actors (Kiely, 2008).[18]

The RSE policy and programme roll-out exemplified key characteristics of a State-led corporatist exercise (Kiely, 2008).[19] As they were required by the State to move the policy and programme along, particular stakeholders in the education community were brought on board to make the programme work.[20] At a distance from the RSE policy-making partnership were student representatives, who were never actively encouraged, nationally or locally, to play any significant part and did not even have to be consulted.[21] Organisations or groups in civic society that had a tradition of providing sex education or support to particular constituencies of young people were also kept at a distance from the policy and programme development, though at least one of these organisations articulated a wish to take part or to be consulted.[22] The official Catholic Church's and the religious school managers' tacit support for the programme were vital for rolling it out in a predominantly Catholic-controlled system. It may have been thought that their co-option might have been jeopardised by the participation of groups more strongly associated with the promotion of a more liberal or secular agenda in Irish society. The Catholic conservative groups were also kept at a distance from RSE policy-making circles and they relied mainly on the media and other opportunities provided in the public sphere to express their determined opposition to the introduction of State-led sex education in Irish schools, and to generate the controversy necessary to force programme withdrawal, if at all possible.

An assemblage of political rationalities, technologies, resources and trade-offs were deployed by the programme planners to keep the key stakeholders aligned, because they were required to roll out the programme (Kiely, 2008). Teachers who had conscientious objections to the programme could be excused from teaching it and parents who did not wish their children to participate in the programme were facilitated by the introduction of what has become known as the 'opt out' clause. This highlighted how children's sexual agency was subjugated, made a private affair to be determined by parents. While the programme was made compulsory and became embedded in the Social and Personal Health Education (SPHE) curriculum, the content was not mandatory and each school community (comprising the local board of management, parents and teacher representatives) was afforded an opportunity, at local level, to decide on its RSE policy and to deliver a RSE programme that it deemed appropriate for its school ethos and environment.

The RSE Programme: A Brief Overview

The aim of the RSE programme in Ireland is, according to the policy guidelines (Department of Education, 1997: 4), to help students 'acquire a knowledge and understanding of human relationships and sexuality through processes which will enable them to form values and establish behaviours within a moral, spiritual and social framework'. The programme covers primary and post-primary schooling in Ireland (ages five to eighteen years). There are published resource materials that accompany the programme. These materials are not prescriptive, but instead provide a range of options in relation to the delivery of the programme in each individual school. While schools are expected to deliver all elements of RSE, which is in keeping with the programme's emphasis on relationships and on students' holistic development, how the resource materials are used is dependent on many factors, including what is stated in the local school RSE policy. This means that students in Ireland do not have equal opportunities in their sex education learning, a fact that has been made increasingly evident in a number of research studies to date. For example, single-sex boys' schools have been found to spend less time than other schools on programme implementation, homosexuality seems to be a neglected topic in RSE teaching and early school-leavers have been found to have received little or no sex education (O'Carroll and Szalacha, 2000; Mayock and Byrne, 2004; Mayock et al., 2007; McBride et al., 2012).

Public Reaction to the RSE Programme

Opposition to the RSE programme emanated from a relatively small number of Catholics, who reviled the programme for many of the same reasons as those put forward by the opponents of life skills and Stay Safe.[23] They deployed a variety of tactics and strategies to articulate their opposition to the programme and to stymie its implementation, in the hope of forcing its withdrawal. Much of what can be loosely interpreted as support for the introduction of the programme came from members of the public and agencies who took issue with what was being articulated by Catholic conservatives in the local media or at public events. In the public discussion that ensued in the media between opponents and proponents of RSE, conceptions of Irish childhood, family, school and nation were strongly debated (Kiely, 2004).

What follows is a summary of the debate between the opponents and proponents of RSE that was played out in the Irish media during this time.[24] Anti-RSE campaigners argued that school-based sex education exposed innocent children to sexual arousal and tempted them to sin. As it was a programme that included children of primary schoolgoing age (five to twelve years), it disrupted the latency period.[25] It used psychological techniques that would have such damaging effects, these effects would stay with persons throughout their lives. They considered the programme content and pedagogical style entirely inappropriate for children whose parents wished to impart moral absolutes informed by Catholic teachings. Its material was considered too intrusive and explicit to render it compatible with the ethos of the majority of Irish schools, which were Catholic.

Proponents of the programme, on the other hand, argued that childhood ignorance could be a factor in child sexual abuse, teenage pregnancy and sexually transmitted infection and that children had a right to be educated about sexual matters in the school context. The programme's supporters viewed school as the best site so as to ensure that all children were afforded some level of sex education; furthermore, they considered teachers to be the most suitable educators. Those who opposed the programme considered the private domain of the family to be the best and only appropriate site for such an education and parents to be the best educators, because of their close relationships with their children. In this regard opponents viewed sex education teachers as usurping and undermining parents' endeavours rather than complementing them. To support their resistance, they identified other countries where there already existed school-based sex education programmes as places of rampant promiscuity, sexual disease and violence (Kiely, 2004). Claiming that RSE was really a foreign import being assimilated into Ireland by organisations seeking to secularise Irish society, the implications, they argued, were that it would contaminate Irish family values and ways of living and ultimately destroy the moral fabric of Irish society. In response, proponents of RSE argued that many of the problems anti-RSE campaigners associated with other countries were also evident in Ireland, and they rejected notions that the Irish nation was morally superior to others at any point in its history.

The introduction of the RSE programme into Irish schools provided a vehicle for the expression of competing, and sometimes polarised, views on a range of social issues at the time. What is evident in the public debate that ensued, however, is that students' sexual citizenship is still conceptualised in very restricted terms by programme opponents and proponents alike. For instance, contributions to the public debate by proponents of the programme revealed that nothing more than nominal improvements of a very regulatory kind were envisaged, i.e. reduction in STIs, teenage pregnancies and abortions and the provision of an alternative discourse to counteract a sexualised popular culture (Kiely, 2004). Similarly, the dominant discourse in both houses of government when the programme was discussed was that it would provide appropriate education to facilitate responsible decision-making by teenagers (Kiely, 2004).[26]

The RSE programme survived the virulent attacks in the public sphere by Catholic conservative interests and the tactics they employed to force its withdrawal, but as the following section shows, the politics of Irish sex education continues.

RSE Delivery and Implementation

To date, RSE has been subjected to many studies to gauge its implementation in schools, predominantly post-primary schools throughout the country. Overall, these studies have revealed that implementation has been increasing, but at a very slow pace (Morgan, 2000; Mayock et al., 2007). While RSE is a mandatory programme at primary and post-primary levels, in a 2011 report the Crisis Pregnancy Agency (CPA) estimated that about 10 per cent of schools are not implementing it (Wayman, 2011). One study of delivery and implementation at post-primary level indicates that the timetabling and delivery of RSE decreases from first year in post-primary schooling through to third year (Mayock et al., 2007). This study identified a range of issues relating to RSE and provided an account of the barriers and facilitators pertaining to its effective delivery and implementation in schools. It found that school leadership was crucial in facilitating or disabling good RSE imple-mentation (Mayock et al., 2007).

Overall, it seems from the study's findings that the programme delivery and implementation is diverse and inconsistent across schools and that this is due to a range of factors. A consistent finding is a very low rate of RSE implementation in the senior cycle, possi-bly reflecting the shifting emphasis towards examination subjects. The study also reiterated the earlier finding that less time is devoted to RSE planning and teaching in single-sex boys' schools (Geary & Mannix McNamara, 2003; Mayock et al., 2007). Mayock et al. (2007) made a significant number of recommendations to improve the rate and quality of programme implementation in post-primary schools. By comparison to other studies, lower rates of implementation, particularly in the senior cycle, were found in a study of SPHE and RSE implementation that surveyed students and was conducted by Dáil na nÓg delegates (Roe, 2010). The main recommendations put forward by survey participants were mandatory RSE classes and a wider curriculum, with more detailed coverage of topics and better trained teachers to deliver RSE.

Despite a number of studies which found dissatisfaction amongst young people with the sex education they received in Irish schools since the programme was introduced (Hyde and Howlett, 2004; Mayock and Byrne, 2004), a recent survey of the general popula-tion conducted for the HSE Crisis Pregnancy Programme revealed that a higher percentage (86 per cent) of respondents in the 18–25 age range than in older age groups reported that they had received sex education. Of those who had received sex education, 90 per cent reported having received it at school; 70 per cent reported that what they had learned in school they found helpful in their adult relationships (McBride et al., 2012).[27] Coupled with the apparent recent decline in the abortion rate (IFPA, 2012), this evidence points to the more consistent use of contraception among young people having their first experience of full sexual relations (McBride et al., 2012). This and the decline in the teenage pregnancy rate (HSE Crisis Pregnancy Programme, 2011) all bodes well for the produc-tion of heteronormative 'good' sexual citizens and the mandatory introduction of a school-based sex education programme in the Irish context. As discussed in greater detail in the next section, it is also useful data for all those who argued that school-based sex education was required to address the 'problems' generated by young people's sexualities.

School-Based Sex Education and RSE: A Discussion of Some Key Issues

Sexuality education programmes comprise a mix of diverse discourses, but in their entirety they constitute a coherent discursive framework prescribing possibilities and limits. For instance, the RSE set of resource materials used for programme implementation reveals that the dominant health-promoting discourse was supplemented by the inclusion of other discourses (including a Catholic discourse), where they were also compatible with health-promoting objectives. A key issue pertaining to school-based sex education generally is that it tends to be oriented towards addressing the 'problems' of students' sexualities, so that children and young people's sexualities are rarely conceptualised or discoursed without this problem focus, a point also acknowledged in Chapter 8 of this book, 'Hiding in Plain Sight? Male Heterosexuality in the Irish School Context'. Writing in 1992, Kiernan (1992) accepted that there was considerable disagreement among the key agents (parents, Church authorities and educators) in Irish society on the specifics of what young people should be taught about sexualities, but at the same time she pointed out that they all were broadly united in their acceptance of the need for a problem preventive approach. This was evident in much of the public discourse surrounding RSE, when advocates of the programme tended to limit its potential impact to reducing teenage pregnancy, abortion and STI rates and to challenging the sexualisation of children in popular culture. Whenever data is made available indicating increasing rates of any of these 'problems', journalists and other commentators promptly raise questions about the RSE programme and its effectiveness. As observed by Diorio (1985), any curriculum field that is closely tied to a set of social problems can easily come under the control of these problems.

In the Irish context, the problem focus might be mediated by the reality that very often RSE is being imparted in Catholic-controlled schools, where elements of the prescribed health education discourse informing students on how to prevent problems may be curtailed. For instance, talk about artificial modes of contraception might be ruled out by the RSE policy in a school with a Catholic ethos, or a teacher may consider it to be off-limits in such a school. Indeed, tensions between Catholic morality and public health pragmatism are undoubtedly played out in Irish schools, as revealed in studies of RSE implementation (Morgan, 2000; Mayock et al., 2007). The problem focus may also have been mediated by the programme planners, who constantly emphasised RSE's broader focus on relationships in order to obscure negative commentary from Catholic conservatives about the teaching of matters sexual in the school curriculum. Yet the problem focus is made evident by the absence of what Fine (1988: 29) called a 'discourse of desire' in the six manuals of resource materials circulated to schools (*see* Kiely, 2005). In her article, Fine was referring to sex education's tendency to emphasise female sexual victimisation at the expense of a discourse about female sexual desire and pleasure. Indeed, since Fine's influential article, a discourse of pleasure is still notably absent in many sex education curricula (Allen, 2004; Fine and McClelland, 2006). In the case of RSE in Ireland, non-procreative and non-penetrative sexual activities (e.g. masturbation) receive virtually no mention and the developing female body is very strongly conceptualised in terms of functions relating to child-bearing and child-rearing. The emphasis placed on the procreative aspects of human sexuality in the context of committed, typically married, heterosexual relationships actively privileges heterosexuality and obscures other conceptions and practices of sexuality that are about fun and pleasure. In many lessons, adult relationships, particularly adult marital relationships, are presented as the only legitimate sexual sites (Kiely, 2005).[28] Teachers are encouraged to speak about sexuality only in terms that accord with how it is officially discoursed in the programme, so that students learn the socially acceptable language and associated vocabulary. The programme is also packaged into lessons according to what adults have decided children need to know and at what stage in their development they need to know it. This packaging of the information for delivery at the adult-defined appropriate ages possibly explains why early school-leavers, among others, report a lack of sex education in Ireland (Mayock and Byrne, 2004). Another significant problem with this approach is that the students' everyday articulations of their lived sexualities and the pleasures they generate tend to be left outside the classroom. This means that valuable opportunities are lost to explore issues pertaining to sexual pleasure, or indeed sexual oppression, as they are witnessed and experienced by students in real-life contexts. Furthermore, there is plentiful evidence in the Irish context that gay students are afforded little opportunity to express themselves sexually and that they experience persecution in some school environments (GLEN/Nexus, 1995; Lynch and Lodge, 2002; Norman et al., 2006; Mayock et al., 2008).

A key feature of the Irish RSE programme is the notable shift away from a religious discourse in favour of a pragmatic public health discourse, which places the onus on the individual student to manage and care for him/herself in line with narrowly selected public health outcomes. One very strident example of this is the way in which students are made very familiar with the list of requirements prescribed for the pregnant woman, who is expected to reproduce in a dutiful manner in accordance with the latest health-promoting advice (Department of Education and Science, 1998: 125, 127–8; 1999: 98). Throughout the programme's lessons, a certain kind of liberal version of the good sexual subject as capable of rational thinking and ultimately responsible for his/her own sexual health and wellbeing is promoted. While it can be assumed that certain students may respond in the ways envisaged, it is unlikely that this kind of conception of self-management is well within the capacity of all students when they make decisions in real-life, power-saturated relational contexts, when the exercise of cognitive competencies may at times elude them. This approach also risks putting students perceived to be making irrational choices in danger of experiencing isolation, stigma and a lack of support from their peers or school authorities. The pragmatic, individualistic, health-promoting approach may obscure the cultivation of strong communitarian values, which can be fostered and promoted in the programme and in the school to very good effect. The RSE discourse does little in itself to inspire confidence that the Irish school environment might become a safer, more comfortable place for the pregnant, gay or gender non-conforming students.[29]

Following Foucault (1981), when talk about sex is subject to regulation and taboo, it does not automatically follow that sex is exorcised or absent. Likewise, the more speechifying there is about sex and the more settings in which sex is discussed does not necessarily mean that sexualities are less repressed or controlled. There are commentators who argue that educational pedagogies are deeply embedded in discourses of social regulation and that the more dimensions of a learner that are made known, the more space there is for the exercise of power and control (Usher and Edwards, 1994; Thorogood, 2000). According to Thorogood (2000), sex education is a technique of governance, and 'empowering' models of sex education generate their own micro-techniques of power and are not unequivocally liberating or resisting. In a similar vein, Rasmussen (2012) urged consideration of the implications of how much of the research on pleasure and desire in sex education is framed by secular thinking, arguing instead for research and practice that complicates to a greater extent the role of pleasure and desire in such education. Yet power in schools, as in other settings, is not one-directional and, as Foucault (1980) observed, where there is power there is resistance. These points are very relevant for thinking about sex education and about young people's sexualities in the Irish context. As highlighted by Thomson (2004: 117), 'sex education is quite different from learning about sex'. There is what is taught now in the formal school curriculum, but there is the influence of the hidden curriculum – the school rituals, culture and ethos, as well as the family, the mass media, the social networking sites, etc. where dominant views about sexualities are further bolstered and sometimes challenged. There is also a growing body of work advancing different ideas about how the limitations of sex education curricula may be transcended in a myriad of ways in school environments. This is aimed at challenging the taboos put in place by dominant discourses, disrupting common sense notions about sex, utilising sexual learning occurring in different school spaces to 'leak into' formal sex education, building alliances across difference or seeking more effective ways of preventing sexual violence (e.g. Kehily, 2002; Allen, 2004; Mayo, 2004; Carmody, 2005; Rogow & Haberland, 2005; Allan et al., 2008; Blaise, 2009; Ivinson, 2007; Powell, 2010). While this body of work cannot be discussed in detail in this chapter, I think it may be very useful for thinking about and analysing critically how we teach sex education in the Irish context.

Conclusion

There have been disruptive moments in the Irish sex education landscape in recent decades, which have shifted the discourses away from protectionism (which constructs children as innocents, who can be damaged by explicit information on sexuality) and towards sexual citizenship (where children are given formal sexual education so that they can keep themselves safe and healthy). It is a limited version of sexual citizenship, however; one that is individualistic in focus and narrowly conceived. Though the official RSE discourse tends to be represented as progressive – primarily because of the challenge it posed to the dominance of a Catholic discourse in the field of sexuality education – it, too, has its limits. It is limited in its discursive framework, in the kinds of sexual subjectivities it makes available to young people to take up and in the kind of ethical project it can facilitate. In the formation and teaching of the programme, students were not afforded the recognition granted to other stakeholders. The programme opt-out clause made available to parents constructed students as illegitimate sexual subjects in the public sphere. The curriculum contains silences and omissions aimed at keeping different forms of sexual agency out of reach of students and it is built on fear-based, rather than sex-positive or pleasure-oriented, messages about sex. Furthermore, by being prescriptive and foreclosing particular possibilities, the programme promotes a narrow vision of what children's sexualities are and what they could be in their adult lives.

In terms of considering how we might move towards greater appreciation of children's sexual citizenship, Egan and Hawkes (2009) make some useful recommendations in this regard. They argue that the sexual rights of children need to be seen as part of a broad collective and collaborative endeavour to create a social setting that promotes children's self-determination and the exercise of sexual agency. They call for the recognition of children as reflexive and thoughtful social actors, capable of dynamic and ideological exchange on their sexualities. To take children seriously as legitimate social actors requires children's sexualities not be to be confined to the private sphere and limited to parental prerogative because children's sexual agency is as much a public as it is a private affair (Egan & Hawkes, 2009). They suggest that we move away from adult-prescribed and adult-centred models of children's sexual subjectivity and towards engaging in a deconstructive project, one that would enable us to critically interrogate and challenge all the ways in which children's sexual lives are being defined and constrained.[30] Finally, they appreciate that changing dominant cultural conceptions of children's sexualities is not an easy project, but they argue that it is a necessary one if the sexual citizenship of children is to be advanced. To facilitate such a transformative project in the Irish context, we could explore what might be made possible within the existing RSE framework and what it might be feasible to teach about sexualities in the broader curriculum. We could also consider what might be changed or introduced in the wider school cultural environment to make it a more exciting and democratising learning environment and a more pleasant place to be for all students.

Notes

[1] Poststructuralism is a complex skein of thought that encompasses a number of diverse intellectual currents (Peters, 1998). A poststructuralist approach destabilises unitary conceptions of identity/self and unsettles claims to truth, opening up alternative meanings and readings. For more discussion of this approach, *see* Peters (1996, 1998) and Sarup (1998).

[2] Critical discourse analysis seeks 'to unmask ideologically permeated and often obscured structures of power, political control and dominance as well as strategies of discriminatory inclusion and exclusion in language use' (Wodak et al., 2009: 8). The critical discourse analytic approach is very concerned with the relationship between discourse and power. For greater insight into the use of this approach for research purposes, *see* Wodak (1996), Fairclough (1995) and Van Dijk (1993).

[3] As David Held noted, 'the nation-state is the entity to which the language of citizenship refers, and within which the claims of citizenship, community and participation are made' (Held, 1991: 24). However, as Denise Riley (1992: 208) has written: 'The common cultural standard embodied in the ideal of citizenship is tested again and again by the realities of a pluralist society in which cultural differences abound.'

[4] In June 2012 the Minister for Justice, Alan Shatter TD, announced his intention to bring proposals on the age of sexual consent before the Irish government in the context of Bills updating the law on sexual offences. The Oireachtas Committee on the Constitutional Amendment recommended, in 2009, reducing the legal age of sexual consent from seventeen to sixteen years (Carbery, 2012).

[5] In 1949 a priest, Jerome O'Hea, wrote that 'an honest confession of ignorance' on sexual matters by parents 'helps immensely to draw the child closer to that parent. The child comes to realise that it shares ignorance with the most important person in the world' (O'Hea, 1949: 2–3).

[6] Filas, writing in 1964, wrote about the very special authority and insight of the clergyman to give advice to his flock and to act as a kind of 'family counsellor' (Filas, 1964: 6–7).

316

[7] The Irish novelist Edna O'Brien commented: 'I don't think I have any pleasure in any part of my body, because my first and initial bad thoughts were blackened by fear of sin and therefore I think of my body as a vehicle for sin, a sort of tabernacle of sin' (Ferriter, 2009: 347).

[8] Key social changes in Irish society during this period include: the emergence of the second wave of the women's movement; significant improvements in the status of women in Irish society; the legalisation of limited access to contraception; the growth of international television, which made secular ideas more accessible; the emergence of the gay and lesbian movements; the impact of Ireland's entry into the EEC; the expansion of education for girls; the changing requirements of the Irish labour market and the economic modernisation project of the Irish State.

[9] Ógra Chorcaí (a voluntary youth work organisation in Cork) produced a social and health education handbook in 1976 for use in youth organisations. In 1984 a teacher was seconded to the Health Education Bureau (HEB) to develop a sex education programme, an initiative supported by the then Minister for Education Gemma Hussey, but the programme developed as a result of this initiative was not implemented. Instead, the HEB developed a life skills programme for use by teachers, which included sexuality and personal relationships, among other issues (Kiernan, 1992).

[10] Donal O'Mahony (1987) advised parents and teachers that Hopson and Scally's books for teaching life skills could be utilised in Catholic schools, but only if they were adapted to meet Catholic schools' policy on the permanence of marriage and family life and if they were used in addition to other Catholic resource material. In an essay in the same publication, Bishop Donal Murray (1987) wrote that life skills programmes, if taught in schools, could be underpinned by an examination of different values, as long as Catholic values were endorsed as the correct values. Inglis (1998) has also distinguished between very traditional and more progressive discourses on sex education evident in the Catholic discursive framework, indicating that there has always been some variation in attitudes and approaches within this framework.

[11] Values clarification refers to the process whereby a specific set of values are not taught, but through exercises students come to know their own values and how they compare with the values of family members, friends and others in society. It is anticipated that the result of this process of review and exploration is that students reject values they do not strongly hold and hold stronger those values they think are important, *see* Simon et al., 1972.

[12] The Health Education Bureau was established by the government in 1974 to undertake a health education remit; training teachers and others to deliver life skills programmes was a significant part of its work. It was dissolved by government in 1987 and the Health Promotion Unit was established some years later.

[13] The IFPA was established by a small group of volunteers in 1969 to address the problems encountered by people in Ireland as a result of the State's ban on contraception. The agency has been to the fore in campaigning for sexual health and reproductive rights in Ireland, and it also provides a range of sexual health services.

[14] Alice Glenn, an elected Fine Gael party member known for her socially conservative views, raised suspicion in the Irish parliament about the activities of the Health Education Bureau (Kiely, 2004). The Irish Branch of the Responsible Society, Family and Youth Concern closely monitored the activities of a range of agencies (e.g. IFPA, HEB, the Campaign to Separate Church and State, Gay Health Action, the Rape Crisis Centre) it perceived as threatening to have a secularising influence in Irish society (Kiely, 2004).

[15] In 1987 the Irish National Teachers' Organisation Congress adopted a resolution that instructed the Executive Committee to seek in-service training for teachers to assist them to respond to incidences of child abuse (Irish National Teachers' Organisation, 1993).

[16] Fianna Fáil came into power in 1986 and the position it adopted was that sex education was a matter between schools and parents (*see* Kiely, 2004). The Catholic conservative lobby was strong in the 1980s in Ireland, after it successfully campaigned to have a constitutional ban on abortion introduced in 1983.

[17] In one Catholic conservative publication, *Response*, the changed legislative and policy climate that emerged as a result of the emergence of the AIDS virus was lamented: 'On the pretext of AIDS, the epidemic that never was, Ireland endured offensive safe-sex programmes, the legislation of homosexual acts, offensive AIDS programmes in the schools and condoms on sale in every outlet' (Irish Branch of the Responsible Society, Family and Youth Concern, 1995: 39). The State introduced optional AIDS educational materials for use in schools in 1990 and around this time there were also calls from parliamentarians for increased access to contraception and for the climate of moralism to give way to realism in order to address the challenges posed by the transmission of AIDS (Kiely, 2004).

[18] The members of the Expert Advisory Group appointed by the Minister were Emer Egan (Chairperson and Primary Inspector with the Department of Education) Sr Pat Murray (Vice Chairperson of the NCCA), Fionnuala Kilfeather and Ruth Brennock (National Parents' Council), Siobhan Cluskey and Aidan Herron (teachers with an interest in sex education), Brian McAuley (school principal), Tony Gorman (senior psychologist, Department of Education) and John Lahiff (guidance counsellor). It was reported that the composition of the Expert Advisory Group was perceived by teachers' unions at the time as signifying a (re)positioning of interest groups in education policy (Walshe, 1999). For a more thorough discussion of the RSE policy-making process, *see* Kiely (2004).

[19] 'Corporatist', in this instance, refers to the relationship between State agents and certain groups' representatives, where the groups selected by State agents receive *ad hoc* benefits or greater recognition for guarantees by the groups' representatives that their members will behave in certain ways. *See* Crouch and Dore (1990) for more discussion of corporatist policy-making arrangements. A partnership model permeated policy-making generally and education policy-making in Irish society at the time RSE was being planned (*see* Walshe 1999; O'Carroll, 2002).

[20] The members of the RSE implementation group included representatives of the government Departments of Education and Health, the teachers' unions, the National Parents' Council, the National Council of Curriculum and Assessment and the various managerial bodies in schools.

[21] In the *Expert Advisory Group Report* (Government of Ireland, 1995: 11) it was stated that the local school RSE policy-making committee 'could consult with students' and then, only 'as appropriate'. Early evaluations of RSE implementation, which surveyed all the stakeholders, did not access student views, though students have been consulted in more recent studies of implementation.

[22] When one voluntary organisation, Lesbians Organising Together (LOT), requested to have an input into the RSE policy process, it was '... met with a wall of silence at programme level' (O'Carroll & Szalacha, 2000).

[23] Groups who publicly opposed the RSE programme in Irish society included Parents and Teachers for Real Education (PATRE), the National Parent Teacher Alliance, the Christian Democrats, Positive Action for Children (PACh), the Irish Family League and the National Party. PATRE produced an undated booklet entitled *The Case Against RSE*.

[24] For a detailed account of the public debate that was played out in the letters pages of the *Irish Times* and the *Irish Examiner* in the late 1990s and early 2000s, *see* Kiely (2004).

[25] The latency period refers to the fourth stage of Freud's five stages of psychosexual development, extending from approximately three years of age until the onset of puberty, during which time a child's sexual urges are supposed to lie dormant. For more discussion, *see* Lehrer (1984).

[26] This finding is based on a detailed analysis of the discourse on RSE in the two houses of parliament in Ireland, the Dáil and Seanad, between 1 January 1997 and 31 December 2002 (*see* Kiely, 2004).

[27] Mayock and Byrne (2004) and Mayock et al. (2007) highlighted the evidence that early school-leavers reported receiving very little sex education. In is interesting to note that the McBride et al. (2012) survey found that the basic biological information on sexual intercourse was the topic in which the majority of respondents received their sex education and education pertaining to homosexuality was the topic on which respondents reported receiving least education.

[28] For example, in a reference sheet for parents' use on the subject of boy/girl relationships, it is stated that 'Sex is a gift, a most sacred act and

full sexual intimacy belongs in a totally adult relationship where there is equal trust, respect, acceptance and understanding of both partners – as in marriage' (Department of Education and Science, 1998: 8).

[29] The assumption of heterosexuality pervades the resource materials; the students engaging with the materials are assumed to be heterosexual and the discrete lessons on sexual orientation teach tolerance. It has been found in studies that homophobic and sexist harassment often goes unchallenged in Irish schools (Norman et al., 2006; Mayock et al., 2008) and that sexist attitudes and behaviours are such a part of the ethos in some schools that they go unnoticed (Lynch & Lodge, 2002). While sexual harassment in Irish schools has received little research attention (Lynch & Lodge, 2004), a successful legal case was taken by two teachers who were sexually harassed by students (Lynch & Lodge, 2004). It is worth noting that in 2012 the Ombudsman for Children in Ireland, Emily Logan, described as 'wholly unacceptable' the decision of a school to refuse to enrol a pregnant girl and that she called on the school to apologise for the treatment of the sixteen-year-old. In correspondence between her office and the school authorities, the school principal remained defiant, saying that 'This school is not a haven for young pregnant people or for young mothers, who in particular, have been in two other post-primary schools' (McGreevy, 2012). It was also reported in the media that in his correspondence, the principal said that his duty was to protect the honourable majority of his pupils (*Sligo Today*, 2012).

[30] By this deconstructive project, Egan and Hawkes (2009: 396) mean that we need to interrogate all the terms by which the sexual life of children is defined and constrained, because these terms narrow complex discussions by predetermining outcomes and they unwittingly reconstruct hegemonic boundaries.

CHAPTER 13

Children's Constructions of 'Porn' in an Irish Primary School: Implications for Boys

Alison Afra and Jean Quigley

Introduction

This chapter is a qualitative exploration of children's constructions of internet 'porn' in the contexts of mobile phone technology and an Irish primary school. The chapter is based on a broader study,[1] which explored sixth class[2] girls' and boys' gender and sexual identities. The overall aim of the study, developed in tandem with what the participants presented as being important to them, was to foreground children's constructions of 'childhood sexuality'. The study has proved timely, given the recent heightening of anxieties surrounding children from within the 'sexualisation of culture' discourse (e.g. DCYA, 2012).

The Return to Porn Studies

During the 1980s and 1990s a large body of research into the effects of pornography was conducted in social psychology. It was assumed that porn caused misogynistic attitudes to develop in men, attitudes that in turn caused men to be sexually violent against women. For example, male research participants would have their attitudes and/or behaviours towards women measured before and after viewing pornography, to test how the latter affected the former. Furthermore, the effects of different types of pornography were measured by varying the conditions for participants; for example some might be exposed to violent porn, others to non-violent porn (*see*, for example, Malamuth et al., 1980; Donnerstein

& Berkowitz, 1981; Marshall et al., 1991; Demaré et al., 1993). The methods and methodologies guiding these types of porn studies have been critiqued at length (e.g. King, 1993; Rubin, 1993; Segal, 1993; Jensen, 1998; Cameron & Frazer, 2000).[3] The critiques most relevant to the current chapter are considered here.

Experimental and/or correlational social psychological porn studies imbue pornography with special properties. In these studies it is assumed that pornography can directly penetrate the mind of the viewer, then proceed to implant and fossilise fixed and stable attitudes in his mind, which then deterministically control his subsequent behaviours. It is plausible, however, that men can engage with pornography for private pleasure (albeit problematically), but reject its ideology in interpersonal life (Hardy, 1998). Yet porn studies within mainstream social psychology tend to ignore the active participation of the viewer in determining the meaning of the porn viewed, preferring instead to pathologise men who engage with it (Attwood, 2005).

Thus far, social and/or developmental psychologists have been unable to test for a cause–effect relationship between porn and sexual violence in boys/young men, mainly because it would be unethical to conduct experiments on minors that involve pornography. Therefore research on adult men has recently, albeit problematically, been drawn upon to speculate on how pornography may be affecting younger populations (e.g. Flood, 2009; 2010). Again due to ethical limitations, findings from studies on the effects of 'sexual content' in mainstream media have been used to speculate on what the effects of actual pornography might be (e.g. Flood, 2009; 2010). Despite contextual differences, it is argued, again problematically, that pornography can only intensify the effects linked to mere sexual content because of its sexual explicitness (Flood, 2009; 2010).

Although there is an ethical obstruction to experimental research on the effects of pornography on minors, some survey questionnaire research has been conducted with young people (e.g. Bonino et al., 2006).[4] Female viewers of porn have also been studied to determine whether porn might cause them to inadvertently consent to their own victimisation (e.g. Bonino et al., 2006). Social and/or developmental psychology's conceptualisation of porn as harmful has been challenged, however, by recent research findings on children's and young people's experiences of viewing porn. For example, the majority of those young Greek people aged 9–18 who did report disgust at the pornography they had viewed on the internet did not consider that they had been harmed by it (Tsaliki, 2011). Yet there is an increasing interest in the topic of porn and younger populations (e.g. Flood, 2009; 2010), including teenage girls as well as teenage boys (e.g. Lo & Wei, 2005; Bonino, 2006). This is arguably a consequence of what has been described as the 'sexualisation of culture'.

The 'Sexualisation of Culture'

That contemporary western culture has become sexualised is evident in the 'proliferation of bodies "on display" … via mediums such as film, television, advertising, fashion, music videos, lad mags and internet pornography' (Bale, 2010: 824). Sex, especially porn-style sex, has become commercialised and mainstream (Attwood, 2009). One of the ways in which this is happening is through the unprecedented accessibility of pornography, often claimed to be only 'a mouse click away' (Attwood, 2009: xiii). Whilst there is a 'surprising degree of consensus' on the existence of an empirical phenomenon, the 'sexualisation of culture' (Gill, 2009: 140), there is much less agreement among the media, popular writers and academics with regard to its impact on individuals and society (Bale, 2010), hence the 'sexualisation debates' (Gill, 2009, *see also* Barker, 2011). The discourse surrounding impact is particularly dominant in relation to children (Bale, 2010).

In Ireland, of the 6 per cent of eleven- and twelve-year-olds who had seen 'sexual images' online, 4 per cent reported feeling 'bothered' (O'Neill et al., 2011: 32) by what they saw. Of the 3 per cent of eleven- and twelve-year-olds who experienced 'sexting' (defined [by the authors as opposed to the respondents] as receiving sexual messages online [and originating with the spread of mobile phone messaging]), 2 per cent were bothered by it (O'Neill et al., 2011). Considering that distress among children and young people who have viewed pornography is not necessarily related to the pornography *per se* but can be due to guilt for having accidentally encountered it online or fear of the risk of losing internet privileges (Mitchell et al., 2003), opportunities for open exploration of issues that might be bothersome are likely foreclosed (Hope, 2006).

Boys and the Missing Discourse of Concern

Where boys are concerned, it is often assumed that the sexualisation of culture conditions a hyper-sexual masculinity that overly objectifies girls and women whilst condoning male violence (e.g. Rush and La Nauze, 2006; APA Task Force, 2007; Papadopoulos, 2010; Bailey, 2011). Similar to the criticisms of the social psychological approaches to porn studies outlined above, the panic[5] about sexualisation imbues popular culture with special properties that allow it to override boys as active interpreters, positioning them instead as cultural dupes (Bale, 2010; Bragg et al., 2011). Some developmental psychologists would argue that sexualisation in general (Else-Quest & Shibley Hyde, 2009) and pornography more specifically (Cameron et al., 2005) need to be understood through a developmental lens because of how cognitive, emotional, physical, social and sexual development vary with age. However, scholars of childhood studies claim that children navigate popular culture in complex and contradictory ways and, like adults, actively reproduce and resist it (Egan & Hawkes, 2008). Furthermore, it has been argued that what influences behaviours is a much more complex combination of elements than just the media, such as 'previous experiences, opinions, values and suggestions from various sources' (Bale, 2010: 835).

Some boys (aged fourteen to seventeen – Cameron et al., 2005) and young men (Johansson and Hammaren, 2007) do report finding pleasure in pornography. The small minority of young men who retrospectively reported that viewing internet pornography before the age of eighteen had strong effects on their emotions reported feeling sexual excitement (Sabina et al., 2008). Porn can also be constructed negatively, however. For example, fourteen- to seventeen-year-old boys have described it as 'sick' (Cameron et al., 2005), while some young men recall it as arousing shock, surprise, guilt and shame for them before they had reached adulthood (Sabina et al., 2008). The same young men also spoke of how porn could turn them off sexual activity and give way to unwanted thoughts, as well as feelings of unattractiveness and inadequacy, again before reaching the age of eighteen (Sabina et al., 2008). What is more, porn can be experienced by young men ambivalently in addition to either positively or negatively (Johansson and Hammaren, 2007).

It is likely that sexualised culture and pornography, in particular, provide discourses from within which misogyny is made acceptable, but, as discussed above, there are more options available to boys than incorporating sexual violence into interpersonal relationships. Some developmental psychological research does refrain from demonising boys by acknowledging that it is difficult to conclude what the effects of pornographic media might be. On the contrary, it is implied that turning to internet porn is a natural effect of male pubertal development (*see* Skoog et al., 2009). The Skoog et al. (2009) research may be considered exceptional in that the rationale for study is not strictly situated in a pathologising, harms-based discourse but rather in a naturalising, biological one. Elsewhere, porn is assumed to be harmful, particularly in terms of how it affects boys' behaviours towards girls.

If the focus is solely on how boys using porn might be a threat to girls, boys' vulnerabilities may be rendered invisible. Segal (2010) argues that framing sexualisation as a dangerous thing and associating it with girls shores up symbolic machismo by downplaying boys' susceptibility to fear, abuse and violence, as experienced during the maintenance of gender and other hierarchies. For example, an ethnographic study in primary schools in the UK highlighted the power of hegemonic heterosexual masculinity to punish those boys positioned as 'failed males' (Renold, 2005). There is, of course, a place for pornography and/or sexualisation in a discussion on violence against girls and women (VAGW) (*see* Afra, 2013). However, the missing discourse of concern for boys in the sexualisation debates, apart from their behaviours toward girls, implies that the ability of boys to cope with male heterosexuality is innate, hence the assumption that there is no need to protect them (Egan & Hawkes, 2008). The normalisation of (hetero)sexuality for boys has left their everyday sexual cultures under-theorised and neglected, at least outside pathologising discourses (Renold, 2005). It is 'violent' boys and not 'sexual/ised' boys whom society positions as 'deviant' (Walkerdine, 1999). Boys-as-sex-abusers are of concern (in addition to boys-as-homosexual), but heterosexual masculinities are otherwise 'unproblematic' and, therefore, unproblematised (Renold, 2005).

Ireland, Sexualisation and the Future

In 2012 the Minister for Children and Youth Affairs, Frances Fitzgerald TD, launched a new National Children's Funded Research

Programme in which the 'sexualisation and commercialisation of childhood in Ireland' was identified as an area of research concern (DCYA, 2012). This focus on the sexualisation and commercialisation of childhood reflects recent political developments in the UK, where the UK government recently commissioned an 'independent'[6] review of the evidence on this topic (Bailey, 2011). The assessment was to be informed, in part, by the findings of pre-existing reviews, making the Bailey review, *Letting Children Be Children* (2011), one of several of its kind to be produced in the UK alone within a short number of years. This has led academics there to question the repeated government focus on sexualisation when young people have not been consulted about their concerns regarding their own lives. The political agenda of 'sexualisation' dominates, while risks in relation to health, housing, poverty and education are sidelined (Attwood et al., 2011).

Although O' Neill et al. (2011: 9) concluded that Ireland is relatively low, compared to other countries, in terms of overall exposure to online pornography and in terms of the degree to which children report feeling upset or bothered by their exposure to online sexual images, the current chapter is timely given the recent emergence of 'sexualisation' discourses in Ireland. In addition to contributing to understandings of boys' sexual cultures,[7] its methods are arguably more sophisticated than the standardised methods of experimental and survey social psychology, which ignore how audiences actively interpret, rather than passively soak up, various media (Attwood, 2005; Egan & Hawkes, 2008; Bragg et al., 2011). The chapter also foregrounds children's discussions about and reflections upon issues that are deemed to be endangering them, at a time when their opportunities to discuss such issues are limited (*see* Vanwesenbeeck, 2009; Attwood & Smith, 2011; Duits & van Zoonen, 2011; Lemish, 2011).

The Current Study

Participants

There were 24 participants in total: eleven boys and thirteen girls, aged eleven and twelve years and all forming one group of sixth class. Two of the boys identified as British and the rest as settled Irish. All eleven boys were white. Of the thirteen girls, one was

South-East Asian–Irish, a second was white continental European–Irish and a third girl was black African–Irish. The remaining ten girls were white and settled Irish. All participants were physically and intellectually normatively abled. To the best of the authors' knowledge, none of the participants identified as non-heterosexual. The large primary school where fieldwork took place was located in a high economic status suburb of Dublin and was under the patronage of the Catholic Church.

Postmodern Feminism: Conceptualising, Heterosexualising and Generationing 'Gender'

This study locates itself within critical social psychology, the aim of which is to highlight and challenge discourse and practice implicated in the oppression of individuals and groups, including those reproduced within the discipline of traditional social psychology (Gough & McFadden, 2001). The strand of critical social psychology that underpins the current study is postmodern feminism, which deconstructs the male/female binary that portrays men and women as inherently and essentially different (Stainton Rogers & Stainton Rogers, 2001). Rather than masculinity and femininity being caused by biological sex, gender identity is perceived as being constituted during social interaction (Butler, 2006). 'Gender' is therefore performative, i.e. it is something that we do rather than something that we already just are, hence the scare quotes to signify that 'gender' cannot and must not be taken for granted as a natural phenomenon.

Postmodernist feminist analyses recognise that power is not operated in any straightforward way. It is not simply the case that males hold power over females. Women have certain kinds of power, for example over children, who are also discriminated against, excluded and oppressed. Consequently, analyses of power must go beyond a preoccupation with gender to acknowledge other systems of oppression (Stainton Rogers & Stainton Rogers, 2001).

Butler (2006) argues that gender is performed within a 'heterosexual matrix', meaning that only those masculinities and femininities aligning with heterosexuality are culturally intelligible. In fact, when Renold (2005) set out on her ethnographic research with primary school children, the original aim had been to study how children construct 'gender', but as gendered subject positions were being taken up within a heteronormative framework, the study developed into one of children's sexual, as well as gender, identities (Renold, 2005). For example, boys who disliked football or who enjoyed romantic ballads were discriminated against for not being 'proper' boys. This describes the process of 'othering'. The interpretation of the data presented in the current chapter was influenced by Butler's theory of performativity and the 'heterosexual matrix'.

Conceptualising 'Porn'

In keeping with the social constructionist epistemologies of critical social psychology and postmodern feminism, 'porn' was conceptualised as an ongoing discursive object constructed by individuals in social interaction. Participants' constructions of 'porn' were understood to be surrounded by wider discourses, for example on 'gender', 'sexuality' and 'age'. It is common practice for pornography to be clearly defined in traditional social psychology by the research psychologists rather than by the research participants. It seems that once this obligation has been met, the authors can get on with the real business of interpreting 'findings' regarding the effects of a phenomenon, even though there is not necessarily a general consensus on the meaning of the phenomenon. Meaning is therefore imposed upon the content by the researcher, on behalf of the participant.

Postmodern feminism problematises assumptions of the fixedness and singularity of 'porn', but some anti-pornography feminists interpret this as playing intellectual games about 'polysemic texts', while the real issue of violence against women within the porn industry is being 'dodged' (e.g. Dines, 1998; Jensen, 1998). We see the troubling of the meaning of 'porn' as an important critique of one of the most influential sources of 'knowledge' available to society about pornography, i.e. the 'findings' produced within mainstream psychology. Such problematisation is indicative of neither a 'pro-porn' nor an 'anti-porn' stance. Rather, it is the rejection of 'tired binaries' (Attwood, 2009) in favour of acknowledging and 'holding the tension' (Barker, 2011) that emerges from the complexity and multiplicity of lived experience.

Procedure

Ethical approval was granted by the School of Psychology Research Ethics Committee of Trinity College Dublin for the study conducted. Informed consent was given by the school, by the participants' parents and by the sixth-class girls and boys who participated. The fieldwork was conducted during the academic year of 2009/2010. There were 32 observational visits in total. The number of visits per month ranged from one to five, with an average of 3.5 visits per month over a nine-month period. In addition to observations, the fieldworker (first author) asked the class to write stories and emails, to draw pictures and to do some drama activities. Each of these activities contributed to the entire data corpus. There were a total of seventeen focus group discussions and 30 pair-interviews, which were recorded and transcribed. Focus group discussions involved three to seven 'same' gender and/or 'mixed'[8] gender participants, depending on the children's preferences on any given day. Pair-interviews involved only two participants, which were always 'same' gender – again by choice of the children – and were intended to simulate one-to-one interviews as the school's insurance policy prohibited the interviewing of children individually.

Although a semi-structured interview schedule informed by previous observations and containing open-ended, non-leading questions was often prepared in advance of recorded sessions, participants were also encouraged to introduce topics of their own choosing for discussion. This was to ensure that participants' priorities were kept in the foreground. The dataset relevant for this chapter comprised: transcripts from two pair-interviews, each with two girls; one pair-interview with two boys; and one focus group discussion involving three boys. Observation diary notes and retrospective journal notes that were systematically recorded subsequent to fieldwork visits as part of researcher reflexivity are also included.

All names used herein are pseudonyms. The transcripts were subjected to Carla Willig's version of Foucauldian discourse analysis (FDA) (see Willig, 2008a: 112–28, 2008b for guidelines). FDA was the analytic 'method' of choice for the current dataset because it attempts to combine micro- and macro- levels of analysis. FDA can therefore be used to understand both social constraints placed upon individuals-in-social-interaction and how individuals-in-social-interaction actively reproduce and/or resist those constraints. FDA seeks to uncover how certain constructions of 'reality' benefit some individuals and groups while disadvantaging others. In other words, it allows us to see how individuals are positioned within systems of difference and inequality. This linking of power to discourse is helpful to critical social psychology as it facilitates the aim of this research, which is to highlight and challenge the oppression of individuals and groups and to promote social change (Gough & McFadden, 2001).

Contextualisation of 'Findings'[9]

'Porn' had been discovered by school staff as a result of a violent fight between two boys (David and Anthony), which involved an escalation of one boy taunting the other with 'gay porn' (Anthony's words) from a mobile phone to imply that he was 'gay' (participants' word). While discussing during interviews a recently delivered anti-bullying programme, some children talked about the 'porn fight', thus leading to an extended discussion of 'porn'.[10] However, one of the ways to construct 'porn' was as 'unspeakable' (note: opening square brackets preceding text indicate overlapping speech):

Interviewer:	What was the fight about? … Or how did it get started?
Mikey:	David just kept on, like, like, it wasn't the first time David had ever, like, annoyed Anthony.
Graham:	He just [kept on doing it
Mikey:	[annoying him and annoying him [and annoying him
Graham:	[and then Anthony just acted out. He acted and then just …
Interviewer:	And what exactly was David doing to annoy Anthony do you know? …
Mikey:	Calling him names and just … just calling him gay and like all that [----------------------------]
Mikey:	I think he was texting him stuff, was he?
Graham:	Yeah, I don't know.

The specific details about how David was 'annoying' Anthony, i.e. by watching 'porn' in the classroom and by taunting him with 'gay porn', were omitted from Graham and Mikey's accounts. When probed, Mikey diverted attention away from 'porn' by emphasising the end to which David had been using 'porn' as a means, namely to ridicule Anthony as 'gay'. The 'just' of 'just calling him gay' functioned to reassure the researcher, an adult woman, that there was nothing more to know about. Shortly after, Mikey conspires to share the 'secret' of 'porn' when he says, 'I think he was texting him stuff, was he?' Graham refuses to take the discussion in this direction by explicitly claiming ignorance: 'Yeah, I don't know.'

Five boys in total spoke about 'porn' and even then, two out of the five subsequently withdrew the relevant sections from their transcripts.[11] Consequently, the co-production of verbal data that was explicitly about 'porn' was extremely challenging. In an effort to address this issue, the children were invited to write stories entitled 'my mobile phone', in case they should feel more inclined to discuss 'porn' in this context. Although nobody did actually write about 'porn' during this task, the stories were consulted to help interpret the more overtly 'porn' data. Other discussions from the stories that were drawn upon included 'awkwardness' between children and adults, for example, when adults want to ask children about girlfriends/boyfriends, going to the disco, or recreational drugs.

Ethics

The vice-principal was notified about the emergence of porn-related data in the project. This step was deemed necessary because in not knowing precisely what it was that the girls and boys had seen in their lives, let alone on the day of the 'porn fight', it was impossible to know if they had been illegally downloading material rated 18.[12] Interestingly, the vice-principal disagreed that what he had seen on the phone involved in the 'porn fight' was 'porn', and suggested that the children were exaggerating by calling it that. He considered whatever he had seen to be typical of what boys 'that age' would be 'naturally' curious about. Even so, he was compelled to add that he had advised the boys to be more 'respectful' toward women. The teacher (a woman) who had been on yard (playground) duty the day of the 'porn fight' referred to the images that she saw as 'unsavoury'.

To what exactly the participants, the yard duty teacher or the vice-principal were referring can neither be confirmed nor disconfirmed. In any case, it is precisely these contentious meanings that get drawn out by discourse analysis. The vice-principal, who held the view that the 'children of today' were becoming older at a younger age than previous generations, was satisfied that the project include the theme of 'porn' if that was what the children were presenting as important in their lives.

Findings

The 'Technologisation of Childhood' Discourse

One of the ways to construct 'porn' was as an inevitable feature of boyhood, and this was done within the 'technologisation of childhood' discourse:

Extract 1:[13]

Interviewer:	Ok. So how do kids your age manage to get pornography?
Brian:	Emmm …
Rory:	That's David
Brian:	That's David
Anthony:	It's called –
Brian:	No one else has porn on the phone
Interviewer:	Ok
Anthony:	It's pretty sick like literally this is all you have to do [takes his phone out of his pocket]
Interviewer:	Don't get it now
Rory:	[laughs]
Anthony:	I'm not. Oh yeah, like I'd do that. All you have to do is go into your browser. Go into Home and connect. And when it finally connects you just type in 'porn'.
Interviewer:	And is –
Anthony:	And then you just go down and you click on whatever you want and then you're able to like maybe copy and paste it or something
Interviewer:	Ok. So it's very easy to get from the internet basically?
Brian:	[yeah
Anthony:	[yeah.

'Porn' is available on demand, 'literally this is all you have to do [takes his phone out of his pocket]', and easily downloadable, 'all you have to do is', 'you just type it in', and so on. These ways of constructing 'porn' depart drastically from the claims of secondary school students of a rural town in Ireland twelve years previously. Then, 'porn' was difficult to obtain and few of the students had ever seen a porn film (Inglis, 1998). They do resonate, however, with findings that emerged in a more recent Swedish grounded theory study of young people's (aged 16–23) thoughts about pornography, which noted: 'The informants claimed that "It is everywhere", referring not only to easily available pornographic material but also to other media with a sexualized content, implying that pornography was almost impossible to avoid' (Haegsstrom-Nordin et al., 2006: 389).

The 'technologisation of childhood' discourse informed constructions of contemporary childhood as radically different from past childhoods, primarily because of the presence of mobile phone technology:

Extract 2:[14]

Interviewer:	Ok mmm. Em, but weren't your parents your age before? [laughs]
Luke:	Yeah
Matthew:	Yeah
Alison:	That doesn't help, no?
Matthew:	No
Luke:	No
Interviewer:	[laughs] So tell me a bit about that then, why that isn't helpful
Matthew:	Just they're not that age now
David:	Yeah. See, things are different now than when they were like kids. Mobile phones, and like you talk about phones and stuff
Interviewer:	Yeah
Matthew:	Inboxes
Interviewer:	In boxes?
Matthew:	Yeah you know your inbox on your mobile phone?
Interviewer:	Oh sorry!
Matthew:	And your Mam wants to see your messages

Extract 2, above, shows how the boys constructed 'intergenerational incomprehensibility', where parents and children had little hope of empathising with each other because of the difference mobile phones have made to growing up today. This notion of impossibility for mutual understanding informed the practice of keeping intergenerational communication to a minimum, and likely gave rise to a sense of alienation from adults.

Extract 3:[15]

Anthony:	I remember, em, one of my friends he was looking it up. And I was like, 'aw stop that's sort of perverted' and, like, he said, 'aw it's grand' and I took his phone and … somehow or other I went in. I took the phone for the whole night, like, off him and I went in to settings and I eh deleted his eh browser so he couldn't look it up coz I said, 'eventually one day your mam and your dad are going to take your phone and look at the addresses.' Like you're able to enter addresses.
Interviewer:	Yeah
Anthony:	Then all of a sudden they're going to see like porn horn[16] and all this crazy cack[17] so

With reference to the above extracts, parental surveillance of text messages and internet usage is expected and encouraged in contemporary society. Therefore, the notion that 'porn' was simply sitting in one's pocket is contradicted by the need to avoid or delete it. This apparent dilemma can be addressed by taking up the subject position of being more technologically savvy than adults. When asked to write a piece entitled 'My Mobile Phone', one boy, who chose to remain anonymous, wrote: 'My mam and dad check my texts on my old phone but they don't know how to work my new one'. Refer back also to Extract 3, where Anthony is aware of the storage of an internet history on the mobile device and claims to know how to delete any incriminating evidence against his friend. It is noteworthy that he is not concerned with how his friend might be harmed by 'porn' *per se*. Rather, and similar to boys and young men in a recent UK study on the use of the internet at school (Hope, 2006), his priority is to avoid getting caught.

The seeming ease with which 'porn' can be accessed, along with any desire to do so, is obstructed by more than merely getting caught. Anthony has pathologised the downloading of 'porn' on to a phone as 'sort of perverted', as well as describing the actual contents as 'crazy cack'. Through his construction of it as being only 'sort of perverted' and not absolutely so, while his friend defines it as not at all perverted, 'aw, it's grand', we are witness to the pushes and pulls of 'porn' as produced by overlapping and competing discourses. This is a further point of similarity with the existing literature in that it is normative to admit to familiarity with mobile-phone 'porn', whilst simultaneously denying possession of it on one's own phone (Bond, 2010).

The chapter now turns to a presentation of the remaining discourses that inform these contradictory ways to talk about 'porn'.

The 'Male Adolescent (Hetero)sexual Curiosity' Discourse

There was evidence in the current study of the naturalisation of boys' interest in 'porn'. However, being a boy was insufficient grounds upon which sexual curiosity could be legitimated. Instead, if boys were too young to be securely positioned as adolescent, their interest in 'porn' was difficult to convincingly construct as natural:

Extract 4:[18]

Sophie:	They [the boys in the class] get caught by their mam [laughing] and they don't care. They just keep doing it.
Anna:	My brother got caught, but he's sixteen, so it's kind of different
Sophie:	[laughs] I caught my brother doing it
	[--]
Alison:	And how old was he?
Sophie:	He is thirteen but he was, like, twelve at the time

Although so compelling that it cannot be quelled by getting caught – 'they don't care. They just keep doing it' – maleness must be combined with adolescence for the watching of 'porn' to be legitimated. That is why Anna's sixteen-year-old brother did not fully get caught, 'it's kind of different', whereas Sophie's did, because he was a twelve-year-old pre-adolescent at the time and not the thirteen-year-old adolescent that he is today. The 'but' in 'but he was like twelve at the time' shows incongruence between her brother's position as pre-adolescent and his adolescent action of watching 'porn' at that time. In other words, masculinity had to intersect with the 'age-grade' (James & Prout, 1998, cited in Renold, 2005) of adolescence for an interest in 'porn' to be acceptable, hence the labelling of the discourse as 'male adolescent (hetero)sexual curiosity' rather than merely 'male sexual curiosity'. What is more, '(hetero)' precedes 'sexual' as a reminder that heterosexuality as opposed to homo- or bi-sexualities is the identity privileged as natural for adolescent boys. From within the discourse of 'male adolescent (hetero)sexual curiosity', boys still located in middle childhood can be positioned as sexually precocious for demonstrating an interest in 'porn'.

The idea that a boy can be sexually precocious is uncommon in the literature on childhood sexuality. It is the girl-child who is chastised for becoming sexual before it is considered appropriate for her to do so, even though girl-child innocence is fetisised. Whilst boys do not have to take up overtly heterosexual practices to validate their hetero-masculinity but can instead do so through sports, girls are already expected to define themselves in terms of romantic investment in boys during the primary school years (Thorne, 1993). However, when boys do start to take up the subject position of boyfriend, adult anxiety is less likely to be roused. It is presumed that boys can innately cope with being (hetero)sexual. Recall from the introduction how this is similar to the missing discourse of concern for boys within the sexualisation debates.

The original discussion, from which this next extract comes, was about how 'awkward' it is when adults and children talk to each other about embarrassing topics, such as drugs or the disco. The three boys have just informed the interviewer that mothers sometimes check the inboxes of boys' mobile phones:

Extract 5:

Interviewer: What? [surprised] Do they want to see your messages really?

David: Yeah

Matthew:	Yeah
Interviewer:	And what do you think they want to see your messages for?
David:	To see who you've been talking to and that
Matthew:	A girlfriend
David:	Yeah and what have you been talking about and stuff
Interviewer:	Ok and what would happen if they saw a message from a girlfriend?
Matthew:	Probably –
Luke:	Give out to you
Matthew:	Yeah
David:	And ask you, like, give out to you and ask you loads of questions, 'Who is she?'

Through the positioning of mothers as 'superintendents', monitoring (hetero)sexual relations, and the construction of having a girlfriend as punishable, 'give out to you', the boys reproduce the notion of boyhood as a time of sexual innocence. They concurrently problematise this notion, however, by virtue of claiming that having a girlfriend is something that mothers consider a possibility in their lives. The blurring of age-grade, i.e. whether to identify as 'child', 'adolescent' or something else, is further evident here:

Extract 6:

Matthew:	I don't think my mam would give out to me. She'd just be asking me loads of questions like, 'Who is she?', 'Is she cute?' 'Is she pretty?' All them kind of questions.
David:	Yeah, that's the same with my mom. She'd do that.
Interviewer:	And would your mum give out to you?
Luke:	No … em … no she wouldn't. She'd just …
Matthew:	Curious
Luke:	My brother's, em, he was in first year and he had a girlfriend and, like, she gave out to him but I wouldn't really say she'd give out to me.

The uncertainty surrounding whether or not having a girlfriend is punishable, evident in Matthew's abrupt shift from agreement to disagreement, 'I don't think my mam would give out to me', shows the ambiguity surrounding the il/legitimate identification as (hetero)sexual. Can the boys be positioned as 'children' who are still 'sexual innocents', or as 'adolescents' and therefore naturally '(hetero)sexual'? Why would a first-year boy (one year older than these boys and already in secondary school) be too young but a sixth-class boy not: 'she gave out to *him*, but I wouldn't really say she'd give out to me'? The boys are struggling to negotiate their current age-grade in terms of whether that stage can legitimate identifying as (hetero)sexual or not, a discursive practice coined 'sexual generationing' (Renold, 2005: 25).

Are they 'sexually innocent children', and/or '(hetero)sexual adolescents', and/or are they perhaps drawing on a 'premature sexualisation of childhood' discourse to position themselves as children who have been prematurely (hetero)sexualised? Renold (2005) argues that boys are rarely subject to a 'he's growing up too soon' discourse in terms of masculine heterosexuality yet Extracts 5 and 6 show the boys responding to a dilemma of, 'Am I old enough?' Despite their similar age in years and in spite of each belonging to sixth class, multiple and competing discourses render their age-grade grouping fragmented and unclear, as age-grade groupings tend to be (Renold, 2005: 25). Furthermore, the notion that male (hetero)sexual curiosity in 'porn' or interest in girlfriends is activated by the onset of puberty, and not before, is developmentalist. It allows the discourse of childhood sexual innocence to determine the in/appropriateness of the psycho-sexual development of a boy rather than boys' diverse experiences determining multiple understandings of what so-called normality might look like.

Turning the focus to contexts where the boys were less constrained by the dilemma of sexual generationing, the discussion now turns to how the discourse of 'male adolescent (hetero)sexual curiosity' implicated 'porn' in the execution of school-based sexual harassment. If engagement with 'porn' is driven by a natural male (hetero)sexual curiosity, then it can function as a marker of hetero-masculinity. By implication, failure to engage with 'porn' can be a marker of failed masculinity and/or homosexuality:

Extract 7:[19]

Interviewer: And was it a case of well how was Anthony involved in this phone with porn on it?

Katie: I think he was kind of being nosey kind he[20] was like 'what are you looking at?' and stuff even though they weren't showing it to him.

Pauline: Yeah he was trying to stop them from watching it because they were going to get into trouble so practically Anthony was just trying to protect them.

Extract 8:[21]

Sophie: David was watching porn [laughs] and Anthony goes 'Stop' and he was like 'Oh you just don't want to watch it because you're gay' and then he was like 'You want to watch gay porn' and all this and then –

In the extracts above, the girls position the boys in the class as othering Anthony. Anthony's advice to the boys to not watch 'porn' results in his masculinity being called into question. In being positioned as a failed boy for preferring to avoid 'porn', 'porn' is instrumental in his heterosexist harassment. In addition, his heterosexuality is questioned, thus implicating 'porn' in his homophobic harassment also.

In his account of the 'porn-fight', Anthony confirms being on the receiving end of David's homophobic harassment: 'he was showing me gay porn and calling me gay, like'. He omits, however, that his discouraging the boys from watching 'porn' was what had led to the fight in the first place. This omission may have been to avoid an 'abnormal' presentation of his masculinity during the interview in which the account was produced, abnormal since, as a boy, he should have wanted to join the boys in watching 'porn'.

Even so, ostensibly approving of 'porn' could not guarantee the consolidation of hetero-masculinity. Refer back to Extract 1, for how David was othered for being in possession of it, 'that's David', though this may well have been the speaker's strategy to avoid self-incrimination, 'no one else has porn on the phone'.

Also, where Anthony had been harassed on the grounds of fearing getting caught, it would seem that anxiety around 'porn' was not a stable signifier of 'other' for all of the boys. For example, Pauline reported, 'and, em, they sent it to all the boys. And then I heard Matthew say, "Oh thank God I deleted it".' Whereas it was acceptable for Matthew to reject 'porn' so as to uphold adults' expectations of sexual innocence, thereby avoiding punishment, similarly motivated actions had been detrimental for Anthony. Since Anthony was subjected to perpetual harassment at school and since Matthew had the privilege of a 'popular boy' identity, the events described in these paragraphs are unsurprising.

In addition to the issues of heterosexist and homophobic harassment was the issue of heterosexual harassment of boys by boys. When a 'popular boy' like Matthew, who is often (though not always) acknowledged and acknowledgeable as 'proper' and heterosexual, prefers not to receive 'porn' texts, demanding that he enjoy 'porn' at school by sending him pornographic downloads is an example of heterosexual harassment. It would be unreasonable to conclude, however, that the various instances of sexual harassment outlined in this chapter have become part of boys' experiences because of 'porn' on mobile phone technology. Different types of sexual harassment of boys were observed in primary schools before ownership of mobile phones with internet access had become normative for children (e.g. Renold, 2005).

The 'Porn as Misogynistic' Discourse

An additional overlapping discourse of 'porn as misogynistic' emerged, but was only explicit from within girls' accounts:

Extract 9:[22]

Interviewer:	What was on the picture?
Katie:	A naked woman
Interviewer:	Her whole body or just her breasts?
Pauline:	[Her whole body
Katie:	[Her whole body. But like –
Pauline:	They're so rude. They have no respect for girls.
Katie:	I know.
	[---]

Katie: Yeah [laughs] and then like I was talking to Gary about it and I was like, 'do you not realise how gross that is? Why did you watch it?'

The practice of disapproving of 'porn', which had been unavailable to Anthony, was more readily available to the girls, as was the judging of boys for their engagement with it – 'why did you watch it?' – along with their stigmatisation as 'misogynists' – 'they have no respect for girls.' In extreme circumstances (*see* Afra, 2013), a boy could even be dehumanised as a 'dirty pig' or 'dirty animal' (Anna's words). Being associated with 'porn' offered boys embarrassing or shameful subject positions:

Extract 10:[23]

Katie: And em then Ashley was laughing coz she found it funny [the question of why 'boobs' are 'so interesting for boys']. I don't know why. Maybe she thought I was trying to be funny or something. So then she asked Mikey [why 'boobs' were 'so interesting for boys'] and Mikey was blushing and he was like 'I don't know. They just are.'

The boys' reluctance to discuss 'porn' with girl peers or a woman researcher should therefore come as little surprise.

Summary of 'Findings' and Conclusion

To construct 'porn', participants drew on the 'adolescent male (hetero)sexual curiosity' discourse, which in turn helped consolidate 'hetero-masculinity', either through normalisation of 'porn' or the 'othering' of those preferring to reject it. The overlapping discourse of 'childhood innocence' did, however, in some circumstances, provide respite from any imperative to watch 'porn', especially in the context of school. The subject position of 'innocent child' was not always readily aligned with the identity of 'sixth-class boy' due to the precariousness of 'sexual generationing' (Renold, 2005). Nonetheless, the subject position of 'adolescent' was not sufficiently available to the boys such that they could openly discuss 'porn'. If they had been securely pubertal, the discourse of 'porn as misogynistic' may have obstructed channels of communication anyway. Although the 'technologisation of childhood' discourse facilitated some discussion of 'porn' – probably because of how mobile phone technology rendered 'porn' inevitable, thus removing responsibility from the boys and on to a technologised culture – the discourse alone was not enough to smash the silences, secrecies and erasures of 'porn'. This discourse likely alienated the boys from adults because of how it differentiated the lives of today's children from those of the past.

Consequently, issues of consent pertaining to the heterosexist, homophobic and heterosexual harassment of boys by boys also passed by more or less unnoticed, with little space to openly deal with the pains, pleasures and ambivalences experienced through 'porn'.

Future research needs to include participants from more diverse social backgrounds in order to explore how 'class', 'race', 'ethnicity' and 'disability' intersect with 'age', 'gender' and 'sexuality' when constructing 'porn'. In the meantime, the complexity of boys' sexual cultures needs urgent recognition if gender and sexual equality among primary school boys is to be taken seriously. It is hoped that the current chapter has contributed towards bringing boys' vulnerabilities into view. The chapter has initiated consideration of the impact of the 'sexualisation of culture' on boys in terms of implications for *boys*.

Notes

A special thanks to all the children who kindly and generously participated in the study.
[1]   The study was conducted for the first author's non-funded doctoral research, which the second author supervised.
[2]   Sixth class is the final year of primary school in Ireland and consists of children aged eleven and twelve.
[3]   For a general critique of the methods and methodologies of traditional/ mainstream social psychology, *see* Gough and McFadden (2001).
[4]   Some commentators have recommended that experimental research be conducted with young people in the future; *see*, for example, Lo and Wei, 2005.
[5]   This panic may be further understood as a moral panic. In order to avoid violence, girls must avoid attracting sexual attention. The onus is therefore on girls to avoid inflaming male desire in a blame-the-victim

logic, while displays of female sexual desire and pleasure are contained (*see* Egan & Hawkes, 2008).

[6]   The review was overseen by Reg Bailey, who is Chief Executive of the Mothers' Union – a Christian charity.

[7]   Although there has been little academic output in Ireland to date, a rudimentary glance at media coverage suggests that the construction of boys-as-a-danger-to-girls-but-otherwise-fine is reproduced by Irish society also. For example, Herald.ie journalist Sinead Ryan (2011) criticises newsagents for placing little boys' magazines, e.g. *Bob the Builder*, in juxtaposition with what are supposed to be 'top-shelf' lads' mags. This is considered harmful for how it encourages boys to value and practise female sexual objectification, presumably normalising VAGW in the process. *Irish Times* journalist Sheila Wayman does not say why sexualisation is bad for boys, but merely asserts that it is in one article (Wayman, 2010), before arguing in a later article (Wayman, 2011) that Irish boys are now victims of the sexually zealous Irish alpha-female girl-child. Given the prevalence of the sexual double standard among teenagers in Ireland, where girls must curtail their sexual desire in interpersonal relationships and sexual violence against them is justified as an inevitable offshoot of male sexuality (Hyde & Howlett, 2004), Wayman's (2012) assertion that girls come out on top is gravely dismissive of the dangers girls face. Female violence against boys does exist (Renold, 2005). Together with male violence against boys, it tends to be played down (e.g. Bonino et al., 2006). Wayman's (2012) positioning of boys as sexually victimised by girls would appear to be a particularity, indeed peculiarity, of the Irish media. While it may contain some merit, it unfortunately comes with a price, namely the insidious obscuring of male sexual violence against girls (*see* Hyde & Howlett, 2004), as well as male violence against and sexual harassment of boys (*see* Renold, 2005).

[8]   The scare quotes signify how 'same' and 'mixed' cannot be taken for granted since an all-boy group, for example, could consist of masculine, feminine and androgynous boys, who furthermore might do hegemonic masculinity in one instance but fail to uphold it or even deliberately resist it in the next.

[9]   Scare quotes are used to highlight how the discourse analyst's reading of the data is but one interpretation. Although every effort is made to offer a credible interpretation and support the 'findings' with empirical evidence (e.g. in the form of participants' quotes), the 'findings' remain unapologetically open to re-interpretation. Indeed, the reader is invited to scrutinise them (*see* Gough & McFadden, 2001).

[10]   It was hoped that raising the anti-bullying programme during recorded sessions would encourage the children to talk about 'porn'. The decision not to confront participants more directly about the topic was based on previous discussions during the year about kissing (called 'meeting') and the relationships and sexuality education (RSE) curriculum, which had

led some children to feel 'awkward'. This short extract exemplifies the necessity to have allowed individual children to take control over whether to talk about 'porn' or not:

Interviewer:	What was the talk about?
Ava:	About the word in, I don't like saying it. The word in, em ...
Lily:	[laughs]
Ava:	[laughs] It's a bit weird.
Lily:	[laughs]
Interviewer:	What was the word? Sex?
Lily:	Yeah
	[------------------]
Lily:	Remember, we're twelve.

[11] Once the fieldworker had transcribed interviews, participants were provided with the transcripts so that they could read over them and withdraw any sections about which they had a change of mind. The point of this was to increase comfort during recorded discussions in the knowledge that subsequent regrets or worries could be redressed. It is an ethical requirement of the Psychological Society of Ireland (PSI) and the British Psychological Society (BPS) that participants be advised, as part of the informed consent procedure, that they are entitled to withdraw participation at any point and that they are not required or expected to provide an explanation for withdrawal.

[12] It had been a condition of the Ethics Committee of the School of Psychology, Trinity College Dublin that any disclosures by children to the researcher about illegal activities were to be reported to a gatekeeper. The fieldworker might have been obliged to report the possibility that children accessing materials from the internet may have been doing so illegally. On the one hand, since the vice-principal was already aware of the fight and therefore of the circulation of 'porn', the fieldworker was not obliged to report on it. But as some of the interviews involved discussions of 'porn' beyond the 'porn' that was particular to 'the fight', the fieldworker judged it best to advise the gatekeepers about a more generalised circulation of 'porn'. It can be assumed that the boys did not trust fully in the procedure of anonymity and feared being identified by adults as knowing about or watching 'porn'.

[13] Focus group discussion: extract immediately follows Anthony telling his story about the 'porn-fight'.

[14] Focus group discussion: extract in the middle of a discussion about 'awkwardness' in 'child–adult relations'.

[15] Focus group discussion: extract during explanation of how to access 'porn'.

[16] It cannot be said for certain, but 'porn horn' was presumably a slang phrase for 'porn erection'.

[17] 'Cack' is a slang word to refer to something as being 'shit' or excrement.

[18] Pair-interview: discussion that followed after recounting the 'porn fight'.

[19] Pair-interview: talking about the 'porn fight' in the context of 'bullying'.

[20] This is transcribed *verbatim*.

[21] Pair-interview: talking about the 'porn fight' in the context of 'bullying'.

[22] Pair-interview: continuation of talking about the 'porn fight'.

[23] Pair-interview: continuation of talking about the 'porn fight'.

Section 7

Sexualities and Disabilities – Rights and Recognition

CHAPTER 14

Constructing the Sexualities of People with Intellectual Disabilities

Grace Kelly

Introduction

In this chapter I explore the ongoing difficulties faced by people with intellectual disabilities in Ireland in relation to exercising their sexual rights. Drawing on staff and family discussions of the sexuality of intellectually disabled people, I demonstrate the routine infantalisation of people with intellectual disabilities and the failure to recognise them as having sexual or romantic desires. Informed by a social constructionist perspective, I tease out the multiple discursive and material practices through which staff and parents construct the sexualities of people with intellectual disabilities. The chapter is based on findings from focus groups with parents and staff in a disability service in the Irish midlands. These were completed as part of my doctoral research, exploring sexuality and intellectual disability in Ireland.[1] The data presented here explores how the parents and staff understood and talked about the sexuality of people with intellectual disabilities.

Background to the Research

Historically, the sexuality and fertility of intellectually disabled people has caused anxiety. While discourses of people with intellectual disabilities as childlike and sexually innocent abounded (e.g. 'holy innocent', 'God's special children'), these discourses competed with others that constructed people with intellectual disabilities as sexually threatening (Carlson, 2001). There were characterisations of intellectually disabled people as sexually uncontrollable and promiscuous and this, combined with a belief that intellectual disability is genetically inherited and that women with intellectual disabilities would produce large families they would be unable to care for, meant that the sexuality of people with intellectual disabilities was constructed as a social problem. Across America and Western Europe, a solution to this perceived problem was the forced sterilisation and institutionalisation of disabled people (Priestley, 2003). In Ireland, this eugenic ideology can be detected in the comments of Frederick Rainsford, Medical Superintendent of St Stewart's Institution, Dublin, who, in 1906, recommended the building of large training institutions because of concerns about 'the number of weak-minded persons who, being at large are a source of danger to the State, either as criminals or as profligates adding unfit units to the population yearly' (cited in Conneally, 1988: 130).

Since the 1970s there have been progressive moves from institutionalisation to normalisation, community integration and rights (Owen et al., 2009). But progress in supporting intellectually disabled people to lead a normal sexual life has been notably slower (Lesseliers & Van Hove, 2002; Hamilton, 2009; Wilson et al., 2011). In Ireland, legislation that aims to protect people who are 'mentally impaired' from sexual exploitation (section 5, Criminal Law (Sexual Offences) Act 1993) manages to provide inadequate protection to those who might need it, while at the same time being over-paternalistic and creating uncertainty regarding whether two people with intellectual disabilities can legally have sexual intercourse with each other (Law Reform Commission, 2005; 2011). It has been suggested that this legislation is impeding the provision of proactive supports for people with intellectual disabilities (Foley & Kelly, 2009). Research highlights that there is 'no national structured approach' to the provision of sex education to people with intellectual disabilities (Allen & Seery, 2007: 6) and that there is 'inconsistency' across disability services in terms of whether they have a policy on relationships and sexuality and what the content of this is (Foley & Kelly, 2009: 21). Staff members say that they are not adequately trained or supported in this area (Simpson et al., 2006; Allen & Seery, 2007).

The UN Convention on the Rights of Persons with Disabilities (2006) (UNCRPD) provides an important stimulus for action with regard to disability rights issues. With regard to sexuality, Article 23 commits governments to taking 'effective and appropriate measures to eliminate discrimination against persons with disabilities in all matters relating to marriage, family, parenthood and relationships, on an equal basis with others'. Ireland signed the Convention in 2007 and the current Minister for Justice and Equality, Alan Shatter TD, noted the State's intention to ratify it once the government was 'in a position to comply with the obligations imposed' (Shatter, 2012a). In particular, he acknowledged that modern legal capacity legislation needs to be enacted in Ireland (Shatter, 2012a).[2]

The challenge facing professionals is articulated as one of needing to balance the protection of vulnerable adults from exploitation and abuse with the promotion of their sexual rights (e.g. Dukes & McGuire, 2009). However, research with people with intellectual disabilities suggests that the issue is more complicated than this. A previous article based on another aspect of my PhD research – focus groups with people with intellectual disabilities – found that intellectually disabled people experience a range of barriers in this area of their lives (Kelly et al., 2009). The people with intellectual disabilities whom I spoke with had huge deficits in their knowledge about sexual matters, experienced many restrictions at home and in their services and, unsurprisingly, many believed that relationships were not allowed (Kelly et al., 2009). In addition, while many of my research participants had been in relationships and others wanted to be in one, the majority had no real awareness that they had rights in this area and were instead resorting to having relationships in secret. My findings correspond with previous Irish and international research with people with intellectual disabilities (Heyman & Huckle, 1995; Lesseliers & Van Hove, 2002; Evans, 2002; Scior, 2003; Simpson et al., 2006; Hollomotz & the Speakup Committee, 2008; Hollomotz, 2011; Bane et al., 2012), and suggest that the difficulties intellectually disabled people experience in relation to sexuality, vulnerability and/or inappropriate behaviour may be as much to do with the social circumstances of their lives as with individual deficiencies.

Research on attitudes towards the sexuality of people with intellectual disabilities suggests that there is at least some acceptance of their sexuality (Ryan & McConkey, 2000; Oliver et al., 2002; Karellou, 2003a; Cuskelly & Bryde, 2004; Cuskelly & Gilmore, 2007; Insight Statistical Consulting, 2007), although attitudes remain more conservative than towards the sexuality of non-disabled people (Scotti et al., 1996; Oliver et al., 2002; Cuskelly & Gilmore, 2007; Gilmore & Chambers, 2010). Attitudes are less positive the more sexually intimate the relationship (Evans, 2002), with the least accepting attitudes being in relation to people with intellectual disabilities as parents (Cuskelly & Gilmore, 2007; Wilkenfeld & Ballan, 2011). In line with this, contraceptive use has the most significant effect on attitudes towards sexual intercourse (Esterle et al., 2008; Morales et al., 2010; 2011). Studies suggest that it is difficult for women with intellectual disabilities to be seen as sexually willing and competent (Hamilton, 2010); and although men with intellectual disabilities are perceived as having greater sexual needs (Hamilton, 2010), their sexuality is often articulated within a 'problematised' male discourse that focuses on inappropriate and problematic sexual behaviour (Wilson et al., 2011).

Research specifically exploring parent/guardian attitudes suggests that while they want their intellectually disabled relative to develop friendships (Caffrey, 1992; Redmond, 1996; Simpson et al., 2006), few are positive about the idea of their relative having an intimate relationship, getting married or having children (Heyman & Huckle, 1995; Redmond, 1996; Evans, 2002; Simpson et al., 2006; Swango-Wilson, 2009). Often they do not perceive their relative as capable of intimate relationships (Evans, 2002) and they are concerned about the risk of pregnancy (Heyman & Huckle, 1995; Redmond, 1996; Swango-Wilson, 2009), and/or that their relative is vulnerable and may be exploited (Heyman & Huckle, 1995; Redmond, 1996; Simpson et al., 2006; Swango-Wilson, 2009; Rogers, 2009; 2010). Family members often have a high degree of control over the relationships and experiences of their relatives with intellectual disability,[3] and studies suggest that they expect disability services to continue this supervisory and protective role (Evans, 2002; Simpson et al., 2006). Research with staff suggests that education (Murray & Minnes, 1994; Drummond, 2006) and training (Ryan & McConkey, 2000) influence their attitudes, but, significantly, the setting in which they work seems to have a more dominant effect (Bazzo et al., 2007; Grieve et al., 2009). Staff working in community group homes have more supportive attitudes towards intellectually disabled people having relationships than staff working in larger or medically orientated facilities (Grieve et al., 2009). This finding may relate to a number of specific factors: service user characteristics, which are linked to the service setting (such as intellectual ability level); staff–client ratios, which facilitate more individualised supports; and service culture, including training for staff around sexuality and policies that support relationships for service users. Although there is a lack of cross-cultural studies comparing attitudes towards the sexuality of people with intellectual disabilities (Griffiths et al., 2004; Karellou, 2003b),[4] in general it would appear that attitudes in Ireland are broadly similar to those in other Western countries.

Research Approach

This research adopts a social constructionist framework to explore why families and disability services have difficulties supporting the sexual autonomy of intellectually disabled people. Social constructionism allows us to question taken-for-granted assumptions and what we define as a 'problem', showing us that how we label things affects how we perceive and respond to them. This perspective is influenced by the work of Michel Foucault,[5] who argued that objects are constituted through discourse. Discourses can be thought of as groups of related statements – text, speech and images – which 'systematically form the object of which they speak' (Foucault, 1972: 49). Foucault (1972) suggests that discourses are associated with relations of power, and that dominant discourses exercise power by claiming to speak the truth. With respect to current understandings of intellectual disability, medical discourse dominates. This discourse positions doctors, psychologists and psychiatrists as 'experts' on the diagnosis, treatment and care of disabled people. The focus is on the individual and their impairment, rather than the social or structural contexts that dis-able some people over others (Gillman et al., 2000). There is a tendency to think of people with intellectual disabilities as a homogenous group, but in fact there are huge variances in the abilities of those with this label (Davies, 1998). Moreover, the category is unstable and context-dependent. Jenkins (1998) argues that the majority of people labelled as having an intellectual disability have no physical cause associated with their diagnosis, and that the numbers being diagnosed have increased since the influence of industrialisation.

Like disability, sexuality can be thought of as socially constructed and historically and culturally specific (Foucault, 1976 and 1990).

Our sexual expression is highly bound up with normative expectations regarding who should be having sex, how, where and with whom. For example, we take for granted that sex is wrong for children, and that it is 'natural' for a person to be attracted to someone of the opposite sex. Heterosexuality and, particularly, married family life is constructed as 'normal' and 'natural', and these norms are institutionalised in law, social policy and media representations (Carabine, 2004). Although lesbian and gay relationships have achieved greater acceptance, they are still not accorded equal legal status in many countries.

Hamilton (2009) argues that it is precisely the narrow conceptions of how a normal sexual life should be lived, combined with constructions of people with intellectual disabilities as incapable, unable or childlike, which lie behind the lack of progress in supporting intellectually disabled people's sexuality. She suggests that we need to understand that staff (and family) practices are influenced by the ways in which 'intellectual disability' and 'sexuality' are constructed within society. Recent qualitative research with staff in disability services highlights that they predominantly construct people with intellectual disabilities as 'conditionally sexual' (Wilson et al., 2011: 278). In Hamilton's study (2009), staff perceptions of a person with intellectual disability as sexually 'able' were linked to individuals exhibiting behaviours that conform to socially desirable ways of doing/being sexual, for example, private, coitus-based, heterosexual sex within a monogamous relationship. When people were deemed incapable of meeting these requirements, no assistance around sexuality was deemed necessary, or offered.

Brown (1994) believes that the dual stereotypes of people with intellectual disabilities as asexual and vulnerable or sexually threatening/promiscuous continue to wield influence, and as a result there is no consensus about appropriate sexual behaviour for people with intellectual disabilities and no consensus about support. Constructions of people with intellectual disabilities as inherently vulnerable (Hollomotz, 2011) and in need of protection and guardianship (Scior, 2003), combined with practices that focus on risk minimisation (Wilson et al., 2011) and the need to demonstrate prerequisite skills before sexual participation (Brown, 1994), all serve to provide continuing challenges for people with intellectual disabilities who want to make their own choices regarding relationships and sexuality.

Research Method

The findings presented here were gathered through four focus groups (FG) carried out in an intellectual disability service in the Irish midlands. Two of the focus groups were with staff members in the service, a third focus group was with the service's 'sexuality committee', and the fourth was with parents of service users. The service caters primarily to people labelled as having moderate to severe levels of intellectual disability, and provides a full range of school, day, residential and respite services. Focus groups with parents and staff took place in January and April 2007.

Participants in Staff FG1 belonged to the activation unit in the service and were asked to participate by their manager. There were seven participants, one male and six females. The majority were frontline staff. Participants in Staff FG2 responded to a service-wide call for participants. There were four in this group: one male and three female. One was a member of frontline staff; the other three had more senior roles. The service's 'sexuality committee' is made up of parent and staff representatives, who are responsible for the development of a service policy on relationships and sexuality. For the focus group with this committee, all members were available, except the two parent representatives. There was one male and six females in this group; all in supervisory or management roles. Participants in the parents' focus group responded to a letter sent out to all family members asking them to participate; three mothers participated. Two of the mothers had sons with intellectual disability, the other mother had a daughter with intellectual disability. Their adult children were in their thirties and forties. The low number of family participants is arguably a reflection of the challenges some parents experience talking about this sensitive topic (Redmond, 1996), combined with general difficulties recruiting participants for research on sexuality and intellectual disability (Hamilton, 2010; Simpson et al., 2006).

Each focus group was approximately one hour long and loosely followed a topic guide, covering attitudes toward sexuality and intellectual disability, experiences with regard to the relationships and sexuality of people with intellectual disability, and supports that might help parents or staff in this area. All focus groups were recorded and transcribed *verbatim*. Transcripts were analysed using a discourse analytic approach, which focused on 'how social categories, knowledges and relations are shaped by discourse' (Tonkiss, 2004: 373). To protect anonymity, all names used here are pseudonyms.

Findings

Lack of Sexual Interest or Capacity

One of the dominant themes to emerge from the focus groups was that people with intellectual disabilities were frequently seen by staff and family members as sexually uninterested, or sexually incapable. Both staff and mothers expressed the view that because the service caters mainly to people who are categorised as having moderate to profound intellectual disabilities, relationships were not something that concerned the vast majority of people. One member of staff was of the opinion that, 'There aren't that many boyfriends and girlfriends' (Jackie, sexuality committee), while another was of the view that those relationships that exist are 'quite harmless' (Liz, Staff FG1). Likewise, the mothers believed that their adult sons and daughters are not interested in romantic/sexual relationships. As one mother put it, they aren't 'inclined to make friends with each other' and 'don't mingle much' (Patricia). The mothers frequently constructed their adult sons and daughters as children. Men and women were referred to as 'girls' and 'boys', and the mothers' descriptions of the social activities of their adult children revealed gender-segregated, childlike and at times religiously oriented leisure practices. One mother indicated that the service runs staff-supervised weekends away, which are gender segregated: 'boys go on one weekend, and the girls go on another' (Claire), while another spoke about the role of a religious charity organisation, CASA, in organising monthly socials for service users:

> **Patricia:**   [F]irst they have a Mass and they say all kinds of little prayers for this, that and the other – and they love that. And then they have the party – the tea and the sandwiches, and after that then there's a disco and then [...] if they've time, they might break off from the disco and have a bingo and a few prizes [...] There's a social

> now every month [...] [N]ext week now, they're
> bringing them to Knock for the day, and then
> in June they'll have the outing – bring them off
> on a surprise trip – to the zoo or that. They get
> helpers [...] Mostly they get children in second-
> ary school [...] to volunteer to help them.

Here we see that supporting social opportunities for people with intellectual disabilities has been identified as a goal by CASA, and the organisation's work is spoken of positively by the mothers. However, while social opportunities are being facilitated, there is little sense here of the men and women with intellectual disabilities being treated as adults, or of the service being influenced by the philosophies of normalisation or rights. Rather, the talk of the 'little prayers' and trips to Knock, combined with school children being recruited to support intellectually disabled adults, recalls the traditional view of people with intellectual disabilities as dependent, childlike and 'holy innocents'.

A recurring theme was the mothers and staff not regarding an intellectually disabled person's attractions or relationships as serious desire. Sometimes there was laughter about an intellectually disabled person having a relationship that would be deemed inappropriate in any other context. For example, in Staff FG1, staff members talked about whether or not a couple in the service are engaged:

Liam:	Are they currently engaged? I think it's called off.
Liz:	[Surprised] Is it?!
Sandra:	[Gently laughing] I think it's off, yeah.

If the couple referred to in this conversation had been non-disabled, one cannot imagine the ending of their engagement being a subject of humour. But laughter about an intellectually disabled person's desires or relationships was not uncommon – as if the person in question was a child experiencing a crush.

Related to this, there were some suggestions that people with intellectual disabilities might be imitating romantic conventions or social norms. Margaret, for example, said that her son sends Valentine's cards because 'he hears this going on', but did not believe her son was interested in romance himself. Similarly, staff identified what one described as 'long-term engagements' (Paula, sexuality committee) between two or three couples in the service. These engagements were constructed not as evidence of a mature decision to progress a committed intimate relationship towards marriage but rather as a strategy used by parents to placate a couple who wanted to move their relationship to a more serious level. It was suggested that a person getting engaged might be less interested in the sexual aspect of the relationship and more interested in 'feeling normal, feeling that you belong, that you have a boyfriend and girlfriend relationship and the next step is a ring' (Paula, sexuality committee).

None of the parents believed that people with intellectual disabilities in the service had a romantic/sexual interest in staff. However, attraction to female staff was a common theme in the focus groups I conducted with men with intellectual disabilities in the service (Kelly et al., 2009). Staff members were aware of service users having such attractions, but they did not construct or respond to these attractions as serious adult attractions. Service users saying they love a member of staff was described as the type of love that a person has for a 'parent kind of figure' (Martha, sexuality committee), while a female service user who had become very focused on a male staff member and had been telling him she loves him 'consistently every single day' was described as 'quite besotted', and this was ignored 'because it's so frequent now, you could time her' (Pam, sexuality committee). These types of comments suggest an infantalisation of service users and a denial, or minimisation, of expressed sexual or romantic interest.

In addition to being constructed as lacking sexual interest, some people with intellectual disabilities in the service were constructed as lacking capacity to understand sexuality. I was told that sex education 'wouldn't be applicable to all service users' (Pam, sexuality committee) and that there were some people in the service 'who don't really need to know about sex' because they don't have the capacity to understand (Sandra, Staff FG1). Likewise, in the parents' focus group, the mothers agreed with the provision of sex education to those who are 'able to take in' the information (Patricia and Margaret), but the issue was that they doubted that many people with intellectual disabilities have the capacity to understand such information: 'they don't really grasp it' (Margaret).

Inappropriate Sexual Behaviour

Staff members suggested that inappropriate sexual behaviour is the most common type of sexual behaviour among service users. As one respondent commented: 'it'd be more masturbation in an inappropriate place [...] that I would deal with, more so than any other kind of relationship issues' (Liam, Staff FG1). These cases of inappropriate sexual expression almost always concerned men with intellectual disabilities: 'it's not just one person [...] [Inappropriate masturbation]'s not uncommon amongst male clients [...] in a canteen setting or, during break time, or whatever' (Peter, Staff FG2). Here is an example of males being characterised as more sexually active, but this sexual behaviour is constructed primarily within a problematised sexual discourse (Wilson et al., 2011). In many cases, where staff talked about inappropriate sexualised behaviour, they continued to construct the person with intellectual disability involved as lacking sexual awareness. The person was constructed as doing something that seemed sexual, but as not really understanding this or doing it in a conscious way.

> **Liz (Staff FG1):** I work with someone who doesn't [...] particularly know the difference between a girl – like [...] instead of saying 'she', he would refer to them as 'he', and I actually recently read in a file that he was trying to kiss another man [...] But [...] I don't think he realises [...] then he actually went over towards one of the staff and tried to kiss her. But no, he doesn't [...] know the difference.

There is no sense here of this man having sexual desire or a questioning of whether he might be sexually attracted to both men and women, let alone the staff member. Rather, his behaviour is constructed as random and as demonstrating what Wilson et al. (2011: 282) refer to as 'lack of insight'. Because the man appears to lack insight into what he's doing, his behaviour is not seen as sexual.

There was some sense of inappropriate behaviours being constructed as more of a problem when they occurred in public. For example, both Sandra (Staff FG1) and Bernie (Staff FG2) referred to the 'problem' of male service users touching people's bums in public.

As in the earlier example, neither woman saw these behaviours as necessarily sexual. Sandra suggested that the touching 'seems to be fun', while Bernie suggested the behaviour was random: 'it doesn't matter *who* it was […] I don't think he sees anything wrong with it, or […] doesn't *know* what he's doing'. Regardless, both staff members saw the behaviour as posing a problem 'out in public' because the men 'would do it to strangers' (Sandra) and someone could complain. Thus, while neither staff member saw these behaviours as sexual, they were aware that outside the service, others would deem the behaviour as sexual and, indeed, as inappropriately sexual. When I asked if a training intervention would help the man Bernie supports, another staff member, Peter (Staff FG2), said: 'Well how do you train somebody like that? Because he's, you know, his memory [is poor] […] he's been […] corrected on it when it happens […] But he still does it'. Thus, the inappropriate behaviour was seen as a consequence of the man's cognitive limitations, but it could also be argued that he was receiving contradictory messages about sexual norms, and insufficient training support.

Risky Sexuality

Even though staff and parents suggested that people with intellectual disabilities are not sexually interested, there was an equally dominant construction of their (potential) sexual expression as risky. Earlier I highlighted that the mothers said that their adult children were not interested in romantic relationships. Some of the stories they told, however, called this stated lack of interest into question. Often, it seemed as if the issue was not so much their adult children's level of interest in intimate relationships but the fact that the mothers viewed such relationships as risky. Patricia, for example, related a story about her daughter, Eimear, having had 'what she called a boyfriend' many years ago.

> It was grand for her, like, to have company […] he'd ring her on the phone now and she'd just talk to him as simple as I'm talking to you now; no way shy or … Normally if she got excited, she'd be kind of stuttery and stammery and this, but she'd talk to him straight out and ask him questions and that, so I thought it was […] grand for her, like, at the time. But if it kept, […] if it stayed at that level […] But, just, I was afraid it might go too far so I kind of discouraged it.

This story highlights that Patricia's daughter had been interested in having a boyfriend. It also suggests that Patricia could see the benefits of the relationship for her daughter's confidence and social skills, and would have been fine with a relationship that would stay at a companionate or platonic level. Her fear was that the relationship might 'go too far' and this fear was so great, it led her to discourage the relationship.

For Margaret, even a non-intimate relationship was unacceptable. Margaret commented that she 'wouldn't like' her son to have a relationship, believing that people with intellectual disabilities are 'better off' without them and expressing that view that her son is 'quite happy and […] has a full life'. Although Margaret implied that her son is engaging in masturbation and admitted that he notices girls and likes looking at pictures of scantily clad women in magazines ('the less clothes they have, the better'), she continued to say that he 'wouldn't be interested in' relationships. Margaret doesn't allow her son to go to parties where he might meet a romantic partner. She said: 'he's got invitations from like, say, this neighbour and her daughters to go to parties where they have tea parties, and I would not be on for that because, ya know […] it is for, like, friendships and that they could meet someone.' For Margaret, there seems to be some recognition of her son's physical sexual needs – she acknowledges some physical desire and a need for physical release through masturbation – but there is no recognition of a right to intimacy with a partner. Her son's life is described as 'full' without this.

The mothers' language consistently indicated that they viewed the development of a relationship for their sons and daughters as a danger that was to be avoided. When I asked Patricia had her daughter ever had another relationship after the first, her immediate reply was: 'No, no, I never had any problems since.' And when I asked Patricia what she would have done if her daughter had wanted to continue her relationship, she replied: 'I don't know! […] I was wishing it wouldn't happen, so it didn't. I was very lucky. [Pause] I'd be in a sweat with it, wouldn't I?' Her daughter having a relationship was something stressful for Patricia, something she didn't know how to handle and would rather not happen. A series of comments from the mothers made it clear that their dominant concern was of pregnancy occurring:

Patricia:	I don't think now that [marriage] is a good thing [...]
Margaret:	I don't either.
Patricia:	Well I've enough to look after her [...] And I think every other mother is the same. [...] And to think that [...] she'd have a child.
Margaret:	Mmm, that is where the problems would arise!

The mothers did not see people with intellectual disabilities as capable of parenting a child. They talked about a woman with intellectual disability in the service who had her child taken into State care:

Patricia:	Her idea was if the child went near the fire, you put his hand into the fire and let him find out that you don't go near the fire [...] So, I think eventually the child was taken away [...] and put into foster care. But she'd be talking about [her child] [...] but I don't think she had a bit of interest in him at the same time [...]
Margaret:	Ya see, that's the thing, [...] they don't have the same interest.

This story, shared by mothers of service users, served as a warning of what can go wrong if people with intellectual disabilities have children. They are constructed as incapable, neglectful and as not having a real or 'normal' parental interest in their children.

When I asked the mothers in the focus groups did they have any concerns about abuse, they said that although they felt their adult children's trusting natures made them more vulnerable, most of the time this was not a dominant concern as their whereabouts were closely monitored: 'Eimear wouldn't be any place like that – as far as I know [...] She's safe enough' (Patricia). The sexuality of their relatives was thus constructed as risky, not primarily because they are perceived as vulnerable to exploitation but because if people with intellectual disabilities have relationships that go beyond the companionate level, this might lead to a pregnancy that parents believe the person with intellectual disability will be unable to cope with, and which will extend the commitment on them as grandparents. Emphasising that pregnancy was the parents' most pressing concern, contraception was seen as a way of making a woman with intellectual disability safer: 'Well, I think with girls [contraception] would be right [...] They'd be safe then, ya know, if something did happen to them' (Margaret).

Staff, too, articulated a risk discourse. Paula (sexuality committee) stated that the first response of staff to a service user developing a relationship would be concern. Jackie elaborated: 'I would say that people's immediate reaction would be, "Oh, I wonder if this happens, then what will happen [...] and I wonder what the parents will say?", rather than "Oh, isn't that nice".' I was told that pregnancy was the main concern for the service, 'abuse in some situations' (Paula, sexuality committee), and also that there might be 'concerns about the emotional effect [...] – say if one person is into the relationship more than the other' (May, sexuality committee). Both staff and management were ambiguous about whether relationships are allowed in the service: 'yes, relationships are allowed [...], but I wouldn't say that we actually encourage it' (Pam, sexuality committee). It appeared that relational intimacy was only allowed up to a certain level. Liz (Staff FG1) said: 'flirting, holding hands [...], sitting together in the unit or something' is 'fine', but 'You can't let it go any further!' The intimate couple was constructed as something potentially unsafe. For example, Sandra said: 'you were saying the word relationship – like, it can be the couple that just want to hold hands and be friends, right up to the couple that want to have sex ... You'd love to facilitate it all, but when it gets to that safety point, you have to monitor to a certain extent and that's different.' I was told that service users 'don't have unsupervised time' (Peter, Staff FG2) and that two service users going for a walk together 'would never really happen here, because you're not letting them out of your sight [...] I mean, if they're out of your sight for two minutes: "Where are they?"' (Bernie, Staff FG2). Both Alice and Peter (Staff FG2) said this is 'because there's a potential for danger if you let them off' and 'we have a duty to make sure that there's no danger, or as little as can be perceived to be no danger.' One of the risks staff highlighted was the 'possibility of exploitation' of one partner by another who might be 'more knowledgeable' (Peter, Staff FG2). However, in the case where this was mentioned, it was also noted that the individuals in the relationship are 'very comfortable together [...] they enjoy each other's company' (Peter, Staff FG2). Thus, exploitation was being considered, even though there were no signs of this and no complaints by either party. The sexuality committee noted that in the past there had been 'four to five' allegations of abuse made to the service (Paula, sexuality committee).

Service users having choices around parenthood is not something most staff members saw as realistic. Some staff saw this as something that might only be possible for people with mild intellectual disability, and said: 'It would depend on their ability, whether they're able to cope' (Pam, sexuality committee). They acknowledged that parenting is something they 'would have some concerns about' (Paula, sexuality committee) and felt that a person/couple with intellectual disability would need family or outside supports. There were comments that indicated an ongoing construction of intellectual disability as a devalued identity, tied to incapacity and dependency. For example, one staff member questioned whether a person with intellectual disability was 'capable of loving' a child and suggested that the child of a parent(s) with intellectual disability could experience stigma or feel negatively about his/her parents: 'when the child'd be in the world, like, how would it feel with both its parents …?' (Alice, Staff FG2). In Staff FG1 there were questions about the likelihood of a person with a condition like Down's syndrome having a child with the same condition. There was a more positive view from one manager. She agreed that the issue of parenthood would have to be looked at on an 'individual case [basis]', but emphasised that 'just because you have a disability doesn't mean you shouldn't ever be allowed to have children […] There are a lot of people without any disabilities that shouldn't have children' (Jackie, sexuality committee).

Earlier, I highlighted that staff (and parents) queried whether all people with intellectual disabilities in the service needed or had the capacity to understand sex education. Although the vast majority of staff articulated a positive attitude to the provision of sex education, the risk discourse meant there were still some underlying concerns as to where such education might lead. For example, Sandra (Staff FG1) said: '[if] everyone gets sex education and everyone's aware of their body … then do you get all these cases of, oh, oh [small laugh], "We want to be a couple and we want to go off for a while"'; while Bernie (Staff, FG2) said: 'Well I mean, if you were delivering a sex education programme and we'll say the next week then, there's … you know, everyone was out trying it, someone gets pregnant …' Such comments seem to tie in with Brown's assertion

(1994) that there is no consensus about appropriate sexual behaviour for people with intellectual disabilities, and thus no consensus about appropriate support.

Support for the sexuality of service users was seen as being contingent on them demonstrating capacity: 'how much support we can give the individual will always be dictated by them' (Paula, sexuality committee). It was stated that people should be allowed to have 'any kind of relationship of their choosing', once both parties have 'an understanding of what they're going to undertake' (Liam, Staff FG1) and 'can consent to it' (Peter, Staff FG2). However, challenges were still envisaged. For some staff, it seemed that support for intimate relationships was something that might only happen 'in an ideal world' (Ted, sexuality committee). Peter (Staff FG2), for example, commented: 'Do they have the right [to relationships and sexuality]? Prob ... Yes, because we all have the right. Whether they ever get the knowledge and the opportunity or the capacity to reach a level where it would become a reality for them ...?' Some staff continued to see supervision as being necessary as a safety measure, while others envisaged difficulties, such as people being at 'different levels [of ability] and one person it was okay for and the other ...' (Paula, sexuality committee). A further difficulty was that staff members were unclear how capacity to consent to relationships could be assessed: 'who's going to decide whether they're capable or not?' (Peter, Staff FG2). They acknowledged that even if they could confirm that a person had capacity to consent to a relationship, parents and staff members might still object.

Staff and management said that they work in conjunction with families regarding the care of people with intellectual disabilities in the service. As part of this, they inform guardians about every aspect of the person's care and send home permission slips for people to do special trips or activities. In the area of sexuality and relationships, the practice is no different. In all three of the staff focus groups, staff members reported that they would never provide any support in the area of relationships and sexuality without getting permission from parents or guardians first: 'we're always going to have to answer to parents first, so we're always going to have to get their consent to do anything as far as sexuality is concerned' (Liam, Staff FG1). Even when it relates to a service user wanting to know something about sexuality, staff members were unsure what, if anything, they could say. One staff member said: 'I wouldn't just answer, I'd have to ask' (Meg, Staff FG1). I was told that when there are objections from families or staff to a service user's relationship, a team meeting with the family, social worker and psychologist would be held, where a decision would be made as to what is in the 'best interest for the individual' (Paula, sexuality committee). Members of the sexuality committee admitted that at these meetings the intellectually disabled person's view 'would be taken into consideration, but it wouldn't be a priority' (Jackie). Furthermore, it was noted that while the person/couple should have an advocate at these meetings, in practice this did not happen. Staff members acknowledged the challenges service users face in asserting their wishes: 'Apart from us influencing them, they'd be very strongly influenced by their parents and they know exactly what was going to be said – that […] this was the relationship and they were going to be supervised' (Paula, sexuality committee).

There are a number of issues highlighted by these staff comments. First, it is clear that relationships or intimacy between service users is viewed by staff as something of a concern rather than as something positive. Potential danger or risk, even when not apparent, is factored in and people in the service are constantly supervised. A guardianship discourse (Scior, 2003), which constructs people with intellectual disabilities as vulnerable and in need of protection, is evident and so too is the emphasis on risk minimisation (Wilson et al., 2011). Staff members believe they have a duty to ensure that there is no danger, which means that opportunities to support personal relationship development are sacrificed in the course of ensuring safety. Staff suggest that service users who have been deemed to have the capacity to make their own decisions should be allowed relationship autonomy, but this is seen as unlikely or unrealistic at present, when people with intellectual disabilities are often presumed not to know what is in their best interests and when parents/guardians make decisions regarding the type of service the person with intellectual disability receives.

Having Needs and Rights

I specifically explored whether there were any constructions of people with intellectual disabilities as having needs, desires and rights around sexuality. From the material above, we can see that there is some recognition of needs and rights. As for the parents,

Patricia could recognise her daughter's emotional intimacy needs and see the benefits of a companionate relationship on her daughter's self-confidence, while Margaret could recognise her son's physical desires and accept his need for masturbation. However, none of the mothers accepted that their adult children had rights around relationships and sexuality. Their fear of the potential consequences of pregnancy didn't make this possible. Although staff members largely constructed people with intellectual disabilities as not having the same romantic/sexual interest or capacity as non-disabled people and were concerned about vulnerability, there was also a suggestion that service users' needs were being ignored or suppressed. This attitude was more apparent in Staff FG1, where the staff had a manager who encouraged them to support clients in this area of their lives: 'Jackie would [...] be all on for you to answer questions or explain to them if there were issues they wanted to discuss' (Liz). In this group, one staff member suggested that the seeming disinterest of people with intellectual disabilities in relationships might not necessarily be their choice: 'I think we suppress a lot of wants, to be honest – we don't even see what they want because we suppress that so much' (Sandra). Another felt that people with intellectual disabilities would be 'so much ... happier if they had someone romantic in their lives' (Liz). A male member of their group spoke about a man he supports who is 'mad about' a particular woman in the service and is engaging in 'inappropriate masturbation' (Liam). Liam believes that this man wants the same thing that his brothers have with their girlfriends: 'he wants the kind of intimacy, and the kind of holding hands kind of thing [...] there is a strong sexual side to him, but he does want the relationship.' However, this man communicates through signs, and is unable to talk to the woman he likes: 'he can't seem to get it across that, "I fancy ya"' [...] he can sign, but she won't understand' (Liam). In contrast to the dominant construction of people with intellectual disabilities as sexually uninterested, incapable or inappropriate, Liam constructs this man as romantically and sexually interested, and suggests that the difficulties he faces are as much a result of social factors as his impairment.

[W]e all learn by trial and error [...] the chat-up lines that don't work [...] but how does *he* learn by trial and error? [...] The way this man operates [...] he's given the knowledge and given the tools to do what he does, be it making tea or trying to have a small conversation about his evening with somebody. But he isn't given the tools to communicate what he wants from another person [in a romantic sense].

Liam suggested that this man needs 'the tools to ask this person, "Do you want to go to the cinema? Do you want to have coffee?"'

It is important to note that many staff felt that there was a difference between how they personally might like to respond to a service user's relationship and how they felt they were expected to respond: 'what staff might want to do, and what we're expected to do, will not always coincide with each other' (Peter, Staff FG2). One of the managers articulated the difficult position in which the service found itself:

[B]ecause it's such a new area for this organisation, the whole thing of having [...] boyfriends and girlfriends over to houses, and the whole issue of sexual relationships within houses, and what have you, is really a door that has not been opened [...]. And that would cause a lot of *uproar*, I'd say, in terms of people's fears and concerns and where they stood in terms of responsibility and that sort of stuff. (Jackie, sexuality committee)

In the sexuality committee, staff and managers talked about their difficulties developing a policy in this area, both because of difficulties with knowing what such a policy should contain and because of anticipated objections from parents, other staff and the service's management committee: 'We would have some of the management committee that would feel that [...] we're totally off the wall thinking that somebody would have a relationship [...] – even to suggest that they would be having relationships or allowing them into the room on their own [...] That would be the strongest opposition we'd have.' (Paula, sexuality committee). Such comments highlight the influence of various service stakeholders on responses to intellectually disabled people's sexuality. Such findings resonate with research that indicates it is a service's setting and culture, more than staff education and training, which influences staff attitudes and practices around the sexuality of people with intellectual disabilities (Grieve et al., 2009).

Discussion and Conclusions

My findings highlight ongoing challenges for parents and staff in seeing people with intellectual disabilities as romantically or sexually interested or capable. People with intellectual disabilities are perceived as childlike and as having childlike (non-serious) crushes or relationships. Additionally, while inappropriate sexualised behaviour (masturbation, touching) is recognised as occurring in the service, people are not necessarily perceived as understanding what they are doing. In part, we can see that the perception of people with intellectual disabilities as not sexually interested is achieved through denial or minimisation of signs of interest, or through a containment of interest. Both parents and staff are containing relationships that go beyond a platonic or companionate level: people are supervised all the time; they're not allowed, or supported, to have opportunities to meet someone; and relationships are discouraged. This is because of an anxiety about what might result from more intimate relationships. People with intellectual disabilities are predominantly perceived as incapable parents and there is some concern about a child also having a disability. As well as this, there is a construction of intellectually disabled people as vulnerable to exploitation and requiring protection. There have been allegations of abuse in the past in the service, and now all relationships are considered in these terms.

In line with dominant constructions of incapacity or risk, not all people with intellectual disabilities in the service are seen as needing, or being capable of understanding, sex education, and although such education is seen as important, there are concerns about the content of any such programme and what it might facilitate. Support for relationships of service users is deemed to be contingent on their level of capacity. At the moment, however, there are no structures in place to determine such capacity and because people with intellectual disabilities are not necessarily seen as knowing what is in their own best interests, it is guardians who have the most say in determining the service the person receives and the person's views on these matters are not prioritised. The findings of the focus groups with people with intellectual disabilities in the service (Kelly et al., 2009) correspond with these findings, and highlight the challenges for intellectually disabled people in getting information about sexuality and making their own decisions around relationships and sexuality.

I believe that the data discussed in the section on needs and rights, above, provides some guidance as to how we could begin to move between the position of people with intellectual disabilities, and those of their parents and support staff. The mothers in the focus groups did acknowledge some level of desire/need/ benefit for their son/daughter around relationships and sexuality – whether this was recognition of physical need or of an emotional, companionate need. Likewise, some staff recognised that service users' needs and desires are being contained, and recognised that service users may require supports in this area of their life. Importantly, having a supportive manager influenced how staff viewed this aspect of service users' lives. There are challenges for the sexuality committee in developing a policy in this area. Clearly, there are many staff and parental voices urging caution and few moving beyond mere recognition of service inadequacies to a call for dramatic changes in practice. The committee seem unclear how to balance within one policy the various discourses of sexuality operating in the service. This service is not alone in facing challenges in this area (Foley and Kelly, 2009), with the consequent response of 'inertia' (Simpson et al., 2006: 91). While no one will want to see a person with intellectual disability exploited or dealing with an unwanted pregnancy they are unprepared to cope with, a move towards rights, equality and respect for the voice of people with intellectual disabilities means that Irish society can no longer deny such people opportunities to develop to the fullest of their capacity because of societal fears.

I believe that the key to moving forward lies in listening to what people with intellectual disabilities have to say and facilitating them to take leadership roles in legislative reform, policy development and training and awareness programmes. I suggest a five-pronged approach, underpinned by the UNCRPD (2006) and supported by a national agency. First, alongside specific supports in the area of sexuality, Ireland needs modern legal capacity legislation and supportive decision-making structures that recognise the right of people with intellectual disabilities to make their own decisions.[6] Second, all services should have a policy, written in accessible format, outlining service users' entitlements and responsibilities with regard to relationships and sexuality. To assist services in this area, and to ensure greater consistency between services' policies, a working group (which includes self-advocates) should be set up to develop a national relationships and sexuality template policy for disability services. Third, training and discussion opportunities, ideally co-facilitated by trained self-advocates, should be made available to parents/guardians. Fourth, a national, accredited, standardised disability and sexuality training program needs to be rolled out to all professionals working with disabled people. This training should be at two levels – basic level training for all staff, and advanced training for those who will provide sex education and related supports. Finally, modular sex education should be made available to all people with intellectual disabilities in all schools and disability services.

Notes

[1] My doctoral research involved focus groups with people with intellectual disabilities, parents and staff from one disability service, and interviews with external informants who have personal, advocacy, educational and/or policy development experience in this area. This research is funded by scholarships from the National Disability Authority and Central Remedial Clinic.

[2] The existing Irish approach to legal capacity utilises the Ward of Court system, which is based on the Lunacy Regulation (Ireland) Act 1871 (*see* NAMHI (National Association for the Mentally Handicapped of Ireland), 2003; Law Reform Commission, 2006a). The current Programme for Government includes a commitment to introduce a Mental Capacity Bill. *See* Government of Ireland (2011: 38).

[3] This may be because they are only happy with relationships that take place within '*very safe and supervised boundaries*' (Redmond, 1996: 58) and/or because they may be required to support such opportunities (Rogers, 2009).

[4] Morales et al. (2011), who compared attitudes in France and Mexico, is a notable exception.

[5] For an introduction to Foucault's key concepts of power, knowledge, discourse and identity, *see* Sara Mills' *Michel Foucault* (2003).

[6] A good approach developed by a consortium of disability and other rights-based groups is outlined in *Essential Principles: Irish Legal Capacity Law*, Dublin: Amnesty International Ireland (2012).

CHAPTER 15

Towards Sexual Citizenship:
Dispelling the Myth of Disabled People's Asexuality

Selina Bonnie

Introduction

In 1992 disabled American activist and author Anne Finger said that 'Sexuality is often the source of our deepest oppression; it is also often the source of our deepest pain' (Finger, 1992: 9). Sadly, twenty years on this statement is still somewhat relevant. The aim of this chapter is to introduce the various issues relating to sexual expression and disabled people in Ireland, the history of which is similar to that of disabled people across the globe and includes many myths, challenges, milestones and successes.

Due to the ease with which disabled people can now research and communicate, the current issues and the way forward in relation to the rights of disabled people to sexual expression and family life are, in fact, more influenced by global developments and understanding of equality than at any other time in history. This chapter, therefore, reflects both the Irish and the international experience, interpreted through the lens of my own personal experience as a disabled woman. I am a wife and mother, activist and academic, leader of two personal assistants and wheelchair user. I work full-time outside the home and I am fiercely proud of my Indian/Irish heritage. I am an eternal optimist: I believe anything is possible and there is always a way around/under/over/through any problem or barrier. Basically, I am a twenty-first-century disabled woman.

This chapter is an introduction to the complex issue of disability and sexuality and it is no way a complete representation.[1] I have not addressed the additional, specific issues that relate particularly to people with learning difficulties, as these have already been discussed in the previous chapter. This chapter is underpinned by the social model's definition of impairment and disability (UPIAS, 1975: 3–4), which is a two-tier classification defining disability as being socially constructed and not as the result of an individual's impairment. This is not, however, the definition used in Ireland's equality legislation (O'Donnell, 2002: 2, 8).

The confinement of many disabled people in either the parental home or large institutions has left its legacy in the mindset of many people today. The fundamental result of the historical, widespread 'invisibility' of disabled people in everyday life is that myths such as those explored below have continued to impact on the lives of disabled people in modern-day Ireland. For example, as a disabled person, on a number of occasions I have been sitting in the street with friends, or canvassing at a local supermarket for the political party to which I am affiliated, and a member of the general public has approached me and tried to put money into my coffee. On most occasions when this has happened it has been an older person proffering their money, and I believe that this is so because, historically, many impairment-specific charities have run fundraising campaigns that have portrayed disabled people as passive 'recipients' of care services and as victims suffering from their impairments and incapable of looking after themselves. As disabled author, activist and politician Baroness Jane Campbell,[2] states in her critique of charity images of disabled people: '99.9% of charity advertising is negative, personally insulting and a lie' (Campbell, 1990).

Historical Overview

It is generally accepted that at any given time, approximately 10 per cent of a population are disabled people. In countries where war has been prevalent this figure is, of course, much higher. According to Census 2011, 13 per cent of the population of Ireland are disabled people, 60 per cent of whom are living with more than one impairment. Of the 595,335 disabled people enumerated in Census 2011, 51 per cent were female and 49 per cent were male (Central Statistics Office, 2011).

There are, and have been, many challenges that disabled people have had to overcome, not only to be recognised as sexual beings but to be recognised as people who have a right to be active, valued members of society. For example, in early Roman and Greek times, deformed, blind or weak infants were left exposed to the elements to die. St Augustine claimed that impairment was a 'punishment for the fall of Adam and other sins' (Ryan & Thomas, 1980: 87). The Nazi euthanasia programme saw disabled people as 'useless eaters' (Coleridge, 1993: 45), and in the first half of the twentieth century most Western countries had a policy of sterilising disabled people. Although such practices have been widely discredited, the practice of administering contraception to disabled people without permission or informed consent continues. Due to the lack of accessible employment, housing and transport and the absence of personal assistance, disabled people did not have opportunity or choice to achieve independent living. Therefore, many disabled people grew up in hospitals, institutions or the family home where the 'carers' were family or medical professionals (Charlton, 1998: 58). In a qualitative study in the UK of 42 young adults with physical impairments, many of the respondents were quoted as saying that 'the parental care situation extended parental control over their lives, keeping them as children despite their years' (Hendey & Pascall, 1998: 423). While engaging in research for my master's degree, I was told of a young disabled girl in her early twenties, who, due to lack of access to personal assistance, still had her personal care carried out by her parents, to the extent that her father inserted her tampons. One can only imagine the impact such intimate personal care from a male relative must have had on that young woman's sense of self and bodily integrity. Unfortunately, I have been unable to source any Irish research exploring the impact that dependency on family carers has had on disabled people. In stark contrast, however, there has been a significant focus on the impact of caring on carers. In May 2011 a current affairs programme on RTÉ (Ireland's national television and radio broadcaster), entitled *Prime Time Investigates*, broadcast an investigation into *The Human Price of Cutbacks*.[3] This programme profiled six different stories, demonstrating the negative impact that health cutbacks were having on family carers. One of the stories was about an eighteen-year-old disabled man (a wheelchair user who had cerebral palsy) and his mother, who was his sole carer. It showed them living in an inaccessible house and his mother having to carry him upstairs and bathe him. I found it very offensive, the way that he was shown being undressed and carried up the stairs and washed in his boxer shorts and the fact that not once did the interviewer address him or ask his thoughts and opinions, until a very brief reference was made to the fact that sometimes the young man gets depressed. I was left wondering how he felt about being on national TV in his underwear and what impact has this and his enforced dependency on his mother had on his dignity and sense of self-worth.

Another particular offender in advertising, both at home and abroad, is road safety awareness campaigning. Quite often these campaigns use extremely disempowering images of disabled people as examples of the negative outcomes of dangerous driving. A recent advertisement on RTÉ television clearly implied that significant impairment was a worse outcome than death. *Crashed Lives* was a road safety campaign featuring true-life case studies in which people speak about the consequences of a crash, how it has changed their lives forever – and robbed them of their dreams (Road Safety Authority, 2007 and 2008).

In Ireland, the majority of long-stay institutions for disabled people have been run by religious orders or by the State. The key focus in these institutions has been to meet basic needs and as many of these places were also hospitals, there was a high instance of medical intervention to 'cure' the disabled residents of their impairments (Doyle, 1989; Harnett, 2007; Conroy, 2010). Basically, disabled people were something to be fixed or rehabilitated or were genetic mistakes to be terminated or euthanased[4] (Rioux, 1994). The appalling treatment of disabled children and adults in Irish industrial schools and hospitals only started to come to light in 1999, after the documentary *States of Fear*, produced and researched by Mary Raftery, was broadcast on RTÉ. The book *Suffer the Little Children*, by Mary Raftery and Eoin O'Sullivan (1999), accompanied the documentary. *States of Fear* was shown in three parts, and part two dealt specifically with the treatment of disabled children and young adults in Irish industrial schools and hospitals from the 1920s right up to the 1970s. In this programme we saw how disabled children underwent unnecessary surgical procedures, were physically, mentally and sexually abused and, in the case of people with physical impairments, were forced to use calipers to walk on limbs and joints that were too weak to support them (Doyle, 1989; Harnett, 2007; Commission of Inquiry into Child Abuse, 2009). Disabled children were also isolated in special schools, away from their non-disabled peers and from society in general.

Cultural Influences: Historical Myths and Media

Prejudice comes from a perception of difference from what is considered 'normality'. In order to recognise difference, people need to have a concept of normality from which they can then calculate 'difference'. Speaking of disabled people, disabled writer Pam Evans stated that 'normal implies that which is average within any social structure ... the degree to which they [disabled people] fail to conform indicated the scale on which they will be mistrusted, feared and finally rejected' (cited in Morris, 1991: 16).

So what is the standard and who sets it? Erving Goffman suggests that 'the notion of a "normal human being" may have its origins in a medical approach or as a rationale for equal treatment by the State, but it is also very much a normative system of grading people. This categorisation system to confer a social identity exists prior to social interaction, and is established by "society"' (Goffman, 1968: 11). It is interesting that Goffman's notion of the normal human being has its origins in the medical approach, considering that society is still emerging from an era that believed in a very medicalised model of disability and that viewed disabled people as medical 'problems' who needed to be fixed. In 'I Accept Myself with Pride', Penny Boot addresses the issue of normalcy, stating that 'During my teenage years attempts were made to "normalise" me. Surgery and drugs, the doctors hoped, would fix my "deformed" body. Drab clothes would deal with my quiet rebelliousness, so various social work folk believed' (Boot, 1999).[5]

In *Exploring the Divide*, Mike Oliver states that '... the disability movement throughout the world is rejecting approaches based upon the restoration of normality and insisting on approaches based upon the celebration of difference' (Oliver, 1996: 44). I agree with this approach and I often point out that I do not necessarily wish to be seen as 'normal' or conforming to the 'norm' as I prefer to be, and to be seen to be, an individual. I also believe that the twenty-first century is a time of cultural, social, political and economic diversity and that the concept of normality is something that should be left in the twentieth century.

Historically, many myths have been generated about disabled people, our worth and our abilities. For example, it is often assumed that disabled people are incapable of self-determination and are totally dependent on non-disabled care-givers and professionals, and that all disabled people have the same needs. In this chapter, I am going to focus on the impact that these myths have had on disabled people's sexuality and sexual expression. In my opinion, the most fundamental impacts are the following assumptions: that all disabled people are heterosexual; that all disabled people are asexual and devoid of sexual feelings and desires; that information and education about sex will encourage 'inappropriate' sexual behaviour or create unreasonable expectations of sexual ability in disabled people; that people with physical impairments are unable to have sex; that disabled people cannot/should not be parents; and, finally, that disabled people should be grateful for any type of sexual relationship (McNutt, 2004).

As Jenny Morris (1989: 80) has pointed out, 'many people assume we are asexual, often in order to hide embarrassment about the seemingly incongruous idea that such "abnormal" people can have "normal" feelings and relationships.' The impact of these widely held myths has been that disabled people's basic human rights have historically been denied and that disabled people's sexuality and sexual expression have been oppressed in a variety of ways. As stated by one respondent in a research project conducted on the topic of independent and community living, 'They don't treat people with disabilities like adults and when it comes to relationships, it manifests itself as you can't do that. Just because you have a physical disability, that you can't have a sexual relationship. I think there is a presumption out there that just because you have a disability, it is not plausible. That is where society needs to change' (Weafer, 2010: 42–3). Disabled people were often and are still viewed as childlike and therefore asexual. Disabled children and teenagers have been dressed in androgynous or babyish clothes, denied relationships and sexuality education, and placed in segregated, 'special' institutions and schools. Displays of sexual feelings were seen as deviant and inappropriate. Parental and professional overprotection has led to disabled adults being infantilised, sterilised, prohibited from engaging in sexual activity and marriage, and excluded from mainstream social and leisure activities (Baker and Donnelly, 2001; Women with Disabilities Australia,

2011). Traditionally, there has been a taboo around discussing sex and related matters in public. Sex was for procreation and was only acceptable within a heterosexual marriage. Disabled people were not expected or encouraged to marry or procreate and they certainly were not expected to be anything other than heterosexual. Society, at best, finds the sexual thoughts/urges of disabled people to be repulsive and, at worst, presumes that we are asexual. As a disabled person, this can be a very difficult reality to acknowledge; however, I would rather that someone considered the thought of me being sexually active as distasteful rather than believing me to be asexual. In general, disabled people are rarely portrayed in radio, film, television, print media and advertising. When we are, it is often as the recipients of charity, evil characters in movies, super-heroes or tragic victims of illness or accident (Barnes, 1992; Flynn and Ging, 2009). We are rarely, if ever, portrayed in everyday situations, in relationships or as sexually active people or parents. In 1994, Lamb and Layzell stated that:

> There is an unspoken taboo about relationships and disabled people. Disabled people's sexual and emotional needs are rarely included in any discussion or representation in everyday life, whether this is in the papers and magazines we read, or the movies we watch. This reinforces the public's attitudes and expectations towards disabled people as seeing them as 'sick and sexless' rather than participating in full sexual and family relationships. (Lamb & Layzell, 1994: 21)

Disability activist and scholar Bethany Stevens also explores the impact of media representations of disabled people on sexual health (an impact not to be underestimated in today's media-driven world) and she warns that 'a person who is represented as pitiful or sexually abnormal may believe that they deserve dehumanising treatment [...] stereotypes serve as more than just rhetorical and representational methods to sell media; they also reflect and distort reality for many individuals – including those represented' (Stevens, 2010: 65). Overall, there has been a significant lack of positive role models and positive representations of disabled people in the media, but there are some media projects that have focused specifically on disabled people. There have been movies produced which portray disabled people in various empowering and disempowering ways, e.g. *Whatever Happened to Baby Jane?* (1962), *Children of a Lesser God* (1986), *My Left Foot* (1989), *Born on the Fourth of July* (1989), *Inside I'm Dancing* (2004), *Murderball* (2005), etc. There are two films that I believe are of particular note with regard to portraying an empowering image of disabled sexuality (albeit only disabled male sexuality). These are *Coming Home* (1978), a portrayal in film of a disabled person as a sexual being and having a relationship with a non-disabled woman, and *Uneasy Riders/National 7* (2000), a story about a group of disabled men in a residential institution accessing sex workers.

In the sphere of television programmes, the BBC and Channel 4 in the UK have produced a few interesting shows that have portrayed a more empowered and sensual image of disabled people. *Britain's Missing Top Model* (2008) followed eight young disabled women who competed for a modelling contract (which including a photo shoot with the English portrait and fashion photographer Rankin and a cover photo in the women's magazine *Marie Claire*). The eventual winner was Kelly Knox, who was born without a left forearm and is now a successful model. One of the judges, Lara Masters, is a very strong, beautiful, disabled woman who has a really individual and inspiring sense of style. Then there was *Dancing on Wheels* (2010), where non-disabled celebrities partnered wheelchair users and competed to represent the UK in the European Wheelchair Dancesport Championships. The choreographers for the show were two professional dancers from *Strictly Come Dancing* and one of the judges was Ade Adepitan, who is a disabled athlete and TV presenter. His flowing dreadlocks and appearance in the PlayStation *Double Life* advert have made him instantly recognisable, and he presents a very strong, charismatic image. The CBeebies channel, from the BBC suite of channels, is an excellent example of inclusive programming. Disabled presenters are shown on an equal basis with their non-disabled colleagues and disabled children are often included in the programmes. Overall, disabled people are included in a completely uncontrived way in the channel's programmes.

Metrosexuality was a UK drama that was aired on Channel 4 in 2001 as a short-run series of six episodes. It followed the interactions of a racially and sexually diverse group of friends and family living in Notting Hill. The show was hailed by critics for its diversity; it depicted a social setting relatively free of racism or homophobia. It was also noted for its inclusion of actor and activist Mat Fraser,[6] a thalidomide survivor with phocomelic[7] arms, in a role where the fact that he is a disabled person was simply part of the show's fabric rather than an inherent focus of his character.

The portrayal of disabled people in radio and television in Ireland is limited, but there are some notable exceptions. *Outside the Box*, a weekly programme on RTÉ Radio 1, highlights issues of broad concern to disabled people and has in the past featured shows dedicated to discussing relationships, parenting and sexuality. In the past five years television shows exploring issues of relationships, sexuality and parenting for disabled people have also featured on RTÉ and Dublin Community TV (DCTV). *Access for All* was a four-part series on DCTV in 2009, which looked at some of the issues facing the disabled community in Dublin. Each episode explored a particular issue from the viewpoint of disabled people. Participants spoke candidly about their experiences in the areas of education, family, media and disability, and sexuality and relationships. The aim of the series was to facilitate disabled people to become more visible and to present their own experiences and views on the issues that matter most to them. I participated in the 'Sexuality and Relationships' episode and I was very pleased with the way the topic was addressed. *Three 60* was an RTÉ show developed to explore and challenge attitudes about disability and disabled people in Ireland. Both series (2006 and 2007) were presented by disabled journalists and featured issues as diverse as a London-based comedian living with Tourette's syndrome, and teenage sexuality. A recent series on RTÉ, *Two for the Road* (2011), followed six well-known public figures who accompanied six disabled people as they embarked on a variety of highly challenging adventures across the globe. This was an interesting concept for a show, but I have severe reservations about the 'impairment simulation' element, where in each challenge the non-disabled celebrity had to simulate the conditions facing their disabled companion, in an effort to understand their perspective as well as their own.

In 2007, RTÉ embarked on a unique experiment with a show called *21st Century Child*. They began to follow the lives of twelve children and their families from birth until six years of age. A core mistake often made by non-disabled people is to underestimate the potential of disabled people to support a loved one or family. Quite often, in a relationship where one of the partners is non-disabled, the disabled partner is seen by concerned parents and friends as a burden on the non-disabled partner. My husband and I decided to take part in this project because we believed that it would be an invaluable opportunity to portray a positive, realistic, everyday image of a mixed ability family (Flynn and Ging, 2009).

Photography constitutes another form of media representation, and it has produced some powerfully positive imaging of the sexuality of disabled people. *Intimate Encounters – Disability and Sexuality* is a touring photographic exhibition featuring two installations and 30 photographic images, with essays by 40 people who collaborated with photographer Belinda Mason-Lovering, expressing their desires, needs, love and affection, reflecting the diversity of their experiences of disability through the lens. This is an excellent exhibition, which I would like to see presented in Ireland. I believe it would be a wonderfully empowering celebration of disabled people as sexual beings and would certainly help to challenge society's widespread denial of disabled sexuality. We live in a multimedia-driven world, and the power of images transmitted across broadcast, print and social media should not be underestimated. Therefore, the disability rights movement and its allies must ensure that honest, realistic and dignified images/portrayals of disabled people are included across all fora.

Challenges to Achieving Sexual Freedom

Societal attitudes are the greatest barrier to disabled people realising their sexual and reproductive potential[8] and desires. The other access barriers that impact on disabled people's abilities and opportunities for sexual expression can be categorised as: environmental and service; communication and information; and educational.

Attitudinal Barriers

Disabled people experience many barriers in relation to sexual and reproductive freedom. Historically, there has been a worldwide practice of forcibly sterilising disabled people (particularly women) and administering contraceptives without consent (*see* Commission on the Status of People with Disabilities, 1996: sections 17 and 18). Although women with learning difficulties have been particularly targeted by these eugenic practices, many people with physical, mental or sensory impairments have also had to endure these abuses.

Many mothers with significant impairments have had their children taken from them by social services because they have been deemed unable to look after the children (O'Toole, 2002). For the majority of these mothers, the provision of adequate personal assistance and support services would have enabled them to care for their children, thus negating the need for the children to be removed. In a 2002 paper, Liz Crow tells the story of Penny, a full-time employer of personal assistants:

> ... when she became pregnant, social services stepped in and announced that the turnover of personal assistants would not be in the best interests of the child-to-be and that, under the Children's Act, it [the child] would be removed into local authority 'care'. Until four days before her caesarean was due, Penny had no idea whether she would in fact have a baby. (Crow, 2002)

Disabled people with genetic/hereditary impairments (particularly women) often meet significant resistance from the medical profession when attempting to access assisted fertility services. I have personally experienced this discrimination. I have a gynaecological condition that is very common in women and totally unconnected with my impairment. As a result of this I am classed as sub-fertile, which means that I can only get pregnant with medical intervention. When my first phase of fertility treatment failed in 1996, I was referred to the then top Irish specialist in this area. On my first (and only) visit to him, he refused to assist me and the key reason given by him was that he could not be guaranteed that I would not give birth to a disabled child. Despite being devastated by his attitude, I refused to be deterred and thankfully, albeit eleven years later, we found some excellent doctors and we are the proud parents of a wonderful five-year-old. It is interesting to note, though, that in its section exploring the potential implications of the Equal Status Acts 2000–2004 for Assisted Human Reproduction (AHR), the Report of the Commission on Assisted Human Reproduction (CAHR) states that sub-section 4 (of the Acts):

… provides that where a person has a disability that could cause harm to that person or to others, treating the person differently to the extent necessary to prevent such harm shall not constitute discrimination. In the present context, this last provision would presumably protect a service provider who refused to provide AHR services to a person with a disability where the disability was such that the person could cause harm to any child conceived as a result of the provision of AHR services. (Commission on Assisted Human Reproduction, 2005: 136)

I understand this to imply that had we legally challenged the fertility specialist over his attitude and refusal to treat me, we would not have been successful in our endeavour.

Environmental and Service Barriers

Access to built environment and services is a key issue in all areas of life for disabled people, but in an area as sensitive as sexuality and sexual expression, access barriers coupled with the already outlined myths have had (and in many ways continue to have) a detrimental effect on disabled people's sexual health and fulfilment. The key pieces of equality legislation enacted in Ireland over the past decade (Equal Status Acts 2000–2011 and Disability Act 2005) have had a significant impact in this area, but there are still many barriers to be addressed. For example:

- Reproductive, maternity and sexual health services should have adapted toilets, induction hearing loops, height-adjustable examination couches, level or ramped access
- All stores, regardless of whether they sell clothes, cosmetics or adult products, should have adapted changing rooms, lowered shelves and counters
- Any place that provides parenting facilities, such as baby-changing stations, should ensure they are accessible to disabled care-givers and stores that sell nursery equipment should either stock or be able to source accessible nursery equipment

Many service providers never consider that disabled people also require access to services related to sexual expression, such as adult shops, family planning clinics, adult websites, pubs and clubs and other places where social relationships are formed, or services are provided.

Communication and Information Barriers

With regard to communication and information, there are a number of access issues to consider:

- People with visual impairments miss out on a lot of the visual cues and body language that sighted people take for granted when out socialising, which means that they can find it more difficult to make connections and form relationships.
- People with speech impairments or hearing loss can find it very difficult to communicate in noisy places, such as pubs and nightclubs.
- Sexual and reproductive health leaflets should be available in alternative formats and in plain language. In Ireland, the best example I have seen of information written to suit the needs of disabled people is the safe sex booklet that was written specifically for gay learning-disabled men, produced by the Gay Men's Health Project in the mid-1990s.
- All websites, regardless of their purpose or content, should be accessible, at a minimum Level 1 compliant, with Web Content Accessibility Guidelines (WCAG).[9] A recent positive example I found of a relevant accessible website is the Ann Summers Ireland website.

Educational Barriers

Although relationships and sexuality education (RSE) (the subject of Chapter 12) is delivered in most mainstream schools where the majority of students are non-disabled, there is a dearth of information or relevant resource material that is of specific use to young disabled people. For example, information on contraception should include information such as that presented in Table 1.1 of *The Baby Challenge: A Handbook on Pregnancy for Women with a Disability* (Campion, 1990: 8–9). The chart on 'Reproductive and Contraceptive Considerations for Women with Physical Disabilities' lists the various types of contraception available and outlines how each type might react with various impairments (Campion, 1990: 8–9).

Historically, relationships and sexuality education was not delivered in 'special' schools, residential institutions or training centres and disabled students/residents/trainees were prohibited from forming relationships (as discussed in Chapter 14). 'Rose', one of the interviewees for my master's research, commented in relation to access to appropriate education and peer contact: 'There was never any education in terms of sexuality. The one thing in the institution was there were the female "wards" and the male "wards" and we never really got to see each other, except in school maybe, or across in the corridor' (Bonnie, 2002: 51). The lack of sex education had a detrimental effect on the lives of many disabled people because it left them vulnerable to abuse. They were not taught to recognise inappropriate touching and as many disabled people grow accustomed, from an early age, to being examined by various adults, such as parents or members of the medical profession, it made it very difficult for the young person to distinguish between appropriate and abusive behaviour. In recent years, however, this situation has started to change. Many training and residential centres have adopted policies aimed at empowering their disabled trainees/residents to explore their sexualities, while giving them the appropriate education and information to ensure that they protect themselves from harm and abuse, e.g. Cheshire Ireland's *Policy on Independence and Choice* (Cheshire Ireland, 2005).

Disabled people are also guilty of a denial of disabled sexuality. We all know that there is more to disabled people's lives than just employment, health care or education, so why is it only in the past ten years that some disabled people's organisations in Ireland have started to highlight and discuss the issue? Historically, access to transport, housing, personal assistance, employment, education and getting our rights enshrined in legislation have been the priority for the disabled people's movement (Centre for Independent Living, 2009: 6–8). Social life and leisure, relationships and sexual expression have been pushed way down the list of priorities as disabled people have fought to achieve a better quality of life and independent living. This can also be related to the distinction between fighting for public rights and private rights, an issue that has been much debated in the women's movement. During the theoretical research I engaged in for my master's dissertation,

I noticed that sexual relief was often referred to as a need, which is similar to pain relief, whereas sexual expression was referred to as pleasure and a want or desire (Earle, 1999; Dagblad, 2001; Owens, 2009). Therefore, one of the questions I asked the interviewees in the study I conducted was: 'Is sexual expression a need or a want?' All eight of the disabled people I interviewed believed that sexual expression is a need.

Disabled women's needs and desires to express their sexuality are recognised even less than those of disabled men, and disabled women are more likely to be viewed as passive, vulnerable recipients of unwanted sexual attention (Hamilton, 2010: 121). This is further evidenced in the international context, where disabled men are widely documented as customers of the sex industry, but it is very rare to find similar accounts of disabled women.

Milestones and Successes

Legislation

Although, until the late 1990s, there was a dearth of rights-based legislation relevant to disabled people's lives, this has begun to change. The impact of socio-cultural barriers on disabled people's abilities to participate in education and employment have been widely discussed, with a variety of measures being put in place to address them. The Americans with Disabilities Act was introduced in the USA in 1995, and in the same year the UK passed the Disability Discrimination Act (subsequently rolled in to the new Disability and Equality Act 2010), followed in 1996 by the Direct Payments Act. However, the Irish Disability Act was only enacted in 2005. Policy-makers and lobby groups, etc. often take action aimed at fostering active citizenship, but the concept of disabled people realising sexual citizenship (Sherry, 2004; Shildrick, 2004; Sanders, 2010) is a new and very powerful concept and it situates the whole issue of disability and sexuality firmly within a rights setting.

A key milestone in Irish policy history came in 1996, when the Commission on the Status of People with Disabilities produced its landmark document, *A Strategy for Equality* (1996). This included a chapter on relationships and sexuality that emphasised 'the right of people with disabilities to the same degree of fulfillment through relationships and sexuality as anyone else must be included in any list of equal rights' (Commission on the Status of People With Disabilities, 1996: 18.1). Chapter 18 contained fifteen recommendations for what the government should provide or fund in order for disabled people's sexual and relationship needs to be met. The Equal Status Act 2000 (later amended by the Equality Act 2004) relates to discrimination based on nine grounds: gender, civil status, family status, age, race, religion, disability, sexual orientation and membership of the Traveller community. The Act applies to people who provide goods and services, obtain or dispose of accommodation, or attend at, or are in charge of, educational establishments. A number of disabled people have taken cases under this Act against pubs and other venues with regard to access and discrimination, with varying results.

The Disability Act 2005 provides a statute-based right for disabled people to an assessment of disability-related health, personal social service and education needs. It also provides a statutory basis for accessible public services. Sections 26, 27 and 28 of the Act place obligations on public bodies to make their buildings, services and information accessible to disabled people. I believe that this piece of legislation has the potential to be used to improve disabled people's sexual health and opportunity for social interactions, because a key function of this Act is that it gives disabled people a statutory basis for expecting improved access to health and public services, ergo greater access to maternity and sexual health services, and social and leisure facilities provided by public bodies. On the international front, the rights of disabled people to sexual expression and family life, i.e. procreation, are enshrined in Standard Rules[10] and Conventions.[11] Rule 9.2 of the UN Standard Rules for the Equalisation of Opportunities for Persons with Disabilities (United Nations, 1994), which deals with family life and personal integrity, states: 'Persons with Disabilities must not be denied the opportunity to experience their sexuality, have sexual relationships and experience parenthood. [...] Persons with Disabilities must have the same access as others to family-planning methods, as well as to information in accessible form on the sexual functioning of their bodies' (United Nations, 1994: 9.2).

In March 2007, Ireland signed the UN Convention on the Rights of People with Disabilities (CRPD), which allows for the rights of disabled persons to 'decide freely and responsibly on the number and spacing of their children [...] to have access to age-appropriate information, reproductive and family planning education' and the 'means necessary to enable them to exercise these rights' (United Nations, 2006: Article 23). However, the existence of the rights identified above does not mean that disabled people are being afforded the opportunities to exercise or realise these rights. Legislation is only as effective as its enforcement and although Ireland signed the CRPD five years ago, in 2008, it has yet to incorporate it into domestic law.[12] Furthermore, it is obvious from reports available from both the Ombudsman's Office (Ombudsman, 2001) and the Equality Tribunal (Murphy, 2012)[13] that there is still a long way to go before disabled people will truly realise equal rights in Ireland.

Recognition of Sexual Diversity Among Disabled People

The news is not all bad, though. There have been many developments and successes, particularly over the past ten years. In this section I outline what I consider to be some of the key achievements to date. Research that has explored the area of sexuality and disability has primarily been controlled by professionals from medical, psychological and sexological backgrounds and has tended to portray sexuality for disabled people mainly as a 'problem' for service providers (Shuttleworth, 2010), as discussed extensively by Kelly, in Chapter 14. There has been a focus on interventions, such as preventing pregnancy and abuse, rather than informing, enabling, facilitating and empowering disabled people. According to Shakespeare, Gillespie-Sells and Davies (1996: 3): 'A medical tragedy model predominates, whereby disabled people are defined by deficit, and sexuality is either not a problem because it is not an issue, or is an issue, because it is seen as a problem.' They suggest that 'the voice and experience of disabled people is absent in almost every case' (Shakespeare et al., 1996: 3).

Over the past twenty years, however, a number of key disabled activists and academics have researched and written about issues of disabled people, disability and sexuality from a rights-based perspective (Morris, 1989, 1991; Shakespeare et al., 1996; Davies, 2000; Tepper, 2000; Shakespeare, 2000, 2001). Nonetheless, it took the groundbreaking text *The Sexual Politics of Disability*, by Shakespeare, Gillespie-Sells and Davies (1996), to truly recognise the complexity of disabled people's sexuality. In 2010 *Sex and Disability: Politics, Identity and Access* (Shuttleworth and Sanders, 2010) was published. It featured a collection of papers from around the globe covering topics as diverse as sex workers, disabled women's sexual expression, and disability and masculinity. Learning-disabled people's capacity to consent to sexual activities and the role the media plays in disabled people's sexual expression were also dealt with in an open and frank way, and this book provides an excellent insight into many different facets of disabled sexuality. Not all disabled people have the same needs or desires and many live with multiple identities, such as disabled and gay or disabled and female. Therefore any discussion of disabled people and sexuality would not be complete without acknowledging the fact that many also experience multiple oppressions in their lives. For example, disabled women have experienced exclusion by the women's movement because of the feminist desire to shift away from the traditional notion of women as carers, and by the disabled people's movement because the movement is still very patriarchal (Begum, 1992: 74).

A pivotal event in the history of disability and sexuality in Ireland, which sought to recognise the existence of diverse sexualities among disabled people, was the 1995 All Different All Sexual Conference. This was the first rights-based conference to address this issue and it was developed by the APIC (Awareness, Publishing, Information and Communication) Arts and Disability Centre. It came about because the centre was engaged in various arts projects with groups such as the Gay Men's Health Project, Dublin AIDS Alliance, etc. and it became very obvious that disabled people's experiences and needs were being omitted from all the talk at the time on AIDS and safe sex. No one was considering disabled people when it came to meetings or literature on 'sexual health' and the pervading attitude was that disabled people are not sexual. So the managers of APIC decided to 'shake things up a little' and provide something that would put a spotlight on the fact that disabled people could be and were sexual, and therefore needed to know about AIDS, pregnancy and STIs, just like everyone else. I worked for APIC during this time and can remember the incredible excitement and energy in the Round Room (which was filled to capacity) of the Mansion House on the day of the conference. It is interesting to note, though, that although the response to the initiative from the disabled people's movement was incredibly positive, the APIC managers were the recipients of many negative phone calls and letters from organisations and people who thought they were doing something 'wrong' and 'nasty'.

Since 1997 the Irish Family Planning Association (IFPA) has undertaken a significant amount of work to ensure that their services and policies are inclusive of disabled people. In 2007 the IFPA produced a briefing paper on the main policy issues related to sexuality and disability in Ireland, published a briefing guide for healthcare professionals on sexuality and disabilities, and developed relevant training resources and programmes (IFPA, 2007).

Another significant Irish initiative that reflected growing recognition of the diverse sexualities of disabled people was Greenbow[14] (founded in 1996), an organisation established by deaf people for deaf lesbian, gay, bisexual and transgender (LGBT) adults all over Ireland. A key aspect of Greenbow's mission is to promote self-determination of, and provide educational information to, deaf LGBTs with regard to their sexuality, Irish sign language (ISL), communication, social organisation and culture. Greenbow's core services are advocacy and the organisation of social events, workshops, classes and information evenings. Unfortunately, the attempt, in 2001, to establish a similar support structure, Delicious, led by gay disabled people who were not part of the deaf community, was not as successful. However, Delicious did play a major part in the Identity at the Crossroads seminar (June 2001), organised by the Equality Authority and the Forum of People with Disabilities, which focused on sexual orientation and disability. A very encouraging initiative, which took place in November 2011, is the Full Spectrum Project (LGBT Diversity, 2011). This project provides an opportunity for disabled people (and other minority groupings) who are part of LGBT groups in the northwest of Ireland, and those who represent or work with them, to have their voices, experiences and needs heard and understood by the broader LGBT community.

In 2003 a project was initiated by the Forum of People with Disabilities (no longer in existence) in partnership with Inclusion Ireland[15] (formerly the National Association for the Mentally Handicapped of Ireland/NAMHI), which aimed to promote the sexual rights of all disabled people. This project was called Sexuality Disability and Relationships (SDR). The project involved a conference, aimed at disabled people, where they could discuss issues relating to sexuality and relationships, highlight barriers to sexual expression and make recommendations as to how services and organisations could be improved. Following the conference, a *Sexuality Disability and Relationships Discussion Paper* was produced, which took recommendations from the SDR conference and directed them at particular sectors (such as health services, sex education providers, disability organisations, parental support groups, etc.). Unfortunately, this paper has never been published. Other important research relating to sexuality and disability has been produced by the National Disability Authority[16] (NDA), an independent state body providing expert advice to government on disability policy and practice, and promoting universal design[17] in Ireland. Since its establishment in 1999, it has commissioned a vast array of research documenting the experiences of disabled people in Ireland. Three key pieces of research worth noting here are the *Disability and Sexual Orientation Report* (QE5, 2005), the Pregnancy, Childbirth and Early Motherhood Project (Begley et al., 2009a, 2009b and 2010) and *The Provision of Appropriate and Accessible Support to People with Intellectual Disabilities Experiencing Crisis Pregnancy* (O'Connor, 2010). The NDA has funded research on sexual violence against disabled people, which is currently being conducted by the Rape Crisis Network of Ireland.[18] Women's Aid has also undertaken work over the past few years to address the issue of violence against disabled women and they produced the booklet, *Responding to Violence Against Women with Disabilities*, which is available on their website (Women's Aid, undated).

Current Debates

In this section I highlight four issues that merit attention because they relate to disabled people and sexual expression everywhere.

1. Facilitated Sexual Expression

In 2002 I conducted research into the area of facilitated sexual expression for disabled people in the Irish Independent Living Movement. This aspect of personal assistance was first brought to my attention in 1996 (Shakespeare et al., 1996) and it intrigued me. If a disabled person (leader) who uses the services of a personal assistant (PA) has a significant impairment and needs their PA to assist them with tasks such as eating or washing and so on, isn't it likely that they may also need assistance with sexual activity (Ratzka, 1998)? This form of assistance has many implications attached, particularly legal, ethical and moral. For example, a PA who facilitates his/her leader by soliciting a prostitute, or assisting with masturbation, could find him/herself in a very difficult legal situation. Equally, the leader, as an employer, could be in breach of employment law and public policy by bringing facilitated sexual expression into the working relationship. One of the key recommendations emanating from my research was that a code of practice for facilitated sexual expression should be developed and that leaders should be supported to develop individual grades of facilitation, which can then be negotiated with their PA, as this will help to protect both the leader and the PA (*see* Bonnie, 2002 for further discussion).

2. Devotees and Disabled Women

Devotees are non-disabled men who are specifically sexually attracted to women who are amputees or who have other physical impairments. The devotee community is particularly big in the USA, with numerous websites and magazines devoted to the issue.[19] This has also been referred to as 'disability fetishism' (Kafer, 2000) and has been the subject of much debate, both in non-disabled society and in the disabled people's movement (*see* Shakespeare, 2006).

There are many sides to this debate. Two key arguments have been that many people find devotees and their organisations distasteful and believe them to be exploitative of disabled women (Smith, 2009). However, many disabled women who are active in this community find the experience of being desired and considered more beautiful than non-disabled women extremely empowering (Waxman-Fiduccia, 1999; Kafer, 2004). They believe that society should not judge the devotees as deviant just because they explicitly desire disabled women.

3. Sex Surrogates

Sex surrogates are trained professionals who engage in sexual activity with people who experience difficulties with sexual expression or performance. The surrogate works at the direction of a therapist, who prescribes this form of 'treatment/therapy' for the client. This system operates in many countries and is regulated by the *Code of Ethics and the Code of Practice* from the World

Association for Sexology (WAS) and the International Professional Surrogates Association (IPSA) (WAS and IPSA, 2002). These services are not specifically designed for disabled people, but do provide a supported opportunity for disabled people to explore sexual expression (Shapiro, 2002). I personally would not advocate for disabled people to use this type of service because I believe it medicalises disabled people's sexual needs. However, if a disabled person is sexually oppressed and has the opportunity to access such a service, maybe surrogacy can be a positive way of addressing his/her sexual need or desire.

4. Access to Adult Material

Whatever one thinks about adult material, it is important to point out that, overall, there is a lack of adult material available in alternative formats and most adult websites are not designed with universal access in mind. While working as a reporter on *Outside the Box*, a weekly show on RTÉ Radio 1 in the early 'noughties', I interviewed the owner of the Utopia chain of adult stores in Ireland to discuss issues of accessibility of adult materials for disabled people. I asked him if he knew of any publications for sale in alternative formats, e.g. Braille or tactile, and he replied that he had not considered such an issue and had never heard of any such materials. I later found out that in 1970, *Playboy* was the first adult publication to be issued in Braille, and the US National Library Service for the Blind and Physically Handicapped (NLS) has published a Braille edition of *Playboy* since then (excludes pictorial representations).[20] In 2010, *Tactile Minds*, a pornographic book complete with explicit text and raised pictures of naked men and women, was launched by Canadian artist Lisa Murphy, to be 'enjoyed' by blind and visually impaired people. Murphy said that she had made the book after realising that blind and visually impaired people 'have been left out in a culture saturated with sexual images' (Murphy, 2010).

The Way Forward/Towards Sexual Citizenship

Despite the difficult history, myths, challenges and barriers that I have outlined in this chapter, it is important to remember that a lot of positive things have happened, too. Many milestones have been passed, successes achieved and there are some very interesting discussions and debates currently taking place. Disabled people are taking control of the debates and research agenda, having fun and fulfilling sex lives, becoming parents, forming lasting relationships and becoming more visible in TV, film and the print media.

Historically, the sexual oppression of disabled people has caused untold damage and misery and destroyed countless lives and in this, the twenty-first century, not one person should have to endure enforced celibacy. In 2000, US academic and activist Mitch Tepper stated: 'Pleasure is an affirmation of life. […] Pleasure adds meaning to our lives. Sexual pleasure is particularly powerful in making one feel alive' (Tepper, 2000: 288). Thirteen years on, I believe that Tepper captures the essence of why disabled people, and indeed all people, should be afforded sexual freedom and the right to safe, fulfilling and fun sexual expression and exploration. I am a strong believer that every person has the power within them to effect change. My personal action to effect change is to continue developing the website I have created (<http://www.sexualcitizens.com>) and to grow it into a key resource on disability and sexual expression in Ireland. I am not creating this on behalf of any organisation or company; this website is a labour of love, and my way of making a tiny contribution to the sexual emancipation and citizenship of fellow disabled people.

I conclude this chapter with a brief list of some core actions that I consider necessary in order to keep the issue of sexual rights and access for disabled people on the agenda in Ireland:

- The Convention on the Rights of People with Disabilities should be ratified and any associated legislative changes should be addressed without any further delay.
- Research should be carried out to document the impact of dependence on family carers of young disabled people, i.e. the impact of care on sense of self and sexuality.
- Relationships and sexuality education that is inclusive of the needs and abilities of disabled people should be available to all young disabled people.
- Positive representations of disabled people should be included in mainstream sexual health education.
- Sexual and reproductive health clinics, adult services and shops should be fully accessible.

- The Intimate Encounters exhibition should be brought to Ireland and perhaps accompanied by a disability and sexuality film festival.
- Harmful myths and stereotypes should be challenged by raising awareness of the fact that disabled people are, and have a basic human right to be, treated as sexual beings.

Recommended Resources

This chapter has included a comprehensive range of references and there is a wealth of online resources available in relation to this subject matter. Two key websites to which I would direct readers are the Disability Archive, which is hosted by the Centre for Disability Studies[21] at the University of Leeds, and the National Disability Authority's website, which has downloadable copies of all research reports published by the NDA and an online database of materials held in its library.

Notes

[1] I would strongly urge readers to engage in further exploration in the area. To assist with this, I have provided a detailed list of endnotes and references. Furthermore, there are two key international academic publications of note. The journal *Sexuality and Disability* is an international publication of peer-reviewed, original, interdisciplinary academic papers addressing the psychological and medical aspects of sexuality in relation to rehabilitation. *Disability and Society* is an international journal that provides a focus for debate about such issues as human rights, discrimination, definitions, policy and practices. This journal publishes articles that represent a wide range of perspectives, including the perspectives of disabled people.

[2] Baroness Jane Campbell of Surbiton's website is <http://www.baronesscampbellofsurbiton.com>

[3] The *Prime Time Investigates* programme, *The Human Price of Cutbacks*, is available for viewing at <http://www.rte.ie/news/av/2111/0531/media-2968230.html>.

[4] *See Carrie Buck v. James Hendren Bell*, Superintendent of State Colony for Epileptics and Feeble Minded, USA, 1927, which can be accessed at <http://supreme.justia.com/cases/federal/us/274/200/case.html> [accessed 17 January 2013].

[5] Penny Pepper (aka Penny/Pam Boot) is a spoken word performer, all round writer and veteran disability arts activist. Her work is described

as subversive, saucy and provocative, visit <http://pennypepper.word-press.com>.

[6] To find out more about Mat Fraser, visit <http://www.matfraser.co.uk>.

[7] From the Greek, meaning 'seal limb'. The term was coined in 1836 by Étienne Geoffroy Saint-Hilaire to describe the congenital absence or abnormal shortening of arms or legs, often with only short, flipperlike limbs projecting from the body.

[8] In 2007 the National Disability Authority (NDA) commissioned research, in a joint initiative with the National Women's Council of Ireland, to explore the strengths and weaknesses of publicly funded Irish health services provided to disabled women in relation to pregnancy, childbirth and early motherhood. The research was carried out by a team of researchers from the School of Nursing and Midwifery in Trinity College Dublin.

[9] WCAG explain how to make web content accessible to disabled people. The guidelines are intended for all web content developers (page authors and site designers) and for developers of authoring tools. The primary goal of these guidelines is to promote accessibility. Following the guidelines will, however, also make web content more available to *all* users, whatever user agent they are using (e.g. desktop browser, voice browser, mobile phone, automobile-based personal computer, etc.) or constraints they may be operating under (e.g. noisy surroundings, under- or over-illuminated rooms, in a hands-free environment, etc.). Following these guidelines will also help people find information on the web more quickly. These guidelines do not discourage content developers from using images, video, etc. but rather explain how to make multimedia content more accessible to a wide audience. Visit <http://www.w3.org> for more information.

[10] Among the major outcomes of the Decade of Disabled Persons was the adoption, by the General Assembly, of the *Standard Rules on the Equalization of Opportunities for Persons with Disabilities* in 1993. Although not a legally binding instrument, the *Standard Rules* represent a strong moral and political commitment of governments to take action to attain equalisation of opportunities for disabled persons. The Rules serve as an instrument for policy-making and as a basis for technical and economic co-operation.

[11] The Convention on the Rights of Persons with Disabilities and its Optional Protocol was adopted on 13 December 2006 at the United Nations Headquarters in New York, and was opened for signature on 30 March 2007. There were 82 signatories to the Convention, 44 signatories to the Optional Protocol, and one ratification of the Convention. This is the highest number of signatories in history to a UN Convention on its opening day. It is the first comprehensive human rights treaty of the twenty-first century and is the first human rights convention to be open for signature by regional integration organisations. The Convention entered into force on 3 May 2008. Although Ireland was one of the first countries to sign the Convention, it is yet to ratify it.

[12] This means that until ratification, Ireland must refrain from acts that would defeat the purpose of the CRPD, but is not legally bound by its terms.

[13] To access a variety of relevant reports, and case studies, etc. visit: <http://www.ombudsman.ie/en/Publications/> and <http://www.equalitytribunal.ie/Database-of-Decisions/>.

[14] For more information, *see* <http://www.greenbowdeaf.com>.

[15] *See* Inclusion Ireland website at <http://www.inclusionireland.ie>.

[16] For more information, *see* the Authority's website at <http://www.nda.ie>.

[17] Universal design is the design and composition of an environment so that it can be accessed, understood and used to the greatest extent possible by all people, regardless of their age, size, ability or disability. Universal design assumes that every person experiences barriers, reduced functioning, or some form of disability – temporary or permanent – at some stage in life. Visit <http://www.universaldesign.ie> for more information.

[18] When the first *National Rape Crisis Statistics 2004* were released by the Rape Crisis Network Ireland (RCNI, 2005), they showed that 4.4 per cent of survivors of rape were disabled people (RCNI, 2005).

[19] <http://devguide.org> and <http://www.disaboom.com/> are examples of two current web resources. *See also* Fulbright (2012).

[20] National Library Service for the Blind and Physically Handicapped (NLS) publishes a large variety of magazines in Braille, including *Playboy*; visit <http://www.loc.gov/nls/reference/circulars/magazines.html>.

[21] Visit <http://www.leeds.ac.uk/disability-studies/>.

Section 8

Commercialised and Commodified Sexualities

CHAPTER 16

The Cheap Lock and the Master Key: Raunch Culture's Double Standard and Its Impact on Irish Women's Sexual Lives

Sara Stokes

Introduction

I was ten years old in 1994, at the height of what Susan Faludi (1992) called the feminist backlash, and at the beginning of what would soon become known as 'laddism' (Whelehan, 2000), with its associated 'ladette' culture. Despite the fact that women had spent the previous thirty years enjoying greater freedoms of access to education and the workplace, it was a time during which the voices of the first- and second-wave feminists[1] who had fought for those very freedoms began to be drowned out by a disparaging popular culture and an overwhelming pressure to discard what were now being portrayed as outdated and unnecessary feminist ideals. I was a product of this culture and, ignorant to the plight that preceded it, I embraced this 'postfeminist' rhetoric in exactly the fashion it was marketed to be embraced: as a glitzy, colourful whirlwind of 'girl power'.

This 'girl power' was a form of pseudo-feminism, which was disseminated most notably through the pop group the Spice Girls and proved to be a stroke of marketing ingenuity that was more successful in generating vast amounts of revenue for the businesses behind the group than for the empowerment of the girls and women of the time. It was a rhetoric that promoted girlishness and frivolity, pigtails and push-up bras: a far cry from the mythical, underwear-burning feminists of the 1960s. Combined with the coinciding 'ladette' phenomenon, which encouraged women to drink as much as men, to have sex 'like men' and to be as sexist as men, the 1990s was a seemingly carefree decade during which everyone appeared equal, empowered and strong.

The end of the millennium brought with it further reinforcement of this rhetoric, and in 1998 the airing of the HBO series *Sex and the City* marked the dawn of a new female sexuality. I was fourteen years old and my peers and I idolised the show's characters and aspired, like them, to wear designer shoes and clothes, to be sexy and confident and, perhaps most significantly, to accept the new millennium's insistence that sex and emotion be completely separated from one another. In fact, it was only in my mid-twenties that I first began reflecting on the notion of female sexuality and the ways in which it had been represented in cultural texts since the early 1980s, when I was born. It was at this time that I became aware that the cultural embodiment of the socio-sexual norms I had witnessed growing up could be classified under what academics and social commentators were now calling 'raunch culture', and I began to question the sexual choices I had made throughout early adulthood and, furthermore, to question whether I had ever felt I had a choice to begin with.

This chapter, then, is based on the findings of a 2011 study, which involved an exploration of 'raunch culture' and its capacity to influence the lived sexualities of young Irish women. The research itself spanned three years and used two distinct research methods: a large-scale quantitative questionnaire with 1,764 young Irish women[2] and a series of twelve qualitative face-to-face interviews with a voluntary sub-sample of that group. The following is a brief overview of the findings of that research and an introduction to the argument that raunch culture has the capacity to impede and inhibit the sexual freedom of young Irish women.

Raunch Culture and Irish Sexuality

But what exactly *is* raunch culture? The term itself was first coined by Ariel Levy in her 2006 investigation of the overt or *hyper*-sexualisation of contemporary popular culture (Levy, 2006). It is a phenomenon that has been much debated over the last decade and has been analysed and investigated under a number of different guises, including 'striptease culture' (McNair, 2002), the 'pornification of culture' (Paul, 2005), the 'sexualisation of culture' (Gill, 2009) and the 'mainstreaming of sex' (Attwood, 2009). In her book *Female Chauvinist Pigs: Women and the Rise of Raunch Culture*, Levy (2006) uses the term to describe the infiltration into mainstream society and culture of contrived sexualities that once existed solely in the realm of the 'sex industry' and pornography. It is a culture, therefore, in which the image of the sex worker (the prostitute, the stripper, the 'glamour model' and, more recently, the 'porn star') embodies ideal female sexuality and is represented as a figure of aspiration in the media and in popular cultural texts.

The phenomenon's infiltration of Irish mainstream popular media has been subtle in its approach, but rapid and extremely pervasive in its influence over the past thirty years. In that time, the Irish socio-cultural landscape has been transformed from one synonymous with censorship and guilt-induced austerity to one in which these sexualised messages have been accepted as part of the technological sophistication of post-Celtic Tiger Ireland. Our reaction to this change as a nation has been to publicly reject all things associated with our repressive sexual history and to instead embrace its antithesis, raunch culture, which embodies all that is not traditionally Irish, parochial, insular and controlled.

In fact, in order to see the prevalence of raunch culture in Irish society, one need only look to the number of advertising campaigns launched by Irish companies between 2011 and 2012 that promote a fetishised image of female sexuality and the female body. Among these is the recent promotional campaign by airline Ryanair, which included images of female cabin crew members dressed in underwear bearing slogans such as, 'Red Hot Fares and Crew'. These images were part of a wider campaign that included an underwear calendar modelled by female staff members and promotional images of the middle-aged male owner, Michael O'Leary, with his hands placed on the young women's bottoms.

Similarly, in 2011 Irish snack brand 'Hunky Dory' ran a campaign that included television, billboard, print and online advertising that depicted female models as rugby and Gaelic football players, dressed in underwear. Many of the campaign's central images focused on their legs, bottoms and breasts and some included scenes of fetishised lesbianism similar to that portrayed in pornography.

This pornographic representation of women as objects of the male gaze and of male pleasure in Irish culture over the last ten years has now become the 'norm' and can be seen, for example, in the surge in popularity of pole-dancing classes, which can be found, using a very quick Google search, in every county in the Republic of Ireland. Such is the extent of this popularity that since 2006, Ireland has played host to an annual 'Pole Championships', which takes place in September each year and all the proceeds of which are donated to Crumlin Children's Hospital. This union between a 'sport' that originated as a facet of the sex industry and a children's charity is significant in terms of the escalation of raunch culture in Ireland and the extent to which it has been normalised and accepted by Irish people.

It is this normalising influence that is of central concern to this study and further evidence of it can be seen in the continued growth and popularity of texts such as Irish 'reality' television show *Tallafornia*, which boasted ratings of over 450,000 viewers for its first episode in December 2011 (*Daily Edge*, 2011) and which, like its American and UK equivalents, *Jersey Shore* and *Geordie Shore*, depicts men whose central function it is to 'pull birds' and women who are primarily driven by their desire to be seen as 'hot' and 'sexy' by men.

'Pornified'

This sexualisation of culture is heavily linked to processes of pornification, which include not just the mainstreaming and normalising of pornographic material but the rebranding of pornography as something 'sexy' and fun that can be both exciting and empowering for women. Despite raunch culture's assertion that pornography has evolved and developed over the past twenty years to encompass the needs and desires of both men and women, the majority of images and audio-visual representations of sexuality found in mainstream pornography are laden with commercial agendas, gendered assumptions and sexual stereotypes. Free internet sites, such as YouPorn or RedTube, provide access to thousands of videos showcasing visual representations of how patriarchal power structures are reproduced and normalised through pornographic material. This is achieved using a standard template for heterosexual pornography, which includes three key elements: a hypermasculine male; an ultra-feminine female; and a dominant, phallocentric, male-normative and coitus-centric vision of sexuality.

The Hypermasculine Male in Pornography

This 'hypermasculine' or macho model of masculinity is inextricably linked to heterosexuality and is propagated through raunch culture by the image of a man with an insatiable libido who engages in sexual activity with women at any given opportunity. His sexual success, then, can be measured by the number of women with whom he has had sex, and he is often characterised by his ability to separate emotion or social connection from the physical elements of sex. Recent textual examples of this male include the TV characters 'Charlie Harper' (*Two And A Half Men*), 'Jason Stackhouse' (*True Blood*) and 'Barney Stinson' (*How I Met Your Mother*), whose roles and scripts are based almost entirely on their (hetero)sexual encounters.

In her 2005 book *Pornified*, Pamela Paul asserts that within this model, '... men tend to find themselves placed in the role of playboy or gigolo, the superficial stud whose status is attained according to the quantity and quality of women he beds' (Paul, 2005: 81). Pornography not only exhibits this image as a contemporary ideal for masculinity through the sexual acts and roles portrayed by its male performers but also reinforces it as a model to be aspired to by its predominantly male audiences. As Jackson and Scott put it:

> Pornography draws on wider cultural narratives through which masculinity and male sexuality are constructed and itself contributes to their construction and reconstruction. It helps to circulate and perpetuate particular versions of these narratives such as the mythology of women as sexually available, deriving pleasure from being dominated and possessed and a model of masculinity validated through sexual mastery over women. (Jackson & Scott, 1996: 23)

In a substantial amount of pornographic material, the male performer dominates and his pleasure is central to the structure of most pornographic videos. Consequently, these videos almost always end in what the industry has termed the 'money shot' (Attwood, 2007) because these shots, which show the male performer ejaculating (often on the face/breasts/anus of the female performer(s)) is the pivotal shot upon which the commercial success of a particular video hinges.

The pleasure of the female performer, on the other hand, is less integral to the success of these videos and although realistic female pleasure is *sometimes* represented therein, more often than not the female orgasm takes the form of either a histrionic pantomime of screams and affirmations of the male performer's sexual prowess, or is exhibited as 'other' or fetishistically, for example where female ejaculation is recorded.

The Ultra-Feminine Female in Pornography

This hypermasculine caricature of 'maleness' is not the only gendered stereotype to be found in raunch culture. Accompanying this 'ideal' of hypermasculinity is what Laura Kipnis (2007) calls 'ultrafemininity', which is a passive, playful and girly femininity that is frequently reinforced in popular culture. This model of femininity has emerged from the patriarchal stereotypes of female sexuality as portrayed in mainstream heterosexual pornography. However, the development of raunch culture has led to further dissemination, mainstreaming and eventual normalising of this model as the 'ideal' femininity of twenty-first-century society.[3]

In pornography, this stereotypical model is firmly upheld and its female performers are portrayed as passive actors in the sexual acts it showcases. They are often depicted as empty receptacles of male sexual pleasure and usually described by pornographers as having sex acts *done to* them, as opposed to being active participants in acts. Evidence of this can be seen in the short taglines that accompany many of the top-rated videos on the website YouPorn, which include descriptions of women being 'nailed', 'pounded' or 'fucked'. When a video *does* show a woman initiating a sexual act, even when the sole purpose of the act is to pleasure a *man*, she is often described in the taglines as a 'whore', 'horny bitch', 'slut', etc. This rigid, one-dimensional view of female sexuality has contributed to the reinforcement of archaic sexual double standards and the normalisation of an extremely narrow version of female sexuality through channels of popular culture and the media.

Raunch Culture's Sexual Rulebook

The reinforcement of such narrowly defined parameters of modern masculinity, femininity and sexuality has led to the establishment of a 'sexual rulebook' in twenty-first-century Western society, which has, over the past twenty years, been implemented steadily and pervasively by raunch culture through popular cultural texts. This is a rulebook that is driven by phallocentric and coitus-centric sexual standards and which, using a model of sex based in pornography, is blatantly patriarchal, not only in its origins but also in its divisive and isolating treatment of women.

Rule #1: Reject Feminism

This divisiveness has been investigated in the studies of researchers such as Rúdólfsdóttir and Jolliffe (2008), who describe the recent palpable shift in the young female imagination away from feminism. According to their research, this distancing involves not only a rejection of the term itself but also a stereotyping of feminists as old-fashioned, dogmatic and man-hating. This is accompanied by a move *towards* a neo-liberal individualism that, via the media, encourages a culture of competition among woman and the uptake of 'ironic', 'naughty', 'one-of-the-lads' sexisms. In raunch culture, this shift has not only been *encouraged*, but any divergence from it is seen as an automatic *convergence* with feminism, which is regarded as 'the preserve of only the unstable, mannish, unattractive woman who has a naturally difficult relationship with her own femininity' (Whelehan, 2000: 18).

Within this phenomenon, femininity is *embodied* and women are scrutinised *for* and judged *by* their looks; pitted against one another by the media as competition or as enemies. This scrutiny is perhaps at its most intense in media aimed exclusively at women. Glossy magazines, such as *Cosmopolitan*, for example, generate vast amounts of revenue each month by promoting the constant need for female self-improvement. This is a phenomenon that Kipnis calls the 'Professional Girlfriend' (Kipnis, 2007: 10), due to the fact that these media, under the guise of dispatching friendly advice and guidance (e.g. '10 Ways to be Better in Bed'/'Look Younger in One Week'), are in fact communicating the message that the female reader is not good enough, attractive enough, sexual enough, etc.

As Durham asserts: 'The media teach us to find pleasure in approximating the unreachable ideal, but because the Barbie body is a myth, we can never fully acquire it and the anxieties remain with us. The pleasure of pursuing a beauty regime is always linked with self-doubt' (Durham, 2009: 104). The reinforcement of these messages, not only in magazines but in film, television and online media aimed at women, is constant, and is a successful tool used, ultimately, to make money by making women feel flawed; 'your self-loathing and neurosis are somebody else's quarterly profits' (Kipnis, 2007: 10).

Rule #2: Be 'Hot'

This contemporary focus in popular culture on female self-improvement is often predicated on a scale of measurement that gauges how 'hot' a woman is. This is linked to the argument that sexual attractiveness can be analysed as a form of social capital and the notion that, within this culture, as M.G. Durham put it in her book *The Lolita Effect*, 'Hot is the highest accolade a girl can get' (Durham, 2009: 67).

'Hotness' in this context, however, is not objective or 'in the eye of the beholder', but relies heavily on a woman's ability to meet a list of physical standards and criteria set out in popular culture. In 'lad's mag' FHM's annual *100 Sexiest Women in the World List 2011*, for example, over 90 per cent of the women listed were white and a further 65 per cent were blonde. All were slimmer than the average Irish woman (whose dress size is estimated at between 14 and 16) and all but one were under the age of 40.

The reinforcement of this image as 'ideal' in Western popular culture and its inextricable links to the *ultrafeminine* mean that non-adherence to this model is often equated with ugliness, unat-tractiveness and a lack of femininity. The pressure that exists for women to conform to this standard is thus linked not only to their level of sexual attractiveness but to the extent to which they feel 'normal' or 'like a woman'.

Rule #3: Embrace 'Sex'

Further to this focus on the importance of being 'hot', is raunch culture's emphasis on the importance of sex, and of being seen to enjoy and embrace the sexualised messages put forward in the media. This includes, for example, a trend wherein Irish women align themselves with aspects of the sex industry, e.g. through strip-tease and pole-dancing classes, in the name of sexual freedom and empowerment. This definition of 'sex', however, is laden with ideals and standards that ultimately focus on pornified manifestations of female sexuality and sexiness as *positive*, while simultaneously rejecting sexualities that fall outside of these pornified parameters as *disempowered* and *unsexy*. This point is reinforced by Levy, who observes that within raunch culture's narrow definition of positive sexuality, '*everyone* who is sexually liberated ought to be imitating strippers and porn stars' (Levy, 2006: 27). Pamela Paul further supports this argument in her work:

> Popular culture promotes the wild fun and whimsy of the girl who loves pornography. She is Carmen Electra ... she sells exercise videos based on strip club routines. She is Pamela Anderson, *Playboy* centrefold, who has her own column in the teenage bible *Jane* magazine. The porn girl is every celebrity who accompanies her boyfriend to a strip club, playing along and plying a few bills to get lap dances herself. (Paul, 2005: 109)

This model, and its reinforcement through popular culture, has proved an immensely successful exercise in patriarchy due to its ability to seduce women into consumption while simultaneously communicating messages to them that ultimately encourage their submission. These messages are based on three key principles: that women exist as objects of male desire; that women are imperfect but should seek perfection through consumption; and that female sexuality exists primarily for men's pleasure. The success of these messages, then, and their penetration into the female sexual habitus is reliant on the fact that they are packaged and sold to women as a form of 'sexual empowerment'.

Rule #4: Be 'Empowered'

The term 'empowerment' is one that is usually synonymous with concepts such as agency, autonomy and a power that is free from coercion. In raunch culture, it is used to denote a form of 'power' that comes with an adherence to a rigid set of socio-sexual rules, such as those discussed above. The vision of female sexual empowerment portrayed through this culture is therefore intrinsically flawed in its prioritisation of female *sexiness* over female *pleasure*, and also in the many falsehoods and contradictory versions of female sexuality that it perpetrates. It is, for example, a form of empowerment accessible only by those who conform (or who *can* conform) to a strict set of physical and sexual standards, a fact that makes it exclusionary and, by extension, automatically *disempowering*.

As well as this, raunch culture's narrow definition of 'good sex' is one that glorifies coitus and male sexual fantasy and that restricts the sexual choices of women who, for example, wish to explore the possibility of sex with other women outside the heterosexual male gaze, or of women who wish to engage in alternative sexual acts or to seek pleasure outside these parameters.

The 'sexually empowered woman', then, is one who is represented prolifically within popular cultural texts. What these women (e.g. *Sex and the City*'s Samantha Jones) *lack*, however, is any acknowledgment of the existence of a double standard. Instead, these texts usually portray women as living in a socio-cultural vacuum that transcends the legacy of patriarchal power structures and inequality. In raunch culture, empowered women are shown to engage in a wide range of sexual activities with a wide range of partners, free from social pressures, negative labelling and sexual double standards.

The Impact of Raunch Culture on Irish Women's Sexual Lives

Despite their absence in popular culture, it is precisely the *presence* of these three under-represented social influences that was identified as the key inhibitor to sexual autonomy in the experiences of the young female participants in the study I undertook. In fact, in their reported experiences, it was the conflicting standards and messages communicated to them by the media that were cited as the primary source of their sexual insecurities, anxieties and fears, which, in turn, led to processes of self-correction and self-regulation that were at odds with their own pleasures and desires. This self-regulatory behaviour, on the part of almost all of the women interviewed, included actively altering the way they look (through dress, diet, exercise, etc.) in order to fit the 'hot' mould. It also involved, at a more inhibitive level, a process of sexual self-correction and regulation that extended to their participation in and consent to unwanted sex or sexual acts and, conversely, their refusal to engage in some sex or sexual acts that *were* wanted.

Pressure to Be 'Hot'

In order to establish the reasons for the first of these self-regulatory behaviours, each of the interview participants was asked the question: 'What does the term "hot" mean to you?' Overwhelmingly, what emerged from the data was the notion that to be considered 'hot', a woman needs to meet a narrow set of physical attributes and criteria, encompassing not just the way she looks but her level of sexual attractiveness to the opposite sex.

Each participant, in her definition of the term, cited an almost identical list of criteria ('slim', 'good hair', 'nice skin', 'big boobs', etc.), a fact that suggests that 'hotness' is not an abstract concept, such as 'beauty' or 'prettiness', but is instead a tangible status that can be accessed by those who meet a set list of physical attributes and a willingness to exhibit themselves as sexual above all else. As Ann[4] asserts, for example: 'it's not even good-looking or beautiful because I think that's separate from describing someone as hot. I suppose its kind of a level of their sexual attractiveness or how appealing they are to somebody.' This sentiment is echoed by Laura, 'hot mightn't always mean beautiful or pretty ... she has sex appeal', and by Louise, who equates 'hot' with looking good, but 'more in a sexual way than a sort of cute or pretty sort of way'.

What is significant in these interviews is not the accepted standards and demanding criteria of 'hotness' as instituted by raunch culture, but the aspiration towards this standard and resultant pressure experienced by these young women to conform to those criteria. This is a pressure that is in evidence throughout the interview transcripts: 'there's a norm of how girls, when they want to be attractive, they have to look a certain way' (Ann). Of the twelve women interviewed, when asked whether they felt that they fit their own description of 'hotness', ten said no outright and some laughed at the idea. Of the two who did not flatly reject the possibility that they might be considered 'hot', their responses were not emphatic. Claire, for example, said, 'Hmmmmmm ... sometimes, maybe'.

A similar level of response was given to the question about whether the women felt pressure to conform to the 'hot' ideal. Some, such as Claire and Erica, embraced 'hotness' as an ideal: 'Yeah ... you think, "Oh wow! I'd love to look like that"' (Claire); 'I would love to look like that. And I do try, like, I work out and I do Weight Watchers' (Erica). Others *acknowledged* the pressure, but demonstrated a reluctance to accept it: 'Yeah, I'd love to say, "no I don't", but I think I have felt that pressure from as long as I can remember' (Daisy).

Most striking, however, were the responses of women who indicated a need on their part to *self-regulate* in order to conform to this 'hot' standard, despite it going against their nature: 'I think I'm trying to get there, but it's far from my personality' (Paula); 'There's definitely pressure there … I try and resist it and, like, the way I dress or whatever doesn't really conform … but the pressure's still there, you feel it and you're constantly questioning what you're wearing and how you look and I think you have to keep constantly reinforcing your own, like, em … belief that you don't need to be like that' (Emer); 'Yeah, I think it sort of creeps up now and again … I would like to have lighter hair or clearer skin … these are very often seen as what is the epitome of hotness and you can't help going, "Yeah, I wouldn't mind, like"' (Louise); 'Yeah, I suppose. I mean, one example, you know, growing up I would have been bordering on tomboy in my clothes and my activities and that, so, em, if I was going to a disco, I would have been, "Right, I have to change things here. I have to dress up in some way"' (Paula).

This self-regulation extends to actively seeking to alter the way they look, from superficial changes like 'dressing up, putting on make-up, getting my hair done' (Claire) to rigorous exercise regimes and restrictive diets: 'That's what drives us all to the gym and what drives us all to keep our diets' (Daisy).

Pressure to Be Seen as 'Sex Positive' or to Be 'Good' at Sex

The pressure to be sexy and hot is not based solely on physical appearance but extends to a pressure to be 'good' at sex, something that was shared by 70 per cent of those surveyed within the study and by eleven of the twelve interview participants. While some of the women stated that this pressure stemmed from a desire to please their partners sexually – 'I guess pleasing the guy you're with' (Emer) – others alluded to the emphasis placed on 'performance' in popular culture. Ruth, for example, cites 'the portrayal of Sam from *Sex and the City*' as typical of raunch's focus on female sexuality as performative and discusses the suggestion, in televisual texts, that sexually satisfied and empowered women are 'meant to be amazing, no matter who [they are] with' (Ruth). Emer and Michelle also support this point, describing the women portrayed in such texts as 'sexual dynamos' (Emer), who 'have to have a screaming orgasm the entire time' (Michelle). This emphasis on performance in mainstream cultural portrayals of female sexuality increases pressure on women to adhere to it: 'you have to be really adventurous and really wild and, you know, be up for all these different positions, sexual positions ... em ... you have to enjoy giving a blow-job ... you have to be good a giving a hand-job, to have techniques or something' (Erica).

This pressure to perform, then, is one that is heavily linked to raunch culture's pornified, coitus-centric definition of 'good sex', a point Erica illustrates as follows: 'that's what society says we should do ... that's what happens on TV, a couple gets into bed and they don't just masturbate each other. They have sex. Em ... in magazines, they mostly talk about having sex and how to get the most out of it, hmmm ... I'm not really sure why, it just seems to be the inevitable, the be-all and end-all and that's how you show you care about someone.' Erica goes on to explain that this act is seen as 'real sex', particularly in media representations of sexuality, and that the end of sex and intimacy is signalled, in her experience, by male ejaculation (as it is in the money-shots of pornographic videos). This portrayal of coitus as 'real' or 'good' sex contradicts the experiences of the survey respondents, only 9 per cent of whom stated that they 'always' experienced orgasm through this method, where no further stimulation was offered.

Despite the experiences of these women, coitus continues to be normalised as 'sex' in popular texts and discourses, thereby deprioritising sex acts that give women more pleasure and focusing on *male* heterosexual pleasure instead. In fact, within the questionnaire data it became clear that, particularly in the context of casual sex or one-night stands, the women surveyed hugely devalued and deprioritised their own pleasure. When questioned about the importance of *their* orgasm and the importance of their *partner*'s orgasm in a long-term relationship, for example, almost 50 per cent stated that they would see their *partner*'s orgasm as 'extremely important', while only half that number granted *their own* orgasm the same level of importance.

These data were supported by the interview findings in which interviewees such as Emer, when asked whether her own pleasure was central to her past decisions to engage in casual sex, answered; 'No … I was just really worried about what it would be like and if I'd be good actually and if he'd get mad if I said no and yeah … I was just … I wasn't really thinking about "would it be good?" at all.' These sentiments are echoed by Ann, who, when discussing her experiences of casual sex, said that she doesn't think 'pleasure really comes into it'.

Consenting to Unwanted Sex and Refusing Sex that Is Wanted

These inadequate negotiations of female pleasure, and an expectation that their male partner will get pleasure even if they don't, extends also to the issue of consent. Several of the women interviewed described situations where they had consented to sex that was ultimately unwanted. Erica, for example, describes her recent relationship with a man who insisted she must have some form of sexual dysfunction because she couldn't orgasm through coitus alone. Within this relationship, she engaged in coitus and other acts, such as performing oral sex, purely to please her male partner, but she conceded that it was a chore: 'it's a job – it's called a job for a reason.'

Many of the women interviewed alluded to the fact that their experiences of casual sex were not always pleasurable nor were they always driven by desire. Both Ann and Emer, for example, explain their engagement in unwanted consensual sex with casual partners and the driving forces behind their decisions to consent. Emer describes her experience, at nineteen, of being set up on a date with an older man (aged 27), who coerced her into going home with him. In this description, she blames herself for getting herself 'into that situation' and explains that 'things moved on a lot faster than I thought and I just sort of went along with it and thought it was fine in the moment and then sort of felt crap afterwards'. She asserts that 'he didn't push me further than I wanted to go, but he was very insistent … I think he expected something else from me.' When asked if she considered her own pleasure in this encounter, she explained that she was concerned about her performance and her partner's reaction to that performance and that her own pleasure had not occurred to her at that moment.

Ann, too, has had similar experiences of unwanted consensual sex, which she describes as follows: 'I've often ended up doing things with people that you wouldn't really have intended at all, but when you're put in that situation it's hard to say "no"... it's nearly easier to say "yes"... you're kind of going with the flow ... I don't think pleasure would come into it much'. Like Emer, she explains that although she did not want to engage sexually with these men, at that particular point in time a variety of different pressures influenced her decision to ultimately consent: 'well, why couldn't I say "no"? Because you seem a bit of prude if you do.'

This fear of judgement and of being negatively labelled (e.g. as 'prude', 'slut', etc.) also imposes further restrictions on female sexual autonomy by encouraging a self-imposed silencing among women who engage in and consent to sex that they want and find pleasurable. This is true in the cases of Daisy and Erica, who had both experienced judgement by partners, friends and family members in the past. Erica explains, for example, that she is more likely to enjoy *illicit* relationships (e.g. her affair with a man who was engaged to be married, or sex with a friend of her ex-boyfriend) due to the fact that both she and her partners *must* not disclose any details of their sexual relationships. Daisy echoes these sentiments and describes her perceived need to keep her sexual encounters and sexual past a secret, due to a fear of being judged by others and by her belief that disclosure might hinder her chances of having a successful committed relationship in the future.

Raunch Culture's Sexual Double Standard

Within this 'prude'/'slut' dichotomy that labels women according to their sexuality, an obvious double standard exists, of which the female participants of the study are extremely aware. Daisy, for example, summarises this standard as follows: 'we all know the double standard exists right? If a girl sleeps with loads of guys, she's a slut; if a guy does it, he's a hero and that's always the way it was.' Laura supports this point and, using the words of one of her male friends, describes the widespread acceptance and proliferation of this double standard: '... a key that can open up loads of locks is a master key, but ... a lock that can be opened up by many keys is a cheap lock' and that's what he was describing girls who have a one-night stand as.'

The interviews in the study highlighted an acknowledgment on the part of these female participants that this attitude, among young men in particular, is widespread, as is an acceptance by the young women that, however unjust, this is the way it is. The internal conflict these young women experience between the benefits of being seen as sexually 'empowered' and as 'embracing sex', and the stigma of being negatively labelled as a 'slut' was palpable within the transcripts. Ann describes this conflict as follows: 'you know it's kind of hard, we're expected to be one thing and we're expected to be another.' Similarly, Orla discusses the importance of discretion and the delicate balance that exists between the 'slut' and 'prude' labels: 'I think it's harder, much harder for girls and I think they have to be … I think they're forced to be more discreet, like, they're expected to be open about sex, but not too open, you know, there's this kind of grey area and it's really tricky to kind of, to get that balance right. You know, to nearly "appear" to do it, but not actually do it.' Within this grey area, then, women feel they are forced to perform; there is no room for discussion of female sexual pleasure, choice, agency or autonomy. In fact, throughout the study's findings, this 'line' that the participants felt they needed to tread was of greater concern to them than their own sexual pleasures, desires, behaviours and choices.

Conclusion

In this chapter, several issues have been discussed that threaten the development of an autonomous Irish female sexuality. This includes the prevalence and influence of raunch culture's sexual rulebook, which imposes a set of rules and standards that are rigid in their definitions of 'sex', 'sexuality', 'empowerment', 'femininity' and 'masculinity', and which are enforced through the social stigmatising, labelling and judgement of those who do not adhere to them. The pressure that exists to adhere is palpable throughout both the questionnaire and interview findings from the study and has manifested itself, as previously discussed at length, in the self-correction and self-regulation of the female participants, whose sexual choices are often dictated by forces that are external to them, such as the media, their partner, peers, etc.

In fact, even where the presence of sexual choice *is* perceived, the choices available to many of the women interviewed have been subject to coercive and restrictive social standards propagated through media messages by raunch culture. In these cases, the young women involved have been forced to make sexual decisions based not on their own sexual gratification, satisfaction or pleasure, but on achieving the least damaging outcome of a sexual situation, e.g. in consenting to unwanted sex to avoid being labelled 'prudish' (e.g. Ann) or to ensure that their sexual partner will not be angry or upset (e.g. Emer).

This data confirms the effect of raunch culture's reinforcement of archaic sexual double standards, and its institution of a rigid and pornified sexual rulebook has been shown to have a profound impact on the sexual lives of young Irish women, such as those interviewed in this study. Thus, rather than acting as a vehicle for female sexual empowerment, raunch culture acts as an oppressive force that ultimately inhibits the development of an autonomous Irish female sexuality.

Notes

[1] First-wave feminism is the term associated with the feminist movement that was most evident during the nineteenth century and early twentieth century and that focused primarily on women's suffrage. Once this goal had been achieved in the majority of Western societies, a 'second' wave of feminists emerged in the 1960s who were eager to build on the achievements of the first wave by focusing on gender equality and so-called 'women's issues', such as their sexual, property and reproductive rights. Postfeminism, on the other hand, is in my opinion best described by Angela McRobbie (2004), who asserts that it refers to an 'active process by which feminist gains of the 1970s and 80s come to be undermined. It proposes that through an array of machinations, elements of contemporary popular culture are perniciously effective in regard to this undoing of feminism, while simultaneously appearing to be engaging in a well-informed and even well-intended response to feminism' (McRobbie, 2004: 255).

[2] The survey sample was made up of 1,764 women who identified as 'ethnically Irish' (i.e. had been born and had lived over 90 per cent of their lives in Ireland), were aged 18–34 and were staff and student members of National University of Ireland, Galway. The interview sample was made up of a voluntary sub-sample of this group and of the twelve women who were interviewed, nine were aged 18–24 and three were aged 25–34. In terms of sexual orientation, six of the twelve identified as 'exclusively heterosexual', with a further five identifying as 'mainly heterosexual' and one as 'bisexual'. Half of the participants said that, at the time of interview, they were 'in a relationship', two were cohabiting, one was married

and one identified her relationship status as 'single but engage in casual relationships'.

[3] This vision of femininity is represented prolifically in 'reality' programming; recent examples include the women involved in television shows such as *Girls of the Playboy Mansion* and *The Only Way is Essex* and, in the Irish context, *Tallafornia*.

[4] The names given for interview participants are codenames used for purposes of anonymity.

CHAPTER 17

Redefining Prostitution as
Sex Work on the Irish Agenda[1]

Teresa Whitaker

Introduction

Discourses about sex work – like those about other sexuality-related phenomena, such as abortion or homosexuality – are deeply informed by concerns for personal and public morality. Sexuality-related issues strike at the heart of our sense of self and identity (Inglis, 2005) and are not easily resolved. At the time of writing, the criminal law in relation to prostitution or sex work is under review in Ireland. In June 2012 the Minister for Justice, Equality and Defence published a *Discussion Document on Future Direction of Prostitution Legislation* (Department of Justice and Equality, 2012) and initiated a consultation process in which interested parties were invited to make submissions to the Joint Oireachtas Committee on Justice, Equality and Defence. In June 2013 the *Report on hearings and submissions on the Review of Legislation on Prostitution* (Houses of the Oireachtas Joint Committee on Justice, Defence and Equality, 2013) was published. It recommended a legal approach that would criminalise those seeking to purchase sex and introduce serious deterrents for those who coerce people into the sex industry. This approach is defined as one of 'partial decriminalisation', similar to that adopted in Sweden (Houses of the Oireachtas Joint Committee on Justice, Defence and Equality, 2013: 15.)

Legislative and social responses to prostitution have varied over time. Under the Brehon Laws (ancient Irish laws operating from the first century BC until the twelfth century), prostitutes were seen to occupy a lower stratum in Irish society (Thurneysen et al., 1936).

After the foundation of the Irish State, the best efforts of Church, government and public opinion failed to eradicate prostitution (Luddy, 2007b). Today, sex workers continue to trade their services in brothels, as independent escorts and on the streets. Modern communications technology has changed how sexual services are traded: buyers can use the internet to engage a sex worker to come to their home or to an agreed venue; even street-based sex workers have regular clients, who may contact them by mobile phone. Potential for secrecy is hugely enhanced. Given the clandestine, stigmatised and criminalised nature of sex work, it is impossible to determine accurately the number of sex workers working in Ireland. Nonetheless, the Irish *Discussion Document on Future Direction of Prostitution Legislation* (Department of Justice and Equality, 2012: 6) estimates that 'more than 1,000 women, mainly migrants, are available or are made available for paid sexual services on a daily basis throughout Ireland'. Data on detected prostitution-related offences available from the Garda PULSE database indicate that in 2011, there were 50 detected cases of brothel-keeping, ten detected cases of organisation of prostitution and 176 detected cases of soliciting (Department of Justice and Equality, 2012: 7).

Due to the varying circumstances and environments in which they work, sex workers may have little in common with each other, apart from the fact that they exchange money for sexual services. Sex workers are not a homogenous group; they comprise women, men, transgender, older and younger people; some may engage in it intermittently, others may make a career of it. O'Neill (1997) argues that prostitution cannot be divorced from the socio-historical, cultural, economic and political contexts that mediate and give rise to prostitution. In countries where sex work is decriminalised, legalised or unionised, sex workers work within a regulated industry; in countries where prostitution is outlawed, they work as part of the informal economy, or the black market. A cohort of individuals also exists who are not voluntarily involved in sex work, but rather are abducted, trafficked and exploited for criminal advantage.[2] The *Discussion Document on Future Direction of Prostitution Legislation* (Department of Justice and Equality, 2012: 7), citing figures from the Anti-Human Trafficking Unit, notes that between 2008 and 2011, 201 alleged[3] reports of trafficking were made to the Gardaí, with 134 (67%) of these relating to victims of trafficking for sexual exploitation. Of these, 102 (76%) were adult females and 31

(23%) were minors (Department of Justice and Equality, 2012: 7). The discussion of sex workers in this chapter refers to those who are voluntarily involved in sex work.

This chapter will begin with a brief overview of various discourses (religious, medical, legal, feminist, harm reduction and human rights) through which prostitution has been socially constructed. This will be followed by consideration of the historical and current situation of sex work in Ireland, and the different kinds of service provision for sex workers in Dublin. Then the focus will shift to give voice to illicit drug-using sex workers in Dublin, to identify how they construct meaning in terms of their work and how they exercise personal agency and control in the sex work setting. Focusing on a micro study of one cohort of sex workers allows for a detailed understanding of the motivations and experiences of women engaged in sex work and allows for the emergence of an alternative discourse, or understanding, of sex work, which is grounded in empirical experiences rather than moral or political concerns. Kesler (2005), in her analysis of feminist approaches to sex work, highlights the value of feminist postmodernist approaches, arguing that ' ... the integration of the voices and stories of prostitutes and sex workers by postmodern feminist theory challenges modern feminist notions of the experiences and oppression of sex workers and prostitutes' (Kesler, 2005: 42).[4] The voices of one cohort of sex workers are included in this chapter, for the purpose of revealing how they exercise agency in their working lives.

The use of the terms 'prostitute' and 'sex worker' in this chapter will reflect usage in the literature and the time period being discussed. 'Prostitute' was the term used historically. Radical feminist commentators (such as Dworkin, 1997), who raised the issue of prostitution as a political concern, predominantly use the term 'prostitute'. The term 'sex worker' is used by other commentators, who consider it to be more respectful and less stigmatising (Whitaker et al., 2011) and also believe that it reflects the economic nature of the transaction between buyer and seller. The term 'sex worker' was coined in 1980 by the sex workers' rights activist Carol Leigh (Koken, 2010). This term is used by international organisations, such as the World Health Organization (WHO, 2005) and the United Nations (UNAIDS, 2010). The diverse use of terminology is evident in the current Irish debate. The government discussion document uses the word 'prostitution', as does the Turn Off the Red Light campaign, a coalition of charities, interest groups, professional associations and political parties that are advocating for more stringent regulation of the purchasers of sex.[5] In contrast, the Turn Off the Blue Light campaign, an opposing interest group, favours the term 'sex worker' and defines itself as a 'sex worker led association campaigning against calls to criminalise the purchase of sex, and for the health, safety, human, civil and labour rights of sex workers in Ireland'.[6] Kesler (2005), in her discussion of femninist responses to prostitution/sex work, uses both terms, with 'prostitute' employed to describe those who are coerced into prostitution and 'sex worker' to describe those who enter sex work voluntarily.

Regulatory and Interpretative Discourses

Current understandings of sexuality and prostitution are rooted in a long history of multiple, often contradictory, discourses. Foucault (1978) explores the regime of power-knowledge-pleasure that sustains the discourse on human sexuality in the Western world. In *The History of Sexuality*, Volume 1 (Foucault, 1978), he argues that sexuality is a social construct and an historical invention. Our sexual definitions, beliefs, identities and behaviours have been shaped within defined power relationships. In the early seventeenth century people spoke frankly and openly about sex, as social norms regarding what was seen as coarse or obscene were lax compared to those of the nineteenth century: 'It was a time of direct gestures, shameless discourse, and open transgressions, when anatomies were shown and intermingled at will, and knowing children hung about amid the laughter of adults: it was a period when bodies "made a display of themselves"' (Foucault, 1978: 3). Foucault (1978) argues, however, that from the end of the sixteenth century, a new concern emerged with classifying and fixing different sexual types and characteristics and defining normal and abnormal sexuality. The day of permissiveness died during what Foucault (1978: 3) describes as '... the monotonous nights of the Victorian bourgeoisie'. Sexuality became officially confined to the conjugal family in the home, sex was for reproduction and it was subjected to a triple edict of taboo, non-existence and silence. Foucault (1978) examines the development of a science of sexuality that was socially constructed through religious, medical and legal discourses.

Religious Discourses

How we think about prostitution is heavily influenced by religious discourses, with both male and female prostitutes condemned in the Bible.[7] In Western Europe, the Christian Churches defined the division between illicit and licit sex and prescribed rules and matrimonial obligations for its regulation (Foucault, 1978). Luddy (2007) provides extensive insight into social and religious attitudes towards prostitution in Ireland in the nineteenth and early twentieth centuries. Historically, both the Catholic and Protestant Churches intervened in the lives of Irish prostitutes (Luddy, 2007). Prostitutes were targeted in the late 1800s by vigilance and purity associations, such as the White Cross Vigilance Association (WCVA), run by the Church of Ireland, which organised patrols targeting women engaging in prostitution (Luddy, 2007: 39). By 1765 at least 41 Magdalene asylums, based on similar asylums in London, existed in Ireland to rescue 'fallen women' (Luddy, 2007: 39). Some of these asylums were established by laypeople; others by religious orders. Typically, these institutions were run as laundries; the larger these were, the better their chance of economic survival through attracting financial contributions from the public. Between 1851 and 1899 a total of 10,674 women were catered for, some of whom entered more than once (Luddy, 2007: 95). Most (7,110, or over 66 per cent) entered by choice, and some possibly stayed on because the asylum offered better access to food and an ordered, secure way of life and was therefore preferable to the workhouse or destitution (Luddy, 2007: 95).[8]

As the name 'Magdalene' suggests, a religious model of repentance and spiritual regeneration underpinned the regime of the asylums (Luddy, 2007: 77). The asylum agendas reflected contradictory opinions about the inmates. On the one hand, the institutions were designed to show the woman the error of her ways and to encourage her to 'loathe her former vileness', while on the other hand she was perceived as not being evil but rather as keeping bad company (Luddy, 2007: 85).

With the foundation of the Irish Free State in 1922, an alliance of Church and State emerged in which women's sexuality was seen as highly dangerous (Luddy, 2007) and in need of control (Inglis, 2005). The only legitimate expression of sexuality was within heterosexual marriage. Sexually active unmarried women and prostitutes were conflated and seen as 'fallen women'. In 1923 Dublin's Monto area (derived from the name Montgomery Street and now known as Foley Street), which housed the greatest number of brothels (most of them run by women), was the target of a religious crusade by Frank Duff and the Legion of Mary,[9] on the basis that it was the site of both moral and physical contagion and was responsible for the spread of venereal disease. In March 1925 the police raided the brothels in the Monto and 45 prostitutes, twelve pimps and 50 customers were arrested. Women were encouraged to leave prostitution and to enter new hostels run by the Legion of Mary (Luddy, 2007). In the hostel the women were subjected to religious indoctrination to improve their morality. The Legion of Mary grew to over 2,000 members by 1934 and its work extended to providing homes for unmarried mothers (Luddy, 2007). Prostitution continued to be a reality in Ireland throughout the twentieth century, as evidenced by fights between pimps for control in Dublin in the 1970s and Lyn Madden's harrowing tale of her life as a prostitute for over twenty years in Dublin (Madden and Levine, 1987).

Attitudes towards sexuality in Ireland were changing in the second half of the twentieth century (Inglis, 2005) and although Magdalene laundries have gone, the belief still persists that sex workers need rescue and rehabilitation. In 1989 the Good Shepherd Sisters and Our Lady of Charity Sisters established Ruhama to work with prostitutes in Dublin. Ruhama uses the term 'prostitute', rather than 'sex worker'. Its position is that prostitution constitutes violence against women (Lawless et al., 2005) and staff encourage and support women to exit prostitution.[10] While there is nothing wrong with this rescue approach in itself, in my view it generalises the experiences of some marginalised or trafficked women to all sex workers; it denies sex workers any agency and depicts them as 'hapless victims' (Luddy, 2007: 16) of male lust and does not acknowledge women's agency.

Medical Discourses

Medical discourses have also influenced how we see sex work. According to Foucault (1978), the severity of the codes relating to sexual offences diminished in the nineteenth century and the law often deferred to medicine. The medical profession created/

identified mental pathologies arising out of 'incomplete' sexual practices (homosexuality, masturbation) and reflected middle-class values and norms around sexual behaviour. Non-marital, non-heterosexual sexuality was excoriated and women's sexuality was severely regulated. Nonetheless, there was widespread prostitution and venereal disease was rampant.

In Ireland, these values and beliefs informed a series of Contagious Diseases Acts in 1864 (Luddy, 2007), the aim of which was to ensure that soldiers did not contract venereal disease from prostitutes. Controls were placed on women rather than on men. The Acts permitted compulsory inspection of suspected prostitutes within a five-mile radius of the Cork, Cobh and Curragh military camps, with women refusing examination being liable to imprisonment for a month. Those found to be infected were forcibly detained in a Lock hospital for up to three months, and moral reform initiatives were part of the treatment regime (Luddy, 2007). Over 60,491 women were treated for venereal disease in Lock hospitals between 1792 and 1810, and 99,982 women were treated as outpatients between 1792 and 1818. The Acts were finally suspended in 1883 (Luddy, 2007). Sexually transmitted diseases, which became a significant public health concern for government and rescue workers in the 1920s and 1930s, also kept the focus on prostitution. A government interdepartmental inquiry, which produced a report into venereal disease (Riordan, 2007), concluded that the disease was being carried by a much broader section of the community than prostitutes, but argued for the suppression of prostitution by utilising more prison sentences rather than fines (Ferriter, 2009). At the same time, it rejected the need to enhance police powers to deal with brothels. The report's recommendations were to have little impact, however. (Ferriter, 2009).

Sex workers' exposure to disease remains a current concern. From the 1980s, acquired immunodeficiency syndrome (AIDS)/human immunodeficiency virus (HIV) emerged as one of the biggest threats to human health worldwide. The Joint United Nations Programme on HIV/AIDS (UNAIDS, 2002) states that sex workers and their clients have higher rates of HIV infection than other social groups. However, it is impossible to estimate the true extent of HIV transmission from sex workers to clients: while, on the one hand, sex workers are the group most likely to protect themselves and their clients by using condoms, on the other hand, certain factors increase sex workers' vulnerability to and risk of HIV infection. These factors include:

- Stigmatisation and marginalisation
- Limited economic options, particularly for women
- Limited access to health, social and legal services
- Limited access to information and prevention means
- Gender-related differences and inequalities
- Sexual exploitation and trafficking
- Harmful, or a lack of protective, legislation and policies
- Exposure to lifestyle-related risks (e.g. violence, substance use, mobility) (UNAIDS, 2002: 2)

In 2010, UNAIDS stated that policies and programmes aimed at reducing the demand for sex work, while ignoring the voices of sex workers, result in unintended harms, including increased risk for sex workers and their clients. To increase the effectiveness of HIV strategies and to respect human rights, UNAIDS (2010: 137) states that 'countries should now take action to decriminalize sex workers, people who use drugs, men who have sex with men and transgender people, and reform other laws that block effective responses to HIV.'

In Dublin, a number of health interventions are directed at sex workers. In the late 1980s, the role of sex workers in spreading the HIV virus resulted in initiatives from both voluntary and statutory services (Cox & Whitaker, 2009). In 1991 a statutory service, the Women's Health Project (WHP), was established; it provides support services for women sex workers, through outreach to streets and massage parlours and distribution of free condoms. It also provides free health screening for HIV, hepatitis and sexually transmitted infections (STIs), and addiction services, such as methadone and needle exchange programmes. The Gay Men's Health Service provides similar services to men who have sex with men.[11]

Dublin AIDS Alliance (DAA) was established in 1987. It is a voluntary organisation that works to improve conditions for people living with HIV and AIDS. It conducts outreach work and distributes free condoms to those who cannot afford to purchase them and to those at higher risk of HIV and STIs. In 2011, it distributed 63,451 condoms (Dublin AIDS Alliance, nd). The Alliance also provides condoms to the Chrysalis Community Drug Project, which offers a range of harm reduction services to drug-using women sex workers in Dublin's north inner city (Chrysalis Community Drug Project, nd).

In 2008 the National AIDS Strategy Committee (NASC) devised a four-year HIV and AIDS education plan (National AIDS Strategy Committee, 2008), which aims to reduce new infections through education and prevention measures. In its mid-term review (2011), NASC suggests that there has been progress in the implementation of actions targeting sex workers, such as enhanced condom-distribution mechanisms, screening and testing interventions for HIV and STIs. It suggests that there is a need for research into appropriate methodologies for HIV and AIDS education and prevention for indoor sex workers. The National Drugs Strategy 2009–2016 also refers to drug-using sex workers as an 'at risk' group, and identifies the importance of improving harm reduction services to them by providing access to needle exchange and condoms (Department of Community, Rural and Gaeltacht Affairs, 2009).

A mobile health clinic operated by the Safetynet Network and staffed by medical and outreach staff provides services to street workers in Dublin. However, Cusick et al. (2011) argue that harm reduction strategies are being frustrated by the discourses of lobbyists, who exclusively favour 'exiting' and who depict sex workers as victims of their circumstances rather than as persons who make choices to address their circumstances. Cusick et al. claim that the strong focus on the exit strategy, underpinned by a moralist stance, denies sex workers personal agency and drives them further underground and exposes them to even greater risks than 'the risks prohibitionists wish to save them from' (Cusick et al., 2011: 38). Cusick et al. (2011) draw on research conducted by the NACD (Cox & Whitaker, 2009), which revealed that some healthcare professionals employed in statutory organisations experienced unease with harm reduction strategies because they believe that they aid and abet the perpetuation of prostitution and the exercise of male violence against women (Cox & Whitaker, 2009; Cusick et al., 2011). This is evident in the following quotation from a health service provider, who sees the exit strategy as the optimum strategy when responding to women engaged in sex work.

I feel we are almost facilitating them to go out and to have sex. It is not them, if you take the focus off them and look at the demand for sex, what we are facilitating is actually the men out there to have sexual gratification on some poor young girl's body, that is what I see more and more and I feel very unsettled about that. We are quite unusual in providing harm reduction services within a health promotion context; however, our experience and analysis of the personal trauma to women in prostitution and the effects on women of the globalised sex industry, leave us in no doubt that prostitution is exploitative and very harmful to women and to that end we seek routes out/exit strategies (Cox & Whitaker, 2009: 149).

This analysis is similar to that put forward by radical feminists (Dworkin, 1997; Farley and Barkan, 1998; Farley and Kelly, 2000) who draw attention to the intimidation, violence and psychological damage sex workers can experience. Radical feminist scholarship understands sex work as the outcome of the intersection of capitalism and patriarchy and as the epitome of male dominance.

Legal Discourses

Legal discourses have constructed prostitution as a crime in Ireland. Historically, the most common legislation used to arrest women deemed to be prostitutes was the Vagrancy Act 1824 (Luddy, 2007).[12] The Police Clauses Act 1847 gave the police the power to arrest a woman believed to be a 'common prostitute or night walker loitering or importuning passengers for the purpose of prostitution' (Luddy, 2007: 29). Concern about young, vulnerable, working-class and country girls led to the Criminal Law Amendment Act 1912, referred to as the 'White Slavery Act', which increased police powers to prosecute procurers and brothel-keepers. However, there was no evidence of slavery, with Irish newspapers reporting, in 1913, that stories about white slavery were 'wild and unauthenticated' (Luddy 2007: 166). The perceived need to contain the spread of venereal diseases prompted further legislation. Regulation 40D of the Criminal Law Amendment Act 1917 made it a criminal offence for any woman with venereal disease to solicit or have sexual relations with a member of the armed forces (Luddy, 2007), while the Criminal Law Amendment Act 1935 was enacted to protect the youth of the country by raising the age of consent to seventeen years (Luddy, 2007).

No further legislation was enacted until the 1990s. From the 1960s to the 1990s there was a growth in off-street prostitution, brothels and massage parlours, all of which advertised openly without interference from the Gardaí (Reynolds, 2003; Ward, 2010b). By the early 1990s, however, a number of factors combined to create a momentum for changes in the law on prostitution. Ward (2010a) identifies these as: the murder of an ex-prostitute in the late 1970s; the growth of HIV in the late 1980s; and the growth of second-wave feminism and its concern with exploitation of women in prostitution. In 1993 the Criminal Law (Sexual Offences) Act was introduced, with eight sections dealing with prostitution. The criminal category of 'common prostitute' was removed, but new crimes were proposed, such as kerb-crawling, managing prostitution and living off the earnings of prostitution (Ward, 2010a). Garda powers and penalties were increased and courts could impose sentences of up to and including five years' imprisonment for violations. Within one year of the enactment of this legislation, there were more prosecutions than there had been in the previous ten years (Ward, 2010a). In the current legal framework, the emphasis is on the prostitute as a criminal. That said, the actual exchange of sexual services for money between consenting adults is not a crime, but soliciting and brothel-keeping are criminalised. In the public debate around prostitution/sex work, demands are being made (e.g. Turn Off the Red Light campaign) to shift the criminality away from the sellers of sex and on to the purchasers (clients/punters), an approach that is used in Sweden and has been recommended in the *Report on Hearings and Submissions on the Review of Legislation on Prostitution* (Houses of the Oireachtas Joint Committee on Justice, Defence and Equality, 2013).

Criminalisation of the purchasers of sexual services has been the cornerstone of Swedish legislation since 1999 (Swedish Institute, 2010). The effect of this legislation is questionable. The Swedish National Board of Health and Welfare, which has published three reports on prostitution in Sweden, highlights that it is difficult to ascertain the number of people involved in prostitution and whether it has increased or decreased. It does assert, however, that street prostitution is slowly returning, and has returned to two-thirds of its pre-criminalisation level (National Board of Health and Welfare of Sweden, 2008: 33). There is also some evidence from Swedish sex workers that the new law has put them at much greater physical risk from dangerous clients and has increased the number of pimps

(National Board of Health and Welfare of Sweden, 2008). It has also been claimed that the criminalisation of buyers means that workers have less time to assess or negotiate with the buyer because the deal takes place very hurriedly (Ministry of Justice and the Police of Norway, 2004: 19–20).

The question of whether the sale of sexual services should be understood as a fundamental abuse of human rights or as a viable sphere of work for some people is at the core of debates about how governments and societies should respond to the issue. It is argued that in patriarchal, capitalist societies, there are unequal relationships between genders, which propel women, predominantly, into prostitution (*see* Pateman, 1999). In radical feminist thinking, prostitution is viewed as violence against women (*see* Jeffreys, 1997); women never actually choose prostitution, but are victims of patriarchy in an unequal set of societal power relations. Radical feminists typically use the terms 'prostitutes' and 'prostituted women' and claim that prostitution is 'paid rape' and cannot, by definition, be chosen: prostitution is 'violence against women' (Koken, 2010).

Human Rights and Harm Reduction Discourses

In recent times the sale of sexual services has also been constructed as an issue of rights and choice. Sex workers are seen as similar to many other low-skilled workers and it is argued that they should be guaranteed their full human and labour rights under law (Bindman, 1997). In 2005, 120 sex workers and 80 allies from 30 countries participated in the European Conference on Sex Work, Human Rights, Law and Migration in Brussels. From this conference, two documents were published: *Sex Workers in Europe Manifesto* and *Declaration of the Rights of Sex Workers in Europe* (Garofalo Geymonat, 2010). There is now a global network of sex work projects. During the writing of the United Nations Protocol on Trafficking, two opposing positions were presented. Lobbyists from the Coalition Against Trafficking in Women (CATW) argued that all sex work is a form of trafficking, whereas the Human Rights Caucus, representing the International Human Rights Law Group and the Asian Women's Human Rights Council, advocated for the analysis of sex work as labour (Koken, 2010). UNAIDS endorses both a human rights and a harm reduction perspective (Hope Ditmore, 2010; UNAIDS, 2012).

In Ireland, a number of groups are taking a human rights perspective to sex work. The Turn Off the Blue Light campaign[13] states that sex workers need human rights, not legal wrongs. Sex Workers Alliance Ireland (SWAI) also takes a human rights approach and promotes the social inclusion, health, safety, civil rights and the right to self-determination of female, male and transgender sex workers.

That said, sex work is also a high-risk occupation, particularly for street workers. The harm reduction approach acknowledges that sex work exists and that governments should take steps to reduce the most harmful aspects of it (Rekart, 2005; Cusick et al., 2010). These harms include criminalisation, stigmatisation, spread of diseases and violence. To reduce the risk of violence, initiatives were trialed in Liverpool. Police treated crimes against sex workers as hate crime and introduced a specialist Independent Sexual Violence Adviser to support sex workers who were victims of crime (Campbell & Stoops, 2010). The Association of Chief Police Officers (ACPO) (2011) endorses a harm reduction approach to prostitution by introducing schemes such as the 'Ugly Mugs' scheme to improve safety and by working with the United Kingdom Network of Sex Work Projects (UKNSWP). Sex workers are encouraged to report violent incidents, and the records are used to identify dangerous individuals and to disseminate the information accordingly.

The next section will present the voices of sex workers working in Dublin. While a significant number of the sample are persons living in adverse circumstances with limited opportunities, the data illustrates that they do make choices about entering and exiting sex work and they do exercise some control over who they work with and the conditions of their work. The data also reveals that these sex workers see themselves as agents who make choices, rather than as victims, and their comments reveal the extent to which they actively manage their working lives.

Sex Workers' Discourses

In 2008–9 the Irish National Advisory Committee on Drugs (NACD) internally commissioned research on drug users who engage in prostitution because they are considered an 'at risk' group. In order to design intervention strategies to reduce the risk of harm to them, forty professionals across sectors (community, voluntary and statutory) and from a range of disciplines, who work either directly or indirectly with drug-using sex workers, were interviewed in order to elicit their perspectives. Interviews were conducted with those at the coalface, as well as those in managerial positions.

Interviews were also conducted with drug users who engage in, or had engaged in, sex work to ascertain what risks they were taking and what risk reduction strategies they engaged in. The sample was accessed through agencies that provide support to drug-using sex workers. (For a comprehensive description of the study, *see* Cox and Whitaker, 2009.) The Drug Treatment Board gave ethical permission for the study.

As lead researcher, I was aware of the importance of reflexivity, which means being aware not only of the effect of the researcher on the research but also being aware of my own prejudices and biases as a researcher and of the different power relations between the researcher and researched (Bondi, 2009; Hammersley & Atkinson, 1996; Mason, 1996; Marshall & Rossman, 2006). Prior to conducting the research, my view on prostitution, informed by radical feminism, was that it was exploitative of women and that they should be encouraged and supported to leave (Whitaker et al., 2011). The very first interview I conducted changed my mind, and subsequent interviews reinforced my position that the men and women interviewed were a diverse group of people, with their own individual ways of seeing and interpreting their working lives. The first woman I spoke to had previously worked in a brothel, and she described sex work as 'an act of human kindness'; other respondents also saw their work as a typical, everyday activity. Four of the participants had been coerced into sex work; the others (including four men) had entered voluntarily, mostly through family or friendship networks. Those who had been coerced into prostitution either exited or managed to extricate themselves from pimps and continued working independently. This is not to argue that all sex workers are able to disentangle themselves from pimps; some may be unable or too fearful to free themselves from exploitative or abusive relationships.

Profile of Sample

The sample of drug-using sex workers interviewed comprised 31 women and four men, three of whom self-identified as being gay.

The average age was 32 years (the median age was 29 years). All were white, indigenous Irish people and the majority came from Dublin. Most of them worked on the street, if not at the time of the interview, then previously in their sex work careers. This group was marginalised in that they were dependent on illicit substances, had criminal records, were infected with HIV or the hepatitis C virus (HCV), and many were living in emergency accommodation or renting in the private sector. In addition, most were parents (24 mothers and one father); many of the mothers did not have custody of their children, which for some added substantially to their distress. More than half of the sample was actively involved in sex work. The data indicated that the men and women interviewed move in and out of sex work, often as a response to economic need and/or changing patterns of drug use. In this study, participants' motivation for exiting sex work included: pregnancy and/or the birth of a child; becoming involved in new romantic relationships; accessing drug treatment; forced 'exiting' as a result of receiving a custodial sentence in prison or negative life event; and maturation – 'it was time to move on' (Cox & Whitaker, 2009; Whitaker et al., 2011).

Why Sex Work?

A brief review of sex workers' accounts is presented, explaining why they engage in sex work, where they work, who their clients are, how they organise their work and certain work practices (Cox & Whitaker, 2009). Simply put, they worked to make money. The participants had poor employment prospects: most were early school-leavers and lacked job skills; some had a criminal record. A few had low-paid jobs, such as cleaning. Some tried to make money through drug dealing, shoplifting, etc. before turning to sex work to supplement their welfare benefits or incomes. Their sex work income paid not only for drugs but for extras for their children: for one it funded private childcare for her twins; for another it funded a holiday abroad and a new car. Most viewed sex work as a job. Finola stated: 'There have been times that I wasn't on drugs that I did work. Now you see because I have the kids, I have much higher expenses, so if I was working, it would specifically be for money for them rather than for me.'

Karen (mother of two-year-old twins) tried working for an escort agency, but found being told what to do by the agency bosses oppressive:

> Then, a girl I knew, she was working in an escort agency. So, I started working there and, like, it was grand, and we were making €2,000 a week. But, it was just the bosses were assholes, telling you what to do, telling you, you have to be here at this time. Then they'd send you on call-outs and if you didn't want to go on them, 'cause I was driving and you'd have to go down to Co. Meath and all this …

Irene was adamant that there was no relationship between her drug (heroin and methadone) use and her sex work. She was operating from an apartment:

> I don't think the drugs has anything to do with the work that I do, to be honest, going back years ago, I had to work to support me habit before I met him, now, I could stop work tomorrow and still live the life that I live today, and still continue the habit I have today, still have me car, me apartment, and still go on me foreign holidays and I could still do all of that because he has his own business and I don't want for anything, so in that sense I don't need to work to have that kind of lifestyle.

Sex work allowed her to exercise some autonomy and freedom in other areas of her life:

> More money basically, more money, I like to have my own separate bank account, away from [X], my partner, we have a joint bank account, and I can go to the bank whenever I want and take what I want, but I like to have a bank account of my own, … that money gets put aside and that's for a rainy day and that's for me. Because you just don't know what's down the road.

Finola also felt that she didn't have to work to buy drugs because she is on methadone maintenance. She had plans to go to college:

> I won't use today, like, I don't know when I'll use again, because I have had my Phi [methadone], so I am not going to

be sick [suffer withdrawal symptoms], the last time I was out working, and working to buy gear [heroin] was, like, probably, over a year ago, that's what I am trying to get across to you. I don't have to go out to work to, I might still buy drugs.

Where to Work?

Donna described the street as her 'place of work': 'It's just a job, you go to your place of work, and if people want to avail of it and use your service, that's what they're going to do.' Some women progressed from selling sex on the street to going out to the clients' houses. A club owner approached Mary with the offer of 'background' work, but she declined because she would lose her independence; she decided to stay working with her regular clients:

> I'd go out to their houses now. I used to do it in cars and lanes. I've just been asked: 'Do I want to work over in Leeson Street' by a Polish guy. I'm not into it, to tell you the truth, too risky. A girl told me all about it. I said I heard they're looking for girls, for backgrounds, whatever backgrounds means. I know now what it is [laughs]. It's for business. You do a dance and businessmen come in. This guy, Polish guy, he gets, say, €1,000, you'd probably only get €350–400 if you're lucky. And then you have to do what they want: for two hours? No way! ... Now I'd probably get three or phone calls off clients, where I'd go out to people's houses, now I don't have to go down the streets, thanks be to God.

Although sex workers may have regular clients, some preferred the freedom and autonomy that working on the street provided. Iseult stated: 'I just work up at the Pepper Canister or Baggot Street.' Áine also took her chances on the street:

> Some people would have my phone number. But I'd really just get ready, go down to Baggot Street. Go down and people in their cars there and they're driving and they'd look at you and you'd nod your head, like. And they'd know what that would mean like ... Or if somebody's walking and you'd say to them: 'Are you looking for business?' And they'd say, 'yes'. Or else they'd say to you, 'Are you doing business?' Like that, does that make any sense?

Regulars and Friends

Contrary to popular assumption that sex workers' clients are always complete strangers to them, some, like Irene, have clients they know and trust: 'I work on the phone now, and I work out of an apartment. More or less, the customers that I deal with now would be all customers that I dealt with over the last six or seven years, so some of them, I count as friends now. I've know them that long, they're all safe.' Carmel formerly worked on the streets:

> Now, I have regulars, but often it used to be every day, like, every night, without fail. And then sometimes, at the start, I used to just walk through, but I used to still end up with about three or four hundred pounds for even walking through, and I used to be in tracksuits and all and I still used to get them. And then, when I started dressing up, then I used to come out with over a grand, like, for really putting the work in, but it used to be always every night.

Mary could ask her clients for an advance if she was stuck for money.

> They've been good to me and I've been good to them. I can ring them if I'm stuck for money, rather than do work, they'll give me €50. And the next time I do business, then €50 will be knocked off.

Working in Pairs

It is illegal for two sex workers to rent an apartment and work from it because legally this constitutes a brothel. Nevertheless, some sex workers do work together to minimise risks; for example, Gemma and friend: 'We wouldn't really work on the streets, we work over the phone and we kinda work together, we'd go down on the street maybe four times in the last three months.' Grace and her friend (young married women with children) also team up:

> Me and X always work together. There was one night that we were frightened, there was a few fellows, they sort of got round me, but I felt claustrophobic. They were surrounding

you, but we got away with it. We have never actually been in a violent [situation], ... I would always know where X was and she would always know where I was and because we kept it so secretive.

Being Able to Say 'No'

These participants didn't simply accept all offers of work. For example, when Karen had a heavy cold, she had to turn down a client: 'one of my regulars rang me last night and he asked me to go in to him last night and I said no. So, he was saying if I felt better, to go in to him maybe, like, Friday and Saturday or Saturday and Sunday, like that would be €300 or €400.' Iseult could take control and give her client instructions:

There was sometimes that even I just had my bus fare into work, I'd get the bus in, I'd wait for the punter to come along, and I'd say, 'Right, we have to stop to get condoms on the way' because I had no money for them, 'cause I couldn't get to the exchange, 'cause the exchange give out the free condoms. So I would just, right, 'Right, you have to stop and get condoms.' That's the way I worked it.

Finola was very clear about what services were for sale and what she kept for an intimate relationship.

And I know a lot of people think, 'how can they do what they do?' but I'll tell you, when you are getting £1,000 or £1,500 into your hand every day, it's very hard to stop. And you don't give a shit, it's sex! The way I look at it is, there is a condom there, and I'm not really touching them. I know we all rationalise ourselves, but that is my way of looking at it, there is no intimacy whatsoever, ... I don't kiss ... I know some girls go on, 'Oh the *Pretty Woman* thing!', it's not that to me. There are certain things I think you keep for relationships and there are certain things you don't mind doing in work. There are certain things I would have done in work that I would never dream of doing in a relationship. And if a guy asked me to do that I'd be like, 'Excuse me, what do you think I am?' Then I would feel a bit bad because I think I'm doing this in work, like, domination and stuff, not a chance would I do that for a boyfriend. But in work, yeah, I'll beat the shit out of you, no problem. You don't really mind.

The above quotations illustrate that these sex workers had the capacity to take control of the sexual encounter and to determine the boundaries between work and their personal, intimate relationships. It also shows how they organised their work in mindful and pragmatic ways.

Discussion and Conclusion

A multitude of competing discourses (religious, legal, medical, human rights, harm reduction and feminist) have influenced our knowledge and understanding of prostitution and sex work. In Ireland, a radical feminist or abolitionist position gained momentum recently, as evidenced in the Turn Off the Red Light campaigning position, and it campaigned to abolish sex work through criminalising the purchasers of sexual services. The Minister for Justice, Equality and Defence, Alan Shatter TD (2012b), decided to take a cautious approach to tightening legislation and he entered into public consultations on the issue. The *Report on Hearings and Submissions on the Review of Legislation on Prostitution*, published in June 2013 (Houses of the Oireachtas Joint Committee on Justice, Defence and Equality, 2013), seems to have been heavily influenced by the Turn Off the Red Light position, and the evidence given by those opposing the Swedish approach of criminalising the client seems to have been ignored. While I consider the report overall to be a well-written and thoughtful response to the eight hundred submissions received by the Joint Committee on Justice, Defence and Equality, in recommending the Swedish approach it raises serious concerns about the health and welfare of sex workers, who may continue to work despite the fact that their clients will be criminalised. On the positive side, it has made a number of recommendations relating to legal changes, which if introduced could pose serious deterrents for those who groom children for work in the sex industry or coerce people into it (Houses of the Oireachtas Joint Committee on Justice, Defence and Equality, 2013: 79). Positive policy initiatives are also recommended for the State and a number of agencies. For instance, the report proposes that 'the Criminal Assets Bureau is specifically tasked to focus on the finances of the prostitution industry in Ireland and the flow of money to criminal organisations in the state and abroad' (Houses of the Oireachtas Joint Committee on Justice, Defence and Equality, 2013: 80). Also advocated in the report is independent research to increase our understanding of prostitution and trafficking, to evaluate the effectiveness of legal and policy measures in this area and to identify any changes required over time (Houses of Oireachtas Joint Committee on Justice, Defence and Equality, 2013: 80).

Calling for the same treatment by law for persons accessing escort sites as for persons accessing child pornography is, in my opinion, not a good recommendation as it infantilises those who sell sex and may not be possible to resource. Sex workers who use the internet to advertise their services may also, as a consequence of this suggested legal reform, resort to other modes of advertising, which present more risks and dangers for them. It also seems inappropriate that it is the Irish police service, and not health and caring agencies, that is charged with consulting '… with men and women in prostitution on how their health and well-being can be protected in the context of a ban on the purchase of sexual services' (Houses of the Oireachtas Joint Committee on Justice, Defence and Equality, 2013: 80). While there are positive policy changes proposed to help sex workers, including immigrant sex workers, to access State provisions in relation to education, health and housing in an effort to reduce the risk the work poses and to help them to exit sex work, the author is sceptical as to whether these policies will actually be introduced and adequately resourced.

Only time will tell whether the Minister for Justice, Equality and Defence will implement the recommendations of this report, and even if implemented, whether the necessary policing and welfare agencies will receive funding to put laws and policies into practice. On the one hand, it argues that it is decriminalising the seller of sexual services; on the other hand, it is criminalising their access to clients. While the report notes that it is proposing a partial decriminalisation approach, such as that adopted by Sweden, in my view the agenda of this report is to abolish prostitution and all the activities that surround it. It remains to be seen if this can be achieved.

Acknowledgments

The author gratefully acknowledges the courage of the sex workers who participated in the research notwithstanding the stigma attached to sex work and illicit drug use in Irish society. The opinions expressed in this paper are those of the author and do not necessarily reflect the views of the National Advisory Committee on Drugs; appreciation is expressed to the Committee for permission to use the data. This paper is based on original research carried out by Gemma Cox, Paul Ryan and Teresa Whitaker for the National Advisory Committee on Drugs. Sincere thanks are extended to Prof. Tom Inglis, who gave constructive feedback, and to Dr Máirín Kenny, who also helped to clarify the arguments and assisted with editing the chapter.

Notes

[1] This title is adapted from a report by Bindman (1997) entitled *Redefining Prostitution as Sex Work on the International Agenda*. She argues against the identification of prostitution as a human rights violation or slavery, as defined by the 1949 Convention on the Suppression of the Traffic in Persons and of the Exploitation of the Prostitution of Others. Her research shows that men and women sex workers face the same abuses as those working in low-status jobs in the informal economic sector.

[2] In 2008 the Criminal Law Human Trafficking Act was enacted in Ireland. The main purpose of this legislation is to criminalise trafficking in persons aged eighteen years or over for the purposes of their sexual or labour exploitation (Department of Justice, Equality and Law Reform, 2009: 40). It also criminalises the selling, offering for sale or purchase of any trafficked person. The National Action Plan to Prevent and Combat Trafficking in Ireland (Department of Justice, Equality and Law Reform, 2009), while acknowledging that the scale of trafficking into Ireland is unknown, argues that trafficking is fuelled by demand for its victims' services, and that targeting the clients of trafficked victims is one of the most effective means of ending trafficking.

[3] It is important to note that alleged reports do not necessarily result in convictions.

[4] For a discussion of various feminist analyses of prostitution, *see* Overall, 1992; Dworkin, 1997; Jeffreys, 1997; Pateman, 1999; Farley and Barkan, 1998; Farley and Kelly, 2000; Kesler, 2002, 2005; Koken, 2010.

[5] For more information on this campaign, *see* its website at http://www.turnofftheredlight.ie/.

[6] For more information on this campaign, *see* its website at http://www.turnoffthebluelight.ie/.

[7]   In the Bible, 'a man who loves wisdom brings joy to his father, but a companion of prostitutes squanders his wealth' (Proverbs 29:2–4).

[8]   The Magdalene laundry inmates were largely forgotten until the early 1990s, when the bodies of 133 women were exhumed from the cemetery in Our Lady of Charity of Refuge, Drumcondra, Dublin (which was closed in 1996) (Luddy, 2007). There was a public outcry. Newspaper articles and television documentaries denounced the way the women had been treated. In 2004 a survivor's advocacy group, Justice for Magdalenes (JFM), was established to promote and represent the interests of the Magdalene women and to seek justice for them. *See* Justice for Magdalenes' website at <http://www.magdalenelaundries.com>.

[9]   The Legion of Mary was founded in Dublin on 7 September 1921. It is a lay Catholic organisation, whose members give service to the Church on a voluntary basis throughout Ireland. *See* Legion of Mary website at <http://www.legionofmary.ie/>.

[10]   *See* Ruhama's website at <http://www.ruhama.ie/>.

[11]   For more information on these health projects, *see* the Health Service Executive's website at http://www.hse.ie/.

[12]   From enactment of the Act of Union in 1801 until independence in 1922, Ireland was directly subject to parliament in Westminster and its laws (Lydon, 1998).

[13]   *See* the campaign's website at <http://www.turnoffthebluelight.ie/>.

References

Afra, A. (2013), 'Primary School Sexualities: A Critical Social Psychological Foregrounding of Children's Constructions of Childhood Sexuality', PhD thesis, Trinity College Dublin.

Ahmed, F. (2009), 'The European Society for Paediatric Endocrinology Disorder of Sex Development Registry; Protocol for a Research Database', *ESPE DSD Registry*, University of Glasgow, available from: <http://www.eurodsd.eu/en/media/02_UOG_The_ESPE_DSD_Registry_SOP160609.pdf> [accessed 16 April 2012].

Ahmed, F. (2012), 'The International Disorder of Sex Development Registry; Protocol for a Research Database', *I-DSD Registry*, University of Glasgow, available from: <https://tethys.nesc.gla.ac.uk/idsd/docs/sop/The%20I-DSD%20Registry%20SOP%20240212.pdf> [accessed 7 May 2012].

AISSG (Androgen Insensitivity Syndrome Support Group) (2011), *Personal Stories*, available from: <http://www.aissg.org/41_STORIES.HTM> [accessed 13 November 2011].

Allan, A., Atkinson, E., Brace, E., dePalma, R. and Hemingway, J. (2008), 'Speaking the Unspeakable in Forbidden Places: Addressing Lesbian, Gay, Bisexual and Transgender Equality in the Primary School', *Sex Education*, 8(3): 315–28.

Allen, L. (2004), 'Beyond the Birds and the Bees: Constituting a Discourse of Erotics in Sexuality Education', *Gender and Education*, 16(2): 151–67.

Allen, L. (2003), 'Girls Want Sex, Boys Want Love: Resisting Dominant Discourses of (Hetero) Sexuality', *Sexualities*, 6(2): 215–36.

Allen, M. and Seery, D. (2007), *The Current Status of Relationships and Sexuality Education Practice for People with an Intellectual Disability in Ireland*, Dublin and Cork: Irish Sex Education Network and Sexual Health Centre, available from: <http://www.sexualhealthcentre.com/PUBLICATIONS/SHC%20Disability%20Report2.pdf> [accessed 26 October 2012].

All-Party Oireachtas Committee on the Constitution (2006), *Tenth Progress Report: The Family*, Dublin: Stationery Office.

References

American Psychiatric Association (1987), *Diagnostic and Statistical Manual of Mental Disorders (DSM) III-R*, Washington, DC: American Psychiatric Association.

American Psychiatric Association (1994), *Diagnostic and Statistical Manual of Mental Disorders (DSM) IV*, Washington, DC: American Psychiatric Association.

American Psychological Association (2012), 'What Is Sexual Orientation?' in *Answers to Your Questions for a Better Understanding of Sexual Orientation and Homosexuality*, available from: <http://www.apa.org/topics/sorientation.html#whatis> [accessed 30 August 2012].

Amnesty International Ireland (2012), *Essential Principles: Irish Legal Capacity Law*, Dublin: Amnesty International Ireland.

APA Task Force (2007), *Report of the APA Task Force on the Sexualization of Girls*, American Psychological Association, available from: <http://www.apa.org/pi/women/programs/girls/report-full.pdf> [accessed 10 October 2011].

Ardagh, J. (1995), *Ireland and the Irish: Portrait of a Changing Society*, London: Penguin.

Arensberg, C.M. and Kimball, T. (1968), *Family and Community in Ireland* (2nd edn), Cambridge, MA: Harvard University Press.

Armesto, J.C. (2002), 'Developmental and Contextual Factors that Influence Gay Fathers' Parental Competence: A Review of the Literature', *Psychology of Men and Masculinity*, 3(2): 67–78.

Association of Chief Police Officers (2011), *ACPO Strategy for Policing Prostitution and Sexual Exploitation*, available from: <http://www.acpo.police.uk/documents/crime/2011/20111102%20CBA%20Policing%20Prostitution%20and%20%20Sexual%20Exploitation%20Strategy_Website_October%202011.pdf> [accessed 14 May 2012].

Attwood, F. (ed.) (2009), *Mainstreaming Sex: The Sexualisation of Western Culture*, London: I.B. Tauris & Co.

Attwood, F. (2007), 'No Money Shot? Commerce, Pornography and New Sex Taste Cultures', *Sexualities*, 10: 441–57.

Attwood, F. (2005), 'What Do People Do with Porn? Qualitative Research into the Consumption, Use and Experience of Pornography, and Other Sexually Explicit Media', *Sexuality and Culture*, 9(2): 65–86.

Attwood, F., Arthurs, A., Bale, C., Barker, M., Boynton, P., Brooks Gordon, B., Fae, J., Ingham, R., Hoyle, A., Hancock, J., Light, B., Petley, J., Renold, E., Ringrose, J., Russell, R., Segal, L., Mac Sithigh, D., Slack, S., Smith, C., Willet, R., and van Zoonen, L. (2011), 'Disservice to Young People', *Times Higher Education*, 13 June, available from: <http://www.timeshighereducation.co.uk/story.asp?storyC ode=416673&sectioncode=26> [accessed 3 October 2011].

Attwood, F. and Smith, C. (2011), 'Lamenting Sexualization: Research, Rhetoric and the Story of Young People's "Sexualization" in the UK Home Office Review', *Sex Education*, 11(3): 327–37.

Auchmuty, R. (2004), 'Same-Sex Marriage Revived: Feminist Critique and Legal Strategy', *Feminism and Psychology*, 14(1): 101–26.

Bacik, I. (2004), *Kicking and Screaming: Dragging Ireland into the Twenty-First Century*, Dublin: O'Brien Press.

Bailey, R. (2011), *Letting Children Be Children. Report of an Independent Review of the Commercialisation and Sexualisation of Childhood*, UK: Stationery Office.

Baker, K. and Donnelly M. (2001), 'The Social Experiences of Children with a Disability and the Influence of Environment: A Framework for Intervention', *Disability and Society*, 16(1): 71–85.

Bale, C. (2010), 'Sexualised Culture and Young People's Sexual Health: A Cause for Concern?', *Sociology Compass*, 4(10): 824–40.

Bane, G., Dooher, M., Flaherty, J., Mahon, A., McDonagh, P., Wolfe, M., Deely, M., Hopkins, R., Minogue, G., Curry, M., Donohoe, B., Tierney, E., Garcia Iriarte, E., O'Doherty, S. and Shannon, S. (2012), 'Relationships of People with Learning Disabilities in Ireland', *British Journal of Learning Disabilities*, 40(2): 109–22.

Bar On, B. (1997), 'Sexuality, the Family, and Nationalism' in H.L. Nelson (ed.) *Feminism and Families*, New York: Routledge, 221–34.

Barker, M. (2011), *Making Sense of the Sexualisation Debates*, Onscenity.org, available from: <http://www.onscenity.org/ sexualization/#blogp> [accessed 3 October 2011].

Barnes, C. (1992), *Disabling Imagery and the Media: An Exploration of Media Representations of Disabled People*, Halifax: British Council of Organisations of Disabled People.

Barnes, C. (2011), 'A Discourse of Disparagement: Boys' Talk about Girls in School', *Young*, 19(1): 5–23.

Baum, M. and Fishman, J.M. (1994), 'AIDS, Sexual Compulsivity, and Gay Men: A Group Treatment Approach' in S.A. Cadwell and R.A. Burnham (eds) *Therapists on the Front Line in the Age of AIDS*, Washington, DC: American Psychiatric Press.

Bauman, Z. and May, T. (2001), *Thinking Sociologically*, Oxford: Blackwell.

Bazzo, G., Nota, L., Soresi, S., Ferrari, L. and Minnes, P. (2007), 'Attitudes of Social Service Providers toward the Sexuality of Individuals with Intellectual Disability', *Journal of Applied Research in Intellectual Disabilities*, 20(2): 110–15.

BBC News (2004), '"Better Rights" for Gay Couples' [online], available from: <http://news.bbc.co.uk/2/hi/uk_news/northern_ireland/4012713.stm>.

Beck, M. (2001), 'My Life as an Intersexual' in *Nova Beta*, available from: <http://www.pbs.org/wgbh/nova/body/intersexual-life.html> [accessed 13 November 2011].

Begley, C., Higgins, A., Lalor, J., Sheerin, F., Alexander, J., Nicholl, H., Lawlor, D., Keenan, P., Touhy, T. and Kavanagh, R. (2009a), *Women with Disabilities: Barriers and Facilitators to Accessing Services During Pregnancy, Childbirth and Early Motherhood*, Pregnancy, Childbirth and Early Motherhood Project, Dublin: Report by Trinity College Dublin and University College Dublin for the National Disability Authority.

Begley, C., Higgins, A., Lalor, J., Sheerin, F., Alexander, J., Nicholl, H., Lawlor, D., Keenan, P., Tuohy, T. and Kavanagh, R. (2009b), *Women with Disabilities: Policies Governing Procedure and Practice in Service Provision in Ireland During Pregnancy, Childbirth and Early Motherhood*, Pregnancy, Childbirth and Early Motherhood Project, Dublin: Report by Trinity College Dublin and University College Dublin for the National Disability Authority.

Begley, C., Higgins, A., Lalor, J., Sheerin, F., Alexander, J., Nicholl, H., Lawlor, D., Keenan, P., Tuohy, T. and Kavanagh, R. (2010), *The Strength and Weakness of Publicly Funded Irish Health Services Provided to Women with Disabilities in Relation to Pregnancy, Childbirth and Early Motherhood*, Pregnancy, Childbirth and Early Motherhood Project, Dublin: Report by Trinity College Dublin and University College Dublin for the National Disability Authority.

Begum, N. (1992), 'Disabled Women and the Feminist Agenda', *Feminist Review*, 40, 70–84.

Beiner, G. (2004), 'Remembrance of Things Past: On the Compatibility of History and Memory' in M.S. O'Neill, C. Cullen and C.A. Dennehy (eds) *History Matters: Selected Papers from the School of History Postgraduate Conferences, 2001–2003*, Dublin: School of History, University College Dublin, 1–12.

Bell, A.P. and Weinberg, M.S. (1978), *Homosexualities: A Study of Diversity Among Men and Women*, New York: Simon and Schuster.

Bell, D. and Binnie, J. (2000), *The Sexual Citizen: Queer Politics and Beyond*, Cambridge: Polity Press.

Benotsch, E.G., Kalichman, S.C. and Pinkerton, S.D. (2001), 'Sexual Compulsivity in HIV-Positive Men and Women: Prevalence, Predictors and Consequences of High-Risk Behaviors', *Sexual Addiction and Compulsivity*, 8(2): 83–99.

Bergner, R.M. (2002), 'Sexual Compulsion as Attempted Recovery from Degradation: Theory and Therapy', *Journal of Sex and Marital Therapy,* 28, 373–87.

Berkowitz, D. (2006), 'Deconstructing Essentialism: A Feminist Analysis of Gay and Lesbian Families', Conference paper presented at the American Sociological Association Annual Meeting, 10 August, Montreal, QU.

Berkowitz, D. (2008b), 'Gay Parenting: Situated in a Straight World', Conference paper presented at the American Sociological Association Annual Meeting, 31 July, Boston, MA.

Berkowitz, D. (2008a), 'A Sociohistorical Analysis of Gay Men's Procreative Consciousness', *Journal of GLBT Family Studies,* 3(2): 157–90.

Berkowitz, D. and Marsiglio, W. (2007), 'Gay Men: Negotiating Procreative, Father and Family Identities', *Journal of Marriage and Family,* 69, 366–81.

Better, A. (2005), 'Best of Two Worlds: An Exploration of Identity Issues Among Gay Fathers', Conference paper presented at the American Sociological Association Annual Meeting, 13 August, Philadelphia, PA.

Bindman, J. (1997), *Redefining Prostitution as Sex Work on the International Agenda,* available from: <http://www.walnet.org/csis/papers/redefining.html> [accessed 14 May 2012].

Black, D.W., Kehrberg, L.L., Flumerfelt, D.L. and Schlosser, S.S. (1997), 'Characteristics of 36 Subjects Reporting Compulsive Sexual Behavior', *American Journal of Psychiatry,* 154, 243–9.

Blackwood, E. and Wieringa, S.E. (eds) (1999), *Female Desires: Same-Sex Relations and Transgender Practices Across Cultures,* New York: Columbia University Press.

Blaise, M. (2009), '"What a Girl Wants, What a Girl Needs": Responding to Sex, Gender and Sexuality in the Early Childhood Classroom', *Journal of Research in Childhood Education,* 23(4): 450–60.

Bloustien, G. and Baker, S. (2003), 'On Not Talking to Strangers. Researching the Microworlds of Girls through Visual Auto-ethnographic Practices', *Social Analysis,* 47(3): 64–79.

Blumstein, P. and Schwartz, P. (1983), *American Couples: Money, Work, Sex,* New York: Morrow.

Blumstein, P.W. and Schwartz, P. (1977), 'Bisexuality: Some Social Psychological Issues', *Journal of Social Issues,* 33(2): 30–45.

Bond, E. (2010), 'The Mobile Phone = Bike Shed? Children, Sex and Mobile Phones', *New Media and Society,* 13(4): 587–604.

Bondi, L. (2009), 'Teaching Reflexivity: Undoing or Reinscribing Habits of Gender?', *Journal of Geography in Higher Education,* 33(3): 327–37.

Bonino, S., Ciairano, S., Rabaglietti, E. and Cattelino, E. (2006), 'Use of Pornography and Self-reported Engagement in Sexual Violence among Adolescents', *European Journal of Developmental Psychology*, 3 (3): 265–88.

Bonnie, S. (2002), 'Facilitated Sexual Expression in the Independent Living Movement in Ireland', MA thesis in Disability Studies, University of Leeds.

Boot, P. (1999), 'I Accept Myself with Pride', *Disability Now*, available on request from: <http://www.disabilitynow.org.uk>

Bornstein, S. (2005), 'The Social Construction of Family in the Gay and Lesbian Community', Conference paper presented at the American Sociological Association Annual Meeting, 13 August 2005, Philadelphia, PA.

Bozett, F.W. (1980), 'Gay Fathers: How and Why they Disclose their Homosexuality to their Children', *Family Relations*, 29: 173–9.

Bozett, F.W. (1981), 'Gay Fathers: Identity Conflict Resolution through Integrative Sanctioning', *Alternative Life-styles*, 4, 90–107.

Bozett, F.W. (1982), 'Heterogenous Couples in Heterosexual Marriages: Gay Men and Straight Women', *Journal of Marital and Family Therapy*, 8(1): 81–9.

Bradford, J. and Sartwell, C. (1997), 'Addiction and Knowledge: Epistemic Disease and the Hegemonic Family' in H.L. Nelson (ed.) *Feminism and Families*, New York: Routledge, 116–27.

Bragg, S., Buckingham, D., Russell, R. and Willett, R. (2011), 'Too Much, Too Soon? Children, "Sexualization" and Consumer Culture', *Sex Education*, 11(3): 279–92.

Bramhill, N. (2012), 'Surge in Sex Addicts Seeking Help after "Shame"', *Irish Examiner*, 6 February, 3.

Braun, V. and Clarke, V. (2006), 'Using Thematic Analysis in Psychology', *Qualitative Research in Psychology*, 3, 77–101.

Brazil, P. (2011), 'Applications for Asylum by Lesbian, Gay, Bisexual, Transgender and Intersex (LGBTI) Persons', *The Researcher*, 6(1): 8–14.

Brinamen, C.F. and Mitchell, V. (2008), 'Gay Men Becoming Fathers: A Model of Identity Expansion', *Journal of GLBT Family Studies*, 4(4): 521–41.

British Medical Journal ADC Online (2006), *Electronic Letters to: I A Hughes, C Houk, S F Ahmed, P A Lee LWPES/ESPE Consensus Group*, available from: <http://adc.bjm.com/content/91/7/554.extract/reply#archdeschildel2460> [accessed 16 January 2013].

Brod, H. and Kaufman, M. (1994), 'Introduction' in H. Brod and M. Kaufman (eds) *Theorizing Masculinities*, London: Sage, 1–10.

Brody, H.A., Meghani, Z., Greenwald, K. (2009), *Michael Ryan's Writings on Medical Ethics*, New York: Springer.

Brook, B. (1999), *Feminist Perspectives on the Body*, London: Longman.

Brown, H. (1994), '"An Ordinary Sexual Life?": A Review of the Normalisation Principle as it Applies to the Sexual Options of People with Learning Disabilities', *Disability and Society*, 9(2): 123–40.

Bush, M.L. (1998), *What Is Love? Richard Carlisle's Philosophy of Sex*, London and New York: Verso.

Butler, J. (1990, 2006), *Gender Trouble: Feminism and the Subversion of Identity*, New York: Routledge.

Butler, J. (2004), *Undoing Gender*, New York: Routledge.

Byrne, A. (2000), 'Singular Identities: Managing Stigma, Resisting Voices', *Women's Studies Review Oral History and Biography*, 7, Galway: Women's Studies Centre, NUIG, 13–34.

Byrne, S. (1995), 'Glimpses' in Í. O'Carroll and E. Collins (eds) *Lesbian and Gay Visions of Ireland: Towards the Twenty-First Century*, London: Cassell, 138–43.

Caffrey, S. (1992), 'S.A.M. & S.U.E. Sexual Attitudes Measured and Sexual Understanding Explored', PhD thesis, Trinity College Dublin.

CAHR (Commission on Assisted Human Reproduction) (2005), *Report of the Commission on Assisted Human Reproduction*, Dublin: Department of Health and Children.

Calhoun, C. (1997), 'Family's Outlaws: Rethinking the Connections between Feminism, Lesbianism and the Family' in H.L. Nelson (ed.) *Feminism and Families*, New York: Routledge, 131–50.

Cameron, D. and Frazer, E. (2000), 'On the Question of Pornography and Sexual Violence: Moving Beyond Cause and Effect' in C. Drucilla (ed.) *Feminisim & Psychology*, New York: Open University Press, 240–53.

Cameron, K., Salazar, L., Bernhardt, J., Burgess-Whitman, N., Wingood, G. and DiClemente, R. (2005), 'Adolescents' Experience with Sex on the Web: Results from Online Focus Groups', *Journal of Adolescence*, 28(4): 535–40.

Campbell, J. (1990), 'Developing Our Image – Who's in Control', presented at the *Cap-in-Hand* Conference, February 1990, also held in the Disability Archive UK, available from: <http://www.leeds.ac.uk/disability-studies/archiveuk/archframe.htm> [accessed 23 April 2012].

Campbell, R. and Stoops, S. (2010), 'Taking Sex Workers Seriously: Treating Violence as Hate Crime in Liverpool', *Research for Sex Work*, 12: 9–12, available from: <http://www.nswp.org> [accessed 22 March 2012].

Campion, M.J. (1990), *The Baby Challenge: A Handbook on Pregnancy for Women with a Physical Disability*, London: Routledge.

Canning, K. (1999), 'The Body as Method? Reflections on the Place of the Body in Gender History', *Gender & History*, 11(3): 499–513.

Carabine, J. (2004), 'Sexualities, Personal Lives and Social Policy' in J. Carabine (ed.) *Sexualities: Personal Lives and Social Policy*, Bristol: Policy Press and Open University Press, 1–48.

Carbery, G. (2012), 'Proposals Soon on Age of Consent', *Irish Times*, 1 June, available from: http://www.irishtimes.com/newspaper/ireland/2012/.../1224317059529.htm...> [accessed 10 July 2012].

Carlson, L. (2001), 'Cognitive Ableism and Disability Studies: Feminist Reflections on the History of Mental Retardation', *Hypatia*, 16(4): 124–46.

Carmody, M. (2005), 'Ethical Erotics; Reconceptualizing Anti-Rape Education', *Sexualities*, 8: 465–80.

Carnes, P. (1983), *Out of the Shadows: Understanding Sexual Addiction*, Center City, MN: Hazelden.

Carnes, P. (1992), *Don't Call it Love: Recovery from Sexual Addiction*, London: Bantam.

Carolan, E. (2007), 'Committed Non-Marital Couples and the Irish Constitution' in W. Binchy and O. Doyle (eds) *Committed Relationships and the Law*, Dublin: Four Courts Press, 239–66.

Carr, C.L. (2009), 'The New (Essentialist) Sexual Fluidity', *Sex Roles*, 61: 130–2.

Carter, H. (2003), 'Marriage Falls Out of Fashion . . . Or Does It?' *The Guardian*, 21 March 2003, 3.

Cashin, D. (2008), 'Queer Times', *Irish Independent*, 21 June, available from: <http://www.independent.ie/lifestyle/queer-times-1417776.html> [accessed 14 June 2012].

Central Statistics Office (2011), *This Is Ireland: Highlights from Census 2011, Part One*, Dublin: Stationery Office.

Centre for Independent Living (2009), *Strategic Plan 2009–2014*, Dublin: Centre for Independent Living, 6–8.

Charlton, J. (1998), *Nothing About Us Without Us: Disability Oppression and Empowerment*, Los Angeles, CA: University of California Press.

Chase, C. (2006), 'Disorders of Sex Development Similar to More Familiar Disorders', *British Medical Journal* ADC Online, *Electronic Letters to: I A Hughes, C Houk, S F Ahmed, P A Lee LWPES/ESPE Consensus Group*, available from: <http://adc.bjm.com/content/91/7/554.extract/reply#archdeschild_el_2460> [accessed 16 January 2013].

Chase, C. (2002), 'What Is the Agenda of the Intersex Patient Advocacy Movement?' Paper prepared for the First World Congress:

Hormonal and Genetic Basis of Sexual Differentiation, available free from: <http://www.isna.org/pdf/gubbio.pdf> [accessed 13 November 2011] or in *Endocrinologist*, March/April 2003, 13: 240–42.

Cheshire Ireland (2005), *Policy on Independence and Choice*, available from: <http://www.cheshire.ie/staffinfo_policies_service.php> [accessed 4 May 2012].

Chodorow, N. (1994), *Femininities, Masculinities, Sexualities: Freud and Beyond*, London: Free Association Books.

Chrysalis Community Drug Project (nd), available from: <http://www.chrysalisdrugproject.org/> [accessed 14 May 2012].

Chughtai, B., Scullio, D., Khan, S.A., Rehman, H., Mohan, E. and Rehman, J. (2010), 'Etiology, Diagnosis and Management of Hypersexuality: A Review', *Internet Journal of Urology*, 6, 2.

Clark, T. (2008), "We're Over-Researched Here": Exploring Accounts of Research Fatigue within Qualitative Research Engagements', *Sociology*, 42(5): 953–70.

Coen, M. (2008), 'Religious Ethos and Employment Equality: A Comparative Irish Perspective', *Legal Studies*, 28(3): 452–74.

Cohen, N.L. (2012), *Delirium: How the Sexual Counterrevolution Is Polarizing America*, Berkeley, CA: Counterpoint.

Colapinto, J. (2000), *As Nature Made Him: The Boy Who Was Raised as a Girl*, New York: Harper Collins.

Coleman, D. (2011), 'When Sex Becomes the Addiction', *Wicklow People*, 22 November, 8.

Coleman, E. (1986), 'Sexual Compulsion vs. Sexual Addiction: The Debate Continues' *SIECUS Report*, 14, 7–11.

Coleman, E. (2003), 'Compulsive Sexual Behavior: What to Call It, How to Treat It?', *SIECUS Report*, 31, 12–16.

Coleridge, P. (1993), *Disability, Liberation and Development*, Oxford: Oxfam.

Colker, R. (1991), 'Marriage', *Yale Journal of Law and Feminism*, 3: 321–6.

Collins, P.H. (2004), 'Learning from the Outsider Within: The Sociological Significance of Black Feminist Thought' in S. Harding (ed.) *The Feminist Standpoint Theory Reader: Intellectual and Political Controversies*, New York: Routledge, 103–26.

Combahee River Collective (1994), 'The Combahee River Collective Statement' in A.C. Herrmann and J.A. Stewart (eds) *Theorising Feminism: Parallel Trends in the Humanities and Social Sciences*, Oxford: Westview, 26–33.

Commission of Inquiry into Child Abuse (2009), 'Special Needs Schools and Residential Services', *Commission to Inquire About Child*

Abuse Report – Confidential Committee Volume III, Dublin: Government Publications.

Commission on the Status of People with Disabilities (1996), *A Strategy for Equality*, available from: <http://www.nda.ie/cntmgmtnew.nsf/0/9007E317368ADA638025718D00372224/$File/strategy_for_equality_21.htm > [accessed 4 May 2012].

Committee of Ministers of the Council of Europe (2010), *Recommendation on Measures to Combat Discrimination on Grounds of Sexual Orientation or Gender Identity* (CM/Rec(2010)5), available from: <https://wcd.coe.int/ViewDoc.jsp?id=1606669> [accessed 30 August 2012].

Conneally, S. (1988), 'Developing the Sexuality of People with a Handicap' in R. McConkey and P. McGinley (eds) *Concepts and Controversies in Services for People with Mental Handicap*, Galway and Dublin: Woodlands Centre Renmore & St. Michael's House, 129–49.

Connell, R.W. (1987), *Gender and Power: Society, the Person and Sexual Politics*, Cambridge: Polity Press.

Connell, R.W. (2005), 'Growing Up Masculine: Rethinking the Significance of Adolescence in the Making of Masculinities', *Irish Journal of Sociology*, 14(2): 11–28.

Connell, R.W. (1995), *Masculinities*, Berkeley, CA: University of California Press.

Connell, R.W. (2000), *The Men and the Boys*, Cambridge: Polity Press.

Connell, R.W. (1994), 'The State, Gender and Sexual Politics: Theory and Appraisal' in H.L. Radtke and H.J. Stam (eds) *Power and Gender: Social Relations in Theory and Practice*, London: Sage, 136–73.

Connolly, L. (2003), *The Irish Women's Movement: From Revolution to Devolution*, Dublin: Lilliput Press.

Conolly, A. (2008), 'Challenges of Generating Qualitative Data with Socially Excluded Young People', *International Journal of Social Research Methodology*, 11(3): 201–14.

Conrad, K.A. (2004), *Locked in the Family Cell: Gender, Sexuality, and Political Agency in Irish National Discourse*, Madison, WI: University of Wisconsin Press.

Conroy, P. (2010), *Disability, Difference and Democracy: Some Rights and Wrongs*, Dublin: TASC.

Consortium on the Management of Disorders of Sex Development (2006a), *Clinical Guidelines for the Management of Disorders of Sex Development in Childhood* , Accord Alliance, available from: <http://www.dsdguidelines.org/files/clinical.pdf > [accessed 2 May 2012].

Consortium on the Management of Disorders of Sex Development (2006b), *Handbook for Parents*, Accord Alliance, available from:

<http://www.accordalliance.org/dsdguidelines/parents.pdf> [accessed 2 May 2012].

Cook, H. (2004), *The Long Sexual Revolution. English Women, Sex and Contraception 1800-1975* (2007 reprint), Oxford: Oxford University Press.

Corish, P.J. (1981), *The Catholic Community in the Seventeenth and Eighteenth Centuries*, Dublin: Helicon.

Cork Family Planning Clinic (nd), available from: <http://www.corkfamilyplanning.com/index1.htm> [accessed 9 August 2012].

Council of Europe Commissioner for Human Rights (2011), *Discrimination on Grounds of Sexual Orientation and Gender Identity in Europe*, Strasbourg: Council of Europe.

Coventry, M. (1998), 'Finding the Words' in A.D. Dreger (ed.), *Intersex in the Age of Ethics*, Hagerstown, MD: University Publishing Group, 71-6.

Cox, G. and Whitaker, T. (2009), 'Drug Use, Sex Work and the Risk Environment in Dublin', Dublin: National Advisory Committee on Drugs, available from <http://www.nacd.ie/publications/Druguse_SexWork-Web.pdf> [accessed 14 May 2012].

Crompton, L. (1981), 'The Myth of Lesbian Impunity: Capital Laws from 1270 to 1791', *Journal of Homosexuality*, 6: 11–25.

Crone, J. (1988), 'Lesbian Feminism in Ireland' in A. Smyth (ed.) *Feminism in Ireland Women's Studies International Forum*, 11(4): 343–7.

Crone, J. (1995), 'Lesbians: The Lavender Women of Ireland' in Í. O'Carroll and E. Collins (eds) *Lesbian and Gay Visions of Ireland: Towards the Twenty-First Century*, London: Cassell, 60–70.

Crouch, C. and Dore, R. (1990), 'Whatever Happened to Corporatism?' in C. Crouch and R. Dore (eds) *Corporatism and Accountability*, Oxford: Clarendon, 1–44.

Crow, L. (2002), 'Invisible and Centre Stage: A Disabled Woman's Perspective on Maternity Services', *Midwives, the Official Journal of the Royal College of Midwives* available from: <http://www.roaring-girl.com/wp-content/documents/maternity.pdf> [accessed 25 April 2012].

Crowley, U. and Kitchin, R. (2008), 'Producing "Decent Girls": Governmentality and the Moral Geographies of Sexual Conduct in Ireland', *Gender, Place and Culture*, 15(4): 355–72.

Curtis, M. (2010), *A Challenge to Democracy: Militant Catholicism in Modern Ireland*, Dublin: History Press Ireland.

Cusack, D.O. (2009), *Come What May*, Dublin: Penguin.

Cusick, L., McGarry, K., Perry, G., Kilcommons, S. (2010), 'Drug Services for Sex Workers – Approaches in England and Ireland', *Safer Communities*, 9(4): 32–9.

Cuskelly, M. and Bride, R. (2004), 'Attitudes Towards the Sexuality of Adults with an Intellectual Disability: Parents, Support Staff and a Community Sample', *Journal of Intellectual and Developmental Disability*, 29(3): 255–64.

Cuskelly, M. and Gilmore, L. (2007), 'Attitudes to Sexuality Questionnaire (Individuals with an Intellectual Disability): Scale Development and Community Norms', *Journal of Intellectual and Developmental Disability*, 32(3): 214–21.

Dagblad, B. (2001), 'Council Funds Prostitute for Disabled Man', *Santa-Banta*, available from: <http://www.santabanta.com/newsmaker.asp?catid=249&catname=Newsmaker > [accessed 23 April 2012].

Dáil Éireann (1977), *Dáil Debates*, 302, No. 8, 13 December.

Dáil Éireann (2010), *Civil Partnership Bill 2010; Fifth Stage*, 714, 2, 1 July, available from: <http://debates.oireachtas.ie/dail/2010/07/01/00012.asp> [accessed 5 January 2012].

Daily Edge (2011), 'Over 450,000 Tune In to *Tallafornia*', 12 December, available from: <http://www.dailyedge.ie/over-450000-tune-into-tallafornia-302835-Dec2011/> [accessed 4 April 2012].

Daly, A. (2012), '"Veiled Obscenity": Contraception and the *Dublin Medical Press* in the Second Half of the Nineteenth Century' in E. Farrell (ed.) *'She Said She Was in the Family Way': Pregnancy and Infancy in Modern Ireland*, London: Institute of Historical Research, 15–33.

Daly, E. (2012), 'Same Sex Marriage Doesn't Need a Referendum', 15 July, available from: <http://www.humanrights.ie/index.php/2012/07/15/same-sex-marriage-doesnt-need-a-referendum/> [accessed 18 July 2012].

Daly, M. (1997), '"Oh, Kathleen Ni Houlihan, Your Way's a Thorny Way!" The Condition of Women in Twentieth-Century Ireland' in A. Bradley and M.G. Valiulis (eds) *Gender and Sexuality in Modern Ireland*, Amherst, MA: University of Massachusetts Press, 102–26.

Davies, C.A. (1998), 'Constructing Other Selves: (In)Competences and the Category of Learning Difficulties' in R. Jenkins (ed.) *Questions of Competence: Comparative Perspectives,* Cambridge: Cambridge University Press, 102–24.

Davies, D. (2000), 'Facilitating Sex and Relationships for People with Disabilities', *The Right to Be Sexual – A Radical Proposal*, available from: <http://www.bentvoices.org/culturecrash/daviessarfp.htm> [accessed 20 April 2012].

DCYA (Department of Children and Youth Affairs) (2012), *Speaking Notes for Minister Frances Fitzgerald,* available from: <http://www. dcya.gov.ie/viewdoc.asp?Docid=1864&CatID=12&mn=&StartDate =1+January+2012> [accessed 14 May 2012].

DeLamater, J. (1981), 'The Social Control of Sexuality', *Annual Review of Sociology, 7,* 263–90.

Demaré, D., Lips, H.M. and Briere, J. (1993), 'Sexually Violent Pornography, Anti-women Attitudes, and Sexual Aggression: A Structural Equation Model', *Journal of Research in Personality, 27,* 285–300.

Dentith, A.M., Measor, L. and O'Malley, M.P. (2009), 'Stirring Dangerous Waters: Dilemmas for Critical Participatory Research with Young People', *Sociology,* 43(1): 158–68.

Department of Community, Rural and Gaeltacht Affairs (2009) *National Drugs Strategy (Interim) 2009-2016,* Dublin: Department of Community, Rural and Gaeltacht Affairs, available from: <http://www. drugsandalcohol.ie/12388/1/DCRGA_Strategy_2009-2016.pdf >

Department of Education (1992), *Education for a Changing World* (Green Paper), Dublin: Stationery Office.

Department of Education (1997), *Relationships and Sexuality Education, Going Forward Together. An Introduction to Relationships and Sexuality Education for Parents,* Dublin: Government of Ireland.

Department of Education and Science (1998), *Resource Materials for Relationships and Sexuality Education, Post-Primary: Junior Cycle,* Dublin: Government of Ireland.

Department of Education and Science (2007), *Sé/Sí: Gender in Irish Education,* Dublin: Government of Ireland.

Department of Finance (1988), *Circular 21/88,* 22 June.

Department of Health and Children (2009), *National Men's Health Policy 2008-2013,* Dublin: Government of Ireland.

Department of Justice and Equality (2012), *Discussion Document on Future Direction of Prostitution Legislation,* available from: <http:// www.inis.gov.ie/en/JELR/Discussion%20Document%20on%20 Future%20Direction%20of%20Prostitution%20Legislation. pdf/Files/Discussion%20Document%20on%20Future%20 Direction%20of%20Prostitution%20Legislation.pdf> [accessed 1 July 2012].

Department of Justice, Equality and Law Reform (2009), *National Action Plan to Prevent and Combat Trafficking in Ireland (2009–2012),* Dublin: Government of Ireland.

Devore, H. (1998), 'Growing Up in the Surgical Maelstrom' in A.D. Dreger (ed.) *Intersex in the Age of Ethics,* Hagerstown, MD: University Publishing Group, 79–81.

Dhikav, V., Anand, K. and Aggarwal, N. (2007), 'Grossly Disinhibited Sexual Behavior in Dementia of Alzheimer's Type', *Archives of Sexual Behavior*, 36, 133–4.

Diamond, L.M. (2006), 'Careful What You Ask For: Reconsidering Feminist Epistemology and Autobiographical Narrative in Research on Sexual Identity Development', *Signs: Journal of Women and Culture and Society*, 31: 471–92.

Diamond, L.M. (2004), 'Emerging Perspectives on Distinctions Between Romantic Love and Sexual Desire', *Current Directions in Psychological Science*, 13: 116–19.

Diamond, L.M. (2005), 'A New View of Lesbian Subtypes: Stable vs. Fluid Identity Trajectories Over an 8-Year Period', *Psychology of Women Quarterly*, 29: 119–28.

Diamond, L.M. (2009), *Sexual Fluidity: Understanding Women's Love and Desire*, Cambridge, MA: Harvard University Press.

Diamond, L.M. (2000), 'Sexual Identity, Attractions, and Behavior among Young Sexual-Minority Women Over a Two-Year Period', *Developmental Psychology*, 36: 241–50.

Diamond, L.M. (2003), 'What Does Sexual Orientation Orient? A Biobehavioral Model Distinguishing Romantic Love and Sexual Desire', *Psychological Review*, 110(1): 173–92.

Diamond, M. (1965), 'A Critical Evaluation of the Ontogeny of Human Sexual Behaviour', *Quarterly Review of Biology*, 44: 147–75.

Diamond, M. (1999), 'Pediatric Management of Ambiguous and Traumatised Genitalia', *Journal of Urology*, 162, 1021–8.

Diamond, M. and Beh, H.G. (2006), 'Variations of Sex Development Instead of Disorders of Sex Development', *British Medical Journal ADC Online, Electronic Letters to: I A Hughes, C Houk, S F Ahmed, P A Lee LWPES/ESPE Consensus Group*, available from: <http://adc.bjm.com/content/91/7/554.extract/reply#archdeschild_el_2460> [accessed 16 January, 2013].

Diamond, M. and Sigmundson, K. (1997a), 'Sex Reassignment at Birth: Long-Term Review and Clinical Application', *Archives of Pediatric and Adolescent Medicine*, 151: 298–304.

Diamond, M. and Sigmundson, K. (1997b), 'Management of Intersexuality: Guidelines for Dealing With persons of Ambiguous Genitalia', *Archives of Pediatric and Adolescent Medicine*, 151: 1046–50.

Dines, G. (1998), 'Living in Two Worlds: An Activist in the Academy' in G. Dines, R. Jensen and A. Russo (eds) *Pornography: The Production and Consumption of Inequality*, New York and London: Routledge.

Diorio, J.A. (1985), 'Contraception, Copulation Domination and the Theoretical Barrenness of Sex Education Literature', *Educational Theory*, 35(3): 239–54.

Dodge, B., Reece, M., Herbenick, D., Fisher, C., Satinsky, S. and Stupiansky, N. (2008), 'Relations Between Sexually Transmitted Infection Diagnosis and Sexual Compulsivity in a Community-based Sample of Men who have Sex with Men', *Sexually Transmitted Infections*, 84, 324–7.

Donnerstein, E. and Berkowitz, L. (1981), 'Victim Reactions in Aggressive Erotic Films as a Factor in Violence Against Women', *Journal of Personality and Social Psychology*, 41, 710–24, and in M.C. Seto, A. Maric and H.E. Barbaree (2001), 'The Role of Pornography in the Etiology of Sexual Aggression', *Aggression and Violent Behaviour*, 6, 35–53.

Dorcey, M. (1995), 'Interview with Mary Dorcey' in I. O'Carroll and E. Collins (eds) *Lesbian and Gay Visions of Ireland: Towards the Twenty-First Century*, London: Cassell, 25–44.

Doyle, P. (1989), *The God Squad*, London: Corgi.

Dreger, A. D. (1998), 'A History of Intersex: From the Age of Gonads to the Age of Consent' in A.D. Dreger (ed.) *Intersex in the Age of Ethics*, Hagerstown, MD: University Publishing Group, 5–22.

Dreger, A.D. (2006), 'Intersex and Human Rights: The Long View' in S.E. Sytsma (ed.) *Ethics and Intersex: International Library of Ethics, Law, and the New Medicine*, The Netherlands: Springer, 73–86.

Drennan, J. (2011), 'Norris Still the People's First Choice as President', *Irish Independent*, 3 July.

Drummond, E. (2006), 'Attitudes Towards Sexuality: A Pilot Study in Ireland', *Learning Disability Practice*, 9(4): 28–34.

Dublin AIDS Allliance (nd), *Dublin AIDS Alliance*, available from: <http://www.dublinaidsalliance.ie/index.php?page=services> [accessed 24 January 2013].

Duits, L. and van Zoonen, L. (2011), 'Coming to Terms with Sexualisation', *European Journal of Cultural Studies*, 14(5): 491–506.

Dukes, E. and McGuire, B.E. (2009), 'Enhancing Capacity to Make Sexuality-Related Decisions in People with an Intellectual Disability', *Journal of Intellectual Disability Research*, 53: 727–34.

Dunphy, R. (1997), 'Sexual Identities, National Identities: The Politics of Gay Law Reform in the Republic of Ireland', *Contemporary Politics* (3)3: 247–65.

Durham, M.G. (2009), *The Lolita Effect*, London: Duckworth.

Dworkin, A. (1997), *Life and Death*, New York: Free Press.

Earle, S. (1999), 'Facilitated Sex and the Concept of Sexual Need: Disabled Students and their Personal Assistants', *Disability and Society*, 14(3): 309–23.

Earner-Byrne, L. (2007), *Mother and Child: Maternity and Child Welfare in Dublin, 1922-60,* Manchester: Manchester University Press.

Edger, K. (2012), 'Evangelicalism, Sexual Morality, and Sexual Addiction: Opposing Views and Continued Conflicts', *Journal of Religion and Health,* 51, 162–78.

Egan, R.D. and Hawkes, G.L. (2008), 'Endangered Girls and Incendiary Objects: Unpacking the Discourse on Sexualization', *Sexuality and Culture,* 12(4): 291–311.

Egan, R.D. and Hawkes, G.L. (2009), 'The Problem with Protection: Or Why We Need to Move Towards Recognition and the Sexual Agency of Children', *Journal of Media and Cultural Studies*, 23(3): 389–400.

Elliott, I. (2010), *Voices of Children: Report on Initial Research with Children of LGBT Parents,* Dublin: Marriage Equality.

Else-Quest, N.M. and Shibley Hyde, J. (2009), 'The Missing Discourse of Development: Commentary on Lerum and Dworkin', *Journal of Sex Research,* 46(4): 264–7.

Epstein, D. (1997), "Boyz" Own Stories: Masculinities and Sexualities in School', *Gender and Education,* 9(1): 105–15.

Epstein, D. and Johnson, R. (1998), *Schooling Sexualities,* Buckingham: Open University Press.

Epstein, S. (2003), 'An Incitement to Discourse: Sociology and the History of Sexuality', *Sociological Forum,* 18(3): 485–502.

Equality Authority (2002), *Implementing Equality for Lesbians, Gays and Bisexuals,* Dublin: Equality Authority.

Errante, A. (2004), 'But Sometimes You're Not Part of the Story: Oral Histories and Ways of Remembering and Telling' in N. Hesse-Bibers and M.L. Yaiser (eds) *Feminist Perspectives on Social Research,* New York: Oxford University Press, 411–34.

Eskridge Jr, W.N. and Spedale, D.R. (2006), *Gay Marriage: For Better or Worse? What We've Learned from the Evidence,* New York: Oxford University Press.

Esterle, M., Munoz Sastre, M.T. and Mullet, E. (2008), 'Judging the Acceptability of Sexual Intercourse Among People with Learning Disabilities: French Laypeople's Viewpoint', *Sexuality and Disability,* 26, 219–27.

Ettelbrick, P. (1989), 'Since When Is Marriage a Path to Liberation?' in R.M. Baird and S.E. Rosenblum (eds) *Same-Sex Marriage: The Moral and Legal Debate,* Amherst, MA: Prometheus Books, 164–8.

EuroDSD (2008), 'EuroDSD Standard Operating Procedure (SOP) for Handling and Coding of Biological Samples', available from: <http://www.eurodsd.eu/en/bilder/EuroDSD_Standard_Operating_Procedure_for_Biomaterials_mitLogo.pdf> [accessed 16 April 2012].

EuroDSD (2009a), 'Standard Operating Procedure WP2 Identification of Novel Genetic Markers for DSD: DNA Extraction for Array CGH Procedures and Control Samples', available from: <http://www.eurodsd.eu/en/bilder/03_WP02_SOP_DNA_extraction.pdf> [accessed 16 April 2012].

EuroDSD (2009b), 'EuroDSD WP05-1 Urine and Plasma Collection SOP', available from: <http://www.eurodsd.eu/en/media/EuroDSD_WP051_Overview_Urine_Plasma_SOPs.pdf> [accessed 7 May 2012].

EuroDSD (nd–a), 'Project Impact', available from: <http://www.eurodsd.eu/en/project-impact.php> [accessed 16 April 2012].

EuroDSD (nd–b), 'Possibilities for Sponsors', available from: <http://www.eurodsd.eu/en/9400.php > [accessed 16 April 2012].

European Union (2000), Council Directive 2000/78/EC of 27 November, Establishing a General Framework for Equal Treatment in Employment and Occupation, *Official Journal of the European Union*, L303, 2 December 2000, 16–22, available from: http://eurlex.europa.eu/LexUriServ/LexUriServ.do?uri=CELEX:32000L0078:en:HTML [accessed 17 January 2013].

Evans, D. (2002), *The Development of Personal Relationship and Sexuality Guidelines for People with Learning Disabilities*, Galway, Western Health Board, available from: <http://lenus.ie/hse/bitstream/10147/43787/1/4289.pdf > [accessed 26 October 2012].

Evans, D. (1993), *Sexual Citizenship: The Material Construction of Sexualities*, London: Routledge.

Faderman, L. (1991), *Odd Girls and Twilight Lovers: A History of Lesbian Life in Twentieth-Century America*, Harmondsworth: Penguin.

Fagan, P. (2011), *Missing Pieces*, Dublin: Marriage Equality.

Fahey, T. (1995), 'Family and Household in Ireland' in P. Clancy, S. Drudy, K. Lynch and L. O'Dowd (eds) *Irish Society: Sociological Perspectives*, Dublin: Institute of Public Administration, 205–34.

Fahey, T. (1999), 'Religion and Sexual Culture in Ireland' in F.X. Eder, L.A. Hall and G. Hekma (eds.) *Sexual Cultures in Europe*, Manchester: Manchester University Press, 53–70.

Fairclough, N. (1995), *Critical Discourse Analysis: The Critical Study of Language*, London and New York: Longman.

Faller, G. (2012), 'Anseo! How a New Generation of Gay Teachers Is Fighting Back', *Irish Times*, 27 March, available from: <http://www.irishtimes.com/newspaper/education/2012/0327/1224313956760.html> [accessed 18 July 2012].

Faludi, S. (1992), *Backlash: The Undeclared War Against Women*, London: Vintage Press.

Farley, M. and Barkan, H. (1998), 'Prostitution, Violence against Women, and Post-traumatic Stress Disorder', *Women and Health*, 27(3): 37–49.

Farley, M. and Kelly, V. (2000), 'Prostitution: A Critical Review of the Medical and Social Sciences Literature', *Women and Criminal Justice*, 11(4): 29–64.

Fausto-Sterling, A. (2000), *Sexing the Body: Gender Politics and the Construction of Sexuality*, New York: Basic Books.

Fearing, J. (1998), 'Intervention and the Sexually Addicted Patient', *Sexual Addiction and Compulsivity*, 5, 15.

Featherstone, B. (2004), *Family Life and Family Support: A Feminist Analysis*, Hampshire: Palgrave Macmillan.

Feder, E. (nd), 'Letter of Concern from Bioethicists' in *Fetaldex.org*, available from: <http://www.fetaldex.org/letter_bioethics.html> [accessed 13 November 2012].

Ferriter, D. (2009), *Occasions of Sin: Sex and Society in Modern Ireland*, London: Profile Books.

Ferriter, D. (2005), *The Transformation of Ireland 1900–2000*, London: Profile Books.

Fetaldex.org (2012), *Exploring the Ethics of Prenatal Dexamethasone Usage*, available from: <http://www.fetaldex.org/home.html> [accessed 10 May 2012].

Fianna Fáil (1993), *Fianna Fáil/Labour Programme for a Partnership Government 1993–1997*, Dublin: Fianna Fáil.

Filas, F.L. (1964), *Telling Your Children: A Moderate View*, Dublin: Catholic Truth Society of Ireland.

Fine, M. (1988), 'Sexuality, Schooling and Adolescent Females: The Missing Discourse of Desire', *Harvard Educational Review*, 58(1): 29–53.

Fine, M. and McClelland, S. (2006), 'Sexuality Education and Desire; Still Missing after all These Years', *Harvard Educational Review*, 76: 297–338.

Fineman, M.A. (2009a), 'Evolving Images of Gender and Equality: A Feminist Journey', *New England Law Review*, 43: 437–60.

References

Fineman, M.A. (2009b), 'The Sexual Family' in M.A. Fineman, J.E. Jackson, and A.P. Romero (eds) *Feminist and Queer Legal Theory: Intimate Encounters, Uncomfortable Conversations*, Farnham: Ashgate.

Fineman, M.A. (2008), 'The Vulnerable Subject: Anchoring Equality in the Human Condition', *Yale Journal of Law and Feminism*, 20(1): 1–23.

Finger, A. (1992), 'Forbidden Fruit', *New Internationalist*, 233, 8–10.

Finkelhor, D. (1986), *A Sourcebook on Child Sexual Abuse*, London: Sage.

Finlayson, A.J.R., Sealy, J. and Martin, P.R. (2001), 'The Differential Diagnosis of Problematic Hypersexuality', *Sexual Addiction and Compulsivity*, 8, 241–51.

Fitzgerald, T. (1956), 'The Irish Parish and the Emigrant', *Christus Rex*, X(4): 346.

Fleury, M.J., Imboua, A., Aubé, D., Farand, L. and Lambert, Y. (2012), 'General Practitioners' Management of Mental Disorders: A Rewarding Practice with Considerable Obstacles', *BioMedCentral Family Practice*, 13, 1–12.

Flood, M. (2009), 'The Harms of Pornography Exposure among Children and Young People', *Child Abuse Review*, 18, 384–400.

Flood, M. (2010), 'Young Men using Pornography' in K. Boyle (ed.) *Everyday Pornography*, Oxford: Routledge, 164–78.

Flood, R.R. (2003), 'Disruptive (M)Others: Lesbian Parenting in Sweden and Ireland', PhD thesis, London School of Economics and Political Science.

Flynn, L. (1995) 'The Irish Supreme Court and the Constitution of Male Homosexuality' in E.D. Herman and C. Stychin (eds) *Legal Inversions: Lesbians, Gay Men, and the Politics of Law*, Philadelphia, PA: Temple University Press, 29–45.

Flynn, R. and Ging, D. (2009), *The Representation and Portrayal of People with Disabilities in Irish Broadcasting*, Dublin: Broadcasting Commission of Ireland and the National Disability Authority.

Foley, S. and Kelly, G. (2009), *Friendships and Taboos: Research on Sexual Health Promotion for People with Mild to Moderate Intellectual Disabilities in the 18–25 Age Range: Results of a Consultation Process and Literature Review*, Cork: HSE South.

Foucault, M. (1972), *The Archaeology of Knowledge*, London: Routledge.

Foucault, M. (1981) [1978], *The History of Sexuality, Volume 1: An Introduction*, Harmondsworth: Pelican.

Foucault, M. (1990) [1978], *The History of Sexuality, Volume 1: An Introduction* (translated from the French by R. Hurley), New York: Vintage.

Foucault, M. (1980), 'Truth and Power' in C. Gordon (ed.) *Power / Knowledge: Selected Interviews and Other Writings 1972–1977*, New York and Toronto, ON: Pantheon Books.

Foucault, M. (1976) and (1990), *The Will to Knowledge: The History of Sexuality: 1* (translated by R. Hurley), London: Penguin Books.

Francis, B. and Skelton, C. (2001), 'Introduction' in B. Francis and C. Skelton (eds) *Investigating Gender: Contemporary Perspectives in Education*, Buckingham: Open University Press, 1–7.

Francis, B. and Skelton, C. (2005), *Reassessing Gender and Achievement: Questioning Contemporary Key Debates,* London: Routledge.

Freedman, V. (1995) *The Cities of David: The Life of David Norris*, Dublin: Basement Press.

Freud Loewenstein, S. (1985), 'On the Diversity of Love Object Orientations among Women', *Journal of Social Work and Human Sexuality,* 3: 7–24.

Frosh, S., Phoenix, A. and Pattman, R. (2002), *Young Masculinities: Understanding Boys in Contemporary Society,* London: Palgrave.

Fulbright, Y.K. (2012), *Understanding Disability Fetishes and "Devotees",* available from: <http://www.disaboom.com/sexuality-and-disability/understanding-disability-fetishes-and-devotees> [accessed 1 May 2012].

Fuss, D. (1989), *Essentially Speaking: Feminism, Nature and Difference,* London: Routledge.

Gabb, J. (1999), 'Imag(in)ing the Queer Lesbian Family', *Lesbian Mothering,* 1(2): 9–20.

Gabb, J. (2005), 'Locating Lesbian Parent Families: Everyday Negotiations of Lesbian Motherhood in Britain', *Gender, Place and Culture,* 12(4): 419–32.

Gabb, J. (2013), 'Qualitative Research on LGBT-Parent Families' in A.E. Goldberg and K.R. Allen (eds) *LGBT-Parent Families: Possibilities for New Research and Implications for Practice,* New York: Springer, 325–42.

Gabb, J. (2001), 'Querying the Discourses of Love. An Analysis of Contemporary Patterns of Love and the Stratification of Intimacy within Lesbian Families', *European Journal of Women's Studies,* 8(3): 313–28.

Gagnon, J. and Simon, W. (1974), *Sexual Conduct,* London: Hutchinson.

Galligan, Y. (1998), *Women in Politics in Contemporary Ireland: From the Margins to the Mainstream,* London: Pinter.

Gantly, D. (2011), 'A New Perspective on Sex Addiction', *Irish Medical Times,* Dublin: MPL Media.

References

Garofalo Geymonat, G. (2010), 'Sex Workers' Rights Activism in Europe: Orientations from Brussels' in M. Hope Ditmore, A. Levy and A. Willman (eds) *Sex Work Matters: Exploring Money, Power, and Intimacy in the Sex Industry*, London: Zed Books, 221–38.

Garvin, T. (2005), *Preventing the Future: Why Was Ireland so Poor for so Long?*, Dublin: Gill and Macmillan.

Geary, T. and Mannix McNamara, P. (2003), *Implementation of Social, Personal and Health Education at Junior Cycle*, University of Limerick, Report commissioned by the SPHE Support Service.

Gender Recognition Advisory Group (2011), *Report of the Gender Recognition Advisory Group*, Dublin: Stationery Office.

Gianino, M. (2008), 'Adaptation and Transformation: The Transition to Adoptive Parenthood for Gay Male Couples', *Journal of GLTB Family Studies*, 42(2): 205–43.

Giddens, A. (1991), *Modernity and Self-Identity: Self and Society in the Late Modern Age*, Cambridge: Polity Press.

Giddens, A. (1994), *The Transformation of Intimacy: Sexuality, Love and Eroticism in Modern Societies*, Cambridge: Polity Press.

Giddens, A. and Pierson, C. (1998), *Conversations with Anthony Giddens: Making Sense of Modernity*, Cambridge: Polity Press.

Giles, J. (2006), 'No Such Thing as Excessive Levels of Sexual Behavior', *Archives of Sexual Behavior*, 35, 2.

Gill, R. (2009), 'Beyond the Sexualisation of Culture Thesis: An Intersectional Analysis of "Sixpacks", "Midriffs" and "Hot Lesbians" in Advertising', *Sexualities*, 12(2): 137–60.

Gilligan, A.L. and Zappone, K. (2008), *Our Lives Out Loud: In Pursuit of Justice and Equality*, Dublin: O'Brien Press.

Gilliland, R., South, M., Carpenter, B.N. and Hardy, S.A. (2011), 'The Roles of Shame and Guilt in Hypersexual Behavior', *Sexual Addiction and Compulsivity*, 18, 12–29.

Gillis, J.R. (1996), *A World of Their Own Making: Myth, Ritual, and the Quest for Family Values*, Cambridge, MA: Harvard University Press.

Gillman, M., Heyman, B. and Swain, J. (2000), 'What's in a Name? The Implications of Diagnosis for People with Learning Difficulties and their Family Carers', *Disability and Society*, 15(3): 389–409.

Gilmore, L. and Chambers, B. (2010), 'Intellectual Disability and Sexuality: Attitudes of Disability Support Staff and Leisure Industry Employees', *Journal of Intellectual and Developmental Disability*, 35(1): 1–22.

Giugliano, J. (2009), 'Sexual Addiction: Diagnostic Problems', *International Journal of Mental Health and Addiction*, 7, 283–94.

GLEN/Nexus (1995), *Poverty: Lesbians and Gay Men, The Economic and Social Effects of Discrimination,* Dublin: Combat Poverty Agency.

Global Action for Trans Equality (GATE) (2012), *English Translation of Argentina's Gender Identity Law as approved by the Senate of Argentina on May 8, 2012,* available from: <http://globaltransaction.files.wordpress.com/2012/05/argentina-gender-identity-law.pdf> [accessed 30August 2012].

Goffman, E. (1968), *Stigma: Notes on the Management of Spoiled Identity,* Harmondsworth: Penguin.

Gold, S.N. and Heffner, C.L. (1998), 'Sexual Addiction: Many Conceptions, Minimal Data', *Clinical Psychology Review,* 18, 367–81.

Golden, C. (1987), 'Diversity and Variability in Women's Sexual Identities' in Boston Lesbian Psychologies Collective (ed.), *Lesbian Psychologies: Explorations and Challenges,* Urbana, IL: University of Illinois Press, 19–34.

Golden, C. (2003), 'Improbable Possibilities', *Psychoanalytic Inquiry,* 23(4): 624–42.

Goldmeier, D. and Petrak, J. (2011), 'How to Recognise Sexual Addiction in the Sexual Health Clinic Setting?', *Sexually Transmitted Infections,* 87, 370–71.

Goodman, A. (1998), *Sexual Addiction: An Integrated Approach,* Madison, CT: International Universities Press.

Gordon, L. (2007), *The Moral Property of Women: A History of Birth Control Politics in America,* Urbana and Chicago, IL: University of Illinois.

Gough, B. and McFadden, M. (2001), *Critical Social Psychology: An Introduction,* Basingstoke: Palgrave.

Government of Ireland (2011), *Government for National Recovery 2011-2016,* Dublin: Stationery Office.

Government of Ireland (1995), *Report of the Expert Advisory Group on Relationships and Sexuality Education,* Dublin: Stationery Office.

Gowran, S. (2004), 'See No Evil, Speak No Evil, Hear No Evil: The Experiences of Lesbian and Gay Teachers in Irish Schools' in J. Deegan, D. Devine and A. Lodge (eds) *Primary Voices: Equality, Diversity and Childhood in Irish Primary Schools,* Dublin: Institute of Public Administration, 37–55.

Gray, B. (2004), *Women and the Irish Diaspora,* London and New York: Routledge.

Gray, B. and Ryan, L. (1997), '(Dis)locating "Woman" and Women in Representations of Irish Nationality' in A. Byrne and M. Leonard (eds) *Women and Irish Society,* Belfast: Beyond the Pale Publishers.

Green, A. (2004), 'Individual Remembering and "Collective Memory": Theoretical Presuppositions and Contemporary Debates', *Oral History*, 32(2): 35–44.

Grieve, A., McLaren, S., Lindsay, W.R. and Culling, E. (2009), 'Staff Attitudes Towards the Sexuality of People with Learning Disabilities: A Comparison of Different Professional Groups and Residential Facilities', *British Journal of Learning Disabilities*, 37: 76–84.

Griffin-Shelley, E. (2009), 'Ethical Issues in Sex and Love Addiction Treatment', *Sexual Addiction and Compulsivity*, 16, 32–54.

Griffin-Shelley, E. (ed.) (1993) *Outpatient Treatment of Sex and Love Addicts*, Westport, CT: Praeger.

Griffin-Shelley, E. (1997), *Sex and Love Addiction, Treatment and Recovery*, Westport, CT: Praeger.

Griffiths, D.M., Watson, S., Lewis, T. and Stoner, K. (2004), 'Sexuality Research and Persons with Intellectual Disabilities' in E. Emerson, C. Hatton, T. Thompson, and T.R. Parmenter (eds) *The International Handbook of Applied Research in Intellectual Disabilities*, Chichester: John Wiley & Sons Ltd., 311–34.

Groneman, C. (2001), *Nymphomania: A History*, New York: W.W. Norton.

Grosz, E. (1994), *Volatile Bodies: Towards a Corporeal Feminism*, St Leonards: Allen and Unwin.

Grov, C., Parsons, J. and Bimbi, D. (2010), 'Sexual Compulsivity and Sexual Risk in Gay and Bisexual Men', *Archives of Sexual Behavior*, 39, 940–49.

Haegsstroem-Nordin, E., Sandberg, J., Hanson, U. and Tyden, T. (2006), "It's Everywhere!" Young Swedish People's Thoughts and Reflections about Pornography', *Scandinavian Journal of Caring Science*, 20: 386–93.

Hagedorn, W.B. (2009), 'Preparing Competent Clinicians: Curricular Applications Based on the Sexual Addiction Counselling Competencies', *Sexual Addiction and Compulsivity*, 16, 341–60.

Hamer, D., Hu, S., Magnuson, V.L., Hu, N. and Pattatucci, A.M.L. (1993), 'Linkage Between DNA Markers on the X Chromosome and Male Sexual Orientation', *Science* 261 (5119): 321–7.

Hamilton, C. (2010), '"But Rachel Was Enjoying It Too, Wasn't She?" A Learning Disability and Sexuality Case Study' in R. Shuttleworth and T. Sanders (eds) *Sex and Disability: Politics, Identity and Access*, Leeds: Disability Press, 121–36.

Hamilton, C. (2009), '"Now I'd Like to Sleep with Rachel" – Researching Sexuality Support in a Service Agency Group Home', *Disability and Society*, 24(3): 303–15.

References

Hammack, P.L. and Cohler, B.J. (2011), 'Narrative, Identity and the Politics of Exclusion: Social Change and the Gay and Lesbian Life Course', *Sexuality Research and Social Policy*, 8 (3): 162–82.

Hammersley, M. and Atkinson, P. (1996), *Ethnography: Principles in Practice*, London: Routledge.

Hantrais, L. (2004), *Family Policy Matters: Responding to Family Change in Europe*, Bristol: Policy Press.

Harding, S. (2004), *The Feminist Standpoint Theory Reader: Intellectual and Political Controversies*, New York: Routledge.

Harding, S. (1991), 'Thinking from the Perspective of Lesbian Lives' in S. Harding, *Whose Science? Whose Knowledge? Thinking from Women's Lives*, Milton Keynes: Open University Press, 249–67.

Hardy, S. (1998), *The Reader*, the *Author, His Woman and Her Lover: Soft-Core Pornography and Heterosexual Men*, London and Washington, DC: Cassell.

Harnett, N. (2007), *Polio and Us – Personal Stories of Polio Survivors in Ireland*, Dublin: Post Polio Support Group.

Harper, C. (2007) *Intersex*, Oxford: Berg.

Haslam, T.J. [Oedipus] (1868), *The Marriage Problem*, copy in Hull History Centre: Correspondence of Thomas and Anna Haslam, presented to the library by Marie Stopes, DX/66/3.

Hawkes, G. (2004), *Sex and Pleasure in Western Culture*, Cambridge: Polity Press.

Hayman L.A., Rexer, J.L., Pavol, M.A., Strite, D. and Meyers, C.A. (1998), 'Kluver-Bucy Syndrome after Bilateral Selective Damage of Amygdala and its Cortical Connections', *Journal of Neuropsychiatry and Clinical Neurosciences*, 10, 354–8.

Heasley, R. and Crane, B. (2012), 'Queering Classes: Disrupting Hegemonic Masculinity and the Effects of Compulsory Heterosexuality in the Classroom' in J.C. Landreau and N.M. Rodriquez (eds) *Queer Masculinities: A Critical Reader in Education*, 1, 21, New York: Springer, 99–116.

Heath, D. (2010), *Purifying Empire: Obscenity and the Politics of Moral Regulation in Britain, India and Australia*, Cambridge: Cambridge University Press.

Hebdige, D. (1988), *Hiding in the Light. On Images and Things*, London: Routledge.

Held, D. (1991), 'Between State and Civil Society' in G. Andrews (ed.) *Citizenship*, London: Lawrence and Wishart, 19–25.

Hemphill, Rev. S. (1908), *The Murderess of the Unseen: A Tract on Race-Suicide*, Dublin: Hodges Figgis & Co. and London: Simpkin, Marshall & Co.

Hendey, N. and Pascall, G. (1998), 'Independent Living: Gender, Violence and the Threat of Violence', *Disability and Society*, 13(3): 415–27.

Herek, G.M. (2004), 'Beyond "Homophobia": Thinking About Sexual Prejudice and Stigma in the Twenty-First Century', *Sexuality Research and Social Policy*, 1(2): 6–24.

Herman, D. (1993), 'The Politics of Law Reform: Lesbian and Gay Rights into the 1990s' in J. Bristow and A.R. Wilson (eds) *Activating Theory: Lesbian, Gay, Bisexual Politics*, London: Lawrence and Wishart, 246–63.

Herman, J.L. and Hirschman, L. (2000), *Father-Daughter Incest*, Cambridge, MA: Harvard University Press.

Herring, B. (2001), 'Ethical Guidelines in the Treatment of Compulsive Sexual Behaviour', *Sexual Addiction and Compulsivity*, 8, 13–22.

Hesketh, T. (1990) *The Second Partitioning of Ireland? The Abortion Referendum of 1983*, Dublin: Brandsma Books.

Hesse-Biber, S.N. (2007), 'The Practice of Feminist In-Depth Interviewing' in S. Hesse-Biber and P.L. Leavy, *Feminist Research Practice: A Primer*, Thousand Oaks, CA: Sage, 111–48.

Heyman, B. and Huckle, S. (1995), 'Sexuality as a Perceived Hazard in the Lives of Adults with Learning Difficulties', *Disability and Society*, 10(2): 139–56.

Hicks, S. (2005a), 'Is Gay Parenting Bad for Kids? Responding to the "Very Idea of Difference" in Research on Lesbian and Gay Parents', *Sexualities*, 8(2): 153–68.

Hicks, S. (2005b), 'Queer Genealogies: Tales of Conformity and Rebellion amongst Lesbian and Gay Foster Carers and Adopters', *Qualitative Social Work*, 4(3): 293–308.

Hilliard, B. (2003), 'The Catholic Church and Married Women's Sexuality: Habitus Change in Late 20th Century Ireland', *Irish Journal of Sociology*, 12(2): 28–49.

Hinkle, C.E. (nd–a), 'Why Is OII Not Using the Term DSD or "Disorders of Sex Development?"' *Organisation Intersex International*, available from: <http://www.intersexualite.org/Response_to_Intersex_Initiative.html > [accessed 8 October 2011].

Hinkle, C.E. (nd–b), 'Mutilations or Non-Consensual Normalisation Treatments?' *Organisation Intersex International*, available from: <http://www.intersexualite.org/Intersex_treatments.html> [accessed 9 October 2011].

Hiort, O. (2009), 'Brief Project Description', *EuroDSD*, available from: <http://www.eurodsd.eu/en/bilder/briefdescription_EuroDSD.pdf> [accessed 16 April 2012].

Hiort, O. (2010), 'Project Periodic Report', *Cordis*, available from: <http://cordis.europa.eu/documents/documentlibrary/11723 9041EN6.pdf> [accessed 16 April 2012].

Hockey, J., Meah, A. and Robinson, V. (2009), 'Fast Girls, Foreigners and GIs: An Exploration of the Discursive Strategies Through Which the Status of Pre-Marital (Hetero)sexual Ignorance and Restraint Was Upheld During the Second World War', *Sociological Research Online*, 14(5): available from: <http://0-www.socresonline.org.uk.library. ucc.ie/14/5/14.html.> [accessed 9 August 2012].

Hoff, C. and Beougher, S. (2010), 'Sexual Agreements Among Gay Male Couples', *Archives of Sexual Behavior*, 39, 774–87.

Holland, J., Ramazanoglu, C., Sharpe, S. and Thompson, R. (1994), 'Power and Desire: The Embodiment of Female Sexuality', *Feminist Review*, 46: 21–38.

Hollomotz, A. (2011), *Learning Difficulties and Sexual Vulnerability: A Social Approach*, London and Philadelphia, PA: Jessica Kingsley.

Hollomotz, A. and the Speakup Committee (2008), '"May We Please Have Sex Tonight" – People with Learning Difficulties Pursuing Privacy in Residential Group Settings', *British Journal of Learning Disabilities*, 37(2): 91–7.

Holt, M. (2004) '"Marriage-Like" or Married? Lesbian and Gay Marriage, Partnership and Migration', *Feminism and Psychology*, 14(1): 30–6.

Hook, J.N., Hook, J.P. and Hines, S. (2008), 'Reach Out or Act Out: Long-Term Group Therapy for Sexual Addiction', *Sexual Addiction and Compulsivity*, 15, 217–32.

hooks, b. (2000), *Feminist Theory: From Margin to Centre*, London: Pluto.

Hope, A. (2006), 'School Internet Use, Youth and Risk: A Socio-Cultural Study of the Relation between Staff Views of Online Dangers and Students' Ages in UK School', *British Educational Research Journal*, 32(2): 307–29.

Hope Ditmore, M. (2010), 'Conclusion: Pushing Boundaries in Sex Work Activism and Research' in M. Hope Ditmore, A. Levy and A. Willman (eds) *Sex Work Matters: Exploring Money, Power, and Intimacy in the Sex Industry*, London: Zed Books, 239–42.

Hopkins, P.E. (2010), *Young People, Place and Identity*, New York: Routledge.

Houses of the Oireachtas Joint Committee on Justice, Defence and Equality (2013), *Report on hearings and submissions of the Review of Legislation on Prostitution*, available from: <http://www.oireachtas. ie/parliament/mediazone/pressreleases/name-17366-en.html> [accessed 19 July 2013].

Howe, B. and Covell, K. (2005), *Empowering Children: Children's Rights as a Pathway to Citizenship*, Toronto, ON: University of Toronto Press.

Howes, M. (2002), 'Public Discourse, Private Reflection, 1916–70' in A. Bourke, S. Kilfeather, M. Luddy, M. MacCurtain, G. Meaney, M. Ní Dhonnchadha, M. O'Dowd and C. Wills (eds) *The Field Day Anthology of Irish Writing, Vol. IV: Irish Women's Writing and Traditions*, Cork: Cork University Press, 923–30.

HPSC (Health Protection Surveillance Centre) (2010), *Annual Report*, Dublin: Health Protection Surveillance Centre.

HPSC (Health Protection Surveillance Centre) (2011a), *Trends in Sexually Transmitted Infection (STI) Notifications, 1995–2009*, Dublin: Health Protection Surveillance Centre.

HPSC (Health Protection Surveillance Centre) (2011b), *Health Protection Surveillance Centre Annual Report 2010*, Dublin: Health Protection Surveillance Centre.

HSE (2012a), 'Ambiguous Genitalia', available from: <http:/www.hse.ie/eng/health/az/A/Ambiguous-genitalia/> [accessed 11 April 2012].

HSE (2012b), 'Androgen Insensitivity Syndrome', available from: <http://www.hse.ie/eng/health/az/A/Androgen-insensitivity-syndrome/> [accessed 11 April 2012].

HSE (2012c), 'Treating Androgen Insensitivity Syndrome', available from: <http://www.hse.ie/eng/health/az/A/Androgen-insensitivity-syndrome/Treating-androgen-insensitivity-syndrome.html> [accessed 11 April 2012].

HSE (2012d), 'Diagnosing Androgen Insensitivity Syndrome', available from: http://www.hse.ie/eng/health/az/A/Androgen-insensitivity-syndrome/Diagnosing-androgen-insensitivity-syndrome.html> [accessed 11 April 2012].

HSE (2012e), 'Turner Syndrome', available from: <http://www.hse.ie/eng/health/az/T/Turner-syndrome/> [accessed 11 April 2012].

HSE (2012f), 'Symptoms of Turner Syndrome', available from: <http://www.hse.ie/eng/health/az/T/Turner-syndrome/Symptoms-of-Turner-syndrome.html> [accessed 11 April 2012].

HSE (2012g), 'Diagnosing Turner Syndrome', available from: <http://www.hse.ie/eng/health/az/T/Turner-syndrome/Diagnosing-Turner-syndrome.html> [accessed 11 April 2012].

HSE Crisis Pregnancy Programme (2011), *Annual Report 2010*.

Hubbard, P. (2000), 'Desire/Disgust: Mapping the Moral Contours of Heterosexuality', *Progress in Human Geography*, 24(2): 191–217.

Hubbard, P. (2001), 'Sex Zones: Intimacy, Citizenship and Public Space', *Sexualities*, 4(1): 51–64.

Hug, C. (2001), 'Moral Order and the Liberal Agenda in the Republic of Ireland', *New Hibernia Review / Iris Éireannach Nua*, 5, 22–41.

Hug, C. (1999), *The Politics of Sexual Morality*, Basingstoke: Palgrave Macmillan.

Hughes, A.I., Houk, C., Ahmed, S.F., Lee, P.A., LWPES1/ESPE2 Consensus Group (2006), 'Consensus Statement on the Management of Intersex Disorders', *Archive of Disease in Childhood* [online] 91:554–63, PMC (PubMed Central), available from: <http://www.ncbi.nlm.nih.gov/pmc/articles/PMC2082839/pdf/554.pdf> [accessed 7 May 2012].

Hyde, A. and Howlett, E. (2004), *Understanding Teenage Sexuality in Ireland*, Dublin: Crisis Pregnancy Agency.

ICJ (International Commission of Jurists) (2007), *Yogyakarta Principles – Principles on the Application of International Human Rights Law in Relation to Sexual Orientation and Gender Identity*, available at: <http://www.refworld.org/docid/48244e602.html>.

IFPA (Irish Family Planning Association) (2007), *Sexuality & Disability*, available from: <http://www.ifpa.ie/Hot-Topics/Sexuality-Disability> [accessed 18 July 2012].

ILGA (International Lesbian and Gay Association) Europe (2011), *Rainbow Europe Map & Index 2011: Legal Situation of Lesbian, Gay, Bisexual & Trans People in Europe*, available from: <http://www.ilga-Europe.org/home/news/for media/media releases/rainbow Europe map index 2011 legal situation of lesbian gay bisexual trans people in Europe> [accessed 6 September 2012].

Inglis, T. (1997), 'Foucault, Bourdieu and the Field of Irish Sexuality', *Irish Journal of Sociology*, 7: 5–28.

Inglis, T. (2006), 'From Self-Denial to Self-Indulgence: The Clash of Cultures in Contemporary Ireland', *Irish Review*, 34, 34–43.

Inglis, T. (1998a), *Lessons in Irish Sexuality*, Dublin: University College Dublin Press.

Inglis, T. (1987/1998b), *Moral Monopoly: The Rise and Fall of the Catholic Church in Modern Ireland*, Dublin: University College Dublin Press.

Inglis, T. (2005), 'Origins and Legacies of Irish Prudery: Sexuality and Social Control in Modern Ireland', *Eire-Ireland*, 40 (3 and 4): 9–37.

Inglis, T. (2002a), 'Pleasure Pursuits', in M. Corcoran and M. Peillon (eds) *Ireland Unbound*, Dublin: Dublin Institute of Public Administration, 25–35.

Inglis, T. (2002b), 'Sexual Transgression and Scapegoats: A Case Study from Modern Ireland', *Sexualities*, 5, 5–24.

Insight Statistical Consulting (2007), *Public Attitudes to Disability in Ireland*, Dublin: National Disability Authority.

Irigaray, L. (1985), *This Sex Which Is Not One*, Ithaca, NY: Cornell.

Irish Branch of the Responsible Society, Family and Youth Concern (1992a), *Response*, 11(1), Dublin.

Irish Branch of the Responsible Society, Family and Youth Concern (1992b), *Response*, 11(4), Dublin.

Irish Branch of the Responsible Society, Family and Youth Concern (1994), *Response*, 13(4) Dublin.

Irish Branch of the Responsible Society, Family and Youth Concern (1995), *Response*, 14(1), Dublin.

Irish Council for Civil Liberties (2006), *Equality for all Families*, Dublin: ICCL.

Irish Educational Research (1995), *Education or Manipulation: What's Going on in Irish Schools Today? Part 1, A New Concept of Education*, Staffordshire: Trentmaker.

Irish National Teachers' Organisation (1993), 'INTO Support "Stay Safe"', *Tuarascáil*, 4: 3.

Irvine, J.M. (1995), 'Reinventing Perversion: Sex Addiction and Cultural Anxieties', *Journal of the History of Sexuality*, 5, 429–50.

ISNA – Intersex Society of North America (1993–2008), 'Our Mission', *ISNA.org*, available from: <http://www.isna.org>[accessed 13 November 2011].

Ivinson, G. (2007), 'Pedagogic Discourse and Sex Education; Myths, Science and Subversion', *Sex Education*, 7(2): 201–16.

Jackson, C. (2006), *Lads and Ladettes in School: Gender and a Fear of Failure*, Maidenhead: Open University Press.

Jackson, L. (2000), *Child Sexual Abuse in Victorian England*, London: Routledge.

Jackson, S. and Scott, S. (eds) (1996), *Feminism and Sexuality: A Reader*, Edinburgh: Edinburgh University Press.

Jackson, S. and Scott, S. (1996), 'Sexual Skirmishes and Feminist Factions: Twenty-Five Years of Debate on Women and Sexuality' in S. Jackson and S. Scott (eds) *Feminism and Sexuality: A Reader*, Edinburgh: Edinburgh University Press, 35–58.

Jackson, S. and Scott, S. (2010), *Theorizing Sexuality*, Maidenhead: Open University Press/McGraw Hill.

James, A. and Prout, A. (1998), 'Constructing and Reconstructing Childhood: Contemporary Issues in the Sociological Study of Childhood' in E. Renold (2005), *Girls, Boys and Junior Sexualities*, Oxford: Routledge Falmer.

References

Jeffreys, S. (1997), *The Idea of Prostitution*, Melbourne, VIC: Spinifex.

Jenkins, R. (1998), 'Culture, Classification and (In)Competence' in R. Jenkins (ed.) *Questions of Competence: Comparative Perspectives*, Cambridge: Cambridge University Press, 1–24.

Jensen, R. (1998), 'Introduction. Pornographic Dodges and Distortions' in G. Dines, R. Jensen and A. Russo (eds) *Pornography. The Production and Consumption of Inequality*, New York and London: Routledge, 1–8.

Johansson, T. and Hammaren, N. (2007), 'Hegemonic Masculinity and Pornography: Young People's Attitudes Toward and Relations to Pornography', *Journal of Men's Studies*, 15(1): 57–70.

Jordan-Young, R.M. (2011), *Brainstorm: Flaws in the Science of Sex Differences*, Cambridge, MA: Harvard University Press.

Jütte, R. (2008), *Contraception: A History*, Cambridge: Polity Press.

Kafer, A. (2000), 'Amputated Desire, Resistant Desire: Female Amputees in the Devotee Community', Paper presented to the Society for Disability Studies Conference, June, Chicago, available from: <http://mailman2.u.washington.edu/pipermail/amp-l/2001-April/ 006350.html> [accessed 1 May 2012].

Kafer, A. (2004), 'Inseparable Gender and Disability in the Amputee-Devotee Community' in B.G. Smith and B. Hutchison (eds) *Gendering Disability*, New Brunswick, NJ: Rutgers University Press, 107–14.

Kafka, M. (2010), 'Hypersexual Disorder: A Proposed Diagnosis for DSM-V', *Archives of Sexual Behavior*, 39, 377–400.

Kamikaze, I. (1995), '"I Used To Be An Activist, But I'm Alright Now"' in Í. O'Carroll and E. Collins (eds), *Lesbian and Gay Visions of Ireland: Towards the Twenty-First Century*, London: Cassell, 110–21.

Kaplan, M.S. and Krueger, R.B. (2010), 'Diagnosis, Assessment, and Treatment of Hypersexuality', *Journal of Sex Research*, 47, 181–98.

Karellou, J. (2003b), 'Development of the Greek Sexuality Attitudes Questionnaire–Learning Disabilities (GSAQ-LD)', *Sexuality and Disability*, 21(2): 113–35.

Karellou, J. (2003a), 'Laypeople's Attitudes Towards the Sexuality of People with Learning Disabilities in Greece', *Sexuality and Disability*, 21(1): 65–84.

Keane, H. (2004), 'Disorders of Desire: Addiction and Problems of Intimacy', *Journal of Medical Humanities*, 25, 189–204.

Keating, A. (2004), 'Church, State, and Sexual Crime against Children in Ireland after 1922', *Radharc*, 5/7, 155–80.

Kehily, M.J. (2001), 'Issues of Gender and Sexuality in School' in B. Francis and C. Skelton (eds) *Investigating Gender: Contemporary Perspectives in Education*, Buckingham: Open University Press, 116–25.

Kehily, M.J. (2002), *Sexuality, Gender and Schooling: Shifting Agendas in Social Learning*, London: Routledge Falmer.

Kelly, G., Crowley, H. and Hamilton, C. (2009), 'Rights, Sexuality and Relationships in Ireland: "It'd Be Nice to Be Kind of Trusted"', *British Journal of Learning Disabilities*, 37: 308–15.

Kennedy, P. (2004), *Motherhood in Ireland: Creation and Context*, Cork: Mercier Press.

Keogh, D. (1986), *The Vatican, the Bishops and Irish Politics, 1919–39*, Cambridge: Cambridge University Press.

Kesler, K. (2002), 'Is a Feminist Stance in Support of Prostitution Possible? An Exploration of Current Trends', *Sexualities*, 5(2): 219–35.

Kesler, K. (2005), 'The Voices of Sex Workers (Prositutes?) and the Dilemma of Feminist Discourse', MA thesis, University of South Florida, available from: <http://scholarcommons.usf.edu> [accessed 24 January 2012].

Kessler, S.J. (1998), *Lessons from the Intersexed*, London: Rutgers University Press.

Kiely, E. (2008), 'Relationships and Sexuality Education in the Irish Context: An Analysis of Policy and Programme Implementation' in P. Hermann (ed.) *Governance and Social Professions*, New York: Nova Science, 61–78.

Kiely, E. (2004), 'Sexing the Curriculum: A Poststructuralist Interrogation of the Politics of Irish Sexuality Education 1960–2002', PhD thesis, University College Cork.

Kiely, E. (2005), 'Where Is the Discourse of Desire? Deconstructing the Irish Relationships and Sexuality Education (RSE) Resource Materials', *Irish Educational Studies*, 24(2–3): 253–66.

Kiernan, K. (1992), 'School Sex Education in Ireland – Towards a Feminist Perspective', MPhil thesis, Trinity College Dublin.

Kimmel, M. (1994), 'Masculinity as Homophobia: Fear, Shame, and Silence in the Construction of Gender Identity' in H. Brod and M. Kaufman (eds) *Theorizing Masculinities*, Thousand Oaks, CA: Sage, 119–41.

King, A. (1993), 'Mystery and Imagination: The Case of Pornography Effects Studies' in A. Assiter and A. Carol (eds) *Bad Girls and Dirty Pictures: The Challenge to Reclaim Feminism*, London: Pluto Press, 18–40.

Kingston, D.A. and Firestone, P. (2008), 'Problematic Hypersexuality: A Review of Conceptualization and Diagnosis', *Sexual Addiction and Compulsivity*, 15, 284–310.

Kinlen, D. (2003), *Report of the Inspection of Mountjoy Prison and the Dochas Centre by the Inspector of Prisons and Places of Detention 2002–2003*, available at: <http://www.justice.ie/en/JELR/Mountjoy%20 Prison%20inspection%200203.pdf/Files/Mountjoy%20Prison%20 inspection%200203.pdf> [accessed 6 September 2012].

Kinsey, A., Pomeroy, W.B. and Martin, C.E. (1948), *Sexual Behaviour in the Human Male*, Philadelphia, PA and London: W.B. Saunders Company.

Kinsman, G. (1987), *The Regulation of Desire: Sexuality in Canada*, Montreal: Black Rose Books.

Kipnis, K. and Diamond, M. (1998) 'Pediatric Ethics and the Surgical Assignment of Sex' in A.D. Dreger (ed.) *Intersex in the Age of Ethics*, Hagerstown, MD: University Publishing Group, 173–94.

Kipnis, L. (2007), *The Female Thing: Dirt, Sex, Envy, Vulnerability*, London: Serpent's Tail.

Kirby, P. (1987), 'Skilful Offensive on Life-Skills', *Magill*, September: 35–8.

Kirkpatrick, B. (1990), *The Cassell Paperback English Dictionary*, London: Cassell Publishers Ltd.

Kitzinger, C. (2003), 'Heteronormativity in Action: Reproducing the Heterosexual Nuclear Family in After-Hours Medical Calls', *Social Problems*, 52(4): 477–98.

Kitzinger, C. and Wilkinson, S. (2004) 'The Re-Branding of Marriage: Why We Got Married Instead of Registering a Civil Partnership', *Feminism and Psychology*, 14(1): 127–50.

Kitzinger, C. and Wilkinson, S. (1995), 'Transitions from Heterosexuality to Lesbianism: The Discursive Production of Lesbian Identities', *Developmental Psychology*, 31(1): 95–104.

Klassen, A.D., Williams, C.J., Levitt, E.E. and O'Gorman, H.J. (1990), *Sex and Morality in the U.S.: An Empirical Enquiry under the Auspices of the Kinsey Institute*, Middleton, CT: Wesleyan University Press.

Klein, F., Sepekoff, B. and Wolf, T.J. (1985), 'Sexual Orientation: A Multi-Variable Dynamic Process', *Journal of Homosexuality*, 11(1–2): 35–49.

Klein, M. (2006), *America's War on Sex: The Attack on Law, Lust and Liberty*, Wesport, CT: Praeger.

Knowlton, C. (1832), *Fruits of Philosophy* (1891 San Francisco Readers' Library edition), C. Bradlaugh, and A. Besant (eds), 1(3), October, available at: <http://archive.org/stream/fruitsphilosoph00kno goog#page/n42/mode/2up> [accessed 4 October 2012].

Koken, J. (2010), 'The Meaning of the "Whore": How Feminist Theories on Prostitution Shape Research on Female Sex Workers' in M. Hope Ditmore, A. Levy and A. Willman (eds) *Sex Work Matters: Exploring*

Money, Power, and Intimacy in the Sex Industry, London: Zed Books, 28–64.

Koyama, E. (2008), 'Frequently Asked Questions about the "DSD" Controversy', *Intersex Initiative*, available from <http://www.ipdx.org/articles/dsdfaq.html> [accessed 12 April 2012].

Lamb, B. and Layzell, S. (1994), *Disabled in Britain: A World Apart*, London: SCOPE.

Lancaster, R.N. (2006), 'Sex, Science, and Pseudoscience in the Public Sphere', *Identities: Global Studies in Culture and Power*, 13: 101–38.

Latt, N., Conigrave, K., Marshall, E.J. and Nutt, D. (2009), *Addiction Medicine*, Oxford: Oxford University Press.

Law Reform Commission (2004), *Consultation Paper on the Rights and Duties of Cohabitees*, LRC-32-2004, Dublin: Law Reform Commission.

Law Reform Commission (2011), *Consultation Paper on Sexual Offences and Capacity to Consent*, LRC CP 63-2011, Dublin: Law Reform Commission.

Law Reform Commission (2005), *Consultation Paper on Vulnerable Adults and the Law: Capacity*, LRC- CP 37-2005, Dublin: Law Reform Commission.

Law Reform Commission (1990), *Report on Child Sexual Abuse*, LRC-32-1990, Dublin: Law Reform Commission.

Law Reform Commission (2010), *Report on Legal Aspects of Family Relationships*, LRC-101-2010, Dublin: Law Reform Commission.

Law Reform Commission (2006a), *Report on Vulnerable Adults and the Law*, LRC-83-2006, Dublin: Law Reform Commission.

Law Reform Commission (2006b), *The Rights and Duties of Cohabitants*, LRC-82-2006, Dublin: Law Reform Commission.

Lawless, K., Wayne, A., Murphy Lawless, J. and Lalor, T. (2005), *Ruhama, The Next Step Initiative, Research Report on Barriers Affecting Women in Prostitution*, Dublin: Ruhama.

Layte, D.R., McGee, P.H., Quail, A., Rundle, K., Cousins, G., Donnelly, D.C., Mulcahy, P.F. and Conroy, D.R. (2006), *The Irish Study of Sexual Health and Relationships*, Dublin: Crisis Pregnancy Agency and Department of Health and Children.

Leane, M. (1999), 'Female Sexuality in Ireland 1920–1940: Construction and Regulation', PhD thesis, University College Cork.

Leane, M., Duggan, H. and Chambers, P. (2002), 'Feminist Research Practice: Learning from Older Women', *Education and Ageing*, 17(1): 35–53.

Leathard, A. (1980), *The Fight for Family Planning. The Development of Family Planning Services in Britain 1921–74*, Basingstoke: Macmillan.

Lees, S. (1993), *Sugar and Spice: Sexuality and Adolescent Girls*, London: Penguin.

Lehrer, S. (1984), 'Modern Correlates of Freudian Psychology, Infant Sexuality and the Unconscious', *American Journal of Medicine*, 77, 977–80.

Lemish, D. (2011), '"Can't Talk About Sex": Producers of Children's Television Around the World Speak Out', *Sex Education*, 11(3): 267–77.

Lesseliers, J. and Van Hove, G. (2002), 'Barriers to the Development of Intimate Relationships and the Expression of Sexuality Among People with Developmental Disabilities: Their Perceptions', *Research and Practice for Persons with Severe Disabilities*, 27(1): 69–81.

LeVay, S. (1991), 'A Difference in Hypothalamic Structure between Heterosexual and Homosexual Men', *Science*, 253: 1034–7.

Levine, M. and Troiden, R. (1988), 'The Myth of Sexual Compulsivity', *Journal of Sex Research*, 25, 347–63.

Levine, S.B. (2010), 'What Is Sexual Addiction?', *Journal of Sex and Marital Therapy*, 36, 261–75.

Lévi-Strauss, C. (1996), 'Preface' to *A History of the Family*, Cambridge, MA: Belknap.

Levy, A. (2006), *Female Chauvinist Pigs: Women and the Rise of Raunch Culture*, New York: Pocket Books.

Lewin, E. (1995), 'On the Outside Looking In: The Politics of Lesbian Motherhood' in F.D. Ginsberg and R. Rapp (eds) *Conceiving the New World Order: The Politics of Global Reproduction*, Berkeley, CA: University of California Press, 103–21.

Ley, D. (2012), *The Myth of Sex Addiction*, Lanham, MA: Rowman and Littlefield.

LGBT Diversity (2011), 'NW Pride's "Full Spectrum" Project Starts This Coming Sunday', posted by Hayley Fox Roberts, available from: <http://www.lgbtdiversity.com/region-blog-post.aspx?contentid=35&blogid=461> [accessed 12 November 2011].

Linneman, T. (2008), 'How Do You Solve a Problem Like Will Truman? The Feminization of Gay Masculinities on *Will & Grace*', *Men and Masculinities*, 10(5): 583–603.

Lister, R. (1997), *Citizenship: Feminist Perspectives*, London: Macmillan.

Lo, V. and Wei, R. (2005), 'Exposure to Internet Pornography and Taiwanese Adolescents' Sexual Attitudes and Behavior', *Journal of Broadcasting and Electronic Media*, 49(2): 221–37.

Lodge, A. (2005), 'Gender and Children's Social World: Esteemed and Marginalised Masculinities in the Primary School Playground', *Irish Journal of Sociology*, 14(2): 177–92.

Luddy, M. (2007b), *Prostitution and Irish Society, 1800–1940*, Cambridge: Cambridge University Press.

Luddy, M. (2007a), 'Sex and the Single Girl in 1920s and 1930s Ireland', *Irish Review*, 35: 79–91.

Lyder, H. (2003), 'Silence and Secrecy: Exploring Female Sexuality During Childhood in 1930s and 1940s Dublin', *Irish Journal of Feminist Studies*, 5 (1 and 2): 77–88.

Lydon, W. (1998), *The Making of Ireland: From Ancient Times to the Present*, London: Routledge.

Lynch, K. (2000), 'Emancipatory Research in the Academy' in A. Byrne and R. Lentin (eds) *(Re)searching Women: Feminist Research Methodologies in the Social Sciences in Ireland*, Dublin: Institute of Public Administration, 73–104.

Lynch, K. (1999), *Equality in Education*, Dublin: Gill and Macmillan.

Lynch, K. (2001), 'Equality in Education', *Studies: An Irish Quarterly Review*, 90(360): 395–411.

Lynch, K. and Lodge, A. (2002), *Equality in Power in Schools, Redistribution, Recognition and Representation*, London: Routledge Falmer.

Lynch, P. (2009), 'What Ever Happened to Ireland's Sexual Health Strategy?' *Irish Medical News*.

Mac an Ghaill, M. (1994a), '(In)visibility: Sexuality, Race and Masculinity in the School Context' in D. Epstein (ed.) *Challenging Gay and Lesbian Inequalities in Education*, Buckingham: University Press, 152–76.

Mac an Ghaill, M. (1994b), *The Making of Men: Masculinities, Sexualities and Schooling*, Buckingham: Open University Press.

Mac an Ghaill, M. and Haywood, C. (2012), 'The Queer in Masculinity: Schooling, Boys, and Identity Formation' in J.C. Landreau and N.M. Rodriguez (eds) *Queer Masculinities: A Critical Reader in Education* 1(21): 69–84.

Mac Greil, M. (1978), *Prejudice and Tolerance in Ireland: Based on a Survey of Intergroup Attitudes of Dublin Adults and Other Sources*, Maynooth: Survey Research Unit, St Patrick's College, Maynooth.

Madden, L, and Levine, J. (1987), *Lyn: A Story of Prostitution*, Dublin: Attic Press.

Malamuth, N.M., Haber, S. and Feshbach, S. (1980), 'Testing Hypotheses Regarding Rape: Exposure to Sexual Violence, Sex Differences and the "Normality" of Rapists', *Journal of Research in Personality*, 14, 121–37.

Mallon, G.P. (2004), *Gay Men Choosing Parenthood*, New York: Columbia University Press.

Manley, G. and Koehler, J. (2001), 'Sexual Behavior Disorders: Proposed New Classification in the DSM-V', *Sexual Addiction and Compulsivity*, 8, 253–65.

Manly, D. (1986), 'Part 1' in D. Manly, L. Browne, K. Cox, N. Lowry, *The Facilitators*, Dublin: Brandsma Books.

Marshall, C. and Rossman, G. (2006), *Designing Qualitative Research* (4th edn), London: Sage.

Marshall, J. (1980), 'The Politics of Tea and Sympathy' in Gay Left Collective (eds) *Homosexuality: Power and Politics*, London: Allison and Busby, 77–84.

Marshall, W.L., Seidman, B.T. and Barbaree, H.E. (1991), 'The Effects of Prior Exposure to Erotic and Nonerotic Stimuli on the Rape Index', *Annals of Sex Research*, 4, 209–20.

Martin, J.I. and Knox, J. (2000), 'Methodological and Ethical Issues in Research on Lesbians and Gay Men', *Social Work Research*, 24(1): 51–9.

Martino, W. and Pallotta-Chiarolli, M. (2005), *Being Normal Is the Only Way to Be: Adolescent Perspectives on Gender and School*, Sydney, NSW: University of New South Wales Press.

Martino, W. (1999), '"Cool Boys", "Party Animals", "Squids" and "Poofters": Interrogating the Dynamics and Politics of Adolescent Masculinities in School', *British Journal of Sociology*, 20(2): 239–63.

Mason, J. (1996), *Qualitative Researching*, London: Sage.

Mayo, C. (2004), *Disputing the Subject of Sex, Sexuality and Public School Controversies*, Lanham: Rowman and Littlefield.

Mayock, P., Bryan, A., Carr, N. and Kitching, K. (2009), *Supporting LGBT Lives: A Study of the Mental Health and Well-Being of Lesbian, Gay, Bisexual and Transgender People*, Dublin: GLEN and BeLonG To Youth Service.

Mayock, P. and Byrne, T. (2004), *A Study of Sexual Health Issues, Attitudes and Behaviours: The Views of Early School Leavers*, Dublin: Crisis Pregnancy Agency.

Mayock, P., Kitching, K. and Morgan, M. (2007), *RSE in the Context of SPHE: An Assessment of the Challenges to Full Implementation of the Programme in Post-Primary Schools*, Dublin: Crisis Pregnancy Agency.

McAvoy, S. (1999), 'The Regulation of Sexuality in the Irish Free State, 1929-35' in G. Jones and E. Malcolm (eds) *Medicine, Disease and the State in Ireland 1650 –1940*, Cork: Cork University Press, 253–66.

McBride, O., Morgan, K. and McGee, H. (2012) *Irish Contraception and Crisis Pregnancy Study 2010 (ICCP – 2010), A Survey of the General Population, Crisis Pregnancy Programme Report No. 24*, Dublin: HSE and the Crisis Pregnancy Programme.

McCafferty, N. (1975), 'In the Eyes of the Law: Two Consenting Adults Learn that it's an Offence Over Here', *Irish Times*, 12 September, 13.

McCafferty, N. (1987), *In the Eyes of the Law*, Dublin: Poolbeg Press.

McCarroll, J. (1987), *Is the School Around the Corner Just the Same?*, Dublin: Brandsma Books.

McGee, H., Garavan, R., de Barra, M., Byrne, J. and Conroy, R. (2002), *The SAVI Report: Sexual Abuse and Violence in Ireland*, Dublin: Dublin Rape Crisis Centre.

McGreevy, R. (2012), 'Department Inquiry into Exclusion of Pregnant Girl', *Irish Times*, 1 May, available from: <http://www.irish times.com/newspaper/ireland/2012/.../1224315408434.htm...> [accessed 10 July 2012].

McIlroy, C. (2009), *Transphobia in Ireland*, Dublin: TENI.

McIlroy, L. (1923), 'The Harmful Effects of Artificial Contraceptive Methods', *The Practitioner*, July, 25–35.

McIntyre, B. (2011), 'Working it Out', *Gay Community News*, 30–31 December.

McLaren, A. (1999) *Twentieth-Century Sexuality: A History*, Oxford: Blackwell.

McLaughlin, J. (1997), 'Feminist Relations with Postmodernism: Reflections on the Positive Aspects of Involvement', *Journal of Gender Studies*, 6(1), 5–15.

McLoughlin, M.T. (1996), 'Crystal or Glass?: A Review of Dudgeon v. United Kingdom on the Fifteenth Anniversary of the Decision', *Murdock University Electronic Journal of Law*, 3(4), available from: <http://www.murdoch.edu.au/elaw/issues/v3n4/mclough.html> [accessed 10 December 2012].

McNair, B. (2002), *Striptease Culture: Sex, Media and the Democratisation of Desire*, Harvard: Harvard University Press.

McNutt, H. (2004), 'Hidden Pleasures', *The Guardian*, 13 October, available from: <http://www.guardian.co.uk/society/2004/oct/13/disability.socialcare> [accessed 1 May 2012].

McPhail, B.A. (2004), 'Questioning Gender and Sexuality Binaries: What Queer Theorists, Transgendered Individuals, and Sex Researchers can Teach Social Work', *Journal of Gay and Lesbian Social Services*, 17(1): 3–21.

McRobbie, A. (2004), 'Postfeminism and Popular Culture', *Feminist Media Studies*, 4(3): 255–64.

Meah, A., Hockey, J. and Robinson, V. (2008), 'What's Sex Got To Do With It? A Family-based Investigation of Growing Up Heterosexual During the Twentieth Century', *Sociological Review*, 56(3): 454–73.

Mee, J. (2007), 'Cohabitation, Civil Partnership and the Constitution' in O. Doyle and W. Binchy (eds) Committed Relationships and the Law, Dublin: Four Courts Press, 181–214.

Meeks, C. (2006), 'Gay and Straight Rites of Passage' in S. Seidman, N. Fisher and C. Meeks (eds) Introducing the New Sexuality Studies: Original Essays and Interviews, London: Routledge.

Miller, B.L., Cummings, J.L., McIntyre, H., Ebers, G. and Grode, M. (1986), 'Hypersexuality or Altered Sexual Preference Following Brain Injury', Journal of Neurology, Neurosurgery and Psychiatry, 49, 867–73.

Mills, S. (2003), Michel Foucault, London: Routledge.

Ministry of Justice and the Police of Norway (2004), Purchasing Sexual Services in Sweden and the Netherlands: Legal Regulation and Experiences, available from: <http://www.regjeringen.no/upload/kilde/jd/rap/2004/0034/ddd/pdfv/232216-purchasing_sexual_services_in_sweden_and_the_nederlands.pdf > [accessed 7 December 2011].

Mitchell, K.J., Finkelhor, D. and Wolak, J. (2003), 'The Exposure of Youth to Unwanted Sexual Material on the Internet: A National Survey of Risk, Impact and Prevention', Youth and Society, 34(3): 330–58.

Moane, G. (1996), 'Legacies of Colonialism for Irish Women', Irish Journal of Feminist Studies, 1(1): 100–18.

Moane, G. (1997), 'Lesbian Politics and Community' in A. Byrne and M. Leonard (eds) Women and Irish Society: A Sociological Reader, Belfast: Beyond the Pale Publications, 431–46.

Moane, G. (1995), 'Living Visions' in Í. O'Carroll and E. Collins (eds) Lesbian and Gay Visions of Ireland: Towards the Twenty-First Century, London: Cassell, 86–98.

Money, J. (2002), A First Person History of Pediatric Psychoendocrinology, New York: Kluwer Academic/Plenum Publishers.

Money, J. (1965a), 'Psychosocial Differentiation' in J. Money (ed.) Sex Research: New Developments, New York: Holt, Rinehart and Winston, 3–23.

Money, J. (1965b), Sex Research: New Developments, New York: Holt, Rinehart and Winston.

Money, J. and Ehrhardt, A. (1972), Man & Woman, Boy & Girl, Baltimore: Johns Hopkins University Press, Baltimore.

Money, J., Hampson, J.G. and Hampson, J.L. (1955), 'Hermaphroditism: Recommendations Concerning Assignment of Sex, Change of Sex, and Psychologic Management', Bulletin Johns Hopkins University Hospital, 97: 284–300.

Money, J., Hampson, J.G. and Hampson, J.L. (1957), 'Imprinting and the Establishment of Gender Role', *American Medical Association Archives of Neurology and Psychiatry*, 77: 333–6.

Money, J., Hampson, J.G. and Hampson, J.L. (1956), 'Sexual Incongruities and Psychopathology: The Evidence of Human Hermaphroditism', *Bulletin Johns Hopkins University Hospital*, 98: 43–57.

Moraga, C. (1994), 'From a Long Line of Vendidas: Chicanas and Feminism' in A.C. Hermann and A.J. Stewart (eds) *Theorising Feminism: Parallel Trends in the Humanities and Social Sciences*, Boulder, CO: Westview, 34–48.

Morales, G.E., Lopez, E.O. and Mullet, E. (2011), 'Acceptability of Sexual Relationships Among People with Learning Disabilities: Family and Professional Caregivers' Views in Mexico', *Sexuality and Disability*, 29: 165–74.

Morales, G.E., Lopez Ramirez, E.O., Esterle, M., Munoz Sastre, M.T. and Mullet, E. (2010), 'Judging the Acceptability of Sexual Intercourse Among People with Learning Disabilities: A Mexico-France Comparison', *Sexuality and Disability*, 28: 81–91.

Morgan, D.H.J. (1996), *Family Connections: An Introduction to Family Studies*, Cambridge: Polity Press.

Morgan, M. (2000), *Relationships and Sexuality Education: An Evaluation and Review of Implementation*, Dublin: Stationery Office.

Morgan, P. (2002), *Children as Trophies: Examining the Evidence on Same-Sex Parenting*, Newcastle-Upon-Tyne: Christian Institute.

Morris, J. (1989), *Able Lives: Women's Experiences of Paralysis*, London: Women's Press.

Morris, J. (1991), *Pride Against Prejudice: Transforming Attitudes to Disability*, London: Women's Press.

Moya, P.M.L. and Hames-Garcia, M.R. (2000), *Reclaiming Identity: Realist Theory and the Predicament of Postmodernism*, Berkeley, CA: University of California Press, available from: <http://clogic.eserver.org/3-1&2/moya.html> [accessed 4 August 2010].

Murphy, E. (2012), *Dec-S2012-004-Full Case Report*, available from: <http://www.equalitytribunal.ie/Database-of-Decisions/2012/Equal-Status-Decisions/DEC-S2012-004-Full-Case-Report.html> [accessed 20 July 2012].

Murray, D. (1987), 'Education in Love' in D. O'Mahony (ed.), *A Teacher's Guide to Resource Material on Relationships/Sex Education*, Dublin: Veritas.

Murray, J.L. and Minnes, P.M. (1994), 'Staff Attitudes Toward the Sexuality of Persons with Intellectual Disability', *Australian and New Zealand Journal of Developmental Disabilities*, 19: 45–52.

NAMHI (National Association for the Mentally Handicapped of Ireland) (2003), *Who Decides and How? People with Intellectual Disabilities – Legal Capacity and Decision Making*, Dublin: NAMHI (Inclusion Ireland).

Narayan, U. (2004), 'The Project of Feminist Epistemology: Perspectives from a Non-Western Feminist' in S. Harding (ed.) *The Feminist Standpoint Theory Reader: Intellectual and Political Controversies*, New York: Routledge, 213–24.

Nast, H.J. (1998), 'Unsexy Geographies', *Gender, Place and Culture*, 5, 191–206.

Nathan, S. (1995), 'Sexual Addiction: A Sex Therapist's Struggle with an Unfamiliar Clinical Entity' in R. Rosen and S. Lieblum (eds) *Case Studies in Sex Therapy*, New York: Guilford Press.

National AIDS Strategy Committee (2008), *HIV and AIDS Prevention Plan 2008–2012 Mid Term Review*, available from: <http://www.drugsandalcohol.ie/15513/1/HIV_AIDS_education_and_prevention_plan_08-12.pdf> [accessed 14 May 2012].

National Board of Health and Welfare of Sweden/Socialstyrelsen (2008), *Prostitution in Sweden 2007*, available from: <http://www.socialstyrelsen.se/Lists/Artikelkatalog/Attachments/8806/2008-126-65_200812665.pdf> [accessed 14 May 2012).

Nayak, A. and Kehily, M.J. (1997), '"Lads and Laughter": Humour and the Production of Heterosexual Hierarchies', *Gender and Education*, 9(1): 69–87.

Nayak, A. and Kehily, M.J. (1996), 'Playing It Straight: Masculinities, Homophobias and Schooling', *Journal of Gender Studies*, 5(2): 211–30.

Neary, A. (2012), 'Lesbian and Gay Teachers' Experiences of "Coming Out" in Irish Schools', *British Journal of Sociology of Education*, iFirst article, 1–20, available from: <http://www.tandfonline.com/doi/abs/10.1080/01425692.2012.722281> [accessed 21 January 2013].

Neill, M. (undated), *Recollections of the Parish of Drumbeg, Diocese of Down*, available from: <http://lisburn.com/books/drumbeg/drumbeg2.html> [accessed 27 July 2012].

Nelson, C.D. (2009), *Sexual Identities in English Language Education: Classroom Conversations*, New York: Routledge.

Nelson, R.J. (2000), *An Introduction to Behavioral Endocrinology* (2nd edn), Sunderland, MA: Sinauer Associates.

NESF (National Economic and Social Forum) (2003) 'Equality Policies for Lesbian, Gay and Bisexual People: Implementation Issues', Dublin: NESF.

Nicholson, L. (1997), 'The Myth of the Traditional Family' in H.L. Nelson (ed.) *Feminism and Families*, New York: Routledge, 27–42.

Nicholson, L.J. (1990), *Feminism/Postmodernism*, London: Routledge.

Ní Mhuirthile, T. (2008), 'Declaring Irish Law Incompatible with the Law of the ECHR – Where to Now?', *Independent Law Review*, 4(1): 2–8.

NLGF (National Lesbian and Gay Federation) (2009) 'Civil Partnership Option Flawed', press release, 3 December, Dublin: NLGF.

Norman, J. and Galvin, M. (2006), *Straight Talk: An Investigation of Attitudes and Experiences of Homophobic Bullying in Second Level Schools*, Dublin: Dublin City University.

Norman, J., Galvin, M. and McNamara, G. (2006), *Straight Talk: Researching Gay and Lesbian Issues in the School Curriculum*, Dublin: Centre for Educational Evaluation, School of Education Studies, Dublin City University.

Norris, D. (1977), 'Homosexual Law Reform in Ireland – A Progress Report', *Dublin University Law Journal*, 2: 27–36.

Nussbaum, M.C. (1997), 'Commentary on Parts III and IV' in D.M. Estlund and M.C. Nussbaum (eds) *Sex, Preference and Family: Essays on Law and Nature*, New York: Oxford University Press, 319–38.

Nussbaum, M.C. (1999), *Sex and Social Justice*, Oxford: Oxford University Press.

O'Brien, C. (2010), 'Two-Thirds Support Gay Marriage, Poll Finds', *Irish Times*, 15 September.

O'Carroll, I. and Szalacha, L. (2000), *A Queer Quandary: The Challenges of Including Sexual Difference Within the Relationships and Sexuality Education Programme*, Dublin: LOT / LEA.

O'Carroll, J.P. (2002), 'Culture Lag and Democratic Deficit in Ireland: Or Dat's Outside de Terms of d'Agreement', *Community Development Journal*, 37(1): 10–19.

Ó Cinnéide, C. (2005), *Equivalence in Promoting Equality*, Dublin/Belfast: Equality Authority/Equality Commission for Northern Ireland.

O'Connor, P. (1998), *Emerging Voices: Women in Contemporary Ireland*, Dublin: Institute of Public Administration.

O'Connor, P. (2008), *Irish Children and Teenagers in a Changing World: The National Write Now Project*, Manchester: Manchester University Press.

O'Connor, P. (2009), 'Irish Young People's Narratives: The Existence of Gender Differentiated Cultures?', *Irish Journal of Sociology*, 17(9): 95–114.

O'Connor, W. (1995), 'Prelude to a Vision: The Impact of AIDS on the Political Legitimacy and Political Mobilization of Gay Men in Ireland' in I. O'Carroll and E. Collins (eds) *Lesbian and Gay Visions of Ireland: Towards the Twenty-First Century*, London: Cassell, 183–96.

O'Donnell, P. (2002), 'Regulating "Problem People": Discourse in Disability', Public Lecture Series, Equality Studies Centre, Dublin, University College Dublin.

O'Flaherty, M. and Fisher, J. (2008), 'Sexual Orientation, Gender Identity and International Human Rights Law: Contextualising the Yogyakarta Principles', *Human Rights Law Review*, 8(2): 207–48.

Ó Gráda, C. and Duffy, N. (1995), 'The Fertility Transition in Ireland and Scotland c.1880–1930' in S.J. Connolly, R.A. Houston and R.J. Morris (eds), *Conflict, Identity and Economic Development: Ireland and Scotland, 1600–1939*, Preston: Carnegie Publishing, 89–102.

O'Hea, J. (1949), *Sex and Innocence: A Handbook for Parents and Educators*, Cork: Mercier Press.

O'Higgins Norman, J., Goldrick, M. and Harrison, K. (2010), *Addressing Homophobic Bullying in Second-Level Schools*, Dublin: Equality Authority.

O'Leary, B. (2008), '"We Cannot Claim Any Particular Knowledge of Homosexuals, Still Less of Iranian Homosexuals..." The Particular Problems Facing Those Who Seek Asylum on the Basis of Their Sexual Identity', *Feminist Legal Studies*, 16: 87–95.

O'Mahony, C. (2012), 'Constitution Is Not an Obstacle to Legalising Gay Marriage', *Irish Times*, 16 July, available from: <http://www.irishtimes.com/newspaper/opinion/2012/0716/1224320203659.html> [accessed 18 July 2012].

O'Mahony, C. (2010), 'Societal Change and Constitutional Interpretation', *Irish Journal of Legal Studies*, 1(2): 71–115.

O'Mahony, D. (1987), *A Teacher's Guide to Resource Material on Relationships / Sex Education*, Dublin: Veritas.

O'Neill, B., Grehan, S., and Olafsson, K. (2011), *Risks and Safety for Children on the Internet: The Ireland Report. Initial Findings from the EU Kids Online Survey of 9–16 Year Olds and Their Parents*, London School of Economics and Political Science, available from: <http://www2.lse.ac.uk/media@lse/research/EUKidsOnline/EU%20Kids%20Online%20reports.aspx> [accessed 3 October 2011].

O'Neill, M. (1997), 'Prostitute Women Now' in G. Scambler and A. Scambler (eds) *Rethinking Prostitution: Purchasing Sex in the 1990s*, Abingdon: Routledge, 3–28.

O'Reilly, E. (1992), *Masterminds of the Right*, Dublin: Attic Press.

O'Shea, M. (2007), *The Don't Panic Guide to Sexual Health*, Dublin: Dublin AIDS Alliance.

O'Toole, C. (2002), 'Sex, Disability and Motherhood: Access to Sexuality for Disabled Mothers', *Disability Studies Quarterly*, 22(4): 87–108.

Office of the Ombudsman (2011), *Annual Report 2010*, Dublin: Government of Ireland.

Okin, S.M. (1997), 'Families and Feminist Theory: Some Past and Present Issues' in H.L. Nelson (ed.), *Feminism and Families*, New York: Routledge, 13–26.

Okin, S.M. (1998), 'Gender, the Public and the Private' in A. Phillips (ed.) *Feminism and Politics*, Oxford Readings in Feminism series, Oxford: Oxford University Press, 67–90.

Okin, S.M. (1989), *Justice, Gender, and the Family*, New York: Basic Books.

Oliver, M.G. (1996), 'Defining Impairment and Disability: Issues at Stake' in C. Barnes and G. Mercer (eds) *Exploring the Divide: Illness and Disability*, Leeds: Disability Press, 39–54.

Oliver, M.N., Anthony, A., Leimkuhl, T.T. and Skillman, G.D. (2002), 'Attitudes Toward Acceptable Socio-Sexual Behaviours for Persons with Mental Retardation: Implications for Normalization and Community Integration', *Education and Training in Mental Retardation and Developmental Disabilities*, 37(2): 193–201.

Ombudsman for Children (2010), *Advice of the Ombudsman for Children on the Civil Partnership Bill July 2010*, available from: <http://www.oco.ie/publications/advice-to-government.html> [accessed 18 February 2011].

Orford, J. (1978), 'Hypersexuality: Implications for a Theory of Dependence', *British Journal of Addiction (to Alcohol and Other Drugs)*, 73, 299–310.

Overall, C. (1992), 'What's Wrong With Prostitution? Evaluating Sex Work', *Signs*, 17(4): 705–24.

Owen, F., Griffiths, D., Tarulli, D. and Murphy, J. (2009), 'Historical and Theoretical Foundations of the Rights of Persons with Intellectual Disabilities: Setting the Stage' in F. Owen and D. Griffiths (eds), *Challenges to the Human Rights of People with Intellectual Disabilities*, London and Philadelphia, PA: Jessica Kingsley, 23–42.

Owens, T. (2009), 'Helping Disabled People Meet Their Emotional and Sexual Needs', *Filament Magazine*, available from: <http://www.filamentmagazine.com/2011/09/helping-disabled-people-meet-their-emotional-and-sexual-needs/> [accessed 1 May 2012].

Packard, J. (2008), '"I'm Gonna Show You What It's Really Like Out Here": The Power and Limitations of Participatory Visual Methods', *Visual Studies*, 23(1): 63–77.

Papadopoulos, L. (2010), *Sexualisation of Young People Review*, London: Home Office, available from: <http://www.wrc.org.uk/includes/documents/cm_docs/2010/s/sexualisationyoungpeople.pdf> [accessed 30 July 2012].

Parsons, J., Kelly, B., Bimbi, D., Dimaria, L., Wainberg, M. and Morgenstern, J. (2008), 'Explanations for the Origins of Sexual Compulsivity Among Gay and Bisexual Men', *Archives of Sexual Behavior*, 37, 817–26.

Pasterski, V., Prentice, P. and Hughes, I.A. (2010b), 'Consequences of the Chicago Consensus on Disorders of Sex Development (DSD): Current Practices in Europe', *Archives of Disease in Childhood*, 95: 618–23.

Pasterski, V., Prentice, P. and Hughes, I.A. (2010a), 'Impact of the Consensus Statement and the New DSD Classification System', *Best Practice and Research Clinical Endocrinology and Metabolism*, 24: 187–95.

Pateman, C. (1999) 'What's Wrong with Prostitution?', *Women's Studies Quarterly*, 27(1/2): 53–64.

Patterson, C.J. (2000), 'Family Relationships of Lesbians and Gay Men', *Journal of Marriage and Family*, 62(4): 1052–70.

Patterson, C.J. (2009), 'Lesbian and Gay Parents and their Children: A Social Science Perspective' in D.A. Hope (ed.) *Contemporary Perspectives on Lesbian, Gay and Bisexual Identities*, New York: Springer 141–82.

Patterson, C.J. and Redding, R.E. (1996), 'Lesbian and Gay Families with Children: Implications of Social Science Research for Policy', *Journal of Social Issues*, 52(3): 29–50.

Paul, P. (2005), *Pornified: How Pornography Is Damaging Our Lives, Our Relationships, and Our Families*, New York: Holt.

Paul VI, Pope (1983), *Humanae Vitae: Encyclical Letter of His Holiness Pope Paul VI on the Regulation of Births*, San Francisco, CA: Ignatius Press.

Peplau, L.A. and Garnets, L.D. (2000), 'A New Paradigm for Understanding Women's Sexuality and Sexual Orientation', *Journal of Social Issues*, 56(2): 329–50.

Peters, M. (1998), *Naming the Multiple: Poststructuralism and Education*, Westport, CT: Bergin and Garvey.

Peters, M. (1996), *Poststructuralism, Politics and Education*, Westport, CT and London: Bergin and Garvey.

Peterson, L.M., Butts, J. and Deville, D.M. (2000), 'Parenting Experiences of Three Self-Identified Gay Fathers', *Smith College Studies in Social Work*, 70(3): 513–21.

Phillips, A. (1991), 'Citizenship and Feminist Theory' in G. Andrews (ed.) *Citizenship*, London: Lawrence and Wishart, 76–88.

Phoenix, A. and Frosh, S. (2001), 'Positioned by "Hegemonic" Masculinities: A Study of London Boys' Narratives of Identity', *Australian Psychologist*, 36(1): 27–35.

Place, F. (1822), *Illustrations and Proofs of the Principles of Population*, London: Longman, Hurst, Rees, Orme and Brown, available from: <http://www.archive.org/stream/illustrationspro00plac#page/n3/mode/2up> [accessed 18 November 2011].

Plummer, K. (2003), *Intimate Citizenship: Private Decisions and Public Dialogues*, Washington, DC: University of Washington Press.

Plummer, K. (2001), 'The Square of Intimate Citizenship: Some Preliminary Proposals', *Citizenship Studies*, 5 (3): 237–53.

Plummer, K. (1995), *Telling Sexual Stories: Power, Change and Social Worlds*, London: Routledge.

Polikoff, N.D. (1987), 'Lesbians Choosing Children: The Personal Is Political Revisited' in S. Pollack and J. Vaughan (eds) *Politics of the Heart: A Lesbian Parenting Anthology*, New York: Firebrand Books, 49–54.

Pope, C. (nd), 'Lost Liturgies File: The Churching of Women', available from: <http://blog.adw.org/2010/02/lost-liturgies-file-the-churching-of-women/ and http://irishfamilyhistory.ie/blog/?p=218> [accessed 9 August 2012].

Powell, A. (2010), *Sex, Power and Consent, Youth Culture and the Unwritten Rules*, Melbourne, VIC: Cambridge University Press.

Preves, S.E. (2003), *Intersex and Identity: The Contested Self*, London: Rutgers University Press.

Priestley, M. (2003), *Disability: A Life Course Approach*, Cambridge: Polity Press.

QE5 (2005), *Disability and Sexual Orientation Report*, Dublin: National Disability Authority.

Quinlan, C. (2001), '"Dark and Obscure to the Average Wife": Marie Stopes, Anna and Thomas Haslam, and the Birth Control Question' in C. Murphy, 'Women and Ireland: A Historical Perspective'

(Special Issue), *Women's Studies: An Interdisciplinary Journal*, 30 (6): 779–96.

Quinlan, C. (2002), *Genteel Revolutionaries: Anna and Thomas Haslam and the Irish Women's Movement*, Cork: Cork University Press.

Radcliffe-Brown, A.R. (1952), *Structure and Function in Primitive Society*, Glencoe, IL: Free Press.

Radicalesbians (1970), 'The Woman-Identified Woman', available from: <http://scriptorium.lib.duke.edu/wlm/womid> [accessed 17 January 2012].

Raftery, M. and O'Sullivan, E. (1999), *Suffer the Little Children: The Inside Story of Ireland's Industrial Schools*, Dublin: New Island Books.

Raftery, M. and O'Sullivan, E. (2002), *Suffer the Little Children: The Inside Story of Ireland's Industrial Schools*, New York: Continuum.

Ramrakha, S., Caspi, A., Dickson, N., Moffitt, T.E. and Paul, C. (2000), 'Psychiatric Disorders and Risky Sexual Behaviour in Young Adulthood: Cross-Sectional Study in Birth Cohort', *British Medical Journal*, 321, 263–6.

Rasmussen, M.L. (2012), 'Pleasure/Desire, Sexularism and Sexuality Education', *Sex Education*, 12(4): 469–81.

Ratzka, A. (1998), *Sexuality and People with Disabilities: What Experts Often Are Not Aware Of*, available from: <http://www.independentliving.org/docs5/sexuality.html> [accessed 4 May 2012].

Raymond, N., Grant, J. and Coleman, E. (2010), 'Augmentation with Naltrexone to Treat Compulsive Sexual Behavior: A Case Series', *Annals of Clinical Psychiatry*, 22, 56–62.

Raymond, N.C., Coleman, E. and Miner, M.H. (2003), 'Psychiatric Comorbidity and Compulsive/Impulsive Traits in Compulsive Sexual Behavior', *Comprehensive Psychiatry*, 44, 370–80.

RCNI (Rape Crisis Network Ireland) (2005), *National Rape Crisis Statistics 2004*, Dublin: Rape Crisis Network Ireland.

RCPI (Royal College of Physicians of Ireland) (2011), *Submission of the RCPI Policy Group on Sexual Health to 'Your Health Is Your Wealth: A Policy Framework for a Healthier Ireland 2012–2020'*, Dublin: Royal College of Physicians of Ireland.

Reay, B., Attwood, N. and Gooder, C. (2012), 'Inventing Sex: The Short History of Sex Addiction', *Sexuality and Culture*, 16, 1–19.

Redmond, B. (1996), *Listening to Parents: The Aspirations, Expectations and Anxieties of Parents about their Teenager with Learning Disability*, Dublin: University College Dublin.

Reid, R.C. (2010), 'Differentiating Emotions in a Sample of Men in Treatment for Hypersexual Behavior', *Journal of Social Work Practice in the Addictions*, 10, 197–213.

Reis, E. (2007), 'Divergence or Disorder?: The Politics of Naming Inter-sex', *Perspectives in Biology and Medicine*, 50(4): 535–43, available from: <http://aissg.org/PDFs/Reis-Divergence-Disorder-2007.PDF> [accessed 9 April 2012].

Rekart, M.L. (2005), 'Sex-Work Harm Reduction', *Lancet*, 366(9503): 2123–34.

Renold, E. (2005), *Girls, Boys and Junior Sexualities*, Oxford: Routledge Falmer.

Reynolds, P. (2003), *Sex in the City: The Prostitution Racket in Ireland*, London: Pan Books.

Reynolds, S. (2007), 'Changing Marriage? Messing with Mr. In-Between? Reflections Upon Media Debates on Same-Sex Marriage in Ireland', *Sociological Research Online*, 12(1), available from: <http://www.socresonline.org.uk/12/1/reynolds.html> [accessed 15 February 2012].

Rich, A. (1980a), 'Compulsory Heterosexuality and Lesbian Existence', *Signs*, 5(4): 631–60.

Rich, A. (1980b), 'Compulsory Heterosexuality and Lesbian Exist-ence' in C. Stimpson and E. Person (eds) *Women: Sex and Sexuality*, Chicago, IL: University of Chicago Press, 62–91.

Rich, A. (1992), *Of Woman Born: Motherhood as Experience and Institution* (2nd edn), London: Virago.

Richardson, D. (2000), 'Constructing Sexual Citizenship: Theorizing Sexual Rights', *Critical Social Policy*, 20(1): 105–35.

Richardson, D. (1998), 'Sexuality and Citizenship', *Sociology*, 32(1): 83–100.

Riley, D. (1992), 'Citizenship and the Welfare State' in J. Allen, P. Braham and P. Lewis (eds) *Political and Economic Forms of Moder-nity*, Cambridge: Polity Press, Blackwell and Open University Press, 179–228.

Rinehart, N.J. and McCabe, M.P. (1997), 'Hypersexuality: Psychopa-thology or Normal Variant of Sexuality?', *Sexual and Marital Therapy*, 12, 45–60.

Riordan, S. (2007), 'Venereal Disease in the Irish Free State: The Politics of Public Health', *Irish Historical Studies*, 35(139): 345–64.

Rioux, M. (1994), 'Towards a Concept of Equality of Well-Being: Over-coming the Social and Legal Construction of Inequality' in M. Rioux and M. Bach (eds) *Disability Is Not Measles: New Research Paradigms in Disability*, Toronto, ON: Roeher Institute, 67–108.

Road Safety Authority (2007, 2008), *Crashed Lives*, available from: <http://www.rsa.ie> [accessed 4 May 2012].

Robb, M. (2007), 'Gender' in M.J. Kehily (ed.) *Understanding Youth: Perspectives, Identities and Practices*, London: Sage, 109–45.

Robinson, K.H. (2012), 'Difficult Citizenship': The Precarious Relationships Between Childhood, Sexuality and Access to Knowledge', *Sexualities*, 15(3/4): 257–76.

Robinson, V., Hockey, J. and Meah, A. (2007), '"What I Used to Do … On my Mother's Settee": Spatial and Emotional Aspects of Heterosexuality in England', *Gender and Culture: A Journal of Feminist Geography*, 11(3): 417–35.

Robson, C. (1995), 'Anatomy of a Campaign' in Í. O'Carroll and E. Collins (eds) *Lesbian and Gay Visions of Ireland in the Twenty-First Century*, London: Cassell, 47–59.

Roche, J. (1999), 'Children: Rights, Participation and Citizenship', *Childhood*, 6(4): 475–93.

Roe, S. (in co-operation with Dáil na nÓg) (2010), *Life Skills Matter Not Just Points: A Survey of Implementation of Social, Personal and Health Education (SPHE) and Relationships and Sexuality Education (RSE) in Second-level Schools*, Dublin: Office of the Minister for Children and Youth Affairs.

Rogers, C. (2010), 'But It's Not All About the Sex: Mothering, Normalisation and Young Learning Disabled People', *Disability and Society*, 25(1): 63–74.

Rogers, C. (2009), '(S)excerpts From a Life Told: Sex, Gender and Learning Disability', *Sexualities*, 12(3): 270–88.

Rogow, D. and Haberland, N. (2005), 'Sexuality and Relationships Education: Towards a Social Studies Approach', *Sex Education*, 5(4): 333–4.

Ronayne, K. and Mee, J. (2000), *Partnership Rights of Same-Sex Couples*, Dublin: Equality Authority.

Roosevelt, T. (1905), *On American Motherhood* (speech before the National Congress of Mothers, available from: <http://www.nationalcenter.org/TRooseveltMotherhood.html> [accessed 27 July 2012].

Rose, K. (1994), *Diverse Communities: The Evolution of Lesbian and Gay Politics in Ireland*, Undercurrents series, Cork: Cork University Press.

Rose, K. (1995), 'The Tenderness of the Peoples' in Í. O'Carroll and E. Collins (eds) *Lesbian and Gay Visions of Ireland: Towards the Twenty-First Century*, London: Cassell, 71–85.

Rose, N. and Miller, P. (1992), 'Political Power Beyond the State: Problematics of Government', *British Journal of Sociology*, 43(2): 173–202.

Rotello, G. (1998), *Sexual Ecology: AIDS and the Destiny of Gay Men*, New York: Plume.

RTÉ (2010) 'Bishops Want Free Civil Partnership Vote' [online], available from: <http://www.rte.ie/news/2010/0616/132280-civilpartnerships/> [accessed 18 December 2012].

RTÉ (2008) 'Brady Criticised over Remarks on Civil Unions' [online], available from: <http://www.rte.ie/news/2008/1104/marriage.html&gt> [accessed 17 December 2012].

RTÉ (2009) 'O'Gorman Criticises Civil Partnership Bill' [online], available from: <http://www.rte.ie/news/2009/0628/118940-civilpartnerships/>, accessed 18 December 2012.

RTÉ (2012), *Two for the Road,* available from: <http://www.rte.ie/tv/programmes/two_for_the_road.html> [accessed 3 February 2012].

Rubin, G. (1993), 'Misguided, Dangerous and Wrong: An Analysis of Anti-Pornography Politics' in A. Assiter and A. Carol (eds), *Bad Girls and Dirty Pictures: The Challenge to Reclaim Feminism,* London: Pluto Press.

Rubin, G. (2007), 'Thinking Sex: Notes for a Radical Theory of the Politics of Sexuality' in R. Parker and P. Aggleton (eds) *Culture, Society and Sexuality, A Reader,* New York: Routledge.

Rúdólfsdóttir, A. and Jolliffe, R. (2008), '"I Don't Think People Really Talk about It That Much": Young Women Discuss Feminism', *Feminism and Psychology,* 18: 268–74.

Rundle, K., Leigh, C., McGee, H. and Layte, R. (2004), *Irish Contraception and Crisis Pregnancy (ICCP) Study: A Survey of the General Population: Summary,* Dublin: Crisis Pregnancy Agency.

Rush, E. and La Nauze, A. (2006), 'Corporate Paedophelia: Sexualisation of Children in Australia', Discussion Paper 90, Australia Institute, available from: <https://www.tai.org.au/index.php?q=node%2F19&pubid=433&act=display> [accessed 30 July 2012].

Rust, P.C. (2000a), 'Bisexuality: A Contemporary Paradox for Women', *Journal of Social Issues,* 56(2): 205–21.

Rust, P.C. (2002), 'Bisexuality: The State of the Union', *The Annual Review of Sex Research,* 13: 180–240.

Rust, P.C. (1993), '"Coming Out" in the Age of Social Constructionism: Sexual Identity Formation Among Lesbian and Bisexual Women', *Gender and Society,* 7(1): 50–77.

Rust, P.C. (1992), 'The Politics of Sexual Identity: Sexual Attraction and Behavior Among Lesbian and Bisexual Women', *Social Problems,* 39(4): 366–86.

Rust, P.C. (2000b), 'Two Many and Not Enough', *Journal of Bisexuality,* 1(1): 31–68.

Ryan, F. (2012b), 'Are Two Irish Mammies (Even) Better than One? Heteronormativity, Homosexuality and the 1937 Constitution' in

E. Carolan (ed.) *The Constitution of Ireland: Perspectives and Prospects,* Dublin: Bloomsbury Professional, 425–52.

Ryan, F. (2011), *Civil Partnership and Certain Rights and Obligations of Cohabitants Act 2010,* Round Hall Annotated Legislation, Dublin: Round Hall.

Ryan, F. (2009), *Civil Partnership: Your Questions Answered, A Comprehensive Analysis of the Civil Partnership Bill,* Dublin: GLEN.

Ryan, F. (2007), 'From Stonewall(s) to Picket Fences: The Mainstreaming of Same-Sex Couples in Contemporary Legal Discourses' in W. Binchy and O. Doyle (eds) *Committed Relationships and the Law,* Dublin: Four Courts Press, 1–60.

Ryan, F. (2012a), 'Out of the Shadow of the Constitution: Civil Partnership, Cohabitation and the Constitutional Family', *Irish Jurist,* 48: 201–48.

Ryan, F. (1997), '"Queering" the Criminal Law: Some Thoughts on the Aftermath of Homosexual Decriminalisation', *Irish Criminal Law Journal,* 7(1): 38–47.

Ryan J. and Thomas, F. (1980), *The Politics of Mental Handicap,* Harmondsworth: Penguin.

Ryan, L. (2008), 'Constructing "Irishwoman": Modern Girls and Comely Maidens', *Irish Studies Review,* 6(3): 263–72.

Ryan, L. (2002a), *Gender, Identity and the Irish Press, 1922–1937: Embodying the Nation,* Lampeter: Edwin Mellen Press.

Ryan, L. (2002b), 'Sexualising Emigration: Discourses of Irish Female Emigration in the 1930s', *Women's Studies International Forum,* 25(1): 51–65.

Ryan, M. (1837), *The Philosophy of Marriage in its Social, Moral, and Physical Relations; with an account of the Diseases of the Genito-Urinary Organs, Which Impair or Destroy the Reproductive Function, and Induce a Variety of Complaints; with the Physiology of Generation in the Vegetable and Animal Kingdoms; Being Part of a Course of Obstetric Lectures Delivered at the North London School of Medicine, Charlotte Street, Bloomsbury, Bedford Square,* London: John Churchill, available from: <http://books.google.ie/books?id=x0kEAAAAQAAJ&printsec=frontcover&source=gbs_ge_summary_r&cad=0#v=onepage> [accessed 22 January 2012].

Ryan, P. (2011b), *Asking Angela Macnamara: An Intimate History of Irish Lives,* Dublin: Irish Academic Press.

Ryan, P. (2003), 'Coming Out, Fitting In: The Personal Narratives of Some Irish Gay Men', *Irish Journal of Sociology,* (12)1: 68–85.

Ryan, P. (2006), 'Coming Out of the Dark: A Decade of Gay and Lesbian Mobilisation in Ireland, 1970–80' in L. Connolly and N. Hourigan (eds) *Social Movements in Ireland,* Manchester: Manchester University Press, 86–105.

Ryan, P. (2011a), 'Love, Lust and the Irish: Exploring Intimate Lives through Angela Macnamara's Problem Page, 1963–1980', *Sexualities,* 14(2): 218–34.

Ryan, P. (2005), 'Strangers in Their Own Land: The Everyday Lives of Gay Men and Irish Society 1970–80', PhD thesis, University College Dublin.

Ryan, S. (2011), 'Bringing Lads' Mags to Heel Is a Start in Battle to Protect Our Children', Herald.ie, 8 June, available from: <http://www.herald.ie/opinion/columnists/sinead-ryan/sinead-ryan-bringing-lads-mags-to-heel-is-a-start-in-battle-to-protect-our-children-2668981.html> [accessed 23 August 2011].

Ryan-Sheridan, S. (1994), *Women and the New Reproductive Technologies in Ireland,* Undercurrents series, Cork: Cork University Press.

Sabina, C., Wolak, J. and Finkelhor, D. (2008), 'The Nature and Dynamics of Internet Pornography Exposure for Youth', *CyberPsychology and Behavior,* 11(6): 691–3.

Salazar, C. (2008), 'Knowledge and Discipline – Knowledge as Discipline: Aspects of the Oral History of Irish Sexuality', *Journal of the Royal Anthropological Institute,* 14, 135–51.

Samenow, C.P. and Finlayson, A.J.R. (2010), 'A Psychiatrist's Approach to a Case of Problematic Sexual Behavior', *Sexual Addiction & Compulsivity,* 17, 173–84.

Sanders, D. (2008) *'The Role of the Yogyakarta Principles',* International Gay and Lesbian Human Rights Commission, 4 August 2008, at *'The Yogyakarta Meeting',* available from: <http://www.iglhrc.org/cgi-bin/iowa/article/takeaction/partners/22.html> [accessed 6 September 2012].

Sanders, T. (2010), 'Sexual Citizenship, Commercial Sex and the Right to Pleasure' in R. Shuttleworth and T. Sanders (eds) *Sex and Disability: Politics, Identity and Access,* Leeds: Disability Press, 139–53.

Sandland, R. (2005), 'Feminism and the Gender Recognition Act 2004', *Feminist Legal Studies,* 13: 43–66.

Sandoval, C. (2004), 'U.S. Third World Feminism: The Theory and Method of Differential Oppositional Consciousness' in S. Harding (ed.) *The Feminist Standpoint Theory Reader: Intellectual and Political Controversies,* New York: Routledge, 195–209.

Sarup, M. (1988), *An Introductory Guide to Post-Structuralism and Post-modernism,* London: Harvester Wheatsheaf.

Sawicki, J. (1991), *Disciplining Foucault: Feminism, Power and the Body,* London: Routledge and Kegan Paul.

Schacher, S.J., Auerbach, C.F. and Silverstein, L.B. (2005), 'Gay Fathers Expanding the Possibilities for Us All', *Journal of GLTB Family Studies*, 1(3): 31–52.

Scheper-Hughes, N. (2001), *Saints, Scholars and Schizophrenics: Mental Illness in Rural Ireland* (20th anniversary edn), Berkeley, CA: University of California Press.

Schiebinger, L. (2000), *Feminism and the Body*, Oxford: Oxford University Press.

Schneider, J.P. (2005), 'Guidelines for Psychiatrists Working with Patients with Sexual Addiction', *Psychiatric Times*, 22, 64–71.

Schwartz, M.F. and Bradsted, W.S. (1985), 'Sexual Addiction', *Medical Aspects of Human Sexuality*, 19, 103–7.

Scior, K. (2003), 'Using Discourse Analysis to Study the Experiences of Women with Learning Disabilities', *Disability and Society*, 18(6): 779–95.

Scott, J. (1998), 'Changing Attitudes to Sexual Morality: A Cross-National Comparison', *Sociology*, 32, 815–45.

Scotti, J.R., Slack, B.S., Bowman, R.A. and Morris, T.L. (1996), 'College Student Attitudes Concerning the Sexuality of Persons with Mental Retardation: Development of the Perceptions of Sexuality Scale', *Sexuality and Disability*, 14(4): 249–63.

Segal, L. (1993), 'Does Pornography Cause Violence? The Search for Evidence' in P. Church Gibson and R. Gibson (eds) *Dirty Looks: Women, Pornography, Power*, London: BFI.

Segal, L. (2010), 'Feminism Did Not Fail', *Radical Philosophy*, available from <http://www.radicalphilosophy.com/commentary/feminism-did-not-fail> [accessed 8 August 2012].

Seidman, S. (1992), *Embattled Eros: Sexual Politics and Ethics in Contemporary America*, New York: Routledge.

Sevenhuijsen, S. (1998), *Citizenship and the Ethics of Care: Feminist Considerations on Justice, Morality and Politics*, London: Routledge.

Seward, R.R., Stivers, R.A., Igoe, D.G., Amin, I. and Cosimo, D. (2005), 'Irish Families in the Twentieth Century: Exceptional or Converging?', *Journal of Family History*, 30, 410–31.

Shakespeare, T. (2001), 'Coming Out and Coming Home', *Equality News*, Equality Authority of Ireland, Autumn Issue, 17–18.

Shakespeare, T. (2000), 'Disabled Sexuality: Towards Rights and Recognition', *Disability and Society*, 18(3): 159–66.

Shakespeare, T. (2006), *Hopelessly Devotee'd to You*, available from: <http://www.bbc.co.uk/ouch/opinion/hopelessly_devoteed_to_you.shtml#> [accessed 3 February 2012].

Shakespeare, T., Gillespie-Sells, K. and Davies, D. (1996), *The Sexual Politics of Disability*, London: Cassell.

Shanley, M.L. (2001), *Making Babies, Making Families: What Matters Most in an Age of Reproductive Technologies, Surrogacy, Adoption, and Same-Sex and Unwed Parents*, Boston, MA: Beacon Press.

Shapiro, L. (2002), 'Incorporating Sexual Surrogacy into the Ontario Direct Funding Program', *Disability Studies Quarterly*, 22(4): 78–87.

Sharpe, A. (2002), *Transgender Jurisprudence: Dysphoric Bodies of Law*, London: Cavendish Publishing.

Shatter, A. (2012a), 'Rights of People with Disabilities', *Dáil Debates: Written Answers Nos. 66-82*, available from: <http://oireachtasdebates.oireachtas.ie/debates%20authoring/DebatesWebPack.nsf/takes/dail2012121100079> [accessed 17 January 2013].

Shatter, A. (2012b), 'Statement by the Minister for Justice, Equality and Defence, Alan Shatter, T.D. Debate on Independent Senators' Private Members' Motion on Criminalising the Purchase of Sex in Ireland to Curb Prostitution and Trafficking' *Seanad*, 18 April 2012, available from: <http://www.merrionstreet.ie/index.php/2012/04/statement-by-the-minister-for-justice-equality-and-defence-alan-shatter-t-d-debate-on-independent-senators-private-members-motion-on-criminalising-the-purchase-of-sex-in-ireland/?cat=11> [accessed 14 May 2012].

Sherry, M. (2004), 'Overlaps and Contradictions between Queer Theory and Disability Studies', *Disability and Society*, 19(7): 769–83.

Sherwin Bailey, D. (1955), *Homosexuality and the Western Christian Tradition*, London: Longmans Green.

Shildrick, M. (2007), ' Contested Pleasures: The Sociopolitical Economy of Disability and Sexuality', *Sexuality Research and Social Policy: Journal of NSRC*, 4(1): 53–66.

Shildrick, M. (2004), 'Silencing Sexuality: The Regulation of the Disabled Body' in J. Carabine (ed.) *Sexualities – Personal Lives and Social Policy*, Bristol: Policy Press, 123–58.

Shipman, B. and Smart, C. (2007), '"It Made a Huge Difference": Recognition, Rights and the Personal Significance of Civil Partnership', *Sociological Research Online*, 12(1), available from: <http://www.socresonline.org.uk/12/1/shipman.html> [accessed 19 January 2012].

Shuttleworth, R. (2010), 'Towards an Inclusive Sexuality and Disability Research Agenda' in R. Shuttleworth and T. Sanders (eds) *Sex and Disability: Politics, Identity and Access*, Leeds: The Disability Press, 1–4.

Shuttleworth, R. and Sanders, T. (eds) (2010), *Sex and Disability: Politics, Identity and Access*, Leeds: Disability Press.

Siedlberg, S. (2009), 'The Euro DSD Project', *Intersexualite.org*, available from: <http://www.intersexualite.org/Eueo-DSD.html> [accessed 16 April 2012].

Siegel, R.M. (2011), 'A Review of Sexual Health in Drug and Alcohol Treatment: Group Facilitator's Manual', *American Journal of Sexuality Education*, 6, 217–26.

Simmonds, M. (2006), 'Was Variations of Reproductive Development Considered?', *British Medical Journal* ADC Online, *Electronic Letters to: I.A. Hughes, C. Houk, S.F. Ahmed, P.A. Lee LWPES/ESPE Consensus Group*, available from: <http://adc.bjm.com/content/91/7/554.extract/reply#archdeschild_el_2460> [accessed 16 January 2013].

Simon, S.B., Howe, L.W. and Kirschenbaum, H. (1972), *Values Clarification: A Handbook of Practical Strategies for Teachers and Students*, New York: Hart Publishing.

Simon, W. (1996), *Postmodern Sexualities*, New York: Routledge.

Simon, W. (2003), 'The Postmodernization of Sex' in J. Weeks, J. Holland and M. Waites (eds) *Sexualities and Society*, Oxford: Polity Press, 22–32.

Simpson, A., Lafferty, A. and McConkey, R. (2006), *Out of the Shadows – 'Our Voices Aren't Going to go Quietly into the Dark Anymore': A Report of the Sexual Health and Wellbeing of People with Learning Disabilities in Northern Ireland*, London and Belfast: Family Planning Association.

Skeggs, B. (1997), *Formations of Class and Gender: Becoming Respectable*, London: Sage.

Skoog, T., Stattin, H. and Kerr, M. (2009), 'The Role of Pubertal Timing in what Adolescent Boys do Online', *Journal of Research on Adolescence*, 19(1): 1–7.

Sligo Today (2012), 'Ombudsman Slams School Principal for Refusing to Accept Pregnant Girl', National News Briefs, 30 April, available from: <http://www.sligotoday.ie/details.php?id=19853&PHPSESSID...> [accessed 14 June 2012].

Smart, C. and Neale, B. (1999), *Family Fragments?* Cambridge: Polity Press.

Smith, D.E. (2005), *Institutional Ethnography: A Sociology for People*, the Gender Lens series, Lanham: Alta Mira Press.

Smith, J.A., Flowers, P. and Larkin, M. (2009), *Interpretative Phenomenological Analysis: Theory, Method and Research*, London: Sage.

Smith, J.M. (2004), 'The Politics of Sexual Knowledge: The Origins of Ireland's Containment Culture and the Carrigan Report (1931)', *Journal of the History of Sexuality*, 13(2): 208–33.

References

Smith, S.E. (2009), *Disabled Sexuality and Disempowerment through Fetishization*, 17 November, available from: <http://disabledfeminists.com/2009/11/17/disabled-sexuality-and-disempowerment-through-fetishization/> [accessed 23 April 2012].

Smith, T. (1999), 'Attitudes Toward Sexual Permissiveness: Trends, Correlates, and Behavioral Connections' in A.S. Rossi (ed.) *Sexuality Across the Life Course*, Chicago, IL: University of Chicago Press.

Smith, T.W. (1990), 'The Sexual Revolution?', *Public Opinion Quarterly*, 54, 415–35.

Spivak, G. (1990), *Post-Colonial Critic*, London: Routledge.

Stacey, J. (1996), *In the Name of the Family: Rethinking Family Values in the Postmodern Age*, New York: Basic Books.

Stacey, J. (1993), 'Untangling Feminist Theory' in D. Richardson and V. Robinson (eds) *Introducing Women's Studies*, London: Macmillan, 49–73.

Stacey, J. and Davenport, E. (2002), 'Queer Families Quack Back', in D. Richardson and S. Seidman (eds), *Handbook of Lesbian and Gay Studies*, London: Sage, 355–74.

Stainton Rogers, W. and Stainton Rogers, R. (2001), *The Psychology of Gender and Sexuality*, Buckingham: Open University Press.

Stein, E. (1992), *Forms of Desire: Sexual Orientation and the Social Constructionist Controversy*, New York: Routledge.

Stevens, B. (2010), 'Cripsex: Sk(r)ewed Media Representation' in R. Shuttleworth and T. Sanders (eds) *Sex and Disability: Politics, Identity and Access*, Leeds: Disability Press, 59–78.

Stychin, C.F. (1995), *Law's Desire: Sexuality and the Limits of Justice*, London: Routledge.

Stychin, C.F. (2000), '"A Stranger to Its Laws": Sovereign Bodies, Global Sexualities and Transnational Citizens', *Journal of Law and Society*, 27(4): 601–25.

Summerfield, P. (2000), 'Dis/composing the Subject: Intersubjectivities in Oral History' in T. Cosslet, C. Lury, and P. Summerfield (eds) *Feminism and Autobiography: Texts, Theories, Methods*, London/New York: Routledge, 91–106.

Sullivan, A. (1995), *Virtually Normal: An Argument About Homosexuality*, London and New York: Picador Press.

Swain, J. (2003), 'Needing to Be "In the Know": Strategies of Subordination Used by 10–11-Year-Old Schoolboys', *International Journal of Inclusive Education*, 7(4): 305–24.

Swango-Wilson, A. (2009), 'Perception of Sex Education for Individuals with Developmental and Cognitive Disability: A Four Cohort Study', *Sexuality and Disability*, 27, 223–8.

Swedish Institute (2010), *Selected Extracts of the Swedish Government Report SOU 2010:49: The Ban against the Purchase of Sexual Services. An Evaluation 1999–2008,* available from: <http://www.turnofftheredlight.ie/wp-content/uploads/2011/02/Swedish-evaluation-summary.pdf> [accessed 4 June 2012].

Swisher, S.H. (1995), 'Therapeutic Interventions Recommended for Treatment of Sexual Addiction/Compulsivity', *Sexual Addiction and Compulsivity,* 2, 31–9.

Swyer, G. (1975), 'Endocrine Disorders and Sexual Function', *British Journal of Sexual Medicine,* 2, 29–31.

Sytsma, S.E. (2006), 'Introduction' in S.E. Sytsma (ed.) *Ethics and Intersex: International Library of Ethics, Law, and the New Medicine,* The Netherlands: Springer, xvii–xxv.

Szasz, T.S. (1991), *Ideology and Insanity: Essays on the Psychiatric Dehumanization of Man,* New York: Syracuse University Press.

Tasker, F. and Patterson, C.J. (2008), 'Research on Gay and Lesbian Parenting', *Journal of GLBT Family Studies,* 3(2), 9–34.

Taylor, C. (2011) 'Aras Candidates Set Out Positions in First Debate', *Irish Times,* 28 September.

Telegraph, The (2010), 'Pornographic Magazine for the Blind Launched', 12 April, available from: <http://www.telegraph.co.uk/news/uknews/7581230/Pornographic-magazine-for-the-blind-launched.html> [accessed 12 November 2011].

Tepper, M. (2000), 'Sexuality and Disability: The Missing Discourse of Pleasure', *Sexuality and Disability,* 18(4): 283–90.

Thapar-Bjorkert, S. and Ryan, L. (2002), 'Mother India/Mother Ireland: Comparative Gendered Dialogues of Colonialism and Nationalism in the Early 20th Century', *Women's Studies International Forum,* 25(3): 301–13.

Thomas, B. (2006), 'Report on Chicago Consensus Conference October 2005', Androgen Insensitivity Syndrome Support Group website, available from: <http://www.aissg.org/PDFs/Barbara-Chicago-Rpt.pdf> [accessed 2 May 2012].

Thomas, D. (2011), 'The Children We Fostered Didn't Care If We Were Gay or Straight', *Irish Times,* Wednesday, 30 March 2011, available from: <http://www.irishtimes.com/newspaper/features/2011/0330/1224293350640.html> [accessed 17 January 2013].

Thomson, R. (2004), 'Sexuality and Young People: Policies, Practices and Identities' in J. Carabine (ed.) *Sexualities, Personal Lives and Social Policy,* Milton Keynes: Open University Press in association with Policy Press, 85–122.

Thorne, B. (1993), *Gender Play: Girls and Boys in School*, Buckingham: Open University Press.

Thorogood, N. (2000), 'Sex Education as Disciplinary Technique: Policy and Practice in England and Wales', *Sexualities*, 3(4): 425–38.

Thurneysen, R., Power, N., Dillon, M., Mulchrone, K., Binchy, D., Knoch, A. and Ryan, S. (1936), *Studies in Early Irish Law*, Dublin: Royal Irish Academy and Hodges Figgis.

Tiefer, L. (2007), 'Beneath the Veneer: The Troubled Past and Future of Sexual Medicine', *Journal of Sex and Marital Therapy*, 33, 473–7.

Tiefer, L. (1996), 'The Medicalization of Sexuality: Conceptual, Normative, and Professional Issues', *Annual Review of Sex Research*, 7, 252.

Tiefer, L. (2000), 'Sexology and the Pharmaceutical Industry: The Threat of Co-Optation', *Journal of Sex Research*, 37, 273–83.

Tobin, B. (2012), 'Law, Politics and the Child-Centric Approach to Marriage in Ireland', *Irish Jurist*, 47: 210–25.

Tobin, B. (2008), 'Relationship Recognition for Same-Sex Couples: The Proposed Models Critiqued', *Irish Journal of Family Law*, 11(1): 10–15.

Tonkiss, F. (2004), 'Analysing Text and Speech: Content and Discourse Analysis' in C. Seale (ed.) *Researching Society and Culture*, London: Sage, 367–81.

Torres, H. and Gore-Felton, C. (2007), 'Compulsivity, Substance Use, and Loneliness: The Loneliness and Sexual Risk Model (LSRM)', *Sexual Addiction and Compulsivity*, 14, 63–75.

Trall, R.T. (1866), *Sexual Physiology*, New York: Wood and Holbrook Hygiene Institute, available from: <http://books.google.com/books?id=IAQAAAAAQAAJ&printsec=frontcover&source=gbs_ge_summary_r&cad=0#v=onepage> [accessed 18 November 2011].

Tsaliki, L. (2011), 'Playing with Porn: Greek Children's Explorations in Pornography', *Sex Education*, 11(3): 293–302.

Turner, V. (2009 [1969]), *The Ritual Process: Structure and Anti-Structure*, London: Aldine Transaction.

Turner, W.B. (2000), *A Genealogy of Queer Theory*, Philadelphia, PA: Temple University Press.

UNAIDS (2010), 'Global Report on the Global AIDS Epidemic 2010', *Joint United Nations Programme on HIV/AIDS (UNAIDS)*, Geneva: United Nations.

UNAIDS (2002), *Sex Work and HIV/AIDS*, UNAIDS Technical Update, UNAIDS Best Practice Collection, Geneva: UNAIDS.

UNAIDS (2012), *UNAIDS Guidance Work on HIV and Sex Work*, available from: <http://www.unaids.org/en/media/unaids/contentassets/documents/unaidspublication/2009/JC2306_UNAIDS-guidance-note-HIV-sex-work_en.pdf.> [accessed 1 July 2012].

United Nations (2006), 'Article 23 Respect for Home and Family', *UN Convention on the Rights of People with Disabilities*, available from: <http://www.un.org/disabilities/default.asp?navid=14&pid=150> [accessed 18 July 2012].

United Nations General Assembly (2008a), *Annex to the Note Verbale Dated 19 December 2008 from the Permanent Mission of the Syrian Arab Republic to the United Nations Addressed to the Secretary-General* (UN Doc A/63/663), available from: <http://documentsddsny.un.org/doc/UNDOC/GEN/N08/669/79/pdf/N0866979.pdf?OpenElement> [accessed 30August 2012].

United Nations General Assembly (2008b), *Letter Dated 18 December 2008 from the Permanent Representatives of Argentina, Brazil, Croatia, France, Gabon, Japan, the Netherlands and Norway to the United Nations Addressed to the President of the General Assembly* (UN Doc A/63/635), available from: <http://www.sxpolitics.org/wp-content/uploads/2009/03/un-document-on-sexual-orientation.pdf> [accessed 30 August 2012].

United Nations Human Rights Council (2011), *Human Rights, Sexual Orientation and Gender Identity* (UN Doc A/HRC/17/L.9/Rev.1), available from: <http://www.scribd.com/doc/58106434/UN-Resolution-on-Sexual-Orientation-and-Gender-Identity> [accessed 6 September 2012].

UPIAS (1975), 'Introduction' in *Fundamental Principles of Disability*, available from <http://www.leeds.ac.uk/disability-studies/archiveuk/UPIAS/fundamental principles.pdf> [accessed 4 May 2012].

Usher, R. and Edwards, R. (1994), *Postmodernism and Education*, London: Routledge.

Valiulis, M. (1995), 'Power, Gender and Identity in the Irish Free State', *Journal of Women's History*, 6/7: 117–36.

Van Dijk, T. (1993), 'Principles of Critical Discourse Analysis', *Discourse and Society*, 14(2): 249–83.

Van Gennep, A. (1909), *Les Rites de Passage*, Paris: E. Nourry.

Vanwesenbeeck, I. (2009), 'The Risks and Rights of Sexualization: An Appreciative Commentary on Lerum and Dworkin's "Bad Girls Rule"', *Journal of Sex Research*, 46 (4): 268–70.

Vilain, E. and Sandberg, D.E. (2009), 'Disorders of Sex Development: Nomenclature', Letters to the Editor, *Growth, Genetics and Hormones Journal*, 25(1): 9, available from <http://www.gghjournal.com/volume25/1/pdf/toTheEditor.pdf> [accessed 1 April 2012].

References

Waites, M. (2005), 'The Fixity of Sexual Identities in the Public Sphere: Biomedical Knowledge, Liberalism and the Heterosexual/ Homosexual Binary in Late Modernity', *Sexualities*, 8(5): 539–69.

Walby, S. (1997), *Gender Transformations*, London: Routledge.

Walby, S. (1994), 'Is Citizenship Gendered?', *Sociology*, 28: 379–95.

Walkerdine, V. (1999), 'Violent Boys and Precocious Girls: Regulating Childhood at the End of the Millennium', *Contemporary Issues in Early Childhood* 1(1): 3–23.

Walsh, J. and Ryan, F. (2006), *The Rights of De Facto Couples*, Dublin: Irish Human Rights Commission.

Walshe, J. (1999), *A New Partnership in Education: From Consultation to Legislation in the Nineties*, Dublin: Institute of Public Administration.

Ward, E. (2010a), 'Prostitution and the Irish State: From Prohibitionism to a Globalised Sex Trade', *Irish Political Studies*, 25(1): 47–65.

Ward, E. (2011b), 'Prostitution Law May Cause Harm to Women', *Irish Times*, 19 October, available from: <http://www.irishtimes.com/ newspaper/opinion/2011/1019/1224306074609.html> [accessed 14 May 2012].

Warne, G.L. (1997), 'Complete Androgen Insensitivity Syndrome', Parkville, VIC: Department of Endocrinology and Diabetes, Royal Children's Hospital.

Warne, G.L. and Raza, J. (2008), 'Disorders of Sex Development (DSDs), Their Presentation and Management in Different Cultures', *Reviews in Endocrine and Metabolic Disorders*, 9(3): 227–36.

WAS (World Association for Sexology) and IPSA (International Professional Surrogates Association) (2002), *Code of Ethics and Code of Practice*, available from: <http://surrogatetherapy.org> and <http://www.worldsexology.org> [accessed 23 April 2012].

Washton, A.M. and Boundy, D. (2000), *Willpower Is Not Enough: Understanding and Overcoming Addiction and Compulsion*, New York: Harper Collins.

Waxman-Fiduccia, B.F. (1999), 'Sexual Imagery of Physically Disabled Women: Erotic? Perverse? Sexist?', *Sexuality and Disability*, 17(3): 277–82.

Wayman, S. (2012), 'Are We Living in a Girls' World?' IrishTimes.com, 7 August, available from: <http://www.irishtimes.com/news paper/health/2012/0807/1224321615473.html> [accessed 8 August 2012.

Wayman, S. (2011), 'Let's Talk About Sex ... and Teenagers', *Irish Times Health Plus*, 27 September, 1.

Wayman, S. (2010), 'Primark Row Signals Backlash Against Unsuitable Marketing', *Irish Times*, 17 April.

Weafer, J.A. (2010), 'Difficulties Experienced by People with a Physical and Sensory Disability' in J.A. Weafer Research Associates, *Independent and Community Living – the Views of People with Disabilities, Families and Frontline Staff, Focus Group Consultation Report*, Dublin: National Disability Authority, 42–3.

Weeks, J. (1990), *Coming Out: Homosexual Politics in Britain from the Nineteenth Century to the Present* (revised edn), London: Quartet.

Weeks, J. (1996), 'The Construction of Homosexuality' in S. Seidman (ed.) *Queer Theory/Sociology*, Cambridge: Blackwell, 41–63.

Weeks, J. (2000), *Making Sexual History*, Cambridge: Polity Press.

Weeks, J. (2003), 'Necessary Fictions: Sexual Identities and the Politics of Diversity' in J. Weeks, J. Holland and M. Waites (eds) *Sexualities and Society: A Reader*, Cambridge: Polity Press, 122–31.

Weeks, J. (1987), 'Questions of Identity' in P. Caplan (ed.) *The Cultural Construction of Sexuality*, London: Tavistock, 31–51.

Weeks, J. (1989), *Sex, Politics, and Society: The Regulation of Sexuality Since 1800*, London: Longman.

Weeks, J. (1998), 'The Sexual Citizen', *Theory, Culture and Society*, 15(3–4): 35–52.

Weeks, J., Heaphy, B. and Donovan, C. (2001), *Same-Sex Intimacies: Families of Choice and Other Life Experiments*, London: Routledge.

Weston, K. (1991), *Families We Choose: Lesbians, Gays, Kinship*, New York: Columbia.

Whelan, C. and Fahey, T. (1996), 'Religious Change in Ireland 1981–1990' in E.G. Cassidy (ed.) *Faith and Culture in the Irish Context*, Dublin: Veritas.

Whelehan, I. (1995), *Modern Feminist Thought: From the Second Wave to Post-Feminism*, Edinburgh: Edinburgh University Press.

Whelehan, I. (2000), *Overloaded: Popular Culture and the Future of Feminism*, London: Women's Press.

Whitaker, T., Ryan, P. and Cox, G. (2011), 'Stigmatization among Drug-using Sex Workers Accessing Support Services in Dublin', *Qualitative Health Research*, 21(8): 1086–100.

Whittle, S. (2006), 'Foreword' in S. Stryker and S. Whittle (eds) *The Transgender Studies Reader*, New York: Routledge, xi–xvi.

Whittle, S. (2002), *Respect and Equality: Transsexual and Transgender Rights*, London: Cavendish Publishing.

Whyte, J.H. (1971) *Church and State in Modern Ireland, 1923–1970*, Dublin: Gill and Macmillan.

Whyte, J.H. (1980), *Church and State in Modern Ireland, 1923–1979* (2nd edn), Dublin: Gill and Macmillan.

WHO (World Health Organisation) (2004), 'Sexual Health – A New Focus for WHO', *Progress in Reproductive Health Research,* 67, 1.

WHO (World Health Organization) (2005), *Toolkit for Targeted HIV/ AIDS Prevention and Care in Sex Work Settings,* available from: <http://whqlibdoc.who.int/publications/2005/9241592966.pdf> [accessed 14 May 2012].

Wilkenfeld, B.F. and Ballan, M.S. (2011), 'Educators' Attitudes and Beliefs Towards the Sexuality of Individuals with Developmental Disabilities', *Sexuality and Disability,* 29(4): 351–61.

Willig, C. (2008b), 'Discourse Analysis' in J.A. Smith (ed.), *Qualitative Psychology: A Practical Guide to Research Methods* (2nd edn), London: Sage: 160–85.

Willig, C. (2008a), *Introducing Qualitative Research in Psychology,* Maidenhead: Open University Press.

Willis, P. (1977), *Learning to Labour,* Hampshire: Gower Publishing.

Wilson, N.J., Parmenter, T.R., Stancliffe, R.J. and Shuttleworth, R.P. (2011), 'Conditionally Sexual: Men and Teenage Boys with Moderate to Profound Intellectual Disability', *Sexuality and Disability,* 29(3): 275–89.

Wilton, T. (2000), *Sexualities in Health and Social Care. A Textbook,* Buckingham: Open University Press.

Wines, D. (1997), 'Exploring the Applicability of Criteria for Substance Dependence to Sexual Addiction', *Sexual Addiction and Compulsivity,* 4, 195–220.

Winters, J., Christoff K. and Gorzalka, B. (2010), 'Dysregulated Sexuality and High Sexual Desire: Distinct Constructs?', *Archives of Sexual Behavior,* 39, 1029–43.

Wise, S. and Stanley, L. (2003), Review Article: 'Looking Back and Looking Forward: Some Recent Feminist Sociology Reviewed', *Sociological Research Online,* 8(3), available from: <http://www.socresonline.org.uk/8/3/wise.html> [accessed 7 January 2008].

Wittig, M. (1981), 'One Is Not Born a Woman', *Feminist Issues* 1(2): 47–54.

Wittig, M. (1992), *The Straight Mind and Other Essays,* Boston, MA: Beacon Press.

Wodak, R. (1996), *Disorders of Discourse,* London and New York: Addison Wesley Longman.

Wodak, R., de Cillia, R., Reisigl, M. and Liebhart, K. (2009), *The Discursive Construction of National Identity* (2nd edn), Edinburgh: Edinburgh University Press.

Wolf, N. (1991), *The Beauty Myth: How Images of Beauty Are Being Used Against Women*, Vintage: London.

Wolfenden Report (1968), *Report of the Committee on Homosexual Offences and Prostitution*, Cmnd. 247, London: HMSO.

Women with Disabilities Australia (2011), *Sterilization of Women and Girls with Disabilities – A Briefing Paper*, available from: <http://www.wwda.org.au/Sterilization_Disability_Briefing_Paper_October2011.pdf> [accessed 4 May 2012].

Women's Aid (nd), *Responding to Violence Against Women with Disabilities*, available from: <http://www.womensaid.ie/> [accessed 23 April 2012].

Working Group on Domestic Partnership (2006), *Options Paper: Presented by the Working Group on Domestic Partnership to the Tánaiste and Minister for Justice, Equality and Law Reform, Mr. Michael McDowell T.D.* , Dublin: Stationery Office.

Wouters, C. (2004), *Sex and Manners: Female Emancipation in the West 1890–2000*, London: Sage.

Yoshino, K. (2002), 'Covering', *Yale Law Journal*, 111(4): 769–939.

Yoshino, K. (2007), *Covering: The Hidden Assault on Our Civil Rights*, New York: Random House.

Zack, N. (1997), '"The Family" and Radical Family Theory' in H.L. Nelson (ed.) *Feminism and Families*, New York: Routledge, 43–51.

Zapf, J.L., Greiner, J. and Carroll, J. (2008), 'Attachment Styles and Male Sex Addiction', *Sexual Addiction and Compulsivity*, 15, 158–75.

Zola, I.K. (1972), 'Medicine as an Institution of Social Control', *Sociological Review*, 20, 487–504.

Index